CONFLICT &
COOPERATION

THIRD EDITION

CONFLICT & COOPERATION

Documents on Modern Global History

Edited by
Tracey J. Kinney

OXFORD
UNIVERSITY PRESS

OXFORD
UNIVERSITY PRESS

Oxford University Press is a department of the University of Oxford.
It furthers the University's objective of excellence in research, scholarship,
and education by publishing worldwide. Oxford is a registered trade mark of
Oxford University Press in the UK and in certain other countries.

Published in Canada by
Oxford University Press
8 Sampson Mews, Suite 204,
Don Mills, Ontario M3C 0H5 Canada

www.oupcanada.com

Library and Archives Canada Cataloguing in Publication
Conflict and cooperation : documents on modern global
history / edited by Tracey J. Kinney. — Third edition.

Includes bibliographical references and index.
ISBN 978-0-19-544934-1 (pbk.)

1. History, Modern—20th century—Sources. 2. History,
Modern—21st century—Sources. I. Kinney, Tracey Jane, 1966-,
editor of compilation II. Title.

D411.C63 2014   909.82   C2013-907179-2

Cover image: Paula Bronstein/Staff/Getty News/Getty Images.com

Printed and bound in the United States of America

1 2 3 4 — 16 15 14

Contents

4 | The Appeal of Revolutionary Change   71

5 | The Authoritarian Alternative   98

6 | Global Depression   124

7 | Global War and Genocide   149

8 | A New World Order?   178

9 | Origins and Implications of the Cold War   205

10 | China and Japan: The Re-emergence of Asian Power   232

11 | Anti-colonial Movements and Independence   257

12 | The Postwar Era in the Middle East   282

Geographical Table of Contents

Africa

Canada

Central and South America

Russia (The Soviet Union)

South and Southeast Asia

Southwestern Asia and the Middle East

The United States

International Organizations and Movements

From the Publisher

Essential updates found in this new edition of

Conflict and Cooperation:
Documents on Modern Global History

1. The text opens with **A Note on the Analysis of Primary Documents** to guide students through the task of interpreting primary-source documents.
2. The 41 new readings include new coverage of Asia, Central and South America, as well as the topics such as developing economies, radical movements, and international organizations, reflecting the significance of these regions and themes from the twentieth century to the present.
3. These new readings include perspectives from influential figures such as Saddam Hussein, Raúl Castro, Gro Harlem Brundtland, and Dilma Vana Rousseff.
4. Chapters have been reorganized to clarify the chronology of the readings and events.
5. The original publication date and source line now appear with each reading for ease of reference.
6. **Study Questions** have been revised to enhance the student's ability to understand and analyze the readings.
7. The companion website features an updated **Image Bank** and **Instructor's Manual** containing sample syllabi, chapter summaries, review questions with answers, and a new chronological table of contents.

Preface

The twentieth century was profoundly shaped both by the threat and the reality of war. As a result, conflict must be seen as one of the defining issues of the twentieth century. However, this was also the century that witnessed genuine attempts to build cooperative global institutions. These institutions and organizations were designed to prevent war, to facilitate communication among all peoples, and to improve the human condition in a meaningful way. These two seemingly contradictory impulses—conflict and cooperation—are thus the defining themes that weave together this collection of documents. For example, conflict among the nations of Europe fueled the drive for colonies; however, cooperative efforts among the colonized peoples, as evidenced at the 1955 Bandung Conference, accelerated the breakdown of colonialism.

In creating this collection, I was motivated by the realization that, increasingly, students find themselves generations removed from many of the critical developments that shaped the twentieth century. Even the end of the Cold War occurred before most first-year undergraduates were born. I have found it essential, therefore, to provide a means by which students can meaningfully connect to the past. Primary documents can serve this function by allowing students to "witness" essential moments in history through the words of the men and women who experienced these events. The chapter on war and genocide, for example, includes the testimony of Holocaust survivors who recall the terror, the deprivation, and the utter hopelessness of their situation in a way that enables contemporary readers to make a personal connection to what might otherwise have been simply an event in the increasingly distant past. Above all, this compilation seeks to show students that history can be studied as a collection of living documents, all of which represent human experience at moments of profound importance, moments which continue to shape the world in which we live.

In the process of creating the third edition of *Conflict and Cooperation*, I have rearranged documents to provide a greater chronological consistency. The chapter on the environment is now more comprehensive and the collection addresses omissions relating to the development of international organizations, as well as the post-Cold War era. The closing chapter on the early twenty-first century world has also been substantially revised and updated. As always, the process of removing documents was difficult, but in the end I was able to eliminate some of the duplication that had crept into the second edition, while tightening the chronological and thematic organization of the book.

Historians often debate whether undergraduates—particularly first-year students—have the necessary analytical tools to interpret primary documents in a meaningful way. I have found that any reader can work successfully with primary sources if guided by several simple analytical questions. Please see **A Note on the Analysis of Primary Documents** following this preface. As in the earlier editions, each of the documents in this collection is accompanied by the information necessary to read the document in a critical and informed way: the author's background and the document's context are reviewed in each introduction; informational notes clarify unfamiliar references in the text of the document; the original source of the document has been provided; and study questions reinforce key issues and alternate interpretations. Students will finish this book better informed about modern global history and better able to work critically with a wide variety of historical sources.

This collection focuses not only on the politicians and diplomats who shaped the twentieth century, but also, wherever possible, on the testimony of ordinary men and women who witnessed crucial moments in history. The documents are arranged in thematic chapters, each corresponding to a major issue or development in the twentieth century. The chapters progress in a broadly chronological narrative, though thematic consistency at times has necessitated breaks within a strict chronological progression. The chapter introductions are intended to provide a brief history of the events under consideration and to summarize the documents that follow. In each chapter, an attempt has been made to include a number of different viewpoints so that readers might begin to understand the many sides of any given issue. The study question at the end of each document also encourages the reader to challenge commonly held assumptions and to consider alternative viewpoints. Finally, each chapter concludes with a list of key Internet resources along with suggested reading and viewing material that, though by no means definitive, is intended to provide additional insights into the themes under discussion. In selecting websites I have been mindful of the fact that web addresses change frequently and links can often become outdated. I have therefore tried as far as possible to include only long-standing sites with stable URLs.

This collection of documents has been a number of years in the making. Earlier versions included different documents, alternate study questions, and different formatting. In producing the third edition I have once again taken into account the candid responses of my students, past and present, to the earlier collections. In most cases, I have chosen the documents and questions that evoked the strongest student reactions—both positive and negative—and those that produced the greatest debate. As a result, this collection is strongly informed by my interactions with students, and I thank all who provided input. Many of my colleagues at Kwantlen Polytechnic University have also contributed helpful advice and feedback on different parts of the manuscript. Any errors that remain are, of course, my own.

I would also like to thank Julia Jevmenova, formerly at Oxford University Press, who brought the manuscript of the first edition to the attention of the

Higher Education Division. Thanks also to the many people at OUP who have provided assistance on the earlier editions of *Conflict and Cooperation*, including Peter Chambers and Jessie Coffey. Meg Patterson and Leah-Ann Lymer have offered invaluable guidance in the preparation of the current edition. Julia Frohn-Nielsen patiently edited the final draft of the manuscript. The digital photograph archives at the US National Archives and Records Office and the Library of Congress provided a vital source for many of the photographs and illustrations that accompany the documents. Finally, thanks to my husband, Jonathan, whose support and patience has made possible the completion of this, the third edition.

A Note on the Analysis of Primary Documents

Primary sources offer us an invaluable window on the past. They allow the people and the organizations that made history to speak directly to us. When studying history, the student is often presented with the opinions of other historians and analysts, written many years after the events under consideration took place. Primary sources take us back in time and allow us to form our own opinions based on the first-hand observations of the men and women who witnessed key moments in history. As with any document, however, a primary source cannot be read uncritically. We must consider the author, his or her biases, the nature of the document, the author's intent, and the contemporaneous influences acting on her or him, among other key issues. Once these factors have been taken into consideration, the reader can begin to assess more difficult questions such as reliability and authenticity.

The following note offers a number of practical questions which readers should ask as they approach a primary source. Mindful of the fact that we cannot stand directly in the shoes of the history-makers—the passage of time and our own subjectivity render this impossible—it is possible to analyze primary sources in such a way as to gain a much deeper understanding of the past and its impact on the present. Remember though, that no single source can provide a complete history of any given time or place.

Consider the Author

Any analysis of a primary document must begin by considering the author. Ask yourself these key questions:

- Who is the author?
- What is his or her background?
- When did the author live?
- When in the author's life was the document written?

This will allow you to consider the events that the author experienced in his or her life. If the document was written early in a person's life consider her or his experiences to that point. If the document was written very late in a person's life consider the issue of memory and the impact of the events that have intervened between the writing of the document and the events under discussion. If you do not know who the author is you can still determine important information from the text itself by asking these subsidiary questions:

- Are key events mentioned?
- Did the author experience these events?

If it is clear that the author experienced the events discussed then you have already determined some basic information about the person, as well as the time and place of the document.

Consider Bias

No writer can be entirely objective; therefore, the author will be influenced by his or her upbringing, education, and experiences. Identifying possible biases on the part of the author will allow you better to understand the way he or she approaches the topic. You can begin to identify bias by asking yourself:

- What is the author's position in society?
- What does the author know about the wider world?
- What are the author's interests?
- Does the author express a clear ideological position?

Consider the Type of Document

The next step is to consider what type of document you are reading and what insights it provides into the time period. It is also useful to note how the document came to be written. The nature of the document often alters the way in which it is written. An international treaty will be written in a very different way than a personal diary entry, which will likely be written in the first person. Read the document closely. The author will provide specific insights into the time period that will add to your understanding. Ask yourself these questions:

- What type of document is this?
- To what aspects of the time period does it relate to?
- What insights into these events or developments does the document provide?
- Was this originally a written piece, or a speech?
- Was it a first-hand account, or a second-hand reflection?

Remember that speeches are often crafted to influence an audience to favour a certain policy or to support a particular viewpoint. Therefore, always consider what the speaker is leaving out and the ways in which this can manipulate the listener. If the author did not experience the events first-hand, consider how this may have altered his or her perception of the event. If the account was written many years after the event took place, note too the impact of the passage of time.

Consider Motivation

A critical reading of primary source material must always include an assessment of the author's motivation in writing the document.

- Was it written for political purposes?
- Is it a legal document?
- Was the piece simply written for personal remembrance?
- Was it written for a future audience to ensure that an event is not forgotten?

In each case the author's motivations will have a substantial impact on the way the document is constructed. Often, there will be more than one motive.

Consider Location

Also ask yourself where the document was written and whether or not it was written to be sent to another place.

- Was the author in the country about which he or she writes?
- Was he or she there during the events discussed?
- Was the document written from another location?

If the author was not present in the country under consideration, ask yourself what was taking place in the author's location that might have influenced the way he or she views the events. If it was sent somewhere else, evaluate the ways in which this might have affected both the tone of the document and its reliability.

Consider the Time Period

Finally, it is necessary to consider the time period in which the document was written. The time period is one of the most important keys to reading a document critically. If the document was written as the events happened the author had only a limited amount of information. If it was written many years after the fact the author would have had more information to work with, but would have been influenced by intervening events and the benefit of hindsight. No author can remove themselves entirely from the influences of the time period in which they are writing. Ask yourself these questions:

- When was the document written?
- Was it written at the time the events were taking place?
- What other events were taking place as the author was writing the document?

- What could the author have known at the time?
- Was the author writing in the middle of a series of events, or had the situation been resolved?

The context in which a document is written and the information available to the author is a vitally important factor, both in understanding the author's motivation and the influences shaping the events under discussion.

Determining Authenticity

Determining the authenticity of a document is a somewhat more difficult process, especially when you have only one primary source in front of you. Even here, however, some simple questions will help to guide you:

- Is there information in the document that the author could not have known?
- Is the document consistent with what is known about this person?
- Is the document consistent with what is known about this time and place?

If you still have doubts about the authenticity of a source then locate other sources by the same author and by additional authors on the same topic and compare them for consistency. The more sources you consider, the closer you will come to a reliable and comprehensive summary of the situation under consideration.

While this may seem like an awful lot of questions to apply to every single primary source, the basic principles of primary source analysis are very simple:

Who? What? How? Why? Where? When?

1

The World and the West

THE RHODES COLOSSUS
STRIDING FROM CAPE TOWN TO CAIRO.

A Punch Cartoon entitled "The Rhodes Colossus" reflects the British desire for an African Empire stretching from the Cape in the south to Cairo in the north.

Photo: © Punch Limited

The western world has come to view the turn of the twentieth century as a pivotal transitional point in human history. Western power had reached a high point as a result of early industrialization and its resulting technological and military advantages. Western optimism seemed boundless. At the 1893 Chicago World's Fair Nikola Tesla's alternating current (AC) had illuminated the buildings and grounds and introduced the public to the idea of inexpensive, widespread electrical power. In 1895 Guglielmo Marconi sent the first wireless signal over a distance of one and a half miles. The age of radio had been born, and with it a revolution in global communications. In 1896 Thomas Edison presented the first publicly projected motion picture in New York City, thereby transforming popular entertainment. In 1903 at Kitty Hawk, North Carolina, Orville Wright flew a man-made craft 37 metres for 12 seconds and revolutionized international transportation in the process. Finally, in 1905 Albert Einstein, then a patent clerk in Switzerland, published his special theory of relativity, and altered the very foundations of the modern scientific worldview.

Yet the turn of the century holds little importance for non-western nations. The most profound changes for the nations of Asia, Africa, and South America had been initiated much earlier in the nineteenth century. In China, the Opium Wars (1839–42 and 1856–60) had triggered a decisive confrontation with western power and western ideas. The consequences of China's increasing loss of sovereignty would preoccupy the Qing emperors for the remainder of the nineteenth century, finally culminating in the Xinhai Revolution in 1911. In Japan, the closed society of the late Tokugawa era was forced open by the steady pressure of foreign efforts to negotiate new trade treaties, beginning in the 1850s. The resulting era of reform—known as the Meiji Restoration—stretched well into the twentieth century. In Africa, the arrival of the industrialized powers of the West, beginning in the 1870s, brought profound change to some nations and the consequences of colonial conquest would be felt for nearly 100 years. The Ottoman Empire had begun its decline long before the turn of the new century. The clash between those who looked to an Islamic revival to secure change and those who looked to the West as a source of modernization would continue even as the Ottoman Empire itself disintegrated in the wake of the First World War. Finally, in South and Central America the challenge of building new national identities and functional political systems, which had begun in the 1820s and 1830s, continued well into the twentieth century.

Nonetheless, intellectuals and political leaders around the world were confronted by the challenge of western power during the nineteenth and early twentieth centuries. Many modernizers in Asia and the Middle East looked favourably upon western education and western political systems as a means to achieve comprehensive reforms in their own countries. However, political leaders often struggled to find ways to meet the challenge of the West while retaining their distinctive cultures and traditions. Chinese reformers phrased this struggle in terms of preserving "ti" (the essence of Chinese culture) while focusing on "yong" (that which was useful from the "barbarians"). Intellectuals who embraced the need to reform also differed over the best way to achieve this goal. In Meiji Japan (1868–1912) political, economic, and military systems were imported wholesale from the West, though the resulting Japanese equivalents managed to retain many uniquely Japanese elements, such as the divinity of the emperor. In China, demands for reform often met strong resistance from those who sought to preserve the traditional imperial system, even in the face of ongoing foreign intervention. Other reformers sought strength through cooperation, as in the case of the pan-Islamist and pan-Africanist movements. Yet those who advocated unity and cooperation often found that national and ethnic divisions worked against the core goals of their movements.

This chapter examines a variety of responses to the challenge posed by the West. The chapter opens with one of the foremost statements of the dominant western view: Cecil Rhodes' 1877 "Confession of Faith." Thereafter, Dadabhai Naoroji reflects on the advantages that British rule had brought to India; Rabindranath Tagore, in contrast, laments the lack of true understanding between India and Britain (and more generally between the East and the West). Kido Takayoshi, a Japanese reformer, explains the advantage of western political models and their applicability in Japan. Itō Hirobumi's commentary on the new Japanese Constitution reveals the degree of Western influence on its formulation. Sayyid Jamal al-Din al-Afghani calls on Islamic leaders to recognize the importance of western science, rather than fearing its impact in the Muslim world. Both Kang Youwei and Wu Tingfang recognize the need for substantive reforms in late-Qing China. Kang argues that the institutions of the West are too remote to be of use in China; however, the methods of the Meiji reformers could be beneficial. Writing some ten years later Wu sees many positive strides towards "the awakening of China."

Cecil Rhodes

Cecil Rhodes (1853–1902) was born in Great Britain, but made his fortune in southern Africa. He first travelled to British South Africa as a teenager in the 1870s and was soon attracted to the lucrative diamond fields in Kimberley. By 1880 Rhodes had amassed enough money to establish his own mining company—which later merged to become De Beers Consolidated Mines in 1888. In 1889 Rhodes established the British South Africa Company (BSAC) which would establish effective control over much of

Africa south of the Limpopo River, including present-day Zimbabwe (originally named Rhodesia, in recognition of Rhodes' role in securing the territory). Rhodes also served in the parliament of the Cape Colony, from 1880 onwards, and was prime minister of the Cape from 1890 to 1896. The document that follows was appended to Rhodes' will, written in 1877 when he was just twenty-four years old.

Document Source: John Flint, *Cecil Rhodes* (London: Hutchinson, 1976), 248–52.

Confession of Faith

It often strikes a man to inquire what is the chief good in life; to one the thought comes that it is a happy marriage, to another great wealth, and as each seizes on his idea, for that he more or less works for the rest of his existence. To myself thinking over the same question the wish came to render myself useful to my country. I then asked myself how could I and after

reviewing the various methods I have felt that at the present day we are actually limiting our children and perhaps bringing into the world half the human beings we might owing to the lack of country for them to inhabit that if we had retained America there would at this moment be millions more of English living. I contend that we are the finest race in the world and that the more of the world we inhabit the better it is for the human race. Just fancy those parts that are at present inhabited by the most despicable specimens of human beings what an alteration there would be if they were brought under Anglo-Saxon influence, look again at the extra employment a new country added to our dominions gives. I contend that every acre added to our territory means in the future birth to some more of the English race who otherwise would not be brought into existence. . . .

At the present day I become a member of the Masonic order. I see the wealth and power they possess the influence they hold and I think over their ceremonies and I wonder that a large body of men can devote themselves to what at times appear the most ridiculous and absurd rites without an object and without an end.

The idea gleaming and dancing before one's eyes like a will-of-the-wisp at last frames itself into a plan. Why should we not form a secret society with but one object the furtherance of the British Empire and the bringing of the whole uncivilised world under British rule for the recovery of the United States for the making the Anglo-Saxon race but one Empire. What a dream, but yet it is probable, it is possible. I once heard it argued by a fellow in my own college, I am sorry to own it by an Englishman, that it was good thing for us that we have lost the United States. There are some subjects on which there can be no arguments, and to an Englishman this is one of them, but even from an American's point of view just picture what they have lost, look at their government, are not the frauds that yearly come before the public view a disgrace to any country and especially theirs which is the finest in the world. Would they have occurred had they remained under English rule great as they have become how infinitely greater they would have been with the softening and elevating influences of English rule, think of those countless 000's of Englishmen that during the

last 100 years would have crossed the Atlantic and settled and populated the United States. Would they have not made without any prejudice a finer country of it than the low class Irish and German emigrants? All this we have lost and that country loses owing to whom? Owing to two or three ignorant pig-headed statesmen of the last century, at their door lies the blame. Do you ever feel mad? Do you ever feel murderous. I think I do with those men. I bring facts to prove my assertion. Does an English father when his sons wish to emigrate ever think of suggesting emigration to a country under another flag, never—it would seem a disgrace to suggest such a thing I think that we all think that poverty is better under our own flag than wealth under a foreign one.

Put your mind into another train of thought. Fancy Australia discovered and colonised under the French flag, what would it mean merely several millions of English unborn that at present exist we learn from the past and to form our future. We learn from having lost to cling to what we possess. We know the size of the world we know the total extent. Africa is still lying ready for us it is our duty to take it. It is our duty to seize every opportunity of acquiring more territory and we should keep this one idea steadily before our eyes that more territory simply means more of the Anglo-Saxon race more of the best the most human, most honourable race the world possesses. . . .

For fear that death might cut me off before the time for attempting its development I leave all my worldly goods in trust to S.G. Shippard and the Secretary for the Colonies at the time of my death to try to form such a Society with such an object.

Study Question

What are the implications of such an ambitious vision of imperial expansion?

Dadabhai Naoroji

Dadabhai Naoroji (1825–1917) was educated in British schools in India and spent time in England in the 1850s and 1860s. He played an important role in the founding of the Indian National Congress and consistently advocated a moderate position with respect to British rule in India. In the 1890s, after returning again to England, he was elected to Parliament, representing both his local constituency and the broader issues facing the people of India. Naoroji was particularly concerned with the impact of British economic policies in India. In 1906 he began to argue for Swaraj *or home rule for India, but remained determined that this would be achieved through moderate means. The speech that follows was the presidential address at the opening of the second session of the Indian National Congress in 1886. The response of the audience is noted in parentheses.*

Document Source: Dadabhai Naoroji, *Essays, Speeches, Addresses, and Writings (on Indian Politics) of the Hon'ble Dadabhai Naoroji* (Bombay: Caxton Printing Works, 1887), 331–3.

The Blessings of British Rule

The assemblage of such a Congress is an event of the utmost importance in Indian history. I ask whether in the most glorious days of Hindu rule, in the days of Rajahs like the great Vikram, you could imagine the possibility of a meeting of this kind, where even Hindus of all different provinces of the kingdom could have collected and spoken as one nation. Coming down to the later empire of our friends, the Mahomedans,[1] who probably ruled over a larger territory at one time than any Hindu monarch, would it have been, even in the days of the great Akbar himself, possible for a meeting like this to assemble composed of all classes and communities, all speaking one language, and all having uniform and high aspirations of their own?

Well, then, what is it for which we are now met on this occasion? We have assembled to consider questions upon which depend our future, whether glorious or inglorious. It is our good fortune that we are under a rule which makes it possible for us to meet in this manner. (*Cheers*) It is under the civilizing rule of the Queen and people of England that we meet here together, hindered by none, and are freely allowed to speak our minds without the least fear and without the least hesitation. Such a

thing is possible under British rule and British rule only. (*Loud cheers*) Then I put the *question* plainly: Is this Congress a nursery for sedition and rebellion against the British Government (*cries of "no, no"*); or is it another stone in the foundation of the stability of that Government (*cries of "yes, yes"*)? There could be but one answer, and that you have already given, because we are thoroughly sensible of the numberless blessings conferred upon us, of which the very existence of this Congress is a proof in a nutshell. (*Cheers*) Were it not for the blessings of British rule I could not have come here, as I have done, without the least hesitation and without the least fear that my children might be robbed and killed in my absence; nor could you have come from every corner of the land, having performed, within a few days, journeys which in former days would have occupied as many months. (*Cheers*) These simple facts bring home to all of us at once some of those great and numberless blessings which British rule has conferred upon us. But there remain even greater blessings for which we have to be grateful. It is to British rule that we owe the education we possess; the people of England were sincere in the declarations made more than half a century ago that

India was a sacred charge entrusted to their care by Providence, and that they were bound to administer it for the good of India, to the glory of their own name, and the satisfaction of God. (*Prolonged cheering*) When we have to acknowledge so many blessings as flowing from British rule—and I could descant on them for hours, because it would simply be recounting to you the history of the British Empire in India—is it possible that an assembly like this, every one of whose members is fully impressed with the knowledge of these blessings, could meet for any purpose inimical to that rule to which we owe so much? (*Cheers*)

The thing is absurd. Let us speak out like men and proclaim that we are loyal to the backbone (*cheers*); that we understand the benefits English rule has conferred upon us; that we thoroughly appreciate the education that has been given to us, the new light which has been poured upon us, turning us from darkness into light and teaching us the new lesson that kings are made for the people, not people for their kings; and this new lesson we have learned amidst the darkness of Asiatic despotism only by the light of free English civilization. (*Loud cheers*)

Note

1. Muslims.

> **Study Question**
>
> Do you believe that Naoroji's flattery of the British was more or less effective than more violent challenges to British rule in India?

Rabindranath Tagore

Rabindranath Tagore (1861–1941) was a Bengali writer who was particularly renowned for his poetry. Tagore spent some time in England in his late teenage years and travelled widely after his literary works became well-known. In 1913 he received the Nobel Prize in Literature. In addition to his poetry, Tagore wrote numerous essays and was, at times, involved in the Indian *nationalist movement. The document that follows was written later in Tagore's life, after he had renounced the knighthood conferred upon him by King George V, in protest over the massacre at Amritsar in 1919. (See also the documents on the Amritsar Massacre).*

Document Source: Rabindranath Tagore, *Creative Unity* (London: Macmillan and Company, 1922), 97–100.

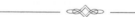

East and West

Lately I went to visit some battlefields of France which had been devastated by war. The awful calm of desolation, which still bore wrinkles of pain—death-struggles stiffened into ugly ridges—brought before my mind the vision of a huge demon, which had no shape, no meaning, yet had two arms that could strike and break and tear, a gaping mouth that could devour, and bulging brains that could conspire and plan. It was a purpose, which had a living body, but no complete humanity to temper it. Because it was passion—belonging to life, and yet not having the wholeness of life—it was the most terrible of life's enemies.

Something of the same sense of oppression in a different degree, the same desolation in a different aspect, is produced in my mind when I realize the effect of the West upon Eastern life—the West which, in its relation to us, is all plan and purpose incarnate, without any superfluous humanity.

I feel the contrast very strongly in Japan. In that country the old world presents itself with some ideal of perfection, in which man has his varied opportunities of self-revelation in art, in ceremonial, in religious faith, and in customs expressing the poetry of social relationship. There one feels that deep delight of hospitality which life offers to life. And side by side, in the same soil, stands the modern world, which is stupendously big and powerful, but inhospitable. It has no simple-hearted welcome for man. It is living; yet the incompleteness of life's ideal within it cannot but hurt humanity.

The wriggling tentacles of a cold-blooded utilitarianism, with which the West has grasped all the easily yielding succulent portions of the East, are causing pain and indignation throughout the Eastern countries. The West comes to us, not with the imagination and sympathy that create and unite, but with a shock of passion—passion for power and wealth. This passion is a mere force, which has in it the principle of separation, of conflict.

I have been fortunate in coming into close touch with individual men and women of the Western countries, and have felt with them their sorrows and shared their aspirations. I have known that they seek the same God, who is my God—even those who deny Him. I feel certain that, if the great light of culture be extinct in Europe, our horizon in the East will mourn in darkness. It does not hurt my pride to acknowledge that, in the present age, Western humanity has received its mission to be the teacher of the world; that her science, through the mastery of laws of nature, is to liberate human souls from the dark dungeon of matter. For this very reason I have realised all the more strongly, on the other hand, that the dominant collective idea in the Western countries is not creative. It is ready to enslave or kill individuals, to drug a great people with soul-killing poison, darkening their whole

Rabindranath Tagore, photographed three years after he received the Nobel Prize for Literature.

Courtesy of the Library of Congress, Prints and Photographs Division (LC-USZ62-123106)

future with the black mist of stupefaction, and emasculating entire races of men to the utmost degree of helplessness. It is wholly wanting in spiritual power to blend and harmonize; it lacks the sense of the great personality of man.

The most significant fact of modern days is this, that the West has met the East. Such a momentous meeting of humanity, in order to be fruitful, must have in its heart some great emotional idea, generous and creative. There can be no doubt that God's choice has fallen upon the knights-errant of the West for the service of the present age; arms and armour have been given to them; but have they yet realised in their hearts the single-minded loyalty to their cause which can resist all temptations of bribery from the devil? The world to-day is offered to the West. She will destroy it, if she does not use it for a great creation of man. The materials for such a creation are in the hands of science; but the creative genius is in Man's spiritual ideal.

Study Question

Contrast Tagore's view of British rule with that of Naoroji in the previous document. Whose assessment of the intentions of the West seems more accurate?

Kido Takayoshi

Kido Takayoshi (also known as Kido Kōin) (1833–1877) was a Choshu[2] Samurai who opposed the Tokugawa refusal to open Japan to western influences. During the Meiji period Kido was an active participant in the creation of a modern Japanese state. In 1871 he travelled throughout the United States and Europe as part of an official fact-finding mission studying a variety of governmental systems. He returned more convinced than ever of Japan's relative lack of development

and the need for constitutional reform. Believing it would take many years to bring Japan up to the level of the western powers, Kido advocated avoiding foreign conflicts in order to concentrate on internal development. In the following report, written in 1873, Kido reflected on the roles of the Emperor and of the citizen in Japan and in the nations that he had visited.

Document Source: Wm. Theodore deBary, ed., *Sources of Japanese Tradition*, Vol. 2 (New York: Columbia University Press, 1958), 143–5.

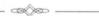

Observations on Returning from the West

It was thought advisable, as early as the spring of 1868 when the northern provinces were still subdued, to summon together at the palace all the officials and nobles of the empire. The Emperor then prayed to the gods of heaven and earth and pronounced an Oath containing five clauses, which was thereupon published throughout the empire, indicating to what end the Constitution should tend, and guiding the ideas of the people in one fixed direction. The heading of this Oath states: "By this Oath We set up as Our aim the establishment of the national weal[2] on a broad basis and the framing of a constitution and laws." This led at last to granting the petitions for leave to restore the fiefs to the Emperor, which occasioned the abolition of feudal titles and the unification of the divided national authority. Is not all this consonant with the prevailing view in the powerful countries

of the five great continents? And if this be so, then surely we must consider those five clauses as the foundation of our Constitution. Now the Constitution is a thing which sets on a firm basis the weal of the entire nation, which prevents officials from taking unauthorized steps on their own judgment, and which by placing under one control all the business of administration, renders it necessary that all measures conform to it. Is not there at the present time any subject of the empire who does not gratefully acknowledge its profound and farsighted policy and admire the loftiness of the Emperor's views?

However, in enlightened countries, though there may be a sovereign, still he does not hold sway in an arbitrary fashion. The people of the whole country give expression to their united and harmonious wishes, and the business of the State is arranged accordingly, a department (styled the government) being charged with the execution of their judgments, and officials appointed to transact business. For this reason all who hold office respect the wishes of the whole nation and serve their country under a deep sense of responsibility, so that even in extraordinary crises, they take no arbitrary step contrary to the people's will. The strictness [of the constitution] of these governments is such as I have just described, but as an additional check upon illegal acts, the people have parliamentary representatives whose duty it is to inspect everything that is done and to check arbitrary proceedings on the part of officials. Herein lies the best quality of these governments. But if the people are not yet sufficiently enlightened, it becomes necessary, at least for a time, that the Sovereign should by his superior discernment anticipate their unanimous wishes and act for them in arranging the affairs of State and in entrusting to officials the execution of their wishes. By this means he will gradually lead them forward in the path of enlightenment. Such a course is consonant with natural principles, and I am inclined to believe that the thought of the Emperor when he inaugurated by an oath his energetic policy was based on this idea. My belief is that although Japan is not yet ready for parliamentary inspection of the affairs of state, in the importance of its laws and the magnitude of its affairs it is no different from those countries of Europe and America the conduct of whose governments embodies the will of the people. It is important that our officials should not be forgetful of their responsibility and should take as their model our five-clause Constitution. . . .

Every citizen's object in life is to preserve his natural liberty by exercising his rights, and to assist in carrying on the government by sharing its obligations. Therefore, [these rights and obligations] are specified in writing and men bind themselves by a solemn promise to permit no infringement of them, but to act as mutual checks on each other in maintaining them. These writings are what we call laws. The laws grow out of the Constitution, for the Constitution is the root of every part of the government, and there is nothing which does not branch out from it. For this reason, every country, when the time comes for changing its constitution, bestows on it the greatest care and the ripest consideration and ascertains to the full the general wishes. No new measures are put in force unless they are imperatively called for by the circumstances, [nor are any adopted] lightly or hastily. In a country whose sovereign generously decides to meet the wishes of the people, the greatest care must be taken to ascertain them with accuracy, the internal conditions of the country must be profoundly studied, what the people produce must be taken into account, and, most important of all, policies must be suited to the degree of civilization of the people.

Again, in ordering the affairs of a nation, its strength must be taken into account. If not, one good will be converted into a hundred evils. The poor man's son who tries to rival the son of the rich man ruins his property and his house, and in the end does not make a show equal to his rival. Those who order the affairs of a nation should remember, before taking action, to consider the due sequence of measures, and should proceed by gradual steps in nourishing its strength, for no nation ever attained to a perfect state of civilization in a single morning. . . .

When I consider the results of the measures of the past few years with reference to the present condition of our country it appears to me that the trend of the times still lacks direction. The people's minds are perversely turned in one direction, and instead of exercising their rights, many of them mimic idly the arts of civilization; instead of discharging their responsibilities to the state, they are much given to ill-judged pretensions to enlightenment. The consequence is that although they are gradually acquiring the outward appearance of refinement, and the old rustic coarseness is gradually changing, they have not suddenly become enlightened in their hearts.

> **Study Question**
>
> Briefly summarize the political structure outlined by Kido. What are the strengths and weaknesses of this system?

Notes

1. Choshu Samurai were strongly anti-foreign when western ships made their first appearance in Japan. However, they soon realized that Japan as it existed in the 1850s and 1860s would be unable to resist the advancing foreign forces. Thus, many of the Choshu Samurai abandoned their isolationist sentiments and would play a prominent role in the Meiji era.
2. Literally the "national welfare."

Itō Hirobumi

Like Kido Takayoshi, Itō Hirobumi (1841–1909) was also a Choshu samurai. Despite the self-enforced isolation of the Tokugawa period, he had travelled to Europe in the early 1860s, working as a deckhand on a British ship. After the Meiji Restoration, Itō became one of the leading advocates of westernization. He served the Meiji Emperor in the ministries of foreign affairs, finance, and industry. Entrusted with the task of preparing a new constitution, Itō established a constitutional commission that again travelled to the West in search of suitable models. His admiration of the newly unified German State led Itō to draw heavily on the German Constitution of 1871 when drafting Japan's new constitution in 1889. In the commentary on the constitution which follows, the degree of western influence is clearly evident.

Document Source: Itō Hirobumi, *Commentaries on the Constitution of the Empire of Japan*, transl. Itō Miyoji (Tokyo: Government Printing Office, 1889), 26–8.

Commentaries on the Constitution: Articles XIII & XIV

[Article XIII] The Emperor declares war, makes peace, and concludes treaties.

Declaration of war, conclusion of peace and of treaties with foreign countries, are the exclusive rights of the Sovereign, concerning which no consent of the Diet is required. For, in the first place, it is desirable that a Monarch should manifest the unity of the sovereign power that represents the State in its intercourse with foreign powers; and in the second, in war and treaty matters, promptness in forming plans according to the nature of the crisis, is of paramount importance. By "treaties" is meant treaties of peace and friendship, of commerce, and of alliance.

(NOTE.) According to the old usage of the middle ages in Europe, every Sovereign seems to have personally attended to his own diplomatic affairs. William III. of England took upon himself the functions of Foreign Secretary, and his special talents for diplomacy were greatly lauded at the time. But with the gradual development of constitutional principles in modern times, diplomatic affairs also have been merged into the functions of responsible Ministers of State, and the Sovereign's rights relating to these subjects have come to be exercised, like all other administrative matters, only by the advice of the Ministers. When Napoleon Bonaparte was First Consul of France, he addressed to the King of England a communication containing proposals of peace between France and England, but on the British side it was acknowledged and answered by the Foreign Secretary. In the diplomatic usage of the present day, it is a recognized principle in every country, that a Minister of State should be made the channel of communication of matters relating to diplomatic affairs and to treaties with foreign powers, except in cases of the Sovereign's personal letters of congratulation or of condolence. The principal object of the present Article is to state that the Emperor shall dispose of all matters relating to foreign intercourse, with the advice of His Ministers, but allowing no interference by the Diet therein.

> [Article XIV] The Emperor declares a state of siege. The conditions and effects of a state of siege shall be determined by law.

A state of siege is to be declared at the time of a foreign war or of a domestic insurrection for the purpose of placing all ordinary law in abeyance and of entrusting part of the administrative and judicial powers to military measures. The present Article expressly provides, that the conditions requisite for the declaration of a state of siege and the effect of the declaration shall be determined by law, and that, in pursuance of the provisions thereof, it appertains exclusively to the sovereign power of the Emperor, under stress of circumstances, to declare or to revoke a state of siege. By "conditions" is meant the nature of the crisis when a state of siege is to be declared, the necessary limits as to the territorial extent affected, and rules needful for making the declaration. By "effect" is meant the limit of the power called into force as the result of the declaration of a state of siege.

The exercise of the right of warfare in the field, or of the declaration of a state of siege as the exigency of circumstances may require, may be entrusted to the commanding officer of the place, who is allowed to take the actual steps his discretion dictates, and then to report to the Government. This is to be regarded as a delegation of the sovereign power of the Emperor to a General in command of an army, in order to meet the stress of emergencies, according to the provisions of the law (Notification No. 36 issued in the 15th year of Meiji—1882 AD).[1]

Note

1. The Meiji calendar corresponds to the reign of the Meiji Emperor Mutsuhito; therefore, the fifteenth year of Meiji would be 1882 by western convention.

> **Study Question**
>
> What are the strengths and weaknesses of vesting the power to declare war in the hands of the emperor, rather than parliament?

Sayyid Jamal al-Din al-Afghani

Sayyid Jamal al-Din al-Afghani (1838/1839–97)[1] was an Islamic reformer and proponent of Islamic nationalism (or pan-Islamism). He had travelled widely and visited many of the major western capitals including London, Paris, and St Petersburg. His experiences overseas led him to conclude that advances in scientific knowledge were essential to a thriving civilization. Thus, successful resistance to the colonial rulers who dominated nations such as India and Egypt would depend upon a new attitude towards scientific education. The lecture that follows was delivered in November 1882 at the Albert Hall in Calcutta.

Document Source: Sayyid Jamal al-Din al-Afghani, *An Islamic Response to Imperialism: Political and Religious Writings of Sayyid Jamal al-Din al-Afghani*, transl. Nikki Keddie (Berkeley: University of California Press, 1968), 105–6.

———————— ◁◇▷ ————————

Lecture on Teaching and Learning

The Ottoman Government and the Khedivate of Egypt have been opening schools for the teaching of the new sciences for a period of sixty years, and until now they have not received any benefit from those sciences. . . .

The first Muslims had no science, but, thanks to the Islamic religion, a philosophic spirit arose among them, and owing to that philosophic spirit they began to discuss the general affairs of the world and human necessities. This was why they acquired in a short time all the sciences with particular subjects that they translated from the Syriac, Persian, and Greek into the Arabic language at the time of Mansūr Davānaqi.[2]

It is philosophy that makes man understandable to man, explains human nobility, and shows man the proper road. The first defect appearing in any nation that is headed toward decline is in the philosophic spirit. After that, deficiencies spread into the other sciences, arts, and associations.

. . . Muslims these days do not see any benefit from their education. For example, they study grammar, and the purpose of grammar is that someone who has acquired the Arabic language be capable of speaking and writing. The Muslims now make grammar a goal in itself. For long years they expend philosophic thought on grammar to no avail, and after finishing they are unable to speak, write, or understand Arabic.

Rhetoric, which they call *literature*, is the science that enables man to become a writer, a speaker, and poet. However, we see these days that after studying that science they are incapable of correcting their everyday speech.

Logic, which is the balance for ideas, should make everyone who acquires it capable of distinguishing every truth from falsehood and every right from wrong. However, we see that the minds of our Muslim logicians are full of every superstition and vanity, and no difference exists between their ideas and the ideas of the masses of the bazaar.

Philosophy is the science that deals with the state of external beings, and their causes, reasons, needs, and requisites. It is strange that our ulama[3] . . . call themselves sages, and despite this they cannot distinguish their left hand from their right hand, and they do not ask: Who are we and what is right and proper for us? They never ask the causes of electricity, the steamboat, and railroads. . . .

The strangest thing of all is that our ulama these days have divided science into two parts. One they call Muslim science, and one European science. Because of this they forbid others to teach some of the useful sciences. They have not understood that science is that noble thing that has no connection with any nation, and is not distinguished by anything but itself. Rather, everything that is known is known by science, and every nation that becomes renowned becomes renowned through science. Men must be related to science, not science to men.

How very strange it is that the Muslims study those sciences that are ascribed to Aristotle with the greatest delight, as if Aristotle were one of the pillars of the Muslims. However, if the discussion relates to Galileo, Newton, and Kepler, they consider them infidels. The father and mother of science is proof, and proof is neither Aristotle nor Galileo. The truth is where there is proof, and those who forbid science and knowledge in the belief that they are safeguarding the Islamic religion are really the enemies of that religion. The Islamic religion is the closest of religions to science and knowledge, and there is no incompatibility between science and knowledge and the foundation of the Islamic faith. . . .

The first education obtained by man was religious education, since philosophical education can only be obtained by a society that has studied some science and is able to understand proofs and demonstrations. Hence we can say that reform will never be achieved by the Muslims except if the leaders of our religion first reform themselves and gather the fruits of their science and knowledge.

If one considers, he will understand this truth, that the ruin and corruption we have experienced first reached our ulama and religious leaders, and then penetrated the rest of the community.

> **Study Question**
>
> Al-Afghani argues that there is no incompatibility between science and faith. On what basis does he make this claim?

Notes

1. There is substantial debate regarding al-Afghani's birth. Scholars differ as to whether he was born in 1838 or 1839; there is even less consensus as to his place of birth—Afghanistan or Iran. For more information on this debate see Roderic H. Davison, "Jamal al-Din Afghani: A Note on his Nationality and on his Burial", *Middle Eastern Studies* 24, 1 (Jan. 1988): 110–12.

2. The Abbasid caliph Mansūr Davānaqi ruled from 754–775 CE.

3. The Ulama [ulema] are Muslim scholars, though the term is often used to describe Islamic clerics.

Kang Youwei

Kang Youwei (1858–1927) was one of the best known reformers in late-Qing China. He played a major role in the Hundred Days Reform movement (June to September 1898), which was launched shortly after this document was produced. Kang's works called for a thorough reform of traditional institutions, using the ideas of Confucius as the basis of his reform program. Like many other reformers of this era Kang was troubled by China's defeat in the Sino-Japanese War (1894–95) but he looked favourably on the Meiji reforms which had so strengthened Japanese power. The document which follows was addressed to the reform-minded Guangxu emperor in January 1898.

Document Source: Wm. Theodore de Bary, et al. eds, *Sources of Chinese Tradition: From 1600 through the Twentieth Century* (New York: Columbia University Press, 2001), 269–70.

Comprehensive Consideration of the Whole Situation

A survey of all states in the world will show that those states that undertook reforms became strong while those states that clung to the past perished. The consequences of clinging to the past and the effects of opening up new ways are thus obvious. If Your Majesty, with your discerning brilliance, observes that trends in other countries you will see that if we can change, we can preserve ourselves; but if we cannot change, we shall perish. Indeed, if we can make a complete change, we shall become strong, but if we only make limited changes, we shall still perish. If Your Majesty and his ministers investigate the source of the disease, you will know that this is the right prescription.

Our present trouble lies in our clinging to old institutions without knowing how to change. In an age of competition between states, to put into effect methods appropriate to an era of universal unification and laissez-faire is like wearing heavy furs in summer or riding a high carriage across a river. This can only result in having a fever or getting oneself drowned. . . .

It is a principle of things that the new is strong but the old weak; that new things are fresh but old things rotten; that new things are active but old things static. If the institutions are old, defects will develop. Therefore there are no institutions that should remain unchanged for a hundred years. Moreover, our present institutions are but unworthy vestiges of the Han, Tang, Yuan, and Ming dynasties; they are not even the institutions of the [Manchu] ancestors. In fact, they are the products of the fancy writing and corrupt dealing of petty officials rather than the original ideas of the ancestors. Furthermore, institutions are for the purpose of preserving one's territories. Now that the ancestral territory cannot be preserved, what good is it to maintain the ancestral institutions? . . .

Although there is a desire to reform, yet if the national policy is not fixed and public opinion not united, it will be impossible for us to give up the old and adopt the new. The national policy is to the state just as the rudder is to the boat or the pointer is to the compass. It determines the direction of the state and shapes the public opinion of the country.

Nowadays the court has been undertaking some reforms, but the action of the emperor is obstructed by the ministers, and the recommendations of the able scholars are attacked by old-fashioned bureaucrats. If the charge is not "using barbarian ways to change China", then it is "upsetting the ancestral institutions". Rumours and scandals are rampant, and people fight each other like fire and water. To reform in this way is as ineffective as attempting a forward march by walking backward. It will inevitably result in failure. Your Majesty knows that under the present circumstances reforms are imperative and old institutions must be abolished. I beg Your Majesty to make up your mind and to decide on the national policy. . . .

After studying ancient and modern institutions, Chinese and foreign, I have found that the institutions of the sage kings and three dynasties [Xia, Shang, and Zhou] were excellent, but that the ancient times were different from today. I hope Your Majesty will daily read Mencius[1] and follow his example of loving the people. The development of the Han, Tang, Song, and Ming dynasties may be learned, but it should be remembered that the age of universal unification is different from that of sovereign nations. I wish Your Majesty would study *Guanzi*[2] and follow his idea of managing the country. As to the republican governments of the United States and France and the constitutional governments of Britain and Germany, these countries are far away and their customs are different from ours. Their changes occurred a long time ago and can no longer be traced. Consequently I beg Your Majesty to adopt the purpose of Peter the Great of Russia as our purpose and to take the Meiji Reform of Japan as the model for our reform. The time and place of Japan's reform are not remote and her religion and customs are somewhat similar to ours. Her success is manifest; her example can be easily followed.

Notes

1. Mencius lived during the fourth century BCE. His interpretations of the writings of Confucius are considered, by many, to be definitive.
2. Guanzi [Guan Zhong] (~725–645 BCE) was a minister in the State of Qi who successfully carried out a number of reforms to the administrative and economic structure of the state. Guanzi advocated rigid control over the population (legalism).

> **Study Question**
>
> Why does Kang reject the governments of the West as a suitable model for China?

Wu Tingfang

Wu Tingfang (1842–1922) served in the diplomatic corps of the late Qing dynasty. He held posts in the United States, Spain, Mexico, Peru, and Cuba. In 1914 Wu wrote America through the Spectacles of an Oriental Diplomat. *Prior to his diplomatic work he had been a lawyer and journalist. After the 1911 Revolution Wu became minister of foreign affairs and minister of justice in the provisional republican government. The following speech, which reflects favourably on the reforms achieved during the latter years of the Qing dynasty, was given in New York City on 5 May 1908.*

Document Source: Wu Tingfang, "The Awakening of China: An Address Delivered before the Civic Forum in Carnegie Hall, New York City, 5 May 1908" (New York: The Civic Forum, 1908), 3–13.

The Awakening of China

The mere mentioning of this subject—"The Awakening of China"—is sufficient to make my countrymen thrill with pleasure and flush with pride. China, the country which made the dying Missionary, the famous Xavier,[1] exclaim in 1552, "O Rock, Rock, when wilt thou open?" is at last, indeed, opened, and changes are taking place in that hoary Empire, which bid fair to constitute the miracle of the Twentieth Century.

China has been dubbed "The Sick Man of the Far East," "The Sleeping Lion," "The Tottering Empire"; and other names more or less picturesque and complimentary have been bestowed upon her. With some people it is the conviction that China has only a historical interest, that her glory is of the past, that the leopard may change its spots, but China remains forever in her ruts, the same yesterday, to-day, and to-morrow.

But while this gloomy picture of the state of affairs might have been partly true of China of a few decades ago, it is no longer true now. The "Sick Man" is rapidly convalescing, the "Sleeping Lion" is awake, and the hoary and tottering Empire has had new blood injected into her system. China is moving, and she is moving with a rapidity difficult for one who has not personally witnessed the wonderful changes to understand and realize. . . .

First and foremost, is the spread of education—and by this I mean the diffusion of general knowledge, knowledge of men, and of affairs of the world. It is a far cry from the time when high officials in Peking, to whom the wonderful performance of the Morse telegraph apparatus was shown and explained, expressed simply their opinion that China got along without it for four thousand years; to the present day when every official residence and department in Peking is connected by the telephone and every provincial yamen, or administrative office, is supplied with the telegraph service.

Repeated defeats at the hand of the foreign powers soon convinced our people of the futility of matching bows and arrows against modern guns and explosives, while our wooden junks went down before the onslaught of armored cruisers and battleships like wheat before the scythe. The inability of our former so-called modern army and navy to encounter those of other nations demonstrated to us clearly that modern weapons of war without the properly trained men to handle them and without scientific leaders to direct and control are of no more

Wu Tingfang during his tenure as a Qing diplomat, photographed in New York City.

value than bows and arrows and wooden junks. . . .

Students poured into foreign countries by the hundreds, and particularly those that went to Japan devoted a large part of their time to the editing of magazines and the translation of books, a veritable flood of literature thus pouring back to their fatherland, and reaching every nook and corner of the Empire. Some of this literature, flowing from the pens of young men flushed with the new learning and burning with patriotism, was naturally somewhat violent in tone and made sensational reading, but it produced its effect on our people who needed something unusual to wake them out of their lethargy.

Nor must I omit to mention the services of the missionary body, particularly the American branch of it, whose indefatigable efforts in the establishment of educational institutions and in the diffusion of literature of general knowledge, formed a part of the leaven which has leavened the whole Empire of China. The onward movement derived great impetus and received much encouragement from the successes of our island neighbor, Japan. The cry was that what Japan could do, China by adopting similar reforms and taking similar steps can and will do. . . .

The anxiety of young men and women to acquire a modern education in schools at home and abroad, and the joyful sacrifice on the part of parents and elders of luxuries and comforts, to which they have been accustomed for years, in order that the younger generation may receive a liberal education, costing ten or twenty times more than the old method, affords a sight unparalleled in our history. Female education, very much neglected in the past, is recognized as work of the first importance, and the position of women is approaching, though at present slowly, the ideal of that in the west.

A movement of striking significance, on account of the remarkable success it has met, is that started by the Anti-Foot-Binding Society. Foot-binding, originally only intended to check the feet of young women from attaining abnormal and disfiguring size, grew into a most horrible custom,

through the perverted ideas of beauty, until it became the exception rather than the rule for women to possess a pair of natural feet. I could never bring myself to see the beauty of human feet, compressed and arbitrarily shaped by artificial means, and from my boyhood I always expressed my strong condemnation of the absurd fashion. I remember I agitated in my early days the question by exposing the absurdity and cruelty of the practice, and with a view of its gradual discontinuance I endeavored to persuade my friends and relatives to join with me in forming a league pledging ourselves to prohibit the compression of our daughters' feet. But to my dismay I could not induce anyone to become a member of my proposed association. It was, therefore, with genuine pleasure and agreeable surprise that some years ago I learned that an anti-foot-binding society was organized by a few foreign ladies, whose object was to accomplish the same thing that I had previously aimed to do. Through the instrumentality of public meetings, pamphlets and leaflets, which were supported by official proclamations and Imperial decrees, the people in a short time have been awakened to the folly and injuriousness of the custom and the appeal has met with a response that must be gratifying to all the people who would hold their bodies as sacred. Today, one walks the streets of the larger cities and hardly ever sees a girl of ten or under with bound feet, and ladies of middle age, whose extremities have been cramped for a score of years, deem it their patriotic duty to liberate themselves from their bondage. Recently the work of the committee of that society has been handed over to a group of prominent Chinese gentlemen, who, it was believed, could better advance the interests of the society now that it has passed its period of infancy.

Another popular movement, which has given great joy to all friends and well-wishers of China, has been the efforts for the suppression of opium. No event in China has given more and better evidence of the hopeful vitality and the solid moral character of our people than the enthusiastic and energetic manner in which the vice of opium smoking is being attacked. On the part of the Government, the highest officials in Peking have been suspended from office for not curing themselves of the habit, creating a sensation in mandarindom.[2] Decrees and proclamations have been issued commanding an annual decrease in the cultivation of the poppy, the closing of public opium dens, the registration of smokers, and other measures which will result in the wiping out of the national curse in eight or ten years. Only a few days ago, I received by cable two Imperial Decrees issued on the 7th and 10th of last month which strengthen the growing conviction that my Government is thoroughly in earnest in its efforts to suppress the opium habit. By the first decree Prince Kung and three other high officials in Peking have been appointed members of an Imperial Commission whose duty is to find out and to see that all officials addicted to the use of the drug in Peking and in all the provinces are cured of the habit, and that in case any opium-smoking official should be discovered, he and his superior for failing to report the same should be both punished. The second commands that all the members of the diplomatic and consular corps abroad must give up their noxious habit at once, while those too old in age or too inveterate in the use of the drug to do so must retire from the service. Our people in foreign countries are also urged to exert themselves in putting an end to the use of opium. But the more encouraging feature is the attitude of the people towards the opium question. A few years ago, opium smoking was no more condemned than cigars or cigarettes, and it was the fashion for giddy youths to sleep and eat with the deadly drug. Today an opium smoker confesses his habit with shame, and all society regards him as more or less an outcast. And it is this healthful change in public opinion that will liberate my country from the chain of the opium devil. At the recent closing of the opium dens in the important cities, the students turned out *en masse*, with their flags and banners and musical instruments, celebrating the occasion as if it were a victory in war, and so earnest were the people in their efforts to suppress the evil that the very keepers of the dens themselves gathered together their vile instruments of smoking and made a huge bonfire of them. . . .

What does this awakening of China mean to the world? To my mind, it means, in the first place, true and lasting peace in the Far East. The moment China becomes strong enough after her awakening to maintain her sovereign rights and protect herself from aggression, the Far Eastern question will have been solved. Again, the awakening of China means the development of commerce, and the day is not distant when the Pacific Ocean will rival the Atlantic with the number of ships that sail on its surface. The world will then witness an expansion of trade never before known in its history, and this trade will also be a safeguard in the interests of universal peace.

Notes

1. St Francis Xavier (1506–1552).
2. The traditionally powerful scholarly elite, schooled in the teachings of Confucius.

Study Question

What does Wu believe to be the most important signs of China's awakening?

Web Resources

Internet Modern History Sourcebook: The Long Nineteenth Century
        http://www.fordham.edu/halsall/mod/modsbook3.html
Perry-Castañeda Library Map Collection
        http://www.lib.utexas.edu/maps

Internet East Asian History Sourcebook
   http://www.fordham.edu/halsall/eastasia/eastasiasbook.html
The Middle East Network Information Center
   http://library.csusm.edu/subject_guides/history/online_primary.asp

Recommended Reading

Arthur Conan Doyle, *The Lost World* (New York: Tor Classics, 1997). *The Lost World* remains a classic adventure story. Many of the attitudes that drove British imperialism are captured: the excitement of discovery, love of adventure, and scientific curiosity, as well as the less noble attitudes towards indigenous populations.

Lafcadio Hearn (Koizumi Yakumo), *Kokoro: Hints & Echoes of Japanese Inner Life* (New York: Routledge, 2002). This collection of essays from Hearn, a European-born naturalized citizen of Japan, reflects on the inner workings of Japanese society during the pivotal encounter between traditional Japan and the rapid modernization of the Meiji Era. Hearn attempts to capture the essential elements of Japanese culture that seemed to be disappearing.

Eric Liu, *The Travels of Lao Can* (Honolulu, HI: University Press of the Pacific, 2001). Set in the latter years of the Qing dynasty, Liu's novel considers the possibility of political reform through a radical revision of Confucian values. Condemning the decadence of the late-Qing era, the author examines the conflict between traditional China and its Confucian values, and the forces of modernization.

Junichiro Tanizaki, *Some Prefer Nettles* (New York: Vintage, 1995). Tanizaki's *Some Prefer Nettles*, written in 1928, examines the conflict between traditional and modern Japanese culture during the Meiji era. The cities of Tokyo and Osaka appear as contrasting symbols of modern and traditional Japan. As Tanizaki himself had done, the novel's main character eventually abandons the modern world.

Recommended Viewing

Empress Dowager (Hong Kong, 1975). Director: Li Han-hsiang. Against the backdrop of late Qing China and the instabilities caused by foreign intervention, Westernization, and internal unrest, Li Han-hsiang dramatizes the life of the Empress Dowager Cixi, and the machinations that installed and maintained her position of power.

The Opium War (China, 1997). Director: Xie Jin. Xie Jin's film begins in 1838 with the first large-scale importation of opium into China. The film provides a balanced look at the events that resulted in the humiliating Treaty of Nanjing, including the reaction of Commissioner Lin and the attitudes of British officials.

Age of Hope (UK/USA, 1999). Director: Jonathan Lewis/WGBH Boston/BBC (Documentary). *Age of Hope* opens with the 1900 Paris Exposition and examines the sources of both turn-of-the-century optimism and disillusionment. Interviews and contemporary film footage create a fascinating narrative.

The Last Samurai (USA, 2003). Director: Edward Zwick. Set in late-nineteenth-century Japan, the film portrays the struggle between Meiji reformers, who wanted to create a modern conscript army, and the Samurai, who attempted to preserve the old order. The film is not historically accurate, but it does capture some of the conflict within Japanese society regarding the turn towards western models.

2

Global Capitalism and Imperialism

In the early part of the twentieth century the British Empire ruled over some 400 million people. This was by far the greatest proportion of the almost 80 per cent of the world that found itself under direct or indirect colonial control. However, France, Germany, Portugal, Belgium, the Ottoman Turks, and Japan also dominated substantial territories. Additionally, the United States had asserted, through the 1823 Monroe Doctrine and the 1904 Roosevelt Corollary, its right to influence political and economic developments throughout the Americas. This "informal" influence would lay the foundations for American neo-colonialism in Central and South America throughout the twentieth century. On rare occasions, US ambitions led to formal colonial involvement, as in the case of the Philippines.

Around the world resistance to the attitudes and consequences of colonial control was quick to form. In India, members of the Indian National Congress condemned the economic and social consequences of colonial control. Writers such as W.E.B. Du Bois drew attention to the fate of the black population around the world, calling for a cooperative effort to achieve liberation, and Vladimir Lenin denounced imperialism as the last gasp of global capitalism. The success or failure of these early efforts to break the hold of global imperialism very often depended upon the attitude and policies of the colonial power.

This chapter considers a broad range of opinions on global imperialism. Both Jules Ferry and the Earl of Cromer defend the need for European control over foreign territory. E.D. Morel, in contrast, decries the brutality and inhumanity of Belgian occupation of the Congo, while B.G. Tilak offers a persuasive argument against British rule in India and proposes the boycott as an effective weapon in the fight to regain indigenous control. Documents on the Amritsar Massacre reveal the degree to which some in the British administration would go to retain their power over colonized peoples. W.E.B. Du Bois points to the emerging pan-African movement as the key to freedom for the black peoples of the world. Emilio Aguinaldo pleads for the US to resist the lure of colonial power and to grant full independence to the Philippines in the wake of the Spanish-American War. Turning to neo-colonialism, Brazilian historian Caio Prado Júnior explains the vulnerability of the cash-crop economies of South America. Finally, Lenin's assessment of imperialism as "the highest stage of capitalism" offers an important explanation for the rapid rise of the colonial empires of the late nineteenth century.

Colonial Occupation

- Independent
- Belgium
- France
- Germany
- Great Britain
- Italy
- Portugal
- Spain

Africa at the height of colonial control. Note the vast size of the territories controlled by France and Great Britain.

Jules Ferry

Jules Ferry (1832–1893) served as minister of instruction, minister of foreign affairs, and was twice premier of France (1880–1, 1883–5). During his tenure he mandated that secular education be provided at the primary level at no charge, and barred members of Catholic orders from serving as public school teachers. Believing that France required a powerful colonial empire, Ferry oversaw the occupation of Tunis, Tonkin, and Madagascar, and ordered French expansion into both the Niger region and the Congo. Ferry was assassinated in 1893. In the following address before the French Chamber of Deputies in July 1885 Ferry defended colonialism on

political, economic, and moral grounds.

Document Source: Paul Robiquet, ed., *Discours et Opinions de Jules Ferry*, Vol. 5. (Paris: Armand Colin & Cie., 1897), 199–218.

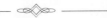

Speech Before the French Chamber of Deputies

I offer for your consideration namely that, in fact, as we say, the policy of colonial expansion is a political and economic system; I said that it could be connected to three sets of ideas: economic ideas; the most far-reaching ideas of civilization; and ideas of a political and patriotic sort.

In the area of economics, permit me to place before you, with the support of some statistics, the considerations that justify the policy of colonial expansion, as seen from the perspective of a need, felt more and more urgently by the industrialized population of Europe and especially the people of our rich and hardworking country of France: the need for outlets. Is this a fantasy? Is this a concern of the future? Or is this not a pressing need, one may say a crying need, of our industrial population? I merely express in a general way what each one of you can see for himself in the various parts of France. Yes, that which our major industries, irrevocably steered by the treaties of 1860 into exports, lack more and more are outlets. Why? Because next door Germany is setting up trade barriers; because across the ocean the United States of America have become protectionists, and extreme protectionists at that; because not only are these great markets—I won't say closed—but they are shrinking, becoming more and more difficult to access, but these great states are beginning to pour into our own markets products not seen there before. This is not only a reality for our agriculture, which has been so cruelly tried, and for which competition is no longer limited to the circle of large European states. . . . Today, one cannot ignore competition, the law of supply and demand, freedom of trade, the effects of speculation, all of these radiate in a circle that

reaches to the ends of the earth. (*Bravo! Bravo!*) That is a great complication, a great economic difficulty; . . . an extremely grave problem. It is so serious, gentlemen, so acute, that the least informed persons must already glimpse, foresee, and take precautions against the time when the great South American market that has, in a manner of speaking, belonged to us forever will be disputed and perhaps taken away from us by North American products. Nothing is more serious; there is no social problem more grave; and these matters are linked intimately to colonial policy. I do not need to push this demonstration further. . . .

It is certain that there is in Germany, a great movement in colonial policy, and this preoccupation with seizing, with taking possession of all that remains of African territory, is a response to something, to a need, to a policy, to a necessity. This German colonial policy should strike you, as it strikes me; when I consider that this German empire which was, until recently, an exclusively continental power, and, further, a careful government, not adventurist for some fifteen years. Well, when I see Germany embark on this colonial policy, I wonder as to the reason . . . .

I repeat, that it is a right for the superior races, because they have a duty. They have the duty to civilize the inferior races (*Accolades from the benches on the left—New interruptions from the extreme-left and the right*). . . .

In the history of earlier centuries these duties, gentlemen, have often been misunderstood; and certainly when the Spanish soldiers and explorers introduced slavery into Central America, they did not fulfill their duty as men of a higher

Contract labourers in Saigon. Ferry's outspoken advocacy of colonialism led the French to consolidate their hold on Indochina and its resources.

Frank and Frances Carpenter Collection. Courtesy of the Library of Congress, Prints and Photographs Division (LC-USZ62-120614).

race. (*Bravo! Bravo!*) But, in our time, I maintain that European nations acquit themselves with generosity, with grandeur, and with sincerity of this superior civilizing duty.

I say that French colonial policy, the policy of colonial expansion, the policy that has taken us under the Empire, to Saigon, to Cochinchina [French Indochina], that has led us to Tunisia, that has brought us to Madagascar—I say that this policy of colonial expansion was inspired by a truth that I need to call to your attention for a moment: the fact that a navy such as ours cannot do without safe harbours, defences, supply centres on the high seas. (*Bravo! Bravo! and considerable*

applause from the left and the centre) Are you unaware of this? Look at a map of the world. . . .

Gentlemen, these are considerations that merit the full attention of patriots. The conditions of naval warfare have greatly changed. (*Bravo! Bravo!*)

At present, as you know, a warship, however perfect its design, cannot carry more than two weeks' supply of coal; and a vessel without coal is a wreck on the high seas, abandoned to the first occupier. Hence the need to have places of supply, shelters, ports for defence and provisioning. (*Applause from the centre and the left—many interruptions*) And that is why we needed Tunisia; that is why we needed Saigon and Indochina;

that is why we need Madagascar, and why we are at Diego Suarez and Volemar, and why we shall never leave them! (*Applause from a great many of the benches*) Gentlemen, in Europe such as it is today, in this competition of the many rivals we see rising up around us, some by military or naval improvements, others by the prodigious development of a constantly growing population; in a Europe, or rather in a universe thus constituted, a policy of withdrawal or abstention is simply the high road to decadence! In our time nations are great only through the activity they deploy; it is not by spreading the peaceable light of their institutions . . . (*Interruptions from the extreme-left and to the right*) that they are great, in the present day.

Spreading light without acting, without taking part in the affairs of the world, keeping out of all European alliances and seeing as a trap, an adventure, all expansion into Africa or the Orient—for a great nation to live this way, believe me, is to abdicate and, in less time than you may think, to sink from the first rank to the third and fourth. . . .

Study Question

Why did Ferry believe that every nation needed to take part in the scramble for colonies or risk falling irrevocably behind?

Evelyn Baring, Earl of Cromer

Evelyn Baring, 1st Earl of Cromer (1841–1917), was a diplomat who served as controller-general in Egypt during the period in which the British established control over the weak Egyptian monarchy. Baring believed that British rule would bring Egypt into a new era of modernization and progress, whereas a victory by Arab forces would have plunged the country into an "age of ignorance." The following excerpt was taken from Baring's 1908 history of modern Egypt, which was written after he was dismissed from the Egyptian administration.

Document Source: The Earl of Cromer, *Modern Egypt*, Vol. I (London: Macmillan & Co., Ltd., 1908), 324–30.

British Rule in Egypt

It is always a somewhat unprofitable proceeding to speculate on what might have been in politics, but I cannot close this portion of the narrative without hazarding conjecture as to whether any foreign occupation of Egypt could have been avoided. Mistakes were, without doubt, committed. The true nature of the Arábi revolt[1] was misunderstood. It was more than a mere military mutiny. It partook in some degree of the nature of a bona fide national movement. . . . It was, in a great degree, a movement of the Egyptians against Turkish rule. . . . I ask myself, where were the elements for the formation of any stable government to have been found when, in pursuance of the policy of "Egypt for the Egyptians," there had been eliminated, as would probably have been the case, first, the Europeans, with all their intelligence, wealth, and governing power; secondly, the Khedive in whose place some illiterate Egyptian, of the type of Arábi or Mahmoud Sami, would have been appointed; thirdly, the Syrians and Armenians, with all their industry and capacity for sedentary employment; fourthly, the native aristocracy, largely composed of Turks, who were at that time the principal large landowners in the country, and amongst whom, in spite of many defects, the habits and traditions of a governing class still lingered; when, in fact, the nationalists and mutineers had got rid of all the classes, who then governed, and who for

The Suez Canal in 1898. Within a few years of the canal's opening in 1869 it became a vital shipping link for European and American interests.

Courtesy of the Library of Congress, Prints and Photographs Division (LC-USZ62-103002).

several centuries had governed the country? The residue would have consisted, first, of the mass of the fellaheen population who were sunk in the deepest ignorance. . .; secondly, of a certain number of small proprietors, village Sheikhs, Omdehs, etc., who constituted the squirearchy of the country, and who, in point of knowledge and governing capacity, were but little removed from the fellaheen; thirdly, of the Copts, whose religion would certainly, sooner or later, have prevented them from acting in complete harmony with the Arábists, and who, even if tolerated by the Mohammedan population, could neither have obtained any influence over the Mohammedans, nor, even if that influence had been obtained could have used it to the general advantage of the country; fourthly, of the hierarchy, consisting principally of the Ulema of the El-Azhar Mosque. . . . They would have been the Jacobins of the movement, which, whether nationalist or military, would certainly have been reactionary in so far as it would have tended to destroy whatever germs of civilisation had been implanted into Egypt. . . . An attempt would have been made to regulate, not only the government, but also the social life of the country upon those principles of the Mohammedan faith which are most antiquated, obsolete, and opposed to the commonplace ideas of modern civilisation.

Egypt may now almost be said to form part of Europe. It is on the high road to the Far East. It can never cease to be an object of interest to all the powers of Europe, and especially to England. A numerous and intelligent body of Europeans and of non-Egyptian Orientals have made Egypt their home. European capital to a large extent has been sunk in the country. The rights and privileges of Europeans are jealously guarded, and, moreover, give rise to complicated questions, which it requires no small amount of ingenuity and technical knowledge to solve. Exotic institutions have sprung up and have taken root in the country. . . . The population is heterogeneous and cosmopolitan to a degree almost unknown elsewhere. Although the prevailing faith is that of Islam, in no country in the world is a greater variety of religious creeds to be found amongst important sections of the community. . . .

Is it probable that a government composed of the rude elements described above, and led by men of such poor ability as Arábi and his coadjutors, would have been able to control a complicated machine of this nature? Were the Sheikhs of the El-Azhar Mosque likely to succeed where Tewfik Pasha and his Ministers, who were men of comparative education and enlightenment, acting under the guidance and inspiration of a first-class

European power, only met with a modified success after years of patient labour? There can be but one answer to these questions. . . . Neither is it in the nature of things that any similar movement should, under the present conditions of Egyptian society, meet with any better success. The full and immediate execution of a policy of "Egypt for the Egyptians," as it was conceived by the Arábists in 1882, was, and still is, impossible.

History, indeed, records some very radical changes in the forms of government to which a State has been subjected without its interests being absolutely and permanently shipwrecked. But it may be doubted whether any instance can be quoted of a sudden transfer of power in any civilised or semi-civilised community to a class so ignorant as the pure Egyptians, such as they were in the year 1882. These latter have, for centuries past, been a subject race. Persians, Greeks, Romans, Arabs from Arabia and Baghdad, Circassians, and finally, Ottoman Turks, have successively ruled over Egypt, but we have to go back to the doubtful and obscure precedents of Pharaonic times to find an epoch when, possibly, Egypt was ruled by Egyptians. Neither, for the present, do they appear to possess the qualities which would render it desirable, either in their own interests, or in those of the civilised world in general, to raise them at a bound to the category of autonomous rulers with full rights of internal sovereignty.

If, however, a foreign occupation was inevitable or nearly inevitable, it remains to be considered whether a British occupation was preferable to any other. From the purely Egyptian point of view, the answer to this question cannot be doubtful. The intervention of any European power was preferable to that of Turkey. The intervention of one European power was preferable to international intervention. The special aptitude shown by Englishmen in the government of Oriental races pointed to England as the most effective and beneficent instrument for the gradual introduction of European civilization into Egypt. . . .

By the process of exhausting all other expedients, we arrive at the conclusion that armed British intervention was, under the special circumstances of the case, the only possible solution of the difficulties which existed in 1882. Probably also it was the best solution. The arguments against British intervention, indeed, were sufficiently obvious. It was easy to foresee that, with a British garrison in Egypt, it would be difficult that the relations of England either with France or Turkey should be cordial. With France, especially, there would be a danger that our relations might become seriously strained. Moreover, we lost the advantages of our insular position. The occupation of Egypt necessarily dragged England to a certain extent within the arena of Continental politics. . . .

There can be no doubt of the force of these arguments. The answer to them is that it was impossible for Great Britain to allow the troops of any other European Power to occupy Egypt. When it became apparent that some foreign occupation was necessary, that the Sultan would not act save under conditions which were impossible of acceptance, and that neither French nor Italian cooperation could be secured, the British government acted with promptitude and vigour. A great nation cannot throw off the responsibilities which its past history and its position in the world have imposed upon it. English history affords other examples of the government and people of England drifting by accident into doing what was not only right, but was also most in accordance with British interests.

Note

1. Modern transliteration: Ahmed Orabi (Egyptian)/Ahmed Urabi, leader of a revolt against foreign control in Egypt.

Study Question

Baring claims that "Egypt for the Egyptians" was an impossible goal. Based on this document, what were the main obstacles to this aim (apart from the British presence)?

Edmund Dene (E.D.) Morel

*E.D Morel (1873–1924) was a French-born natur-
alized British citizen. While working for a shipping
company in Liverpool he became aware of the enormous quantities of rubber and ivory being extracted
from Congo. Concluding that only a criminal level of
exploitation could produce such enormous returns,
Morel set out to publicize the conditions in Leopold's
Congolese territory. When newspapers refused to publish his meticulously documented accounts, he founded*
*his own paper in 1903, the West African Mail. Morel's
activism led to the establishment of a formal enquiry
into the conditions in Congo, and, ultimately, to the
transfer of control over Congo from King Leopold to
the Belgian Government. The following excerpt was
published in 1904 in a lengthy monograph detailing
the effects of Leopold's rule in Congo.*

Document Source: Edmund Dene Morel, *King Leopold's Rule in Africa*
(London: William Heinemann, 1904), 242–8.

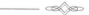

King Leopold's Rule in Africa

But depopulation, after all, is only an outward and
visible sign of inward causes. What a sum total
of human wretchedness does not lie behind that
bald word "depopulation"! To my mind, the horror of this curse which has come upon the Congo
peoples reaches its maximum of intensity when
we force ourselves to consider its everyday con-
comitants; . . . the gradual elimination of everything in the daily life of the natives which makes
that life worth living. Under the prevailing system, every village is a penal settlement. Armed
soldiers are quartered in every hamlet; the men
pass nearly the whole of their lives in satisfying
the ceaseless demands of the "Administration," or
its affiliates the Trusts; whether it be in the collection of rubber, of gum-copal, of food-stuffs,
or forced labour in Government plantations, or
in the construction of those "fine brick houses"
on which the apologists of the State are for ever
harping. Women and children do not enjoy as
much protection as a dog in this country. They
are imprisoned, flogged, left at the mercy of the
soldiery, taxed beyond endurance, regarded as
lower than the beasts. Native industries die out.

Intercommunication between native communities
ceases. The people who are taxed in what may be
termed sedentary taxation can never leave their
homes, where they reside under the vigilant eye
of a sentry, loaded rifle or cap-gun in hand, the
real king of the village, omnipotent and insolent. Monstrous fines are inflicted for the slightest shortage in taxes, and punishments varying in
degree from murder and mutilation to the chain-
gang, the "houses of hostages," and the *chicotte*.[1]
. . . Floggings are perpetual; for insufficient supplies of rubber; for inadequate supplies of food;
as a punishment for lack of activity or ability in
forced labour; on the most trivial pretexts, sparing
neither age nor sex. . . . It is one unending, heart-
rending story of odious brutality from first to last.

Chiefs are shamelessly degraded in the eyes
of their people; made to fetch and carry for the
soldiers; cast in the chains, and flogged for re-
missness in village taxes; flung into the "prisons"
often to die of neglect, ill-treatment, and starvation; forced to the commitment of unspeakable
bestialities[2] by their "moral and material" re-
generators. . . .

The European defenders of the conception of tropical African "development" which the Sovereign of the Congo State has so logically and ruthlessly carried out, allege that in his natural condition, the native of tropical Africa is content to smoke and drink all day, while his wife labours. It is either grossly exaggerated, or totally untrue; but even were it true to the very letter, then the male African is an angel of light by comparison with those who, on the Congo, profess (in Europe) to lead him into better ways. . . .

If this is not the slave trade, what is it? How much longer will the civilised world tolerate these things?

It would need a volume in itself to deal in a thorough manner with the exotic abominations introduced into the Congo territories under King Leopold's sway. One labours under the weight of well-nigh overpowering testimony. These short extracts I have quoted can give no adequate account of the full misery upon the peoples which such measures entail.

The cumulative effects of depopulation and infantile mortality by dragging women away from their homes for forced labour requisitions—seizing them as "hostages," and "tying them up," whether virgins, wives, mothers, or those about to become mothers, in order to bring pressure to bear upon brothers, husbands, and fathers for the adequate supply of rubber or food taxes; flinging them into "prison," together with their children, often to die of starvation and neglect; flogging them, sometimes even unto death; leaving them at the mercy of the soldiers; distributing them after punitive raids among hangers-on—must be enormous. There we have depopulation through the infamous torture of women—often enough shot outright or mutilated—and the neglect and mutilation of young children and boys; most of whom, it may be presumed, when so mutilated do not survive the operation, in order to have "the bad taste to show their stumps to the missionaries," as one of the Belgian deputies said in the course of the Congo debate in the Belgian House last year.

What has come over the civilised people of the globe that they can allow their Governments to remain inactive and apathetic in the face of incidents which recall in aggravated form the worst horrors of the overseas slave trade. . . .

Notes

1. A whip made of hippopotamus hide.
2. [Morel] The Chief Lisanginya, of Mbenga, was compelled to drink from the white man's latrine—Whitehead to Governor-General, Africa, No. I, 1904.

> **Study Question**
>
> In what ways would Congo's future be affected by the conditions which Morel describes under Belgian colonial rule?

Keshav Bal Gangadhar (B.G.) Tilak

B.G. Tilak (1856–1920) was a prominent Indian nationalist and a key member of the Indian National Congress. Tilak argued that British rule depended on the active cooperation of the Indian population; therefore, boycotts would cripple the ability of the British to maintain their hold. Branded an extremist by the British, Tilak was arrested in 1908 and imprisoned in Burma until 1914. He remained a lifelong advocate of Swaraj (home rule). The speech which follows was delivered in Calcutta in January 1907. Tilak contrasts his views with those of Dadabhai Naoroji (see Chapter One) and those of the so-called "moderates" in Congress.

Document Source: Bal Gangadhar Tilak, *His Writings and Speeches* (Madras: Ganesh, 1919), 54–6 and 63–7.

The Tenets of the New Party

Two new words have recently come into existence with regard to our politics, and they are *Moderates* and *Extremists*. These words have a specific relation to time, and they, therefore, will change with time. The Extremists of today will be Moderates tomorrow, just as the Moderates of today were Extremists yesterday. When the National Congress was first started and Mr Dadabhai's views, which now go for Moderates, were given to the public, he was styled an Extremist, so that you will see that the term Extremist is an expression of progress. We are Extremists today and our sons will call themselves Extremists and us Moderates. Every new party begins as Extremists and ends as Moderates. The sphere of practical politics is not unlimited. We cannot say what will or will not happen 1,000 years hence—perhaps during that long period, the whole of the white race will be swept away in another glacial period. We must, therefore, study the present and work out a program to meet the present condition.

It is impossible to go into details within the time at my disposal. One thing is granted, namely, that this government does not suit us. As has been said by an eminent statesman—the government of one country by another can never be a successful, and therefore, a permanent government. There is no difference of opinion about this fundamental proposition between the old and new schools. One fact is that this alien government has ruined the country. In the beginning, all of us were taken by surprise. We were almost dazed. We thought that everything that the rulers did was for our good and that this English government has descended from the clouds to save us from the invasions of Tamerlane and Chingis Khan, and, as they say, not only from foreign invasions but from internecine warfare, or the

internal or external invasions, as they call it. We felt happy for a time, but it soon came to light that the peace which was established in this country did this, as Mr Dadabhai has said in one place— that we were prevented from going at each other's throats, so that a foreigner might go at the throat of us all. *Pax Britannica* is being gradually realized in these days. It was an unhappy circumstance that it was not realized sooner. We believed in the "benevolent intentions of the government," but in politics there is no benevolence. Benevolence is used to sugar-coat the declarations of self-interest and we were in those days deceived by the apparent benevolent intentions under which rampant self-interest was concealed. That was our state then. But soon a change came over us. English education, growing poverty, and better familiarity with our rulers, opened our eyes and our leaders; especially, the venerable leader who presided over the recent Congress was the first to tell us that the drain from the country was ruining it, and if the drain was to continue, there was some great disaster awaiting us. . . .

We have come forward with a scheme which if you accept, shall better enable you to remedy this state of things than the scheme of the old school. Your industries are ruined utterly, ruined by foreign rule; your wealth is going out of the country and you are reduced to the lowest level which no human being can occupy. In this state of things, is there any other remedy by which you can help yourself? The remedy is not petitioning but boycott. We say prepare your forces, organize your power, and then go to work so that they cannot refuse you what you demand. A story in Mahabharata tells that Sri Krishna was sent to effect a compromise, but the Pandavas and Kauravas were both organizing their forces to meet the contingency of failure of the compromise. This is politics. Are you prepared in this way to fight if your demand is refused? If you are, be sure you will not be refused; but if you are not, nothing can be more certain than that your demand will be refused, and perhaps, for ever. We are not armed, and there is no necessity for arms either. We have a stronger weapon, a political weapon, in boycott. We have perceived one fact, that the whole of this administration, which is carried on by a handful of Englishmen, is carried on with our assistance. We are all in subordinate service. This whole government is carried on with our assistance and they try to keep us in ignorance of our power of cooperation between ourselves by which that which is in our own hands at present can be claimed by us and administered by us. The point is to have the entire control in our hands. I want to have the key of my house, and not merely one stranger turned out of it. Self-government is our goal; we want a control over our administrative machinery. We don't want to become clerks and remain [clerks]. At present, we are clerks and willing instruments of our own oppression in the hands of an alien government, and that government is ruling over us not by its innate strength but by keeping us in ignorance and blindness to the perception of this fact. Professor Seeley shares this view. Every Englishman knows that they are a mere handful in this country and it is the business of every one of them to befool you in believing that you are weak and they are strong. This is politics. We have been deceived by such policy so long. What the new party wants you to do is to realize the fact that your future rests entirely in your own hands. If you mean to be free, you can be free; if you do not mean to be free, you will fall and be for ever fallen. So many of you need not like arms; but if you have not the power of active resistance, have you not the power of self-denial and self-abstinence in such a way as not to assist

this foreign government to rule over you? This is boycott and this is what is meant when we say, boycott is a political weapon. We shall not give them assistance to collect revenue and keep peace. We shall not assist them in fighting beyond the frontiers or outside India with Indian blood and money. We shall not assist them in carrying on the administration of justice. We shall have our own courts, and when time comes we shall not pay taxes. Can you do that by your united efforts? If you can, you are free from tomorrow. Some gentlemen who spoke this evening referred to half bread as against the whole bread. I say I want the whole bread and that immediately. But if I can not get the whole, don't think that I have no patience.

I will take the half they give me and then try for the remainder. This is the line of thought and action in which you must train yourself. We have not raised this cry from a mere impulse. It is a reasoned impulse. Try to understand that reason and try to strengthen that impulse by your logical convictions. I do not ask you to blindly follow us. Think over the whole problem for yourselves. If you accept our advice, we feel sure we can achieve our salvation thereby. This is the advice of the new party. Perhaps we have not obtained a full recognition of our principles.

Old prejudices die very hard. Neither of us wanted to wreck the Congress, so we compromised, and were satisfied that our principles were recognized, and only to a certain extent. That does not mean that we have accepted the whole situation. We may have a step in advance next year, so that within a few years our principles will be recognized, and recognized to such an extent that the generations who come after us may consider us Moderates. This is the way in which a nation progresses, and this is the lesson you have to learn from the struggle now going on. This is a lesson of progress, a lesson of helping yourself as much as possible, and if you really perceive the force of it, if you are convinced by these arguments, then and then only is it possible for you to effect your salvation from the alien rule under which you labour at this moment.

Study Question

Why does Tilak believe that boycotts can be such a powerful weapon against British rule in India?

Accounts of the Amritsar (Jallianwala Bagh[1]) Massacre, 1919

In March 1919 the British Government in India passed the Rowlatt Acts, which gave the authorities a wide range of emergency powers to deal with anti-colonial protests. The net result for the Indian population was the loss of a number of hard-won civil rights, including the right to public assembly. In protest Mohandas Gandhi called for a general strike, a call that resonated most strongly in the Punjab, where nationalist leaders had already organized a powerful resistance movement to British rule. In Amritsar a

protest meeting was organized for 13 April, a meeting which would ultimately be attended by some 10,000 men, women, and children. Determined to put an end to such protests British General R.E.H. Dyer (1864–1927) decided to fire on the crowd. Most estimates put the final death toll at 379, with another 1,200 wounded. The documents that follow were written between April 1919 and January 1920.

Document Source: "Accounts of the Amritsar (Jallianwala Bagh) Massacre, 1919." © Embassy of India, Cairo, Egypt.

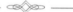

Amritsar Deputy Commissioner's Letter to the Commissioner of Lahore Division

The following letter was sent by Miles Irving, Deputy Commissioner of Amritsar, to A.J.W. Kitchin, Commissioner of the Lahore Division, on 8 April 1919, five days before the massacre, with an advance copy to Michael O'Dwyer, the Lt Governor of Punjab.

This account of the events of last Sunday (6th April) is for your information and that of Government.

It was in the evening about 5 p.m. at a cricket match, that it was suddenly announced by Dr Kitchlew, Dr Satyapal[2] and others that the hartal[3] should take place. It is said that this was a consequence of the belief that the meeting of Honorary Magistrates at my house had promised to stop the hartal, and was intended to show that they could

do nothing. But it is much more likely to have been simply due to Dr Kitchlew not wishing to give us too long a notice. Anyhow a secret meeting was called at Dr Satyapal's house, and by 9:10 a small party, swelled to 200 by sightseers, was going round the town proclaiming the hartal by beat of drum. After 2 a.m. notices were pasted to the same effect.

In the morning all shops were closed. I hear of no violence being offered, but there was the dumb threat of numbers, and the fear of being boycotted. . . .

As for the future in Amritsar, the first point I want to press urgently is the necessity for an increase in the military forces. It is absurd to attempt to hold Amritsar city with a company of

British infantry and half a company of Garrison Artillery. Any resolute action in the city would leave Civil Lines almost undefended. I know what the situation as regards British troops in India is, but another company would be of enormous value. And whether this can be supplied or not, I would earnestly press for a motor machine gun unit, *and some Lewis or Maxim or Vickers Maxim guns* [emphasis added]. We have at present only two machine guns one of which has a parapet mounting only. The problem of holding the railway as the line of defence would be greatly simplified by a machine gun on each bridge while armored motor cars are an ideal arm for so small a force covering an area so great. As it is, we must abandon nine-tenths of the city to a riot, holding only the kotwali [district] communications, and, even so, will be hard pressed to defend the station and Civil Lines.

Secondly, we cannot go indefinitely with the policy of keeping out of the way, and congratulating ourselves that the mob has not forced us to interfere. . . . I think that we shall by prohibiting some strike or procession that endangers the public peace. But for this a really strong force will have to be brought in and we shall have to be ready to try conclusions to the end to see who governs Amritsar. For this I should want a movable column from Lahore available at 6 hours' notice. . . .

General Dyer's Report on the Massacre

I fired and continued to fire till the crowd dispersed, and I considered that this is the least amount of firing which would produce the necessary moral and widespread effect, it was my duty to produce if I was to justify my action. If more troops had been at hand the casualties would have been greater in proportion. It was no longer a question of merely dispersing the crowd, but one of producing a sufficient moral effect from a military point of view, not only on those who were present, but more specially throughout the Punjab. There could be no question of undue severity. . . .

General Dyer's Statements Before the Hunter Committee[4]

The following questions and answers are from the enquiry conducted by the Hunter Commission (Disorders Enquiry Committee) appointed by the British Government; Dyer testified on 19 November, 1919.

Q: I think you had an opportunity to make up your mind while you were marching to decide what was the right course. You came to the conclusion that if there really was a meeting, the right thing for you would be to fire upon them straightaway?

A: I had made up my mind. . . .

Q: No question of having your forces attacked

entered into your consideration at all?

A: No. The situation was very, very serious. I had made up my mind that I will do all men to death if they were going to continue the meeting.

Q: Does it or does it not come to this: you thought that some striking act would be desirable to make people not only in Amritsar but elsewhere to consider their position more correctly?

A: Yes, I had to do something very strong.

Q: When you got into the Bagh, what did you do?

A: I opened fire.

Q: At once?

A: Immediately. I had thought about the matter, and I don't imagine it took me more than 30 seconds to make up my mind as to what my duty was.

Q: Did the crowd at once start to disperse as soon as you fired?

A: Immediately.

Q: Did you continue firing?

A: Yes.

Q: The crowds were making an effort to go away by some of the entrances at the farther end of the Bagh?

A: Yes.

Q: I take it that towards these exits the crowd was rather thick than at other places?

A: Yes.

Q: From time to time you changed your firing and directed it to places where the crowds were thickest?

A: That is so.

Q: Is that so?

A: Yes.

Q: And for the reasons you have explained to us you had made up your mind to open fire at the crowd.

A: Quite right.

Q: When you heard of the contemplated meeting at 12:40 you made up your mind that if the meeting was going to be held you would go and fire?

A: I had made up my mind that I would fire immediately in order to save the military situation. The time had come now when we should delay no longer. If I had delayed any longer, I was liable for court-martial.

Q: Supposing the passage was sufficient to allow the armored cars to go in, would you have opened fire with machine guns?

A: I think, probably, yes.

Q: In that case the casualties would have been very much higher?

A: Yes.

Q: I take it that your idea in taking the action (shooting in the Bagh) was to strike terror?

A: Call it what you like. I was going to punish them. My idea from the military point of view was to make a wide impression.

Q: To strike terror not only in the city of Amritsar but throughout the Punjab?

A: Yes, throughout the Punjab. I wanted to reduce their morale, the morale of the rebels.

Eye-Witness Account of the Massacre

Rattan Devi stated the following before the Congress Enquiry Committee.

I was in my house near the Jallianwala Bagh when I heard the shots fired. I was then lying down. I went as I was anxious because my husband had gone to the Bagh. I began to cry and went to the place accompanied by two women to help me. There I saw heaps of dead bodies and I began to search for my husband. After passing through that heap, I found the dead body of my husband. The way towards it was full of blood and of dead bodies. After a short time, both the sons of Lala Sundar Das came there and I asked them to bring a charpai (cot) to carry the dead body of my husband to home. The boys accordingly went home and sent away the two women also. By this time it was 8 o'clock and no one could stir out of his house because of the curfew order. I stood on, waiting and crying. At about 8:30 a Sikh gentleman came. There were others also who were looking for something amongst the dead. I did not know them. I entreated the Sikh gentleman to help me in removing my husband's body to a dry place, for that place was overflowing with blood. He caught the body by the head and I by the legs, and we carried it to a dry place and laid it down on a wooden block. I waited up to 10 p.m. but no one arrived there. I got up and started towards Ablowa Patra. I thought of asking some students from the Thakurdwara to help me in carrying my husband home. I had not gone far when some men sitting in a window in an adjacent house asked me where I was going at that late hour. I said I wanted some men to carry my husband's body and as it was past 8 p.m. nobody could help me then. . . . So, I went back and seated myself by the side of my dead husband. Accidentally I found a bamboo stick which I kept in my hand to keep off dogs. I saw three men writhing in agony, a buffalo struggling in great pain, and a boy about twelve years old in agony entreated me not to leave the place. I told him that I could not go anywhere leaving

the dead body of my husband. I asked him if he wanted any wrap, and if he was feeling cold, I could spread it over him. He asked for water, but water could not be procured at that place.

I heard the clock striking at regular intervals (of one hour) At 2 o'clock, a Jat belonging to Sultan village, who was lying entangled in a wall, asked me to go near him and to raise his leg. I got up and taking hold of his clothes drenched in blood raised his leg up. After that no one else came till half past five. At about six, L. Sundar Das, his sons, and some people from my street came there with a charpai and I brought my husband home. I saw other people at the Bagh, in search of their relatives. I passed my whole night there. It is impossible for me to describe what I felt. Heaps of dead bodies lay there, some on their backs, and some with their faces turned. A number of them were poor, innocent children. I shall never forget the sight. . . .

British Newspaper on Jallianwala Bagh Massacre

The following excerpts are from the comments made by the British newspaper Daily Herald *on the Jallianwala Bagh massacre, which were reproduced in the* Amrita Bazar Patrika *of 12 January 1920.*

The first detailed account of the April shootings at Amritsar, in the Punjab, shows it to have been one of the most bloody massacres of modern history.

Of the various stories of imperial oppression and the revolt against it by the subject races of the British Empire which we print today, the most amazing and stupefying in its naked horror is that of the massacre of Amritsar. The report of the evidence given by the General Dyer before the Committee of Investigation presided by Lord Hunter is not yet official, but it is so full and so well authenticated that no doubts have been cast upon its authenticity, so far as we know by any-one over here. According to the report of General

Dyer's evidence, over 400 Indians were killed and 1,500 wounded by the deliberate firing on a crowd of 5,000 who were listening to a speech.

No blacker or fouler story has ever been told. General Dyer is reported as admitting that the crowd might have gone away peacefully and without bloodshed, and that his motive for the slaughter was merely that the crowd would in that case have come back again and laughed, and he would have made a fool of himself!

According to his reported evidence, he admits that, with incredible indifference to human suffering, the British authorities left the wounded unattended in the streets. This, we presume, was done in order to teach men and women, of a different civilization and a different religion, what a beautiful and merciful thing Christianity is, and how sacred we British hold the law of Him who said that we were to love our enemies.

Notes

1. The Jallianwala Bagh [garden] had become a public meeting place during the war. It had a limited number of exits and Dyer's forces blocked at least one of the exits so the crowd was essentially trapped.
2. Dr Saifuddin Kitchlu and Dr Satya Pal were both members of the Congress Party and leaders in the nationalist movement.
3. A hartal is an extended demonstration, usually involving a general strike.

4. The findings of the Hunter Commission led to General Dyer being relieved of his command.

> **Study Question**
>
> In what ways would the events described in these documents contribute to the success of the Indian independence movement?

W.E.B. Du Bois

W.E.B. Du Bois (1868–1963) was an historian, sociologist, and activist. Widely travelled and highly educated— Du Bois received a Ph.D. from Harvard in 1895—he devoted his life to the study of the black population of the world. Du Bois was a founding member of the National Association for the Advancement of Colored People (NAACP) and a strong advocate of pan-Africanism as a means to achieve the freedom of all black peoples. Du Bois remained interested in socialist and communist movements throughout his life, but was first and foremost a black nationalist. The following excerpt from Du Bois' book The Negro *was published in 1915.*

Document Source: W.E.B. DuBois, *The Negro* (New York: Holt, 1915), 232–42.

The Negro

What is to be the future relation of the Negro race to the rest of the world? . . . Most persons have accepted that tacit but clear modern philosophy which assigns to the white race alone the hegemony of the world and assumes that other races, and particularly the Negro race, will either be content to serve the interests of the whites or die out before their all-conquering march. This philosophy is the child of the African slave trade and of the expansion of Europe during the nineteenth century.

The Negro slave trade was the first step in modern world commerce, followed by the modern theory of colonial expansion. Slaves as an article of commerce were shipped as long as the traffic paid. When the Americas had enough black laborers for their immediate demand, the moral action of the eighteenth century had a chance to make its faint voice heard. . . .

Finally European capital began to find better investments than slave shipping and flew to them. These better investments were the fruit of the new industrial revolution of the nineteenth century, with its factory system; they were also in part the result of the cheapened price of gold and silver, brought about by slavery and the slave trade to the new world. Commodities other than gold, and commodities capable of manufacture and exploitation in Europe out of materials furnishable by America, became enhanced in value; the bottom fell out of the commercial slave trade and its suppression became possible. . . .

As the emancipation of millions of dark workers took place in the West Indies, North and South America, and parts of Africa at this time, it was natural to assume that the uplift of this working class lay along the same paths with that of European and American whites. This was the *first* suggested solution of the Negro problem. Consequently these Negroes received partial enfranchisement, the beginnings of education, and some of the elementary rights of wage earners and property holders, while the independence of Liberia and Hayti [Haiti] was recognized. However, long before they were strong enough to assert the rights thus granted or to gather intelligence enough for proper group leadership, the new colonialism of the later nineteenth and twentieth centuries began to dawn. The new colonial theory transferred the reign of commercial privilege and extraordinary profit from the exploitation of the European working class to the exploitation of backward races under the political domination of Europe. For the purpose of carrying out this idea the European and white American working class was practically invited to share in this new exploitation, and particularly were flattered by popular appeals to their inherent superiority to "Dagoes," "Chinks," "Japs," and "Niggers."

This tendency was strengthened by the fact that the new colonial expansion centered in Africa. Thus in 1875 something less than one-tenth of Africa was under nominal European control, but the Franco-Prussian War and the exploration of the Congo led to new and fateful things. Germany desired economic expansion and, being shut out from America by the Monroe Doctrine, turned to Africa. France, humiliated in war, dreamed of an African empire from the Atlantic to the Red Sea. Italy became ambitious for Tripoli and Abyssinia. Great Britain began to take new interest in her African realm, but found herself largely checkmated by the jealousy of all Europe. Portugal sought to make good her ancient claim to the larger part of the whole southern peninsula. It was Leopold of Belgium who started to make the exploration and civilization of Africa an international movement. This project failed, and the Congo Free State became in time simply a Belgian colony. While the project was under discussion, the international scramble for Africa began. As a result the Berlin Conference and subsequent wars and treaties gave Great Britain control of 2,101,411 square miles of African territory, in addition to Egypt and the Egyptian Sudan with 1,600,000 square miles. This includes South Africa, Bechuanaland and Rhodesia, East Africa, Uganda and Zanzibar, Nigeria, and British West Africa. The French hold 4,106,950 square miles, including nearly all North Africa (except Tripoli) west of the Niger Valley and Libyan Desert, and touching the Atlantic at four points. To this is added the Island of Madagascar. The Germans have 910,150 square miles, principally in Southeast and South-west Africa and the Kamerun. The Portuguese retain 787,500 square miles in Southeast and Southwest Africa. The Belgians have 900,000 square miles, while Liberia (43,000 square miles) and Abyssinia (350,000 square miles) are independent. The Italians have about 600,000 square miles and the Spanish less than 100,000 square miles.

This partition of Africa brought revision of the ideas of Negro uplift. Why was it necessary, the European investors argued, to push a continent of black workers along the paths of social uplift by education, trades-unionism, property holding, and the electoral franchise when the workers desired no change, and the rate of European profit would suffer?

There quickly arose then the *second* suggestion for settling the Negro problem. It called for the virtual enslavement of natives in certain industries, as rubber and ivory collecting in the Belgian Congo, cocoa raising in Portuguese Angola, and diamond mining in South Africa. This new slavery or "forced" labor was stoutly defended as a necessary foundation for implanting modern industry in a barbarous land; but its likeness to slavery was too clear and it has been modified, but not wholly abolished. . . .

. . . the economic significance of the Negro today is tremendous. Black Africa to-day exports annually nearly two hundred million dollars worth of goods, and its economic development has scarcely begun. The black West Indies export nearly one hundred million dollars worth of goods; to this must be added the labor value of Negroes in South Africa, Egypt, the West Indies, North, Central, and South America, where the result is blended in the common output of many races. The economic foundation of the Negro problem can easily be seen to be a matter of many hundreds of millions to-day, and ready to rise to the billions tomorrow. . . .

What do Negroes themselves think of these their problems and the attitude of the world toward them? First and most significant, they are thinking. There is as yet no great single centralizing of thought or unification of opinion, but there are centers which are growing larger and larger and touching edges. The most significant centers of this new thinking are, perhaps naturally, outside Africa and in America: in the United States and in the West Indies; this is followed by South Africa and West Africa and then, more vaguely, by South America, with faint beginnings in East Central Africa, Nigeria, and the Sudan.

The pan-African movement when it comes will not, however, be merely a narrow racial propaganda. Already the more far-seeing Negroes sense the coming unities: a unity of the working classes everywhere, a unity of the colored races, a new unity of men. The proposed economic solution of the Negro problem in Africa and America has turned the thoughts of Negroes toward a realization of the fact that the modern white laborer of Europe and America has the key to the serfdom of black folk, in his support of militarism and colonial expansion. He is beginning to say to these working-men that, so long as black laborers are slaves, white laborers cannot be free. Already there are signs in South Africa and the United States of the beginning of understanding between the two classes.

In a conscious sense of unity among colored races there is to-day only a growing interest. There is slowly arising not only a curiously strong brotherhood of Negro blood throughout the world, but the common cause of the darker races against the intolerable assumptions and insults of Europeans has already found expression. Most men in this world are colored. A belief in humanity means a belief in colored men. The future world will, in all reasonable probability, be what colored men make it. In order for this colored world to come into its heritage, must the earth again be drenched in the blood of fighting, snarling human beasts, or will Reason and Good Will prevail? That such may be true, the character of the Negro race is the best and greatest hope; for in its normal condition it is at once the strongest and gentlest of the races of men: "Semper novi quid ex Africa!" [Everything new comes out of Africa—Pliny]

> **Study Question**
>
> What were the primary obstacles to the pan-African movement envisioned by Du Bois?

Emilio Aguinaldo y Famy

Emilio Aguinaldo (1869–1964) was active for much of his life in the struggle to gain independence for the Philippines—first from Spain and then from the United States. Though American officials had initially backed Aguinaldo's rebellion against the Spanish, ultimately the US chose to annex the Philippines outright in the treaty that concluded the Spanish-American War in December 1898. In the interim, Aguinaldo had declared the Philippines independent of foreign control on 12 June 1898, and by 1899, the Philippine-American War had begun. The document that follows was written on 23 September 1899, as hostilities between the two countries escalated.

Document Source: Don Emilio Aguinaldo y Famy, *True Version of the Philippine Revolution* (Tarlak, P.I.: 1899), 56–9.

Outbreak of Hostilities

Oh, dear Philippines! Blame your wealth, your beauty for the stupendous disgrace that rests upon your faithful sons.

You have aroused the ambition of the Imperialists and Expansionists of North America and both have placed their sharp claws upon your entrails!

Loved mother, sweet mother, we are here to defend your liberty and independence to the death! We do not want war; on the contrary, we wish for peace; but honourable peace, which does not make you blush nor stain your forehead with shame and confusions. And we swear to you and promise that while America with all her power and wealth could possibly vanquish us; killing all of us; but enslave us, never!!!

No; this humiliation is not the compact I celebrated in Singapore with the American Consul Pratt. This was not the agreement stipulated for with Mr Wildman, American Consul in Hongkong. Finally, it was not the subjection of my beloved country to a new alien yoke that Admiral Dewey promised me.[1]

It is certain that these three have abandoned me, forgetting that I was sought for and taken from my exile and deportation; forgetting, also, that neither of these three solicited my services in behalf of American Sovereignty, they paying the expense of the Philippine Revolution for which, manifestly, they sought me and brought me back to your beloved bosom!

If there is, as I believe, one God, the root and fountain of all justice and only eternal judge of international disputes, it will not take long, dear mother, to save you from the hands of your unjust enemies. So I trust in the honour of Admiral Dewey: So I trust in the rectitude of the great people of the United States of America, where, if there are ambitious Imperialists, there are defenders of the humane doctrines of the immortal Monroe, Franklin, and Washington; unless the race

of noble citizens, glorious founders of the present greatness of the North American Republic, have so degenerated that their benevolent influence has become subservient to the grasping ambition of the Expansionists, in which latter unfortunate circumstance would not death be preferable to bondage?

Oh, sensible American people! Deep is the admiration of all the Philippine people and of their untrained Army of the courage displayed by your Commanders and soldiers. We are weak in comparison with such Titanic instruments of your Government's ambitious Caesarian policy and find it difficult to effectively resist their courageous onslaught. Limited are our warlike resources, but we will continue this unjust, bloody, and unequal struggle, not for the love of war—which we abhor—but to defend our incontrovertible rights of Liberty and Independence (so dearly won in war with Spain) and our territory which is threatened by the ambitions of *a party* that is trying to subjugate us. . . .

Civilized nations! Honourable inhabitants of the United States, to whose high and estimable consideration I submit this unpretentious work, herein you have the providential facts which led to the unjust attack upon the existence of the Philippine Republic and the existence of those for whom, though unworthy, God made me the principal guardian.

The veracity of these facts rests upon my word as President of this Republic and on the honour of the whole population of eight million souls, who, for more than three hundred years have been sacrificing the lives and wealth of their brave sons to obtain due recognition of the natural rights of mankind—liberty and independence.

If you will do me the honour to receive and read this work and then pass judgment impartially solemnly declaring on which side right and justice rests, your respectful servant will be eternally grateful.

Note

1. Aguinaldo believed that both US consuls, Rounceville Wildman and E. Spencer Pratt, along with US Admiral George Dewey, had committed to support Philippine independence during the Spanish-American War.

Study Question

Does Aguinaldo make a convincing case regarding Philippine independence?

Caio Prado Júnior

Caio Prado Júnior (1907–1990) was a Marxist historian and geographer who lived through much of Brazil's twentieth century instability. He argued that the root of Brazil's development problems could be traced to the period of colonial control and the continuing hold of global capitalism. He was impressed with the Soviet Union of the 1930s, a belief that created conflict between Prado and the government of Getúlio Vargas. The following excerpt is taken from Prado's Economic History of Brazil *(1945).*

Document Source: Caio Prado Júnior, *História econômica do Brasil* (São Paulo: Editora Brasilense Ltda., 1945), 237–48.

The Coffee Cycle in Brazil

Coffee holds the first and sovereign place among all modern Brazilian products. In an earlier phase, under the Empire, we observed its ascendant progress, bringing under its sway the best and most important activities of the country. Now, under the Republic, we see it attaining the zenith of its grandiose course and establishing itself on a level that definitely puts in the shade all other Brazilian products. Even in absolute and world terms, coffee acquired an outstanding position. In the twentieth century it was, if not the first, at least among the first food products of international trade; and Brazil, with 70 per cent of the world's coffee production, enjoyed an undisputed supremacy. . . .

Another aspect of coffee production, much more important in its history, as well as in the evolution of the Brazilian economy in general, was its financial vicissitudes in the period that opened with the establishment of the Republic. If the large expansion of production brought the country wealth and progress, it also brought a problem of overproduction that began to plague

Men, women, and children picking coffee berries in Brazil in the early 1920s.

Frank and Frances Carpenter Collection. Courtesy of the Library of Congress, Prints and Photographs Division (LC-USZ62-104097).

Brazil's coffee economy only a few years after the start of its great cycle of growth and that has continued to the present day, with profound and varied repercussions on the general evolution of the Brazilian economy. I have already noted that the first signs of disequilibrium appeared in 1896. It was the result of the extensive plantings made during the first years of the Republic, and which now began to bear fruit (let us recall again that the coffee tree is a plant that begins production at the age of four or five years). At that time appeared the classic symptoms of overproduction: decline in prices, the formation of unsalable stocks. . . .

Commercial speculation intervened in this situation for its own benefit, and this was of great importance, not only in the particular sector of coffee production and commerce but in the economic and financial life of Brazil in general. Dependent as it was on its principal product, the Brazilian economy suffered all the vicissitudes through which coffee passed. I have already indicated how commercial speculation first intervened in the coffee industry in 1896.

From then on, its maneuvers largely conditioned the evolution of the coffee economy. Good harvests were utilized for the formation of reserves that dragged prices down or were doled out later, in years of poor harvests, at advantageous prices. The planters, compelled to dispose of their products without delay in order to pay the costs of production, lost the difference in price to the middlemen, who in the last analysis were large financial houses and international banks operating under cover. Maneuvers of this type were carried out even within the space of a single agricultural year. The coffee harvest in Brazil occupies the relatively short space of four months (May to August), when production flows to the ports, forcing a fall in prices. This is followed by a period of shortages of the product, when prices rise. The commercial middlemen would be buyers in the first phase, sellers in the

second. In this way they monopolized the major part of the profits of the business, to the detriment of the producers. . . .

. . . Brazil's weak national finances were inadequate for such a large-scale operation; an appeal for foreign credit was rejected by Brazil's bankers in Europe (the Rothschild House and group). Directly or indirectly, they were too closely tied to established interests to accept any modification of the existing order in the coffee business. Now there entered upon the scene other financial groups, who took advantage of the opportunity (it may even be that they had prepared that opportunity) to change in their favor the control of the coffee trade. First entered a great German exporting firm, Theodor Wille & Co. This marked the simultaneous entrance of German imperialism, which until that time had played only a modest role in Brazilian affairs. Behind Theodor Wille were aligned the principal financial groups of that country: the Discount Gesellschaft and the Dresden Bank. They were joined by English and French bankers who formed an opposition in their countries to the groups that had held Brazilian finances in their hands. They were J. Henry Schroder and Co. of London, and the Société Générale of Paris. The National City Bank of New York also joined this aggregation. It furnished São Paulo with the necessary means to implement the valorization plan, making credits available to the amount of 4,000,000 pounds.

In the face of this development, Rothschild, seeing that his previous refusal had been without effect and unwilling to remain on the outside and compromise his position, hastened to join the group. Through him São Paulo received 3,000,000 pounds more. The Bank of France, representing the established financial and commercial interests in the coffee business, refused to accept coffee warrants calculated on a basis higher than 40 francs a bag (the price reached by coffee at that time fluctuated around 50 francs);

in this way it hoped to neutralize the maneuvers of valorization.[1] At the same time the importing firms of Havre, the great French center of the coffee trade, unleashed a powerful campaign to discredit the loans being floated by Brazil in Europe.

But the battle was finally won by the "bulls." In order to consolidate the previous loans and carry the operation to a conclusion, fifteen more millions were obtained; intervention in the market continued until 1910, when, tension having eased and prices stabilized, the purchases were finally suspended. During the period 1906–10 nearly 8,500,000 bags had been withdrawn from the free market.

The financial interests involved in the operation thus won the contest. And it was they, much more than the producers in whose name the operation had been conducted, who reaped its best fruits. . . . While the financial agents of the valorization reaped large profits from the operation, the producers, though enjoying better and more stable prices for some years, later had to bear its entire burden. It was they who assumed the responsibility for the large debts contracted in order to execute the plan. For this purpose there was established a new tax of five gold francs per bag of coffee exported. This tax was used to pay the principal and interest of the debt, which even today, more than 30 years later . . . has not been entirely liquidated.

Note

1. Valorization is a Marxist concept that refers to the increase in the value of an asset when labour is applied to it.

Study Question

Is there any way to escape the cycle of debt once a country has become dependent on a single cash crop such as coffee?

V.I. Lenin

Vladimir Ilyich Ulyanov ("Lenin") was born in Simbirsk, Russia, in 1870. He died in January 1924 in Gorki, USSR. After the execution of his brother he was expelled from university for participating in radical student politics. By the 1890s he was studying Marxism in St Petersburg where he was arrested in 1895, tried, and exiled to Siberia until 1900. After 1900 Lenin was an active member of the Russian Social Democratic Labour Party (RSDLP), eventually leading the Bolshevik faction to break with the more moderate Mensheviks in 1903. In 1907 Lenin left Russia once more, this time for Finland. For the next ten years Lenin travelled throughout Europe meeting with various Social Democratic leaders and writing some of his most important theoretical works. The following commentary on imperialism was written between January and June 1916, and published in 1917.

Document Source: V.I. Lenin, *Collected Works*, volume twenty-two (Moscow: Progress Publishers, 1964), 185–204.

Imperialism, the Highest Stage of Capitalism

. . . For the first time the world is completely divided up, so that in the future only redivision is possible, i.e., territories can only pass from one "owner" to another, instead of passing as ownerless territory to an owner. . . .

For Great Britain, the period of the enormous expansion of colonial conquests was that between 1860 and 1880, and it was also very considerable in the last twenty years of the nineteenth century. For France and Germany this period falls precisely in these twenty years. We saw above that the development of premonopoly capitalism, of capitalism in which free competition was predominant, reached its limit in the 1860s and 1870s. We now see that it is precisely after that period that the tremendous "boom" in colonial conquests begins, and that the struggle for the territorial division of the world becomes extraordinarily sharp. It is beyond doubt, therefore, that capitalism's transition to the stage of monopoly capitalism, to finance capital, is connected with the intensification of the struggle for the partitioning of the world.

Hobson, in his work on imperialism, marks the years 1884–1900 as the epoch of intensified "expansion" of the chief European states. According to his estimate, Great Britain during these years acquired 3,700,000 square miles of territory with 57,000,000 inhabitants; France, 3,600,000 square miles with 36,500,000; Germany, 1,000,000 square miles with 14,700,000; Belgium, 900,000 square miles with 30,000,000; Portugal, 800,000 square miles with 9,000,000 inhabitants. The scramble for colonies by all the capitalist states at the end of the nineteenth century and particularly since the 1880s is a commonly known fact in the history of diplomacy and of foreign policy. . . .

. . . at the end of the nineteenth century the British heroes of the hour were Cecil Rhodes and Joseph Chamberlain, who openly advocated imperialism and applied the imperialist policy in the most cynical manner! . . . It is not without interest to observe that even then these leading British bourgeois politicians saw the connection between what might be called the purely economic and the socio-political roots of modern imperialism. Chamberlain advocated imperialism as a "true, wise and economical policy," and pointed particularly to the German, American and Belgian competition which Great Britain was encountering in the world market. Salvation lies in monopoly, said the capitalists as they formed cartels, syndicates and trusts. Salvation lies in monopoly, echoed the political leaders of the bourgeoisie, hastening to appropriate the parts of the world not yet shared out. And Cecil Rhodes, we are informed by his intimate friend, the journalist Stead, expressed his imperialist views to him in 1895 in the following terms: "I was in the East End of London (a working-class quarter) yesterday and attended a meeting of the unemployed. I listened to the wild speeches, which were just a cry for "bread! bread!" and on my way home I pondered over the scene and I became more than ever convinced of the importance of imperialism. . . . My cherished idea is a solution for the social problem, i.e., in order to save the 40,000,000 inhabitants of the United Kingdom from a bloody civil war, we colonial statesmen must acquire new lands to settle the surplus population, to provide new markets for the goods produced in the factories and mines. The Empire, as I have always said, is a bread and butter question. If you want to avoid civil war, you must become imperialists."[1]

The principal feature of the latest stage of capitalism is the domination of monopolist associations of big employers. These monopolies are most firmly established when all the sources of raw materials are captured by one group, and we have seen with what zeal the international capitalist associations exert every effort to deprive their rivals of all opportunity of competing, to buy up, for example, ironfields, oilfields, etc. Colonial possession alone gives the monopolies complete guarantee against all contingencies in the struggle against competitors, including the case of the adversary wanting to be protected by a law establishing a state monopoly. The more capitalism is developed, the more strongly the shortage of raw materials is felt, the more intense the competition and the hunt for sources of raw materials throughout the whole world, the more desperate the struggle for the acquisition of colonies. . . .

In order to finish with the question of the

division of the world, I must make the following additional observation. This question was raised quite openly and definitely not only in American literature after the Spanish-American War, and in English literature after the Anglo-Boer War, at the very end of the nineteenth century and the beginning of the twentieth; not only has German literature, which has "most jealously" watched "British imperialism," systematically given its appraisal of this fact. This question has also been raised in French bourgeois literature as definitely and broadly as is thinkable from the bourgeois point of view. Let me quote Driault, the historian, who, in his book, *Political and Social Problems at the End of the Nineteenth Century*, in the chapter "The Great Powers and the Division of the World," wrote the following: "During the past few years, all the free territory of the globe, with the exception of China, has been occupied by the powers of Europe and North America. This has already brought about several conflicts and shifts of spheres of influence, and these foreshadow more terrible upheavals in the near future. For it is necessary to make haste. The nations which have not yet made provision for themselves run the risk of never receiving their share and never participating in the tremendous exploitation of the globe which will be one of the most essential features of the next century (i.e., the twentieth). That is why all Europe and

America have lately been afflicted with the fever of colonial expansion, of "imperialism," that most noteworthy feature of the end of the nineteenth century." And the author added: "In this partition of the world, in this furious hunt for the treasures and the big markets of the globe, the relative strength of the empires founded in this nineteenth century is totally out of proportion to the place occupied in Europe by the nations which founded them. The dominant powers in Europe, the arbiters of her destiny, are not equally preponderant in the whole world. And, as colonial might, the hope of controlling as yet unassessed wealth, will evidently react upon the relative strength of the European powers, the colonial question—"imperialism," if you will—which has already modified the political conditions of Europe itself, will modify them more and more."[2]

Notes

1. [Lenin] *Die Neue Zeit*, XVI, 1, 1898, S. 304.
2. [Lenin] J.E. Driault, *Problèmes politiques et sociaux*, Paris, 1900, p. 299.

Study Question

How persuasive is Lenin's argument that imperialism, and its economic rationale, was the primary source of conflict in the world?

Web Resources

Internet Resources for Asian History
       http://guides.lib.washington.edu/history-asia
Internet Modern History Sourcebook: Imperialism
       http://www.fordham.edu/halsall/mod/modsbook34.html
History in Focus: Empire
       http://www.history.ac.uk/ihr/Focus/Empire/web.html
Sources and General Resources on Latin America
       http://www.oberlin.edu/faculty/svolk/latinam.htm

Recommended Reading

Joseph Conrad, *Heart of Darkness* (Oxford: Oxford University Press, 2003). Conrad's complex narrative focuses on Charles Marlow's journey up the Congo River to find the reclusive European, Kurtz. The novel, written in 1899, has been condemned as a typical nineteenth-century European view of "the dark continent," but it remains one of the most intriguing commentaries on the dialectical relationship between "civilization" and "barbarism."

E.M. Forster, *Passage to India* (New York: Everyman's Library, 1992). *Passage to India*—the 1924 product of two visits to India in 1912 and 1921—spans a series of key events in the history of British India: the First World War, Gandhi's return, the Rowlatt Acts, and the Amritsar Massacre. Though Forster denied that it was a political novel, it highlights many of the key issues that dominated the struggle for independence.

Amadou Hampate Ba, *The Fortunes of Wangrin* (Bloomington, IN: Indiana University Press, 2000). French West African society in the early part of the twentieth century is the backdrop for Amadou Hampate Ba's examination of the impact of colonization, both on West Africans themselves and on the French citizens of the colonies.

Rudyard Kipling, *Kim* (New York: Penguin Classics, 1992). *Kim*—the story of an Irish soldier's orphan, living on the streets of Lahore amidst the convoluted political and social setting of British India—was created in part from Kipling's memories of his childhood in India. Kipling's novel, originally published in 1901, reflects on the interaction between the British and Indian cultures and the position of those who, like him, had been born in India of European ancestry.

Uwe Timm, *Morenga* (New York: New Directions Publishing, 2003). Historical sources and fictional elements combine in Timm's story of Morenga, the leader of the Nama rebellion against German colonialism in October 1904 (several months after the brutal suppression of the Herero uprising). The novel examines ethnic conflict, colonial prejudices, and the possibility of political freedom in German Southwest Africa.

Recommended Viewing

Sanders of the River (UK, 1935). Director: Zoltan Korda (B&W). Based on a book by Edgar Wallace, *Sanders of the River* (also released under the title *Bosambo*) is a British imperialist film set in Nigeria. With strongly propagandistic overtones, the film portrays the heroism of colonial officials and the values of British imperial rule.

Zulu (UK, 1964). Director: Cy Raker Endfield. During the Battle of Rorke's Drift in 1879 just over 100 British soldiers held off an attack by some 4,000 Zulu warriors. Recognized as one of the finest war movies ever made, the film focuses less on the details of British colonialism in southern Africa and more on the impact of war on all of the participants.

Khartoum (UK, 1966). Director: Basil Dearden. *Khartoum* recreates the fate of General Charles Gordon, administrator of the Sudan between 1874 and 1880, who was sent back to Sudan in 1884 to rescue the British garrison. The film portrays the Arab uprising against British-Egyptian rule and the clash between colonial ideals and Arab nationalism.

Breaker Morant (Australia, 1980). Director: Bruce Beresford. *Breaker Morant* is a dramatization of actual events that occurred during the Boer War. Three Australian soldiers serving in the British army were tried for war crimes allegedly committed against Boer POWs and a German missionary. Beresford's film has strong antiwar overtones and illustrates the complex political situation that existed at the turn of the century.

3

War and Peace

Aggressive nationalism, colonial competition, and a resultant arms race combined in the early part of the twentieth century to create a number of conflicts in Europe. By 1914 three crises involving territorial claims had occurred in Eastern Europe, with war being narrowly averted on each occasion. Military strategists across the continent were so certain that war was imminent that they had already prepared elaborate war plans. There was, however, very little resemblance between the war that so many had anticipated, and the war that actually occurred between 1914 and 1918. Far from resembling the short and decisive wars of the late nineteenth century, the First World War rapidly evolved into a war of attrition in which all national resources had to be mobilized in order to sustain the war effort. Rationing, conscription, censorship, and an unprecedented level of government control over everyday life were the hallmarks of this conflict.

Soldiers attempt to relax in the cold, cramped trenches of the Western Front on 16 June 1916.
Courtesy of the Library of Congress, Prints and Photographs Division (LC-USZ62-55899).

Colonial empires were also drawn in and, in some cases, experienced even greater levels of privation than their colonial overlords.

The mobilization of colonial empires guaranteed that the effects of the war would be felt in most parts of the world. One consequence of this was that, as imperial powers were weakened economically by the war, independence movements in the colonies gained strength and influence. Several of the extensive multi-ethnic empires in Europe—the Austro-Hungarian, Russian, and Ottoman Empires—collapsed completely during the war, releasing previously suppressed tensions. One by-product of this realignment of power and control was the first twentieth century outbreak of genocide as Turks deported and massacred Armenians beginning in 1915. Violence against the Armenian Christian population of the Ottoman Empire predated the First World War, as both the traditionalist Ottoman rulers and the reformist Young Turks had targeted the Armenians; however, the cover of war provided an ideal opportunity for more extremist elements to attempt the wholesale destruction of the Armenian minority.

Another by-product of the war was the creation of numerous small states in Eastern Europe. None of these states was ethnically homogeneous and most contained the basis for future regional conflicts. Meanwhile, in the former Russian Empire the war had ended with the removal of the Tsarist regime and the rise of the Bolshevik Party. Peace with Germany in 1918 led to the secession of vast areas of territory in the West and, ultimately, to war with Russia's former allies.

Perhaps the greatest global impact, however, came from the treaties that formally ended the hostilities: borders were shifted, empires officially dissolved, new leaders were anointed, and colonies redistributed. Predictably, new tensions emerged out of many of the postwar settlements. The mandate system in the Middle East frustrated the ambitions of both Arabs and Zionists and seemed to disregard promises made during the war; decisions regarding former German colonies antagonized Chinese students and reformers; Indian political leaders remained disappointed by the lack of progress towards home rule; and, throughout Central and Eastern Europe, ethnic minorities remained dissatisfied with the power structure in the new states. Even the architects of the postwar settlement soon expressed doubts regarding their new international order.

Despite widespread disappointment with the peace treaties, there was some hope that the League of Nations and the idea of collective security would prevent a repeat of "the war to end all wars." Despite strong congressional opposition in the United States, a great many scholars and diplomats genuinely believed in the power of the League to usher in a new, cooperative era of international relations.

The documents in this section examine the experience of war and the repercussions of the postwar settlement. Excerpts from *All Quiet on the Western Front* reveal some of the horrors of warfare on the Western Front, while "Russian Women in Combat" shows another side of the conflict. The 4th McMahon Letter and the Balfour Declaration provide an idea of the competing promises made during the war. The Armenian genocide is examined through newspaper reports that appeared in the United States and Britain. Woodrow Wilson's "Fourteen Points" document illustrates the illusion of a just peace. Marcus Garvey warns the negotiators not to forget the fate of the black peoples of the world while John Maynard Keynes outlines the reality of the peace settlement. Finally, H.G. Wells defends the potential of the League of Nations, while Henry Cabot Lodge summarizes the American congressional opposition to the League.

Erich Maria Remarque

Erich Maria Remarque (1898–1970), born Erich Paul Remark, published All Quiet on the Western Front *(in German: Im Westen nichts Neues—"In the West, Nothing New") in early 1929. For many years it was believed that the book was a semi-autobiographical account of Remarque's own wartime experiences; however, much controversy remains with respect to Remarque's military career, which was extremely limited. He was conscripted on 21 November 1916, first reached the Western Front on 12 June 1917, and was invalided out of active service on 31 July of the same year. In light of this, much of the story is likely second-hand. Nonetheless, Remarque's fictional account remains one of the most widely accepted accounts of the German trenches during the First World War. The following excerpt takes place in the final months of the war.*

Document Source: Erich Maria Remarque, *All Quiet on the Western Front* (Toronto: Random House of Canada, 1975), 242–8.

All Quiet on the Western Front

Müller is dead. Someone shot him point-blank in the stomach with a Verey Light.[1] He lived for half an hour, quite conscious, and in terrible pain.

Before he died he handed over his pocket-book to me, and bequeathed me his boots—the same that he once inherited from Kemmerich. I wear them, for they fit me quite well. After me Tjaden will get them, I have promised them to him.

We have been able to bury Müller, but he is not likely to remain long undisturbed. Our lines are falling back. There are too many fresh English and American regiments over there. There's too much corned beef and white wheaten bread. Too many new guns. Too many aeroplanes.

But we are emaciated and starved. Our food is bad and mixed up with so much substitute stuff that it makes us ill. The factory owners in Germany have grown wealthy;—dysentery dissolves our bowels. The latrine poles are always densely crowded; the people at home ought to be shown these grey, yellow, miserable, wasted faces here, these bent figures from whose bodies the colic wrings out the blood, and who with lips trembling and distorted with pain, grin at one another and say:

"It is not much sense pulling up one's trousers again."

Our artillery is fired out, it has too few shells and the barrels are so worn that they shoot uncertainly, and scatter so widely as even to fall on ourselves. We have too few horses. Our fresh troops are anaemic boys in need of rest who cannot carry a pack, but merely know how to die. By thousands. They understand nothing about warfare, they simply go on and let themselves be

A field bakery prepares bread for German troops stationed near the Ypres Salient. George Granthan Bain Collection. Courtesy of the Library of Congress, Prints and Photographs Division (LC-DIG-ggbain-17961).

shot down. A single flyer routed two companies of them for a joke, just as they came fresh from the train—before they had ever heard of such a thing as cover.

"Germany ought to be empty soon," says Kat.

We have given up hope that some day an end may come. We never think so far. A man can stop a bullet and be killed; he can get wounded, and then the hospital is his next stop. There, if they do not amputate him, he sooner or later falls into the hands of one of those staff surgeons who, with the War Service Cross in his button-hole, says to him: "What, one leg a bit short? If you have any pluck you don't need to run at the front. The man is A1. Dismiss!"

Kat tells a story that has traveled the whole length of the front from the Vosges to Flanders;— of the staff surgeon who reads the names on the list, and when a man comes before him, without looking up, says: "A1. We need soldiers up there." A fellow with a wooden leg comes up before him,

the staff surgeon again says A1—"And then," Kat raises his voice, "the fellow says to him: 'I already have a wooden leg, but when I go back again and they shoot off my head, then I will get a wooden head made and become a staff surgeon.'" This answer tickles us all immensely. . . .

There are many such stories, they are mostly far more bitter. All the same, they have nothing to do with mutiny or lead-swinging. They are merely honest and call a thing by its name; for there is a very great deal of fraud, injustice, and baseness in the army. It is nothing that regiment after regiment returns again and again to the ever more hopeless struggle, that attack follows attack along the weakening, retreating, crumbling line.

From a mockery the tanks have become a terrible weapon. Armoured they come rolling on in long lines, more than anything else embodying for us the horror of war.

We do not see the guns that bombard us; the attacking lines of the enemy infantry are men like ourselves; but these tanks are machines, their caterpillars run on as endless as the war, they are annihilation, they roll without feeling into the craters, and climb up again without stopping, a fleet of roaring, smoke-belching armour-clads, invulnerable steel beasts squashing the dead and the wounded—we shrivel up in our thin skin before them, against their colossal weight our arms are sticks of straw, and our hand-grenades matches.

Shells, gas clouds, and flotillas of tanks—shattering, corroding, death.

Dysentery, influenza, typhus—scalding, choking, death.

Trenches, hospitals, the common grave—there are no other possibilities. . . .

In one attack our Company Commander, Bertinck, falls. He was one of those superb frontline officers who are foremost in every hot place. He was with us for two years without being wounded, so that something had to happen in the end.

We occupy a crater and get surrounded. The stink of petroleum or oil blows across with the fumes of powder. Two fellows with a flame-thrower are seen, one carries the tin on his back, the other has the hose in his hands from which the fire spouts. If they get so near that they can reach us we are done for, we cannot retreat yet.

We open fire on them. But they work nearer and things begin to look bad. Bertinck is lying in the hole with us. When he sees that we cannot hit them because under the sharp fire we have to think too much about keeping under cover, he takes a rifle, crawls out of the hole, and lying down propped on his elbows, he takes aim. He fires—the same moment a bullet smacks into him, they have got him. Still he lies and aims again;—once he shifts and again takes aim; at last the rifle cracks. Bertinck lets the gun drop and says: "Good," and slips back into the hole. The hindmost of the two flame-throwers is hit, he falls, the hose slips away from the other fellow, the fire squirts about on all sides and the man burns.

Bertinck has a chest wound. After a while a fragment smashes away his chin, and the same fragment has sufficient force to tear open Leer's hip. Leer groans as he supports himself on his arm, he bleeds quickly, no one can help him. Like an emptying tube, after a couple of minutes he collapses.

What use is it to him now that he was such a good mathematician at school. . . .

The months pass by. The summer of 1918 is the most bloody and the most terrible. The days stand like angels in blue and gold, incomprehensible, above the ring of annihilation. Every man here knows that we are losing the war. Not much is said about it, we are falling back, we will not be able to attack again after this big offensive, we have no more men and no more ammunition.

Still the campaign goes on—the dying goes on—

Summer of 1918—Never has life in its niggardliness seemed to us so desirable as now;—the red poppies in the meadows round our billets, the smooth beetles on the blades of grass, the warm evenings in the cool, dim rooms, the black mysterious trees of the twilight, the stars and the flowing waters, dreams and long sleep—O Life, life, life!

Summer of 1918—Never was so much silently suffered as in the moment when we depart once again for the front-line. Wild, tormenting rumours of an armistice and peace are in the air, they lay hold on our hearts and make the return to the front harder than ever.

Summer of 1918—Never was life in the line more bitter and more full of horror than in the hours of the bombardment, when the blanched faces lie in the dirt and the hands clutch at the one thought: No! No! Not now! Not now at the last moment!

Summer of 1918—Breath of hope that sweeps over the scorched fields, raging fever of impatience, of disappointment, of the most agonizing terror of death, insensate question: Why? Why do they make an end? And why do these rumours of an end fly about? . . .

There are so many airmen here, and they are so sure of themselves that they give chase to single individuals, just as though they were hares. For every one German plane there come at least five English and American. For one hungry, wretched German soldier come five of the enemy, fresh and fit. For one German army loaf there are fifty tins of canned beef over there. We are not beaten, for as soldiers we are better and more experienced; we are simply crushed and driven back by overwhelming superior forces.

Behind us lay rainy weeks—grey sky, grey fluid earth, grey dying. If we go out, the rain at once soaks through our overcoat and clothing;—and we remain wet all the time we are in the line. We never get dry. Those who will wear high boots tie sand bags round the tops so that the mud does not pour in so fast. The rifles are caked, the uniforms caked, everything is fluid and dissolved, the earth one dripping, soaked, oily mass in which lie yellow pools with red spiral streams of blood and into which the dead, wounded, and survivors slowly sink down.

The storm lashes us, out of the confusion of grey and yellow the hail of splinters whips forth the child-like cries of the wounded, and in the night shattered life groans painfully into silence.

Our hands are earth, our bodies clay and our eyes pools of rain. We do not know whether we still live.

Note

1. A Verey Light (also Very Light) is a coloured flare fired from a pistol, ordinarily used for signaling.

> **Study Question**
>
> In what ways would returning soldiers have been affected by such an experience?

Novoe Vremya

There has been considerable debate during the past few decades regarding the truthfulness of accounts of Russian women fighting in combat roles during the First World War. These accounts were initially believed to be myths, created to inspire patriotism on the home front. However, there is now substantial research proving that many of these accounts are real. The first all-female unit was called "The Battalion of Death" and was commanded by Maria Botchkareva (1889–1920).

It participated in the defence of Russia's Provisional Government in the months leading up to the Bolshevik uprising. The following account of the military service of a woman named Zoya Smirnov and several of her friends was first printed in Russian newspapers and then reprinted in the New York Times *in 1916.*

Document Source: "Young Girls Fighting on the Russian Front," (*The New York Times Current History: The European War,* April–June 1916): 366.

Russian Women in Combat

Stories are filtering in from the various belligerent countries telling of actual fighting in the ranks by women. . . . A correspondent of the *Novoe Vremya* tells an interesting story of the experiences of 12 young Russian girls who fought in the ranks as soldiers of the line. The story was also authenticated by the Petrograd correspondent of the London *Times*.

She was called Zoya Smirnov. She came to our staff straight from the advanced positions, where she had spent 14 months wearing soldier's clothes and

A photo-montage depicting a Petrograd women's regiment in 1918. Regiments such as this were involved in the Russian Civil War. Courtesy of the Library of Congress, Prints and Photographs Division (LC-USZ62-129088).

fighting with the foe on even terms with the men. Zoya Smirnov was only 16 years old. Closely cropped hair gave her the appearance of a boy, and only a thin girlish voice involuntarily betrayed her sex.

At the beginning Zoya was somewhat shy; she carefully chose her words and replied confusedly to our questions; but later she recovered and told us her entire history, which brought tears to the eyes of many a case-hardened veteran who heard it.

She and her friends decided to go to the war on the eighth day of mobilization—i.e., at the end of July 1914; and early in August they succeeded in realizing their dream.

Exactly twelve of them assembled; and they were all nearly the same age and from the same high school. Almost all were natives of Moscow, belonging to the most diversified classes of society, but firmly united in the camaraderie of school life.

"We decided to run away to the war at all costs," said Zoya. "It was impossible to run away from Moscow, because we might have been stopped at the station. It was therefore necessary to hire *izvozchiks*[1] and ride out to one of the suburban stations through which the military echelons were continually passing. We left home early in the morning without saying a word to our parents and departed. It was a bit terrible at first; we were very sorry for our fathers and mothers, but the desire to see the war and ourselves kill the Germans overcame all other sentiments."

And so they attained the desired object. The soldiers treated the little patriots quite paternally and properly, and having concealed them in the cars, took them off to the war. A military uniform was obtained for each; they donned these and unobstructed arrived at the Austrian frontier, where they had to detrain and on foot proceed to Lemberg. Here the regimental authorities found out what had happened, but not being able to persuade the young patriots to return home allowed them to march with the regiment.

The regiment traversed the whole of Galicia; scaled the Carpathians,[2] incessantly participating in battle, and the girls never fell back from it a step, but shared with the men all the privations and horrors of the march and discharged the duties of ordinary privates, since they were taught to shoot and were given rifles.

Days and months passed.

The girls almost forgot their past, they hardly responded to their feminine names, for each of them had received a masculine surname, and completely mingled with the men. The soldiers themselves mutually guarded the girls and observed each other's conduct.

The battles in which the regiment engaged were fierce and sanguinary, particularly in the Spring, when the Germans brought up their heavy artillery to the Carpathians and began to advance upon us with their celebrated phalanx. Our troops underwent a perfect hell and the young volunteers endured it with them.

"Was it terrible?" an officer asked Zoya. "Were you afraid?"

"I should say so! Who wouldn't be afraid? When for the first time they began to fire with their heavy guns, several of us couldn't stand it and began to cry out."

"What did you cry out?"

"We began to call "Mamma." Shura was the first to cry, then Lida. They were both 14 years old, and they remembered their mothers all the time. Besides, it seems that I also cried out as well. We all cried. Well, it was frightful even for the men."

During one of the Carpathian engagements, at night, one of the 12 friends, the 16-year-old Zina Morozov, was killed outright by a shell. It struck immediately at her feet, and the entire small body of the girl was torn into fragments.

"Nevertheless, we managed to collect her remains," Zoya stated with a tender inflexion in her voice. "At dawn the firing died down and we all—that is, all the remaining high school volunteers—assembled near the spot where Zina had perished, and somehow collected her bones and laid them in a hastily dug grave. In the same grave we laid also all Zina's things, such as she had with her. The grave was then filled up and upon the cross which we erected above it the following inscription was written: "Volunteer of such and such a regiment, Zina Morozov, 16 years old, killed in action on such and such a date in such and such year."

On the following day we were already far away, and exactly where Zina's grave is I don't remember well. I only know that it is in the Carpathians at the foot of a steep rocky incline."

After the death of Zina other of her friends were frequently wounded in turn—Nadya, Zhena, and the 14-year-old Shura. Zoya herself was wounded twice—the first time in the leg, and the second time in the side. Both wounds were so serious that Zoya was left unconscious on the battlefield, and the stretcher-bearers subsequently discovered her only by accident. After the second wound she was obliged to lie at a base hospital for over a month. On being discharged she again proceeded to the positions, endeavoring to find her regiment, but on reaching the familiar trenches she could no longer find a single regimental comrade, nor a single fellow-volunteer; they had all gone to another front, and in the trenches sat absolute strangers. The girl lost her presence of mind, and for the first time during the entire campaign began to weep, thus unexpectedly betraying her age and sex. Her unfamiliar fellow-countrymen gazed with amazement upon the strange young non-commissioned officer with the Cross of St George medal on her breast, who resembled a stripling and finally proved to be a girl. But the girl had with her all necessary documents, not excepting a certificate giving her the right to wear the St George's Cross received for a brave and dashing reconnaissance, and distrustful glances promptly gave place to others full of respect.

Zoya was finally induced to abandon the trenches, at least for the time being, and to try to engage in nursing at one of the advanced hospitals. She is now working at the divisional hospital of the N—— division, in the village of K., ten versts from the Austrian town of Z.

From her remaining friends whom she left with the regiment which went to another front Zoya has no news whatever.

What has befallen them? Do these amazing Russian girls continue their disinterested and heroic service to the country, or do graves already hold them, similar to that which was dug for the remnants of poor little Zina, who perished so gloriously in the distant Carpathians?

Notes

1. Carriages.
2. Galicia was an Austrian province in east central Europe, which is today divided between Poland and Ukraine. Lemberg was the capital of Galicia. The Carpathians are a range of mountains stretching through Eastern Europe.

> **Study Question**
>
> Why would the truth of accounts such as this be called into question?

A. Henry McMahon/Arthur James Balfour

During the First World War, agents of the British government made numerous contradictory statements regarding the postwar fate of the Middle East. Two sets of documents in particular—the McMahon Correspondence and the Balfour Declaration—would prove to be an ongoing source of instability in the region. The Balfour Declaration, dated 2 November 1917, provided a clear indication of support for the idea of a national home for the Jewish people in Palestine. The McMahon Correspondence of 1915–16 between A. Henry McMahon (1862–1949), British High Commissioner to Egypt, and the Sharif of Mecca, Husayn bin Ali (1854–1931), provided a far more detailed blueprint for Arab control of much of the post-war Middle East.

Document Source: Balfour Declaration: http://avalon.law.yale.edu/20th_century/balfour.asp; McMahon Correspondence: http://www.jewishvirtuallibrary.org/jsource/History/hussmac1.html#4

McMahon Letter #4

24 October 1915

I have received your letter of the 29th Shawal, 1333,[1] with much pleasure and your expression of friendliness and sincerity have given me the greatest satisfaction.

I regret that you should have received from my last letter the impression that I regarded the question of limits and boundaries with coldness and hesitation; such was not the case, but it appeared to me that the time had not yet come when that question could be discussed in a conclusive manner.

I have realised, however, from your last letter that you regard this question as one of vital and urgent importance. I have, therefore, lost no time in informing the Government of Great Britain of the contents of your letter, and it is with great pleasure that I communicate to you on their behalf the following statement, which I am confident you will receive with satisfaction.

The two districts of Mersina and Alexandretta and portions of Syria lying to the west of the districts of Damascus, Homs, Hama, and Aleppo cannot be said to be purely Arab, and should be excluded from the limits demanded. With the above modification, and without prejudice to our existing treaties with Arab chiefs, we accept those limits. As for those regions lying within those frontiers wherein Great Britain is free to act without detriment to the interests of her ally, France, I am empowered in the name of the Government of Great Britain to give the following assurances and make the following assurances and make the following reply to your letter:

1. Subject to the above modifications, Great Britain is prepared to recognise and support the independence of the Arabs in all the regions within the limits demanded by the Sherif of Mecca.
2. Great Britain will guarantee the Holy Places against all external aggression and will recognise their inviolability.
3. When the situation admits, Great Britain will give to the Arabs her advice and will assist them to establish what may appear to be the most suitable forms of government for those various territories.
4. On the other hand, it is understood that the Arabs have decided to seek the advice and guidance of Great Britain only, and that such European advisers and officials as may be required for the formation of a sound form of administration will be British.
5. With regard to the vilayets of Bagdad and Basra, the Arabs will recognise that the established position and interests of Great Britain necessitate special administrative

arrangements in order to secure these territories from foreign aggression to promote the welfare of the local populations and to safeguard our mutual economic interests.

I am convinced that this declaration will assure you beyond all possible doubt of the sympathy of Great Britain towards the aspirations of her friends the Arabs and will result in a firm and lasting alliance, the immediate results of which will be the expulsion of the Turks from the Arab countries and the freeing of the Arab peoples from the Turkish yoke, which for so many years has pressed heavily upon them.

I have confined myself in this letter to the more vital and important questions, and if there are any other matters dealt with in your letters that I have omitted to mention, we may discuss them at some convenient date in the future.

It was with very great relief and satisfaction that I heard of the safe arrival of the Holy Carpet and the accompanying offerings which, thanks to the clearness of your directions and the excellence of your arrangements, were landed without trouble or mishap in spite of the dangers and difficulties occasioned by the present sad war. May God soon bring a lasting peace and freedom of all peoples.

I am sending this letter by the hand of your trusted and excellent messenger, Sheikh Mohammed ibn Arif ibn Uraifan, and he will inform you of the various matters of interest, but of less vital importance, which I have not mentioned in this letter.

(Compliments)

(Signed): A. HENRY MCMAHON

--- ◆ ---

The Balfour Declaration

2 November 1917

Dear Lord Rothschild,

I have much pleasure in conveying to you, on behalf of His Majesty's Government, the following

declaration of sympathy with Jewish Zionist aspirations, which has been submitted to, and approved by, the Cabinet.

"His Majesty's Government view with favour the establishment in Palestine of a national home for the Jewish people, and will use their best endeavours to facilitate the achievement of this object, it being clearly understood that nothing shall be done which may prejudice the civil and religious rights of existing non-Jewish communities in Palestine, or the rights and political status enjoyed by Jews in any other country."

I should be grateful if you would bring this declaration to the knowledge of the Zionist Federation.

Yours sincerely,

ARTHUR JAMES BALFOUR

Note

1. McMahon uses the Islamic calendar in his response. The date of the original letter from the Sharif of Mecca was 9 September 1915.

Study Question

Based on your reading of the two documents, which should take precedence?

The Armenian National Institute: Press Reports on the Armenian Genocide

In 1915 a number of reports appeared in American and British newspapers regarding a genocide being carried out by the Ottoman government against the Armenians. These reports continued both during and after the First World War; however, the war and its consequences would mean that the genocide committed against the Armenian people between 1915 and 1920 was largely ignored by history.

Attempts have been made only recently to study this genocide, its origins—which predated the outbreak of war—and its implications. The Turkish government and other nations continue to deny that a genocide occurred.

Document Source: *The New York Times*, found at The Armenian National Institute Press Reports, http://www.armenian-genocide.org/press.html

500,000 Armenians Said to Have Perished

The New York Times, 24 September 1915

Washington Asked to Stop Slaughter of Christians by Turks and Kurds

Special to The New York Times

WASHINGTON, Sept. 23. Charles R. Crane of Chicago, a Director of Roberts College, Constantinople, and James L. Burton of Boston, Foreign Secretary of the American Board of Commissioners for Foreign Missions, visited the State Department today and conferred with Acting

Secretary of State Polk and other officials regarding the slaughter of Armenians by Turks and Kurds in Asia Minor. They will attend a meeting of a general committee, to be held in New York within a few days, to devise a plan for appealing to the American people for funds and aid for as many of the unfortunate Armenians as can be helped.

It was learned, in connection with the conferences held here today, that general representations have from time to time been made to the Ottoman Government by Ambassador Morgenthau[1] for humane treatment of Armenians. Despite these representations, the slaughter of Armenians has continued.

The records of the State Department are replete with detailed reports from American Consular officers in Asia Minor, which give harrowing tales of the treatment of the Armenian Christians by the Turks and the Kurds. These reports have not been made public. They indicate that the Turk has undertaken a war of extermination on Armenians, especially those of the Gregorian Church,[2] to which about 90 per cent of the Armenians belong. The Turkish Government originally ordered the deportation of all Armenians, but, some time ago, after representations had been made by Ambassador Morgenthau, the Ottoman Government gave assurances that the order would be modified so as not to embrace Catholic and Protestant Armenians.

Reports reaching Washington indicate that about 500,000 Armenians have been slaughtered or lost their lives as a result of the Turkish deportation order and the resulting war of extinction. Turkish authorities drove the Gregorian Armenians out of their homes, ordered them to proceed to distant towns in the direction of Baghdad, which could only be reached by crossing long stretches of desert. During the exodus of Armenians across the deserts they have been fallen upon by Kurds and slaughtered, but some of the Armenian women and girls, in considerable numbers, have been carried off into captivity by the Kurds. The reports that have been sent to the State Department by its agents in Asia Minor fully confirm these statements made in the appeal sent to this country by Viscount Bryce, formerly British Ambassador to the United States, to try to stop the slaughter of the Armenians. Viscount Bryce stated that the horrors through which the Armenians have passed have been unparalleled in modern times.

800,000 Armenians Counted Destroyed

The New York Times, 7 October 1915

LONDON, 6 Oct. Viscount Bryce, former British Ambassador to the United States, in the House of Lords today said that such information as had reached him from many quarters showed that the figure of 800,000 Armenians destroyed since May was quite a possible number. Virtually the whole nation had been wiped out, he declared, and he did not suppose there was any case in history of a crime "so hideous and on so large a scale."

"The death of these people," said Lord Bryce, "resulted from the deliberate and premeditated policy of the gang now in possession of the Turkish Government. Orders for the massacres came in every case direct from Constantinople. In some instances local Governors, being humane, pious men, refused to carry out the orders and at least two Governors were summarily dismissed for this reason."

"The customary procedure was to round up the whole of the population of a designated town. A part of the population was thrown into prison and the remainder were marched out of town and in the suburbs the men were separated from the women and children. The men were then taken to a convenient place and shot and bayoneted. The women and children were then put under a convoy of the lower kind of soldiers and dispatched to some distant destination."

They were driven by the soldiers day after day. Many fell by the way and many died of hunger, for no provisions were furnished them. They were robbed of all they possessed, and in many cases the women were stripped naked and made to continue the march in that condition. Many of the women went mad and threw away their children. The caravan route was marked by a line of corpses. Comparatively few of the people ever reached their destination.". . .

Armenians Dying in Prison Camps

The New York Times, 21 August 1916

Hundreds of Thousands Still in Danger from Turks, Refugees Fund Secretary Says.

GERMANS WON'T INTERFERE

About 1,000,000 Victims Deported and 500,000 Massacred, the Rev. Harold Buxton Reports.

Special Cable to *The New York Times*

LONDON, Monday, 21 Aug. The Rev. Harold Buxton, Secretary of the Armenian Refugees Fund, has just returned to England after devoting three months to relief work in the devastated villages. In an interview the Rev. Mr Buxton gave details which entirely confirm the grave statements made by Lord Bryce some months ago in the House of Lords. Asked whether he had any proof that the deportation of Armenians last summer was due to German instigation, he said:

"All I can say is that the German Government did nothing to stop the massacres. During the whole business German influence was supreme at Constantinople, and German Consuls were at their posts in all the chief centres through Asia Minor. Besides, the people were swept away with a methodical thoroughness which one does not expect from the Turk, who, when left to himself, acts rather with sudden spasms of fury."

"I have evidence from an American missionary that certain of the German Consuls did their best on behalf of the Armenian people. For instance, the German Consul at Erzerum wired to his Ambassador in Constantinople vigorously protesting at the order of deportation. He received a reply in these words: "We cannot interfere in the internal affairs of Turkey.""

"I don't think there has been any exaggeration as to losses as published in England. The Armenian race numbered over 4,000,000, of whom 2,000,000 were Turkish Armenians, and of these perhaps 1,000,000 have been deported and 500,000 massacred. Only 200,000 escaped into the mountains, and so across to Russian soil. There are some hundreds of thousands in concentration camps between Aleppo and Mosul and in the neighboring regions of Mesopotamia, where Turkey continues to be supreme over their fate."

"To this considerable population we have no access, and it is still in danger. According to reports which come through, it is being ravaged by sickness, famine, privations of all kinds, outrages, and murder, all of which means high mortality among the victims."

Shall Armenia Perish?

The Independent, 28 February 1920

By Henry Morgenthau, Former Ambassador to Turkey, and National Vice-chairman of Near East Relief

Two hundred and fifty thousand Christian Armenian women enslaved in Turkish harems call to the people of America for liberation! One hundred thousand women already rescued by Near East Relief agents from harems will perish unless support from America is continued! Two hundred and fifty thousand children, orphaned by the unspeakable Turks, are calling in the only English they know, "Bread, Uncle Sam." One million two hundred thousand destitute, homeless, clotheless adults look to the giant in the West for the succor that will keep them from annihilation. What shall our answer be?

If they were good enough to fight and die for us when we needed their help so sorely, are they not good enough to be given some crumbs from our plenty? . . .

The belief, held by some persons, that Turkey has repented and can do no further harm, is without foundation. The group that led Turkey into the war on the side of Germany is now in the saddle. The Turk has not been disarmed and these leaders are now aiding the Tartars. Kurds and Bolshevists are urging them on to kill and rob the surviving Armenians at every opportunity. The deportations and massacres during the war were not spontaneous uprisings of unorganized mobs, but were the working out of a well-plotted plan of wholesale extermination in which regular Turkish officers and troops took part as if in a campaign against an enemy in the field.

More than 2,000,000 persons were deported. The system was about the same everywhere. The Armenians, men, women and children, would be assembled in the marketplace. Then the able-bodied men would be marched off and killed by being shot or clubbed in cold blood at some spot which did not necessitate the trouble of burial.

Next the women would be sorted out. Agents of the Turk officers picked the youngest and fairest for their masters' harems. Next the civil officials had their pick, and then the remainder either were sold for one medjidi—a silver coin valued at about 80 cents—or were driven forth to be seized by the lower class Turks and Kurds.

As a last step, those who remained, mothers, grandmothers, children, were driven forth on their death pilgrimages across the desert of Aleppo, with no food, no water, no shelter, to be robbed and beaten at every halt, to see children slain in scores before their eyes, and babies dashed to death against rocks or spitted on the bayonets of the soldier guards.

If America is going to condone these offenses, if she is going to permit to continue conditions that threaten and permit their repetition, she is party to the crime. These peoples must be freed from the agony and danger of such horrors. They must not only be saved for the present but either thru governmental action or protection under the League of Nations they must be given assurance that they will be free in peace and that no harm can come to them.

Notes

1. Henry I. Morgenthau was the United States Ambassador at Constantinople from 1913–16.
2. The Gregorian Church dates to the late third century CE. It is an independent Christian church.

> **Study Question**
>
> In what ways could the war be seen to have facilitated the Armenian genocide?

Woodrow Wilson

Woodrow Wilson (1856–1924) was a social reformer who entered politics in 1911, winning the governorship of New Jersey on his first attempt. In 1912 a three-way race[1] allowed Wilson to win the presidency of the United States; however, his plans to focus on domestic social reforms were shattered by the outbreak of war in Europe in 1914. Determined to maintain a policy of neutrality, Wilson managed to keep the

US out of the war until April 1917, by which time American commercial interests were being seriously compromised by Germany's unrestricted U-Boat campaign. However, even as the United States was mobilizing for war, Wilson was already envisioning a peace settlement free of punitive damages and arbitrary territorial changes. These sentiments guided the creation of his "fourteen points for peace." On 8 January 1918 Wilson presented the outline of his Fourteen Points to Congress.

Document Source: *The Avalon Project: Documents in Law, History, and Diplomacy:* http://avalon.law.yale.edu/20th_century/wilson14.asp

Fourteen Points Speech

Gentlemen of the Congress:

It will be our wish and purpose that the processes of peace, when they are begun, shall be absolutely open and that they shall involve and permit henceforth no secret understandings of any kind. The day of conquest and aggrandizement is gone by; so is also the day of secret covenants entered into in the interest of particular governments and likely at some unlooked-for moment to upset the peace of the world. It is this happy fact, now clear to the view of every public man whose thoughts do not still linger in an age that is dead and gone, which makes it possible for every nation whose purposes are consistent with justice and the peace of the world to avow now or at any other time the objects it has in view.

We entered this war because violations of right had occurred which touched us to the quick and made the life of our own people impossible unless they were corrected and the world secured once for all against their recurrence. What we demand in this war, therefore, is nothing peculiar to ourselves. It is that the world be made fit and safe to live in; and particularly that it be made safe for every peace-loving nation which, like our own, wishes to live its own life, determine its own institutions, be assured of justice and fair dealing by the other peoples of the world as against force and selfish aggression. All the peoples of the world are in effect partners in this interest, and for our own part we see very clearly that unless justice be done to others it will not be done to us. The program of the world's peace, therefore, is our program; and that program, the only possible program, as we see it, is this:

I. Open covenants of peace, openly arrived at, after which there shall be no private international understandings of any kind but diplomacy shall proceed always frankly and in the public view.

II. Absolute freedom of navigation upon the seas, outside territorial waters, alike in peace and in war, except as the seas may be closed in whole or in part by international action for the enforcement of international covenants.

III. The removal, so far as possible, of all economic barriers and the establishment of an equality of trade conditions among all the nations consenting to the peace and associating themselves for its maintenance.

IV. Adequate guarantees given and taken that national armaments will be reduced to the lowest point consistent with domestic safety.

V. A free, open-minded, and absolutely impartial adjustment of all colonial claims, based upon a strict observance of the principle that in determining all such questions of sovereignty the interests of the populations concerned must have equal weight with the equitable claims of the government whose title is to be determined.

VI. The evacuation of all Russian territory and such a settlement of all questions affecting Russia as will secure the best and freest cooperation of the other nations of the world in obtaining for her an unhampered and unembarrassed opportunity for the independent determination of her own political development and national policy and assure her of a sincere welcome into the society of free nations under institutions of her own choosing; and, more than a welcome, assistance also of every kind that she may need and may herself desire. The treatment accorded Russia by her sister nations in the months to come will be the acid test of their good will, of their comprehension of her needs as distinguished from their own interests, and of their intelligent and unselfish sympathy.

VII. Belgium, the whole world will agree, must be evacuated and restored, without any attempt to limit the sovereignty which she enjoys in common with all other free nations. No other single act will serve as this will serve to restore confidence among the nations in the laws which they have themselves set and determined for the government of their relations with one another. Without this healing act the whole structure and validity of international law is forever impaired.

VIII. All French territory should be freed and the invaded portions restored, and the wrong done to France by Prussia in 1871 in the matter of Alsace-Lorraine, which has unsettled the peace of the world for nearly fifty years, should be righted, in order that peace may once more be made secure in the interest of all.

IX. A readjustment of the frontiers of Italy should be effected along clearly recognizable lines of nationality.

X. The peoples of Austria-Hungary, whose place among the nations we wish to see safeguarded and assured, should be accorded the freest opportunity of autonomous development.

XI. Rumania, Serbia, and Montenegro should be evacuated; occupied territories restored; Serbia accorded free and secure access to the sea; and the relations of the several Balkan states to one another determined by friendly counsel along historically established lines of allegiance and nationality; and international guarantees of the political and economic independence and territorial integrity of the several Balkan states should be entered into.

XII. The Turkish portions of the present Ottoman Empire should be assured a secure sovereignty, but the other nationalities which are now under Turkish rule should be assured an undoubted security of life and an absolutely unmolested opportunity of an autonomous development, and the Dardanelles should be permanently opened as a free passage to the ships and commerce of all nations under international guarantees.

XIII. An independent Polish state should be erected which should include the territories inhabited by indisputably Polish populations, which should be assured a free and secure access to the sea, and whose political and economic independence and territorial integrity should be guaranteed by international covenant.

XIV. A general association of nations must be formed under specific covenants for the purpose of affording mutual guarantees of political independence and territorial integrity to great and small states alike.

In regard to these essential rectifications of wrong and assertions of right we feel ourselves to be intimate partners of all the governments and peoples associated together against the Imperialists. We cannot be separated in interest or divided in purpose. We stand together until the end.

For such arrangements and covenants we are willing to fight and to continue to fight until they are achieved; but only because we wish the right to prevail and desire a just and stable peace such as can be secured only by removing the chief provocations to war, which this program does not remove. We have no jealousy of German greatness, and there is nothing in this program that impairs it. We grudge her no achievement or distinction of learning or of pacific enterprise such as have made her record very bright and very enviable. We do not wish to injure her or to block in any way her legitimate influence or power. We do not wish to fight her either with arms or with hostile arrangements of trade if she is willing to associate herself with us and the other peace-loving nations of the world in covenants of justice and law and fair dealing. We wish her only to accept a place of equality among the peoples of the world—the new world in which we now live—instead of a place of mastery.

Neither do we presume to suggest to her any alteration or modification of her institutions. But it is necessary, we must frankly say, and necessary as a preliminary to any intelligent dealings with her on our part, that we should know whom her spokesmen speak for when they speak to us, whether for the Reichstag majority or for the military party and the men whose creed is imperial domination.

We have spoken now, surely, in terms too concrete to admit of any further doubt or question. An evident principle runs through the whole program I have outlined. It is the principle of justice to all peoples and nationalities, and their right to live on equal terms of liberty and safety with one another, whether they be strong or weak. Unless this principle be made its foundation no part of the structure of international justice can stand. The people of the United States could act upon no other principle; and to the vindication of this principle they are ready to devote their lives, their honor, and everything that they possess. The moral climax of this the culminating and final war for human liberty has come, and they are ready to put their own strength, their own highest purpose, their own integrity and devotion to the test.

Note

1. Theodore Roosevelt and William Howard Taft both ran as Republican candidates, allowing Wilson, the only Democratic challenger, to win the election.

> **Study Question**
>
> Which countries would benefit the most from the ideals established in the Fourteen Points?

Marcus Garvey

Marcus Garvey (1887–1940) was one of the strongest advocates of black nationalism in the first half of the twentieth century. Garvey argued for a "re-segregation" of the races, as Africans around the world would return to Africa and liberate the continent from colonial rule. In 1919 he founded the Black Star Line to facilitate the movement of African-Americans back to Africa. Garvey hoped that the *peace-makers who met in Paris in 1919 would begin the process of decolonizing Africa. The excerpt which follows was taken from an editorial piece written by Garvey just nineteen days after the Armistice in 1918, offering guidance to the diplomats who would assemble in Paris to draft a peace settlement.*

Document Source: Marcus Garvey, "Advice of the Negro to the Peace Conference," *The Negro World* (Saturday 30 November 1918): editorial.

Advice of the Negro to the Peace Conference

Now that the statesmen of the various nations are preparing to meet at the Peace Conference, to discuss the future government of the peoples of the world, we take it as our bounden duty to warn them to be very just to all those people who may happen to come under their legislative control. If they, representing the classes, as they once did, were alive to the real feeling of their respective masses four and one-half years ago, today Germany would have been intact, Austria-Hungary would have been intact, Russia would have been intact, the spirit of revolution never would have swept Europe, and mankind at large would have been satisfied. But through graft, greed and selfishness, the classes they represented then, as some of them represent now, were determined to rob and exploit the masses, thinking that the masses would have remained careless of their own condition for everlasting.

It is a truism that you "fool half of the people for half of the time, but you cannot fool all of the people for all of the time"; and now that the masses of the whole world have risen as one man to demand true equity and justice from the "powers that be," then let the delegates at the Peace Conf[e]rence r[e]alize, just now, that the Negro, who forms an integral part of the masses of the world, is determined to get no less than what other men are to get. The oppressed races of Europe are to get their freedom, which freedom will be guaranteed them. The Asiatic races are to get their rights and a larger modicum of self-government.

We trust that the delegates to the Peace Conference will not continue to believe that Negroes have no ambition, no aspiration. There are no more timid, cringing Negroes; let us say that those Negroes have now been relegated to the limbo of the past, to the region of forgetfulness, and that the new Negro is on the stage, and he is going to play his part good and well. He, like the other heretofore oppressed peoples of the world, is determined to get restored to him his ancestral rights.

When we look at the map of Africa today we see Great Britain with fully five million square miles of our territory, we see France with fully three million five hundred thousand square miles, we see that Belgium has under her control the Congo, Portugal has her sway over Southeast Africa, Italy has under her control Tripoli, Italian Somaliland on the Gulf of Aden and Erythria on the Red Sea. Germany had clamored for a place in the sun simply because she had only one million square miles, with which she was not satisfied, in that England had five millions and France three millions five hundred thousand. It can be easily seen that the war of 1914 was the outcome of African aggrandizement, that Africa, to which the white man has absolutely no claim, has been raped, has been left bleeding for hundreds of years, but within the last thirty years the European powers have concentrated more than ever on the cleaning up of that great continent so as to make it a white man's country. Among those whom they have killed are millions of our people, but the age of killing for naught is passed and the age of killing for something has come. If black men have to die in Africa or anywhere else, then they might as well die for the best of things, and that is liberty, true freedom and true democracy. If the delegates to the Peace Conference would like to see no more wars we would advise them to satisfy the yellow man's claims, the black man's claims and the white man's claims, and let all three be satisfied so that there can be indeed a brotherhood of men. But if one section of the human race is to arrogate to itself all that God gave for the benefit of mankind at large, then let us say human nature has in no way changed, and even at the Peace Conference where from the highest principles of humanity are supposed to emanate there will come no message of peace.

There will be no peace in the world until the white man confines himself politically to Europe, the yellow man to Asia and the black man to Africa. The original division of the earth among mankind must stand, and any one who dares to interfere with this division creates only trouble for himself. This division was made by the Almighty

Power that rules, and therefore there can be no interference with the plans Divine.

Cowardice has disappeared from the world. Men have died in this world war so quickly and so easily that those who desire liberty today do not stop to think of death, for it is regarded as the price which people in all ages will have to pay to be free; that is the price the weaker people of Europe have paid; that is the price the Negro must pay some day.

Let the Peace Conference, we suggest, be just in its deliberations and in its findings, so that there can be a true brotherhood in the future with no more wars.

Study Question

Compare Wilson's Fourteen Points to Garvey's proposal for world peace. What are the major similarities and differences between the two?

J.M. Keynes

John Maynard Keynes (1883–1946) was educated in mathematics at the University of Cambridge and worked briefly in the British Civil Service's India Office. After lecturing at Cambridge he joined the British Treasury and in 1919 served as the Treasury's representative to the Paris Peace Conference. Keynes soon resigned from the negotiations, frustrated with what he perceived to be the greed of the major *leaders and their lack of concern for the impact of the treaty on the global economy. Keynes's analysis of the impact of the peace settlement was published as a monograph in November 1919 under the title,* The Economic Consequences of the Peace. *An excerpt follows.*

Document Source: John Maynard Keynes, *The Economic Consequences of the Peace* (New York: Harcourt, Brace, and Howe, 1920), 98–100.

The Economic Consequences of the Peace

This chapter must be one of pessimism. The treaty includes no provisions for the economic rehabilitation of Europe—nothing to make the defeated Central empires into good neighbours, nothing to stabilise the new states of Europe, nothing to reclaim Russia; nor does it promote in any way a compact of economic solidarity amongst the Allies themselves; no arrangement was reached at Paris for restoring the disordered finances of France and Italy, or to adjust the systems of the Old World and the New.

The Council of Four paid no attention to these issues, being preoccupied with others—Clemenceau to crush the economic life of his enemy, Lloyd George to do a deal and bring home

something which would pass muster for a week, the President to do nothing that was not just and right. It is an extraordinary fact that the fundamental economic problem of a Europe starving and disintegrating before their eyes, was the one question in which it was impossible to arouse the interest of the Four. Reparation was their main excursion into the economic field, and they settled it as a problem of theology, of politics, of electoral chicane, from every point of view except that of the economic future of the states whose destiny they were handling.

I leave, from this point onwards, Paris, the conference, and the treaty, briefly to consider the present situation of Europe, as the war and the peace have made it; and it will no longer be part of my purpose to distinguish between the inevitable fruits of the war and the avoidable misfortunes of the peace.

The essential facts of the situation, as I see them, are expressed simply. Europe consists of the densest aggregation of population in the history of the world. This population is accustomed to a relatively high standard of life, in which, even now, some sections of it anticipate improvement rather than deterioration. In relation to other continents Europe is not self-sufficient; in particular it cannot feed itself. Internally the population is not evenly distributed, but much of it is crowded into a relatively small number of dense industrial centres. This population secured for itself a livelihood before the war, without much margin of surplus, by means of a delicate and immensely complicated organisation, of which the foundations were supported by coal, iron, transport, and an unbroken supply of imported food and raw materials from other continents. By the destruction of this organisation and the interruption of the stream of supplies, a part of this population is deprived of its means of livelihood. Emigration is not open to the redundant surplus. For it would take years to transport them overseas, even, which is not the case, if countries could be found which were ready to receive them. The danger confronting us, therefore, is the rapid depression of the standard of life of the European populations to a point which will mean actual starvation for some (a point already reached in Russia and approximately reached in Austria). Men will not always die quietly. For starvation, which brings to some lethargy and a helpless despair, drives other temperaments to the nervous instability of hysteria and to a mad despair. And these in their distress may overturn the remnants of organisation, and submerge civilisation itself in their attempts to satisfy desperately the overwhelming needs of the individual. This is the danger against which

all our resources and courage and idealism must now co-operate.

On 13 May 1919 Count Brockdorff-Rantzau addressed to the peace conference of the Allied and Associated Powers the Report of the German economic commission charged with the study of the effect of the conditions of peace on the situation of the German population. "In the course of the last two generations," they reported, "Germany has become transformed from an agricultural state to an industrial state. So long as she was an agricultural state, Germany could feed 40 million inhabitants. As an industrial state she could ensure the means of subsistence for a population of 67 millions; and in 1913 the importation of foodstuffs amounted, in round figures, to 12 million tons. Before the war a total of 15 million persons in Germany provided for their existence by foreign trade, navigation, and the use, directly or indirectly, of foreign raw material." After rehearsing the main relevant provisions of the peace treaty the report continues: "After this diminution of her products, after the economic depression resulting from the loss of her colonies, her merchant fleet, and her foreign investments, Germany will not be in a position to import from abroad an adequate quantity of raw material. An enormous part of German industry will, therefore, be condemned inevitably to destruction. The need of importing foodstuffs will increase considerably at the same time that the possibility of satisfying this demand is as greatly diminished. In a very short time, therefore, Germany will not be in a position to give bread and work to her numerous millions of inhabitants, who are prevented from earning their livelihood by navigation and trade. These persons should emigrate, but this is a material impossibility, all the more because many countries and the most important ones will oppose any German immigration. To put the peace conditions into execution would logically involve, therefore, the loss of several millions of persons in Germany. This catastrophe would not be long in coming about, seeing that the health of the population has been broken down during the war by the blockade, and during the armistice by the aggravation of the blockade of famine. No help, however great, or over however long a period it were continued, could prevent these deaths en masse." "We do not know, and indeed we doubt," the Report concludes, "whether the delegates of the Allied and Associated Powers realise the inevitable consequences which will take place if Germany, an industrial state, very thickly populated, closely bound up with the economic system of the world, and under the necessity of importing enormous quantities of raw material and foodstuffs, suddenly finds herself pushed back to the phase of her development which corresponds to her economic condition and the numbers of her population as they were half a century ago. Those who sign this treaty will sign the death sentence of many millions of German men, women, and children."

I know of no adequate answer to these words. The indictment is at least as true of the Austrian, as of the German, settlement. This is the fundamental problem in front of us, before which questions of territorial adjustment and the balance of European power are insignificant. Some of the catastrophes of past history, which have thrown back human progress for centuries, have been due to the reactions following on the sudden termination, whether in the course of Nature or by the act of man, of temporarily favourable conditions which have permitted the growth of population beyond what could be provided for when the favourable conditions were at an end.

> **Study Question**
>
> Was the peace described by Keynes unfairly punitive?

H.G. Wells

H.G. Wells (1866–1946), along with a number of prominent British scholars and diplomats, was a founding member of the League of Free Nations Association, which was formed in 1918 to advance the cause of global unification. Wells and others believed that there must be no more war, as the scale of destruction would devastate the globe. A truly international organization, built on the principle of collective security, could perhaps

avoid such a catastrophe. Many of Wells's fictional works explore his fears of a future dominated by increasingly destructive wars. The document that follows was published in the United States in 1919. In it, Wells and a number of co-authors examine the potential inherent in an association of the nations of the world.

Document Source: Herbert George Wells, *The Idea of a League of Nations* (Boston: The Atlantic Monthly Press, Inc., 1919), 3–18.

The Idea of a League of Nations

Unification of human affairs, to the extent at least of a cessation of war and a worldwide rule of international law, is no new idea; it can be traced through many centuries of history. It is found as

an acceptable commonplace in a fragment, *De Republica*, of Cicero. It has, indeed, appeared and passed out of the foreground of thought, and reappeared there, again and again

Hitherto, however, if only on account of the limitations of geographical knowledge, the project has rarely been truly world-wide, though in some instances it has comprehended practically all the known world. Almost always there has been an excluded fringe of barbarians and races esteemed as less than men.

. . . at the outbreak of the Great War in August, 1914, Europe and the world awoke out of a dream of intensified nationality to a new system of realities which were entirely antagonistic to the continuance of national separations.

It is necessary to state very plainly the nature of these new forces. Upon them rests the whole case for the League of Nations as it is here presented. It is a new case. It is argued here that these forces give us powers novel in history and bring mankind face to face with dangers such as it has never confronted before. It is maintained that, on the one hand, they render possible such a reasoned coordination of human affairs as has never hitherto been conceivable, and that, on the other, they so enlarge and intensify the scope and evil of war and of international hostility as to give what was formerly a generous aspiration more and more of the aspect of an imperative necessity. Under the lurid illumination of the world war, the idea of world-unification has passed rapidly from the sphere of the literary idealist into that of the methodical, practical man, and the task of an examination of its problems and possibilities, upon the scale which the near probability of an actual experiment demands, is thrust upon the world. . . .

And we live to-day in a time of accelerated inventiveness and innovation, when a decade modifies the material of inter-communication far more extensively than did any century before, in range, swiftness, and intensity alike. Within the present century, since 1900, there have been far more extensive changes in these things than occurred in the ten centuries before Christ. Instead of regarding *Around the World in Eighty Days* as an amazing feat of hurry, we can now regard a flight about the globe in fifteen or sixteen days as a reasonable and moderate performance. The teaching of history compels us to recognize in these new facilities factors which will necessarily work out into equally revolutionary social and political consequences. . . .

While all these things, on the one hand, point plainly now to such possibilities of human unification and world unanimity as no one could have dreamed of a hundred years ago, there has been, on the other hand, a change, an intensification, of the destructive processes of war which opens up a black alternative to this pacific settlement of human affairs. The case as it is commonly stated in the propaganda literature for a League of Nations is a choice between, on the one hand, a general agreement on the part of mankind to organize a permanent peace, and on the other, a progressive development of the preparation for war and the means of conducting war which must ultimately eat up human freedom and all human effort, and, as the phrase goes, destroy civilization.

It is not impossible to adumbrate the general nature of the catastrophe which threatens mankind if war-making goes on. Modern warfare is not congenial to the working masses anywhere. No doubt the primitive form of warfare, a murderous bickering with adjacent tribes, is natural enough to uneducated men; but modern warfare, and still more the preparation for it, involves distresses, strains, and a continuity of base and narrow purpose quite beyond the patience and interest of the millions of ordinary men who find no other profit in it but suffering. The natural man is more apt for chaotic local fighting than for large-scale systematic fighting. Hatred campaigns and a sustained propaganda are needed to keep up the combatant spirit in a large modern state, even during actual hostilities; and in the case of Russia we have a striking example of the distaste a whole population may develop for the war-strain, even during the war and with the enemy at its gates.

What is likely to happen, then, when the working masses of Central and Western Europe, being no longer sustained by the immediate excitement of actual war, find themselves still obliged to go on, year after year, producing vast masses of war-material, pledged to carry a heavy burden of war loan *rentiers* on their backs, and subjected to an exacerbated conscription? Possibly, so far as the *rentier* burden on the worker goes, a great rise in prices and wages will relieve the worker to some extent, but only at the cost of acute disappointment and distress at another social level. There is a dangerously narrowing limit now to the confidence of the common man in the intelligence and good faith of those who direct his affairs; and the probability of a cruel confused class-war throughout Europe, roughly parallel in its methods to the Bolshevik revolution in Russia, and released by a similar loss of faith in leaders and government, appears at the end of the vista of waste of directive energy and natural resources, completing that waste of energy and resources into which the belligerent systems of Europe, the German Empire being the chief and foremost, have led mankind. Systematic force, overstrained and exhausted, will then give place to chaotic force, and general disorganization will ensue. Thereafter the world may welter in confusion for many generations, through such ruinous and impoverished centuries as close the Roman imperial story, before it develops the vitality for an effective reorganization.

Such, roughly, is the idea of the phrase "downfall of civilization" as used in discussions like these. It is a vision of the world as a social system collapsing chaotically, not under the assault of outer barbarians, but beneath the pressure of this inevitable hypertrophy of war.

> **Study Question**
>
> How accurate was this assessment of a future without a strong commitment to collective security?

Henry Cabot Lodge

Henry Cabot Lodge (1850–1924) was elected as a Republican member of Congress in 1887. Though he hoped that the United States would play a role in world affairs and he had backed Theodore Roosevelt's ambitions in Latin America, Lodge was best known for his opposition to Woodrow Wilson's policies—in particular, to American participation in the League of Nations. Lodge's objections to the League are made clear in this extract from an August 1919 speech.

Document Source: *Congressional Record*, 66th Cong., 1st sess., 1919, 3779–84.

The League of Nations

For ourselves we asked absolutely nothing. We have not asked any government or governments to guarantee our boundaries or our political independence. We have no fear in regard to either. We have sought no territory, no privileges, no advantages, for ourselves. That is the fact. It is apparent on the face of the treaty. I do not mean to reflect upon a single one of the powers with which we have been associated in the war against Germany, but there is not one of them which has not sought individual advantages for their own national benefit. I do not criticize their desires at all. The services and sacrifices of England and France and Belgium and Italy are beyond estimate and beyond praise. I am glad they should have what they desire for their own welfare and safety. But they all receive under the peace territorial and commercial benefits. We are asked to give, and we in no way seek to take. Surely it is not too much to insist that when we are offered nothing but the opportunity to give and to aid others we should have the right to say what sacrifices we shall make and what the magnitude of our gifts shall be. In the prosecution of the war we have unstintedly given American lives and American treasure. When the war closed we had 3,000,000 men under arms. We were turning the country into a vast workshop for war. We advanced ten billions to our allies. We refused no assistance that we could possibly render. All the great energy and power of the Republic were put at the service of the good cause. We have not been ungenerous. We have been devoted to the cause of freedom, humanity, and civilization everywhere. Now we are asked, in the making of peace, to sacrifice our sovereignty in important respects, to involve ourselves almost without limit in the affairs of other nations and to yield up policies and rights which we have maintained throughout our history. We are asked to incur liabilities to an unlimited extent and furnish assets at the same time which no man can measure. I think it is not only our right but our duty to determine how far we shall go. . . .

Never forget that this league is primarily—I might say overwhelmingly—a political organization, and I object strongly to having the policies of the United States turn upon disputes where deep feeling is aroused but in which we have no direct interest. It will all tend to delay the Americanization of our great population, and it is more important not only to the United States but to the peace of the world to make all these people good Americans than it is to determine that some

piece of territory should belong to one European country rather than to another. For this reason I wish to limit strictly our interference in the affairs of Europe and of Africa. We have interests of our own in Asia and in the Pacific which we must guard upon our own account, but the less we undertake to play the part of umpire and thrust ourselves into European conflicts the better for the United States and for the world.

It has been reiterated here on this floor, and reiterated to the point of weariness, that in every treaty there is some sacrifice of sovereignty we are justified in sacrificing. In what I have already said about other nations putting us into war I have covered one point of sovereignty which ought never to be yielded—the power to send American soldiers and sailors everywhere, which ought never to be taken from the American people or impaired in the slightest degree. Let us beware how we palter with our independence. We have not reached the great position from which we were able to come down into the field of battle and help to save the world from tyranny by being guided by others. Our vast power has all been built up and gathered together by ourselves alone. We forced our way upward from the days of the Revolution, through a world often hostile and always indifferent. We owe no debt to anyone except to France in that Revolution, and those policies and those rights on which our power has been founded should never be lessened or weakened. It will be no service to the world to do so and it will be of intolerable injury to the United States. We will do our share. We are ready and anxious to help in all ways to preserve the world's peace. But we can do it best by not crippling ourselves. . . .

. . . I am thinking of what is best for the world, for if the United States fails the best hopes of mankind fail with it. I have never had but one allegiance—I can not divide it now. I have loved but one flag and I can not share that devotion and give affection to the mongrel banner invented by a league. Internationalism, illustrated by the Bolshevik and by the man to whom all countries are alike provided they can make money out of them, is to me repulsive. National I must remain, and in that way I like all other Americans can render the amplest service to the world. The United States is the world's best hope, but if you fetter her in the interests and quarrels of other nations, if you tangle her in the intrigues of Europe, you will destroy her power for good and endanger her very existence. Leave her to march freely through the centuries to come as in the years that have gone. . . .

We are told that we shall "break the heart of the world" if we do not take this league just as it stands. I fear that the hearts of the vast majority of mankind would beat on strongly and steadily and without any quickening if the league were to perish altogether. If it should be effectively and beneficently changed the people who would lie awake in sorrow for a single night could be easily gathered in one not very large room but those who would draw a long breath of relief would reach to millions.

"If We Were in the League of Nations." A 1920 propaganda poster emphasizes the potential cost to the US of joining the League of Nations.

Courtesy of the Library of Congress, Prints and Photographs Division (LC-USZ62-85742).

Study Question

Can a nation maintain its independence and yet participate in a meaningful way in organizations based on collective security?

Web Resources

A Multimedia History of the First World War
    http://www.firstworldwar.com
Canada and the First World War
    http://www.collectionscanada.gc.ca/firstworldwar/index-e.html
World War I: Trenches on the Web
    http://www.worldwar1.com/trenchesontheweb.htm
Spartacus Educational: First World War Index
    http://www.spartacus.schoolnet.co.uk/FWW.htm

Recommended Reading

Vera Brittain, *Testament of Youth* (New York: Penguin, 1994). *Testament of Youth* is an autobiographical story of the author's coming of age in pre-war England and her service as a nurse, both in Malta and in France near the Western Front during the Great War. Personal losses and the lost generation are interwoven into Brittain's memoir, which is based on letters and diaries written at the time.

Robert Graves, *Goodbye to All That* (New York: Anchor, 1958). *Goodbye to All That* is Graves's autobiography. It speaks of a generation raised in late Victorian Britain and sacrificed on the battlefields of France and Belgium. Considered by many to be the best First World War narrative, it contains observations on society, class, nationalism, and above all, the horrors of the trenches.

Ernest Hemingway, *The Sun Also Rises* (London: Scribner, 1995). Set in Paris, Madrid, and Pamplona, Hemingway's 1926 volume, *The Sun Also Rises*, explores the physical and psychological impact of the Great War on "the lost generation." Key themes include the search for meaning and fulfillment, and the escape from reality through alcohol, sex, and violence.

Aldous Huxley, *Brave New World* (New York: HarperCollins Perennial Classics, 1998). *Brave New World*, written in 1932, tells of life in the futuristic utopia of the year 632 AF (After Ford). Science and technology provide for all needs and have assumed control of all human functions, including reproduction—humans are now tailored genetically to fit their future jobs. Mood-altering drugs and unlimited sexual partners maintain happiness, at the cost of freedom and individuality.

Sinclair Lewis, *Babbitt* (New York: Bantam Classics, 1998). *Babbitt* chronicles American society in the business-driven, capitalist, materialistic, "normalcy" of the 1920s. Through George E. Babbitt of Zenith, Ohio, the values of "normalcy" are tested during a brief period of Bohemian experimentation, after which "normalcy" returns, with Babbitt slightly more tolerant and wiser.

Henry Miller, *Tropic of Cancer* (New York: Grove Press, 1987). *Tropic of Cancer*—banned in the United States from its initial publication in 1934, and for nearly 30 years thereafter due to its graphic sexuality—is Miller's semi-autobiographical account of the economically depressed, bohemian interwar Paris (*Tropic of Capricorn*, 1936, is set in the United States in the same era).

Erich Maria Remarque, *All Quiet on the Western Front* (New York: Ballantine, 1987). Remarque's 1928 antiwar testimony is told through the eyes of Paul Baumer, a German infantryman on the Western Front. The novel captures much of the horror of the war: the senseless slaughter of the trenches and the psychological impact on winners and losers alike.

H.G. Wells, *War of the Worlds* (New York: Signet Books, 1996). Focused on the consequences of a Martian invasion, *War of the Worlds*, written in 1898, remains one of the most famous turn-of-the-century narratives on technological and industrial change, imperialism, war, and destruction.

Recommended Viewing

Metropolis (Germany, 1927). Director: Fritz Lang (Silent, B&W). *Metropolis* is considered to be the most important German expressionist film. Set in the year 2000, the film offers Lang's vision of the future, where the elite live in towering skyscrapers and the masses labour beneath the earth, producing for the elite. Though many versions of *Metropolis* exist, a 2003 Kino Video release restored the film to 124 minutes and returned the original orchestral score by Gottfried Huppertz.

All Quiet on the Western Front (USA, 1930). Director: Lewis Milestone (B&W). Based on Erich Maria Remarque's novel, the movie is a classic depiction of the brutality of trench warfare from the German perspective. Considered one of the finest cinematic antiwar statements, this Academy Award winning film recreates the horrific conditions on the Western Front while revealing the intense patriotism of 1914.

Westfront 1918 (Germany, 1930). Director: G.W. Pabst (B&W). A multinational cast recreates the final few months of the First World War. Pabst's film emphasizes the extreme futility of war and briefly examines the desperate state of the German home front by the end of the war. The film is renowned for its exceptional battle scenes.

Paths of Glory (USA, 1957). Director: Stanley Kubrick (B&W). Set in 1917, Kubrick's film condemns the idiocy of the French military leadership during the First World War and highlights the futility of the war itself. The movie, which was banned in France for many years, focuses on the needless sacrifice of French troops and the consequences of refusing to follow orders.

Cabaret (USA, 1972). Director: Bob Fosse. Based on Christopher Isherwood's novel *Goodbye to Berlin*, this movie is a musical recreation of life in Germany during the early 1930s. Fosse's film—a winner of eight Academy Awards—focuses on the cabaret culture of the era, depicting the hedonism and excess of the late Weimar period and the slow descent of German society into fascism.

Gallipoli (Australia, 1991). Director: Peter Weir. *Gallipoli* dramatizes the catastrophic defeat of Australian and New Zealand forces at the Battle of Gallipoli. The second half of the film recreates the battle itself. Like *All Quiet on the Western Front*, Peter Weir's film makes a strong antiwar statement.

Ararat (Canada, 2002). Director: Atom Egoyan. *Ararat* examines the Armenian genocide and its historical impact. Egoyan creates a non-linear depiction of the impact of the genocide on several generations of Armenian émigrés. A number of different plot lines are interwoven, with the genocide itself standing as the unifying theme.

4

The Appeal of Revolutionary Change

Tsar Nicholas II, the final member of the Romanov dynasty to rule Russia. Tsar Nicholas made what many believe to be a fatal mistake by leaving St Petersburg to command Russian troops at the front.

Photograph courtesy of the University of Texas Libraries , http://www.lib.utexas.edu/exhibits/portraits/index.php?img=332

The late nineteenth and early twentieth centuries witnessed profound political, economic, cultural, and social transformations around the world. Both Russia and China experienced revolutionary changes to their traditional political systems which radically altered the lives of the people in those countries. In Russia, a revolutionary process began in the late nineteenth century and reached its climax during the First World War with the rise to power of Vladimir Lenin and the Bolshevik Party. However, Russia's transformation had only just begun in 1917. From the Bolshevik Revolution until the late 1930s Russian society continued to experience massive socio-economic upheavals, first under Lenin and then, perhaps even more profoundly, under Joseph Stalin.

In China, resentment towards foreign control and its social and economic impact increased throughout the late nineteenth and early twentieth centuries, leading to periodic anti-foreign and anti-dynastic uprisings. By 1911 there had been numerous unsuccessful attempts to topple the Qing dynasty, but on 10 October 1911 a fortuitous set of circumstances, including a revolt by elements of the Qing military, allowed the rebels to secure control over a key region in Central China. In 1912, Puyi, the boy emperor, was forced to abdicate. After several thousand years of monarchical rule China became a republic. Stability, however, would prove to be elusive as the people of China experienced several more decades of revolutionary upheaval before the final victory of the Chinese Communists in 1949.

The appeal of a revolutionary remaking of society was not limited to China and Russia. European intellectuals posited a number of solutions to the problems of the late nineteenth and early twentieth century. Political Zionism emerged as a possible remedy to the widespread discrimination facing Europe's Jewish population. Meanwhile, intellectuals such as Rosa Luxemburg saw socialism as a means both to end the bloodshed of the First World War while simultaneously initiating the final confrontation between proletariat and bourgeoisie. Socialist ideas also made a powerful impact in the colonial world. Leaders such as Jawaharlal Nehru viewed socialism as the key to independence and to a better future for the 400 million people of the Indian subcontinent. The changes initiated in Turkey, where Mustapha Kemal Atatürk set out to transform the last remnant of the Ottoman Empire into a modern, secular, democratic state, were no less revolutionary. Finally, in Mexico, a lengthy period of revolution, beginning in 1911, would lay the foundations for the modern Mexican State.

The documents in this chapter highlight the sweeping changes that took place around the world during the 1910s and 1920s. Theodor Herzl advocates the creation of a Jewish State, either in Palestine or Argentina. Luxemburg's "Junius Pamphlet" invokes the power of the European working class to transform their own lives. Documents by Vladimir Lenin and Nikita Khrushchev reveal both the chaotic situation in Russia in the early years of the twentieth century, and the great hope for the future. Writing in China, Li Dazhao sees in the triumph of Bolshevism in Russia, the best hope for the future of the world's oppressed classes. Sun Yat-sen and Soong Ching-ling propose far-reaching changes for newly republican China. In the concluding documents in this chapter, John Reed assesses the nascent revolutionary ideals building in Mexico; Mustapha Kemal Atatürk discusses the revolutionary changes necessary to create a modern Turkish Republic; and Jawaharlal Nehru reflects on the importance of socialism, both in India and around the world.

Theodor Herzl

Theodor (Binyamin Ze'ev) Herzl (1860–1904) worked as a writer and journalist in Vienna. As a correspondent for the liberal newspaper The New Free Press *he covered the 1884 trial of Alfred Dreyfus, a French Jewish military officer convicted of treason, despite overwhelming evidence of his innocence. During this time Herzl witnessed violent anti-Semitic demonstrations in which participants called for the*

destruction of the Jews. Herzl saw the Dreyfus trial, and many other anti-Semitic outbreaks around the turn of the century, as evidence of the impossibility of assimilation and acceptance in European society. This led him to develop his idea of a separate Jewish State in an 1896 pamphlet excerpts of which follow.

Document Source: Theodor Herzl, *The Jewish State* (New York: American Zionist Emergency Council, 1946), 85–97.

The Jewish State

No one can deny the gravity of the situation of the Jews. Wherever they live in perceptible numbers, they are more or less persecuted. Their equality before the law, granted by statute, has become practically a dead letter. They are debarred from filling even moderately high positions, either in the army, or in any public or private capacity. And attempts are made to thrust them out of business also: "Don't buy from Jews!"

Attacks in Parliaments, in assemblies, in the press, in the pulpit, in the street, on journeys—for example, their exclusion from certain hotels—even in places of recreation, become daily more numerous. The forms of persecution varying according to the countries and social circles in which they occur. In Russia, imposts are levied on Jewish villages; in Rumania, a few persons are put to death; in Germany, they get a good beating occasionally; in Austria, Anti-Semites exercise terrorism over all public life; in Algeria, there are travelling agitators; in Paris, the Jews are shut out of the so-called best social circles and excluded from clubs. Shades of anti-Jewish feeling are innumerable. But this is not to be an attempt to make out a doleful category of Jewish hardships. . . .

Everything tends, in fact, to one and the same conclusion, which is clearly enunciated in that classic Berlin phrase: "*Juden Raus.*" (Out with the Jews!)

I shall now put the Question in the briefest possible form: Are we to "get out" now and where to?

Or, may we yet remain? And, if so, how long?

Let us first settle the point of staying where we are. Can we hope for better days, can we possess our souls in patience, can we wait in pious resignation till the princes and peoples of this earth are more mercifully disposed towards us? I say that we cannot hope for a change in the current of feeling. And why not? Even if we were as near to the hearts of princes as are their other subjects, they could not protect us. They would only fuel popular hatred by showing us too much favour. By "too much," I really mean less than is claimed as a right by every ordinary citizen, or by every race. The nations in whose midst Jews live are all either covertly or openly Anti-Semitic.

The common people have not, and indeed cannot have, any historic comprehension. They do not know that the sins of the Middle Ages are now being visited on the nations of Europe. We are what the Ghetto made us. We have attained pre-eminence in finance, because mediaeval conditions drove us to it. The same process is now being repeated. We are again being forced into finance, now it is the stock exchange, by being kept out of other branches of economic activity. Being on the stock exchange, we are consequently exposed afresh to contempt. At the same time we continue to produce an abundance of mediocre intellects who find no outlet, and this endangers our social position as much as does our increasing wealth. Educated Jews without means are now rapidly becoming Socialists. Hence we are certain to suffer very severely in the struggle between classes, because we stand in the most exposed position in the camps of both Socialists and capitalists. . . .

Causes of Anti-Semitism

We shall not again touch on those causes which are a result of temperament, prejudice, and narrow views, but shall here restrict ourselves to political and economical causes alone. Modern Anti-Semitism is not to be confounded with the religious persecution of the Jews of former times. It does occasionally take a religious bias in some countries, but the main current of the aggressive movement has now changed. In the principal countries where Anti-Semitism prevails, it does so as a result of the emancipation of the Jews. When civilized nations awoke to the inhumanity of discriminatory legislation and enfranchised us, our enfranchisement came too late. It was no longer possible to remove our disabilities in our old homes. For we had, curiously enough, developed while in the Ghetto into a bourgeois people, and we stepped out of it only to enter into fierce competition with the middle classes. Hence, our emancipation set us suddenly within this middle-class circle, where we have a double pressure to sustain, from within and from without. The Christian bourgeoisie would not be unwilling to cast us as a sacrifice to Socialism,

though that would not greatly improve matters.

At the same time, the equal rights of Jews before the law cannot be withdrawn where they have once been conceded. Not only because their withdrawal would be opposed to the spirit of our age, but also because it would immediately drive all Jews, rich and poor alike, into the ranks of subversive parties. . . .

Effects of Anti-Semitism

The oppression we endure does not improve us, for we are not a whit better than ordinary people. It is true that we do not love our enemies; but he alone who can conquer himself dare reproach us with that fault. Oppression naturally creates hostility against oppressors, and our hostility aggravates the pressure. It is impossible to escape from this eternal circle.

"No!" Some soft-hearted visionaries will say: "No, it is possible! Possible by means of the ultimate perfection of humanity."

Is it necessary to point to the sentimental folly of this view? He who would found his hope for improved conditions on the ultimate perfection of humanity would indeed be relying upon a Utopia!

I referred previously to our "assimilation." I do not for a moment wish to imply that I desire such an end. Our national character is too historically famous, and, in spite of every degradation, too fine to make its annihilation desirable. We might perhaps be able to merge ourselves entirely into surrounding races, if these were to leave us in peace for a period of two generations. But they will not leave us in peace. For a little period they manage to tolerate us, and then their hostility breaks out again and again. The world is provoked somehow by our prosperity, because it has for many centuries been accustomed to consider us as the most contemptible among the poverty-stricken. In its ignorance and narrowness of heart, it fails to observe that prosperity weakens our Judaism and extinguishes our peculiarities. It is only pressure that forces us back to the parent stem; it is only hatred encompassing us that makes us strangers once more.

Thus, whether we like it or not, we are now, and shall henceforth remain, a historic group with unmistakable characteristics common to us all.

We are one people—our enemies have made us one without our consent, as repeatedly happens in history. Distress binds us together, and, thus united, we suddenly discover our strength. Yes, we are strong enough to form a State, and, indeed, a model State. We possess all human and material resources necessary for the purpose. . . .

The Plan

The whole plan is in its essence perfectly simple, as it must necessarily be if it is to come within the comprehension of all.

Let the sovereignty be granted us over a portion of the globe large enough to satisfy the rightful requirements of a nation; the rest we shall manage for ourselves.

The creation of a new State is neither ridiculous nor impossible. We have in our day witnessed the process in connection with nations which were not largely members of the middle class, but poorer, less educated, and consequently weaker than ourselves. The Governments of all countries scourged by Anti-Semitism will be keenly interested in assisting us to obtain the sovereignty we want.

The plan, simple in design, but complicated in execution, will be carried out by two agencies: The Society of Jews and the Jewish Company.

The Society of Jews will do the preparatory work in the domains of science and politics, which the Jewish Company will afterwards apply practically.

The Jewish Company will be the liquidating agent of the business interests of departing Jews, and will organize commerce and trade in the new country.

We must not imagine the departure of the Jews to be a sudden one. It will be gradual, continuous, and will cover many decades. The poorest will go first to cultivate the soil. In accordance with a preconceived plan, they will construct roads, bridges, railways, and telegraph installations; regulate rivers; and build their own dwellings; their labour will create trade, trade will create markets, and markets will attract new settlers, for every man will go voluntarily, at his own expense and his own risk. The labour expended on the land will enhance its value, and the Jews will soon perceive that a new and permanent sphere of operation is opening here for that spirit of enterprise which has heretofore met only with hatred and obloquy. . . .

The Society of Jews will treat with the present masters of the land, putting itself under the protectorate of the European Powers, if they prove friendly to the plan. We could offer the present possessors of the land enormous advantages, assume part of the public debt, build new roads for traffic, which our presence in the country would render necessary, and do many other things. The creation of our State would be beneficial to adjacent countries, because the cultivation of a strip of land increases the value of its surrounding districts in innumerable ways.

Palestine or Argentine

Shall we choose Palestine or Argentine? We shall take what is given us, and what is selected by Jewish public opinion. The Society will determine both these points.

Argentine is one of the most fertile countries in the world, extends over a vast area, has a sparse population, and a mild climate. The Argentine Republic would derive considerable profit from the cession of a portion of its territory to us. The present infiltration of Jews has certainly produced some discontent, and it would be necessary to enlighten the Republic on the intrinsic difference of our new movement.

Palestine is our ever-memorable historic home. The very name of Palestine would attract our people with a force of marvelous potency. If His Majesty the Sultan were to give us Palestine, we could in return undertake to regulate the whole finances of Turkey. We should there form a portion of a rampart of Europe against Asia, an outpost of civilization as opposed to barbarism. We should as a neutral State remain in contact with all Europe, which would have to guarantee our existence. The sanctuaries of Christendom would be safeguarded by assigning to them an extra-territorial status such as is well-known to the law of nations. We should form a guard of honour about these sanctuaries, answering for the fulfillment of this duty with our existence. This guard of honour would be the great symbol of the solution of the Jewish question after 18 centuries of Jewish suffering.

> **Study Question**
>
> In what ways does Herzl's argument echo the preconceptions of European colonialists?

Rosa Luxemburg

Rosa Luxemburg (1871–1919) was born in the Polish area of Russia. In 1889 she emigrated to Zurich and joined study groups with other exiled Russian revolutionaries including Alexandra Kollontai and Georgi Plekhanov. In 1898 she joined the German Social Democratic Party (SPD). Between 1907 and 1914 Luxemburg gradually developed a more radical interpretation of Marxist theory, insisting on the necessity of a violent revolution. "The Junius Pamphlet" was written in early 1915 while *Luxemburg was imprisoned for her opposition to the war. It was published in Zurich in February 1916 and was illegally smuggled into Germany for distribution. Luxemburg's ideas became the foundational doctrines of several important communist groups, including the German Communist Party (KPD). She was murdered by right-wing extremists on 15 January 1919.*

Document Source: Rosa Luxemburg, "The Junius Pamphlet: The Crisis of German Social Democracy" (1915); Luxemburg Internet Archive.

The Junius Pamphlet

The scene has changed fundamentally. The six weeks' march to Paris has grown into a world drama.[1] Mass slaughter has become the tiresome and monotonous business of the day and the end is no closer. Bourgeois statecraft is held fast in its own vice. The spirits summoned up can no longer be exorcised.

Gone is the euphoria. Gone the patriotic noise in the streets, the chase after the gold-coloured automobile, one false telegram after another, the wells poisoned by cholera, the Russian students heaving bombs over every railway bridge in Berlin, the French airplanes over Nuremberg, the spy hunting public running amok in the streets, the swaying crowds in the coffee shops with ear-deafening patriotic songs surging ever higher, whole city neighbourhoods transformed into mobs ready to denounce, to mistreat women, to shout hurrah and to induce delirium in themselves by means of wild rumours. Gone, too, is the atmosphere of ritual murder, the Kishinev air where the crossing guard is the only remaining representative of human dignity.[2]

The spectacle is over. German scholars, those "stumbling lemurs," have been whistled off the stage long ago. The trains full of reservists are no longer accompanied by virgins fainting from pure jubilation. They no longer greet the people from the windows of the train with joyous smiles. Carrying their packs, they quietly trot along the streets where the public goes about its daily business with aggrieved visages.

In the prosaic atmosphere of pale day there sounds a different chorus—the hoarse cries of the vulture and the hyenas of the battlefield. Ten thousand tarpaulins guaranteed up to regulations! A hundred thousand kilos of bacon, cocoa powder, coffee-substitute—c.o.d, immediate delivery! Hand grenades, lathes, cartridge pouches, marriage bureaus for widows of the fallen, leather belts, jobbers for war orders—serious offers only! The cannon fodder loaded onto trains in August and September is mouldering in the killing fields of Belgium, the Vosges, and Masurian Lakes where the profits are springing up like weeds. It's a question of getting the harvest into the barn quickly. Across the ocean stretch thousands of greedy hands to snatch it up.

Business thrives in the ruins. Cities become piles of ruins; villages become cemeteries; countries, deserts; populations are beggared; churches, horse stalls. International law, treaties, and alliances, the most sacred words and the highest authority have been torn in shreds. Every sovereign "by the grace of God" is called a rogue and lying scoundrel by his cousin on the other side. Every diplomat is a cunning rascal to his colleagues in the other party. Every government sees every other as dooming its own people and worthy only of universal contempt. There are food riots in Venice, in Lisbon, Moscow, Singapore. There is plague in Russia, and misery

An 1890 portrait of Rosa Luxemburg. At this time she was studying in Zurich with prominent Marxist intellectuals.

Courtesy of the Library of Congress, Prints and Photographs Division (LC-USZ62-122266).

and despair everywhere.

Violated, dishonoured, wading in blood, dripping filth—there stands bourgeois society. This is it [in reality]. Not all spic and span and moral, with pretence to culture, philosophy, ethics, order, peace, and the rule of law—but the ravening beast, the witches' sabbath of anarchy, a plague to culture and humanity. Thus it reveals itself in its true, its naked form.

In the midst of this witches' sabbath a catastrophe of world-historical proportions has happened: International Social Democracy has capitulated. To deceive ourselves about it, to cover it up, would be the most foolish, the most fatal thing the proletariat could do. Marx says: ". . . the democrat (that is, the petty bourgeois revolutionary) [comes] out of the most shameful defeats as unmarked as he naively went into them; he comes away with the newly gained conviction that he must be victorious, not that he or his party ought to give up the old principles, but that conditions ought to accommodate him." The modern proletariat comes out of historical tests differently. Its tasks and its errors are both gigantic: no prescription, no schema valid for every case, no infallible leader to show it the path to follow. Historical experience is its only school mistress. Its thorny way to self-emancipation is paved not only with immeasurable suffering but also with countless errors. The aim of its journey—its emancipation depends on this—is whether the proletariat can learn from its own errors. Self-criticism, remorseless, cruel, and going to the core of things is the life's breath and light of the proletarian movement. The fall of the socialist proletariat in the present world war is unprecedented. It is a misfortune for humanity. But socialism will be lost only if the international proletariat fails to measure the depth of this fall, if it refuses to learn from it.

The last forty-five year period in the development of the modern labour movement now stands in doubt. What we are experiencing in this critique is a closing of accounts for what will soon be half a century of work at our posts. The grave of the Paris Commune ended the first phase of the European labour movement as well as the First International.[3] Since then there began a new phase. In place of spontaneous revolutions, risings, and barricades, after which the proletariat each time fell back into passivity, there began the systematic daily struggle, the exploitation of bourgeois parliamentarianism, mass organizations, the marriage of the economic with the political struggle, and that of socialist ideals with stubborn defence of immediate daily interests. For the first time the polestar of strict scientific teachings lit the way for the proletariat and for its emancipation. Instead of sects, schools, utopias, and isolated experiments in various countries, there arose a uniform, international theoretical basis which bound countries together like the strands of a rope. Marxist knowledge gave the working class of the entire world a compass by which it can make sense of the welter of daily events and by

which it can always plot the right course to take to the fixed and final goal. . . .

One thing is certain. The world war is a turning point. It is foolish and mad to imagine that we need only survive the war, like a rabbit waiting out the storm under a bush, in order to fall happily back into the old routine once it is over. The world war has altered the conditions of our struggle and, most of all, it has changed us. Not that the basic law of capitalist development, the life-and-death war between capital and labour, will experience any amelioration. But now, in the midst of the war, the masks are falling and the old familiar visages smirk at us. The tempo of development has received a mighty jolt from the eruption of the volcano of imperialism. The violence of the conflicts in the bosom of society, the enormousness of the tasks that tower up before the socialist proletariat—these make everything that has transpired in the history of the workers' movement seem a pleasant idyll.

Historically, this war was ordained to thrust forward the cause of the proletariat. . . . It was ordained to drive the German proletariat to the pinnacle of the nation and thereby begin to organize the international and universal conflict between capital and labour for political power within the state.

But to push ahead to the victory of socialism we need a strong, activist, educated proletariat, and masses whose power lies in intellectual culture as well as numbers. These masses are being decimated by the world war. The flower of our mature and youthful strength, hundreds of thousands of whom were socialistically schooled in England, France, Belgium, Germany, and Russia, the product of decades of educational and agitational training, and other hundreds of thousands who could be won for socialism tomorrow, fall and moulder on the miserable battlefields. The fruits of decades of sacrifice and the efforts of generations are destroyed in a few weeks. The key troops of the international proletariat are torn up by the roots.

The blood-letting of the June Days [1848] paralyzed the French workers' movement for a decade and a half. Then the blood-letting of the Commune massacres again retarded it for more than a decade. What is now occurring is an unprecedented mass slaughter that is reducing the adult working population of all the leading civilized countries to women, old people, and cripples. This blood-letting threatens to bleed the European workers' movement to death. Another such world war and the outlook for socialism will be buried beneath the rubble heaped up by imperialist barbarism. . . .

The world war today is demonstrably not only murder on a grand scale; it is also suicide of the working classes of Europe. The soldiers of socialism, the proletarians of England, France, Germany, Russia, and Belgium have for months been killing one another at the behest of capital. They are driving the cold steel of murder into each other's hearts. Locked in the embrace of death, they tumble into a common grave.

"Deutschland, Deutschland über Alles! Long live democracy! Long live the Tsar and Slavdom! Ten thousand tarpaulins guaranteed up to regulations! A hundred thousand kilos of bacon, coffee-substitute for immediate delivery!". . . Dividends are rising, and the proletarians are falling. And with every one there sinks into the grave a fighter of the future, a soldier of the revolution, mankind's saviour from the yoke of capitalism.

The madness will cease and the bloody demons of hell will vanish only when workers in Germany and France, England and Russia finally awake from their stupor, extend to each other a brotherly hand, and drown out the bestial chorus of imperialist war-mongers and the shrill cry of capitalist hyenas with labour's old and mighty battle cry:

Proletarians of all lands, unite!

Notes

1. Germany's war plans anticipated that victory in the West would be complete within six weeks.
2. For three days in April 1903 Kishinev, in the Russian Empire, was the scene of anti-Jewish violence which left more than 50 Jews dead and over 500 injured.
3. At the end of the Franco–Prussian War of 1870–71 Parisians revolted against the French government. For ten weeks representatives of the working class, the Commune, ruled Paris.

Study Question

What do you think were the most important factors which induced soldiers to continue to fight, even when the situation seemed hopeless?

V.I. Lenin

During the February 1917 revolution that overthrew the increasingly inept Romanov dynasty, Lenin remained in exile in Switzerland. He would not return to Russia until April of that year. In the interim he wrote a number of letters, articles, and pamphlets addressing the unfolding situation, and the role that the Bolsheviks would play. The following piece was written in March 1917, immediately before Lenin's return to Russia and the publication of his "April Theses" which famously called for "peace, land, and bread," as well as the transfer of power to the workers' and soldiers' soviets.

Document Source: V.I. Lenin, "The Revolution in Russia and the Tasks of the Workers of All Countries, *Lenin: Collected Works*, Vol. 23 (Moscow: Progress Publishers, 1964), 350–4.

The Revolution in Russia

Comrade workers,

The prediction of the socialists who have remained faithful to socialism and have not succumbed to the savage and beastly war hysteria has proved correct. The first revolution, caused by the world-wide predatory war among the capitalists of various countries, has broken out. The imperialist war, that is, a war for the capitalist division of spoils, for the strangling of weak nations, has *begun* to turn into civil war, that is, a war of the workers against the capitalists, of the toilers and the oppressed against their oppressors, against tsars and kings, landowners and capitalists, a war for mankind's complete liberation from wars, from poverty of the masses, from oppression of man by man!

To the Russian workers has fallen the honour and the good fortune of being the *first* to start the revolution—the great and only legitimate and just war, the war of the oppressed against the oppressors.

The St Petersburg workers have vanquished the tsarist monarchy. Having started the uprising unarmed in face of machine-guns, in their heroic struggle against the police and the tsar's armies, the workers won over the majority of the soldiers of the St Petersburg garrison. The same thing occurred in Moscow and in other cities. Abandoned by his armies, the tsar had to capitulate: he signed an abdication on behalf of himself and his son. He suggested that the throne be transferred to his brother Mikhail.

Owing to the great rapidity of the revolution, the direct assistance of the Anglo-French capitalists, insufficient class-consciousness of the *mass* of the workers and the people in St Petersburg, the organization and preparedness of the Russian landowners and capitalists, *they* succeeded in

seizing power. The key posts, the premiership and the Ministries of the Interior and War, in the new Russian government, the "Provisional Government," have gone to Lvov and Guchkov,[1] the Octobrists who had done their best to help Nicholas the Bloody and Stolypin the Hangman crush the Revolution of 1905, shoot down and hang workers and peasants fighting for land and freedom. The less important ministerial posts have gone to the Cadets: Foreign Affairs to Milyukov, Education to Manuilov, Agriculture to Shingaryov. One quite insignificant post, that of Minister of Justice, has gone to the glib-tongued Trudovik Kerensky, whom the capitalists need to pacify the people with empty promises, fool

W.A. Rogers, an American cartoonist, illustrates Lenin and Trotsky as lizards. Rogers was criticizing the upper-class fascination with Bolshevism.

Accession no. DLC/PP-1932:0042; published in: New York Herald, Nov. 23, 1919, sec. 1, p.4. http://www.loc.gov/pictures/item/2010717818/

them with high-sounding phrases, reconcile them to the government of landlords and capitalists who, in union with the capitalists of England and France, want to continue the predatory war, a war for the seizure of Armenia, Constantinople, Galicia, a war to enable the Anglo-French capitalists to *retain* the booty they have taken from the German capitalists (all Germany's African colonies), and, at the same time, *recover* the spoils seized by the German capitalist robbers (part of France, Belgium, Serbia, Rumania, etc.).

The workers could not, of course, trust such a government. They had overthrown the tsarist monarchy in their fight for *peace, bread* and *freedom*. They immediately saw why Guchkov, Milyukov and Co. succeeded in wresting victory from the hands of the working people. The reason was that the Russian landlords and capitalists were well prepared and organized; that they had on their side the power of capital, the *wealth* both of the Russian capitalists and of the richest capitalists in the world, the English and the French. The workers realized from the very start that in order to fight for peace, bread, and freedom, the labouring classes, the workers, soldiers and peasants, must *organize*, close their ranks, unite *independently* of the capitalists and *against* the capitalists.

Thus the St. Petersburg workers, having overthrown the tsarist monarchy, immediately set up their *own* organization, the *Soviet of Workers' Deputies*, immediately proceeded to strengthen and extend it, to organize *independent* Soviets of Workers' and Soldiers' Deputies. Only a few days after the revolution, the St. Petersburg Soviet of Workers and Soldiers' Deputies comprised *over 1,500* deputies of workers and peasants dressed in soldier's uniform. It enjoyed such wide confidence among the railway workers and the entire mass of the labouring population that it began to develop into a real *people's government*.

And even the most faithful friends and patrons of Guchkov-Milyukov, even the most faithful watchdogs of Anglo-French predatory capital, the staff correspondent of the richest newspaper of the English capitalists, Robert Wilson of *The Times*, and the staff correspondent of the richest paper of the French capitalists, Charles Rivet of *Le Temps*, even they, while hurling curses at the Soviet of Workers' Deputies, have been obliged to admit that *there are two governments in Russia*. One—recognized by "everybody" (actually, by everybody among the *wealthy*), the landlord and capitalist government of the Guchkovs and the Milyukovs. The other—recognized by "nobody" (of the wealthy classes), the government of the workers and the peasants—the St. Petersburg Soviet of Workers' and Soldiers' Deputies that is trying to establish Soviets of Workers' and Soviets of Peasants' Deputies *throughout Russia*. . . .

In none of its programmes has the new government said a *single word* about land for the peasants or higher wages for the workers. No date has as yet been set for convocation of the constituent assembly. No elections to the St. Petersburg City Council have as yet been appointed. The people's militia is being placed under the supervision of rural and urban local government bodies which, in accordance with the Stolypin law, were elected only by capitalists and the richest landowners. Governors are being appointed from the landowning class—and this is "freedom"!

Note

1. Prince Georgy Lvov served as prime minister of the Provisional Government after the abdication of the Tsar; Alexander Guchkov was war minister in the Provisional Government. Both had served in the Duma prior to the February Revolution.

Study Question

How realistic were the goals expressed by Lenin in this document?

Nikita Khrushchev

Nikita Sergeyevich Khrushchev (1894–1971) joined the Bolsheviks in 1918 and became a member of the CPSU Central Committee in 1934. Khrushchev participated in Stalin's purges and earned his complete trust. After 1939 Khrushchev became a full member of the Politburo and remained a loyal supporter until Stalin's death in 1953. In 1956 he emerged victorious from the power struggle that took place after Stalin's death. At the Twentieth Party Congress in 1956 he delivered a secret report denouncing Stalin's policies and personality. The following excerpt from Khrushchev's memoirs, written after he was dismissed from office in 1964, recalls the Fifteenth Party Congress in 1927—the final congress before Stalin's consolidation of power.

Document Source: Nikita Khrushchev, *Khrushchev Remembers*. Strobe Talbott, trans. (Boston, MA: Little, Brown, and Company, 1971), 23–6.

Khrushchev Remembers

In 1927 I attended—again, as a delegate from the Yuzovka Party organization—the Fifteenth Party Congress, at which Stalin and his supporters squared off against the Zinovievites[1] or "Leningrad opposition" as they were then called. I remember we used to say that even the sparrows were chirping the news to the man in the street that a schism had formed in the Party. Our delegation was again quartered in the House of Soviets at Number 3, Karetny Row. Shortly after we arrived in Moscow, we were told that Yakov Arkadyevich Yakovlev was coming by to talk to us about certain developments in the Party and to warn us about the situation that was likely to arise at the Congress. I think Yakovlev was one of Sergo Ordzhonikidze's deputies. We knew Yakovlev must be coming to see us on factional business because we were told not to let anyone into the meeting except members of the Ukrainian delegations. We also realized that Yakovlev was passing on to us confidential information and instructions directly from Stalin himself. Yakovlev explained where we differed with the Zinovievites and told us what we were to do. In other words, he prepared us to carry out factional work against the Zinoviev-Kamenev opposition which was then gathering force. Zinoviev was Chairman of the Comintern, the international Communist organization which steered the course of the world revolution. As the main person in the international Communist movement, Zinoviev commanded much authority and prestige. Yakovlev explained that Zinoviev was to be co-speaker with Stalin at the Congress. (He had given the General Report after Lenin's death and had been co-speaker with Stalin at the previous Party Congress, the Fourteenth, in 1925.) Yakovlev told us that the Leningrad delegation to the Fifteenth Congress had written a letter to the Congress Presidium demanding, on the basis of the Party Statutes, that Zinoviev once again be given equal time with Stalin.

When the Congress began we found that once again we had the central place in the hall. On our left were the Leningraders, and on our right was the Moscow delegation. We were in contact with the Moscow Party workers, coordinating with them our activities against the Leningrad opposition. Discussions and arguments were going on everywhere, formal and informal in large groups and small during the sessions and during the recesses, inside St George's Hall and out in the corridors.

I was distressed to find my old comrade Abramson in the enemy camp. He had been the editor of the newspaper *The Dictatorship of Labour* in Yuzovka when I returned from the army in 1922. Now he was working in Leningrad as the secretary of some district committee. He was a good Communist, but like all Leningraders, he was a Zinovievite. The Zinovievites had also added Badayev and Nikolayeva to their delegation, so that the opposition might swing more weight at the Congress. These were good active Party members. They're all dead now.

Stalin, Rykov, and Bukharin[2] spoke for the Central Committee line—that is, Stalin's line. There was the Central Committee line on one side and the opposition on the other. There was nothing in between.

A word about Bukharin. He was much respected and very popular. I had seen him and heard him speak back in 1919 when I was serving in the Red Army. As Secretary of our unit's Party cell I had been invited to a meeting of the active Party members in Kursk Province at which Bukharin gave a speech. Everyone was very pleased with him, and I was absolutely spellbound. He had an appealing personality and a strong democratic spirit. Later I met some comrades who had worked with him— simple, progressive Communists from Moscow who were more or less at my level of political development. They told me how Bukharin had lived with them in their dormitory and eaten with them at their mess at the same table. This impressed me very much. Bukharin was also the editor of *Pravda*[3]. He was the Party's chief theoretician. Lenin always spoke affectionately of him as "Our Bukharchik." On Lenin's instructions he wrote *The A–B–C of Communism*, and everyone who joined the Party learned Marxist-Leninist science by studying Bukharin's work. In short, Bukharin was much beloved in the Party.

During the Fifteenth Party Congress some delegation or other presented the Congress Presidium with a steel broom. Rykov, who was Chairman of the Presidium, made a speech, saying, "I hereby present this steel broom to Comrade Stalin so that he may sweep away our enemies." There was a burst of appreciative applause and laughter. Rykov himself broke into a smile and

then laughed, too. He obviously trusted Stalin to use the broom wisely, for the good of the Party, against anti-Party elements and opponents of the General Line. Rykov could hardly have foreseen that he, too, would be swept away by this same broom which he handed over to Stalin in 1927.

At the time of the Fifteenth Party Congress we had no doubt in our minds that Stalin and his supporters were right, and that the opposition was wrong. I still think that Stalin's ideological position was basically correct. We realized that a merciless struggle against the opposition was unavoidable. We justified what was happening in a lumberjack's terms: when you chop down a forest, the chips fly. After all, it was no accident that Stalin held the leading position in the Party, and it was no accident that the Party supported him against such powerful opponents as the Trotskyites, Zinovievites and later the right–left bloc of Syrtsov and Lominadze. Stalin was a powerful personality, and he had contributed greatly to the mobilization of the Party's forces for the reconstruction of our industry and agriculture and the strengthening of our army. It shouldn't be overlooked that Stalin's name hadn't been very widely known among the masses in the first years of the Revolution. He had come a long way in a short time, and he had brought our Party and our people with him.

Notes

1. Grigori Zinoviev sided with Lenin in the 1903 Social-Democratic Party split. After the Russian Revolution, he led the Comintern (1919–26) and served in the Politburo (1921–26). In 1936 Zinoviev, Lev Kamenev, and others were tried for treason and executed.
2. Aleksei Rykov succeeded Lenin as prime minister of the Soviet Union. Nikolai Bukharin was the Party's greatest intellectual and a close friend of Lenin. They were tried in 1938, condemned, and shot.
3. *Truth*—the primary newspaper of the Communist Party of the Soviet Union.

Study Question

Assess the validity of Khrushchev's argument regarding the need for a merciless purge of all opposition?

Li Dazhao

Li Dazhao[1] (1888–1927) was drawn to the study of Marxist theory after the Bolshevik victory in Russia. He is recognized as one of the founding members of the Chinese Communist Party (CCP) (along with Chen Duxiu) and maintained close ties between the CCP and the COMINTERN. Like many Chinese modernizers Li had studied in Japan. He taught at Beijing University where *he is credited with greatly influencing Mao Zedong. In the following essay, written in November 1918, Li discusses the global implications of the Bolshevik victory.*

Document Source: Li Dazhao, "The Victory of Bolshevism," *China's Response to the West: A Documentary Survey*, eds Ssu-yü Têng and John King Fairbank (Cambridge, MA: Harvard University Press, 1954/1979), 246–9.

The Victory of Bolshevism

"Victory! Victory! The Allies have been victorious! Surrender! Surrender! Germany has surrendered!" These words are on the national flag bedecking every doorway, they can be seen in colour and can be indistinctly heard in the intonation of every voice. Men and women of the Allied powers run up and down the street in celebration of the victory, and in the city of Peking the soldiers of these nations loudly blast forth their triumphal songs. . . .

But let us think carefully as small citizens of the world; to whom exactly does the present victory belong? Who has really surrendered? Whose is the achievement this time? And for whom do we celebrate? If we ponder over these questions, then not only will our non-fighting generals' show of strength and our shameless politicians' grasping of credit become senseless, but also the talk of the Allied nations, that the end of the war was brought about by their military forces defeating the military force of Germany. . . .

For the real cause of the ending of the war was not the vanquishing of the German military power by the Allied military power, but the vanquishing of German militarism by German socialism. It was not the German

people who surrendered to the armed forces of the Allied powers, but the German Kaiser, militarists and militarism who surrendered to the new tides of the world. It was not the Allied nations, but the awakened minds of the German people that defeated German militarism. . . . The victory over German militarism does not belong to the Allied nations; even less does it belong to our factious military men who used participation in the war only as an excuse [for engaging in civil war], or to our opportunistic, cunningly manipulative politicians. It is the victory of humanitarianism, of pacifism; it is the victory of justice and liberty; it is the victory of Bolshevism; it is the victory of the red flag; it is the victory of the labour class of the world; and it is the victory of the twentieth century's new tide. Rather than give Wilson and others the credit for this achievement, we should give the credit to Lenin, Trotzky [sic], Collontay [Alexandra Kollontai], to Liebknecht, Scheidemann, and to Marx.[2]

Bolshevism is the ideology of the Russian Bolsheviki. . . . it is clear that their ideology is revolutionary socialism; their party is a revolutionary socialist party; and they follow the German socialist economist Marx as the founder of their doctrine. Their aim is to destroy the national boundaries which are obstacles to socialism at present, and to destroy the system of production in which profit is monopolized by the capitalist. Indeed, the real cause of this war was also the destruction of national boundaries. Since the present national boundaries cannot contain the expansion of the system of production brought about by capitalism, and since the resources within each nation are inadequate for the expansion of its productive power, the capitalist nations began depending on war to break down these boundaries, hoping to make all parts of the globe one single, coordinated economic organ.

. . . The Bolsheviki saw through this point; therefore they vigorously protested and proclaimed that the present war is a war of the Tsar, of the Kaiser, of kings and emperors that it is a war of capitalist governments, but it is not their war. Theirs is the war of classes, a war of all the world's proletariat and common people against the capitalists of the world. While they are opposed to war itself, they are at the same time not afraid of it. They hold that all men and women should work. All those who work should join a union, and there should be a central administrative soviet in each union. Such soviets then should organize all the governments of the world. . . . There will be only the joint soviets of labour, which will decide all matters. . . . They will unite the proletariat of the world, and create global freedom with their greatest, strongest power of resistance: first they will create a federation of European democracies, to serve as the foundation of a world federation. This is the ideology of the Bolsheviki. This is the new doctrine of the twentieth-century revolution.

. . . The pattern of the revolutions generally develops along the same line as that in Russia. The red flag flies everywhere, the soviets are established one after another. Call it revolution entirely *à la Russe*, or call it twentieth-century revolution. Such mighty rolling tides are indeed beyond the power of the present capitalist governments to prevent or to stop, for the mass movement of the twentieth century combines the whole of mankind in one great mass. The efforts of each individual within this great mass, following the example of some of them, will then be concentrated and become a great, irresistible social force. Whenever a disturbance in this worldwide social force occurs among the people, it will produce repercussions all over the earth, like storm clouds gathering before the wind and valleys echoing the mountains. In the course of such a world mass movement, all those dregs of history which can impede the progress of the new movement—such as emperors, nobles, warlords, bureaucrats, militarism, capitalism—will certainly be destroyed as though struck by a thunderbolt. . . . Although the word "Bolshevism" was created by the Russians, the spirit it embodies can be regarded as that of a common awakening in the heart of each individual among mankind of the twentieth century. The victory of Bolshevism, therefore, is the victory of the spirit of common awakening in the heart of each individual among mankind in the twentieth century.

Notes

1. Li Ta-chao (Wade-Giles)
2. Karl Liebknecht was a founding member of the German Communist Party, along with Rosa Luxemburg; Philipp Scheidemann was the Social Democrat who proclaimed the creation of the Weimar Republic.

Study Question

What was the most important factor that prevented revolutionary movements around the world from uniting in the years immediately following the First World War?

Sun Yat-sen

Sun Yat-sen (1866–1925) became familiar with Western ideas and religions at an Anglican boys' school in Honolulu. During the early 1890s Sun became increasingly involved in anti-Qing activities, eventually concluding that the dynasty could be overthrown. After ten years of fundraising activities among overseas Chinese communities, Sun settled in Japan in 1905, at which time several anti-Qing groups merged to become the Chinese Revolutionary Alliance.[1] After numerous failed uprisings,[2] on 10 October 1911 a garrison of soldiers in Wuchang rebelled and declared China to be a republic. Sun returned to China in December 1911 and was sworn in as Provisional President of the Chinese Republic. However, he soon resigned his post in favour of Yuan Shikai—a former Qing general. In 1917 Sun established a new government in Canton, but controlled only a small part of China. He wrote Fundamentals of National Reconstruction *in 1923.*

Document Source: Sun Yat-sen, *Fundamentals of National Reconstruction* (Taipei: China Cultural Service, 1953), 76–83.

Fundamentals of National Reconstruction

Following China's war with France (1883–84) I made up my mind to devote myself to the revolution. In 1895 I started the first insurrection in Canton and the revolution of 1911 culminated in the establishment of the Republic. Up to the present the task of revolution, however, has not yet been completed. A span of 37 years of my revolutionary work is to be chronicled by future historians from all manner of facts and incidents. An outline sketch is given below.

I. Principles of Revolution. The term Kemin, or revolution, was first used by Confucius. Incidents of a revolutionary nature repeatedly happened in Chinese history after Tang (founder of the Shang Dynasty, 1766 BCE) and Wu (founder of the Zhou Dynasty, 1122 BCE). In Europe revolutionary tides surged in the seventeenth and eighteenth centuries and they have since spread over the whole world. In due course they created republics, they conferred constitutions on monarchies. The principles which I have held in promoting the Chinese revolution were in some cases copied from our traditional ideals, in other cases modeled on European theory and experience, and in still others formulated according to original and self-developed theories. They are described as follows:

a. Principle of Nationalism. Revelations of Chinese history prove that the Chinese as a people are independent in spirit and in conduct. Coerced into touch with other people, they could at times live in peace with them by maintaining friendly relations and at others assimilate them as the result of propinquity. During the periods when their political and military prowess declined, they could not escape for the time from the fate of a conquered nation, but they could eventually vigorously reassert themselves. Thus the Mongol rule of China (1260–1333 CE), lasting nearly a hundred years was finally overthrown by Tai Tse of the Ming dynasty and his loyal followers. So in our own time was the Manchu yoke thrown off by the Chinese. Nationalistic ideas in China did not come from a foreign source; they were inherited from our remote forefathers. Upon this legacy is based my principle of nationalism, and where necessary, I have developed it and amplified and improved upon it. No vengeance has been inflicted

A US immigration photograph of Sun Yat-sen taken in 1910 upon his arrival in San Francisco from Korea. The immigration department opened an investigation under the Chinese Exclusion Acts.

HB Sun Yat Sen, 40, XPI Korea 3-28-10, File no. 140-C., 03/28/1910, http://research.archives.gov/description/296447

on the Manchus and we have endeavoured to live side by side with them on an equal footing. This is our nationalistic policy toward races within our national boundaries. Externally, we should strive to maintain independence in the family of nations, and to spread our indigenous civilization as well as to enrich it by absorbing what is best in world civilization, with the hope that we may forge ahead with other nations towards the goal of ideal brotherhood.

b. Principle of Democracy. In ancient China we had the Emperor Yao (2357–2258 BCE) and Emperor Shun (2258–2206 BCE) who departed from the hereditary system and chose their successors. We also had Tang and Wu who overthrew kingdoms by revolution. Preserved in our books are such sayings as "Heaven sees as the people see"; "Heaven hears as the people hear"; "We have heard of a person named Zhou having been slain, we have not heard of a monarch having been murdered"; "The people are most

important, while the king is of the least importance." All these sayings ring with democratic sentiments. Since we have had only ideas about popular rights, and no democratic system has been evolved, we have to go to Europe and America for a republican form of government. There some countries have become republics and others have adopted constitutional monarchism, under which royal power has shrunk in the face of the rising demand for popular rights. Though hereditary monarchs have not yet disappeared, they are but vestiges and shadows of their former selves.

All through my revolutionary career I have held the view that China must be made a republic. There are three reasons. First, from a theoretical point of view, there is no ground for preserving a monarchical form of government, since it is widely recognized that the people constitute the foundation of a nation and they are all equal in their own country. In the second place, under Manchu occupation the Chinese were forced into the position of the vanquished and suffered oppression for more than two hundred and sixty years. While a constitutional monarchy may not arouse deep resentment in other countries and can maintain itself for the time being, it will be an impossibility in China. This is from a historical point of view. A third reason may be advanced with an eye on the future of the nation. That in China prolonged periods of disorder usually followed a revolution was due to the desire of every insurgent to be a king and to his subsequent contention for the throne. If a republican government is adopted, there will be no contention. . . .

My second decision is that a constitution must be adopted to ensure good government. The true meaning of constitutionalism was discovered by Montesquieu. The threefold separation of the legislative, judicial, and executive powers as advocated by him was accepted in every constitutional country in Europe. On a tour of Europe and America I made a close study of their governments and laws and took note of their shortcomings as well as their advantages. . . . [T]he system of the people's direct political powers should be adopted in order that the provision that the sovereign power is vested in the people may become a reality. In this way my principle of democracy may be carried out satisfactorily.

c. Principle of Livelihood. With the invention of modern machines, the phenomenon of uneven distribution of wealth in the West has become all the more marked. Intensified by crosscurrents, economic revolution was flaring up more ferociously than political revolution. This situation was scarcely noticed by our fellow-countrymen thirty years ago. On my tour of Europe and America, I saw with my own eyes the instability of their economic structure and the deep concern of their leaders in groping for a solution. I felt that, although the disparity of wealth under our economic organization is not so great as in the West, the difference is only in degree, not in character. The situation will become more acute when the West extends its economic influence to China. We must form plans beforehand in order to cope with the situation. After comparing various schools of economic thought, I have come to the realization that the principle of state ownership is most profound, reliable, and practical. Moreover, it will forestall in China difficulties that have already caused much anxiety in the West. I have therefore decided to enforce the principle of the people's livelihood simultaneously with the principles of nationalism and democracy, with the hope to achieve our political objective and nip economic unrest in the bud.

To sum up, my revolutionary principles in a nutshell consist in the Three Principles of the People and the Five Power Constitution. Those who have a clear knowledge of the general tendency of the world and the conditions in China will agree that my views are practical and must be put in practice.

II. Fundamentals of Revolution. In the age of autocracy, the masses of the people were fettered in spirit and body so that emancipation seemed impossible. Those who worked for the welfare of the people and were willing to sacrifice themselves for the success of revolution not only did not receive assistance from the people but were also ridiculed and disparaged. Much as they desired to be the guides of the people, they proceeded without followers. Much as they desired to be the vanguards, they advanced without reinforcement. It becomes necessary that, apart from destroying enemy influence, those engaged in revolution should take care to develop the constructive ability of the people. A revolutionary program is therefore indispensable.

According to my plan, the progress of our revolution should be regulated and divided into three stages: First, military rule; second, political tutelage; third, constitutional government. The first stage is a period of destruction, during which military rule is installed. The revolutionary army is to break down (as it did) Manchu despotism, sweep away official corruptions, and reform vicious customs.

The second stage is a transitional period, during which a provisional constitution (not the present one) will be promulgated. Its object is to build a local self-government system for the development of democracy. The Hsien or district will be unit of self-government. When disbanded troops are disposed of and fighting ceases, every district should accept the provisional constitution, which will regulate the rights and duties of the people and the administrative powers of the revolutionary government. It will be in force for three years, at the end of which period the people will choose their district magistrates. Even before the expiration of the period, the people in a district may be empowered to choose their own magistrate and become a complete self-governing body. . . .

The third stage, which marks the completion of national reconstruction, will usher in constitutional government. During this period the self-governing bodies in the various districts should exercise the direct political powers of the people. In district political affairs citizens should have the rights of universal suffrage, initiative, referendum, and recall. In national political affairs they should, while directly exercising the right of election, delegate the three other rights to their representatives in the People's Congress. This period of constitutional government marks the completion of national reconstruction and the successful conclusion of the revolution.

Notes

1. T'ung Meng Hui/Tongmeng Hui.
2. The Wuchang uprising of October 1911, which ultimately succeeded, was the 11th attempt to overthrow the Qing.

Study Question

Briefly summarize Sun's "Fundamentals"; to what extent were they applicable in a country with no history of democratic or constitutional government?

Soong Ching-ling

Soong Ching-ling (1893–1981) was born in Shanghai. After graduation she attended Wesleyan College in the United States and received her degree in 1913. Soong took over her sister Ai-ling's job as secretary to Sun Yat-sen upon returning home. Sun and Soong were married in 1915. Her youngest sister Mei-ling eventually married Sun's deputy Chiang Kai-shek. Soong Ching-ling worked alongside her husband both to preserve and to advance the revolution in China.

After Sun's death in 1925 Soong devoted herself to preserving his ideals, a position that brought her into direct opposition to Chiang Kai-shek. The following document was written in August 1927 as Soong and the more radical faction of the Guomindang began to split with Chiang Kai-shek over his recent crackdown on the Chinese Communist Party and its members.

Document Source: Soong Ching-ling, *The Struggle for New China* (Peking: Foreign Languages Press, 1952), 7–11.

The Struggle for New China

If China is to survive as an independent country in the modern struggle of nations, her semi-feudal conditions of life must be fundamentally changed and a modern state created to replace the medieval system that has existed for more than a thousand years. This task needs to be done by the method of revolution, if only because the alternative method of gradualness postulates a period of time which is denied the nation by both the cancerous force of Chinese militarism eating from inside and foreign imperialism ravaging from outside.

To forge a fit instrument of revolution, Sun Yat-sen reorganized the Guomindang on a revolutionary basis in the winter of 1924, and reinforced the "Three People's Principles" by formulating the

"Three Great Policies" of action. The first of these policies calls for the inclusion and support of the nation's workers and peasants in the work of the revolution. These two massive elements of the national population—one carrying on and sustaining the life of organized society and the other producing food on which man lives—represent nearly 90 per cent of the nation. And, in view of their numerical strength and the fact that the masses ought to be the chief beneficiaries of the revolution, they must be drawn into it if there is to be life and reality in the movement.

The second of the policies laid down by Sun recognizes the necessity of cooperation between the Guomindang and members of the Chinese

Communist Party during the period of revolutionary struggle with Chinese militarism and foreign imperialism. The Chinese Communist Party is indubitably the most dynamic of all internal revolutionary forces in China; and its influence over the masses and power of propaganda enabled the Guomindang to control its military elements and subordinate them to the civil authorities.

The third of Sun Yat-sen's policies deals with the profoundly important question of the connection of the Soviet Union with the Guomindang. The connection is sometimes justified on the ground that the Soviet Union has no unequal treaties with China. This, however, was a minor consideration in Sun's view of the matter. In formulating the third policy, he was moved by larger reasons. Just as he regarded the Chinese Communist Party as the most active revolutionary force in China, so he envisaged the Soviet Union as the most powerful revolutionary force in the world; and he believed that a right correlation by the Guomindang of these two outstanding revolutionary forces would signally assist the revolution to realize national independence for China. Sun was not afraid or ashamed to avow this revolutionary thesis, since he knew that the revolutionary role played by France, in the person of Lafayette in the American Revolution, was repeated in many a chapter in the history of freedom.

It was a statesmanlike application of these three policies of Sun and the correlation of the forces deriving from them that enabled the Guomindang power to put an end to ten years of disorder and confusion in Canton, and to create and finance revolutionary armies that conquered their way to the historic line of the Yangtze and—after shattering the main force of the Fengtien army[1] in Honan—penetrated to the bank of the Yellow River. Besides its striking administrative work at Canton and the great military achievement of the Northern Expedition, the Guomindang scored memorable successes in a field in which China has always known defeat and humiliation.

Soong Ching-ling in 1937 after her break with Chiang Kai-shek and the more right wing elements of the Nationalist Party.
New York World-Telegram and the Sun Newspaper Photograph Collection. Courtesy of the Library of Congress, Prints and Photographs Division (LC-USZ62-132824).

It raised the international status of China to a point never attained before, compelling the representatives of great powers to meet the foreign minister of Nationalist China as an equal in council, and causing men in high as well as in the scattered places of the earth to heed his statements on Nationalist aims and aspirations. In those days—it is but three months since—the Guomindang may have been hated and even feared, but none dared to despise it.

Today it is otherwise. The famous name of the Nationalist Government is now sunk to the level of other semi-feudal remnants in the North; and those who have been entrusted by the revolution with leadership are allowing the new militarist clique in the Yangtze to capture and utilize the Guomindang; and they themselves are now becoming or are about to become, the secretaries and clerks of the new Caesar. No one fears and no one respects the Guomindang, which is now despised even by foes who used to blanch and flee at the sound of its armies on the march.

What is the cause for this startling change in values and in men's opinions? The answer is to be found in the work of the reaction in Canton, in Nanking and Shanghai, in Changsha, and lastly in Wuhan. Peasants and their leaders, workers, and their leaders, Communists and their leaders, who laboured in order that the Guomindang power might reach the Yangtze, have been ruthlessly and wantonly killed; and Soviet workers who gave of their best to the Guomindang and who men, in later and juster days, will adjudge to have deserved well of Nationalist China, have been forced to leave, because so-called "leaders" of the Guomindang—petty politicians reverting to type—believe that they can violate Sun Yat-sen's Three Policies and rely on the new militarism to carry out the stupendous task of the revolution.

They will fail and go the way of those before them who have sought to rule in like fashion. But they must not be permitted to involve in their own ultimate ruin the heritage left to us by Sun. His true followers must seek to rescue the real Guomindang from the degradation of becoming a mere secretariat of the new militarist clique emerging out of the intrigues and disloyalties now afoot.

My own course is clear. Accepting the thesis that the Three Policies are an essential part of the thought and technique of the revolution, I draw the conclusion that real nationalist success in the struggle with Chinese militarism and foreign imperialism is possible only by a right correlation, under Guomindang leadership, of the revolutionary forces issuing from the Three Policies. As the reaction led by pseudo-leaders of the Guomindang endangers the Third Policy, it is necessary for the revolutionary wing of the Guomindang—the group with which Sun would today be identified had he been alive—to leave no doubt in the Soviet mind that, though some have crossed over to reaction and counter-revolution, there are others who will continue true and steadfast to the Three Policies enunciated by him for the guidance and advancement of the work of the revolution.

I go, therefore, to Moscow to explain this in person.

Note

1. The Fengtien army was controlled by a Manchurian warlord named Zhang Zuolin.

> **Study Question**
>
> Based on your reading of Sun Yat-sen and Soong Ching-ling, did Soong remain faithful to Sun's original ideas?

John Reed

John Reed (1887–1920) was an American journalist and writer who travelled to Mexico in 1913 to cover the Mexican Revolution. He spent time with the armies of Pancho Villa and came to admire the goals of the more radical Mexican revolutionaries. His reports on the revolution were collected and published in 1914 in the book Insurgent Mexico, *an excerpt from which follows. Reed's sympathies for the working class eventually led him to Russia to report on the*

1917 revolutions. He was thus able to witness firsthand the Bolshevik victory in October. His account of the revolution, Ten Days That Shook the World, *remains widely read. He died of typhus in 1920 and was buried at the Kremlin Wall, an honour reserved for key Bolshevik leaders and a small number of foreign supporters.*

Document Source: John Reed, *Insurgent Mexico* (New York & London: D. Appleton & Company, 1914), 76–9.

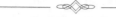

Insurgent Mexico

After a while I slipped away, and I doubt if they even saw me go. They sang around their fire for more than three hours.

But in our cuartel there was other entertainment. The room was full of smoke from the fire on the floor. Through it I dimly made out some thirty or forty troopers squatting or sprawled at full length—perfectly silent as Silveyra read aloud a proclamation from the Governor of Durango[1] forever condemning the lands of the great haciendas to be divided among the poor.

He read:

"Considering: that the principal cause of discontent among the people in our State, which forced them to spring to arms in the year 1910, was the absolute lack of individual property; and that the rural classes have no means of subsistence in the present, nor any hope for the future, except to serve as peons on the haciendas of the great land owners, who have monopolized the soil of the State;

"Considering: that the principal branch of our national riches is agriculture, and that there can be no true progress in agriculture without that the majority of farmers have a personal interest in making the earth produce. . . .

"Considering, finally: that the rural towns have been reduced to the deepest misery, because the common lands which they once owned have gone to augment the property of the nearest hacienda, especially under the dictatorship of Diaz[2]; with which the inhabitants of the State lost their economic, political, and social independence, then passed from the rank of citizens to that of slaves, without the Government being able to lift the moral level through education, because the hacienda where they lived is private property. . . .

"Therefore, the Government of the State of Durango declares it a public necessity that the inhabitants of the towns and villages be the owners of agricultural lands. . . . "

When the paymaster had painfully waded through all the provisions that followed, telling how the land was to be applied for, etc., there was a silence.

"That," said Martinez, "is the Mexican Revolucion."

"It's just what Villa's doing in Chihuahua," I said. "It's great. All you fellows can have a farm now."

An amused chuckle ran around the circle. Then a little, bald-headed man, with yellow, stained whiskers, sat up and spoke.

"Not us," he said, "not the soldiers. After a Revolucion is done it wants no more soldiers. It is the *pacificos* who will get the land—those who did not fight. And the next generation. . . . " He paused and spread his torn sleeves to the fire. "I was a school teacher," he explained, "so I know that Revolucions, like Republics, are ungrateful. I have fought three years. At the end of the first Revolucion that great man, Father Madero[3], invited his soldiers to the Capital. He gave us clothes, and food, and bull-fights. We returned to our homes and found the greedy again in power."

"I ended the war with forty-five pesos," said a man.

"You were lucky," continued the schoolmaster. "No, it is not the troopers, the starved, unfed, common soldiers who profit by the Revolucion. Officers, yes—some—for they get fat on the blood of the Patria. But we—no."

"What on earth are you fighting for?" I cried.

"I have two little sons," he answered. "And *they* will get their land. And they will have other little sons. They, too, will never want for food. . . ." The little man grinned. "We have a proverb in Guadalajara: 'Do not wear a shirt of 11 yards, for he who wants to be a Redeemer will be crucified.'"

"*I've* got no little son," said 14-year-old Gil

Tomas, amid shouts of laughter. "I'm fighting so I can get a 30-30 rifle from some dead Federal, and a good horse that belonged to a millionaire."

Just for fun I asked a trooper with a photo button of Madero pinned to his coat who that was.

"*Pues, quien sabe, señor?* [Well, who knows, sir]" he replied. "My captain told me he was a great saint. I fight because it is not so hard as to work."

"How often are you fellows paid?"

"We were paid three pesos just nine months ago tonight," said the schoolmaster, and they all nodded. "We are the real volunteers. The *gente* [people] of Villa are professionals."

Then Luis Martinez got a guitar and sang a beautiful little love song, which he said a prostitute had made up one night in a *bordel*.

Notes

1. The State of Durango (and its northern neighbour, Chihuahua) played a key role during the Mexican Revolution, providing a safe haven to a number of key revolutionary figures.
2. Porfirio Diaz dominated Mexican politics from 1876 until he was forced from office in 1911.
3. Francisco Madero was a leading Mexican democrat who briefly assumed the presidency in 1911 after Porfirio Diaz was forced to relinquish power. He was assassinated by supporters of the former dictator in February 1913.

Study Question

In the end, the more radical elements of the revolution were utterly defeated. In what ways does the passage above provide insight into the reasons for their failure?

Mustapha Kemal Atatürk

Mustapha Kemal Atatürk (1881–1938)[1] first gained prominence as a military leader. He was involved in the 1908 Young Turk uprising which attempted to modernize the Ottoman Empire along western lines. He fought for the Ottoman Empire during the First World War and, subsequently, for Turkish independence in the early 1920s. In 1923 Atatürk became the leader of the new Turkish Republic and launched an ambitious program of domestic reforms with the goal of creating a secular, modern, and democratic state. In the following excerpt Atatürk addresses the wearing of the fez—a form of head-covering that had become synonymous with the previous Ottoman regime, along with prohibitions against the use of various traditional titles. The original speech was delivered over the course of six days in 1927.

Document Source: Ghazi Mustapha Kemal Pasha, *A Speech* (Leipzig: K.F. Köhler, 1929), 721–3.

October 1927 Speech

Gentlemen, it was necessary to abolish the fez, which sat on our heads as a sign of ignorance, of fanaticism, of hatred to progress and civilization, and to adopt in its place the hat, the customary headdress of the whole civilized world, thus showing, among other things, that no difference existed in the manner of thought between the Turkish nation and the whole family of civilized mankind. We did that while the law for the Restoration of Order was still in force. If it had not been in force we should have done so all the same; but one can say with complete truth that the existence of this law made the thing much easier for us.[2] As a matter of fact the application of the law for the Restoration of Order prevented the morale of the nation being poisoned to a great extent by the reactionaries.

It is true that a deputy of Brusa, who, during his whole time of being deputy, had not once appeared on the speaker's rostrum, nor ever spoken a word in the Chamber in defence of the interests of the nation and the Republic, the deputy of Brusa, I say, Nureddin Pasha, introduced a lengthy motion against wearing hats and mounted the rostrum to defend it.

He asserted that hat-wearing was a "contradiction of the fundamental rights of the national sovereignty, and of the principle of the integrity of personal freedom," and attempted "on no account to let this measure be forced upon the population." But the outbreak of fanaticism and reaction which Nureddin Pasha succeeded, from the tribune, in calling forth, merely led to the sentencing of a few reactionaries by the Courts of Independence.

Gentlemen, while the law regarding the Restoration of Order was in force there took place also the closing of the Tekkes, of the convents, and of the mausoleums, as well as the abolition of all sects and all kinds of titles such as Sheikh, Dervish, "Junger," Tschelebi, Occultist, Magician, Mausoleum Guard, etc.

One will be able to imagine how necessary the carrying through of these measures was, in order to prove that our nation as a whole was no primitive nation, filled with superstitions and prejudices.

Could a civilized nation tolerate a mass of people who let themselves be led by the nose by a herd of Sheikhs, Dedes, Seids, Tschelebis, Babas and Emirs; who entrusted their destiny and their lives to chiromancers [palm-readers], magicians, dice-throwers and amulet sellers? Ought one to conserve in the Turkish State, in the Turkish Republic, elements and institutions such as those which had for centuries given the nation the appearance of being other than it really was? Would one not therewith have committed the greatest, most irreparable error to the cause of progress and awakening?

If we made use of the law for the Restoration of Order in this manner, it was in order to avoid such a historic error; to show the nation's brow pure and luminous, as it is; to prove that our people think neither in a fanatical nor a reactionary manner.

Gentlemen, at the same time the new laws were worked out and decreed which promise the most fruitful results for the nation on the social and economic plane, and in general in all the forms of the expression of human activity . . . the Citizens' Lawbook, which ensures the liberty of women and stabilizes the existence of the family [was introduced].

Accordingly we made use of all circumstances only from one point of view, which consisted therein: to raise the nation on to that step on which it is justified in standing in the civilized world, to stabilize the Turkish Republic more and more on steadfast foundations . . . and in addition to destroy the spirit of despotism for ever.

Notes

1. The surname "Atatürk" was bestowed in 1934; it translates approximately to "father of the Turkish people."
2. The Restoration of Order Law, passed in 1925, allowed Atatürk to govern with sweeping executive authority, to censor the press, and to invoke martial law.

Study Question

Could a modern Turkish State have been created without such sweeping prohibitions against traditional practices?

Jawaharlal Nehru

Jawaharlal Nehru (1889–1964) was educated in Britain, attending Harrow and Cambridge. He became familiar with socialist doctrines while training to become a lawyer. On his return to India Nehru gradually came to appreciate the value of Gandhi's satyagraha campaigns, though a number of ideological differences remained between the two men. In the 1920s he visited Moscow, gaining first-hand knowledge of the revolutionary transformation underway in the Soviet Union. In 1936 Nehru was elected to the leadership of the Indian National Congress, having clearly stated his commitment to Indian independence. In a 1936 speech to the Indian National Congress (INC), Nehru summarized his commitment to progress through socialism.

Document Source: Jawaharlal Nehru, "Presidential Address to the Indian National Congress," *The Labour Monthly*, 18(5) (May 1936): 282–305.

The Socialist Creed

I am convinced that the only key to the solution of the world's problems and of India's problems lies in socialism, and when I use this word I do so not in a vague humanitarian way but in the scientific economic sense. Socialism is, however, something even more than an economic doctrine; it is a philosophy of life and as such also it appeals to me. I see no way of ending the poverty, the vast unemployment, the degradation and the subjection of the Indian people except through socialism. That involves vast and revolutionary changes in our political and social structure, the ending of vested interests in land and industry, as well as the feudal and autocratic Indian states system. That means the ending of private property, except in a restricted sense, and the replacement of the present profit system by a higher ideal of cooperative service. It means ultimately a change in our instincts and habits and desires. In short, it means a new civilization, radically different from the present capitalist order. Some glimpse we can have of this new civilization in the territories of the USSR. Much has happened there which has pained me greatly and with which I disagree, but I look upon that great and fascinating unfolding of a new order and a new civilization as the most promising feature of our dismal age. If the future is full of hope it is largely because of Soviet Russia and what it has done, and I am convinced that, if some world catastrophe does not intervene, this new civilization will spread to other lands and put an end to the wars and conflicts which capitalism feeds.

I do not know how or when this new order will come to India. I imagine that every country will fashion it after its own way and fit it in with its national genius. But the essential basis of that order must remain and be a link in the world order that will emerge out of the present chaos.

Socialism is thus for me not merely an economic doctrine which I favour; it is a vital creed which I hold with all my head and heart. I work for Indian independence because the nationalist in me cannot tolerate an alien domination; I work for it even more because for me it is the inevitable step to social and economic change. I should like the Congress to become a socialist organization and to join hands with the other forces that in the world are working for the new civilization. But I realize that the majority in the Congress, as it is constituted today, may not be prepared to go this far. We are a nationalist organization and we think and work on the nationalist plane. It is evident enough now that this is too narrow even for the limited objective of political independence, and so we talk of the masses and their economic needs. But most of us hesitate, because of our nationalist backgrounds, to take a step which might frighten away some vested interests. Most of those interests are already ranged against us and we can expect little from them except opposition even in the political struggle.

Much as I wish for the advancement of socialism in this country, I have no desire to force the issue on the Congress and thereby create difficulties in the way of our struggle for independence. I shall cooperate gladly and with all the strength in me with all those who work for independence even though they do not agree with the socialist solution. But I shall do so stating my position frankly and hoping in course of time to convert the Congress and the country to it, for only thus can I see it achieving independence.

Study Question

Why did socialism hold so much appeal among colonized nations?

Web Resources

Marxists Internet Archive
   http://www.marxists.org
Marx & Engels WWW Library
   http://www.eng.fju.edu.tw/Literary_Criticism/marxism/marxism_links.html
Project Gutenberg [numerous Marxist writings in electronic form]
   http://www.gutenberg.org/wiki/Main_Page
Internet Modern History Sourcebook: Asia since 1900
   http://www.fordham.edu/halsall/mod/modsbook52.html

Recommended Reading

Boris Pasternak, *Doctor Zhivago* (New York: Everyman's Library, 1991). Pasternak was awarded the Nobel Prize for *Doctor Zhivago* in 1958; he declined the honour due to controversy over the book in his homeland. (The book remained banned in the USSR until the Gorbachev era.) The novel, though not overtly critical, provides an honest look at modern Russian history and the upheavals of the revolutionary era through the life of Iurii Zhivago.

Rabindranath Tagore, *The Home and the World* (New York: Penguin, 1996). Tagore, a Nobel Prize-winning Bengali author, sets *The Home and the World* in 1908 Bengal during the early years of the Swadeshi movement, exploring the first expressions of radical nationalism and the excitement they generated. Originally published in 1916, Tagore examines the impact of political awakening on traditional Indian society, and foreshadows the violent conflicts that erupted at partition.

Su Tong (Tong Zhonggui), "Wives and Concubines," in *Raise the Red Lantern: Three Novellas* (New York: Penguin, 1996). "Wives and Concubines" is an examination of the domestic life and social values in a traditional Chinese household during the Republican era. Tong's novella relates the story of Lotus, a college student who leaves school to become the fourth concubine of a wealthy man.

Mo Yan, *Red Sorghum* (New York: Penguin, 1994). Set in the 1930s after the Japanese invasion of China, as the Chinese Communist Party (CCP) was fighting both the Guomindang (GMD) and the Japanese, Mo Yan's violent and gloomy novel portrays one of the most brutal periods in Chinese history. Rather than presenting an idealized vision of the past, or a clear ideological statement, the author focuses simply on the struggle for survival during this period.

Recommended Viewing

Battleship Potemkin (USSR, 1925). Director: Sergei Eisenstein (Silent, B&W). Commissioned by the Soviet government, Eisenstein recreates the revolution of 1905, as told through the story of the crew of the *Potemkin*. Eisenstein ties the mutiny of the sailors on the battleship to the broader events in Odessa. Considered an early masterpiece of cinematography, the film contains a strong political message about the people's hatred of tsarism.

Mat [*Mother*] (USSR, 1926). Director: Vsevolod Pudovkin (Silent, B&W). *Mat* is Pudovkin's recreation of the revolution of 1905, told on a more personal level while the historical events unfold, for the most part, in the background. The film recounts the story of one family caught up in the political radicalism of the era.

Lawrence of Arabia (UK/USA, 1962). Director: David Lean. Lean's film recreates the Allied campaign in the Middle East during the First World War, under the leadership of T.E. Lawrence. The film focuses in painstaking detail on the British effort to unite an Arab force to fight against the Ottoman Turks. The script was written, in part, from the diaries of T.E. Lawrence.

Sand Pebbles (USA, 1966). Director: Robert Wise. Set in republican China during the pivotal year of 1926, *Sand Pebbles* highlights the ongoing tensions and open warfare between Chiang Kai-shek and the Chinese communists. This was compounded by the American presence along the Yangtze River to defend American interests in China.

Shanghai Triad (China, 1995). Director: Zhang Yimou. Set in Shanghai in the 1930s, Zhang Yimou recreates the clashes among the many gangs that controlled the city during the Republican era. The film captures the atmosphere of the era, though the narrative, told from the perspective of a young boy, is somewhat fragmented.

5

The Authoritarian Alternative

In the aftermath of the First World War traditional liberal democratic political systems seemed increasingly unable to deal with the complex problems facing their citizens. Multi-party systems became mired in endless disputes, which threatened to render parliament effectively useless. In one nation after another people turned to extra-parliamentary alternatives to provide relief from political infighting and paralysis, economic crises, and too-rapid social and cultural change. By the late 1930s a fundamental political transformation had taken place. In Italy and Germany fascist regimes had risen to power; in the Soviet Union Stalin had launched one of the most rapid and comprehensive transformations of a nation ever seen; in South America fragile democracies had given way to new, authoritarian governments; and in Japan the liberal democratic system was supplanted by an aggressively expansionist regime, dominated by the military.

Italy was the first European nation to abandon its democratic system. At the end of the Great War Italy faced a number of systemic problems including underdevelopment in the South, political fragmentation, ultra-nationalist agitation, and unrest among industrial workers. In the first postwar elections socialist and communist parties made dramatic gains, causing considerable alarm among Italian industrialists and landowners. Unable to create sustainable coalitions, the government lurched from one crisis to the next, paralyzed by internal power struggles and ideological divisions. Perceiving a threat to their livelihood, Italian industrialists began to hire private armies of strike-breakers to force their discontented workers back to the factories. In this chaotic situation it was relatively simple for a new political force advocating hyper-nationalism and aggressive activism to gain a substantial following. Clever political manoeuvring and a good deal of luck allowed the *Fasci* to gain power in Italy in 1922.

In contrast, Germany's democratic system was able to survive the 1920s intact, even showing some growth in support in the latter years of the decade as reconstruction loans began to produce real economic improvements. The economic crises of the 1930s, however, would prove insurmountable. Increasingly the German people turned away from liberal-democratic political parties to embrace the extremes—the Communist Party and the National Socialist German Workers' Party. Though Communist support remained strong

A propaganda magazine for young Italian supporters of Fascism. Note the images of strength and militarism evident on the cover.

Courtesy of the University of Wisconsin Digital Collections Center, http://specialcollections.library.wisc.edu/exhibits/Fascism/Images/FRY46.html

throughout the early years of the 1930s, more voters rallied to the aggressively nationalist message of the National Socialists. In the last free election, in November 1932, the communists received almost six million votes; the Nazis, however, received nearly double that number. The German people had clearly expressed their preference. Few, however, could have anticipated the massive social, economic, cultural, and political changes that would follow the National Socialist rise to power.

In the Soviet Union, Lenin's death in 1924 triggered a succession dispute, which Stalin successfully manipulated in order to gain power. He then moved rapidly to dismantle the New Economic Policy (NEP) in order to focus on complete collectivization and a hurried program of industrialization. While the economic results were impressive, the human toll was immense. The Soviet State launched artificial famines, elaborate show trials, and draconian purges in order to gain the total cooperation necessary for such a massive transformation.

Though Stalin's Soviet Union was a largely insular regime during the late 1920s and much of the 1930s, its attention did turn outward during the Spanish Civil War, as the Soviets funneled substantial assistance to the Republican forces. The conflict in Spain is often situated within the pan-European rise of fascism. However, the ideological orientation of the "Nationalist" forces confronting the Republic ranged from traditional monarchists to religious conservatives to true believers in the fascist cause. In the end, the Nationalists emerged victorious and Spain joined the pan-European trend towards authoritarianism.

The appeal of authoritarian governments was not, however, limited to Europe. The political instability of the nineteenth century intensified in South America with the onset of the Great Depression. In nations such as Brazil latent tensions over industrialization and urbanization led to the overthrow of the republican government and the eventual rise of neo-fascist regimes. Fascism also gained a measure of popularity in Argentina, Chile, Peru, and elsewhere throughout the region.

Finally, in Japan frustration with the wartime settlement, the national debt, parliamentary politics, and the perceived injustice of the Washington Naval Limitation Treaty (1922) left many among the public questioning the effectiveness of the so-called Taishō Democracy. By 1930 ultra-nationalism was rising and prominent members of the Japanese military were able to supplant the parliamentary process and increasingly assume all governing functions.

The documents in this chapter examine the appeal of authoritarian doctrines, as well as some of their consequences. Two documents from Joseph Stalin outline his opinions on opposition and the importance of Soviet patriotism. The "Anniversary Statement" of the Amur (Black Dragon) Society lays out some of the ultra-nationalist beliefs which facilitated the rise of Japanese militarism. Benito Mussolini's interpretation of fascism is outlined in "Fascist Doctrines." Turning to National Socialist Germany Joseph Goebbels speaks to the role of propaganda in the new Nazi state. Adolf Hitler describes the role of women in the Nazi New Order, and David Buffum describes *Kristallnacht*, one of the early results of Nazi racial policy. Evgeniia Ginzburg describes the descent into the gulags of the Stalinist era. George Orwell's *Homage to Catalonia* captures much of the complexity of the political situation in Spain. Finally, the "New State" of Getúlio Vargas in Brazil is discussed in an article from *Fortune* magazine.

Joseph Stalin

Josef Vissarionovich Dzhugashvili (1879–1953)[1] sided with Lenin and the Bolshevik faction in 1903. In 1912 he went to St Petersburg, where he was elected to the party's central committee. About this time he took the name Stalin ("steel"). After the Russian Revolution of March 1917, he joined the editorial board of the party paper Pravda. *When the Bolsheviks took power in November 1917 he became the Commissar of Nationalities. In 1922 Stalin was made general secretary of the party,* a relatively minor position at the time. Before his death in 1924, Lenin wrote a testament urging Stalin's removal from the post because of his arbitrary conduct and well-known rudeness; but in the struggle to succeed Lenin, Stalin was victorious. The two passages which follow outline Stalin's views on opposition within the party in 1927 and on the "Socialist Fatherland" in 1931.*

Document Source: Joseph Stalin, *Works*, Vol. 10 (Moscow: Foreign Languages Publishing House, 1954), 379–82 and Vol. 13, 40–4.

On Opposition

From Kamenev's speech it is evident that the opposition does not intend to disarm completely. The opposition's declaration of 3 December indicates the same thing. Evidently, the opposition prefers to be outside the Party. Well, let it be outside the Party. There is nothing terrible, or exceptional, or surprising, in the fact that they prefer to be outside the Party, that they are cutting themselves off from the Party. If you study the history of our Party you will find that always, at certain serious turns taken by our Party, a certain section of the old leaders fell out of the cart of the Bolshevik Party and made room for new people. A turn is a serious thing, comrades. A turn is dangerous for those who do not sit firmly in the Party cart. Not everybody can keep his balance when a turn is made. You turn the cart—and on looking around you find that somebody has fallen out. *(Applause)*

Let us take 1903, the period of the Second Congress of our Party. That was the period of the Party's turn from agreement with the liberals to a mortal struggle against the liberal bourgeoisie, from preparing for the struggle against tsarism to open struggle against it for completely routing tsarism and feudalism. At that time, the Party was headed by the six: Plekhanov, Zasulich, Martov, Lenin, Axelrod, and Potresov. The turn proved fatal to five out of the six. They fell out of the cart. Lenin alone remained. *(Applause)* It turned out that the old leaders of the Party, the founders of the Party (Plekhanov, Zasulich, and Axelrod) plus two young ones (Martov and Potresov) were against one, also a young one, Lenin. If only you knew how much howling, weeping, and wailing there was then that the Party was doomed, that the Party would not hold out, that nothing could be done without the old leaders. The howling and wailing subsided however, but the facts remained. And the facts were that precisely thanks to the departure of the five the Party succeeded in getting on the right road. It is now clear to every Bolshevik that if Lenin had not waged a resolute struggle against the five, if the five had not been pushed aside, our Party could not have rallied as a Bolshevik Party capable of leading the proletarians to the revolution against the bourgeoisie. . . .

Our Party is a living organism. Like every

organism, it undergoes a process of metabolism: the old and obsolete passes away *(Applause)*, the new and growing lives and develops. *(Applause)* Some go away, both at the top and at the bottom. New ones grow, both at the top and at the bottom, and lead the cause forward. That is how our Party grew. This is how it will continue to grow.

The same must be said about the present period of our revolution. We are in the period of a turn from the restoration of industry and agriculture to the reconstruction of the entire national economy, to its reconstruction on a new technical basis, when the building of socialism is no longer merely in prospect, but a living, practical matter, which calls for the surmounting of extremely great difficulties of an internal and external character.

You know that this turn has proved fatal to the leaders of our opposition, who were scared by the new difficulties and intended to turn the Party in the direction of surrender. And if certain leaders, who do not want to sit firmly in the cart, now fall out, it is nothing to be surprised at. It will merely rid the Party of people who are getting in its way and hindering its progress. Evidently, they seriously want to free themselves from our Party cart. Well, if some of the old leaders who are turning into trash intend to fall out of the cart—a good riddance to them! *(Stormy and prolonged applause)*.

The Socialist Fatherland

It is sometimes asked whether it is not possible to slow down the tempo a bit, to put a check on the movement. No, comrades it is not possible! The tempo must not be reduced! On the contrary, we must increase it as much as is within our powers and possibilities. This is dictated to us by our obligations to the workers and peasants of the USSR. This is dictated to us by our obligations to the working class of the whole world.

To slacken the tempo would mean falling behind. And those who fall behind get beaten. But we do not want to be beaten. No, we refuse to be beaten! One feature of the history of old Russia was the continual beatings she suffered for falling behind, for her backwardness. She was beaten by the Mongol khans. She was beaten by the Turkish beys. She was beaten by the Swedish feudal lords. She was beaten by the Polish and Lithuanian gentry. She was beaten by the British and French capitalists. She was beaten by the Japanese barons. All beat her—for her backwardness: for military backwardness, for cultural backwardness, for political backwardness, for industrial backwardness, for agricultural backwardness. She was beaten because to do so was profitable and could be done with impunity. Do you remember the words of the pre-Revolutionary poet: "You are poor and abundant, mighty and impotent, Mother Russia." These words of the old poet were well learned by those gentlemen. They beat her, saying: "You are

An Uzbek weaver works at the Stalin Textile Combine in Tashkent during WWII. Stalin's forced industrialization contributed enormously to the Soviet war effort.

Courtesy of the Library of Congress, Prints and Photographs Division, FSA/OWI Collection (LC-USW33-024239-C).

abundant," so one can enrich oneself at your expense. They beat her, saying: "You are poor and impotent," so you can be beaten and plundered with impunity. Such is the law of the exploiters—to beat the backward and the weak. It is the jungle law of capitalism. You are backward, you are weak—therefore you are wrong; hence, you can be beaten and enslaved. You are mighty—therefore you are right; hence, we must be wary of you.

That is why we must no longer lag behind. In the past we had no fatherland, nor could we have one. But now that we have overthrown capitalism and power is in the hands of the working class, we have a fatherland, and we will defend its independence. Do you want our Socialist fatherland to be beaten and to lose its independence? If you do not want this you must put an end to its backwardness in the shortest possible time and

develop a genuine Bolshevik tempo in building up its Socialist system of economy. There is no other way. That is why Lenin said during the October Revolution: "Either perish, or overtake and outstrip the advanced capitalist countries."

We are fifty or a hundred years behind the advanced countries. We must make good this distance in ten years. Either we do it, or they crush us.

Note

1. There is evidence to suggest that Stalin changed his birth date from 1878 to 1879 after he consolidated power.

> **Study Question**
>
> According to these two documents, what did Stalin believe were the most important steps to preserve and advance the Soviet Union?

The Amur Society

The Amur Society, also known as the Black Dragon Society, was an ultra-nationalistic group founded in 1901, in part to promote Japanese expansionism throughout greater East Asia.[1] After the Japanese defeat of Russia in 1905, the society turned its attention to the perceived weaknesses of the liberal parliamentary system. In particular, the society objected to the ongoing Westernization of Japan. With

the onset of the Great Depression and its impact on the Japanese economy, the Amur Society dedicated itself to the creation of a more aggressive foreign policy. The following statement was issued in 1930 as the society prepared to celebrate its thirtieth anniversary.

Document Source: Wm. Theodore de Bary, ed., *Sources of Japanese Tradition*, Vol. 2 (NY: Columbia University Press, 1958), 255–9.

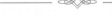

Anniversary Statement

Today our empire has entered a critical period in which great zeal is required on the part of the entire nation. From the first, we members of the Amur Society have worked in accordance with the imperial mission for overseas expansion to solve our overpopulation; at the same time, we have sought to give support and encouragement to the

peoples of East Asia. Thus we have sought the spread of humanity and righteousness throughout the world by having the imperial purpose extend to the neighbouring nations.

Earlier, in order to achieve these principles, we organized the Heavenly Blessing Heroes in Korea in 1894 and helped the Tong Hak rebellion there in order to speed the settlement of the dispute between Japan and China. In 1899 we helped Aguinaldo[2] in his struggle for the independence of the Philippines. In 1900 we worked with other comrades in helping Sun Yatsen start the fires of revolution in South China. In 1901 we organized this Society and became exponents of the punishment of Russia, and thereafter we devoted ourselves to the annexation of Korea while continuing to support the revolutionary movement in China. At all times we have consistently centered our efforts on the solution of problems of foreign relations, and we have not spared ourselves in this cause.

During this period we have seen the fulfillment of our national power in the decisive victories in the two major wars against China and Russia, in the annexation of Korea, the acquisition of Formosa and Sakhalin, and the expulsion of Germany from the Shantung peninsula. Japan's status among the empires of the world has risen until today she ranks as one of the three great powers, and from this eminence she can support other Asiatic nations. While these achievements were of course attributable to the august virtue of the great Meiji emperor, nevertheless we cannot but believe that our own efforts, however slight, also bore good fruit.

However, in viewing recent international affairs it would seem that the foundation established by the great Meiji emperor is undergoing rapid deterioration. The disposition of the gains of the war with Germany was left to foreign powers, and the government, disregarding the needs of national defence, submitted to unfair demands to limit our naval power. Moreover, the failure of our China policy made the Chinese more and more contemptuous of us, so much so that they have been brought to demand the surrender of our essential defence lines in Manchuria and Mongolia. Furthermore, in countries like the United States and Australia our immigrants have

been deprived of rights which were acquired only after long years of struggle, and we now face a highhanded anti-Japanese expulsion movement which knows no bounds. Men of purpose and of humanity who are at all concerned for their country cannot fail to be upset by the situation.

When we turn our attention to domestic affairs, we feel more than deep concern. There is a great slackening of discipline and order. Men's hearts are become corrupt. Look about you! Are not the various government measures and establishments a conglomeration of all sorts of evils and abuses? The laws are confusing, and evil grows apace. The people are overwhelmed by heavy taxes, the confusion in the business world complicates the livelihood of the people, the growth of dangerous thought threatens social order, and our national polity, which has endured for three thousand years, is in danger. This is a critical time for our national destiny; was there ever a more crucial day? What else can we call this time if it is not termed decisive? . . .

Our determination to rise to save the day is the inescapable consequence of this state of affairs. Previously our duty lay in the field of foreign affairs, but when we see internal affairs in disorder how can we succeed abroad? Therefore we of the Amur Society have determined to widen the scope of our activity. Hereafter, besides our interest in foreign affairs, we will give unselfish criticism of internal politics and of social problems, and we will seek to guide public opinion into proper channels. Thereby we will, through positive action, continue in the tradition of our past. We will establish a firm basis for our organization's policy and, through cooperation with other groups devoted to similar political, social, and ideological ideals, we are resolved to reform the moral corruption of the people, restore social discipline, and ease the insecurity of the people's livelihood by relieving the crises in the financial world, restore national confidence, and increase the national strength, in order to carry out the imperial mission to awaken the countries of Asia. In order to clarify these principles, we here set forth our platform to all our fellow patriots:

Principles

We stand for Divine Rulership (*tennō shugi*). Basing ourselves on the fundamental teachings of the foundation of the empire, we seek the extension of the imperial influence to all peoples and places and the fulfillment of the glory of our national polity.

Platform

Developing the great plan of the founders of the country, we will widen the great Way (*tao*) of Eastern culture, work out a harmony of Eastern and Western cultures, and take the lead among Asian peoples.

We will bring to an end many evils, such as formalistic legalism; it restricts the freedom of the people, hampers common sense solutions, prevents efficiency in public and private affairs, and destroys the true meaning of constitutional government. Thereby we will show forth again the essence of the imperial principles.

We shall rebuild the present administrative systems. We will develop overseas expansion through the activation of our diplomacy, further the prosperity of the people by reforms in internal government, and solve problems of labour and management by the establishment of new social policies. Thereby we will strengthen the foundations of the empire.

We shall carry out the spirit of the Imperial Rescript to Soldiers and Sailors and stimulate a martial spirit by working toward the goal of a nation in arms. Thereby we look toward the perfection of national defence.

We plan a fundamental reform of the present educational system which is copied from those of Europe and America; we shall set up a basic study of a national education originating in our national polity. Thereby we anticipate the further development and heightening of the wisdom and virtue of the Yamato race.

Notes

1. The Amur Society (*Kokuryu-kai*) was founded by Ryohei Uchida; in 1901 the group separated from the *Genyōsha* which dated back to 1871.
2. Emilio Aguinaldo y Famy led Philippine resistance against both the Spanish and later the United States (see Chapter Two).

> **Study Question**
>
> After reading this statement, how would you best categorize the ideology of the Black Dragon society?

Benito Mussolini

Benito Mussolini (1883–1945) was raised in a socialist household and trained to be an elementary school teacher. Because the socialist movement promoted pacifism, Mussolini opposed the First World War when it began; however, several months later he abruptly changed his opinion and began to argue in favour of Italian involvement in the war. In November 1914 he founded a new ultra-nationalist newspaper, Il Popolo d'Italia. In 1917 he served briefly in the army and then returned to Italy and eventually organized the Fasci di Combattimento. By 1922 the domestic situation in Italy was approaching crisis levels and King Vittorio Emmanuele III invited Mussolini to form a new government. In 1932 Mussolini co-wrote the following article with philosopher Giovanni Gentile (1875–1944).

Document Source: Adrian Lyttelton, ed., *Italian Fascisms from Pareto to Gentile*, transl. Douglas Parmée (London: Jonathan Cape, 1973), 47–57.

Fascist Doctrines

Above all, Fascism, in so far as it considers and observes the future and the development of humanity quite apart from the political considerations of the moment, believes neither in the possibility nor in the utility of perpetual peace. It thus repudiates the doctrine of Pacifism—born of a renunciation of the struggle and an act of cowardice in the face of sacrifice. War alone brings up to their highest tension all human energy and puts the stamp of nobility upon the peoples who have the courage to meet it. All other trials are substitutes, which never really put a man in front of himself in the alternative of life or death. A doctrine, therefore, which begins with a prejudice in favour of peace is foreign to Fascism; as are foreign to the spirit of Fascism, even though acceptable by reason of the utility which they might have in given political situations, all internationalistic and socialistic systems which, as history proves, can be blown to the winds when emotional, idealistic, and practical movements storm the hearts of the peoples. Fascism carries over this anti-pacifist spirit even into the lives of individuals. The proud motto of the *Squadrista*, "Me ne frego" [It doesn't matter], written on the bandages of a wound, is an act of philosophy not only stoical, it is the epitome of a doctrine that is not only political: it is education for combat, the acceptance of the risks which it brings; it is a new way of life for Italy. Thus the Fascist accepts and loves life, he knows nothing of suicide and despises it; he looks on life as duty, ascent, conquest: life which must be noble and full, lived for oneself, but above all for those others near and far away, present and future. . . .

Such a conception of life makes Fascism the precise negation of that doctrine which formed the basis of the so-called Scientific or Marxian Socialism: the doctrine of historical Materialism, according to which the history of human civilizations can be explained only as the struggle of interest between the different social groups and as arising out of change in the means and instruments of production. That economic improvements—discoveries of raw materials, new methods of work, scientific inventions—should have an importance of their own, no one denies, but that they should suffice to explain human history to the exclusion of all other factors is absurd: Fascism believes, now and always, in holiness and in heroism, that is in acts in which no economic motive—remote or immediate—plays a part. . . . [A]nd above all it is denied that the

Mussolini at the Turin Air Show in July 1932, during celebrations of the party's tenth anniversary in power.

Courtesy of the University of Wisconsin Digital Collections Center, http://specialcollections.library.wisc.edu/exhibits/Fascism/Images/FRY66.html

class struggle can be the primary agent of social changes. . . .

After Socialism, Fascism attacks the whole complex of democratic ideologies, and rejects them, both in their theoretical premises and in their applications of practical manifestations. Fascism denies that the majority, through the mere fact of being a majority, can rule human societies; it denies that this majority can govern by means of a periodical consultation; it affirms the irremediable, fruitful, and beneficent inequality of men, who cannot be leveled by such a mechanical and extrinsic fact as universal suffrage. By democratic regimes we mean those in which from time to time the people is given the illusion of being sovereign, while true effective sovereignty lies in other, perhaps irresponsible and secret, forces. Democracy is a regime without a king, but with very many kings, perhaps more exclusive, tyrannical, and violent than one king even though a tyrant . . .

In face of Liberal doctrines, Fascism takes up an attitude of absolute opposition both in the field of politics and in that of economics. It is not necessary to exaggerate—merely for the purpose of present controversies—the importance of Liberalism in the past century, and to make of that which was one of the numerous doctrines sketched in that century, a religion of humanity for all times, present and future. Liberalism flourished for no more than some fifteen years. . . .

If it is admitted that the nineteenth century has been the century of Socialism, Liberalism, and Democracy, it does not follow that the twentieth century must also be the century of Liberalism, Socialism, and Democracy: political doctrines pass; peoples remain. It is to be expected that this century may be that of authority, a century of the "Right," a Fascist century. If the nineteenth was the century of the individual (Liberalism means individualism) it may be expected that this one may be the century of "collectivism" and therefore the century of the State.

That a new doctrine should use the still vital elements of other doctrines is perfectly logical. No doctrine is born quite new, shining, never before seen. No doctrine can boast of an absolute "originality." It is bound, even if only historically, to other doctrines that have been, and must develop into other doctrines that will be. . . .

The keystone of Fascist doctrine is the conception of the State, of its essence, of its tasks, of its ends. For Fascism the State is an absolute before which individuals and groups are relative. Individuals and groups are "thinkable" in so far as they are within the State. The Liberal State does not direct the interplay and the material and spiritual development of the groups, but limits itself to registering the results; the Fascist State has a consciousness of its own, a will of its own, on this account it is called an "ethical" State. In 1929, at the first quinquennial[1] assembly of the regime, I said: "For Fascism, the State is not the night-watchman who is concerned only with the personal security of the citizens; nor is it an organization for purely material ends, such as that of guaranteeing a certain degree of prosperity and a relatively peaceful social order, to achieve which a council of administration would be sufficient, nor is it a creation of mere politics with no contact with the material and complex reality of the lives of individuals and the life of peoples. The State, as conceived by Fascism and as it acts, is a spiritual and moral fact because it makes concrete the political, juridical, economic organization of the nation and such an organization is, in its origin and in its development, a manifestation of the spirit. The State is the guarantor of internal and external security, but it is also the guardian and the transmitter of the spirit of the people as it has been elaborated through the centuries in language, custom, faith. . . . It is the State which educates citizens for civic virtue, makes them conscious of their mission, calls them to unity; harmonizes their interests in justice; hands on the achievements of thought in the sciences, the arts, in law, in human solidarity; it carries men from the elementary life of the tribe to the highest human expression of power which is Empire. . . .

A State founded on millions of individuals who recognize it, feel it, are ready to serve it, is not the tyrannical State of the medieval lord. It has nothing in common with the absolutist States that existed either before or after 1789. In the Fascist State the individual is not suppressed, but rather multiplied, just as in a regiment a soldier is not weakened but multiplied by the number of his comrades. The Fascist State organizes the nation, but it leaves sufficient scope to individuals; it has limited useless or harmful liberties and has preserved those that are essential. It cannot be the individual who decides in this matter, but only the State. . . .

The Fascist State is a will to power and to government. In it the tradition of Rome is an idea that has force. In the doctrine of Fascism Empire is not only a territorial, military, or mercantile expression, but spiritual or moral. One can think of an empire, that is to say a nation that directly or indirectly leads other nations, without needing to conquer a single square kilometre of territory. For Fascism the tendency to Empire, that is to say, to the expansion of nations, is a manifestation of vitality; its opposite, staying at home, is a sign of decadence: peoples who rise or re-rise are imperialist, peoples who die are renunciatory. Fascism is the doctrine that is most fitted to represent the aims, the states of mind, of a people, like the Italian people, rising again after many centuries of abandonment or slavery to foreigners. But Empire calls for discipline, co-ordination of forces, duty, and sacrifice. . . . If every age has its own doctrine, it is apparent from a thousand signs that the doctrine of the present age is Fascism. That it is a doctrine of life is shown by the fact that it has resuscitated a faith. That this faith has conquered minds is proved by the fact that Fascism has had its dead and its martyrs.

Note

1. Five-yearly.

> **Study Question**
>
> Mussolini discusses "harmful liberties" in the document. Based on your reading of his philosophy, what did he mean by this?

Joseph Goebbels

Joseph Paul Goebbels (1897–1945) was the foremost German National Socialist propagandist. He was one of the few highly educated members of the Party's elite, having graduated from the University of Heidelberg with a Ph.D. in 1921. He joined the National Socialist Party during its formative years and was appointed district party leader in Berlin in 1926. From this position he founded Der Angriff *(The Attack), one of the Party's most successful newspapers. When Hitler came to power in 1933 he appointed Goebbels Propaganda Minister, a position that* gave him complete control over radio, the press, cinema, and theatre. His most virulent propaganda was directed against the Jews. Goebbels remained loyal to Hitler until the end; in April 1945, he and his family committed suicide while Berlin was falling to Soviet troops. In the following speech, delivered on 15 March 1933, Goebbels discusses the aims of the new Ministry of Popular Enlightenment and Propaganda.

Document Source: Jeremy Noakes and Geoffrey Pridham, eds, *Nazism, 1919–1945*, Vol. 2: *State, Economy and Society 1933–1939* (Exeter: University of Exeter Press, 2000), 186–7.

The Reich Ministry of Popular Enlightenment and Propaganda

I see in the setting up of the new Ministry of Popular Enlightenment and Propaganda by the Government a revolutionary act in so far as the new Government no longer intends to leave the people to their own devices. This government is in the truest sense of the word a people's government. It arose out of the people and will always execute the will of the people. I reject most passionately the idea that this government stands for reactionary aims, that we are reactionaries. We want to give the people their due, though admittedly in another form than occurred under parliamentary democracy.

In the newly-established Ministry of Popular Enlightenment and Propaganda I envisage the link between regime and people, the living contact between the national government, as the expression of the people's will, and the people themselves. In the past few weeks we have seen an increasing coordination between Reich policy and the policy of the states, and in the same way I view the first task of the new Ministry as being to establish coordination between the Government and the whole people. If this government is determined never and under no circumstances to give way, then it has no need of the lifeless power of the bayonet, and in the long run will not be content with 52 per cent behind it and with terrorizing the remaining 48 per cent, but will see its most immediate task as being to win over that remaining 48 per cent.

. . . It is not enough for people to be more or less reconciled to our regime, to be persuaded to adopt a neutral attitude towards us, rather we want to work on people until they have capitulated to us, until they grasp ideologically that what is happening in Germany today not only must be accepted but also can be accepted.

Propaganda is not an end in itself, but a means to an end. If the means achieves the end then the means is good. Whether it always satisfies stringent aesthetic criteria or not is immaterial. But if the end has not been achieved then this means has in fact been inadequate. The aim of our movement was to mobilize people, to organize people, to win them for the national revolutionary ideal. This aim— even the most hostile person cannot dispute this— has been achieved and that represents the verdict on our propaganda methods. The new Ministry has no other aim than to unite the nation behind the ideal of the national revolution. If the aim has been achieved then people can pronounce judgment on my methods if they wish; that would be a matter of complete indifference for the Ministry would then by its efforts have achieved its goal. If, however, the aim is not achieved then although I might be able to prove that my propaganda methods satisfied all the laws of aesthetics I would have done better to become a theatre producer or the director of an Academy of Art not the Minister of a Ministry of Popular Enlightenment and Propaganda . . .

The most important tasks of this Ministry must be the following: first, all propaganda ventures and all institutions of public information belonging to the Reich and the states must be centralized in one hand. Furthermore, it must be our task to instill into these propaganda facilities a modern feeling and bring them up to date. We must not allow technology to run ahead of the Reich but rather the Reich must keep pace with technology. Only the latest thing is good enough. We are living in an age when policies must have mass support . . . the leaders of today must be modern princes of the people, they must be able to understand the people but need not follow them slavishly. It is their duty to tell the masses what they want and put it across to the masses in such a way that they understand it too. . . .

Study Question

What were the essential components of successful propaganda according to Goebbels?

Adolf Hitler

Adolf Hitler (1889–1945) gave the following speech to the National Socialist Women's Section (NS Frauenbund) on 8 September 1934, just eighteen months after assuming the chancellorship of Germany. This was during the period in which the Nazis were attempting to consolidate absolute power over the German state. The speech explains the National Socialist view of male and female roles.

Only a small number of women were able to rise to positions of power within the National Socialist women's organizations and very few women were able to retain the powerful positions they had occupied during the Weimar era.

Document Source: Jeremy Noakes and Geoffrey Pridham, eds, *Nazism, 1919–1945*, Vol. 2: *State, Economy and Society 1933–1939* (Exeter: University of Exeter Press, 2000), 255–6.

Speech to the National Socialist *Frauenbund*

The slogan "Emancipation of women" was invented by Jewish intellectuals and its content was formed by the same spirit. In the really good times of German life the German woman had no need to emancipate herself. She possessed exactly what nature had necessarily given her to administer and preserve; just as the man in his good times had no need to fear that he would be ousted from his position in relation to the woman.

In fact the woman was least likely to challenge his position. Only when he was not absolutely certain in his knowledge of his task did the eternal instinct of self and race-preservation begin to rebel in women. There then grew from this rebellion a state of affairs which was unnatural and which lasted until both sexes returned to the respective spheres which an eternally wise providence had preordained for them.

If the man's world is said to be the State, his struggle, his readiness to devote his powers to the service of the community, then it may perhaps be said that the woman's is a smaller world. For her world is her husband, her family, her children, and her home. But what would become of the greater world if there were no one to tend and care for the smaller one? How could the greater world survive if there were no one to make the cares of the smaller world the content of their lives? No, the greater world is built on the foundation of this smaller world. This greater world cannot survive if the smaller world is not stable. Providence has entrusted to the woman the cares of that world which is her very own, and only on the basis of this smaller world can the man's world be formed and built up. The two worlds are not antagonistic. They complement each other, they belong together just as man and woman belong together.

We do not consider it correct for the woman to interfere in the world of the man, in his main sphere. We consider it natural if these two worlds remain distinct. To the one belongs the strength of feeling, the strength of the soul. To the other belongs the strength of vision, of toughness, of decision, and of the willingness to act. In the one case this strength demands the willingness of the woman to risk her life to preserve this important cell and to multiply it, and in the other case it demands from the man the readiness to safeguard life.

The sacrifices which the man makes in the struggle of his nation, the woman makes in the preservation of that nation in individual cases. What the man gives in courage on the battlefield, the woman gives in eternal self-sacrifice, in eternal pain and suffering. Every child that a woman brings into the

DIE FRAUEN VERTRAUEN IHM:

Der Führer begrüßt Krankenschwestern

Adolf Hitler spricht mit einer Frau aus dem Volke

Women and children figured prominently in propaganda pictures of Hitler. Here, Hitler greets German nurses and "a woman of the people."

Image courtesy of Randall Bytwerk, Calvin College.

world is a battle, a battle waged for the existence of her people. And both must therefore mutually value and respect each other when they see that each performs the task that Nature and Providence have ordained. And this mutual respect will necessarily result from this separation of the functions of each.

It is not true, as Jewish intellectuals assert, that respect depends on the overlapping of the spheres of activity of the sexes; this respect demands that neither sex should try to do that which belongs to the sphere of the other. It lies in the last resort in the fact that each knows that the other is doing everything necessary to maintain the whole community. . . .

So our women's movement is for us not something which inscribes on its banner as its programme the fight against men, but something which has as its programme the common fight together with men. For the new National Socialist national community acquires a firm basis precisely because we have gained the trust of millions of women as fanatical fellow-combatants, women who have fought for the common life in the service of the common task of preserving life, who in that combat did not set their sights on the rights which a Jewish intellectualism put before their eyes, but rather on the duties imposed by nature on all of us in common.

Whereas previously the programmes of the liberal, intellectualist women's movements contained many points, the programme of our National Socialist Women's movement has in reality but one single point, and that point is the child, that tiny creature which must be born and grow strong and which alone gives meaning to the whole life-struggle. . . .

> **Study Question**
>
> Based upon Hitler's speech, why would National Socialism appeal to so many women?

David Buffum

On the night of 9–10 November 1938 the National Socialist regime orchestrated a series of attacks on the remaining German-Jewish population. Synagogues were burned, Jewish shops vandalized, and approximately 30,000 Jews were arrested. Ninety-one Jews were killed and the German-Jewish community was forced to pay for the damages. Most of these attacks were carried out by the Sturmabteilung (SA) and the Schutzstaffel (SS). Following Kristallnacht (often translated as the Night of Broken Glass due to the number of shop windows broken *during the night) there was a substantial increase in the number of Jews attempting to emigrate from Germany. At the time David Buffum was the American Consul in the city of Leipzig. His report on the events of* Kristallnacht *was included among the documents introduced by the*

prosecution at the Nuremburg Tribunal. Buffum filed his report on 21 November.

Document Source: Jeremy Noakes and Geoffrey Pridham, eds, *Documents on Nazism 1919–1945*, Vol. 2 (Exeter: University of Exeter Press, 2000), 360–2.

On *Kristallnacht*

The shattering of shop windows, looting of stores and dwellings of Jews, which began in the early hours of 10 November 1938, was hailed subsequently in the Nazi press as a "spontaneous wave of righteous indignation throughout Germany, as a result of the cowardly Jewish murder of Third Secretary von Rath[1] in the German Embassy at Paris." So far as a very high percentage of the German populace is concerned, a state of popular indignation that would spontaneously lead to such excesses, can be considered as nonexistent. On the contrary, in viewing the ruins and attendant measures employed, all of the local crowds observed were obviously benumbed over what had happened and aghast over the unprecedented fury of Nazi acts that had been or were taking place with bewildering rapidity throughout their city. . . .

At 3 AM on 10 November 1938 was unleashed a barrage of Nazi ferocity as had had no equal hitherto in Germany, or very likely anywhere else in the world since savagery began. Jewish buildings were smashed into and contents demolished or looted. In one of the Jewish sections an eighteen-year-old boy was hurled from a three-storey window to land with both legs broken on a street littered with burning beds and other household furniture and effects from his family's and other apartments. This information was supplied by an attending physician. It is reported from another quarter that among domestic effects thrown out of a Jewish building, a small dog descended four flights on to a cluttered street with a broken spine. Although apparently centered in poorer districts, the raid was not confined to the humble classes. One apartment of exceptionally

refined occupants known to this office was violently ransacked, presumably in a search for valuables which was not in vain, and one of the marauders thrust a cane through a priceless medieval painting portraying a biblical scene. Another apartment of the same category is known to have been turned upside down in the frenzied pursuit of whatever the invaders were after. Reported loss by looting of cash, silver, jewellery, and otherwise easily

The synagogue at Aachen after the devastating attacks on *Kristallnacht*, 10 November 1938.

convertible articles, has been apparent.

Jewish shop windows by the hundreds were systematically and wantonly smashed throughout the entire city at a loss estimated at several millions of marks. There are reports that substantial losses have been sustained on the famous Leipzig "Grühl," as many of the shop windows at the time of the demolition were filled with costly furs that were seized before the windows could be boarded up. In proportion to the general destruction of real estate, however, losses of goods are felt to have been relatively small. The spectators who viewed the wreckage when daylight had arrived were mostly in such a bewildered mood that there was no danger of impulsive acts, and the perpetrators probably were too busy in carrying out their schedule to take off a whole lot of time for personal profit. At all events, the main streets of the city were a positive litter of shattered plate glass. According to reliable testimony, the debacle was executed by SS men and Stormtroopers not in uniform, each group having been provided with hammers, axes, crowbars, and incendiary bombs.

Three synagogues in Leipzig were fired simultaneously by incendiary bombs and all sacred objects and records desecrated or destroyed, in most cases hurled through the windows and burned in the streets. No attempts whatsoever were made to quench the fires, the activity of the fire brigade being confined to playing water on adjoining buildings. All of the synagogues were irreparably gutted by flames, and the walls of the two that are close to the consulate are now being razed. The blackened frames have been centres of attraction during the past week of terror for eloquently silent and bewildered crowds. One of the largest clothing stores in the heart of the city was destroyed by flames from incendiary bombs, only the charred walls and gutted roof having been left standing. As was the case with the synagogues, no attempts on the part of the fire brigade were made to extinguish the fire, although apparently there was a certain amount of apprehension for adjacent property, for the walls of a coffee house next door were covered with asbestos and sprayed by the doughty firemen. It is extremely difficult to believe, but the owners of the clothing store were actually charged with setting the fire and on that basis were dragged from their beds at 6 a.m. and clapped into prison.

Tactics which closely approached the ghoulish took place at the Jewish cemetery where the temple was fired together with a building occupied by caretakers, tombstones uprooted, and graves violated. Eyewitnesses considered reliable the report that ten corpses were left unburied at this cemetery for a whole week because all gravediggers and cemetery attendants had been arrested.

Ferocious as was the violation of property, the most hideous phase of the so-called "spontaneous" action has been the wholesale arrest and transportation to concentration camps of male German Jews between the ages of sixteen and sixty, as well as Jewish men without citizenship. This has been taking place daily since the night of horror. This office has no way of accurately checking the numbers of such arrests, but there is very little question that they have run to several thousands in Leipzig alone. Having demolished dwellings and hurled most of the movable effects onto the streets, the insatiably sadistic perpetrators threw many of the trembling inmates into a small stream that flows through the Zoological Park, commanding horrified spectators to spit at them, defile them with mud, and jeer at their plight. The latter incident has been repeatedly corroborated by German witnesses who were nauseated in telling the tale. The slightest manifestation of sympathy evoked a positive fury on the part of the perpetrators, and the crowd was powerless to do anything but turn horror-stricken eyes from the scene of abuse, or leave the vicinity. These tactics were carried out the entire morning of 10 November without police intervention and they were applied to men, women, and children.

There is much evidence of physical violence,

including several deaths. At least half-a-dozen cases have been personally observed, victims with bloody, badly bruised faces having fled to this office, believing that as refugees their desire to emigrate could be expedited here. As a matter of fact this consulate has been a bedlam of humanity for the past ten days, most of these visitors being desperate women, as their husbands and sons had been taken off to concentration camps.

Similarly violent procedure was applied throughout this consular district, the amount of havoc wrought depending upon the number of Jewish establishments or persons involved. It is understood that in many of the smaller communities even more relentless methods were employed than was the case in the cities. Reports have been received from Weissenfels to the effect that the few Jewish families there are experiencing great difficulty in purchasing food. It is reported that three Aryan professors of the University of Jena have been arrested and taken off to concentration camps because they had voiced disapproval of this insidious drive against mankind.

Note

1. Ernst vom Rath was shot on 7 November 1938 at the German Embassy in Paris; he died on 9 November. Herschel Grynszpan, a 17-year-old Polish-German Jew, was accused of the murder. The Nazis used this event as an excuse to attack the German-Jewish community on the night of 9–10 November. Grynszpan's motives remain a subject of controversy.

> **Study Question**
>
> Was the crowd "powerless" to do anything under the circumstances described by Buffum?

Evgeniia Ginzburg

Evgeniia Ginzburg's Journey Into the Whirlwind *is considered one of the most important first-hand accounts of the Stalinist-era purges in the Soviet Union. Ginzburg (1906–77)[1] was by her own account, a loyal supporter of Leninism. She became a professor at the Teacher Training Institute of Kazan University and later was editor of a local communist newspaper, Red Tartary. In February 1937 a colleague denounced her for having failed to attack the work of another colleague whose writings had angered Stalin. Subsequently she was imprisoned, placed on trial, and sent to a series of gulags. She was not released from prison until 1955, even though her original sentence was only ten years.* Journey Into the Whirlwind *along with its sequel,* Within the Whirlwind, *chronicles her entire imprisonment. When Ginzburg was released as part of Nikita Khrushchev's de-Stalinization she continued to express her loyalty to "the great Leninist truths."[2] This excerpt covers Ginzburg's experiences during her arrest, "trial," and sentencing.*

Document Source: Evgeniia Ginzburg, *Journey into the Whirlwind* (New York: Harcourt, Inc., 1967), 60–3, 171–4.

Journey Into the Whirlwind

I have often thought about the tragedy of those by whose agency the purge of 1937 was carried out. What a life they had! They were all sadists, of course. And only a handful found the courage to commit suicide.

Step by step, as they followed their routine directives, they traveled all the way from the human condition to that of beasts. Their faces, as time went by, defied description. I, at any rate, cannot find words to convey the expression on the faces of these un-men.

But all this happened only gradually. That night, Interrogator Livanov, who had summoned me, looked like any other civil servant with perhaps a little more than the usual liking for red tape. Everything about him confirmed this impression—the placid, well-fed face, the neat writing with which he filled the left-hand side (reserved for questions) of the record sheet in front of him, and his local, Kazan accent. Certain turns of speech, provincial and old-fashioned, reminded me of our nurse Fima and aroused a host of memories of home.

In that first moment I had a flash of hope that the madness might be over, that I had left it behind me, down there, with the grinding of padlocks and the pain-filled eyes of the golden-haired girl from the banks of the river Sungari. Here, it seemed, was the world of ordinary, normal people. Outside the window was the old familiar town with its clanging streetcars. The window had neither bars nor a wooden screen, but handsome net curtains. And the plate with the remains of Livanov's supper had not been left on the floor but stood on a small table in a corner of the room.

He might be a perfectly decent man, this quiet official who was slowly writing down my answers to his straight-forward, insignificant questions: Where had I worked between this year and that, where and when had I met this or that person. . . ? But now the first page had been filled and he gave it to me to sign.

What was this? He had asked me how long I had known Elvov,[3] and I had answered, "Since 1932." But here it said, "How long have you known the Trotskyist Elvov?" and my reply was put down as "I have known the Trotskyist Elvov since 1932."

"This isn't what I said."

He looked at me in amazement, as though it really were only a question of getting the definition right.

"But he *is* a Trotskyist!"

"I don't know that."

"But we do. It's been established. The

investigators have conclusive evidence."

"But I can't confirm something I don't know. You can ask me when I met *Professor* Elvov, but whether he is a Trotskyist, and whether I knew him as a Trotskyist—that's a different question."

"It's for me to ask the questions, if you please. You've no right to dictate to me the form in which I should put them. All you have to do is answer them."

"Then put the answers down exactly as I give them, and not in your own words. In fact, why don't we have a stenographer to put them down?"

These words, the height of naïveté, were greeted by peals of laughter—not, of course, from Livanov but from the embodiment of lunacy which had just entered the room in the person of State Security Lieutenant Tsarevsky.

"Well, well, what do I see! You're behind bars now, are you?". . .

"So you're behind bars," he sneered again, in a tone of hatred as intense as though I had set fire to his house or murdered his child.

"You realize of course," he went on more quietly, "that the regional committee has agreed to your arrest. Everything has come out. Elvov gave you away. That husband of yours, Aksyonov—he's been arrested too, and he's come clean. He's a Trotskyist too, of course. . . ."

"Is Elvov here, in this prison?"

"Yes! In the very cell next to yours. And he's confirmed all the evidence against you."

"Then confront me with him. I want to know what he said about me. Let him repeat it to my face."

"Like to see your friend, eh?" He added such a scurrilous obscenity that I could hardly believe my ears.

"How dare you! I demand to see the head of your department. This is a Soviet institution where people can't be treated like dirt."

"Enemies are not people. We're allowed to do what we like with them. People indeed!"

Again he roared with laughter. Then he screamed at me at the top of his voice, banged the table with his fist . . . and told me I'd be shot if I didn't sign the record.

I noticed with amazement that Livanov, so quiet and polite, looked on unmoved. Obviously, he had seen it all before.

"Why do you allow this man to interfere with a case you're in change of?" I asked.

His smile was almost gentle.

"Tsarevsky's right, you know. You can make things better for yourself if you honestly repent and make a clean breast of it. Stubbornness won't help you. The investigators have conclusive evidence."

"Of what?"

"Of your counter-revolutionary activity as a member of the secret organization headed by Elvov. You'd much better sign the record. If you do you'll be treated decently. We'll allow you to have parcels, and we'll let you see your children and your husband."

While Livanov spoke Tsarevsky kept quiet in readiness for his next attack. I thought he had just happened to come into Livanov's office. But after the two of them had been at me for three or four hours, I realized that it was part of a deliberate technique.

The blue light of a February dawn was casting its chill on the room by the time Tsarevsky rang for the warder. The same words ended the interrogation as those of Vevers the day before, but Tsarevsky's voice rose to a falsetto:

"Off to the cell with you! And there you'll sit until you sign."

Going down the stairs, I caught myself hurrying back to my cell. It seemed, after all, that I was better off there, in the human presence of a companion in misfortune—and the grinding of locks was better than the demented screams of un-men.

[Six months passed during which time Ginzburg was subjected to similar treatment. Then, in August, she was summoned to her trial.]

My hour had come. The military tribunal of the Supreme Court—three officers and a secretary—faced me across a table. On either side of me were two warders. Such were the "fully public" conditions in which my "trial" was conducted.

I looked intently at my judges' faces and was struck by the fact that they closely resembled one another and also for some reason reminded me of the official at Black Lake who had taken my watch. They all looked alike, although one of them was dark and another's hair was graying. Yes, I saw what it was they had in common—the empty look of a mummy, or a fish in aspic. Nor was this surprising. How could one carry out such duties day after day without cutting oneself off from one's fellow men—if only by that glazed expression?

Suddenly I found that it was easy to breathe. A summer breeze of extraordinary freshness was blowing through the wide-open window. The room was a handsome one, with a high ceiling. So there were, after all, such places in the world!

Outside the windows there were some large, dark-green trees: their leaves were rustling and I was moved by the cool, mysterious sound. I could not remember having heard it before. It was strangely touching—why had I never noticed it?

And the clock on the wall—large and round, its shiny hands like a gray mustache—how long was it since I had seen anything like it?

I checked the time at the beginning and end of the trial. Seven minutes. That, neither more nor less, was the time it took to enact this tragicomedy.

The voice of the president of the court—Dmitriev, People's Commissar for Justice of the Russian Republic—resembled the expression of his eyes. If a frozen codfish could talk, that is undoubtedly what it would sound like. There was not a trace here of the animation, the zest which my interrogators had put into their performances: the judges were merely functionaries earning their pay. No doubt they had a quota, and were anxious to over-fulfill it if they could.

"You have read the indictment?" said the president in tones of unutterable boredom. "You plead guilty? No? But the evidence shows . . ."

He leafed through the bulky file and muttered through his teeth: "For instance the witness Kozlov . . ."

"Kozlova. It's a woman—and, I may add, a despicable one."

"Kozlova, yes. Or again, the witness Dyachenko . . ."

"Dyakanov."

"Yes. Well, they both state . . ."

But what they stated the judge was too pressed for time to read. Breaking off he asked me: "Any questions you wish to ask the court?"

"Yes, I do. I am accused under section 8, of Article 58, which means that I am charged with terrorism. Will you please tell me the name of the political leader against whose life I am supposed to have plotted?"

The judges were silent for a while, taken aback by this preposterous question. They looked reproachfully at the inquisitive woman who was holding up their work. Then the one with grizzled hair muttered:

"You know, don't you, that Comrade Kirov[4] was murdered in Leningrad?"

"Yes, but I didn't kill him, it was someone called Nikolayev. Anyway, I've never been in Leningrad. Isn't that what you call an alibi?"

"Are you a lawyer by chance?" said the gray-haired man crossly.

"No, I'm a teacher."

"You won't get anywhere by quibbling. You may never have been in Leningrad, but it was your accomplices who killed him, and that makes you morally and criminally responsible."

"The court will withdraw for consultation," grunted the president. Whereupon they all stood up, lazily stretching their limbs . . .

I looked at the clock again. They couldn't even have had time for a smoke! In less than two minutes the worshipful assembly was back in session. The president had in his hand a large sheet of paper of excellent quality, covered with typescript in close spacing. The text, which must have taken at least twenty minutes to copy, was my sentence: the official document setting forth my crimes and the penalty for them. It began with the solemn words: "In the name of the Union of Soviet Socialist Republics," followed by something long and unintelligible. Oh, yes, it was the same preamble as in the indictment, with its "restoration of capitalism," "underground terrorist organization," and all the rest. Only wherever that document had said "accused," this one said "convicted". . . .

Notes

1. There is some debate as to Ginzburg's date of birth, some sources list 1904, others 1906.
2. Evgeniia Semyonovna Ginzburg, *Journey Into the Whirlwind*, transl. Paul Stevenson and Max Hayward (New York: Harcourt, Brace, Jovanovich, 1967), 417.
3. Nikolai Naumovich Elvov's history of the Communist Party had angered Stalin.
4. Sergei Kirov was Secretary of the Central Committee of the CPSU. His assassination in December 1934 provided Stalin with an excuse to launch the wave of purges which followed.

Study Question

Was there any way under the system described by Ginzburg to demonstrate one's loyalty?

George Orwell

Eric Arthur Blair was born in India in 1903 (d. 1950). His parents worked in the Indian civil service and Blair initially found a job with the Indian Imperial Police in Burma. After growing disillusioned with British imperial policies, he resigned from the civil service. Blair published four novels in the 1930s under the pen name George Orwell, and three non-fictional works, including Homage to Catalonia, *which was written between December 1936 and mid-summer 1937. During his time in Spain he sympathized with and fought alongside the Trotskyist Workers' Party of Marxist Unification (POUM),* *instead of the left-wing factions which were directly supported by the Soviet Union.*

Document Source: George Orwell, *Homage to Catalonia* (London: Secker and Warburg, 1938), chapter five.

Homage to Catalonia

To understand the alignment on the Government side one has got to remember how the war started. When the fighting broke out on 18 July it is probable that every anti-Fascist in Europe felt a thrill of hope. For here at last, apparently, was democracy standing up to Fascism. For years past the so-called democratic countries had been surrendering to Fascism at every step. The Japanese had been allowed to do as they liked in Manchuria. Hitler had walked into power and proceeded to massacre political opponents of all shades. Mussolini had bombed the Abyssinians while fifty-three nations (I think it was fifty-three) made pious noises "off." But when Franco tried to overthrow a mildly Left-wing Government the Spanish people, against all expectation, had risen against him. It seemed—possibly it was—the turning of the tide.

But there were several points that escaped general notice. To begin with, Franco was not strictly comparable with Hitler or Mussolini. His rising was a military mutiny backed up by the aristocracy and the Church, and in the main, especially at the beginning, it was an attempt not so much to impose Fascism as to restore feudalism. This meant that Franco had against him not only the working class but also various sections of the liberal bourgeoisie—the very people who are the supporters of Fascism when it appears in a more modern form. More important than this was the fact that the Spanish working class did not, as we might conceivably do in England, resist Franco in the name of "democracy" and the *status quo*; their resistance was accompanied by—one might almost say it consisted of—a definite revolutionary outbreak. Land was seized by the peasants; many factories and most of the transport were seized by the trade unions; churches were wrecked and the priests driven out or killed. The *Daily Mail*, amid the cheers of the Catholic clergy, was able to represent Franco as a patriot delivering his country from hordes of fiendish "Reds". . . .

Meanwhile the workers had weapons in their hands, and at this stage they refrained from giving them up. (Even a year later it was computed that the Anarcho-Syndicalists in Catalonia possessed 30,000 rifles.) The estates of the big pro-Fascist landlords were in many places seized by the peasants. Along with the collectivization of industry and transport there was an attempt to set up the rough beginnings of a workers' government by means of local committees, workers' patrols to replace the old pro-capitalist police forces, workers' militias based on the trade unions, and so forth. Of course the process was not uniform, and it went further in Catalonia than elsewhere. There were areas where the institutions of local government remained almost untouched, and others where they existed side by side with revolutionary committees. In a few places independent Anarchist communes were set up, and some of them remained in being till about a year later, when they were forcibly suppressed by the Government.

In Catalonia, for the first few months, most of the actual power was in the hands of the Anarcho-Syndicalists, who controlled most of the key industries. The thing that had happened in Spain was, in fact, not merely a civil war, but the beginning of a revolution. It is this fact that the anti-Fascist press outside Spain has made it its special business to obscure. The issue has been narrowed down to "Fascism versus democracy" and the revolutionary aspect concealed as much as possible. In England, where the Press is more centralized and the public more easily deceived than elsewhere, only two versions of the Spanish war have had any publicity to speak of: the Right-wing version of Christian patriots versus Bolsheviks dripping with blood, and the Left-wing version of gentlemanly republicans quelling a military revolt. The central issue has been successfully covered up. . . .

The POUM "line" was approximately this:

"It is nonsense to talk of opposing Fascism by bourgeois "democracy." Bourgeois "democracy" is only another name for capitalism, and so is Fascism; to fight against Fascism on behalf of "democracy" is to fight against one form of capitalism on behalf of a second which is liable to turn into the first at any moment. The only real alternative to Fascism is workers' control. If you set up any less goal than this, you will either hand the victory to Franco, or, at best, let in Fascism by the back door. Meanwhile the workers must cling to every scrap of what they have won; if they yield anything to the semi-bourgeois Government they can depend upon being cheated. The workers' militias and police-forces must be preserved in their present form and every effort to "bourgeoisify" them must be resisted. If the workers do not control the armed forces, the armed forces will control the workers. The war and the revolution are inseparable." . . .

I do earnestly feel that on our side—the Government side—this war was different from ordinary, imperialistic wars; but from the nature of the war-propaganda you would never have guessed it. The fighting had barely started when the newspapers of the Right and Left dived simultaneously into the same cesspool of abuse. We all remember the *Daily Mail's* poster: "REDS CRUCIFY NUNS," while to the *Daily Worker* Franco's Foreign Legion was "composed of murderers, white-slavers, dope-fiends, and the offal of every European country". As late as October 1937 the *New Statesman* was treating us to tales of Fascist barricades made of the bodies of living children (a most unhandy thing to make barricades with), and Mr Arthur Bryant was declaring that "the sawing-off of a Conservative tradesman's legs" was "a commonplace" in Loyalist Spain. The people who write that kind of stuff never fight; possibly they believe that to write it is a substitute for fighting. It is the same in all wars; the soldiers do the fighting, the journalists do the shouting, and no true patriot ever gets near a front-line trench, except on the briefest of propaganda-tours. Sometimes it is a comfort to me to think that the aeroplane is altering the conditions of war. Perhaps when the next great war comes we may see that sight unprecedented in all history, a jingo with a bullet-hole in him.

> **Study Question**
>
> Based upon Orwell's description of the Republican supporters, how should we characterize the dominant ideology?

Fortune Magazine

Getúlio Vargas (1882–1954) rose to power in Brazil at the end of a long period of republican rule, in which powerful coffee interests dominated politics. Vargas hoped to end Brazil's reliance on the unstable world market for coffee and usher in a more broadly based program of industrialization. However, opposition from the coffee oligarchs led him to consolidate power in 1934.

Using dictatorial controls, Vargas promoted Brazilian nationalism and cracked down on all leftist movements. The article which follows discusses the nature and impact of the Vargas regime; it appeared in American media mogul Henry Luce's Fortune *magazine in 1939.*

Document Source: *Fortune* Magazine, "South America VI: Brazil," *Fortune*, 19(6) (June 1939): 140–2.

Getúlio Vargas and the *Estado Novo*

The Brazilian Government is a dictatorship, under a constitution that takes effect only as it is implemented by the dictator's decrees. Although there are liberal tendencies in the regime, labor laws, public works, and certain cooperative economic controls—the usual forms of democracy have been abandoned and probably will remain in the discard for some time to come. The reason is quite simple. Brazilian politics are dominated, as are politics in nearly all Latin American countries, by the influence of the leading army officers, whose hold over their troops is based on personal loyalty. In Brazil this group felt a natural affinity for the Integralista movement[1] and its fascist doctrine. They were thoroughly tired of the squabbles and the oratorical displays of the sectional politicians. Getúlio saw early in 1937 that if the choice lay between the Integralistas and a democratic President supported by a popular assembly, then the preponderant weight of the army would be thrown to the Integralistas and Brazil would indeed be delivered over to fascism.

Moved by this perception, and perhaps even more by a politician's desire to hold on to a job, Getúlio took over the government himself. It was the only way to keep the army in line, and how narrowly it succeeded was shown by the Integralista and army plot just described. While putting down fascism with one hand, Getúlio now spares no pains to keep the army happy and to play off its leaders against one another. The new barracks just completed at Recife include a purple swimming pool and a movie auditorium. Integralistas could scarcely do more. The army is kept busy with its own internal feuds and does not have to worry about politics. And so, as long as the threat of fascism remains, Brazil, by ironic circumstance, is being made safe for democracy by dictatorial means.

The man who is preserving this delicate balance came to prominence up the customary political ladder: military academy, law school, small state jobs, deputy in Rio, Cabinet Minister, and Governor of his native state. Now 56 years old, Getúlio is physically a little man, with fine eyes, a strong profile, and a corporeal outline that would at once win him the nickname of "Tubby" in an American university. He laughs often and heartily, and the laughter is not forced. An enthusiastic beginner at golf—he sometimes breaks 110—he gets in a round at least every Sunday. Getúlio has three sons and two daughters, most prominent of whom is the younger daughter, Alzira, who collects a salary for her titular job as lawyer to the Bank of Brazil, works closely with her father, and calls him "boss," for, unlike Getúlio, she speaks English well. Getúlio is genuinely popular, and although there are many in São Paulo who refer to him as "that man" or call him by his full name, Getúlio Vargas, rather than the usual Getúlio, the President is widely liked because of his engaging personality and admired for his uncanny political shrewdness. . . .

Naturally enough, the present regime in Brazil is presented to the people as something a good deal more philosophical than a mere political expedient. Indeed the regime arrogates to itself the best features of all popular systems and proudly labels them the New State, *Estado Novo*. The name came into use just after the *golpe* (coup d'état) of 10 November 1937, when Getúlio seized power and closed both federal and state legislatures; but subsequently the designation *Estado Novo* has been used retroactively on the theory that the *golpe* was a logical, planned step in an evolution that started in 1930. And that evolution presents certain alarming traits: extreme nationalism, Red-baiting, censorship, army control, and the turgid rhetoric of men straining to justify themselves. Let us take up these traits one by one.

The *Estado Novo* is decidedly nationalistic. Two-thirds of all employees in each job category in a foreign company must be Brazilians. Pilots of planes flying on national lines (as contrasted with international through routes) must be Brazilians. Brazilians must be paid the same salary as foreigners if they hold the same jobs. Waterpower and mineral resources can be exploited today only by companies controlled by Brazilians, and oil can be exploited only by the government. The constitution provides that all banks and insurance companies are to be nationalized (but so far foreign banks and insurance companies still operate as before). Twenty per cent of the coal bought by a factory must be national coal, although the quality is so poor that some factories simply buy it and pile it up in a dump heap. Alcohol made from Brazilian sugar must be mixed with all gasoline, the percentage varying in different states. Manioc flour must be mixed with wheat flour. A bachelor's tax is contemplated.

Getúlio has said: "The *Estado Novo* does not recognize individual rights against the collective state. Individuals have no rights, they have duties. The rights belong to the collective state." The worst sin a Brazilian can commit is to be a Communist; or to be what is known in this country as a "fellow traveler." Or even to possess volumes of Karl Marx. A man who is not a Communist may still get a couple of months in jail if someone complains that he is a Communist. . . .

A censor from the police is assigned to every newspaper office and his pencil deletes whatever is construed as prejudicial to the *Estado Novo*. Often his chore includes international news: he will demand soft pedaling of a renewed Nazi drive against Jews, as last winter, or the final absorption of Czechoslovakia by Germany. Part of this is policy, to avoid the appearance of taking sides on international questions; part of it is laziness, the reluctance of the censor to stand up under the accusations of prejudice leveled at him

by local German officials. The censor also has a special interest to see that the military are treated with the utmost respect. Mail is censored to an unknown extent, but most letters from Europe are strictly inspected for communism.

Getúlio has said: "That negligible minority made up of the spiteful, the malcontents, of those who circulate rumors, of those who have been defeated, and of the saboteurs waste their time, and those who dare to disturb the order, under whatever pretext, will be punished." Keeping an eye on malcontents is the job of the police, and there are four different kinds of police in Rio, totaling about 10,000 in all. Besides the police, the army, numbering 65,000 effectives, and on the increase, is always available for real trouble. State police, which in the *Estado Novo* are under federal authority, add at least 30,000 more. The army is trained by a French mission, and the navy, with 12,500 men, has US instruction. Appropriations for the army and navy departments for the current year are officially set at about one-quarter of the total budget, but the amount will probably prove to be an understatement of actual expenditures. The new armament program, projected for ten years, amounts to some $10,000,000 a year, with large orders in England now for six cruisers and other orders totaling $40,000,000 placed with Krupp for the eventual delivery of arms, which, incidentally, will use up a lot of the bloated compensation-mark balance. Over a period of years Brazil's expenditures on the armed forces have taken as much as 50 per cent of the tax revenue remaining after payments on the debt.

Note

1. The *Ação Integralista Brasileira* was a political party formed in 1932. Some of the party's ideological inspiration was drawn from Mussolini's fascist movement.

> **Study Question**
>
> To what extent does the *Estado Novo* described here match Mussolini's description of the ideal fascist state?

Web Resources

Internet Modern History Sourcebook: Fascism (see also Nazism)
   http://www.fordham.edu/halsall/mod/modsbook42.html
Italian Life under Fascism
   http://specialcollections.library.wisc.edu/exhibits/Fascism
German Propaganda Archive
   http://www.calvin.edu/academic/cas/gpa
University of Washington Libraries: Latin American History
   http://www.lib.washington.edu/ /history-latinam

Recommended Reading

Mikhail Bulgakov, *Master and Margarita* (New York: Vintage, 1996). *Master and Margarita* was completed shortly before Bulgakov's death, but remained unpublished for 26 years. Through a complex interweaving of two stories, Bulgakov's satirical novel captures the worst aspects of the Stalinist era: forced collectivization, purges, arbitrary use of terror, and forced atheism.

Hans Fallada, *Little Man, What Now?* (Chicago: Academy Chicago Publishers, 1992). Written in 1932—immediately prior to the Nazi rise to power—Fallada's novel spans the Weimar era. Economic deprivation falls hardest upon the "little man," leading to radicalization, desperation, and the inevitable political choice between communism and National Socialism.

Günter Grass, *The Tin Drum* (New York: Vintage, 1990). *The Tin Drum* chronicles the pivotal events of the First World War, the rise of the Nazis, and the National Socialist regime, including *Kristallnacht*, and the war years. Grass was one of the first German authors to condemn the involvement of ordinary Germans in the activities of the National Socialist regime and to point out the inherent danger of refusing to acknowledge guilt.

Christopher Isherwood, *Goodbye to Berlin* (New York: New Directions Publishing, 1963). Published in 1939, and set amidst the cultural decadence of the late Weimar years, *Goodbye to Berlin*—the inspiration for the musical *Cabaret*—was based on Isherwood's visits to Germany between 1929 and 1933. Sexuality, excess, and the bohemian lifestyle of the late Weimar era stand as the backdrop to the looming rise of National Socialism.

Arthur Koestler, *Darkness at Noon* (New York: Bantam, 1984). Set in 1938, at the height of the Stalinist purges, Koestler's powerful novel tells the story of an innocent man imprisoned for crimes he did not commit, but who was, at the same time, aware that he was guilty of blind loyalty to the system that has now imprisoned him. The novel was based partly on the author's firsthand experiences.

George Orwell, *Animal Farm* and *1984* (New York: Harcourt, 2003). Orwell's fascinating analyses of totalitarianism: the first is told in allegorical form, the second through the eyes of the protagonist Winston Smith, an employee in the "Ministry of Truth." *Animal Farm* is the deceptively simple story of animals that, having overthrown their human masters, must create a new social order. The novel begins with the premise of equality, but concludes "all animals are equal, but some animals are more equal than others." *1984* is Orwell's meditation on truth, reality, ideology, resistance, and conformity.

Alexander Solzhenitsyn, *One Day in the Life of Ivan Denisovich* (New York: Bantam, 1984). Solzhenitsyn's novel—authorized for publication by Nikita Khrushchev—played a key role in the de-Stalinization era. Based partly on the author's experiences in the Stalinist Russian labour camps, the novel delves into the absurdities of life under a system where everything is relative to the whims of an absolute authority.

John Wray, *Right Hand of Sleep* (New York: Vintage, 2002). After a 20-year exile in Soviet Ukraine, a deserter from the Austro-Hungarian armies of the Great War returns to Austria in 1938. There he encounters the desperation of interwar Austria and the implications of the Anschluss. Disillusioned with socialism but uncertain about the future, the protagonist watches Nazism spread slowly through the region.

Recommended Viewing

Zemlya [*Earth*] (USSR/Ukraine, 1930). Director: Alexander Dovzhenko (Silent, B&W). In this highly idealistic vision of collective farming in Ukraine, Dovzhenko demonizes the Kulak class and idealizes life on Stalin's collective farms. The film contains visually stunning imagery. It was created just prior to the artificially induced famines that decimated Ukraine in the early 1930s.

Triumph of the Will (Germany, 1934). Director: Leni Riefenstahl (B&W). *Triumph of the Will* remains both a documentary masterpiece—the template for the modern documentary—and a tremendously controversial film. Set during the Nuremberg Party rally in 1934, the film provides insights into the nature of the regime, the atmosphere of the time, and the mind of the senior Nazi leaders.

Alexander Nevsky (USSR, 1938). Director: Sergei Eisenstein (B&W). Ostensibly a retelling of the thirteenth century Russian defeat of the Teutonic knights, *Alexander Nevsky* was designed to inspire the Soviet people against the looming threat from Hitler's Germany. Despite its propagandistic intent, the film remains impressive for its cinematography and for Sergei Prokofiev's score.

The Great Dictator (USA, 1940). Director: Charles Chaplin (B&W). Chaplin's first talking picture launches a comedic attack on Adolf Hitler, Nazi Germany, and Benito Mussolini. Despite its comedic premise, the film raises vital issues such as anti-Semitism, ghettoization, and discrimination. It closes with Chaplin stepping out of character to plead for peace and humanity.

The Conformist (Italy/France/West Germany, 1970). Director: Bernardo Bertolucci. Bertolucci's psychological drama focuses on the transformation of one man into a loyal fascist. The film links fascist support to a particular personality type, rather than socio-economic causes, but Bertolucci also captures the atmosphere of fascist Italy in this production.

Kaigenrai (Japan, 1973). Director: Yoshishige Yoshida (B&W). *Kaigenrai* is a semi-biographical portrait of the life of Kitta Ikki, whose writings are often seen as being responsible for the rise of radical militarism in the 1930s and 1940s. The film addresses the origins of Japanese militarism, the Emperor system, and racism.

6

Global Depression

By the late 1920s the interconnectedness of the global economy was evident to many observers. Postwar recovery in Europe had been fuelled in large part by on-going loans from the United States and by American demand for European goods. Latin America's economies were also tied to the United States, largely by neo-colonial trade agreements. The economies of the colonial world remained tightly bound to the economies of the mother countries, and Japan had created an entire network of formal and informal economic ties throughout East Asia. In short, any major economic downturn was bound to have a ripple effect around the globe.

As well, despite the outward appearance of economic stabilization and, in some cases, growth, serious structural weaknesses remained. Agriculture found itself in a perpetual crisis throughout the 1920s. Industry struggled to

A Dorothea Lange portrait of Florence Thompson, a 32-year old mother of seven living in a make-shift tent—a common fate for the families of migrant labourers.

New York World-Telegram and the Sun Newspaper Photograph Collection. Courtesy of the Library of Congress, Prints and Photographs Division (LC-USZ62-58355).

modernize—which meant to mechanize—and as a result there were substantial job losses as workers were displaced by assembly lines. At the same time the banking and financial sectors in many nations remained dangerously unregulated. The United States government in particular had adopted a hands-off approach to nearly all facets of the economy; the businessmen, after all, knew best what was good for business, or so many believed.

The first signs of serious financial instability came in the United States in the middle of 1929. Rampant speculation, fuelled by lax margin requirements and easy credit, had driven the stock market to impossible heights. The *New York Times* reported in March 1929 that "[p]laying the stock market has become a major American pastime." Though some well-informed investors were able to pull their profits out of the market in the summer months, most investors stayed in, believing that the market would continue to soar upwards. It did not. The crash came in late October. On the 28th stock prices began to decline precipitously (13 per cent over the day's trading); on the 29th prices fell a further 12 per cent. By the time the bottom was reached in 1932 the market had fallen 89 per cent overall.[1]

The resulting financial crisis in the United States had immediate global repercussions. America called in its loans to Europe and erected an historically high tariff wall that restricted access to the American market. This, in turn, led to retaliatory protectionist measures by its leading trading partners. The net result was a massive decline in global trade: American imports from Europe dropped from $1,334 million in 1929 to $390 million in 1932; exports from the United States had been $2,341 million in 1929 and fell to $809 million in 1932. Total global trade dropped by 66 per cent between 1929 and 1934.[2] European nations, such as Germany, whose recovery had been bankrolled by the United States, were thrown into immediate economic chaos. Other nations, such as Britain, whose economy had been suffering throughout the 1920s, found their social support systems overwhelmed. In the colonial world the level of suffering varied according to the degree to which a country's economy was dependent on the mother country. However, few escaped without feeling any of the Depression's consequences. Japan also suffered and, as a result, began to move away from its reliance on the world market and to seek out new, guaranteed sources of raw materials. Meanwhile, in the United States, the government of Herbert Hoover struggled to find new ways to deal with the economic downturn. Ultimately, despite some successful public works projects, Hoover would be decisively defeated in the 1932 election, allowing Franklin D. Roosevelt to sweep into office with an unprecedented mandate for change.

This set of documents focuses, for the most part, on the Depression's impact on ordinary citizens. US President Franklin D. Roosevelt's inaugural address provides a sense of the condition of the United States in 1933 and the obstacles that had to be overcome. The exploitation of American workers, in some cases created by the Depression and in other cases simply worsened by it, is examined by journalist Paul Comly French. Heinrich Hauser describes life for Germany's unemployed, while George Orwell chronicles life in Depression-era northern England. W.E.B. Du Bois examines the root of the economic problems facing Liberia, while Lázaro Cárdenas provides some sense of the damage wrought by the Depression in Mexico. Finally, Neville Chamberlain and W.L. Mackenzie King discuss the contentious policy of appeasement, which was, to some extent, a product of the economic crises of the 1930s.

Notes

1. Floyd Norris, "Looking Back at the Crash of 1929," *New York Times*, http://www.nytimes.com/library/financial/index-1929-crash.html.
2. "Smoot-Hawley Tariff," *Bureau of Public Affairs*, US Department of State, http://www.state.gov/r/pa/ho/time/id/17606.htm.

Franklin D. Roosevelt

When Franklin D. Roosevelt (1882–1945) took office in 1933, statistics showed that the economy was already beginning to respond to the measures put in place by Herbert Hoover. However, the confidence of the American people was at an all-time low. In his inaugural address, Roosevelt laid out, step-by-step, the approach he would take to deal with the worst effects of the Depression. Note throughout Roosevelt's speech the degree to which he intended to increase the government's power to intervene in the lives of its citizens, as well as the clear warning to Congress regarding the penalty for inaction in the latter part of the speech.

Document Source: Franklin D. Roosevelt, "First Inaugural Address, 1933." From Franklin D. Roosevelt Library, National Archives and Records Administration, ARC Identifier: 197333.

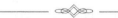

Inaugural Address of the President, 4 March 1933

I am certain that my fellow Americans expect that on my induction into the Presidency I will address them with a candor and a decision which the present situation of our nation impels. This is pre-eminently the time to speak the truth, the whole truth, frankly and boldly. Nor need we shrink from honestly facing conditions in our country today. This great nation will endure as it has endured, will revive and will prosper. So, first of all, let me assert my firm belief that the only thing we have to fear is fear itself—nameless, unreasoning, unjustified terror which paralyzes needed efforts to convert retreat into advance. In every dark hour of our national life a leadership of frankness and vigor has met with that understanding and support of the people themselves which is essential to victory. I am convinced that you will again give that support to leadership in these critical days.

In such a spirit on my part and on yours we face our common difficulties. They concern, thank God, only material things. Values have shrunken to fantastic levels; taxes have risen; our ability to pay has fallen; government of all kinds is faced by serious curtailment of income; the means of exchange are frozen in the currents of trade; the withered leaves of industrial enterprise lie on every side; farmers find no markets for their produce; the savings of many years in thousands of families are gone.

More important, a host of unemployed citizens face the grim problem of existence, and an equally great number toil with little return. Only a foolish optimist can deny the dark realities of the moment.

Yet our distress comes from no failure of substance. We are stricken by no plague of locusts. Compared with the perils which our forefathers conquered because they believed and were not afraid, we have still much to be thankful for. Nature still offers her bounty and human efforts have multiplied it. Plenty is at our doorstep, but a generous use of it languishes in the very sight of the supply. Primarily this is because rulers of the exchange of mankind's goods have failed, through their own stubbornness and their own incompetence, have admitted their failure, and abdicated. Practices of the unscrupulous money changers stand indicted in the court of public opinion, rejected by the hearts and minds of men.

True they have tried, but their efforts have been cast in the pattern of an outworn tradition. Faced by failure of credit they have proposed only the lending of more money. Stripped of the lure of profit by which to induce our people to follow their false leadership, they have resorted to exhortations, pleading tearfully for restored confidence. They know only the rules of a generation of self-seekers. They have no vision, and when there is no vision the people perish.

The money changers have fled from their high seats in the temple of our civilization. We may now restore that temple to the ancient truths. The measure of the restoration lies in the extent to which we apply social values more noble than mere monetary profit.

Happiness lies not in the mere possession of money; it lies in the joy of achievement, in the thrill of creative effort. The joy and moral stimulation of work no longer must be forgotten in the mad chase of evanescent profits. These dark days will be worth all they cost us if they teach us that our true destiny is not to be ministered unto but to minister to ourselves and to our fellow men.

Recognition of the falsity of material wealth as the standard of success goes hand in hand with the abandonment of the false belief that public office and high political position are to be valued only by the standards of pride of place and personal profit; and there must be an end to a conduct in banking and in business which too often has given to a sacred trust the likeness of callous and selfish wrongdoing. Small wonder that confidence languishes, for it thrives only on honesty, on honor, on the sacredness of obligations, on faithful protection, on unselfish performance; without them it cannot live.

Restoration calls, however, not for change in ethics alone. This Nation asks for action, and action now.

Our greatest primary task is to put people to work. This is no unsolvable problem if we face it wisely and courageously. It can be accomplished in part by direct recruiting by the Government itself, treating the task as we would treat the emergency of a war, but at the same time, through this employment, accomplishing greatly needed projects to stimulate and reorganize the use of our natural resources.

Hand in hand with this we must frankly recognize the overbalance of population in our industrial centers and, by engaging on a national scale in redistribution, endeavor to provide a better use of the land for those best fitted for the land. The task can be helped by definite efforts to raise the values of agricultural products and with this the power to purchase the output of our cities. It can be helped by preventing realistically the tragedy of the growing loss through foreclosure of our small homes and our farms. It can be helped by insistence that the Federal, State, and local governments act forthwith on the demand that their cost be drastically reduced. It can be helped by the unifying of the relief activities which today are often scattered, uneconomical, and unequal. It can be helped by national planning for and supervision of all forms of transportation and of communications and other utilities which have a definitely public character. There are many ways in which it can be helped, but it can never be helped merely by talking about it. We must act and act quickly.

Finally, in our progress toward a resumption of work we require two safeguards against a return of the evils of the old order; there must be a strict supervision of all banking and credits and investments; there must be an end to speculation with other people's money, and there must be provision for an adequate but sound currency.

There are the lines of attack. I shall presently urge upon a new Congress, in special session, detailed measures for their fulfillment, and I shall seek the immediate assistance of the several States.

Through this program of action we address ourselves to putting our own national house in order and making income balance outgo. Our international trade relations, though vastly important, are in point of time and necessity secondary to the establishment of a sound national economy. I favor as a practical policy the putting of first things first. I shall spare no effort to restore world trade by international economic readjustment, but the emergency at home cannot wait on that accomplishment.

The basic thought that guides these specific means of national recovery is not narrowly nationalistic. It is the insistence, as a first consideration, upon the interdependence of the various elements in and parts of the United States—a recognition of the old and permanently important manifestation of the American spirit of the pioneer. It is the way to recovery. It is the immediate way. It is the strongest assurance that the recovery will endure.

In the field of world policy I would dedicate this nation to the policy of the good neighbor—the neighbor who resolutely respects himself and, because he does so, respects the rights of others—the neighbor who respects his obligations and respects the sanctity of his agreements in and with a world of neighbors.

If I read the temper of our people correctly, we now realize as we have never realized before our interdependence on each other; that we cannot merely take but we must give as well; that if we are to go forward, we must move as a trained and loyal army willing to sacrifice for the good of a common discipline, because without such discipline no progress is made, no leadership becomes effective. We are, I know, ready and willing to submit our lives and property to such discipline, because it makes possible a leadership which aims at a larger good. This I propose to offer, pledging that the larger purposes will bind upon us all as a sacred obligation with a unity of duty hitherto evoked only in time of armed strife.

With this pledge taken, I assume unhesitatingly the leadership of this great army of our people dedicated to a disciplined attack upon our common problems.

Action in this image and to this end is feasible under the form of government which we have inherited from our ancestors. Our Constitution is so simple and practical that it is possible always to meet extraordinary needs by changes in emphasis and arrangement without loss of essential form. That is why our constitutional system has proved itself the most superbly enduring political mechanism the modern world has produced. It has met every stress of vast expansion of territory, of foreign wars, of bitter internal strife, of world relations.

It is to be hoped that the normal balance of executive and legislative authority may be wholly adequate to meet the unprecedented task before us. But it may be that an unprecedented demand and need for undelayed action may call for temporary departure from that normal balance of public procedure.

I am prepared under my constitutional duty to recommend the measures that a stricken nation in the midst of a stricken world may require. These measures, or such other measures as the Congress may build out of its experience and wisdom, I shall seek, within my constitutional authority, to bring to speedy adoption.

But in the event that the Congress shall fail to take one of these two courses, and in the event that the national emergency is still critical, I shall not evade the clear course of duty that will then confront me. I shall ask the Congress for the one remaining instrument to meet the crisis—broad Executive power to wage a war against the emergency, as great as the power that would be given to me if we were in fact invaded by a foreign foe.

For the trust reposed in me I will return the courage and the devotion that befit the time. I can do no less.

We face the arduous days that lie before us in the warm courage of national unity; with the clear consciousness of seeking old and precious moral values; with the clean satisfaction that comes from the stern performance of duty by old and young alike. We aim at the assurance of a rounded and permanent national life.

We do not distrust the future of essential democracy. The people of the United States have not failed. In their need they have registered a mandate that they want direct, vigorous action. They have asked for discipline and direction under leadership. They have made me the present instrument of their wishes. In the spirit of the gift I take it.

In this dedication of a Nation we humbly ask the blessing of God. May He protect each and every one of us. May He guide me in the days to come.

> **Study Question**
>
> Based upon his inaugural address, what did Roosevelt believe was the key to the nation's recovery? Was he correct?

Paul Comly French

The exploitation of children and women in the textile industry has long been a feature of industrial nations. However, during the 1930s Franklin Roosevelt's supportive attitude towards trade unions—traditionally weak and ineffective in the United States—encouraged some workers to take a stand against the factory owners who exploited them. The conditions described below by journalist Paul Comly French (1890–1956)[1] in 1933 were not particularly unusual in this industry and were only peripherally related to the ongoing economic depression.

Document Source: Paul Comly French, "Children on Strike," *The Nation*, 136(3543) (May 31, 1933), 611.

Children on Strike

Allentown, Pennsylvania, 20 May [1933]

Shocking conditions in the sweatshops of Pennsylvania, where 200,000 men, women, and children work long hours for starvation wages, became front-page news through the efforts of the "baby strikers" of the Lehigh Valley. Aided by the presence of Mrs Gifford Pinchot on their picket line, they won the first skirmish in their fight against intolerable conditions when some of the employers signed an agreement providing for shorter working hours, a minimum-wage scale, and an immediate 10 per cent increase in wages. Unfortunately the agreement does not affect all the mills in Allentown or those in Easton, Northampton, and Catasqua, where the children are still on the picket line.

Another victory against the sweatshop was won in Philadelphia when 5,000 garment workers, encouraged by the public support of the children's strike against the Morris Freezer plant in Allentown

As early as 1909 protests against child labour were common. This protest in New York included many young workers—the signs were written in both English and Yiddish.

George Grantham Bain Collection. Courtesy of the Library of Congress, Prints and Photographs Division (LC-USZ62-22198).

and the D. & D. shirt factory in Northampton, a nearby borough, went on strike. Within two days the operators signed an agreement raising wages 10 per cent, establishing a 44-hour week in place of the previous 54-hour week, and allowing to complete unionization of the shops.

Meanwhile Governor Pinchot's commission for the investigation of sweatshops will continue its hearings with a view to recommending to the next session of the General Assembly legislation which would abolish sweatshops and child labor in Pennsylvania. These hearings have so far produced tales of hideous working conditions, long hours, and miserable wages, comparable only to those which obtained in the earliest years of the Industrial Revolution. They have also revealed the forces of reaction against which the reformers must contend. Much credit for the limited victory

in the children's strike must go to Mayor Fred E. Lewis of Allentown, who has vigorously protested for years against the evils and degradation of the sweatshops. But Charles Fox, burgess of the neighboring borough of Northampton, where the D. & D. plant is located, holds a different view. "If I had my way," he told the Governor's commission, "I'd give no food orders to unemployed persons who urged factory workers to strike." And his wife, who handles unemployment relief in Northampton, has even more amazing ideas. "I don't believe the strikers should be entitled to any unemployment relief," she testified before the commission, "because they don't have souls."

According to a quiet survey which Mrs Pinchot has made in every section of Pennsylvania, sweatshops are not confined to the Lehigh Valley and Philadelphia. And many of the case histories she has collected tell a story of lost youth and saddened childhood. In Gottlieb's Sewing Factory at York the usual wage is $3 or $4 a week, girls in Bernstein's Factory at York reported a payment of $2.90 for two weeks' work—an average of 3 cents an hour. At the York Suit Company button sewers receive from $3 to $4 a week for 50 hours; York tobacco workers said they received $2.50 for a week's work totaling 50 hours, while workers in a second cigar factory in this rich Lancaster County agricultural section said their wages averaged $1.60 for 54 hours. A silk mill in York charged girls $10 for "teaching them how to become operators." Pressers in the Lehigh Valley Shirt Company in Allentown receive $4 a week as against $14 paid for the same work two years ago. At the Adkins Shirt Company in Allentown only three girls in the place were over fourteen; their pay averaged from $1.30 to $2 a week, while one girl, with seven years' experience, earned the munificent salary of $7 a week. One boy in an Allentown shop earned 10 cents a week for a ten-week period; another Allentown shirt company paid 14 cents a dozen for a complicated operation, a high wage compared with the 8 cents paid for the same operation in another shop. The Caddy Shirt Company of Allentown moved out of town in the night owing four weeks' wages.

Hale A. Guss, borough manager of Northampton, told the Governor's commission that either Harry or Nathan Dashefsky—the two operate one of the worst sweatshops in the Lehigh Valley, the D. & D. Shirt Company—suggested having a gun "planted" on a union organizer. Another State official, a woman, said that one of the Dashefskys asked her why he couldn't have national guardsmen to protect his mill against the "baby strikers."

"Why?" she asked. "Aren't the police sufficient protection?" "Yes," he said, "but they won't fight."

One boy said he worked from 7 a.m. until 5 p.m. and then returned to the factory three nights each week to work from 7 p.m. until 3 a.m.; others told of being ordered to hide in the cellar and on fire escapes when State inspectors came to the mill; many of the girls testified they had been forced to accept the attentions of their employers or face instant dismissal. A titian-haired girl receiving 55 cents a week said the mill superintendent offered her a 100 per cent wage increase if she would accept his attentions at least three times weekly. Others, mere children, told of being taken to New York hotels for week-ends as playthings for the owners of the factories and for the purpose of enticing buyers to purchase shirts made in their mills. State officials, aided by the vigorous demands of Mrs Pinchot, plan criminal action against these men for violation of the Mann Act.

Other testimony, offered by fourteen-year-old Martin Kroboth, a trimmer, explained how the Dashefsky brothers saved the two-cent check tax by assessing each employee. The boy said his last check, for six days' work, was 96 cents. But he did not get all of that. An additional 10 per cent was deducted as a wage cut together with the two cents for the check tax. Another Allentown employer developed an even better system. He deducted 33 cents a week from the pay envelopes of each child to repay a fine of $100 assessed by the State for his failure to carry workmen's compensation insurance. Frank Selthofer, considered the "fastest" trimmer in the plant, received $1.73 for two weeks' work.

According to figures of the Bureau of Industrial Relations, many of the children are attempting to support entire families on their meager earnings. "Hours of labor in many of the Pennsylvania sweatshops range from 50 to 90 a week," said Stephen Raushenbush, of the bureau, "and the wages start at 50 cents and go to $10. This deplorable condition is responsible for $1.98 silk dresses, 3-for-10-cent cigars, 39-cent silk hosiery, $10 suits and top coats, and 25 cent shirts and neckties." More than half of the men's garment industry of the State operates on a sweatshop basis. The average in the cigar-making industry is about 70 per cent, while about 85 per cent of the production of men's shirts and pajamas is conducted on a sweatshop basis. "The State is powerless in many cases," Mr Raushenbush said, "because no statutes prevent women from working for $1 a week or men for any figure they'll accept."

Sweatshop conditions affect workers throughout the Commonwealth, from the anthracite coal miners of northeastern Pennsylvania to the soft-coal miners of the southwest, and from the silk and hosiery mills of the east to the shops, factories, and mills of the west. The opening attack on these conditions by the "baby strikers" received immediate support from the Philadelphia *Record* and the Pittsburgh *Press*. The *Record* carried editorials and cartoons depicting the plight of the children, while the *Press*, a Scripps-Howard newspaper, devoted

columns to its campaign to rid the State of the evils of the sweatshop. The editor of the *Press*, Edward T. Leech, spoke over the radio as part of the paper's fight. The minor victories in Philadelphia and Allentown are encouraging, but the war on the sweatshop has only begun.

Note

1. Sources disagree as to whether French died in 1956 or 1960.

> **Study Question**
>
> Given the economic situation of the nation in 1933, was there any way to prevent the abuse of workers who lacked even the most basic of rights?

Heinrich Hauser

Heinrich Hauser (1901–1955) was a journalist and photographer during the Weimar Republic. He left Germany in the late 1930s and relocated to the United States (he returned to Germany in 1948). In the following account, first published in 1933 in a National Socialist magazine based in the city of Jena, Hauser relates the experiences of Germany's unemployed, in

particular the psychological impact of poverty, during the worst years of the Depression—the early 1930s. This was the period in which support for both the National Socialist Party and the German Communist Party increased markedly.

Document Source: Heinrich Hauser, "With Germany's Unemployed," *Die Tat*, 334 (March 1933): 27–38.

With Germany's Unemployed

An almost unbroken chain of homeless men extends the whole length of the great Hamburg–Berlin highway.

There are so many of them moving in both directions, impelled by the wind or making their way against it, that they could shout a message from Hamburg to Berlin by word of mouth. . . .

. . . [m]ost of the hikers paid no attention to me. They walked separately or in small groups, with their eyes on the ground. And they had the queer, stumbling gait of barefooted people, for their shoes were slung over their shoulders.

Some of them were guild members,—carpenters with embroidered wallets, knee breeches, and broad felt hats, milkmen with striped red shirts, and bricklayers with tall black hats,—but they were in a minority. Far more numerous were those whom one could assign to no special profession or craft—unskilled young people, for the most part, who had been unable to find a place for themselves in any city or town in Germany, and who had never had a job and never expected to have one. There was something else that had never been seen before—whole families that had piled all their goods into baby carriages and wheelbarrows that they were pushing along as they plodded forward in dumb despair. It was a whole nation on the march.

I saw them—and this was the strongest impression that the year 1932 left with me—I saw them, gathered into groups, of fifty or a hundred men, attacking fields of potatoes. I saw them digging up the potatoes and throwing them into sacks while the farmer who owned the field watched them in despair and the local policeman looked on gloomily from the distance. I saw them staggering toward the lights of the city as night fell, with their sacks on their backs. What did it remind me of? Of the War, of the worst periods of starvation in 1917 and 1918, but even then people paid for the potatoes. . . .

I saw that the individual can know what is happening only by personal experience. I know what it is to be a tramp. I know what cold and hunger are. I know what it is to spend the night outdoors or behind the thin walls of a shack through which the wind whistles. I have slept in holes such as hunters hide in, in hayricks under bridges, against the warm walls of boiler houses, under cattle shelters in pastures, on a heap of fir-tree boughs in the forest. But there are two things that I have only recently experienced— begging and spending the night in a municipal lodging house.

I entered the huge Berlin municipal lodging house in a northern quarter of the city. Initiates call it "The Palms," a strangely romantic name suggestive of southern landscapes and soft skies. But the sky was not mild and the landscape was not southern when I made my way to this lodging house from the Alexanderplatz.

. . . There was an entrance arched by a brick vaulting, and a watchman sat in a little wooden sentry. His white coat made him look like a doctor. We stood waiting in the corridor. Heavy steam rose from the men's clothes. Some of them sat down on the floor, pulled off their shoes, and

National Socialist election banners appealed to the desperation of Germans during the Depression era. Here the banner indicates that Hitler will bring work and bread.

Reprinted by permission of the United States Holocaust Memorial Museum (98518).

unwound the rags that were bound around their feet. More people were constantly pouring in the door, and we stood closely packed together. Then another door opened. The crowd pushed forward, and people began forcing their way almost eagerly through this door, for it was warm in there. Without knowing it I had caught the rhythm of the municipal lodging house. It means waiting, standing around, and then suddenly jumping up. . .

We arrange ourselves in long lines, each leading up to one of these men, and the mill begins to grind. Each of us rests one arm on the iron railing that keeps us at a respectful distance from the bar. We hold on to it and slowly make headway toward the man in the white smock, scuffling and whispering, each one with a paper in his hand. And as the fact of the man gradually comes nearer it seems to be growing larger and larger, and we feel the power of this man over our whole destiny until he acquires almost super-human dimensions. . . .

As the line passes in single file the official does not look up at each new person to appear. He only looks at the paper that is handed to him. These papers are for the most part invalid cards or unemployment certificates. The very fact that the official does not look up robs the homeless applicant of self-respect, although he may look too beaten down to feel any. There is a process of evaluation going on in which the man is being weighed against his paper. . . .

Now it is my turn and the questions and answers flow as smoothly as if I were an old hand. But finally I am asked, "Have you ever been here before?"

"No."

"No?" The question reverberates through the whole room. The clerk refuses to believe me and looks through his card catalogue. But no, my name is not there. The clerk thinks this strange, for he cannot have made a mistake, and the terrible thing that one notices in all these clerks is that they expect you to lie. They do not believe what you say. They do not regard you as a human being but as an infection, something foul that one keeps at a distance. He goes on. "How did you come here from Hamburg?"

"By truck."

"Where have you spent the last three nights?"

I lie coolly.

"Have you begged?"

I feel a warm blush spreading over my face. It is welling up from the bourgeois world that I have come from. "No."

"Never mind. The day will come, comrade, when there's nothing else to do." And the line breaks into laughter again, the bitterest laughter I have ever heard, the laughter of damnation and despair . . .

Again the crowd pushes back in the kind of rhythm is so typical of a lodging house, and we are all herded into the undressing room. It is like all of the other rooms except that it is divided by benches and shelves like a fourth-class railway carriage. I cling to the man who spoke to me. He is a Saxon with a friendly manner and he has noticed that I am a stranger here. A certain sensitiveness, an almost perverse, spiritual alertness makes me like him very much.

Out of a big iron chest each of us takes a coat hanger that would serve admirably to hit somebody over the head with. As we undress the room becomes filled with the heavy breath of poverty. We are so close together that we brush against each other every time we move. Anyone who has been a soldier, anyone who has been to a public bath is perfectly accustomed to the look of naked bodies. But I have never seen anything quite so repulsive as all these hundreds of withered human frames. For in the homeless army the majority are men who have been defeated in the struggle of life, crippled, old, and sick. There is no repulsive disease of which traces are not to be seen here. There is no form of mutilation or degeneracy that is not represented, and the naked bodies of the old men are in a disgusting state of decline. . .

It is superfluous to describe what follows. Towels are handed out, then nightgowns—long, sack-like affairs made of plain unbleached cotton but freshly washed. Then slippers . . . Distribution of spoons, distribution of enamelware bowls with the words "Property of the City of Berlin" written on their sides. Then the meal itself. A big kettle is carried in. Men with yellow smocks have brought it and men with yellow smocks ladle out the food. These men, too, are homeless and they have been expressly picked by the establishment and given free food and lodging and a little pocket money in exchange for their work about the house. . .

My next recollection is sitting at table in another room on a crowded bench that is like a seat in a fourth-class railway carriage. Hundreds of hungry mouths make an enormous noise eating their food. The men sit bent over their food like animals who feel that someone is going to take it away from them. They hold their bowl with their left arm part way around it, so that nobody can take it away, and they also protect it with their other elbow and with their head and mouth, while they move the spoon as fast as they can between their mouth and the bowl. . . .

We shuffle into the sleeping room, where each bed has a number painted in big letters on the wall over it. You must find the number that you have around your neck, and there is your bed, your home for one night. It stands in a row with fifty others and across the room there are fifty more in a row. . . .

Some people read newspapers and anything else they may have picked up on the street. But there is not much argument. Poverty is nonpolitical. "Hitler or Communism? It's six of one and half a dozen of the other as far as I'm concerned. Both the same kind of dung," says the Saxon beside me. . . .

A cat streaked with grey glides between the beds, seeking affection, and everybody stokes it, for it is a good, comforting proletarian cat, thin, accustomed to being stroked by coarse hands, and grateful for the attention. . . . The air is poisoned with the breath of men who have stuffed too much food into empty stomachs. There is also a sickening smell of Lysol. It seems completely terrible to me, and I am not merely pitying myself. It is painful just to look at the scene. Life is no longer human here.

> **Study Question**
>
> What does Hauser mean when he notes that "poverty is non-political"? Was he correct?

George Orwell

George Orwell's non-fictional account of the Depression, The Road to Wigan Pier, *was commissioned by the socialist publisher Victor Gollancz in Great Britain and was published in 1937. The monograph provides a deeply sympathetic look at the lives of impoverished miners during the Depression in the Lancashire town of Wigan. The impact of the Depression in Great Britain was magnified by pre-existing economic problems, especially in resource sectors such as mining.*

Document Source: George Orwell, *The Road to Wigan Pier* (London: Victor Gollancz, 1937), chapter one.

The Road to Wigan Pier

The first sound in the mornings was the clumping of the mill-girls' clogs down the cobbled street. Earlier than that, I suppose, there were factory whistles which I was never awake to hear.

There were generally four of us in the bedroom, and a beastly place it was, with that defiled impermanent look of rooms that are not serving their rightful purpose. Years earlier the house had been an ordinary dwelling-house, and when the Brookers had taken it and fitted it out as a tripe-shop and lodging-house, they had inherited some of the more useless pieces of furniture and had never had the energy to remove them. We were therefore sleeping in what was still recognizably a drawing-room. Hanging from the ceiling there was a heavy glass chandelier on which the dust was so thick that it was like fur. And covering most of one wall there was a huge hideous piece of junk, something between a sideboard and a hall-stand, with lots of carving and little drawers and strips of looking-glass, and there was a once-gaudy carpet ringed by the slop-pails of years, and two gilt chairs with burst seats, and one of those old-fashioned horsehair armchairs which you slide off when you try to sit on them. The room had been turned into a bedroom by thrusting four squalid beds in among this other wreckage.

My bed was in the right-hand corner on the side nearest the door. There was another bed across the foot of it and jammed hard against it (it had to be in that position to allow the door to open) so that I had to sleep with my legs doubled up; if I straightened them out I kicked the occupant of the other bed in the small of the back. He was an elderly man named Mr Reilly, a mechanic of sorts and employed "on top" at one of the coal pits. Luckily he had to go to work at five in the morning, so I could uncoil my legs and have a couple of hours' proper sleep after he was gone. In the bed opposite there was a Scotch miner who had been injured in a pit accident (a huge chunk of stone pinned him to the ground and it was a couple of hours before they could lever it off), and had received five hundred pounds compensation. He was a big handsome man of forty, with grizzled hair and a clipped moustache, more like a sergeant-major than a miner, and he would lie in bed till late in the day, smoking a short pipe. The other bed was occupied by a succession of commercial travelers, newspaper-canvassers, and hire-purchase touts who generally stayed for a couple of nights. . . .

The shop was a narrow, cold sort of room. On the outside of the window a few white letters, relics of ancient chocolate advertisements, were scattered like stars. Inside there was a slab upon which lay the great white folds of tripe, and the grey flocculent stuff known as "black tripe," and the ghostly translucent feet of pigs, ready boiled. It was the ordinary "tripe and pea" shop, and not much else was stocked except bread, cigarettes, and tinned stuff. "Teas" were advertised in the window, but if a customer demanded a cup of tea he was usually put off with excuses. Mr Brooker, though out of work for two years, was a miner by trade, but he and his wife had been keeping shops of various kinds as a side-line all their lives. At one time they had had a pub, but they had lost their licence for allowing gambling on the premises. I doubt whether any of their businesses had ever paid; they were the kind of people who run a business chiefly in order to have something to grumble about. Mr Brooker was a dark, small-boned, sour, Irish-looking man, and astonishingly dirty. I don't think I ever once saw his hands clean. As Mrs Brooker was now an invalid he prepared most of the food, and like all people with permanently dirty hands he had a peculiarly intimate, lingering manner of handling things. If he gave you a slice of bread-and-butter there was always a black thumbprint on it. Even in the early morning when he descended into the mysterious den behind Mrs Brooker's sofa and fished out the tripe, his hands were already black. I heard dreadful stories from the other lodgers about the place where the tripe was kept. Blackbeetles were said to swarm there. I do not know how often fresh consignments of tripe were ordered, but it was at long intervals, for Mrs Brooker used to date events by it. "Let me see now, I've had in three lots of froze (frozen tripe) since that happened," etc. We lodgers were never given tripe to eat. At the time I imagined that this was because tripe was too expensive; I have since thought that it was merely because we knew too much about it. The Brookers never ate tripe themselves, I noticed.

The only permanent lodgers were the Scotch miner, Mr Reilly, two old-age pensioners, and an unemployed man on the PAC[1] named Joe—he was the kind of person who has no surname. The Scotch miner was a bore when you got to know him. Like so many unemployed men he spent too much time reading newspapers, and if you did not head him off he would discourse for hours about such things as the Yellow Peril, trunk murders, astrology, and the conflict between religion and science. The old-age pensioners had, as usual, been driven from their homes by the Means Test. They handed their weekly ten shillings over to the Brookers and in return got the kind of accommodation you would expect for ten shillings; that is, a bed in the attic and meals chiefly of bread-and-butter. One of them was of "superior" type and was dying of some malignant disease—cancer, I believe. He only got out of bed on the days when he went to draw his pension. The other, called by everyone Old Jack, was an ex-miner aged seventy-eight who had worked well over fifty years in the pits. He was alert and intelligent, but curiously enough he seemed only to remember his boyhood experiences and to have forgotten all about the modern mining machinery and improvements. He used to tell me tales of fights with savage horses in the narrow galleries underground. When he heard that I was arranging to go down several coal mines he was contemptuous and declared that a man of my size (six feet two and a half) would never manage the "travelling"; it was no use telling him that the "travelling" was better than it used to be. But he was friendly to everyone and used to give us all a fine shout of "Good night, boys!" as he crawled up the stairs to his bed somewhere under the rafters. What I most admired about Old Jack was that he never cadged; he was generally out of tobacco towards the end of the week, but he always refused to smoke anyone else's. The Brookers had insured the lives of both old-age pensioners with one of the tanner-a-week companies. It was said that they were overheard anxiously asking the insurance-tout "how long people lives when they've got cancer". . . .

Of course, as I was indoors a good deal, I heard all about the Brookers' woes, and how everyone swindled them and was ungrateful to them, and how the shop did not pay and the lodging-house hardly paid. By local standards they were not so badly off, for, in some way I did not understand,

Mr Brooker was dodging the Means Test and drawing an allowance from the PAC, but their chief pleasure was talking about their grievances to anyone who would listen. Mrs Brooker used to lament by the hour, lying on her sofa, a soft mound of fat and self-pity, saying the same things over and over again. "We don't seem to get no customers nowadays. I don't know 'ow it is. The tripe's just a-laying there day after day—such beautiful tripe it is, too! It does seem 'ard, don't it now?" etc., etc., etc. All Mrs Brookers' laments ended with "It does seem 'ard, don't it now?" like the refrain of a ballade. Certainly it was true that the shop did not pay. The whole place had the unmistakable dusty, flyblown air of a business that is going down. But it would have been quite useless to explain to them why nobody came to the shop, even if one had had the face to do it; neither was capable of understanding that last year's dead bluebottles supine in the shop window are not good for trade. . . .

On the day when there was a full chamber-pot under the breakfast table I decided to leave. The place was beginning to depress me. It was not only the dirt, the smells, and the vile food, but the feeling of stagnant meaningless decay, of having got down into some subterranean place where people go creeping round and round, just like blackbeetles, in an endless muddle of slovened jobs and mean grievances. The most dreadful thing about people like the Brookers is the way they say the same things over and over again. It gives you the feeling that they are not real people at all, but a kind of ghost for ever rehearsing the same futile rigmarole. In the end Mrs Brooker's self-pitying talk—always the same complaints, over and over, and always ending with the tremulous whine of "It does seem 'ard, don't it now?"—revolted me even more than her habit of wiping her mouth with bits of newspaper. But it is no use saying that people like the Brookers are just disgusting and trying to put them out of mind. For they exist in tens and hundreds of thousands; they are one of the characteristic by-products of the modern world. You cannot disregard them if you accept the civilization that produced them. For this is part at least of what industrialism has done for us. Columbus sailed the Atlantic, the first steam engines tottered into motion, the British squares stood firm under the French guns at Waterloo, the one-eyed scoundrels of the nineteenth century praised God and filled their pockets; and this is where it all led—to labyrinthine slums and dark back kitchens with sickly, ageing people creeping round and round them like blackbeetles. It is a kind of duty to see and smell such places now and again, especially smell them, lest you should forget that they exist; though perhaps it is better not to stay there too long.

The train bore me away, through the monstrous scenery of slag-heaps, chimneys, piled scrap-iron, foul canals, paths of cindery mud criss-crossed by the prints of clogs. This was March, but the weather had been horribly cold and everywhere there were mounds of blackened snow. As we moved slowly through the outskirts of the town we passed row after row of little grey slum houses running at right angles to the embankment. At the back of one of the houses a young woman was kneeling on the stones, poking a stick up the leaden waste-pipe which ran from the sink inside and which I suppose was blocked. I had time to see everything about her—her sacking apron, her clumsy clogs, her arms reddened by the cold. She looked up as the train passed, and I was almost near enough to catch her eye. She had a round pale face, the usual exhausted face of the slum girl who is 25 and looks 40, thanks to miscarriages and drudgery; and it wore, for the second in which I saw it, the most desolate, hopeless expression I have ever seen. It struck me then that we are mistaken when we say that "It isn't the same for them as it would be for us," and that people bred in the slums can imagine nothing but the slums. For what I saw in her face was not the ignorant suffering of an animal. She knew well enough what was happening to her—understood as well as I did how dreadful a destiny it was to be kneeling there in the bitter cold, on the slimy stones of a slum backyard, poking a stick up a foul drain-pipe. . . .

Note

1. PACs (Public Assistance Committees) were set up by local governments in the early 1930s to deliver relief payments to the unemployed. Before any assistance was given, however, the recipient had to submit to a humiliating Means Test. "On the PAC" meant that a person was receiving relief from the local authorities.

> **Study Question**
>
> To what extent do the accounts by Orwell and Hauser point to similar conditions in both Great Britain and Germany?

W.E.B. Du Bois

Liberia was one of the few nations to escape formal colonial subjugation during the so-called scramble for Africa in the late nineteenth century. However, as W.E.B. Du Bois clearly demonstrates, it was no less affected by the spread of global capitalism. Writing in 1933 Du Bois reveals the ways in which corporate interests had gained control of Liberia and *focuses on the economic vulnerability which this created during global economic downturns. The essay also reveals the inability of the League of Nations to enforce its authority when confronting the major powers of the era.*

Document Source: W.E.B. Du Bois, "Liberia, the League, and the United States," *Foreign Affairs,* 11 (July 1933): 682–95.

Liberia, the League, and the United States

I remember standing once in a West African forest where thin, silver trees loomed straight and smooth in the air. There were two men with me. One was a black man, Solomon Hood, United States Minister to Liberia; a man of utter devotion, whose solicitude for the welfare of Liberia was like a sharp pain driving him on. And he thought he had found the solution. The solution was the white man beside us. He was a rubber expert sent by the Firestone Corporation of the United States to see if rubber could be grown in Liberia.

Those were rather ticklish times in the rubber situation. England was attempting to corner the world's production and prices were shooting up. Henry Ford flew south to seek plantations. Edison experimented with new plants. Firestone sent his representative to Liberia.

Most people cannot easily visualize the peculiarly helpless position of a small outland in the modern world of industry. It seems that a rich country like Liberia ought easily to be self-supporting and to secure machinery, experts and modern luxuries in return for its raw material. But this is much more easily said than done. In the first place, it must raise the raw materials which the world at the moment demands, and it often finds that the price of its product is so manipulated that absolutely no dependence can be put on it. In fact, between changing and disappearing markets, freight carrying monopolies, high cost of machinery, and absence of expert knowledge, Liberia, like many other small, isolated countries, has been in continual financial difficulties. She needs expert advice; but expert advice from white men, accompanied by invested capital, means loss of political power. And Liberia is jealous of her independence—jealous and proud. Indeed, the record of peace, efficiency and ability made

by this little poverty-stricken settlement of the rejected and despised, sitting on the edge of Africa and fighting the world in order to be let alone, is, despite querulous criticism, one of the most heartening efforts in human history. . . .

Just before the World War industrial aggression began again. The Sunlight Soap interests in Great Britain tried to get a concession which would monopolize the palm oil. When Liberia resisted, England began to press for payment of Liberian debts which had been defaulted. Sedition spread among the frontier force, and it looked as though France or England was on the point of

A 1918 portrait of W.E.B. Du Bois. Shortly after this picture was taken Du Bois began writing on the peace treaty and the proposed League of Nations.

Courtesy of the Library of Congress, Prints and Photographs Division (LC-USZ62-16767).

seizing the country. Liberia moved swiftly. She sent a delegation to America, which appealed to Booker T. Washington. Mr Washington appealed to Theodore Roosevelt. Theodore Roosevelt needed the Negro vote, and he appointed a Liberian commission. The commission went out and made negotiations for a refunding of the Liberian debt. A new loan of $2,000,000 was raised at 5 per cent. It looked as though at last Liberia had got a start, because, while a Financial Adviser with large powers was the string attached to this new loan, nevertheless there was no American disposition to interfere with Liberian independence.

Then suddenly came the World War and smashed all these dreams. Liberia, despite her large German trade, was forced to declare in favor of the Allies. One inducement was a loan promised her by the United States Government. Before this went through, however, the war was over and Congress refused to confirm the loan. Again Liberia was on the rocks. She sent another delegation to the United States, headed by President King, but little was accomplished.

For five or six years Liberia staggered on during the reaction from the World War, but finally began to make progress between 1922 and 1926. "The economic and financial future of the country looked brighter than for many years." But she was handicapped. She needed roads, machinery, local industry. She still feared foreign capital, but she needed it.

Then came Solomon Porter Hood, as United States Minister. He knew Firestone slightly. He corresponded with him. The rubber situation developed. King was reelected President, and at his inauguration, as a gesture of good will, I was designated by cable to act as Special Minister Plenipotentiary and Envoy Extraordinary. The appointment was purely ornamental, but I did all I could to cooperate with Hood and Africa and Liberia and tell them of the tremendous interest which American colored people had in them.

Firestone determined to enter into contract with Liberia to start rubber plantations, and began negotiations. On my return to the United States I wrote to him. I know what modern capital does to poor and colored peoples. I know what European imperialism had done to Asia and Africa; but, nevertheless, I had not then lost faith in the capitalistic system, and I believed that it was possible for a great corporation, headed by a man of vision, to go into a country with something more than the mere ideal of profit. I tried to state this to Mr Firestone. I intimated that the one thing above all which he must avoid was taking capital into a small country and putting it under the control of officials who despised the natives and organized ruthless exploitation. I tried to point out that by using trained American Negroes he might avoid this situation in Liberia, and have a more normal development by putting in the hands of people of the same race, local and immigrant, such power over the invested capital as would divert it, at least to some extent, toward ends of social welfare as well as towards profit. I had no reply to my letter. Perhaps it never got by the assistant secretary. When I heard of the terms which Firestone demanded in Liberia my heart began to fall. The Liberians resisted, and if the leading officials had had their way, the contract would never have been signed.

Firestone presented a contract which gave his company the right to select wherever he wished in Liberia one million acres of land at a nominal rental of only 6 cents an acre, and he insisted that because of certain public improvements Liberia must have more money; particularly, a modern harbor must be built, so that passengers and freight would not have to take that gloriously exciting but dangerous and costly ride in the surf boats over the bar. This insistence upon a loan increased the opposition in Liberia, but the Firestone Company refused to come on any other terms. Moreover, Liberia recognized that her only protection against the territorial and economic aggression of France and England lay in the attitude of America, and she was certain that if an American loan were made the United States would protect Liberia in order to safeguard the loan. In spite, therefore, of bitter opposition on the part of many high officials and without the knowledge of even some of the cabinet officers, the Firestone contract was signed in September 1926. Raymond L. Buell says: "In response to the question why they agreed to this loan in the face of early opposition and manifestly unfavorable terms, all of them gave the same reply: The State Department of the United States told us to accept this loan." . . . .

The sudden influx of cash to Liberia in 1926 started a boom. The country was stirred as never before by a vision of prosperity. Mr Buell, who was there then, wrote: "Business has begun to 'hum.' More hard money is in circulation than ever before. While most of this goes to private interests, the government has already secured a few thousand dollars a year additional revenue. Many American missionaries and educators are enheartened; they now believe that Liberia will survive."

Hardly had apparent prosperity come to Liberia than the shadow of the Great Depression began to move across the world. The British rubber monopoly broke. The price of rubber fell from 72 cents to 5 cents. Far from needing a million acres, Firestone took only 50,000 and cut wages of his laborers in half, from a shilling to 6 pence a day; he did practically nothing about the promised $300,000 harbor. As the commercial and industrial situation began to tighten, opposition began to seethe in Liberia. The former opponents of the loan became vocal. It was pointed out by the opposition that President King was getting rich, not simply by his connection with the Firestone project, but by other transactions; and high government officials were implicated with him. . . .

The League of Nations appointed a committee, headed by Dr Cuthbert Christy, an Englishman. A colored American, Dr Charles S. Johnson, appointed by President Hoover, and the grand old man, the Honorable Arthur Barclay, one of the finest products of Liberia, were the other two members. This Commission made its report in 1930. On the whole it was thorough and frank. The Commission made a careful investigation and proved that domestic slavery existed among the more primitive Liberian tribes; that there was pawning of children; and especially that laborers were recruited among the tribes and sent out of the country to the French colony of Gabon and to the Spanish colony of Fernando Po. Military force had been used, and President King, Vice President Yancy and some other officials were involved in the accusations of profit-sharing from the proceeds of this slave-trade. Members of the frontier force were used in obtaining this labor, and also in extortion and illegal taxation.

The Report of the International Commission of Enquiry was filed at Monrovia on 8 September 1930. The legislature met the second Monday of October, and President King gave his annual message October 30. After the report and various petitions had been received, a select committee of the House of Representatives reported December 2, and on adoption of that report President King, Vice President Yancy and other officials were retired from office. Edwin Barclay, Secretary of State, nephew of Arthur Barclay, one of the Commission, was selected to fill out the unexpired term, and took the oath on December 3. . . .

Despite this, the United States refused to recognize President Barclay and united with the British and German legations on 21 January 1931, to present notes to the Government of Liberia demanding that it ask the Council of the League of Nations to appoint an International Governing Commission to take over Liberia and administer the affairs of the country. President Barclay replied that he could not do this without violating his oath of office, but that he would ask the League of Nations to nominate capable persons to help in reorganizing the country. . . .

Meantime, the full force of the depression had struck Liberia. Prices fell. The value of Liberian exports dropped from $1,497,214 in 1927 to $856,759 in 1930. Salaries of Liberian officials were reduced on three occasions (in one case more than 50 per cent), and the Liberian Secretary of State said in 1932 that "most salaries had not been paid at all during the last seventeen months." At the same time, the debt service was absorbing larger and larger proportions of the whole income of the country.

. . . Liberia is not faultless. She lacks training, experience, and thrift. But her chief crime is to be black and poor in a rich, white world; and in precisely that portion of the world where color is ruthlessly exploited as a foundation for American and European wealth. The success of Liberia as a Negro republic would be a blow to the whole colonial slave labor system. Are we starting the United States Army toward Liberia to guarantee the Firestone Company's profits in a falling rubber market or smash another Haiti in the attempt?

> **Study Question**
>
> In what ways did the Depression solidify the dependent status of countries such as Liberia?

Lázaro Cárdenas

Lázaro Cárdenas (1895–1970) was elected to Mexico's presidency in 1934. Cárdenas redistributed millions of hectares of land, most of which were then transformed into communal farms, and he also introduced compulsory primary education. He next announced the nationalization of Mexico's oil industry, an industry that had been developed by British and American interests—most notably Standard Oil—and had returned virtually no benefits to the people of Mexico. Cárdenas's actions were a drastic attempt to change this situation. In the following radio address, given in March 1938, President Cárdenas discussed the problems created by foreign oil companies in Mexico.

Document Source: Lázaro Cárdenas, "Speech to the Nation," *Readings in Latin-American Civilization: 1492 to the Present* (Boston: Houghton Mifflin, 1955), 363–4.

Speech to the Nation

In each and every one of the various attempts of the Executive to arrive at a final solution of the conflict within conciliatory limits, and which include the periods prior to and following the . . . action which has produced the present situation, the intransigence of the companies was clearly demonstrated.

Their attitude was therefore premeditated and their position deliberately taken, so that the Government, in defense of its own dignity, had to resort to application of the Expropriation Act, as there were no means less drastic or decision less severe that might bring about a solution of the problem.

For additional justification of the measure herein announced, let us trace briefly the history of the oil companies' growth in Mexico and of the resources with which they have developed their activities.

It has been repeated *ad nauseam* that the oil industry has brought additional capital for the development and progress of the country. This assertion is an exaggeration. For many years, throughout the major period of their existence, the oil companies have enjoyed great privileges for development and expansion, including customs and tax exemptions and innumerable prerogatives; it is these factors of special privilege, together with the prodigious productivity of the oil deposits granted them by the Nation often against public will and law, that represent almost the total amount of this so-called capital.

Potential wealth of the Nation; miserably underpaid native labor; tax exemptions; economic privileges; governmental tolerance—these are the factors of the boom of the Mexican oil industry.

Let us now examine the social contributions of the companies. In how many of the villages bordering on the oil fields is there a hospital, or school or social center, or a sanitary water supply, or an athletic field, or even an electric plant fed by the millions of cubic meters of natural gas allowed to go to waste?

What center of oil production, on the other hand, does not have its company police force for the protection of private, selfish, and often illegal interests? These organizations, whether authorized by the Government or not, are charged with innumerable outrages, abuses, and murders, always on behalf of the companies that employ them.

Who is not aware of the irritating discrimination governing construction of the company camps? Comfort for the foreign personnel; misery, drabness, and insalubrity for the Mexicans. Refrigeration and protection against tropical insects for the former; indifference and neglect, medical service and supplies always grudgingly provided, for the latter; lower wages and harder, more exhausting labor for our people.

The tolerance which the companies have abused was born, it is true, in the shadow of the ignorance, betrayals, and weakness of the country's rulers; but the mechanism was set in motion by investors lacking in the necessary moral

Cárdenas (centre) meets with labour leaders from the oil industry in Tamaulipas State in 1938. Support from labour leaders would be essential to successful reforms in the industry.

New York World-Telegram and the Sun Newspaper Photograph Collection. Courtesy of the Library of Congress, Prints and Photographs Division (LC-USZ62-125079).

resources to give something in exchange for the wealth they have been exploiting.

Another inevitable consequence of the presence of the oil companies, strongly characterized by their anti-social tendencies, and even more harmful than all those already mentioned, has been their persistent and improper intervention in national affairs.

The oil companies' support to strong rebel factions against the constituted government in the Huasteca region of Veracruz and in the Isthmus of Tehuantepec during the years 1917 to 1920 is no longer a matter for discussion by anyone. Nor is anyone ignorant of the fact that in later periods and even at the present time, the oil companies have almost openly encouraged the ambitions of elements discontented with the country's government, every time their interests were affected either by taxation or by the modification of their privileges or the withdrawal of the customary tolerance. They have had money, arms, and munitions for rebellion, money for the anti-patriotic press which defends them, money with which to enrich their unconditional defenders. But for the progress of the country, for establishing an economic equilibrium with their workers through a just compensation of labor, for maintaining hygenic conditions in the districts where they themselves operate, or for conserving the vast riches of the natural petroleum gases from destruction, they have neither money, nor financial possibilities, nor the desire to subtract the necessary funds from the volume of their profits.

Nor is there money with which to meet a responsibility imposed upon them by judicial verdict, for they rely on their pride and their economic power to shield them from the dignity and sovereignty of a Nation which has generously placed in their hands its vast natural resources and now finds itself unable to obtain the satisfaction of the most elementary obligations by ordinary legal means.

As a logical consequence of this brief analysis,

it was therefore necessary to adopt a definite and legal measure to end this permanent state of affairs in which the country sees its industrial progress held back by those who hold in their hands the power to erect obstacles as well as the motive power of all activity and who, instead of using it to high and worthy purposes, abuse their economic strength to the point of jeopardizing the very life of a Nation endeavoring to bring about the elevation of its people through its own laws, its own resources, and the free management of its own destinies.

With the only solution to this problem thus placed before it, I ask the entire Nation for moral and material support sufficient to carry out so justified, important, and indispensable a decision.

The Government has already taken suitable steps to maintain the constructive activities now going forward throughout the Republic, and for that purpose it asks the people only for its full confidence and backing in whatever dispositions the Government may be obliged to adopt.

Nevertheless, we shall, if necessary, sacrifice all the constructive projects on which the Nation has embarked during the term of this Administration in order to cope with the financial obligations imposed upon us by the application of the Expropriation Act to such vast interests; and although the subsoil of the country will give us considerable economic resources with which to meet the obligation of indemnization which we have contracted, we must be prepared for the possibility of our individual economy also suffering the indispensable readjustments, even to the point, should the Bank of Mexico deem it necessary, of modifying the present exchange rate of our currency, so that the whole country may be able to count on sufficient currency and resources with which to consolidate this act of profound and essential economic liberation of Mexico.

It is necessary that all groups of the population be imbued with a full optimism and that each citizen, whether in agricultural, industrial, commercial, transportation, or other pursuits, develop a greater activity from this moment on, in order to create new resources which will reveal that the spirit of our people is capable of saving the nation's economy by the efforts of its own citizens.

And, finally, as the fear may arise among the interests now in bitter conflict in the field of international affairs that a deviation of raw materials fundamentally necessary to the struggle in which the most powerful nations are engaged might result from the consummation of this act of national sovereignty and dignity, we wish to state that our petroleum operations will not depart a single inch from the moral solidarity maintained by Mexico with the democratic nations, whom we wish to assure that the expropriation now decreed has as its only purpose the elimination of obstacles erected by groups who do not understand the evolutionary needs of all peoples and who would themselves have no compunction in selling Mexican oil to the highest bidder, without taking into account the consequences of such action to the popular masses and the nations in conflict.

> **Study Question**
>
> In what ways would the issues raised by Cárdenas in the document impact the establishment of effective governance in Mexico?

Neville Chamberlain / William L. Mackenzie King

Neville Chamberlain's (1869–1940) policy of appeasement has been widely condemned as a shortsighted and foolhardy strategy—a strategy that guaranteed that Hitler would try to gain even greater concessions in Europe. However, it had been only twenty years since the Great War had claimed millions of European lives and devastated the economies of victors and vanquished alike. With the effects of the Great Depression still evident around the globe, Chamberlain's decision at the 1938 Munich Conference, to accede to Hitler's demand to annex the Sudetenland from Czechoslovakia, seemed a reasonable approach that, at minimum, brought Great Britain much needed time to prepare its military for a possible future conflict. Foreign leaders, too, hailed Chamberlain's achievement. The second document in this series is a congratulatory telegram sent from Canadian Prime Minister W.L. Mackenzie King (1874–1950) to Chamberlain. Contemporary readers should keep in mind the situation in Canada at this time. The after-effects of the stock market crash had devastated Canada and the country was still struggling to find the correct response to the economic crisis.

Document Sources: Neville Chamberlain, "Speech to the House of Commons." From *Parliamentary Debates*, Commons, HMSO: Vol. 339 (3 October 1938). William L. Mackenzie King, "Telegram from Prime Minister William L. Mackenzie King to British Prime Minister Neville Chamberlain." From Library and Archives of Canada, papers of William L. Mackenzie King, series 4: Memoranda and Notes, 155, C-111226.

Speech to the House of Commons, 3 October 1938

The Prime Minister:

Before I come to describe the Agreement which was signed at Munich in the small hours of Friday morning last, I would like to remind the House of two things which I think it very essential not to forget when those terms are being considered. The first is this: We did not go there to decide whether the predominantly German areas in the Sudetenland should be passed over to the German Reich. That had been decided already. Czechoslovakia had accepted the Anglo-French proposals. What we had to consider was the method, the conditions and the time of the transfer of the territory. The second point to remember is that time was one of the essential factors. All the elements were present on the spot for the outbreak of a conflict which might have precipitated the catastrophe. We had populations inflamed to a high degree; we had extremists on both sides ready to work up and provoke incidents; we had considerable quantities of arms which were by no means confined to regularly organised forces. Therefore, it was essential that we should quickly reach a conclusion, so that this painful and difficult operation of transfer might be carried out at the earliest possible moment and concluded as soon as was consistent, with orderly procedure, in order that we might avoid the possibility of something that might have rendered all our attempts at peaceful solution useless. . . .

Before giving a verdict upon this arrangement, we should do well to avoid describing it as a personal or a national triumph for anyone. The real triumph is that it has shown that representatives of four great Powers can find it possible to agree on a way of carrying out a difficult and delicate operation by discussion instead of by force of arms, and thereby they have averted a catastrophe which would have ended civilisation as we have known it. The relief that our escape from this great peril of war has, I think, everywhere been mingled in this country with a profound feeling of sympathy.

[*Hon. Members*: Shame.] I have nothing to be ashamed of. Let those who have, hang their heads. We must feel profound sympathy for a small and gallant nation in the hour of their national grief and loss.

Mr Bellenger: It is an insult to say it.

The Prime Minister: I say in the name of this House and of the people of this country that Czechoslovakia has earned our admiration and respect for her restraint, for her dignity, for her magnificent discipline in face of such a trial as few nations have ever been called upon to meet.

The army, whose courage no man has ever questioned, has obeyed the order of their president,

as they would equally have obeyed him if he had told them to march into the trenches. It is my hope and my belief, that under the new system of guarantees, the new Czechoslovakia will find a greater security than she has ever enjoyed in the past. . . .

I pass from that subject, and I would like to say a few words in respect of the various other participants, besides ourselves, in the Munich Agreement. After everything that has been said about the German Chancellor today and in the past, I do feel that the House ought to recognise the difficulty for a man in that position to take back such emphatic declarations as he had already made amidst the enthusiastic cheers of his supporters, and to recognise that in consenting, even though it were only at the last moment, to discuss with the representatives of other Powers those things which he had declared he had already decided once for all, was a real and a substantial contribution on his part. With regard to Signor Mussolini, . . . I think that Europe and the world have reason to be grateful to the head of the Italian government for his work in contributing to a peaceful solution.

In my view the strongest force of all, one which grew and took fresh shapes and forms every day was, the force not of any one individual, but was that unmistakable sense of unanimity among the peoples of the world that war must somehow be averted. The peoples of the British Empire were at one with those of Germany, of France and of Italy, and their anxiety, their intense desire for peace, pervaded the whole atmosphere of the conference, and I believe that that, and not threats, made possible the concessions that were made. I know the House will want to hear what I am sure it does not doubt, that throughout these discussions the Dominions, the Governments of the Dominions, have been kept in the closest touch with the march of events by telegraph and by personal contact, and I would like to say how greatly I was encouraged on each of the journeys I made to Germany by the knowledge that I went with the good wishes of the Governments of the

Dominions. They shared all our anxieties and all our hopes. They rejoiced with us that peace was preserved, and with us they look forward to further efforts to consolidate what has been done.

Ever since I assumed my present office my main purpose has been to work for the pacification of Europe, for the removal of those suspicions and those animosities which have so long poisoned the air. The path which leads to appeasement is long and bristles with obstacles. The question of Czechoslovakia is the latest and perhaps the most dangerous. Now that we have got past it, I feel that it may be possible to make further progress along the road to sanity.

Telegram from Prime Minister William L. Mackenzie King to British Prime Minister Neville Chamberlain

Ottawa, 29 September 1938

The Right Honourable Neville Chamberlain, PC, MP
Prime Minister of Great Britain
10 Downing Street,
London, England.

The heart of Canada is rejoicing tonight at the success which has crowned your unremitting efforts for peace. May I convey to you the warm congratulations of the Canadian people, and with them, an expression of their gratitude, which is felt from one end of the Dominion to the other.

My colleagues in the Government join with me in unbounded admiration at the service you have rendered mankind. Your achievements in the past month alone will ensure you an abiding and illustrious place among the great conciliators whom the United Kingdom, the British Commonwealth of Nations and the whole world will continue to honour.

On the very brink of chaos, with passions flaming, and armies marching, the voice of Reason has found a way out of the conflict which no people in their heart desired, but none seemed able to avert.

A turning point in the world's history will be reached if, as we hope, tonight's agreement means a halt to the mad race of arms, and a new start in building the partnership of all peoples. May you have health and strength to carry your great work to its completion.

W.L. Mackenzie King

Study Question

Based upon your reading of the documents in this chapter, why did so many countries support the appeasement policies of Chamberlain and other world leaders?

Web Resources

American Memory—American Life Histories (from the Works Progress Administration)
    http://memory.loc.gov/ammem/wpaintro/wpahome.html
New Deal Network
    http://newdeal.feri.org/index.htm
The History Place—Dorothea Lange
    http://www.historyplace.com/unitedstates/lange/index.html
The Jarrow Crusade
    http://www.bbc.co.uk/history/british/britain_wwone/jarrow_01.shtml#two

Recommended Reading

Harper Lee, *To Kill a Mockingbird* (New York: Warner Books, 1988). A black man is charged with the rape of a white girl in Depression-era Maycomb, Alabama. Harper Lee's 1960 novel examines the prejudice of the American south, intensified by the economic conditions of the Depression, as well as the conscience, compassion, and justice of the main characters and their hope for the future.

George Orwell, *The Road to Wigan Pier* (London: Victor Gollancz, 1937). A journalistic account based on Orwell's experiences in the 1930s, this text provides a portrait of the Depression era, of unemployment, and of the resultant desperation in the industrial towns of Lancashire and Yorkshire. The book is told in two parts: the first relates the misery of life in the northern towns, and the second part is a discourse on the irrelevance of socialist theory in this situation.

Gabrielle Roy, *The Tin Flute* (Toronto: New Canadian Library, 1989). Set in the working class industrial slums of Montreal during the latter years of the Depression, just before the Second World War, this novel provides a compassionate look at lives dominated by poverty and hopelessness, and the effort to find something more.

John Steinbeck, *The Grapes of Wrath* (New York: Penguin, 2002). The Pulitzer Prize–winning *The Grapes of Wrath* was drawn from Steinbeck's experience in the migrant camps of California in 1936. It tells of migrants from the Dust Bowl of Oklahoma who are headed towards an uncertain future in California. Destitution, abandonment, and oppression are contrasted with the basic human dignity of the Joad family.

Recommended Viewing

Modern Times (USA, 1936). Director: Charles Chaplin (Silent, B&W). Set during the Great Depression, Chaplin's *Modern Times* attacks mechanization and the inherent dehumanization of the factory system. The film highlights many of the social problems of the time, including worker riots and communist protests.

You Only Live Once (USA, 1937). Director: Fritz Lang (B&W). Fritz Lang's second American feature film depicts much of the injustice and oppression of the Depression era, including society's attitude towards the poor, the criminals, and the downtrodden.

The Grapes of Wrath (USA, 1940). Director: John Ford (B&W). Many critics believe that John Ford's cinematic adaptation of Steinbeck's novel is the best depiction of the impact of the Depression on rural America. The film illustrates the lives of Dust Bowl migrants: migrant camps, hunger, despair, and inequality. Ford's film contains some of the most famous images of the Great Depression.

Love on the Dole (UK, 1941). Director: John Baxter (B&W). Filmed in the north of England during the 1930s, Baxter created a harrowing depiction of the ravages of the Depression and the extent to which families had to go in order to survive. Black humour punctuates the otherwise bleak narrative.

Bonheur d'occasion [*The Tin Flute*] (Canada, 1982). Director: Claude Fournier. Based on the novel by Gabrielle Roy, *The Tin Flute* is set in 1940, in the aftermath of the Depression during the early part of the Second World War. The film focuses on one family caught in the poverty of the era and the numerous obstacles facing family members as they struggle against unemployment, disease, and war.

7

Global War and Genocide

Damage from the German bombing during the Blitz in London. Some 43,000 Britons died during the aerial bombardment.

Courtesy of the Franklin D. Roosevelt Library, http://docs.fdrlibrary.marist.edu/images/photodb/23-0429a.gif

The ferocity and barbarism of the Second World War was unprecedented in the modern era. Civilians became military targets, entire peoples were targeted for extermination, and new weapons of mass destruction wiped out whole cities in an instant. By the time the war was over more than 60 million people were dead—19 million had been soldiers, while the rest were civilian victims of war, famine, disease, and genocide.[1]

Though few military planners openly admitted to targeting the civilian population, there was little doubt that a total war involved all of a nation's peoples in the war effort. Therefore, the line between legitimate military targets and non-combatants became much harder to establish. In some cases, such as the firebombings of Hamburg, Dresden, and Tokyo and the atomic bombings of Hiroshima and Nagasaki, entire cities were destroyed, killing men, women, and children indiscriminately. As well, racial wars, which were carried out under the cover of the military conflict in a number of countries, targeted civilians without exception. The net result was a greater number of civilian casualties than military in almost every nation that committed forces to the war. Meanwhile, civilians determined to be "enemy aliens" were stripped of their property and interned by ostensibly democratic governments.

Genocide was neither an invention of, nor unique to, the Second World War, but the sheer number and intensity of genocidal acts that occurred during the war was remarkable in and of itself. Adolf Hitler set the destruction of the world's Jewish population as one of his primary wartime goals. Japanese forces were instructed to "kill all captives" when they invaded China. In the former Yugoslavia both the Croats and the Serbs engaged in "ethnic cleansing." Frequently these campaigns were given priority over ongoing military actions. Hitler, for example, refused to allocate railway cars to move troops to the West because they were needed for the war against the Jews. Croatian efforts to wipe out the entire Serbian population as quickly as possible created considerable antagonism between the Croatian government and its German allies.

The collection of documents in this chapter attempts to convey some of the viciousness and brutality that marked the conflict. The chapter opens with an account of the massacres committed by Japanese forces in the Chinese city of Nanjing. The Japanese blueprint for the control of greater East Asia follows. The impact of the internment of Japanese-Canadians is illustrated in the extract from Muriel Kitagawa's letters. The documents continue with accounts collected by the Polish Ministry of Information of German atrocities after the invasion of Poland and with Victor Klemperer's observations on the conditions endured by the surviving German-Jewish population in the 1940s. Stella Wieseltier confronts those responsible for the Holocaust and considers what it means "to rejoin the human race" in the aftermath of war and genocide. In the former Yugoslavia, a police commander details the activities of the infamous Ustaše in purging the region's Serbian population. The horrific effects of aerial bombardment are captured in an eyewitness account of the firebombing of the German city of Dresden in February 1945. The chapter concludes with the draft statement announcing and justifying the dropping of the first atomic bomb on the Japanese city of Hiroshima, and the cable indicating the successful detonation of the bomb.

Note

1. A further seven million people died in China during the early years of the Sino–Japanese War, and at least two million Germans died after the end of the war as populations were being relocated from Eastern Europe.

Harold Timperley

The war in the Pacific began fully two years before the war in Europe. The Japanese had been marshaling forces in Northern China since 1932 in anticipation of a massive invasion. The assault began in July *1937; by mid-December the former Nationalist capital of Nanjing came under attack. The following report was written by Harold Timperley (1898–1954), an Australian who worked as a correspondent for the*

Manchester Guardian. *As with all accounts of massacres committed by Japanese forces, there is substantial debate surrounding Timperley's report. In particular, revisionists have argued that Timperley was not in Nanjing during the Japanese attack.[1] Thus his information may have been drawn from second-hand sources. However, foreign charitable and religious organizations* *did remain in the city in December 1937 and Timperley had established very good contacts among these organizations. In October 2002* The Guardian *(formerly the* Manchester Guardian*) published a detailed defence of Timperley's account and his journalistic integrity.[2]*

Document Source: Harold Timperley, *What War Means: The Japanese Terror in China* (London: Victor Gollancz, 1938), 33–5.

An Eyewitness Account at Nanjing

Friday, 17 December. Robbery, murder, rape continued unabated. A rough estimate would be at least a thousand women raped last night and during the day. One poor woman was raped thirty-seven times. Another had her five months infant deliberately smothered by the brute to stop its crying while he raped her. Resistance means the bayonet. The hospital is rapidly filling up with the victims of Japanese cruelty and barbarity. Bob Wilson, our only surgeon, has his hands more than full and has to work into the night. Rickshaws, cattle, pigs, donkeys, often the sole means of livelihood of the people, are taken from them. Our rice kitchens and rice shop are interfered with. We have had to close the latter.

After dinner I took Bates[3] to the University and McCallum to the hospital where they will spend the night, then Mills and Smythe to Ginling, for one of our group has been sleeping there each night. At the gate of the latter place we were stopped by what seemed to be a searching party. We were roughly pulled from the car at the point of the bayonet, my car keys taken from me, lined up and frisked for arms, our hats jerked off, electric torches held to our faces, our passports and purpose in coming demanded. Opposite us were Miss Vautrin, Mrs Twinem, and Mrs Chen, with a score of refugee women kneeling on the ground. The sergeant, who spoke a little French (about as much as I do), insisted there were soldiers concealed there. I maintained that aside from about fifty domestics and other members of their staff there were no men on the place. This he said he did not believe and said he would shoot all he found beyond that number. He then demanded that we all leave, including the ladies, and when Miss Vautrin refused she was roughly hustled to the car. Then he changed his mind: the ladies were told to stay and we to go. We tried to insist that one of us should stay too, but this he would not permit. Altogether we were kept standing there for over an hour before we were released. The next day we learned that this gang had abducted 12 girls from the school.

Saturday, 18 December. At breakfast Riggs, who lives in the Zone a block away but has his meals with us, reported that two women, one a cousin of a YMCA secretary, were raped in his house while he was having dinner with us. Wilson reported a boy of five years of age brought to the hospital after having been stabbed with a bayonet five times, once through his abdomen; a man with 18 bayonet wounds, a woman with 17 cuts on her face and several on her legs. Between four and five hundred terrorized women poured into our headquarters compound in the afternoon and spent the night in the open.

Sunday, 19 December. A day of complete anarchy. Several big fires raging today, started by the soldiers, and more are promised. The American flag was torn down in a number of places. At the American School it was trampled on and the caretaker told he would be killed if he put it up again. The proclamations placed on all American and other foreign properties by the Japanese Embassy are flouted by their soldiers, sometimes deliberately torn off. Some houses are entered from five to ten times in one day and the poor people looted and robbed and the women raped. Several were killed in cold blood, for no apparent reason whatever. Six out of seven of our sanitation squad in one district were slaughtered; the seventh escaped, wounded, to tell the tale. Toward evening today two of us rushed to Dr Brady's house (he is away) and chased four would-be rapers out and took all women there to the University. Sperling is busy at this game all day. I also went to the house of Douglas Jenkins of our Embassy. The flag was still there; but in the garage his house boy lay dead, another servant, dead, was under a bed, both brutally killed. The house was in utter confusion. There are still many corpses on the streets. All of them civilians as far as we can see. The Red Swastika Society[4] would bury them, but their truck has been stolen, their coffins used for bonfires, and several of their workers bearing their insignia have been marched away.

Smythe and I called again at the Japanese Embassy with a list of fifty-five additional cases of violence, all authenticated, and told Messers Tanaka and Fukui[5] that today was the worst so far. We were assured that they would "do their best" and hoped that things would be better "soon," but it is quite obvious that they have little or no influence with the military whatever, and the military have no control over the soldiers. . . .

Notes

1. Timperley's wife indicated that they had moved to Shanghai by December 1937.
2. John Gittings, "Japanese Re-Write *Guardian* History," *The Guardian* (Friday 4 October 2002); available online at: http://www.guardian.co.uk/japan/story/0,7369,804391,00.html.
3. Most of the Western names refer to American staff members at the University of Nanjing and its hospital.
4. The Red Swastika Society is an organization devoted to educational and charitable projects. In China, Japan, and Tibet the destroverse swastika is a symbol of luck and good fortune.
5. Japanese diplomats.

Study Question

Why do you suppose that the Japanese invaders acted with such ferocity towards the citizens of Nanjing?

Total War Research Institute

On 27 January 1942 the Total War Research Institute[1] prepared a draft outlining the creation of the "Greater East Asia Co-Prosperity Sphere" for the Japanese government. Despite the benevolent language, the Co-Prosperity Sphere proposed to extend the Japanese Empire throughout East Asia, with the vast majority of benefits flowing back to the Japanese mainland. The Sphere itself was made up of an Inner Sphere (Japan, Manchuria,[2] and North China), a Smaller Co-Prosperity Sphere (Eastern Siberia, China, and Southeast Asia), and the Greater East Asia Co-Prosperity Sphere (Australia, India, the Pacific Islands, and New Guinea). The smaller Co-Prosperity Sphere would take approximately 20 years to create.

Document Source: Total War Research Institute, "The Greater East Asia Co-Prosperity Sphere," in Wm. Theodore de Bary, *Sources of Japanese Tradition*, Vol. 2 (New York: Columbia University Press, 2006), 313–15.

The Greater East Asia Co-Prosperity Sphere

Part 1. Outline of Construction

The Plan. The Japanese empire is a manifestation of morality and its special characteristic is the propagation of the Imperial Way. It strives but for the achievement of *Hakkō Ichiu*,[3] the spirit of its founding. . . . It is necessary to foster the increased power of the empire, to cause East Asia to return to its original form of independence and co-prosperity by shaking off the yoke of Europe and America, and to let its countries and peoples develop their respective abilities in peaceful cooperation and secure livelihood.

The Form of East Asiatic Independence and Co-Prosperity. The states, their citizens, and resources, comprised in those areas pertaining to the Pacific, Central Asia, and the Indian Oceans formed into one general union are to be established as an autonomous zone of peaceful living and common prosperity on behalf of the peoples of the nations of East Asia. The area including Japan, Manchuria, North China, lower Yangtze River, and the Russian maritime Province, forms the nucleus of the East Asiatic Union. The Japanese empire possesses a duty as the leader of the East Asiatic Union.

The above presupposes the inevitable emancipation of independence of Eastern Siberia, China, Indo-China, the South Seas, Australia, and India.

Regional Division in the East Asiatic Union and the National Defence Sphere for the Japanese Empire. In the union of East Asia, the Japanese empire is at once the stabilizing power and the leading influence. To enable the empire actually to become the central influence in East Asia, the first necessity is the consolidation of the inner belt of East Asia. . . .

Outline of East Asiatic Administration. It is intended that the unification of Japan, Manchoukuo, and China in neighbourly friendship be realized by the settlement of the Sino-Japanese problems through the crushing of hostile influences in the Chinese interior,[4] and through the construction of a new China in tune with the rapid construction of the Inner sphere. Aggressive American and British influences in East Asia shall be driven out of the area of Indo-China and the South Seas, and this area shall be brought into our defence sphere. The war with Britain and America shall be prosecuted for that purpose.

The Russian aggressive influence in East Asia will be driven out. Eastern Siberia shall be cut off from the Soviet regime and included in our defence sphere. For this purpose a war with the Soviets is expected. It is considered possible that this Northern problem may break out before the general settlement of the present Sino-Japanese and the Southern problems if the situation renders this unavoidable. Next the independence of Australia, India, etc. shall gradually be brought about. . . .

The Building of the National Strength. Since the Japanese empire is the center and pioneer of Oriental moral and cultural reconstruction, the officials and people of this country must return to the spirit of the Orient and acquire a thorough understanding of the spirit of the national moral character.

In the economic construction of the country, Japanese and Manchurian national power shall first be consolidated, then the unification of Japan, Manchoukuo, and China, shall be effected. . . . Thus a central industry will be constructed in East Asia, and the necessary relations established with the Southern Seas.

The standard for the construction of national power and its military force, so as to meet the various situations that might affect the stages of East Asiatic administration and national defence sphere, shall be so set as to be capable of driving off any British, American, Soviet, or Chinese counter-influences in the future. . . .

Chapter 3. Political Construction

Basic Plan. The realization of the great ideal of constructing Greater East Asia Co-Prosperity requires not only the complete prosecution of the current Greater East Asia War but also presupposes another great war in the future. Therefore, the following two points must be made the primary starting points for the next twenty years: 1) Preparation for war with the other spheres of the world; and 2) Unification and construction of the East Asia Smaller Co-Prosperity Sphere.

The following are the basic principles for the political construction of East Asia, when the above two points are taken into consideration:

a. The politically dominant influence of European and American countries in the Smaller Co-Prosperity Sphere shall be gradually driven out and the area shall enjoy its liberation from the shackles hitherto forced upon it.

b. The desires of the peoples in the sphere for their independence shall be made for their fulfillment, but proper and suitable forms of government shall be decided for them in consideration of military and economic requirements and of the historical, political, and cultural elements peculiar to each area.

It must also be noted that the independence of various peoples of East Asia should be based upon the idea of constructing East Asia as "independent countries existing within the New Order of East Asia" and that this conception differs from an independence based on the idea of liberalism and national self-determination.

c. During the course of construction, military unification is deemed particularly important, and the military zones and key points necessary for defence shall be directly or indirectly under the control of our country.

d. The peoples of the sphere shall obtain their proper positions, the unity of the people's minds shall be effected and the unification of the sphere shall be realized with the empire as its center. . . .

Chapter 4. Thought and Cultural Construction

General Aim in Thought. The ultimate aim in thought construction in East Asia is to make East Asiatic peoples revere the imperial influence by propagating the Imperial Way based on the spirit of construction, and to establish the belief that uniting solely under this influence is the one and only way to the eternal growth and development of East Asia.

And during the next twenty years (the period during which the above ideal is to be reached) it is necessary to make the nations and peoples of East Asia realize the historical significance of the establishment of the New Order in East Asia, and in the common consciousness of East Asiatic unity, to liberate East Asia from the shackles of Europe and America and to establish the common conviction of constructing a New Order based on East Asiatic morality. . . .

General Aim in Culture. The essence of the traditional culture of the Orient shall be developed and manifested. And, casting off the negative and conservative cultural characteristics of the continents (India and China) on the other hand, and taking in the good points of Western culture on the other, an Oriental culture and morality, on a grand scale and subtly refined, shall be created.

> **Study Question**
>
> Was it realistic for Japan to assume it could control the enormous expanse of territory envisioned in the Greater East Asia Co-Prosperity Sphere?

Notes

1. The plans drawn up by Japan's Total War Research Institute (Soryokusen Kenkyujo) would form a key part of the prosecution's argument at the Tokyo War Crimes Trial. The draft plan reflected ideas that had been circulating since 1938.
2. The Japanese referred to Manchuria as Manchukuo (spelled Manchoukuo in this document).
3. Literally "all eight corners of the world under one roof"—the belief that the Japanese emperor was mandated to rule the whole world.
4. A reference to the resistance being waged by the Chinese Communist Party and its army.

Muriel Kitagawa

Tsukiye Muriel Kitagawa (1912–1974) was born in Vancouver and spent much of her childhood in New Westminster. After graduation in 1929 Kitagawa wrote for community newspapers and participated in Japanese-Canadian organizations dedicated to gaining "full equal citizenship with the rest of Canada."[1] The bombing of Pearl Harbor on 7 December 1941 would make this goal all but impossible to achieve. On 24 February 1942 the Government of Canada issued a secret order-in-council that allowed "the government to remove all persons of Japanese origin from the 'protected area,' regardless of citizenship.

They are restricted in areas of employment, communication and association with other persons, and denied possession of cameras, firearms and radios."[2] Stripped of their possessions, some 21,000 persons (including 17,000 Canadian citizens) were dispersed throughout the interior of British Columbia and across Canada. The following excerpts are taken from Kitagawa's letters written during the war to her brother Wes, who lived in Toronto.

Document Source: Muriel Kitagawa, *This is My Own: Letters to Wes and Other Writings on Japanese Canadians, 1941–1948,* ed. Roy Miki (Vancouver BC: Talon Books, 1985), 92–5, 114–19.

Letters to Wes

4 March 1942

Dear Wes:

Just got your air-mail letter. I'll try to tell you as much as I can get down on paper.

We are Israelites on the move. The public is getting bloodthirsty and will have our blood Nazi-fashion. Okay we move. But where? Signs up on all highways. . . JAPS KEEP OUT. Curfew. "My father is dying. May I have permission to go to his bedside?"

"NO!" Like moles we burrow within after dark, and only dare to peek out of the window or else be thrown into the hoosegow with long term sentences and hard labour. Confiscation of radios, cameras, cars, and trucks. Shutdown of all business. No one will buy. No agency yet set up to evaluate. When you get a notice to report to RCMP for orders to move, you report or be interned. "Who will guard my wife and daughters?" Strong arm reply. Lord, if this was Germany you can expect such things as the normal way, but this is Canada, a Democracy! And the Nisei, repudiated by the only land they know, no redress anywhere. Sure we can move somewhere on our own, but a job? Who will feed the family? Will they hire a Jap? Where can we go that will allow us to come? The only place to go is the Camp the Government will provide when it gets around to it. Ah, but we are bewildered and bitter and uncertain.

As for Eddie and us, the Bank is worried about us. At any rate, there is so much business that he has to clear up for the removees that no hakujin[3] can do, so though we don't know for certain, he may have to stay till the last. We may stay on with him or move first to wherever we have to go, either to Camp or to some other city where there is a Branch big enough to let Ed do routine work behind the counter, but never at the counter as he is doing now. Perhaps we can move together. I don't know. This uncertainty is more nerve-wracking than anything that can happen. I don't know whether to pack all my stuff or sell it. I can take only the irreplaceables. I hope that by the time we go the twins will be big enough to stand the trip in some discomfort. But again I don't know. I may have to cart 12 bottles and 6 dozen diapers. By myself or with Ed, I don't know. Much as I would hate to sell my books I may have to. My wedding presents, all those little things that are more valuable than furniture or $300 radios, what to do with them? If we go to Camp we shall need more blankets, warm clothes, which we haven't got at all . . . winter or summer I wear cotton dresses. In any case, wherever we go will be colder and hotter than Vancouver. We can't even get around to saying good-bye to friends. Our whole way of life is disrupted. My nights are filled with exodus nightmares. My friends are so sorry for me . . . now that I have four kids, twins at that . . . they daren't phone me for fear of hurting me. So I heard. They are so kind. They come and mind them when I want a bit of time for myself. They wash dishes for me too. But now it's every man for himself and devil take the hindmost. Just the same, I am worried about Eiko and Fumi and Uncle and Aunt Toyofuku, Nobi, and the rest of them. When

shall we ever meet again if we scatter? *Don't you dare come here!!!* I'll lose you for sure if you do, then where will we be? You sit tight and maybe if Ed isn't transferred, he may find a job where you are, even as a house-servant if he has to. At least we will be together. The Nisei would have been so proud to wear the King's uniform! Even die in it.[4] But not as Helots, tied to the chariot wheels of Democracy. "Labour within or without Canada" . . . who knows but the "without" may be the hot sands of Libya, hauled there as front-line ditch-diggers. And you know that most of the people here call this a "damned shame," this treatment especially of the Canadian-born? It's just the few antis who have railroaded Ottawa into this unfairness. Talk about

---

NOTICE TO ALL JAPANESE PERSONS
AND PERSONS OF JAPANESE RACIAL ORIGIN

TAKE NOTICE that under Orders Nos. 21, 22, 23 and 24 of the British Columbia Security Commission, the following areas were made prohibited areas to all persons of the Japanese race:—

LULU ISLAND (including Steveston)	SAPPERTON
SEA ISLAND	BURQUITLAM
EBURNE	PORT MOODY
MARPOLE	IOCO
DISTRICT OF QUEENSBOROUGH	PORT COQUITLAM
CITY OF NEW WESTMINSTER	MAILLARDVILLE
	FRASER MILLS

AND FURTHER TAKE NOTICE that any person of the Japanese race found within any of the said prohibited areas without a written permit from the British Columbia Security Commission or the Royal Canadian Mounted Police shall be liable to the penalties provided under Order in Council P.C. 1665.

AUSTIN C. TAYLOR,
Chairman,
British Columbia Security Commission

Coastal areas of British Columbia were declared off limits to Japanese Canadians. Soon deportations from these areas would begin.

Vancouver Public Library, Special Collections.

opportunists. Was there ever a better excuse for them to kick us out lock stock and barrel?

I'll try to salvage as many of your books as possible, but honest Wes, I can't promise. You see, we don't know what's going to happen next. Maybe we can move everything . . . maybe we can take nothing. Just depends on whether we go to Camp or to some other city. So the saga of the Nisei begins. I, too, mean to survive this. This is the furnace where our worth will be tempered to white-hot resilience or not at all.

Pray for us all, you who are in "safe" areas. For me, whose faith these last few years is sorely tried and wearing thin. Gosh, your first year at school has been a hell of a time. Don't mind my cuss-words . . . we're doing nothing but.

Tommy has bedded down at the NC office since the curfew tolled. We visit in the mornings, and do our housework at night. Every night, when Ed is late getting home and the minute hand gets nearer seven, I sweat blood, wondering whether he'll make it before he's nabbed. He's so busy at the office transferring accounts and helping the Japanese straighten out their affairs, that he stays till the last possible minute. I sweat and sit fuming and helpless. And he can't leave the house before eight either.

So there you have a blurred picture of what life is like here. I'll keep you posted.

Martial law on the coast in the States. 120,000 Japs on the move inland. But there they don't have to join Gangs, or go to Camps . . . which may be better or worse I don't know. The watchword is "I don't know."

I'm glad you are in Toronto.

Love,

Mur.

. . .

20 April 1942

Dear Wes:

I went to the Pool[5] yesterday to see Eiko who is working there as steno. I saw Sab too who is working in the baggage . . . old Horseshow Building. Sab showed me his first paycheque as something he couldn't quite believe . . . $11.75. He's been there for an awful long time. Eiko sleeps in a partitioned stall, she being on the staff, so to speak. This stall was the former home of a pair of stallions and boy oh boy, did they leave their odour behind. The whole place is impregnated with the smell of ancient manure and maggots. Every other day it is swept with dichloride of lime or something, but you can't disguise horse smell, cow smell, sheeps, and pigs, and rabbits, and goats. And is it dusty! The toilets are just a sheet metal trough, and up till now they did not have partitions or seats. The women kicked so they put up partitions and a terribly makeshift seat. Twelve-year old boys stay with the women too. The auto show building, where there was also the Indian exhibit, houses the new dining room and kitchens. Seats 3000. Looks awfully permanent. Brick stoves, 8 of them, shining new mugs . . . very very barrack-y. As for the bunks, they were the most tragic things I saw there. Steel and wooden frames with a thin lumpy straw tick, a bolster, and three army blankets of army quality . . . no sheets unless you bring your own. These are the "homes" of the women I saw. They wouldn't let me into the men's building. There are constables at the doors . . . no propagation of the species . . . you know . . . it was in the papers. These bunks were hung with sheets and blankets and clothes of every hue and variety, a regular gipsy tent of colours, age, and cleanliness, all hung with the pathetic attempt at privacy. Here and there I saw a child's doll and teddy bear . . . There are ten showers for 1,500 women. Hot and cold water. The men looked so terribly at loose ends, wandering around the grounds, sticking their noses through the fence watching the golfers, lying on the grass. Going through the place I felt so depressed that I wanted to cry. I'm damned well not going there. They are going to move the Vancouver women first now and shove them into the Pool before sending them to the ghost towns. . .

The other day at the Pool, someone dropped his key before a stall in the Livestock Building, and he fished for it with a long wire and brought to light rotted manure and maggots!!! He called the nurse and then they moved all the bunks from the stalls and pried up the wooden floors. It was the most stomach-turning nauseating thing. They got fumigators and tried to wash it all away and got most of it into the drains, but maggots still breed and turn up here and there. One woman with more guts than the others told the nurse (white) about it and protested. She replied: "Well, there's worms in the garden aren't there?" This particular nurse was a Jap-hater of the most virulent sort. She called them "filthy Japs" to their faces and Eiko gave her "what-for" and Fumi had a terrible scrap with her, both girls saying: "What do you think we are? Are we cattle? Are we pigs you dirty-so-and-so!" You know how Fumi gets. The night the first bunch of Nisei were supposed to go to Schreiber and they wouldn't, the women and children at the Pool milled around in front of their cage, and one very handsome mountie came with his truncheon and started to hit them, yelling at them, "Get the hell back in there." Eiko's blood boiled over. She strode over to him and shouted at him: "You put that stick down! What do you think you're doing! Do you think these women and children are so many cows that you can beat them back into their place?" Eiko was shaking mad and raked him with fighting words. She has taken it on her to fight for the poor people there, and now she is on the black list and reputed to be a trouble-maker. Just like Tommy and Kunio. I wish I too could go in there and fight and slash around. It's people like us who are the most hurt . . . people like us, who have had faith in Canada, and who have been more politically minded than the others, who have a hearty contempt for the whites.

Notes

1. Muriel Kitagawa, *This Is My Own: Letters to Wes & Other Writings on Japanese Canadians, 1941–1948*, ed. Roy Miki (Vancouver: Talonbooks, 1985), 30.
2. Canada Order-in-Council PC 1486.
3. Literally "white person."
4. Miki, ed.: After Pearl Harbor—and until late 1944—Nisei were not allowed to serve in the armed forces. Opposition came from such powerful political figures as BC Premier T.D. Patullo who wrote to Prime Minister Mackenzie King, ". . . if they are called up for service, there will be a demand they be given the franchise, which we in this province can never tolerate" (Public Archives of Canada, William Lyon Mackenzie King Papers, MG26 J1, 331, T.D. Patullo to W.L.M. King. 25 September 1940).
5. Vancouver's Pacific National Exhibition site—Hastings Park—was rapidly converted from housing livestock into a temporary camp for Japanese-Canadians awaiting transportation to internment camps in the British Columbia interior and elsewhere in Canada. Many were forced into low-paying, menial jobs while living on the PNE grounds.

> **Study Question**
>
> Compare the conditions described by Kitagawa to those discussed by Victor Klemperer later in this chapter. In what ways were they similar?

Polish Ministry of Information

In 1941 Poland's Ministry of Information (in exile in London) published a lengthy summary of atrocities committed by invading German forces in Poland between 1939 and 1941. The accounts included both the territories annexed directly to the German Reich—areas which were targeted for eventual resettlement by German civilians—and those territories under military government. The following excerpt reveals the extent to which certain social groups were targeted for extermination, as well as the ongoing efforts to terrorize the Polish population into submission.

Document Source: Polish Ministry of Information, *The German New Order In Poland* (London: Hutchinson & Co., 1941), chapter two.

Mass Slaughters and Executions under the Occupation

Immediately after their entry into Poland, the Germans set to work to exterminate the Polish intellectual classes. They at once murdered large numbers of Polish priests, landowners, officials, lawyers, professors, teachers and doctors. Then came mass executions, which reached their greatest intensity in the period following October 15, 1939. It appeared that the Germans had determined to exterminate entirely the leading elements in the Western provinces of Poland. In addition to the categories already mentioned, these murders also included merchants, artisans, labour leaders, Trade Union leaders, leaders of peasants' agricultural organizations, etc.

Especially during the first period, these murders were committed without even a parody of court procedure, without even the formulation of a charge. A Pole had only to be indicated as "inimically disposed towards the Germans" (*deutschfeindlich gesinnt*). Poles were executed either publicly, usually in the market-places, or the Gestapo disposed of them secretly, often at night; very many were murdered in the prisons. Hundreds of hostages also were murdered. The most glaring cases in each of the Western provinces of Poland are given below.

Pomerania

At Gdynia, 350 of the leading men were arrested as hostages. First they were taken to Danzig, where they were made to do hard labour, then to Wejherowo. Many of these hostages were shot in the local prison, on the Polish Independence Day, November 11, 1939. Before the executions took place, these men dug their own graves. The shooting was carried out in relays, each group being obliged to witness the deaths of those who preceded them. The Gestapo agents killed their victims by a revolver shot in the head.

The attitude of these unfortunate men was heroic. They died crying: "Long live Poland!" There was not a suggestion of court procedure. No statement was made as to why these massacres took place. . . .

At Grudziądz, a factory town, numbering 60,000 inhabitants, 300 Poles were shot, 30 percent of the population was deported to the "Government General" or to Germany; children between 7 and 14 years old were also deported to Germany.

In the first half of December, 1939, in Inowroclaw, one of the largest cities in Pomerania, a group of drunken German officers visited the local prison, where 70 Poles were interned as hostages, and shot them all with revolvers. With the officers was the Landrat of the County of Inowroclaw, who himself shot some 20 of the prisoners. The Landrat stood higher up the steps, and as the prisoners were brought up one by one from below, he shot them. The Mayor of the city of Inowroclaw, Mr Jankowski, and the deputy mayor, Mr Jungst, were among the victims; others who shared their fate were Messrs. Wlodzimierz Wichlinski, Stanislaw Wichlinski, Count Poninski, Katalowski, Hoppe, all landowners; Knast, proprietor of a book shop; Fajgiel, a merchant, Laubitz, brother of the late Bishop of Gniezno; Reszka, a chemist, whose house had been destroyed by the Germans; and a number of workmen whose names are unknown.

In this city also several hundred young girls of from 14 to 20 years of age were imprisoned. A few days later, the prison guards and members of the German S.A. opened the doors and announced that those who desired could go. As the girls started to file out they were shot down. Over 40 fell thus wantonly murdered. . . .

The total number of Poles shot and murdered in Pomerania down to January 1, 1940, is estimated at 20,000. Of this number more than 10,000, as has been previously stated, were in the city of Bydgoszcz alone. . . .

Silesia

In this area also, immediately after the German Army's invasion of Silesia, mass executions of Poles were carried out. The Gestapo agents slaughtered the members of the Association of Silesian Insurgents, who had fought in 1919–1921 for the liberation of Silesia from the German yoke. The number of persons shot in the courtyard of the House of the Insurgents in Matejko Street, at Katowice, alone was estimated in November, 1939, at 250. In addition many other Katowice Poles were shot including the chemist, Mr Olejniczak, of the Third of May Street, whose body was left for three days in front of his shop in order to terrorise others. . . .

The treatment reserved for the Polish intellectuals of Silesia was especially cruel and brutal. For instance, on September 8, agents of the Gestapo and the S.S. arrested Dr. Olszak and his wife, aged respectively 65 and 60, at Karwina, in Cieszyn Silesia. He was one of the most respected citizens of Karwina, a great philanthropist, and for 40 years had been a leader of local Catholic and social activities.

Dr Olszak and his wife were taken away in a car by night to Frysztat, the county town. At the Gestapo and S.S. headquarters they were both tortured with incredible cruelty. They were beaten with iron rods and kicked while they lay on the ground. This battering with heavy military boots fractured Dr Olszak's skull. The bodies of both the husband and wife were black with bruises. They were taken, unconscious, back to Karwina, where they were abandoned at the door of their house. The executioners, who were 4 in number, feasted in their victims' house. During the evening they violated the maids, one after another. The house was sacked and plundered. The doctor had several fractured ribs, and an internal haemorrhage caused by the skull injury. He died on September 11. . . .

The Massacre in Wawer, and other Mass Murders

. . . One of its cruelest and most inhuman methods is the so-called collective responsibility of the Polish population. This is applied in cases where a German, not necessarily a soldier or even an official, but an ordinary Volksdeutsche, has been wounded or killed, often in a common brawl, or by bandits. Fifty to a hundred times as many entirely innocent residents of those localities who know nothing about the affair are at once shot, including often women and children. These mass repressions frequently have the character of punitive expeditions. Cases are known of people being killed with hand grenades, or of buildings being burned with their inhabitants locked inside them.

A particularly shocking event of this kind took place on December 26, 1939—3 months after the occupation of the country—when inhabitants of the town of Wawer, near Warsaw and of the neighbouring summer resort of Anin were massacred.

In the former town, two German soldiers were killed in a small restaurant by two common criminals, fugitives from justice attempting to evade arrest.

Two hours later, a battalion of Landesschützen arrived at Wawer. At 2 o'clock in the morning soldiers went from house to house, rousing the innocent inhabitants from sleep and dragging them from their beds, though they knew nothing whatever of the affair. Some of them were given no explanation whatever; others were told that as a punitive measure every tenth inhabitant of Wawer and Anin would be shot. Terrible scenes were witnessed. In some houses, where there were several men in the family, the women were ordered to choose who should go; in one case, a mother had to choose between her two sons; another had to choose between husband, brother, and father. From other houses, all the men were taken, including old men over 60 years of age, and boys of 12. Despite the 36 degrees of frost, many of them were dragged out of their homes in overcoats thrown over their shirts. In addition to Wawer and Anin, this raid embraced the neighbouring villages of Marysinek Wawerski and Zastow.

Futhermore, all of the men who arrived by train from the direction of Otwock, to report for work, were held up at the Wawer railway station. These men and those taken from their homes—in all about 170 persons—were assembled in a railway tunnel and obliged to stand in the frost for several hours, with their hands above their heads. At 6 o'clock a dozen or so men were detached from the whole group and led out of the tunnel; a few minutes later the noise of machine-guns was heard. Every few minutes a fresh group of a dozen or so men was led out and conducted to a place where already there were heaps of bodies, lighted by the lamps of the police cars. The unfortunates were placed with their backs to the machine-guns, and ordered to kneel.

Those of the last group were not shot, but were ordered to dig the graves of the murdered men, who numbered 107 in all. Among the victims were 2 doctors, of whom one, 60 years old, was the physician of the Hospital of the Felician Sisters; also a boy of 14, with his father, an engineer, etc. Thirty-four were less than 18 years of age, and 12 were over 60. There were 2 American citizens, a man named Szczygiel, and his son, the latter 16 years old. Mr Przedlacki and his two sons and a 12-year-old boy named Dankowski were also shot.

Mr Bartoszek, the proprietor of the restaurant where the original incident had taken place, was hanged and buried. Not long after, his body was exhumed by the Germans and hanged again. The bodies of the other victims were not returned to their families, but were buried on the spot.

Study Question

Which social classes were specifically targeted by the Nazis and why?

Victor Klemperer

Victor Klemperer (1881–1960) was born into the Jewish faith but at age twenty-two Klemperer was baptized a Protestant. After service during the First World War, Klemperer became a professor of Romance Languages and Literature at Dresden Technical College. However, the Nuremberg Laws of 1935 were also applied to baptized Jews—even those married to "Aryan" wives. Klemperer was suspended from his job, stripped of most of his possessions, and he and his Protestant wife were forced to move into a so-called "Jews' House"

in Dresden. From 1933 onwards, Klemperer recorded every detail of his life under the National Socialists in a series of diaries. Unlike the vast majority of Germans in his situation, Klemperer survived the war and, in 1945, his job and his house were restored to him. He resumed teaching at the universities of Halle, Berlin, and Greifswald until his death in 1960.

Document Source: Victor Klemperer, *I Will Bear Witness 1942–1945: A Diary of the Nazi Years* (Toronto: Random House of Canada, 2001), 64–6, 80–2.

---✧---

I Will Bear Witness

June 2, Tuesday toward evening [1942]

Two hours ago saw dispatch printed in bold letters in the *Dresdener NN.* Germany has just given Turkey a credit of 100 million rei to buy arms in Germany. And that means: Turkey is on Germany's side, or at least: She will give Germany passage (and has *more* confidence in the latter's victory than in that of its opponents!); that means an offensive against Syria, Palestine, Egypt; it means the endless prolongation of the war. Very, very depressed, and since my heart rebels more and more and since our position is becoming ever more precarious, so my hope of seeing the end of this calamity sinks ever lower.

On Sunday evening, after I had sat at home for 48 hours, short walk to Südhöhe, Toll House. Everything in bloom. The last time I was there, had to fight my way uphill in the cold, against a biting wind, to shovel show. *Then* we still had enough to eat, *then* we had not yet been beaten and spat upon by the Gestapo. And even then we already believed that things were going very badly for us. Perhaps in three months we shall say: In June we could still almost live in comfort. There is a big blue patch on Eva's arm from the recent ill-treatment. . . .

Yesterday toward evening to Steinitz for half an hour. He had written to me that he would no longer be able to call on me on Mondays. The interruption of this tiresome regularity is at least one agreeable consequence of the Gestapo terror. When Steinitz was recently caught up in a house search at friends' and was punched on the neck, he was immediately asked: "Where are you working?" Someone who is "working" is supposed to be treated a little more leniently. Steinitz thereupon registered with the Jewish community and is now, like Dr Magnus, employed in an "honourary" capacity at the Jewish cemetery. I met him after his first day at work, in shirtsleeves

and barefoot. His wife, who is not very nice to him, brought him his food and scolded him, because in his blindness he was dribbling on his trousers. He told me that there were a couple of old men under a gardener out there. Each person gets allocated a grave to clean. A whole day is spent killing time like that, but one had an answer to: "Where are you working?" and perhaps even some cover against the next evacuation. At the moment factory work is no longer given to people over sixty. —For my part I shall keep away from such tedium for as long as I possibly can. One is in danger everywhere, with and without "work." My days at home are not very fruitful either—the terrible tiredness!—but yet not completely sterile. I am now working my way into *The Myth of the Twentieth Century.* I am also reading aloud a great deal, usually very early in the morning, at four or five, and for a while following afternoon tea. [. . .] New decrees *in judaeos.* The choker is being pulled ever tighter; they are wearing us down with ever new tricks. All the things, great and small, that have accumulated in the last few years! And a pinprick is sometimes more agonizing than a blow with a club. I shall list the decrees once and for all: 1) To be home after eight or nine in the evening. Inspection! 2) Expelled from one's own house. 3) Ban on radio, ban on telephone. 4) Ban on theaters, cinemas, concerts, museums. 5) Ban on subscribing to or purchasing periodicals. 6) Ban on using public transport: three phases: a) buses banned, only front platform of tram permitted, b) all use banned, except to work, c) to work on foot, unless one lives 2 1/2 miles away or is sick (but it is a hard fight to get a doctor's certificate). Also ban on taxicabs, of course. 7) Ban on purchasing "goods in short supply". 8) Ban on purchasing cigars or any kind of smoking materials. 9) Ban on purchasing flowers. 10) Withdrawal of *milk* ration card.

Deportation from the Siedlce Ghetto to Treblinka in August 1942. Many ghettos were emptied in a matter of days, with few surviving the deportations.

Reprinted by permission of the United States Holocaust Memorial Museum (18789).

11) Ban on going to the barber. 12) Any kind of tradesman can be called only after application to the Community. 13) Compulsory surrender of typewriters, 14) of furs and woolen blankets, 15) of bicycles—it is permissible to cycle to work (Sunday outings and visits by bicycle are forbidden), 16) of deck chairs, 17) of dogs, cats, birds. 18) Ban on leaving the city of Dresden, 19) on entering the railway station, 20) on setting foot on the Ministry embankment, in parks, 21) on using Burgerwiese and the roads bordering the Great Garden (Parkstrasse, Lennéstrasse, and Karcherallee). This most recent restriction since only yesterday. Also, since the day before yesterday, a ban on entering the market halls. 22) Since September 19 [last year] the *Jew's star*. 23) Ban on having reserves of foodstuffs at home. (Gestapo also takes away what has been bought with food coupons.) 24) Ban on use of lending libraries. 25)

Because of the star all restaurants are closed to us. And in the restaurants one can still get something to eat, some "dish of the day," if one has nothing at all left at home. Eva says the restaurants are packed.[1] 26) No clothing card. 27) No fish card. 28) No special rations such as coffee, chocolate, fruit, condensed milk. 29) The special taxes. 30) The constantly contracting disposable allowance. Mine at first 600, then 320, now 185 marks. 31) Shopping restricted to *one* hour (three till four, Saturday twelve till one). I think these 31 points are everything. But all together they are nothing as against the constant threat of house searches, of ill-treatment, of prison, concentration camp, and violent death. . . .

June 19, Friday morning
Wednesday, at about seven o'clock in the evening, furious ringing of the doorbell (the bell

push remained stuck). Gestapo car. I opened up, Frau Kreidl was there also. Two of our tormentors, as well as an officer in army uniform with the Iron Cross, First Class. I was courteously asked a number of questions. I could go, Frau Kreidl was also treated courteously and not molested, they merely unsealed Friedheim's rooms and rummaged around in them for a while, before sealing them again. —Later I said to Frau Kreidl: Only the lower ranks are really bad, when an officer is present, one has a degree of protection. She responded very emphatically: "No!" Immediately after these people, Hirschel came for a moment and announced that the funeral service for Friedheim would take place the next day, Thursday afternoon, at five o'clock. He said the officer was Major Schindhelm, head of the Gestapo here, familiar with all their methods and in agreement with them, occasionally also present at beatings.

After supper we now always sit for a while with Frau Pick, who is still very weak (and who gets on badly with Ida Kriedl—both complain about the other to us). The question arose of who would go to Friedheim's funeral service—a long walk, since we are banned from tram and Great Garden and the cemetery is at the end of Fürstenstrasse. Frau Pick is afraid of being alone [if everyone went to the funeral]. ("If *they* come. . ."). We promised to help, and so yesterday morning, after endless discussions with Frau Pick and Ida Kriedl and Kätchen Sara had already taken place over breakfast, I walked over to the Hirschels'. Wiener Strasse 85, very close to the Marckwalds. A very elegant property, owner Frau Hirschel, née Glauber, a very solid, elegant drawing room with two well-filled bookcases. Frau Hirschel, in her mid-thirties, two small boys, received me, it turned out there were curious connections. She had been an assistant to Walzel, with whom she still corresponded [. . .]. Julius Wahle, with whom I edited

the Walzel Festschrift, was her uncle, and died in this house a year ago at a very great age. Frau Pick was living with the Hirschels before she moved into our Jews' House. Frau Hirschel's attitude: German, emphatically non-Zionist, emphatically aesthetic, Goethe-German—"*we* shall save Goethe!"—but also, no doubt become so under the pressure of the times, emphatically religious, orthodox Jewish. Pleasantly discreet to me. I asked for books. Once she had "neither loaned nor borrowed" books, but now she was happy if "there was a bit of life in her library" as a result. She gave me one volume of *Zionist Writings* by Herzl and lent me three volumes of Dubnow's *Jewish History*. —She organized help for Frau Pick for the afternoon. First she herself would come, then be relieved by a tenant. —She was unambiguous on the cause of Friedheim's death: It was, of course, possible that he had really died of heart failure, but . . . [. . .] There had been an old business pending against Friedheim, which they had probably taken up again. (He was the owner of the Bassenge banking house—God knows what he had tried to save.) . . .

At midday on Thursday I had only a very small Gestapo fright: A man who identified himself as being "from the Geheime Staatspolizei"[2] was courteous apart from that and wanted only to go into Friedheim's rooms. He seemed familiar, and he also asked Ida Kriedl about me: He was one of the group who had gone through my books in Dölzschen and relieved me of some, he was also looking for books in Friedheim's room.

In Shaw's *Saint Joan* there is a wild hunter of heretics, who breaks down in despair when he sees Joan burning. "I did not know. . .!" He was unable to imagine the horror. Until now I had found our situation *just as literally unimaginable*: I had always been told about being beaten and spat upon, of trembling at the sound of a car, at every ring at the door, of disappearing and not coming back again—I had not known it. Now I know it, now the dread is always inside me, deadened for a couple of hours or become habitual or paralyzed by "So far things have always turned out well in the end" and then alive and at one's throat again. . . . It is a thousand times more horrible than all my fear in 1915. —And always being afraid, always running to the window, in case a car . . .

Notes

1. As a non-Jew, even though married to Klemperer, Eva still had access to the restaurants.
2. The Gestapo.

> **Study Question**
>
> What did the Nazis accomplish through the passage of so many discriminatory measures?

Stella Wieseltier

In 1981 historian and author Yaffa Eliach conducted a series of interviews with survivors of the Holocaust and their children. In the following excerpt, entitled "Rejoining the Human Race," Stella Wieseltier (née Backenroth) recalls for Eliach the struggles that she and her formerly well-to-do family experienced after the German invasion of *present-day Ukraine. Wieseltier also explains her attitude towards the captured Nazi war criminals who were summarily hanged at the Madjenek extermination camp after the end of the Second World War.*

Document Source: Yaffa Eliach, *Hasidic Tales of the Holocaust* (New York: Oxford University Press, 1982), 267–70.

Rejoining the Human Race

In Drohobycz,[1] Stella and her family quickly learned that hunger does not discriminate even against a Backenroth. In the Drohobycz of 1941, a table such as Avrumche Backenroth's where the hungry were fed did not exist.

Stella soon realized that her father, Leibele Backenroth, the oil magnate, who returned that night from the pogrom in Schodnica, was a changed man. All his initiative, vigor, and drive were gone. He was a desperate man, unable to cope with the new order of things. Once when Stella scolded her brother for not addressing their father properly, Leibele Backenroth responded: "The child is right. A father is no longer a father if he cannot provide a slice of bread and a pair of shoes for his children. I do not deserve the respect accorded to a father."

The burden of the family's survival was now thrust upon Stella's young shoulders. Under the cover of night she and other young girls would sneak out of Drohobycz, make their way across forest and fields back to Schodnica, and pick vegetables from their own gardens. With loads of fifty pounds and more they would return to Drohobycz. Stella even managed to go back to Schodnica and, in broad daylight, bring to Drohobycz the family cow, parading her under the Gestapo windows! Three days later a decree was issued banning Jews from owning livestock. The cow was confiscated by the Gestapo. Stella did not rest. Nothing was too big, too small, or too difficult for her as long as it brought some food for her darling Zygus, her parents, and her mother's parents, the Tenzers, who had come

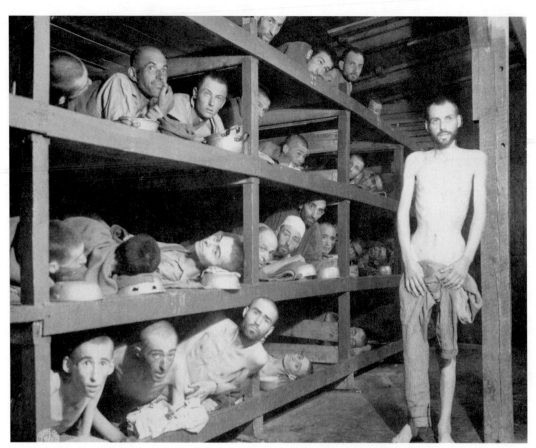

Survivors of the Buchenwald concentration camp. This photograph was taken by the American 80th Division on 16 April 1945 as they liberated the camp.

Courtesy of the National Archives (NWDNS-208-AA-206K-31), http://research.archives.gov/description/535560

with them. Conditions in the ghetto became more difficult with each passing day. Stella's father was taken away to the labour camp of Dachufka. Aktions[2] against the very young and the aged became more frequent. The lives of her brother, mother, and grandparents were in constant danger. And then it happened. In the summer of 1943, Stella's grandfather and grandmother were taken aboard trucks to Bronica. In the evening the trucks returned to Drohobycz with the victims' clothing. On the fifth day of Sivan, 8 May 1943, her mother and brother were murdered in Bronica. On the twentieth day of Tamuz, 23 July 1943, her father was shot there too.

Stella was on one of the trucks going to Bronica but she was pulled down by a member of the *Judenrat*:[3] "You are too young to die," he announced. "You can still serve the Third Reich." As she stood there in a daze, a Gestapo man by the name of Landau was practicing target shooting. Instinctively, she bent down. But Stella was not his target that day. He had a pocket full of lollipops. A group of children who were dragged out of hiding were standing around him. He asked them, one by one, if they would like lollipops, and if they wanted one, they should open their mouths. They did. One by one he shot them in their open mouths.

Stella fainted. (Until today, she feels faint when she sees dolls. To her, they represent the little, lifeless bodies of the innocent children on that Drohobycz street.)

After the liquidation of the ghetto, Stella somehow made her way back to Schodnica and found refuge with Stanislav and Aniela Nendza there in a cellar under a stable on the premises of the Backenroth oil wells. She lived with four more adults: her uncles, Leon and David Thome, Dr Isidor Friedman, a lawyer, and Luisa Mahler. The cellar was six feet long, about four feet wide, and about five feet high. It was filled with water and rats. Above, in freedom and more spacious quarters, were a pig, a goat, rabbits, and chickens. Never did Avrumche Backenroth dream that his beloved granddaughter would use his oil fields in this manner!

On Tuesday, 8 August 1944, at 7:00 AM, Benek, the 16-year-old son of Janiewski, opened the trapdoor to the cellar and brought them the message of freedom: Russian troops had just liberated Schodnica. Stella, with the others, climbed out of the cellar. It was the first time in nine months that she had seen the sky and the sun.

With swollen feet, barely able to walk, Stella decided to see Schodnica once more. The big synagogue was a stable filled with horses. Her own home was occupied by three Ukrainian families. Around Grandfather Backenroth's huge dining-room table were sitting some drunken Ukrainians. Only the Carpathian mountains were as graceful as ever, and the Backenroth pumps were still bringing up oil from the blood-soaked earth of Schodnica. Stella vowed never to return to this cursed town that she had once loved. She left for Warsaw. There she met and married a young man named Mark Wieseltier, an officer in the Polish Army who had spent the war in Siberia. For some time they lived as Christians in a house filled with icons, fearing

that they too would join the ever-growing list of Jewish casualties, Jews who survived the war only to be killed by hostile Poles.

In the fall of 1945 there was a hanging of Nazi war criminals in Majdanek.[4] Stella decided to go there for the occasion. She wanted revenge, revenge for every Jew whom she had buried with her own hands, for each child shot in Drohobycz, for her mother, father, grandparents, for her beloved Zygus, for the world of her youth that was so brutally murdered. She traveled all night to assure herself a choice seat. The hanging began. The noose was placed around the neck of each criminal. The chairs were kicked out from underneath, the bodies dangled, the crowd cheered. Stella closed her eyes in horror. "My God! What am I doing here?' she mumbled to herself. "Cheering death? Death begets more death, hatred more hatred. It will never bring back Father, Mother, and Zygus." Her revenge was short-lived, it had lost all its sweetness. All she wanted was to get away, away from Majdanek, from Warsaw, from Poland, away from this accursed soil—once her ancestral home, now the graveyard of her people.

In that moment, Stella sensed that she had once more joined the human race that still must exist somewhere, someplace—a world like that she once knew in Schodnica.

Notes

1. Now Drogobych, Ukraine.
2. Roundups for deportation.
3. The Jewish administration set up by the Nazis within the ghettos.
4. One of the six Nazi extermination camps, all on Polish territory.

Study Question

Why was it so important for Wieseltier to distance herself from the postwar reprisals against those who had committed genocide?

Sinisa Djuric (translator)

The following document is a report from the commander of the police platoon in Slunj, a Croatian town on the outskirts of Zagreb, in 1941. In the report he discusses the various fates suffered by the region's Serbian population following the creation of the Independent State of Croatia under Ante Pavelic. The author goes to some lengths to distance himself and the rest of the local police forces from the activities of the Ustaše–Croat fascist paramilitary forces. Though the final part of the document, and the author's identity, is missing the report still provides a comprehensive overview of the Ustaše's activities throughout the region.

Document Source: Sinisa Djuric, translator, "Police Report on the Cleansing of Serbs." From *The Pavelic Papers: On the Trail of the Ustaše.* Available online: www.pavelicpapers.com/documents/ndh/ndh002.html

Police Report on the Cleansing of Serbs

Headquarters of the 1st Croatian Police Regiment

Number: 484/j-S.
Report on general situation in the zone of the regiment, in consideration of Communist-Chetnik[1] activity.
TO THE DIRECTION FOR PUBLIC ORDER AND SECURITY ZAGREB OF THE INDEPENDENT STATE OF CROATIA
Dordiceva St., No. 4

Zagreb, 16th of August 1941.

Commander of the police platoon in Slunj, in report Number 89 of 13th of August 1941, reports the following:

"Until the 27th of July of this year conditions were still satisfactory considering the blow for the Serbian population, which they got by the foundation of Independent State of Croatia. A large number of them had already been reconciled with their fate. Many had already asked to convert to Catholicism. It is true that most of them didn't do that out of conviction, but if the goals of real Chetniks were fulfilled—these Serbs who convert to Catholicism would be exposed to even greater danger than the Catholics themselves, because they would be marked as traitors not only nationally but also religiously, therefore it could be concluded that they had good intentions. More importantly, most of them wouldn't act against the state, on the contrary they would in their own benefit work for its preservation.

"The sabotage of railroad tracks in the district Vojnic on the 27th and 30th of July of this year was the work of Communists, and the idea came from Communists from Karlovac, while the execution of these actions was confided to domestic people, but of Communist disposition. The Serbian population was scared knowing that the blame will fall on them as a community, even though the vast majority of them knew nothing of this, and didn't want it to happen. This may not be out of love for the state of Croatia but in their own benefit, because they knew they would be the ones to pay for this.

"As of the 29th of July of this year the cleansing by Ustaše had begun. This caused panic within Serbian population so that they all ran to the forests in fear of being cleansed. That lasted until the 8th of August of this year, but the last few days they failed, because the people knew the real situation and were hiding in the forests. They were in a state of general fear. From a psychological point of view, out of crawling and cowardice, but from a different point of view, from a bestial bitterness.

"The work of the Ustaše was among other things non-tactical, because they cleansed the less dangerous and least responsible people like many old men, women and children of the youngest age, while those with dark conscience, young and stronger fled to the forests. Described in a single sentence: 'NON-FIGHTERS WERE CLEANSED, AND FIGHTERS STAYED IN THE FORESTS.' The more naive ones and those with a clear conscience didn't even run away at first, because they thought no harm will come to them.

"The cleansing operation is completely achieved in Slunj and effectively around Slunj, while in more remote places there was little success.

"The present condition cannot be specified with exact data because the remaining people are still in the forests, but it is certain that a large number of families lost a member.

"The planning for the Ustaše cleansing was almost public, which is one of the main reasons that people hid in the forests. They 'cleansed' in houses, yards, on roads, in the presence of parents, children or vice versa. They plundered houses and property of people in such way that they competed among themselves over who will get a wealthier house and who will be the one to cleanse a wealthier man. During the last cleansing, they took clothing, there were disputes among Ustaše because of that. There was carousing, savage scenes during the 'cleansing' of a child in a cradle, old people, whole families together, sadistic delight in the most horrid tortures before the final cleansing. These kinds of actions caused disfavour even among the honourable and fair Croats and whispers were heard: 'THIS IS DISGRACE FOR THE CROAT PEOPLE, CULTURE AND THE CATHOLIC FAITH.' The pits were mostly

dug earlier. There were cases, that the ones to be cleansed carried the tools for digging pits themselves and the like. The burial of people barely alive, leaving the dead unburied or poorly buried, so that their relatives and the ones who fled to the forests came to see them.

"All this caused fear among people, but also such bitterness that there cannot be even a thought about reconciliation. Even if there were some conditions there could still be a possibility, but there were no conditions here and to this day there still aren't any.

"I—like all policemen in general—was completely powerless. Everything was done without our knowledge and with great distrust towards us. If I would say anything, even insignificant, they would threaten my life, directly or indirectly, there were even words: 'Now it's the policemen's turn.'

"Maybe the main reason for distrust towards policemen was that they didn't stand out in the cleansing even if they favoured it. I explained to the same, that we are an organ of authority and that we have to preserve the reputation of the state. Among the Croatian population (many of them) there was also noted a disfavour for this kind of cleansing operation, because it was known that many who were cleansed didn't do any harm to Croats, on the contrary they were despised by earlier regimes exactly because of that reason, because they favoured Croats. These people would have been useful now, because through them, those who fled could be influenced. . . .

"These people would have accepted everything: expulsion, concentration camps, forced labour, conversion to Catholicism, but not to be cleansed, and they would have liked best if they could stay at home and become whatever it is required of them to become (this of course not all of them, but the majority). The conversion to Catholicism would be most successful through missionaries, because in that way they would have converted with conviction.

"Today, when cleansing began in the Vojnic district, the Italian army was leaving Vojnic, and there were cases that when passing by they told the people: 'Run Serbs, Ustaše are coming and they slit everyone's throats.'

"The situation concerning Communist-Chetnik actions from station to station in the area of this district is as follows:

"SLUNJ: The number of them is negligible, because most of them were cleansed, and the rest of them are harmless and returning to their homes. There is no danger from the domestic ones, and the outsiders will probably not react. Patrols are moving undisturbed throughout the area. . . .

"PRIMISLJE: In the area of this station there were several attacks on policemen, and on the 7th of August of this year policeman Luka Perkovic was murdered and Mate Stankic was wounded. Part of this area is somewhat cleansed, and the rest are in the forests and only few have returned home. Police patrols are not safe in villages if they are of lesser strength. In the forests there are larger groups, and there are probably some of them from the Plaski area. Catholic settlements are in danger. If the return is not successful, the situation will be more critical.

"VELJUN: In the area of this station the most critical condition for now is in Slunj district. The population is mostly of the Greek religion. The most dangerous place is between Veljun and Cvijanovic Brdo. In this area there are larger groups of armed people, and there are probably some of them even from Krstinja. In this area there were three attacks on police patrols and teachers Ivan Sajfar and Martinic have been taken away. Patrols of policemen cannot go to this area without fear for their lives.

"CETINGRAD: The area of this station borders with the stations from Krstinja and V. Kladusa, so the situation is never safe even though nothing is happening for now. Patrols from this station cannot go into some villages of this area, because fugitives are in power there. . . .

"KRSTINJA: The situation in the area of this station is the most critical. The army barracks was attacked for several days in such way that there was no contact with it for 5 days. Now it is mostly liberated, but the situation is still critical. Patrols cannot move through villages at all, and all people are in the forests, or in their villages, but when the authorities come in greater strength, they run to the forests.

"VOJNIC: The same situation as in Krstinja station, except that there were no attacks on army barracks.

"KRNJAK: The population is all of the Greek religion. Most of them are fugitives, but some are returning with distrust. Situation is critical even though there were no significant events.

"VUKMANIC: There have been frequent sabotages of the railroad tracks and also hand grenades have been thrown at the post office in Tusilovac. This was the work of Communists from Karlovac. Like in other places, the people are fugitives, but police patrols are still in contact with those who are at home.

"In the area of this headquarters (districts Slunj and Vojnic) 350 army rifles with the necessary quantity of ammunition were given to endangered Croatian villages for defence. This could be good on the one hand, but dangerous on the other, if Chetniks attack them and disarm them and in that way get the weapons they need. The weapons were given on request of Ustaše station in Slunj. Besides this, a large number of hunting rifles were given to people. . . ."

Note

1. Chetniks were Serbian paramilitary fighters.

Study Question

Do you believe that the author was correct when he noted that there could be no reconciliation after what had happened in Croatia?

Margaret Freyer

The following document was written by Margaret Freyer, a German civilian who provides one of the few first-hand accounts of the effects of the allied fire-bombing of the medieval city of Dresden on the night of 13–14 February 1945. On the night of 13 February the British sent two separate waves of Lancaster bombers to Dresden. The first wave bombed for 17 minutes. The second wave arrived three hours later. Altogether, the British dropped 2,660 tons of bombs. About 50 per cent of the bombs were incendiaries. Ten hours later the Americans dropped 771 tons of explosives on the city's *railway stations and marshalling yards. What made the Dresden attack so extraordinarily destructive was the fact that the city had no air defences. The worst fire occurred within an hour of the RAF bombing, when thousands of separate blazes merged into a 1,500-degree firestorm that engulfed most of the city centre, generating winds of tornado force and incinerating everything and everyone in its path. The firestorm was so intense that counting the victims was an impossible task.*

Document Source: John Carey, ed., *Eyewitness to History* (New York: Harper Perennial, 2003), 608–11.

Eyewitness Account of the Firestorm in Dresden

I stood by the entrance and waited until no flames came licking in, then I quickly slipped through and out into the street. I had my suitcase in one hand and was wearing a white fur coat which by now was anything but white. I also wore boots and long trousers. Those boots had been a lucky choice, it turned out.

Because of the flying sparks and the fire-storm I couldn't see anything at first. A witches' cauldron was waiting for me out there: no street, only rubble nearly a metre high, glass, girders, stones, craters. I tried to get rid of the sparks by constantly patting them off my coat. It was useless. I stopped doing it, stumbled, and someone behind me called out, "Take your coat off, it's started to burn." In the pervading extreme heat I hadn't even noticed. I took off the coat and dropped it. . . .

Suddenly I fall into a big hole—a bomb crater, about six metres wide and two metres deep, and I end up down there lying on top of three women. I shake them by their clothes and start to scream at them, telling them they must get out of here—but they don't move any more. I believe I was severely shocked by this incident; I seemed to have lost all emotional feeling. Quickly, I climbed across the women, pulled my suitcase after me, and crawled on all fours out of the crater.

To my left I suddenly see a woman. I can see her to this day and shall never forget it. She carries a bundle in her arms. It is a baby. She runs, she falls, and the child flies in an arc into the fire. It's only my eyes which take this in; I myself feel nothing. The woman remains lying on the ground, completely still. Why? What for? I don't know, just stumble on. The fire-storm is incredible, there are calls for help and screams from somewhere but all around I see one single inferno. I hold another wet handkerchief in front of my mouth, my hands and my face are burning; I feel as if the skin is hanging down in strips.

On my right I see a big, burnt-out shop where lots of people are standing. I join them, but think, "No, I can't stay here either, this place is completely surrounded by fire." I leave all these people behind, and stumble on. Where to? But every time towards those places where it is dark, in case there is no fire there. I have no conception of what the street actually looked like. But it is especially from those dark patches that the people come who wring their hands and cry the same thing over and over again: "You can't carry on there, we've just come from there, everything is burning there!" Wherever and to whomsoever I turn, always that same answer.

In front of me is something that might be a street, filled with a hellish rain of sparks which look like enormous rings of fire when they hit the ground. I have no choice. I must go through. I press another wet handkerchief to my mouth and almost get through, but I fall and am convinced that I cannot go on. It's hot. Hot! My hands are burning like fire. I just drop my suitcase, I am past caring, and too weak. At least, there's nothing to lug around with me any more.

I stumbled on towards where it was dark. Suddenly, I saw people again, right in front of me. They scream and gesticulate with their hands, and then—to my utter horror and amazement—I see how one after the other they simply seem to let themselves drop to the ground. I had a feeling that they were being shot, but my mind could not understand what was really happening. Today I know that these unfortunate people were the victims of lack of oxygen. They fainted and then burnt to cinders. I fall then, stumbling over a fallen woman and as I lie right next to her I see how her clothes are burning away. Insane fear grips me and from then on I repeat one simple sentence to myself continuously: "I don't want to burn to death—no, no burning—I don't want to burn!"

Once more I fall down and feel that I am not going to be able to get up again, but the fear of being burnt pulls me to my feet. Crawling, stumbling, my last handkerchief pressed to my mouth . . . I do not know how many people I fell over. I knew only one feeling: that I must not burn.

Then my handkerchiefs are all finished—it's dreadfully hot—I can't go on and I remain lying on the ground. Suddenly a soldier appears in front of me. I wave, and wave again. He comes over to me and I whisper into his ear (my voice has almost gone), "Please take me with you, I don't want to burn." But that soldier was much too weak himself to lift me to my feet. He laid my two arms crosswise over my breast and stumbled on across me. I followed him with my eyes until he disappears somewhere in the darkness.

A statue on the cathedral overlooks the destruction of Dresden.
Courtesy of the Library of Congress, Print and Photographs Divison (LC-USZ62-94453 DLC)

I try once more to get up on my feet, but I can only manage to crawl forward on all fours. I can still feel my body, I know I'm still alive. Suddenly, I'm standing up, but there's something wrong, everything seems so far away and I can't hear or see properly any more. As I found out later, like all the others, I was suffering from lack of oxygen. I must have stumbled forwards roughly ten paces when I all at once inhaled fresh air. There's a breeze! I take another breath, inhale deeply, and my senses clear. In front of me is a broken tree. As I rush towards it, I know that I have been saved, but am unaware that the park is the *Burgerwiese*.

I walk on a little and discover a car. I'm pleased and decide to spend the night in it. The car is full of suitcases and boxes but I find enough room on the rear seats to squeeze in. Another stroke of good luck for me is that the car's windows are all broken and I have to keep awake putting out the sparks which drift in. I don't know how long I sat there, when a hand suddenly descended on my shoulder and a man's voice said, "Hello! You must get out of there." I got such a fright, because obviously someone was determined to force me away from my safe hiding place. I said, with great fear in my voice. "Please, allow me to stay here, I'll give you all the money I've got on me." (If I think about this now it almost sounds like a joke.) But the answer was

"No, I don't want your money. The car is on fire."

Good God! I leapt out immediately and could see that indeed all four tires were burning. I hadn't noticed because of the tremendous heat.

Now I looked at the man and recognized him as the soldier who had put my arms across my chest. When I asked him, he confirmed it. Then he started to weep. He continued to stroke my back, mumbling words about bravery, Russian campaign . . . but this here, this is hell. . . .

I spent all the daylight hours which followed in the town searching for my fiancé. I looked for him amongst the dead, because hardly any living beings were to be seen anywhere. What I saw is so horrific that I shall hardly be able to describe it. Dead, dead, dead everywhere. Some completely black like charcoal. Others completely untouched, lying as if they were asleep. Women in aprons, women with children sitting in the trains as if they had just nodded off. Many women, many young girls, many small children, soldiers who were wholly identifiable as such by the metal buckles on their belts, almost all of them naked. Some clinging to each other in groups as if they were clawing at each other. . . .

> **Study Question**
>
> In what ways does this document help us to understand the nature of "total war"?

Arthur W. Page

The following statement was written for US President Harry Truman (1884–1972) by Arthur W. Page (1883–1960), at the end of July 1945, in anticipation of the use of the atomic bomb against Japan. Page, then a vice president at AT&T, was a friend of US Secretary of War Henry Stimson; Stimson requested that Page craft the announcement regarding the atomic bomb. The original draft contained two blank spaces since the timing and final target had yet to be chosen.

These were subsequently hand-written onto the version of the document which appears here. A slightly edited version of this draft was released to the public on 6 August following the bombing of Hiroshima. The brief cable that follows the draft document was sent immediately after the bomb was dropped on 6 August.

Document Source: Draft Statement on the Dropping of the Bomb, July 30, 1945. President's Secretary's File, Truman Papers. Harry S. Truman Library and Museum: www.trumanlibrary.org

Draft Statement on the Dropping of the Atomic Bomb

Draft of 30 July 1945.

_____3_____ hours ago an American airplane dropped one bomb on _HIROSHIMA_ and destroyed its usefulness to the enemy. That bomb has more power than 20,000 tons of T.N.T. It has more than two thousand times the blast power of the British "Grand Slam" which is the largest bomb ever yet used in the history of warfare.

The Japanese began the war from the air at Pearl Harbor. They have been repaid many fold. And the end is not yet. With this bomb we have now added a new and revolutionary increase in destruction to supplement the growing power of our armed forces. In their present form these bombs are now in production and even more powerful forms are in development.

It is an atomic bomb. It is a harnessing of the basic power of the universe. The force from which the sun draws its power has now been loosed against those who brought war to the Far East.

Before 1939, it was the accepted belief of scientists that it was theoretically possible to release atomic energy. But no one knew any practical method of doing it. By 1942, however, we knew that the Germans were working feverishly to find a way to add atomic energy to the other engines of war with which they hoped to enslave the world. But they failed. We may be grateful to Providence that the Germans got the V-1's and the V-2's late and in limited quantities and even more grateful that they did not get the atomic bomb at all.

The battle of the laboratories held fateful risks for us as well as the battles of the air, land and sea, and we have now won the battle of the laboratories as we have won the other battles. . . .

The aftermath of the atomic bombing of Hiroshima.

Truman Library Accession Number 98-2460, http://www.trumanlibrary.org/photographs/printRecord.php?id=21790

We are now prepared to obliterate more rapidly and completely every productive enterprise the Japanese have above ground in any city. We shall destroy their docks, their factories, and their communications. Let there be no mistake; we shall completely destroy Japan's power to make war.

It was to spare the Japanese people from utter destruction that the ultimatum of July 26 was issued at Potsdam. Their leaders promptly rejected that ultimatum. If they do not now accept our terms they may expect a rain of ruin from the air, the like of which has never been seen on this earth. Behind this air attack will follow sea and land forces in such numbers and power as they have not yet seen and with the fighting skill of which they are already well aware. . . .

The fact that we can release atomic energy ushers in a new era in man's understanding of nature's forces. Atomic energy may in the future supplement the power that now comes from coal, oil, and falling water, but at present it cannot be produced on a basis to compete with them commercially. Before that comes there must be a long period of intensive research.

It has never been the habit of scientists of this country or the policy of this Government to withhold from the world scientific knowledge. Normally, therefore, everything about the work with atomic energy would be made public.

But under present circumstances it is not intended to divulge the technical processes of production or all the military applications, pending further examination of possible methods of protecting us and the rest of the world from sudden destruction.

I shall recommend that the Congress of the United States consider promptly the establishment of an appropriate commission to control the production and use of atomic power within the United States. I shall give further consideration and make further recommendations to the Congress as to how atomic power can become a powerful and forceful influence towards the maintenance of world peace.

6 August 1945

FROM: ADMIRAL EDWARDS
TO: ADMIRAL LEAHY (EYES ONLY)
NR: 334
Following information regarding MANHATTAN received:

"Hiroshima bombed visually with only 1–10th cover at 052315Z. There was no fighter opposition and no flak. Parsons reports fifteen minutes after drop as follows:

'Results clear cut successful in all respects. Visible effects greater than any test. Conditions normal in airplane following delivery.'"

Study Question

To what extent does the draft reveal concerns beyond simply ending the war in the Pacific?

Web Resources

Avalon Project: WWII Documents
    http://avalon.law.yale.edu/subject_menus/wwii.asp
Yad Vashem
    http://www.yadvashem.org
US Holocaust Memorial Museum
    http://www.ushmm.org

Historical Text Archive: World War II

>   http://www.historicaltextarchive.com/sections.php?action=list&secid=
>   18&total=38

World War II Archives Foundation

>   http://wwiiarchives.net

Recommended Reading

Louis de Bernières, *Captain Corelli's Mandolin* (New York: Vintage, 1995). Set on the Greek Island of Cephallonia before and after the Italian occupation during the Second World War, *Captain Corelli's Mandolin* takes a darkly comedic look at the complications brought about by the fascist occupation, collaboration, resistance, and the deprivation of war.

Ernest Hemingway, *For Whom the Bell Tolls* (London: Scribner, 1995). Hemingway's story reveals the flaws on both sides of the Spanish Civil War, though it is slightly more sympathetic to the Republican side. *For Whom the Bell Tolls* is a nuanced portrayal of the conflict and is both a war novel and a story of personal honour and love.

Primo Levi, *If Not Now, When?* (New York: Penguin, 1995). Partially based on Levi's experience with the Italian partisans fighting against the Nazi occupation in 1943, this novel confronts the implications of total war and the power of resistance, even in the face of overwhelming odds.

Shohei Ooka, *Fires on the Plain* (Boston: Tuttle Publishing, 2001). Set in Leyte, as Japanese defeat is imminent, *Fires on the Plain* follows one Japanese soldier, abandoned by his unit, as he wanders the island, starving and delirious, and is captured by American forces. The novel's strong antiwar focus is sometimes compared to Remarque's *All Quiet on the Western Front*.

Jean-Paul Sartre, *Iron in the Soul* (London: Penguin, 2002). Sartre's *Iron in the Soul* is set in June 1940, as the Fall of France is imminent. French soldiers, abandoned by their leaders, await their final defeat at the hands of the Nazis. The novel examines thoughts and actions in the face of total loss. This is the third volume of Sartre's *The Roads to Freedom* series, a trilogy based on the author's war experiences.

Elie Wiesel, *The Night Trilogy* (London: Farrar, Strauss and Giroux, 1987). *The Night Trilogy* is Wiesel's exploration of life in the extermination camps and the guilt of survival. *Night* is the autobiographical story of a boy and his father and their struggle to survive in Auschwitz. *Dawn* is set in Palestine, where terrorist acts against the British lead a survivor of the Holocaust to become a potential executioner. In *The Accident*, a Holocaust survivor faces the guilt of having survived while his family died.

Recommended Viewing

A Diary for Timothy (UK, 1945). Director: Humphrey Jennings (Short Documentary). *A Diary for Timothy* is constructed around the life of a baby born in the last year of the Second World War. Written by E.M. Forster, the narrative tells the story of ordinary people and how their lives were affected by the war, in their own words.

Night and Fog (France, 1955). Director: Alain Resnais (B&W/Colour) (Documentary). Drawn from contemporary newsreels, *Night and Fog* conveys all of the horrors of the extermination camps, especially the mechanization of the killing process. The documentary, which was filmed at Auschwitz in 1955, briefly touches on the issue of responsibility and the Nuremberg Trials. The short film provides an important contrast to the approach of Claude Lanzmann's epic documentary, *Shoah*.

Kanal (Poland, 1957). Director Andrzej Wajda. *Kanal* is set during the last days of the Warsaw Ghetto Uprising as the few remaining resistance fighters take to the sewers to try to survive and continue their resistance to the Nazis. The film's script was written by Jerzy Stefan Stawiński, a survivor of the uprising who escaped into the sewers.

Tora! Tora! Tora! (USA, 1970). Directors: Richard Fleischer/Kinji Fukasaku. A $25 million collaboration between American and Japanese filmmakers, *Tora! Tora! Tora!* recreates the attack on Pearl Harbor. The film focuses on Japanese planning and the American refusal to heed warnings that an attack was imminent. The film was recognized for its remarkable battle scenes.

Enemy Alien (Canada, 1975). Director: Jeanette Lerman (Short Documentary). *Enemy Alien* is a Canadian National Film Board documentary focusing on the internment of Japanese-Canadians during the Second World War. The film uses historical news footage and photographs in examining key issues such as immigration, racism, dispossession, and repatriation.

Das Boot (West Germany, 1981). Director: Wolfgang Petersen. This epic film is told entirely from the German perspective. It follows a U-boat captain and his crew as they patrol the Atlantic and Mediterranean, capturing the boredom, monotony, and tension of life on a submarine, punctuated by the brief, intense moments of combat. The 2004 Director's Cut runs almost five hours.

Kuroi Ame [*Black Rain*] (Japan, 1989). Director: Shohei Imamura (B&W and Colour). Adapted from the novel by Masuji Ibuse, *Kuroi Ame* is set amidst the aftermath of the atomic bombing and the radioactive fallout—so-called black rain. The film opens with a realistic depiction of the bombing and the moments after, then moves to the postwar era to examine both the physical and psychological impact of the bombing.

Schindler's List (USA, 1993). Director: Steven Spielberg (Primarily B&W). Spielberg's powerful recreation of the life of Oskar Schindler and his efforts to protect his Jewish workers from the extermination camps of Poland is noted for its powerful cinematography and attempt to remain historically accurate. The film won seven Academy Awards.

In the Name of the Emperor (USA, 1998). Directors: Christine Choy/Nancy Tong (Documentary). Choy and Tong's 52-minute documentary focuses on the Rape of Nanjing. Using eyewitness accounts and small pieces of film shot at the time, the film also draws much material from the diaries of missionaries who witnessed the atrocities that followed the Japanese occupation of the Nationalist capital.

Unmei No Toki [*Pride*] (Japan, 1998). Director: Shunya Ito. *Unmei No Toki* remains a highly controversial film because of its sympathetic depiction of Japanese wartime Prime Minister Hideki Tojo. Ignoring any negative elements of Tojo's life (he was sentenced to death by the 1948 Tokyo war crimes trial), Ito portrays Tojo as a passionate nationalist and heroic leader who was motivated by his determination to eliminate the presence of western imperialism in East Asia.

8

A New World Order?

The destruction wrought by the Second World War ushered in a number of profound changes in the postwar era, most importantly to the global balance of power. The once powerful nations of Europe—Britain, France, and Germany—had been utterly devastated. In Asia, Japan lay in ruins, after a sustained campaign of aerial bombardment, culminating in the detonation of Atomic Bombs over Hiroshima and Nagasaki. Perhaps most importantly, the events of the Second World War seemed to have shaken the foundations of the old world order to its core; no longer would a few great powers be able to enforce their political dominance over the vast majority of the earth's inhabitants. Fascism had been decisively defeated and a commitment to new, democratic political systems secured. Thus, the end of the war seemed to offer the promise of a new cooperative world order based, in the words of the Potsdam Proclamation, on "peace, security, and justice."

The creation of the United Nations was intended to ensure that such high ideals were translated into practice. The problematic League of Nations was to be replaced by a new organization built on the principle that "[t]he only true basis of enduring peace is the willing cooperation of free peoples in a world in which, relieved of the menace of aggression, all may enjoy economic and social security."[1] In 1945, 51 nations signed the Charter of the United Nations, thereby committing their governments to be guided by its principles. Unlike the League, the United Nations, through the Security Council, would have the ability to summon military forces in order to maintain peace and security and to repel aggression. Five permanent members—the Republic of China, France, Great Britain, the Soviet Union, and the United States—along with ten rotating members, were charged with ensuring that the UN Security Council met this obligation.[2]

The reduced power of the major imperial nations—in particular Great Britain and France—seemed to bode well for groups seeking freedom from colonial rule. Though imperialists such as Winston Churchill continued to defend the concept of Empire, the economic reality of the postwar world would refocus Britain's attention on its internal situation. This provided a window of opportunity for independence movements which had gained strength in the 1920s and 1930s to exploit.

The documents in this section focus on the potential for a postwar world free of imperial ambitions and built on cooperative principles. The Atlantic Charter establishes that the postwar world would be constructed on the principles of democracy and self-determination, with justice and security provided to all. Turning to economics, the Bretton Woods Conference established both the principles and the institutions which would govern the postwar economic recovery. The ideal of cooperative economic development is further underscored in the treaty which created the European Coal and Steel Community (ECSC). The Universal Declaration of Human Rights asserts the basic freedoms owing to every individual and condemns prejudice based on gender, race, religion, or political viewpoint. Ho Chi Minh's "Declaration of Independence" affirms the right of all peoples to independent development, free of colonial or neo-colonial influence. An Anglo-American Committee of Inquiry was created to balance the interests of both Arabs and Jewish settlers in Palestine. At the 1955 Bandung Conference, leaders of five newly independent South Asian nations, attempted to foster collaboration and cooperative development among the nations of Africa and Asia. Finally, Lester Pearson reflects both on the potential of the United Nations, and on the frustrations resulting from the UN's early attempts to mobilize the international community in peacekeeping efforts.

Notes

1. The Declaration of St. James Palace, June 1941, http://www.un.org.
2. In practice, the veto power held by the five permanent members often rendered the Security Council impotent in conflicts involving any of the five.

Franklin D. Roosevelt and Winston S. Churchill

In August 1941, American President Franklin D. Roosevelt and British Prime Minister Winston Churchill (1874–1965) met to discuss war aims and a possible postwar settlement. The four-day meeting took place aboard the USS Augusta, anchored off the coast of Newfoundland—at that time still a part of the British Empire. Though the United States had not entered the war at this time, Roosevelt played a

major role in shaping the document created at these meetings—the "Atlantic Charter." Though Stalin was not present during the discussions, the Soviet Union subsequently agreed to the principles embodied in the Atlantic Charter.

Document Source: Franklin D. Roosevelt, and Winston Churchill, "The Atlantic Charter." Available online: http://www.ibiblio.org/hyperwar/Dip/Atlantic.html.

The Atlantic Charter

14 August 1941

The President of the United States of America and the Prime Minister, Mr Churchill, representing His Majesty's Government in the United Kingdom, being met together, deem it right to make known certain common principles in the national policies of their respective countries on which they base their hopes for a better future for the world.

First, their countries seek no aggrandisement, territorial or other.

Second, they desire to see no territorial changes that do not accord with the freely expressed wishes of the peoples concerned.

Third, they respect the right of all peoples to choose the form of government under which they will live; and they wish to see sovereign rights

AUGUST 14—"TWO YEARS AGO TODAY, PRESIDENT ROOSEVELT AND PRIME MINISTER CHURCHILL SIGNED THE ATLANTIC CHARTER."... NEWS ITEM

"A SECOND EMANCIPATION PROCLAMATION !! "

This sketch likened the signing of the Atlantic Charter to Lincoln's emancipation of American slaves.
Courtesy of the National Archives (NWDNS-208-COM-994), http://research.archives.gov/description/535700

and self-government restored to those who have been forcibly deprived of them.

Fourth, they will endeavour, with due respect for their existing obligations, to further the enjoyment by all States, great or small, victor or vanquished, of access, on equal terms, to the trade and to the raw materials of the world which are needed for their economic prosperity.

Fifth, they desire to bring about the fullest collaboration between all nations in the economic field, with the object of securing for all improved labour standards, economic advancement, and social security.

Sixth, after the final destruction of the Nazi tyranny they hope to see established a peace which will afford to all nations the means of dwelling in safety within their own boundaries, and which will afford assurance that all the men in all the lands may live out their lives in freedom from fear and want.

Seventh, such a peace should enable all men to

traverse the high seas and oceans without hindrance.

Eighth, they believe that all the nations of the world, for realistic as well as spiritual reasons, must come to the abandonment of the use of force. Since no future peace can be maintained if land, sea, or air armaments continue to be employed by nations which threaten, or may threaten, aggression outside of their frontiers, pending the establishment of a wider and permanent system of general security,

that the disarmament of such nations is essential. They will likewise aid and encourage all other practicable measures which will lighten for peace-loving peoples the crushing burden of armaments.

Study Question

To what extent did the Atlantic Charter provide a practical and workable framework for the postwar era?

Raymond F. Mikesell

Raymond Mikesell (1913–2006) was an American economist who took part in the 1944 Bretton Woods Conference, a series of discussions that established the broad parameters of the postwar international economy, at least in the capitalist world. With the world economy shattered by the impact of both depression and war, the Bretton Woods Conference created both the International Monetary Fund (IMF) and the International Bank for Reconstruction and Development (IBRD).[1] On the

occasion of the 50th anniversary of the Bretton Woods conference, Mikesell published his recollections of the conference and the significance of the system devised there. The excerpt below explains the broad principles upon which the postwar economic recovery would, at least in theory, be based, as well as the importance of Bretton Woods after 50 years.

Document Source: Raymond F. Mikesell, *The Bretton Woods Debates: A Memoir* (Princeton, NJ: Princeton University, 1994), 44–6 and 62.

The Bretton Woods Debates

After two decades of isolationism promoted by defaults on US World War I loans and discriminatory restrictions against US trade, the American public was not ready to embrace foreign aid, except to allies in a common war. Assistance merely to induce countries to observe the rules of fair trade and to eliminate government control over commerce was not widely accepted. The war had, however, spawned broad support for international cooperation on behalf of peace and collective security. By tying Bretton Woods to the peace movement, the Treasury Department, in collaboration with the rest of the administration, was able to elicit grass-roots support for the Fund and Bank in the face of strong opposition from banking, big-business associations, and

conservative Republicans. There was also considerable support from foreign-trade associations and firms heavily dependent on exports.

The Treasury mounted a massive campaign during the second half of 1944 and the first half of 1945 by sending speakers to foreign-relations organizations, civic economic clubs, foreign-trade associations, and universities. All of the cabinet-level officials of the Treasury and many professional economists in Monetary Research participated, and some of us spent a large part of our time on this campaign. . . .

The lectures and public forums emphasized the advantages to American exporters of stable exchange rates and free access to foreign markets; the exceptions to these objectives contained in the Fund's Articles of Agreement were avoided or treated as unimportant. The transitional provisions were downplayed, as were the perplexities and ambiguities in the provisions on convertibility and changes in exchange rates. The speeches tended to be litanies of unrealistic promises and light dismissals of difficulties. The chaotic monetary and financial conditions following World War I were compared with the orderly regime to be established by the Bretton Woods System. Virtually every speech touted stable monetary conditions and exchange rates as defenses against future dictators and World War III. International monetary cooperation would somehow guarantee world peace.

The bankers, who had at least read summaries of the Bretton Woods Agreement, raised questions about the safety of the Fund's assets, the conditions for initiating exchange-rate changes, and the conditions governing drawings from the Fund. They rightly queried the complex language having to do with convertibility and eligibility for drawings on the Fund. The bankers were also concerned about the extent to which the Fund might interfere with their foreign-exchange operations. They were more comfortable with the Bank's charter, which emphasized the Bank's role as a guarantor rather than a direct lender. A report by the American Bankers Association advocated combining the Fund and Bank, with the function of the Fund largely confined to making currency-stabilization loans to those countries whose currencies were used in international trade. . . .

In light of the changes that have taken place in international financial policies and practices and in the functions and policies of the Fund and Bank,

did the debates of 50 years ago really matter? . . .

The debates at Bretton Woods did not determine the postwar international financial regime, but they did determine the constitutions of the Fund and Bank. The compromises reflected in those constitutions with respect to the powers of the institutions and the obligations of members gave the Fund and the Bank the flexibility to respond to changes in the international economic environment. Moreover, the constitutions set forth important principles, such as free and nondiscriminatory exchange practices, the free international flow of capital, and untied loans, all of which have influenced international economic policy.

Finally, the institutions themselves would not have been established without the Bretton Woods debates, and their activities have had a substantial influence on national financial policies and international cooperation. . . . Whatever the difficulties along the way, the Bretton Woods debates effectively turned the world away from the state controls of the 1930s and toward an international commitment to free and nondiscriminatory markets for currencies, capital, and goods.

Note

1. The IBRD became part of the group of institutions which make up the World Bank.

> **Study Question**
>
> In what way would the system described by Mikesell serve as a defence against "future dictators and World War III"?

Foreign Ministers of Belgium, France, Germany, Italy, Luxembourg, and the Netherlands

In the aftermath of two catastrophic wars involving Germany and France, many postwar leaders concluded that another conflict must be avoided at all costs. One way to ensure cooperation between the two *traditional adversaries was to establish joint economic interests. At the urging of Robert Schuman, the French Foreign Minister, and economist Jean Monnet, the first tentative steps towards economic cooperation were embodied in the treaty which created the six-power European Coal and Steel Community. This agreement is widely seen as the precursor to more ambitious efforts at European unity in the postwar period. The*

Treaty excerpted below was signed on 18 April 1951.

Document Source: Treaty Constituting the European Coal and Steel Community. Council of the European Union. Available at: http://www.consilium.europa.eu

Treaty Constituting the European Coal and Steel Community

THE PRESIDENT OF THE GERMAN FEDERAL REPUBLIC, HIS ROYAL HIGHNESS THE PRINCE ROYAL OF BELGIUM, THE PRESIDENT OF THE FRENCH REPUBLIC, THE PRESIDENT OF THE ITALIAN REPUBLIC, HER ROYAL HIGHNESS THE GRAND DUCHESS OF LUXEMBOURG, HER MAJESTY THE QUEEN OF THE NETHERLANDS,

CONSIDERING that world peace may be safeguarded only by creative efforts equal to the dangers which menace it;

CONVINCED that the contribution which an organized and vital Europe can bring to civilization is indispensable to the maintenance of peaceful relations;

CONSCIOUS of the fact that Europe can be built only by concrete actions which create a real solidarity and by the establishment of common bases for economic development;

DESIROUS of assisting through the expansion of their basic production in raising the standard of living and in furthering the works of peace;

RESOLVED to substitute for historic rivalries a fusion of their essential interests; to establish, by creating an economic community, the foundation of a broad and independent community among peoples long divided by bloody conflicts; and to lay the bases of institutions capable of giving direction to their future common destiny;

HAVE DECIDED to create a European Coal and Steel Community. . . .

TITLE ONE—The European Coal and Steel Community

Article 1

By the present Treaty the HIGH CONTRACTING PARTIES

institute among themselves a EUROPEAN COAL AND STEEL COMMUNITY, based on a common market, common objectives, and common institutions.

Article 2

The mission of the European Coal and Steel Community is to contribute to economic expansion, the development of employment and the improvement of the standard of living in the participating countries through the institution, in harmony with the general economy of the member States, of a common market as defined in Article 4.

The Community must progressively establish conditions which will in themselves assure the most rational distribution of production at the highest possible level of productivity, while safeguarding the continuity of employment and avoiding the creation of fundamental and persistent disturbances in the economies of the member States.

Article 3

Within the framework of their respective powers and responsibilities and in the common interest, the institutions of the Community shall:

(a) see that the common market is regularly supplied, taking account of the needs of third countries;

(b) assure to all consumers in comparable positions within the common market equal access to the sources of production;

(c) seek the establishment of the lowest prices which are possible without requiring any corresponding rise either in the prices charged by the same enterprises in other transactions or in the price-level as a whole in another period, while at the same time permitting necessary amortization and providing normal possibilities of remuneration for capital invested;

(d) see that conditions are maintained which will encourage enterprises to expand and improve their ability to produce and to promote a policy of rational development of natural resources, avoiding inconsiderate exhaustion of such resources;

(e) promote the improvement of the living and working conditions of the labor force in each of the industries under its jurisdiction so as to make possible the equalization of such conditions in an upward direction;

(f) further the development of international trade and see that equitable limits are observed in prices charged on external markets;

(g) promote the regular expansion and the modernization of production as well as the improvement of its quality, under conditions which preclude any protection against competing industries except where justified by illegitimate action on the part of such industries or in their favor.

Article 4

The following are recognized to be incompatible with the common market for coal and steel, and are, therefore, abolished and prohibited within the Community in the manner set forth in the present Treaty:

(a) import and export duties, or charges with an equivalent effect, and quantitative restrictions on the movement of coal and steel;

(b) measures or practices discriminating among producers, among buyers or among consumers, specifically as concerns prices, delivery terms and transportation rates, as well as measures or practices which hamper the buyer in the free choice of his supplier;

(c) subsidies or state assistance, or special charges imposed by the state, in any form whatsoever;

(d) restrictive practices tending towards the division of markets or the exploitation of the consumer. . . .

Article 100

The present Treaty, drawn up in a single copy, shall be deposited in the archives of the Government of the French Republic, which shall transmit a certified copy thereof to each of the governments of the other signatory States.

IN WITNESS WHEREOF the undersigned Plenipotentiaries have placed their signatures and seals at the end of the present Treaty.

Done at Paris, the eighteenth of April one thousand nine hundred and fifty-one.

ADENAUER.
Paul VAN ZEELAND.
J. MEURICE.
SCHUMAN.
SFORZA.
Jos. BECH.
STIKKER.
VAN DEN BRINK.

Study Question

A number of important postwar principles are evident in this document. What do you believe to be the most essential ideals?

United Nations

In response to the horrific experiences of the Second World War and the era of imperialism, the United Nations set out, in 1948, to create a comprehensive statement of global human rights. The result was embodied in the Universal Declaration of Human Rights. Following the proclamation of the Declaration, the General Assembly called on all of its member nations "to cause it to be disseminated, *displayed, read, and expounded principally in schools and other educational institutions, without distinction based on the political status of countries or territories."[1]*

Document Source: United Nations, "The Universal Declaration of Human Rights." From The United Nations. "The Universal Declaration of Human Rights, Adopted and Proclaimed by General Assembly Resolution in December 1948." Available online: http://www.un.org/Overview/rights.html.

The Universal Declaration of Human Rights

Preamble

WHEREAS recognition of the inherent dignity and of the equal and inalienable rights of all members of the human family is the foundation of freedom, justice and peace in the world,

WHEREAS disregard and contempt for human rights have resulted in barbarous acts which have outraged the conscience of mankind, and the advent of a world in which human beings shall enjoy freedom of speech and belief and freedom from fear and want has been proclaimed as the highest aspiration of the common people,

WHEREAS it is essential, if man is not to be compelled to have recourse, as a last resort, to rebellion against tyranny and oppression, that human rights should be protected by the rule of law,

WHEREAS it is essential to promote the development of friendly relations between nations,

WHEREAS the peoples of the United Nations have in the Charter reaffirmed their faith in fundamental human rights, in the dignity and worth of the human person and in the equal rights of men and women and have determined to promote social progress and better standards of life in larger freedom,

WHEREAS Member States have pledged themselves to achieve, in cooperation with the United Nations, the promotion of universal respect for and observance of human rights and fundamental freedoms,

WHEREAS a common understanding of these rights and freedoms is of the greatest importance for the full realization of this pledge,

Now, Therefore, The General Assembly proclaims:

This Universal Declaration of Human Rights as a common standard of achievement for all peoples and all nations, to the end that every individual and every organ of society, keeping this Declaration constantly in mind, shall strive by teaching and education to promote respect for these rights and freedoms and by progressive measures, national and international, to secure their universal and effective recognition and observance, both among the peoples of Member States themselves and among the peoples of territories under their jurisdiction.

Article 1

All human beings are born free and equal in dignity and rights. They are endowed with reason

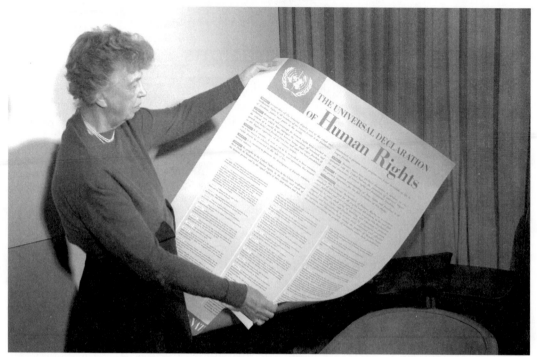

Eleanor Roosevelt reads from the Universal Declaration of Human Rights. Roosevelt was instrumental in securing the passage of the declaration.

Courtesy of the United Nations Photo Library (23783/UN/DPI).

and conscience and should act towards one another in a spirit of brotherhood.

Article 2

Everyone is entitled to all the rights and freedoms set forth in this Declaration, without distinction of any kind, such as race, colour, sex, language, religion, political or other opinion, national or social origin, property, birth or other status.

Furthermore, no distinction shall be made on the basis of the political, jurisdictional or international status of the country or territory to which a person belongs, whether it be independent, trust, non-self-governing or under any other limitation of sovereignty.

Article 3

Everyone has the right to life, liberty and security of person.

Article 4

No one shall be held in slavery or servitude; slavery and the slave trade shall be prohibited in all their forms.

Article 5

No one shall be subjected to torture or to cruel, inhuman or degrading treatment or punishment.

Article 6

Everyone has the right to recognition everywhere as a person before the law.

Article 7

All are equal before the law and are entitled without any discrimination to equal protection of the law. All are entitled to equal protection against any discrimination in violation of this Declaration and against any incitement to such discrimination.

Article 8

Everyone has the right to an effective remedy by the competent national tribunals for acts violating the fundamental rights granted him by the constitution or by law.

Article 9

No one shall be subjected to arbitrary arrest, detention or exile.

Article 10

Everyone is entitled in full equality to a fair and public hearing by an independent and impartial tribunal, in the determination of his rights and obligations and of any criminal charge against him.

Article 11

(1) Everyone charged with a penal offence has the right to be presumed innocent until proved guilty according to law in a public trial at which he has had all the guarantees necessary for his defence.

(2) No one shall be held guilty of any penal offence on account of any act or omission which did not constitute a penal offence, under national or international law, at the time when it was committed. Nor shall a heavier penalty be imposed than the one that was applicable at the time the penal offence was committed.

Article 12

No one shall be subjected to arbitrary interference with his privacy, family, home or correspondence, nor to attacks upon his honour and reputation. Everyone has the right to the protection of the law against such interference or attacks.

Article 13

(1) Everyone has the right to freedom of movement and residence within the borders of each State.

(2) Everyone has the right to leave any country, including his own, and to return to his country.

Article 14

(1) Everyone has the right to seek and to enjoy in other countries asylum from persecution.

(2) This right may not be invoked in the case of prosecutions genuinely arising from non-political crimes or from acts contrary to the purposes and principles of the United Nations.

Article 15

(1) Everyone has the right to a nationality.

(2) No one shall be arbitrarily deprived of his nationality nor denied the right to change his nationality.

Article 16

(1) Men and women of full age, without any limitation due to race, nationality or religion, have the right to marry and to found a family. They are entitled to equal rights as a marriage, during marriage and at its dissolution.

(2) Marriage shall be entered into only with the free and full consent of the intending spouses.

(3) The family is the natural and fundamental group unit of society and is entitled to protection by society and the State.

Article 17

(1) Everyone has the right to own property alone as well as in association with others.

(2) No one shall be arbitrarily deprived of his property.

Article 18

Everyone has the right to freedom of thought, conscience and religion; this right includes freedom to change his religion or belief, and freedom, either alone or in community with others and in public or private, to manifest his religion or belief in teaching, practice, worship and observance.

Article 19

Everyone has the right to freedom of opinion and expression; this right includes freedom to hold opinions without interference and to seek, receive and impart information and ideas through any media and regardless of frontiers.

Article 20

(1) Everyone has the right to freedom of peaceful assembly and association.
(2) No one may be compelled to belong to an association.

Article 21

(1) Everyone has the right to take part in the government of his country, directly or through freely chosen representatives.
(2) Everyone has the right of equal access to public service in his country.
(3) The will of the people shall be the basis of the authority of the government; this will shall be expressed in periodic and genuine elections which shall be by universal and equal suffrage and shall be held by secret vote or by equivalent free voting procedures.

Article 22

Everyone, as a member of society, has the right to social security and is entitled to realization, through national effort and international cooperation and in accordance with the organization and resources of each State, of the economic, social and cultural rights indispensable for his dignity and the free development of his personality.

Article 23

(1) Everyone has the right to work, to free choice of employment, to just and favourable conditions of work and to protection against unemployment.
(2) Everyone, without any discrimination, has the right to equal pay for equal work.
(3) Everyone who works has the right to just and favourable remuneration ensuring for himself and his family an existence worthy of human dignity, and supplemented, if necessary, by other means of social protection.
(4) Everyone has the right to form and to join trade unions for the protection of his interests.

Article 24

Everyone has the right to rest and leisure, including reasonable limitation of working hours and periodic holidays with pay.

Article 25

(1) Everyone has the right to a standard of living adequate for the health and well-being of himself and of his family, including food, clothing, housing, and medical care and necessary social services, and the right to security in the event of unemployment, sickness, disability, widowhood, old age, or other lack of livelihood in circumstances beyond his control.
(2) Motherhood and childhood are entitled to special care and assistance. All children, whether born in or out of wedlock, shall enjoy the same social protection.

Article 26

(1) Everyone has the right to education. Education shall be free, at least in the elementary and fundamental stages. Elementary education shall be compulsory. Technical and professional education shall be made generally available and higher education shall be equally accessible to all on the basis of merit.
(2) Education shall be directed to the full

development of the human personality and to the strengthening of respect for human rights and fundamental freedoms. It shall promote understanding, tolerance and friendship among all nations, racial or religious groups, and shall further the activities of the United Nations for the maintenance of peace.

(3) Parents have a prior right to choose the kind of education that shall be given to their children.

Article 27

(1) Everyone has the right freely to participate in the cultural life of the community, to enjoy the arts and to share in scientific advancement and its benefits.

(2) Everyone has the right to the protection of the moral and material interests resulting from any scientific, literary or artistic production of which he is the author.

Article 28

Everyone is entitled to a social and international order in which the rights and freedoms set forth in this Declaration can be fully realized.

Article 29

(1) Everyone has duties to the community in which alone the free and full development of his personality is possible.

(2) In the exercise of his rights and freedoms, everyone shall be subject only to such limitations as are determined by law solely for the purpose of securing due recognition and respect for the rights and freedoms of others and of meeting the just requirements of morality, public order and the general welfare in a democratic society.

(3) These rights and freedoms may in no case be exercised contrary to the purposes and principles of the United Nations.

Article 30

Nothing in this Declaration may be interpreted as implying for any State, group or person any right to engage in any activity or to perform any act aimed at the destruction of any of the rights and freedoms set forth herein.

Note

1. http://www.un.org/en/documents/udhr/index.shtml.

> **Study Question**
>
> Has the Declaration of Human Rights been an effective means of protecting basic human rights and freedoms in the postwar world? Why or why not?

Ho Chi Minh

Vietnamese President Ho Chi Minh[1] (1890–1969) read the following declaration of independence on 2 September 1945 at a meeting of half a million people in Ba Dinh Square in Hanoi. Though defeated Japanese troops remained in Vietnam and French imperialists were attempting to regain control over the region, Ho Chi Minh, who had fought against the Japanese alongside the Vietminh, believed that Vietnam would finally be able to secure its independence. He was reassured by repeated anti-imperialist proclamations by the United States, believing that the United States would not allow the French to reclaim their Indochinese territories.

Document Source: Ho Chi Minh, "Declaration of Independence of the Democratic Republic of Viet Nam." From *Selected Writings*. Hanoi: Communist Party of Vietnam, 1945. Available online: http://dangcongsan.vn/cpv/index_e.html

Declaration of Independence of the Democratic Republic of Viet Nam

"All men are created equal. They are endowed by their Creator with certain unalienable Rights; among these are Life, Liberty and the pursuit of Happiness."

This immortal statement appeared in the Declaration of Independence of the United States of America in 1776. In a broader sense, it means: All the peoples on the earth are equal from birth, all the peoples have a right to live and to be happy and free.

The Declaration of the Rights of Man and the Citizen, made at the time of the French Revolution, in 1791, also states: "All men are born free and with equal rights, and must always remain free and have equal rights."

Those are undeniable truths.

Nevertheless, for more than eighty years, the French imperialists, abusing the standard of Liberty, Equality, and Fraternity, have violated our Fatherland and oppressed our fellow-citizens. They have acted contrary to the ideals of humanity and justice.

Politically, they have deprived our people of every democratic liberty.

They have enforced inhuman laws; they have set up three different political regimes in the North, the Centre, and the South of Viet Nam in order to wreck our country's oneness and prevent our people from being united.

They have built more prisons than schools. They have mercilessly massacred our patriots. They have drowned our uprisings in seas of blood.

They have lettered public opinion and practised obscurantism.

They have weakened our race with opium and alcohol. In the field of economics, they have sucked us dry, driven our people to destitution, and devastated our land.

They have robbed us of our ricefields, our mines, our forests, and our natural resources. They have monopolized the issue of bank-notes and the import and export trade.

They have invented numerous unjustifiable taxes and reduced our people, especially our peasantry, to extreme poverty. They have made it impossible for our national bourgeoisie to prosper; they have mercilessly exploited our workers.

In the autumn of 1940, when the Japanese fascists invaded Indochina to establish new bases

Ho Chi Minh in 1954, after the defeat of French forces in the battle of Dienbienphu.

New York World Telegram and the Sun Newspaper Photograph Collection. Courtesy of the Library of Congress, Prints and Photographs Division (LC-USZ62-119630).

against the Allies, the French colonialists went down on their bended knees and opened the door of our country to welcome the Japanese in.

Thus, from that date, our people were subjected to the double yoke of the French and the Japanese. Their sufferings and miseries increased. The result was that towards the end of last year and the beginning of this year, from Quang Tri province to the North more than two million of our fellow-citizens died from starvation.

On the 9th of March this year, the French troops were disarmed by the Japanese. The French colonialists either fled or surrendered, showing that not only were they incapable of "protecting" us, but that, in a period of five years, they had twice sold our country to the Japanese.

Before the 9th of March, how often the Viet Minh had urged the French to ally themselves with it against the Japanese! But instead of this proposal, the French colonialists only intensified their terrorist activities against the Viet Minh. After their defeat and before fleeing, they massacred the political prisoners detained at Yen Bai and Cao Bang.

In spite of all this, our fellow-citizens have always manifested a lenient and humane attitude towards the French. After the Japanese putsch of 9 March 1945, the Viet Minh helped many Frenchmen to cross the frontier, rescued others from Japanese jails, and protected French lives and property. In fact, since the autumn of 1940, our country had ceased to be a French colony and had become a Japanese possession.

When the Japanese surrendered to the Allies, our entire people rose to gain power and founded the Democratic Republic of Viet Nam.

The truth is that we have wrested our independence from the Japanese, not from the French.

The French have fled, the Japanese have capitulated, Emperor Bao Dai has abdicated. Our people have broken the chains which have fettered them for nearly a century and have won independence for Viet Nam. At the same time they have overthrown the centuries-old monarchic regime and established a democratic republican regime.

We, the Provisional Government of the new Viet Nam, [a] republic representing the entire Vietnamese people, hereby declare that from now on we break off all relations of a colonial character with France; cancel all treaties signed by France on Viet Nam, and abolish all privileges held by France in our country.

The entire Vietnamese people are of one mind in their determination to oppose all wicked schemes by the French colonialists.

We are convinced that the Allies, which at the Teheran and San Francisco Conferences uphold the principle of equality among the nations, cannot fail to recognize the right of the Vietnamese people to independence.

A people who have courageously opposed French enslavement for more than eighty years, a people who have resolutely sided with the Allies against the fascists during these last years, such a people must be free, such a people must be independent.

For these reasons, we, the Provisional Government of the Democratic Republic of Viet Nam, solemnly make this declaration to the world:

Viet Nam has the right to enjoy freedom and independence and in fact has become a free and independent country. The entire Vietnamese people are determined to mobilize all their physical and mental strength, to sacrifice their lives and property in order to safeguard their freedom and independence.

Note

1. Ho Chi Minh was a pseudonym meaning "the Enlightener"; he was born Nguyen Sinh Cung and also used the name Nguyen Ai Quoc (Nguyen the Patriot).

Study Question

Based only upon the Declaration of Independence how would you characterize Ho Chi Minh's ideology?

Anglo-American Committee of Inquiry

Faced with growing public awareness of the events of the Holocaust, on 13 November 1945 British Foreign Secretary Ernest Bevin and American President Harry Truman announced the creation of the "Anglo-American Committee of Inquiry Regarding the Problems of European Jewry & Palestine." The Committee was to investigate the situation of the remaining Jews of Europe, as well as the current circumstances in Palestine, and to make recommendations to the local British administration. After a series of hearings in April 1946 the Committee recommended that 100,000 Jews be admitted immediately to Palestine, but that the region should become neither an Arab nor a Jewish state. The following excerpts describe the reaction of the Palestinian population, as well as the argument put forth by Chaim Weizmann (1874–1952).

Document Source: Anglo-American Committee of Inquiry, "Testimony by Chaim Weizmann." From Chaim Weizmann, United Nations General Assembly, Working Documentation Prepared by the Secretariat, Volume I, Reference Library on Palestine (A/296, 28 April 1947) / "The Palestinian Arab Case." From Anglo-American Committee of Inquiry, "The Palestine Arab Case," 13 November 1945. Available online: http://www.yale.edu/lawweb/avalon/anglo/angtoc.htm

Testimony on the Creation of the State of Israel

The Palestinian Arab Case

The Committee heard a brief presentation of the Arab case in Washington, statements made in London by delegates from the Arab States to the United Nations, a fuller statement from the Secretary General and other representatives of the Arab League in Cairo, and evidence given on behalf of the Arab Higher [Committee and the Arab Office in Jerusalem]. In addition, subcommittees visited Baghdad, Riyadh, Damascus, Beirut, and Amman, where they were informed of the views of Government and of unofficial spokesmen.

Stopped to the bare essentials, the Arab case is based upon the fact that Palestine is a country which the Arabs have occupied for more than a thousand years, and a denial of the Jewish historical claims to Palestine. In issuing the Balfour Declaration, the Arabs maintain, the British Government were giving away something that did not belong to Britain, and they have consistently argued that the Mandate conflicted with the Covenant of the League of Nations from which it derived its authority. The Arabs deny that the part played by the British in freeing them from the Turks gave Great Britain a right to dispose of their country.[1] Indeed, they assert that Turkish was preferable to British rule, if the latter involves their eventual subjection to the Jews. They consider the Mandate a violation of their right of self-determination since it is forcing upon them an immigration which they do not desire and will not tolerate—an invasion of Palestine by the Jews.

The Arabs of Palestine point out that all the surrounding Arab States have now been granted independence. They argue that they are just as advanced as are the citizens of the nearby States, and they demand independence for Palestine now. The promises which have been made to them in the name of Great Britain, and the assurances concerning Palestine given to Arab leaders by Presidents Roosevelt and Truman, have been understood by the Arabs of Palestine as a recognition of the principle that they should enjoy the same rights as those enjoyed by the neighbouring countries. Christian Arabs unite with Moslems in all of these contentions. They demand that their independence should be recognized at once, and they would like Palestine, as a self-governing country, to join the Arab League. . . .

The suggestion that self-government should be withheld from Palestine until the Jews have acquired a majority seems outrageous to the Arabs. They wish to be masters in their own house. The Arabs were opposed to the idea of a Jewish National Home even before the Biltmore Program and the demand for a Jewish State. Needless to say, however, their opposition has become more intense and more bitter since that program was adopted.

The Arabs maintain that they have never been anti-Semitic; indeed, they are Semites themselves. Arab spokesmen profess the greatest sympathy for the persecuted Jews of Europe, but they point out that they have not been responsible for this persecution and that it is not just that they should be compelled to atone for the sins of Western peoples by accepting into their country hundreds of thousands of victims of European anti-Semitism. Some Arabs even declare that they might be willing to do their share in providing for refugees on a quota basis if the United States, the British Commonwealth and other Western countries would do the same.

The Peel Commission took the view that the enterprise of the Jews in agriculture and industry had brought large, if indirect, benefits to the Arabs in raising their standard of living. Though a very large part of the Jewish purchases of land has been made from absentee landlords, many of them living outside Palestine, it is probable that many Arab farmers who have sold part of their land to the Jews have been able to make use of the money to improve the cultivation of their remaining holdings. The improvement of health conditions in many parts of the country, while due in part to the activities of Government and in part to the efforts of the Arabs themselves, has undoubtedly been assisted by the work of the Jewish settlers. It is also argued that the Jewish population has conferred substantial indirect benefits on the Arabs through its contribution to the public revenue. On the other hand, the Arabs contend that such improvement as there may have been in their standard of living is attributable solely to their own efforts, perhaps with a measure of aid at some points from the Administration. They assert that at least equal improvements have occurred in other Arab countries, and that the action taken by the Government to assist Jewish industry and agriculture has reacted unfavourably on the Arabs. Import duties for the protection of Jewish industries, for example, are said to have confronted Arab consumers with the necessity of buying high priced local products in place of cheaper imported goods. In any event the Arabs declare that, if they must choose between freedom and material improvement, they prefer freedom. . . .

The Arabs of Palestine are overwhelmed by a vague sense of the power of Western capital represented by the Jewish population. The influx of Western capital and the purchase of modern equipment for agriculture and industry excite in the minds of the Arabs a sense of inferiority and the feeling that they are contending against an imponderable force which is difficult to resist. This feeling is accentuated by the fact that they realize that the Jewish case is well understood and well portrayed in Washington and London, and that they have no means comparable in effectiveness of stating their side of the controversy to the Western World. They have particularly resented the resolutions in favour of Zionist aspirations, adopted respectively by the United States Congress and by the British Labour Party. Although the Arab States have diplomatic representation and five of them are members of the United Nations, the Arabs of Palestine feel nevertheless that they have not succeeded in making their case heard. The Western countries have many Jewish but few Arab citizens, and Arabs are less familiar with modern methods of propaganda. They feel that their case is being judged and their fate is being decided by mysterious forces in the Western World, which they do not understand and which do not understand them.

Testimony by Chaim Weizmann

As a people, as a race, as a collectivity, the Jews are homeless, and this homelessness and the unchanging attachment of the Jews to Palestine did not begin with Hitler. It existed many, many years, many centuries before Hitler was ever thought of, and long before this hideous tragedy was enacted, the tragedy which would have seemed utterly incredible fifteen or twenty years ago. . . . the Jews have a right to collective self-expression, like everybody else—that the existence of a "national home," if and when it is established and well-founded, would give poise and satisfaction and would render the Jew less unstable, even in the countries where he enjoys equality of treatment. He would feel that he had found collective self-expression in Palestine. They also realized that Palestine appeals powerfully to the Jews because there has been a connection between them and Palestine unbroken for thousands of years—not only in the moral and religious sense, but literally. With the exception of one or two periods—the period of the Crusades, when the Jews were more or less wiped out, and the subsequent Mongol invasion—there were always Jewish communities in Palestine and a certain amount of Jewish agriculture in Galilee. These communities were not sterile; they showed very considerable intellectual activity, spreading far beyond the confines of Palestine. And whenever there was the faintest possibility of going back, there was a movement, a literal, physical movement for return, even in the

Chaim Weizmann and Rabbi Stephen Wise at a May 1942 emergency meeting of Zionist groups, called to discuss the situation of the European Jewish population.

face of great difficulties. . . .

I am reliably informed by men in whom I have absolute confidence—some of them trusted colleagues who have seen our country and studied it, who I think are unbiased and honest observers who would not mislead us—and they tell us that if the country is developed to the utmost, and the rain waters and the rivers utilized to the fullest extent, there would be room for many hundreds of thousands more. Some of them have named a figure of something like 900,000. As Lord Samuel pointed out, there would seem to be room for double or treble the present population of Palestine without—and I would like to emphasize it—without harm to the present population, Jews or Arabs, and without thinking of displacing anybody. . . .

. . . We are sometimes accused by our Arab friends of having got hold of the best land in Palestine; that you can go round the coast and see the flourishing villages of the Jews, leaving only the poor lands and the hills to the Arabs. There is nothing more false than that accusation. It has become the best of land, but it has been marsh, it has been sand, it has been covered with rocks and with stones, and we have had to clean, to drain, to nurture and to build it up. Along with that, we have had to do the building up of the Jew to the soil, changing him from an urban inhabitant into a man who is attached to soil. We had to build up the soil at the same time, and in this process we are all regenerated. The land which we have now was derelict, it is true, 25 or 30 years ago. . . . To us it is not merely an agricultural or industrial enterprise. To us it is a question of life and death. Only we could ever have achieved this progress in face of the heavy cost of material and moral effort. . . .

I have witnessed the gradual whittling down of our rights in Palestine, and this culminated in the White Paper, which really, with the exception of 75,000 immigrants, put a stop to the "national home". . . .

The British government, in the White Paper of 1939, laid down once and for all that the Jews were to remain a minority of 1/3 until the end of time. . . . This . . . placed urgent problems of survival before us; not merely of salvage but of survival. My brain reels when I think of six million people being killed off in a comparatively short time, and if nothing is done of what can humanly be done to prevent a repetition of such a tragedy, then I fear for the survival of the Jews. . . .

I recognize fully that what I ask for will meet with considerable opposition on the part of the Arabs, and I know there may be Arabs present, opponents or friends or whatever they are—I think probably opponents. But there is no counsel of perfection in this world, and there is no absolute justice in this world. What you are trying to perform, and what we are all trying to do in our small way, is just rough human justice. I think the decision which I should like this committee to take, if I dare to say this, would be to move on the line of least injustice. Injustice there is going to be, but if you weigh up, on the one hand how the Arabs have emerged out of this war—I do not begrudge them—they have emerged with so many kingdoms, at any rate two kingdoms, four republics; they will have six seats in the UNO, one seat in the Security Council. To speak quite frankly, which may be forgiven—for at my age it may be permitted to be frank—I do not know if it is commensurate, what the Arabs have gained during this war. What is the number of their casualties? Have they suffered so much? If you compare it with our suffering, with our casualties, with our contribution. . . . I say that there may be some slight injustice politically if Palestine is made a Jewish state, but individually the Arabs will not suffer. They have not suffered hitherto. On the contrary, economically, culturally, religiously, the Arabs will not be affected. Not because we are so good—though perhaps something may be said for the character of the Jew who has gone through hell for thousands of years, and it would stultify his own history if, when he gets his slight chance, he started persecuting the Arabs. We know what it is to be a minority, we know it only too well, but there are quite different reasons. The Arabs have a perfect guarantee: whatever Palestine may be, it will only be an island in an Arab sea, and the Arabs will not need to appeal or to have separate guarantees inserted in the treaties; the mere weight of their existence in organized states would prevent any Jew from doing them injustice even if he wanted to, and I am sure he does not want to. The position of the Arabs as a people is secure. Their national sentiments can find full expression in Damascus and in Cairo and in Baghdad and in all the great countries which will, I hope, some day build up an Arab civilization which will equal the ancient glories of their people. Palestine is to the Jews what Baghdad, Cairo and Damascus all rolled together are to the Arabs, and I think the line of least injustice demands that we should be given our chance. When carried out, that will, I am sure, eventually lead to understanding and harmony between our two races, which are, after all, akin.

Note

1. [Note in original document] We have not felt it necessary to enter into the historical arguments based upon undertakings given by the British Government to the Sharif Hussein of Mecca and others during the last war and interpreted by the Arabs as promising among other things that Palestine would become an independent Arab country. These undertakings, the most important of which preceded the Balfour Declaration, form an essential part of the Arab case and were examined by an Anglo-Arab Committee in London in February 1939. The report of this Committee, containing statements of both the Arab and the British point of view, is to be found in British Command Paper No. 5974. The documents under examination were printed at the same time in Command Papers Nos. 6967 and 69 (all of 1939).

Study Question

Assess the claims of both the Palestinian Arabs and the points raised by Chaim Weizmann. Was there a way to resolve the situation without creating the potential for future violence?

Indian Delegation

In April 1955 a conference that brought together representatives from 29 nations took place in Bandung, Indonesia. It had been organized by the leaders of Burma, Sri Lanka, India, Indonesia, and Pakistan, countries that had only recently been granted their independence from colonial rule. The conference considered a number of major issues, not least of which was the regional role of the People's Republic of China. The broader theme of the conference was the promotion of co-operative development among all of the nations of Asia and Africa.

Document Source: Statement by the Indian Delegation at the Closing Session of the Bandung Conference, 1955; available at: docenti.unimc.it/docenti/uoldelul-chelati-dirar/2011/history-of-international-relations-2011/bandung/

Statement by the Indian Delegation at the Closing Session (Bandung, 17–24 April 1955)

Mr President,

For seven days we have been in this pleasant city of Bandung, and Bandung has been the focal centre—perhaps I might even say the capital, of Asia and Africa during this period.

All the world's eyes have been upon us. We have laboured for these seven days, as you all know, and we have wrestled with many problems and we have come to certain conclusions that have been placed before you. Why did we meet? Some persons called the Prime Ministers of five countries invited you. Do you think that is the reason why you met? They were the conscious or unconscious agents of other forces. We met because there is an irrepressible urge amongst the people of Asia and Africa for us to meet. We met because mighty forces are at work in these great continents moving millions of people, creating a ferment in their minds, and urges and passions and a desire for a change from their present conditions. So, however big or small we might be, we represented these great forces. We met. What have we achieved? Well, you have seen the draft statement which has been read out to you and I think it represents a considerable achievement. Other delegates have referred to it and you'll read it. But I should like to draw your attention, to direct your minds, not to that statement which is an important statement, but rather to the imponderables, to the fact that we have met and gathered here from thousands of miles, conferred together, seen each other, and in spite of all manner of differences and arguments, made friends with each other.

My friend, the Prime Minister of Burma, referred to our diversities of opinion as our differences and our arguments. We wrestled with each other these many days because we were not all of the same opinion. Because, obviously, the world looks different from where you are. If you are sitting in the Far East of Asia, you have a different perspective of the world and the world's problems. If you are sitting in the Far West of Asia, you have a different perspective again, and if you are in Africa, naturally the problems of Africa overwhelm you. So, we all came with our own perspectives, with our own problems, considering each one, no doubt, his own problem the most important in the world, but, at the same time, trying to understand that big problem, that is the problem of the world; and the second big problem, that is the problem of Asia and Africa, and trying somehow to fit in our little problems in this larger context because in the ultimate analysis all our little problems, however important they might be, are part of this larger problem and can hardly be

solved unless that larger problem is tackled and solved. How will you solve this problem or that problem if peace itself is endangered and thrown overboard? Obviously, you cannot. The very primary consideration is peace. You and I sitting here in our respective countries are passionately eager to advance our countries peacefully. We have been backward; we are backward. We have been left behind in the race, in the world race, and now we have got a chance again to make good. We want to make good and we have to make good rapidly because of the compulsion of events. It is not so much a choice of yours and mine, but a choice dictated by this compulsion of events, because if we do not make good, we fade away or we stumble and fall again, not to rise again for a long time. We are not going to do that; we are determined not to do that. We are determined in this new chapter of Asia and Africa to make good. Not, primarily, not to be dominated in any way by any other country or continent. Secondly to rise in the economic domain, in the social domain; to become prosperous, to bring happiness to our people. To put an end to all the age-old shackles that have tied us; not only political—you call them colonialism, rightly—but the other shackles of our own making, which are tighter.

We criticized other nations in our resolutions, and it is a fact that criticism is just; therefore we advanced it. But in the final analysis the criticism has to be directed against ourselves, because a country falls because of its own failings, not because another attacks it or does anything to it. It is because we failed that we fell, and it is only when we make good that we'll succeed, and not all the resolutions in the world make much difference if we are weak of heart and weak of spirit.

But there is yet another spirit of Asia today, as we all know, for Asia today is not static, Asia is not passive, Asia is not submissive, Asia does not tolerate things which it has tolerated for so long. Asia is dynamic; Asia is alive, full of life. Asia will make mistakes, has made mistakes, but it does not matter so long as life is there. If life is there, every mistake is tolerated and we advance. If life is not there, all our right words and right actions and right eloquence will not hold good. What have we achieved then? I think our achievement has not only been great in the agreements we have arrived at. But much greater is the background of that agreement, because as I said, we wrestled with problems, we have wrestled with our difference, we have argued till we nearly—what shall I say? till fatigue overtook all our bodies and minds. And finally in spite of those differences, we have agreed—that is the main thing. We are not "yes-men" I hope, sitting here saying "Yes" to this country or that country, saying "Yes" even to each other. I hope we are not. There are great countries in the world who rather like having submissive friends; if I may say so, who like to dictate. Well, if there is one thing which Asia wants to tell them it is this: no dictation there is going to be in future; no "yes-men" in Asia, I hope, or in Africa. We have had enough of that in the past. We value the friendship of the great countries and, if I may on your part, I should like to say that we send our greetings to the great countries of Europe and America. It is not in any spirit of hatred or dislike or aggressiveness we meet here with regard to Europe or America; certainly not. We send our greetings to them I hope from all of us here, and we want to be friends with them and to cooperate with them. But, we shall only cooperate in future and we shall obviously only be friends and equals; there is no friendship when nations are not equal, when one has to obey another and when one only dominates another. That is why we raise our voices against the domination and colonialism from which many of us have suffered for so long, and that is why we have to be very careful that any other form of domination does not come in our way. Therefore, we want to be friends with the West and friends with the East and friends with everybody, because if there is something that may be called the approach to the mind and spirit of Asia, it is one of toleration and friendship and cooperation; not one of aggressiveness.

I wish to speak no ill of anybody. In Asia all of us have many faults as countries, as individuals. Our past history shows it. Nevertheless, I say that Europe has been in the past a continent full of conflict, full of trouble, full of hatred, and their conflicts continue, and their wars continue, and we have been dragged in their wars because we were tied to their chariot wheels. Now, are we going to continue to be dragged in, and tie ourselves to Europe's troubles and Europe's hatreds and Europe's conflicts? I hope not. Of course, Europe and Asia and America and Africa and all these countries are all dependent on one another. It is perhaps not quite right to think of them as isolated, because we are not isolated; we have to live together and cooperate together in this modern world which is going up toward the idea of a one world. Nevertheless, Europe has got into the habit of thinking and other great countries in America—whatever political or economic persuasion they may be in America or Europe—got into the habit of thinking that their quarrels are the world's quarrels and therefore the world must submit to them this way or that way. Well, I do not quite follow that reasoning. I do not want anybody to quarrel, to quarrel in Europe, or Asia or America, but if at least others quarrel, why should I quarrel and why should I be dragged into their quarrels and wars? I just do not understand it. Therefore, I hope we shall keep away from those quarrels and exercise our pressure on all others not to quarrel. I realize, as the Prime Minister of Burma said, that we cannot exercise tremendous influence over the world. Our influence will grow, no doubt; it is growing, and we can exercise some influence even today. But whether our influence is great or small, it must be exercised in the right direction, in an independent direction, in a direction which has integrity of purpose and ideals and objectives behind it. It represents the ideals of Asia, it represents the new dynamism of Asia, because if it does not represent that, what are we then? Are we copies of Europeans or Americans or Russians? What are we? We are Asians or Africans. We are none else, and for anybody to tell us that we have to be camp-followers of Russia or America or any country of Europe, is, if I may say so, not very creditable to our new dignity, our new independence, our new freedom and our new spirit and our new self-reliance.

So, we mean no ill to anybody. We send our greetings to Europe and America. We send our greetings to Australia and New Zealand. And indeed Australia and New Zealand are almost in our region. They certainly don't belong to Europe, much less to America. They are next to us and I should like indeed for Australia and New Zealand to come nearer to Asia, where they are. I would welcome them, because I do not want what we say or do to be based on racial prejudices. We have had enough of this racialism elsewhere. We have it today, my friends. We have passed many resolutions etc. about this country and that country. But I think that there is nothing more terrible, there is nothing more horrible, than the infinite tragedy of Africa in the past few hundred years. When I think of it everything else pales into insignificance, all that we have had in Asia. That infinite tragedy of Africa ever since the days when millions of them were carried away in galleys as slaves to America and elsewhere; the way they were treated, the way they were caught, the way they were taken away, 50 per cent dying in the galleys. We have to bear

that burden, all of us. We did not do it ourselves I mean, but the world has to bear it. We talk about this little country and that little country in Africa or outside, but let us remember this Infinite Tragedy. But unfortunately, in a different sense, even now the Tragedy of Africa is greater than that of any other, I venture to say, even today. Whether it is racial, whether it is political, whatever it may be, it is there, and it is up to Asia to help Africa, to the best of her ability, because we are sister continents.

So, Sir, I trust that the achievement that we have had in this Conference has left, I am sure it has, a powerful impress on the minds of all who are here. I am quite sure, that it has left an impress on the minds of the world. We came here, I repeat, consciously or unconsciously as agents of historic destiny, and we have made some history here. And we have to live up to what we have said and what we have thought and, even more so, we have to live up to what the world expects of us, what Asia expects of us, what the millions of these two continents expect of us. I hope that we'll be worthy of the peoples' faith and our destiny.

> **Study Question**
>
> What were the most important obstacles facing the countries of Asia and Africa in 1955?

Lester B. Pearson

Lester B. "Mike" Pearson (1897–1972) was born in Toronto. After service during the Great War, he studied history at Oxford. In 1928 Pearson joined the Department of External Affairs serving in numerous capacities, which included attending the sessions of the League of Nations. He was an active participant in the discussions that led to the creation of both the United Nations and the North Atlantic Treaty Organization (NATO). Elected to parliament as a Liberal in 1948, Pearson served as minister

for external affairs for nine years. During the 1956 Suez Crisis, Pearson proposed a multinational force to keep the peace between Israel and Egypt, an act for which he was awarded the Nobel Peace Prize. The following speech was delivered at Temple University in Philadelphia in 1965.

Document Source: Lester B. Pearson, "On Peacekeeping." From Lester B. Pearson, "On Peacekeeping, 2 April 1965" (National Archives of Canada, Papers of Lester B. Pearson, series 9: Speeches, vol. 33, file, April 1965).

On Peacekeeping

Mr President, honoured guests and members of the Temple University Alumni Association:

With my very deep personal gratitude for this honour go my thanks for the recognition you have given to my country's efforts—as the citation reads—in promoting the cause of peace and understanding among nations and man. I wish also to pay my tribute to the work and the life of the man whom this Award commemorates. . . .

It is an often noted phenomenon that man's inventive ingenuity has out-distanced his sense of moral obligation; that technology and science have left politics and ethics far behind. Like the sorcerer's apprentice, we have set in motion destructive forces we are unable to control. The point, however, can be put another way. It is one thing to conquer space and to perceive, stretching before one without limit, the prospect of unimpeded exploration and advance. It is another to expect, in scientific terms, a quantum jump from immoral men to a world at peace. We must take it as given, I believe, that man's moral nature will continue to be ambiguous, that in Paul Tillich's words: "In the best will there is an element of bad will." The reverse is also true. It is not therefore so much a matter of morality catching up with science, of building a new Jerusalem, while there is something left to build on, but of collectively adjusting our habits of mind and our ways of living to the changing world around us. Surely man's capacity for reason can be applied to international politics as well as to international space and, in the application, strengthen our world community against the consequences of man's inhumanity to man.

As for me, and in spite of current headlines, I remain impressed with the elements of hope in our world as it is today. For one thing, there is a *world* community in a sense that no one would have believed possible 50 years ago, despite the apparent paradox that this community is divided into a greater number of political units than ever before. The paradox is more apparent than real, however, because cultural and racial divisions have always existed. For many years they were hidden by the crust of colonial empires. Now that this quite artificial and imposed unity has been broken, the new nations, as well as the old, are able to judge for themselves how they wish to arrange their relations with each other.

The new nations, also, now share with the old the essentially Western belief in, and pursuit of, material progress. Western technology has spread to the ends of the earth, bringing with it new hope for people long chained to a fatalistic acceptance of poverty, disease and ignorance. They may now hope, with an awakened intensity, that opportunities will exist for their children, if not for themselves, to participate in activities and to share in experience that we, in the West, take for granted. They know that nuclear physics means new sources of energy as well as new means of destruction; that rockets may propel communications satellites into space as well as guided missiles. And we know, as the privileged have never known or admitted before, that our own future and well-being depends on our imaginative capacity to help organize the world's resources and skills so that all may share in its wealth more equitably than in the past.

The most significant and hopeful, if at times the most frustrating, expression of this sense of community is the United Nations. The world organization means different things to different men. It is godparent and mentor to the new nations, some of whom might not be independent if it were not for the United Nations. It is the gangling, awkward child of the old nations who conceived of the United Nations "to safeguard succeeding generations from the scourge of war" even as the guns were still sounding on the battlefields of World War II. For all, it is a meeting place, a centre, as the Charter puts it, "for harmonizing the actions of nations," and an instrument for furthering the common purposes of mankind. It often does just this. Out of the push and pull of debate and negotiation between conflicting interests and ambitions there emerges on many issues what may be thought of as a consensus of world opinion; and, ready to interpret this consensus and to give it form, stands an independent and impartial Secretariat. There has never been anything like it before in history. It is now an indispensable part of human development in a new age.

Keeping the peace is the first and most difficult purpose of the United Nations. I have no doubt it will remain the yardstick by which the United Nations stands or falls, however legitimate and even compelling are the economic, social and ethical purposes which it is also called upon to serve. If we cannot manage our affairs peacefully in the short term, our long-term goals will never be reached.

Threats to peace and the danger of local conflict escalating to nuclear destruction have been responsible in large measure for calling into being the series of UN forces, observer groups and presences that have served to implement what the Secretary-General has described as "the idea of the UN as a representative instrument for promoting and maintaining international order." It is a remarkable advance in world affairs that many thousands of UN military personnel from more than a dozen countries should be able effectively to represent the concern of the world's peoples that conflict shall be prevented or stopped before it engulfs us all in war. Future threats to the peace will provoke similar appeals to the UN to put out the fire before it spreads. Tonight, with a feeling of fear and foreboding, I wish that there could be

such an appeal from North and South Vietnam.

We have now reached a critical stage in the development of the UN's peace-keeping capacity. The organization is quite different from what it was in 1945, or in 1950, when it was able to mobilize under US leadership collective resistance to aggression in Korea. The increase in the membership to more than double the original number, the nature of that increase and the diffusion of power amongst several regional groups have led to a corresponding decrease in the influence and authority of the Western states.

Nevertheless, the leadership in peace-keeping has come from the West, in close cooperation with the Secretary-General and with members of the non-aligned group. I would reject, however, the Soviet charge that, in this leadership, we had some special Western axe to grind. Indeed the Assembly approved by large majorities the assessment resolutions establishing collective financial responsibility for the operations in the Middle East and the Congo. What has happened is that since 1962 the balance of the membership has tended to take a more critical view of Great Power disputes over peace-keeping. They have begun to question whether, in the light of this disagreement, complete collective responsibility is often feasible in practice, however desirable it may always be in principle. . . .

I would like now to turn to peace-keeping outside the United Nations, specifically to Indo-China. Canada has gained much experience in such peace-keeping through its participation, with India and Poland, during nearly eleven years, on the International Supervisory Commissions in the former Indo-China States of Vietnam, Laos, and Cambodia. This experience has taught us to recognize the practical difficulties confronting peace-keeping operations. It has, however, also shown us the contribution—at times the essential contribution—which can be made to peace and stability by international bodies of this kind. . . .

When a savage war broke out between

the two Vietnams, the whole problem entered an even more difficult stage. What had been a Vietnamese war against a colonial power became a Communist attack against a Vietnamese state.

In this tragic conflict, the US intervened to help South Vietnam defend itself against aggression and at the request of the government of the country that was under attack.

Its motives were honourable; neither mean nor imperialistic. Its sacrifices have been great and they were not made to advance any selfish American interest.

The Government and the great majority of the people of Canada have supported whole-heartedly US peace-keeping and peace-making policies in Vietnam. We wish to be able to continue that support. . . .

The universal concern which is being expressed about the tragedy of Vietnam is a reflection both of this fearful possibility and of that sense of world community to which I have referred. All nations watch with deep anxiety the quickening march of events in Vietnam toward a climax which is unknown but menacing. All are seeking solutions to the dilemma confronting us, because all would be involved in the spread of war.

The dilemma is acute and seems intractable. On the one hand, no nation—and particularly no newly-independent nation—could ever feel secure if capitulation in Vietnam led to the sanctification of aggression through subversion and spurious "wars of national liberation."

On the other hand, the progressive application of military sanctions can encourage stubborn resistance; rather than a willingness to negotiate. Continued intensification of hostilities in Vietnam could lead to uncontrollable escalation.

A settlement is hard to envisage in the heat of the battle, but it is now imperative to seek one. . . .

In doing so, we should realize that the crisis in Vietnam is, in part at least, a reflection of a broader conflict, and that a lasting resolution of the specific problem may be possible only within the framework of a much broader settlement. But one thing is certain: without a settlement guaranteeing the independence, neutrality and territorial integrity of North Vietnam's neighbours in Southeast Asia and without a willingness by all parties to respect and protect these, a continuation of the present fear and instability will be inescapable.

The problem, therefore, remains the responsibility of the international community. The members of that community will therefore be obliged to make available the means of supervising any settlement and guaranteeing the fulfilment of its terms in spirit and in letter. The world community will also be obliged to assist in establishing the economic, as well as political, foundations of future understanding and security. In this connection, I was encouraged by President Johnson's expression of the willingness of the United States to help in promoting economic and social cooperation in the whole area. This is important. . . .

We in North America have a special duty and a special opportunity in this struggle for peace. We enjoy a high standard of material well-being and security with freedom. Our good fortune carries with it a corresponding obligation.

At the moment, the most immediate obligation facing the international community—not merely the United States of America—is to restore peace, freedom and security to the people of Vietnam.

If we fail here, the consequence may extend far beyond the area directly concerned. If we succeed, it could make possible new and greater progress toward a better world.

Study Question

What were the barriers to an international settlement of the type envisioned by Lester Pearson?

Web Resources

United Nations Website
   http://www.un.org
The Avalon Project: World War II Documents
   http://avalon.law.yale.edu/subject_menus/wwii.asp
The Pearson Peacekeeping Centre/Centre pour le Maintien de la Paix
   http://www.peaceoperations.org
Foreign and International Law Resources
   http://www.law.harvard.edu/library/research/guides/int_foreign/web-resources/index.html

Recommended Reading

S.Y. Agnon, *Only Yesterday* (Princeton, NJ: Princeton University Press, 2002). *Only Yesterday* focuses on Jewish emigration to Palestine during the early twentieth century. The central character, Isaac Kumer, arrives in Palestine amidst the devotees of Zionism and the ultra-Orthodox Jews who reject Zionist ideology. His own rootlessness, the inability to establish an identity in his new homeland, and absurd twists of fate, lead Kumer to question his long-held beliefs.

Mulk Raj Anand, *Untouchable* (New York: Penguin, 1990). Anand's *Untouchable*, first published in 1935, tells of the life of Bakha, an untouchable, and his struggle against the restrictions of the caste system. The novel stands as a powerful condemnation of caste, and argues that British colonial rule increased the suffering of the "untouchables."

Ghassan Kanafani, *Men in the Sun* (Boulder, CO: Lynne Rienner Publishers, 1998). *Men in the Sun*—set in 1958—is the story of three Palestinians who attempt to escape to Kuwait in order to guarantee their survival. Three generations recollect the Palestinian experience beginning with the war in 1948, offering thoughts on national identity, the refugee question, and survival itself.

Wole Soyinka, *Death and the King's Horseman* (New York: W.W. Norton, 2002). Based on events in the Yoruba village of Oyo in 1946, Soyinka's play examines the clash between traditional values and roles in colonial Nigeria. Following the King's death, his horseman must commit suicide and accompany him, but the British authorities prevent the suicide—with dire consequences.

Rabindranath Tagore, *The Home and the World* (New York: Penguin, 1996). Tagore, a Nobel Prize winning Bengali author, sets *The Home and the World* in 1908 Bengal during the early years of the Swadeshi movement, exploring the first expressions of radical nationalism and the excitement they generated. Originally published in 1916, Tagore's novel examines the impact of political awakening on traditional Indian society, and foreshadows the violent conflicts that erupted at partition.

Recommended Viewing

Hamsin [*Eastern Wind*] (Israel, 1982). Director: Daniel Wachsmann. Set in Galilee, the film provides a balanced look at the tensions that developed when the Israeli army requisitioned Arab land. Wachsmann examines both land disputes and the pre-existing relationships between Arab and Jewish neighbours.

Gandhi (UK/India, 1982). Director: Richard Attenborough. This epic recreation of Mohandas K. Gandhi's life follows its subject from his early life in India, through his experiences in colonial South Africa, to the Indian independence struggle, partition, and death. The film won eight Academy Awards and remains notable for its outstanding cinematography.

Chocolat (France, 1988). Director: Claire Denis. Not to be confused with the 2000 film of the same title, Denis' *Chocolat* is set in Cameroon in 1950s, as a young French woman returns to West Africa during the dying days of French colonial control. The film underscores both the injustices of the system and the complex nature of colonial relationships and racism during the earlier period of colonial rule.

Tsahal (Israel/France, 1994). Director: Claude Lanzmann (Documentary). *Tsahal* is one of three films in Lanzmann's trilogy exploring Jewish life in the twentieth century (*Shoah* and *Pourquoi Israel* are the others). This documentary focuses on the founding of the Israeli state and the role of the military in society and politics.

9

Origins and Implications of the Cold War

Despite optimistic predictions of a postwar world built on cooperation and justice, responsive to the wishes of all of the world's peoples, escalating conflicts between the Western powers and the Soviet Union rendered this vision increasingly unlikely. In the last few months of the war occupying armies began to impose their own vision of the postwar world in the regions that they controlled. The final two wartime conferences—at Yalta and Potsdam—were marked by tensions among the leaders of the "Big Three."

As the war ended, the areas of Europe controlled by the Western nations—Britain, France, and the United States—were designated for rebuilding and reintegration into the capitalist world economy as quickly as possible in order to halt the political trend to the left throughout Western Europe. In the Soviet zones, which included the majority of Eastern Europe and the Balkan states, Communist and Socialist parties tended to dominate weak coalition governments. In all cases, the armies of occupation retained a strong presence in the immediate aftermath of the war.

Xenophobic nationalism reached new heights in both the United States and the Soviet Union during the immediate postwar years. In the United States, Joseph McCarthy's crusade against communists in the American government led to a nationwide Red Scare which far surpassed the wave of anti-communist activity which had followed the First World War. America's quest to root out communism throughout the world would soon embroil the nation in complex conflicts beyond its borders—in Latin America, in Southeast Asia, and in China—conflicts that served to shape the development of the United States for years to come.

In the Soviet Union, Stalin's paranoia regarding Western intentions towards the communist world reached new heights. A renewed round of purges was prevented only by Stalin's death in 1953, an event which ushered in an important period of transition in the Soviet Union. At first the USSR was led by a group of men, most of whom were determined to modernize the nation's economy and reduce the use of the terror and the cult of personality which had marked Stalin's rule. Eventually Nikita Khrushchev emerged from the collective leadership to seize control of the Communist Party of the Soviet Union. In 1956 he spoke to the Twentieth CPSU Congress and systematically denounced the "crimes" of the Stalin era. In the future, he observed, a more moderate, Leninist path would guide the Soviet Union and, indeed, the entire

Soviet Bloc. Nonetheless, even as the level of terror decreased in the USSR, the hold of the Party remained as strong as ever under Khrushchev. Hopes that Cold War tensions might be alleviated by the USSR's new openness largely came to naught as new conflicts continued to create friction between the two global superpowers and soon the Cold War extended beyond the bounds of Earth and into the realm of space.

Meanwhile in Asia, the end of the Pacific War did not bring an end to conflict. Some regions, such as Indochina and India, found themselves embroiled in struggles for national independence. China, on the other hand, slipped rapidly back into a state of civil war between the Nationalist forces of Chiang Kai-shek (Jiang Jieshi) and the Communist forces of Mao Zedong. Other regions, such as the Korean Peninsula, remained occupied by both Soviet and American armies—their future to be determined, once again, by external powers. Japan similarly remained an occupied nation with the American occupation authorities, led by General Douglas MacArthur, determined to remake the country as an outpost of capitalist democracy.

The documents in this section reflect the tensions of the postwar era. Winston Churchill's "Iron Curtain" speech draws attention to the ongoing division of Europe and intimates that the Soviet Union would not be satisfied with the position that it occupied in 1946. Churchill, however, failed to mention his own culpability in the division of Europe, despite having agreed to divide the continent between the Western powers and the Soviets in the 1944 Moscow Accords. Stalin's immediate and contemptuous response follows. President Harry S. Truman's speech to Congress in 1947 commits the US firmly to the containment of communism in Europe, while the excerpt from one of Senator Joseph McCarthy's speeches in 1950 clearly reveals the level of anti-communist hysteria in the US. Similar paranoia and suspicion is evident in a directive from the Central Committee of the Soviet Union to members of the press. Nikita Khrushchev's 1956 "de-Stalinization" speech comprehensively denounces the system created during the Stalin years; contemporary readers should, however, keep in mind the degree to which Khrushchev was complicit in the crimes of the Stalin era. Turning back to the US, Robert McNamara's memorandum on Indochina for newly-elected US President John F. Kennedy is indicative of the degree to which Cold War concerns took precedence when the US assessed its global commitments. Finally, Kennedy's speech announcing the American intention to put a man on the moon by the end of the decade, likewise reflects the determination to best the Soviets in every realm.

Winston Churchill

After the Second World War, despite Winston Churchill's tremendous wartime popularity, Britons voted him out of office and instead chose the left-leaning Labour Party under Clement Attlee to form a government. Churchill's speech that follows, originally entitled "The Sinews of Peace," was delivered in Fulton, Missouri, at Westminster College, where he was granted an honorary degree in 1946. This speech *popularized the phrase "Iron Curtain" to describe the division of Europe between the Western powers and the area controlled by the Soviet Union. Contemporary readers should keep in mind Churchill's own role in*

establishing the divided world that he laments.

Document Source: Winston Churchill, *The Sinews of Peace: Postwar Speeches by Winston S. Churchill*, ed. Randolph S. Churchill (London: Cassell, 1948), 93–105.

Iron Curtain Speech

I am glad to come to Westminster College this afternoon, and am complimented that you should give me a degree. The name "Westminster" is somehow familiar to me. I seem to have heard of it before. Indeed, it was at Westminster that I received a very large part of my education in politics, dialectic, rhetoric, and one or two other things. In fact we have both been educated at the same, or similar, or, at any rate, kindred establishments. . . .

The United States stands at this time at the pinnacle of world power. It is a solemn moment for the American Democracy. For with this primacy in power is also joined an awe-inspiring accountability to the future. As you look around you, you must feel not only the sense of duty done, but also you must feel anxiety lest you fall below the level of achievement. Opportunity is here now, clear and shining, for both our countries. To reject it or ignore it or fritter it away will bring upon us all the long reproaches of the after-time. It is necessary that constancy of mind, persistency of purpose, and the grand simplicity of decision shall rule and guide the conduct of the English-speaking peoples in peace as they did in war. We must, and I believe we shall, prove ourselves equal to this severe requirement. . . .

I have, however, a definite and practical proposal to make for action. Courts and magistrates may be set up but they cannot function without sheriffs and constables. The United Nations

Joseph Stalin and Winston Churchill talk with US President Harry S. Truman at the opening of the Potsdam Conference in July 1945.
US Army Signal Corps, Courtesy of the Harry S. Truman Library.

Organization must immediately begin to be equipped with an international armed force. In such a matter we can only go step by step, but we must begin now. I propose that each of the Powers and States should be invited to delegate a certain number of air squadrons to the service of the world organization. These squadrons would be trained and prepared in their own countries, but would move around in rotation from one country to another. They would wear the uniform of their own countries but with different badges. They would not be required to act against their own nation, but in other respects they would be directed by the world organization. This might be started on a modest scale and would grow as confidence grew. I wished to see this done after the First World War, and I devoutly trust it may be done forthwith.

It would nevertheless be wrong and imprudent to entrust the secret knowledge or experience of the atomic bomb, which the United States, Great Britain, and Canada now share, to the world organization, while it is still in its infancy. It would be criminal madness to cast it adrift in this still agitated and un-united world. No one in any country has slept less well in their beds because this knowledge and the method and the raw materials to apply it, are at present largely retained in American hands. I do not believe we should all have slept so soundly had the positions been reversed and if some Communist or neo-Fascist State monopolized for the time being these dread agencies. The fear of them alone might easily have been used to enforce totalitarian systems upon the free democratic world, with consequences appalling to human imagination. . .

Now I come to the second danger of these two marauders which threatens the cottage, the home, and the ordinary people—namely, tyranny. We cannot be blind to the fact that the liberties enjoyed by individual citizens throughout the British Empire are not valid in a considerable number of countries, some of which are very powerful. In these States control is enforced

upon the common people by various kinds of all-embracing police governments. The power of the State is exercised without restraint, either by dictators or by compact oligarchies operating through a privileged party and a political police. It is not our duty at this time when difficulties are so numerous to interfere forcibly in the internal affairs of countries which we have not conquered in war. But we must never cease to proclaim in fearless tones the great principles of freedom and the rights of man which are the joint inheritance of the English-speaking world and which through Magna Carta, the Bill of Rights, the Habeas Corpus, trial by jury, and the English common law find their most famous expression in the American Declaration of Independence.

All this means that the people of any country have the right, and should have the power by constitutional action, by free unfettered elections, with secret ballot, to choose or change the character or form of government under which they dwell; that freedom of speech and thought should reign; that courts of justice, independent of the executive, unbiased by any party, should administer laws which have received the broad assent of large majorities or are consecrated by time and custom. Here are the title deeds of freedom which should lie in every cottage home. Here is the message of the British and American peoples to mankind. Let us preach what we practice—let us practice what we preach. . . .

Now, while still pursuing the method of realizing our overall strategic concept, I come to the crux of what I have traveled here to say. Neither the sure prevention of war, nor the continuous rise of world organization will be gained without what I have called the fraternal association of the English-speaking peoples. This means a special relationship between the British Commonwealth and Empire and the United States. Fraternal association requires not only the growing friendship and mutual understanding between our two vast but kindred systems of society, but the continuance of the intimate relationship between our military advisers, leading to common study of potential dangers, the similarity of weapons and manuals of instructions, and to the interchange of officers and cadets at technical colleges. . .

A shadow has fallen upon the scenes so lately lighted by the Allied victory. Nobody knows what Soviet Russia and its Communist International organization intends to do in the immediate future, or what are the limits, if any, to their expansive and proselytizing tendencies. I have a strong admiration and regard for the valiant Russian people and for my wartime comrade, Marshal Stalin. There is deep sympathy and goodwill in Britain— and I doubt not here also—towards the peoples of all the Russias and a resolve to persevere through many differences and rebuffs in establishing lasting friendships. We understand the Russian need to be secure on her western frontiers by the removal of all possibility of German aggression. We welcome Russia to her rightful place among the leading nations of the world. We welcome her flag upon the seas. Above all, we welcome constant, frequent and growing contacts between the Russian people and our own people on both sides of the Atlantic. It is my duty, however, for I am sure you would wish me to state the facts as I see them to you, to place before you certain facts about the present position in Europe.

From Stettin in the Baltic to Trieste in the Adriatic, an iron curtain has descended across the Continent. Behind that line lie all the capitals of the ancient states of Central and Eastern Europe. Warsaw, Berlin, Prague, Vienna, Budapest, Belgrade, Bucharest, and Sofia; all these famous cities and the populations around them lie in what I must call the Soviet sphere, and all are subject, in one form or another, not only to Soviet influence but to a very high and in some cases increasing measure of control from Moscow. Athens alone— Greece with its immortal glories—is free to decide its future at an election under British, American, and French observation. The Russian-dominated Polish Government has been encouraged to make enormous and wrongful inroads upon Germany, and mass expulsions of millions of Germans on a scale grievous and undreamed-of are now taking place. The Communist parties, which were very small in all these Eastern States of Europe, have been raised to preeminence and power far beyond their numbers and are seeking everywhere to obtain totalitarian control. Police governments are prevailing in nearly every case and so far, except in Czechoslovakia, there is no true democracy. . . .

The safety of the world requires a new unity in Europe, from which no nation should be permanently outcast. It is from the quarrels of the strong parent races in Europe that the world wars we have witnessed, or which occurred in former times, have sprung. Twice in our own lifetime we have seen the United States, against their wishes and their traditions, against arguments, the force of which it is impossible not to comprehend, drawn by irresistible forces, into these wars in time to secure the victory of the good cause, but only after frightful slaughter and devastation had occurred. Twice the United States has had to send several millions of its young men across the Atlantic to find the war; but now war can find any nation, wherever it may dwell between dusk and dawn. Surely we should work with conscious purpose for a grand pacification of Europe, within the structure of the United Nations and in accordance with its Charter. That I feel is an open cause of policy of very great importance. . .

. . . [I]n a great number of countries, far from the Russian frontiers and throughout the world, Communist fifth columns are established and work in complete unity and absolute obedience to the directions they receive from the Communist center. Except in the British Commonwealth and in the United States where Communism is in its infancy, the Communist parties or fifth columns constitute a growing challenge and peril to Christian civilization. These are somber facts for anyone to have to recite on the morrow of a victory gained by so much splendid comradeship in arms and in the cause of freedom and democracy; but we should be unwise not to face them squarely while time remains. . . .

From what I have seen of our Russian friends and Allies during the war, I am convinced that there is nothing they admire so much as strength, and there is nothing for which they have less respect than for weakness, especially military weakness. For that reason the old doctrine of a balance of power is unsound. We cannot afford, if we can help it, to work on narrow margins, offering temptations to a trial of strength. If the Western Democracies stand together in strict adherence to the principles of the United Nations Charter, their influence for furthering those principles will be immense and no one is likely to molest them. If however they become divided or falter in their duty and if these all-important years are allowed to slip away then indeed catastrophe may overwhelm us all.

Last time I saw it all coming and I cried aloud to my own fellow-countrymen and to the world, but no one paid any attention. Up till the year 1933 or even 1935, Germany might have been saved from the awful fate which has overtaken her and we might all have been spared the miseries Hitler let loose upon mankind. There never was a war in history easier to prevent by timely action than the one which has just desolated such great areas of the globe. It could have been prevented, in my belief, without the firing of a single shot, and Germany might be powerful, prosperous and honoured today; but no one would listen and one by one we were all sucked into the awful whirlpool. We surely must not let that happen again. This can only be achieved by reaching now, in 1946, a good understanding on all points with Russia under the general authority of the United Nations Organization and by the maintenance of that good understanding through

many peaceful years, by the whole strength of the English-speaking world and all its connections. There is the solution which I respectfully offer to you in this Address to which I have given the title "The Sinews of Peace."

Let no man underrate the abiding power of the British Empire and Commonwealth. Because you see the 46 millions in our island harassed about their food supply, of which they only grow one half, even in war-time, or because we have difficulty in restarting our industries and export trade after six years of passionate war effort, do not suppose that we shall not come through these dark years of privation as we have come through the glorious years of agony, or that half a century from now you will not see 70 or 80 millions of Britons spread about the world and united in defence of our traditions, our way of life, and of the world causes which you and we espouse. If the population of the English-speaking Commonwealths be added to that of the United States, with all that such cooperation implies in the air, on the sea, all over the globe, and in science and in industry, and in moral force, there will be no quivering, precarious balance of power to offer its temptation to ambition or adventure. On the contrary there will be an overwhelming assurance of security. If we adhere faithfully to the Charter of the United Nations and walk forward in sedate and sober strength, seeking no one's land or treasure, seeking to lay no arbitrary control upon the thoughts of men, if all British moral and material forces and convictions are joined with your own in fraternal association, the high roads of the future will be clear, not only for us but for all, not only for our time but for a century to come.

Study Question

It is possible to distinguish a number of motives in Churchill's speech. What do you believe to be the most important of these?

Joseph Stalin

The following interview appeared in the 14 March 1946 edition of Pravda, *the official newspaper of the Communist Party of the Soviet Union (CPSU). The interview deals directly with the issues raised by Winston Churchill in his "Iron Curtain" speech. In reading Stalin's response, keep in mind the position* *of both western and Soviet forces in early 1946, as well as all of the prior agreements with respect to the division of Europe.*

Document Source: Joseph Stalin, "Response to Churchill, 14 March 1946." *Pravda*, 14 March 1946. Available online: http://www.cnn.com/SPECIALS/cold.war/episodes/02/

Response to Churchill, 14 March 1946

Recently one of *Pravda's* correspondents turned to Comrade Stalin, asking for an explanation of a series of questions regarding Mr Churchill's speech. Comrade Stalin had given respective explanations, which we publish below in form of the answers to the correspondent's questions.

Question: How do you assess the recent speech of Mr Churchill, which he gave in the United States of America?

Answer: My assessment is, it is a dangerous act, calculated to breed strife between allied countries and make their cooperation more difficult.

Question: Could Mr Churchill's speech be considered as a harm to the progress of peace and security?

Answer: Absolutely, yes. As a matter of fact Mr Churchill is standing now in the position of a warmonger. And here Mr Churchill is not alone—he has many friends not only in England but also in the United States. It ought to be mentioned that in this matter Mr Churchill and his friends strikingly resemble Hitler and his friends. Hitler started the process of unleashing war from the proclamation of a racist theory, according to which only the German-speaking people are a worthy nation. Mr Churchill is starting his process of unleashing war also from a racist theory, stating that only the English-speaking countries are worthy nations,

destined to manage the fate of the world. German racist theory led Hitler and his friends to the conclusion that Germans, as the only worthy nation, should rule the other nations. English racist theory leads Mr Churchill and his friends into the following conclusion: that English-speaking countries, as the only worthy nations, should govern the other nations of the world. As a matter of fact, Mr Churchill and his friends in England and in the United States are presenting the non-English-speaking nations with something like an ultimatum: either voluntarily agree to our rule, and everything will be all right, or a war is unavoidable. But during five years of difficult war nations shed blood for the sake of freedom and independence of their respective countries, and not for the sake of replacing the tyranny of people like Hitler for the tyranny of those like Churchill. Therefore, by all probability, nations which do not speak English, and yet comprise the majority of the world's population, will not conform to the new slavery. The tragedy of Mr Churchill is that he, as a deep-rooted Tory, can not accept this simple and clear truth. Undoubtedly, Mr Churchill's aim is war, a war with the USSR. It is also clear that such a goal of Mr Churchill's is incompatible with the present alliance treaty between England and the USSR. However, Mr Churchill, in order to misguide the readers, has mentioned in between that the term of the Soviet–English Treaty of Mutual Aid and Cooperation could be extended up to 50 years. But how do we combine such a statement of Mr Churchill with his aim to wage war with the USSR, with his prophecy of war against the USSR? It is clear, that those things could not coexist. And if Mr Churchill is simultaneously calling for war against the Soviet Union and mentioning the extension of the Soviet–English treaty for up to 50 years, it means that he is considering this treaty as a piece of paper, needed only as a cover to mask his anti-Soviet position. Therefore, the false announcements of Mr Churchill and his friends in England about extension of the English-Soviet treaty for up to 50 years, and more, could not be taken seriously. Extension of the agreement has no point when one of the sides is violating the treaty and transforming it into only a piece of paper.

Question: How do you assess the part of Mr Churchill's speech where he attacks the democratic governments of our neighboring European countries and where he criticizes good neighborly interrelations established between those countries and the Soviet Union?

Answer: This part of Mr Churchill's speech represents a blend of elements of defamation and elements of rudeness and tactlessness. Mr Churchill states that "Warsaw, Berlin, Prague, Vienna, Budapest, Belgrade, Bucharest, Sophia, all those renowned cities and inhabitants of respective regions are in a Soviet zone and all submit in one way or another not only to the Soviet influence, but also in large degree to the growing control of Moscow." Mr Churchill is qualifying all that as the boundless "expansionist tendencies" of the Soviet Union. There is no need for any special effort to show that Mr Churchill is rudely slandering Moscow and the above-mentioned countries neighboring the USSR. First, it is particularly absurd to talk about the exclusive control of the Soviet Union in Vienna and Berlin, where the Allied Control Councils exist and whose members represent four powers, and where the Soviet Union has only 1/4 of the votes. Occasionally people cannot resist slander, but one must know where to stop. Secondly, the following matters shall not be forgotten. The Germans carried out the invasion into USSR through Finland, Poland, Romania, Bulgaria, and Hungary. Germans were able to carry out the invasion through those countries because at the time, there existed regimes hostile to the Soviet Union. As a result of the German invasion, the Soviet Union irrevocably lost about 7 million people during the conduct of war, German occupation, and due to driving away people for servitude labor. In other words, the Soviet Union lost several times more people than England and United States combined. It is possible that in some places, some are inclined to forget the colossal sacrifices of the Soviet Nation, which ensured the liberation of Europe from Hitler's regime. But the Soviet Union can not forget the sacrifice. Let the question be asked: Is it odd that the Soviet Union, wishing to ensure its safety, in the future works toward having in those countries' governments loyal to the Soviet Union? How could one, in his right mind, qualify those peaceful measures of the Soviet Union as expansionist tendencies of our country? Further Mr Churchill states that the Polish government, being under Russia's rule, was encouraged to greatly and unfairly encroach upon Germany. Here, every single word is rude, offensive slander. Contemporary, democratic Poland is ruled by outstanding people. By their actions they proved their ability to defend the interests and dignity of their Motherland, which their predecessors were unable to do. On what basis does Mr Churchill state that the government of contemporary Poland has allowed their country to be supervised by members of any given foreign regime? Are Mr Churchill's words not slanderous here because he is attempting to breed strife between Poland and the Soviet Union? . . . As to Churchill's attacks against USSR in spite of the expansion of Poland's

Western borders with the territories occupied by Germans in the past, here I think he is clearly trying to confuse us. It is known that the resolution regarding Poland's borders was accepted during the three countries' conference in Berlin based on Poland's needs. The Soviet Union repeatedly announced that it counts Poland's needs as fair and just. It is very likely that Mr Churchill is unhappy with this solution. But why does Mr Churchill, who uses all his cards in his attack against the Russian position on this matter, hide from his readers the fact that this arrangement was unanimously agreed upon during the Berlin conference, that it was voted upon not only by the Russians but also by English and Americans? Why does Mr Churchill feel that it is necessary to mislead the people? Mr Churchill further states that "communist parties, which used to have tiny minorities in all Eastern European countries, have become an exclusive power, much more superior than the number of their members, and rush to establish totalitarian control; and military rule in almost all those countries tends to prevail; with the exception of Czechoslovakia, there is no genuine democracy whatsoever." It is known that right now England is ruled by only one party, the Labour Party, and opposition parties have no right to take part in England's government. This Mr Churchill calls true democracy. In Poland, Romania, Yugoslavia, Bulgaria, Hungary, the power is in the hands of a block that is comprised of four to six parties—and opposition, if only it appears more or less loyal, has a secured part in government. This Mr Churchill calls totalitarianism, tyranny, police state. Why? On what basis? Do not expect Mr Churchill to answer. Mr Churchill does not understand what a silly position he put himself in with his loud speeches about totalitarianism, tyranny, and police states. Mr Churchill would like to see Poland ruled by Sosnkowski and Anders, Yugoslavia by Michajlovic and Pavelic, Romania by Prince Stirbey and Radetzky, and Hungary and Austria by some king from the house of Habsburg,

and so on. Mr Churchill wants us to believe that those gentlemen with fascist leanings are able to secure "true democracy." This is Mr Churchill's way of "democracy." Mr Churchill is close to the truth when he speaks about the growing influence of communist parties in Eastern Europe. But it shall be mentioned that he is not exactly correct. Influence of communist parties grew not only in Eastern Europe but almost in all European countries, where fascism once ruled (Italy, Germany, Hungary, Bulgaria, Romania, Ukraine), or where the German, Italian, or Hungarian occupation took place (France, Belgium, Holland, Norway, Denmark, Poland, Czechoslovakia, Yugoslavia, Greece, Soviet Union, etc.) The growing influence of communists shall not be taken as a coincidence. It represents a fully normal phenomenon. Influence of the communists grows because during the hard years of fascist rule in Europe, communists displayed themselves as dependable, brave, self-sacrificing fighters against the fascist regime, and for freedom of nations. Mr Churchill sometimes mentions in his speeches about "common people from simple houses" brotherly patting them on their shoulders and pretending to be one of them. But those people are not that simple as first impressions suggest. They, the "common people," have their needs, their politics, and they know how to stand for their interests. It was they, the millions of "common people" in England, who balloted out Mr Churchill and his party giving their votes to the Labourites. It was they, the millions of "common people," who isolated the reactionaries, the supporters of cooperation with fascism, and preferred leftist, democratic parties in Europe. It was they, the millions of "common people," who tested the communists in flames of war and resistance against fascism and concluded that communists fully deserve the trust of the nation. This is how the influence of communists in Europe has grown. This is the rule of historic development. Of course, Mr Churchill does not like this kind of development, and he sounds the alarm, appealing to the use of power. But he also did not like the emergence of the Soviet regime in Russia after the First World War. Then he also sounded the alarm and organized the campaign of 14 states against Russia, trying to make true his goal of turning back the wheel of history. But history proved to be stronger than Churchill's intervention; and quixotic attempts of Churchill led to the point where he had experienced full defeat. I don't know if after the Second World War Mr Churchill and his friends will succeed with the new campaign against "Eastern Europe,"

but even if they succeed—which is not very likely, because millions of "common people" are on guard for the cause of peace—it can surely be said that they also will be beaten as they were beaten 26 years ago.

Study Question

Both Churchill and Stalin rely heavily on propaganda and distortion of the truth in their accounts. Based on what is now known of postwar events, whose analysis now seems to contain more valid points?

Harry S. Truman

Harry S. Truman (1884–1972) assumed the presidency of the United States on the death of Franklin Roosevelt in April 1945. He would be elected in his own right in November 1948. Already, at the Potsdam Conference in July 1945, it was evident that Truman would take a less conciliatory approach towards Joseph Stalin and the Soviet Union than had Roosevelt. Truman's growing determination to resist communism led him to consider a far greater degree of overt international involvement

than had been traditional for the United States. The difficulty, however, lay in convincing an increasingly isolationist Congress that far-ranging global commitments were essential to American security and prosperity. On 12 March 1947, faced with the imminent withdrawal of British support to the Greeks, Truman delivered the following speech to Congress.

Document Source: Harry S. Truman, "The Truman Doctrine," Truman Papers. Harry S. Truman Library and Museum. www.trumanlibrary.org

The Truman Doctrine

Mr President, Mr Speaker, Members of the Congress of the United States:

The gravity of the situation which confronts the world today necessitates my appearance before a joint session of the Congress. The foreign policy and the national security of this country are involved. One aspect of the present situation, which I present to you at this time for your consideration and decision, concerns Greece and Turkey. The United States has received from the Greek Government an urgent appeal for financial and

economic assistance. Preliminary reports from the American Economic Mission now in Greece and reports from the American Ambassador in Greece corroborate the statement of the Greek Government that assistance is imperative if Greece is to survive as a free nation. . . .

The very existence of the Greek state is today threatened by the terrorist activities of several thousand armed men, led by Communists, who defy the government's authority at a number of points, particularly along the northern boundaries. A Commission appointed by the United

Nations Security Council is at present investigating disturbed conditions in northern Greece and alleged border violations along the frontiers between Greece on the one hand and Albania, Bulgaria, and Yugoslavia on the other.

Meanwhile, the Greek Government is unable to cope with the situation. The Greek army is small and poorly equipped. It needs supplies and equipment if it is to restore the authority of the government throughout Greek territory. Greece must have assistance if it is to become a self-supporting and self-respecting democracy. The United States must supply that assistance. We have already extended to Greece certain types of relief and economic aid. But these are inadequate. There is no other country to which democratic Greece can turn. No other nation is willing and able to provide the necessary support for a democratic Greek government.

The British Government, which has been helping Greece, can give no further financial or economic aid after March 31st. Great Britain finds itself under the necessity of reducing or liquidating its commitments in several parts of the world, including Greece.

We have considered how the United Nations might assist in this crisis. But the situation is an urgent one, requiring immediate action, and the United Nations and its related organizations are not in a position to extend help of the kind that is required. . . .

Greek's [sic] neighbor, Turkey, also deserves our attention. The future of Turkey, as an independent and economically sound state, is clearly no less important to the freedom-loving peoples of the world than the future of Greece. The circumstances in which Turkey finds itself today are considerably different from those of Greece. Turkey has been spared the disasters that have beset Greece. And during the war, the United States and Great Britain furnished Turkey with material aid.

Nevertheless, Turkey now needs our support. Since the war, Turkey has sought additional financial assistance from Great Britain and the United States for the purpose of effecting that modernization necessary for the maintenance of its national integrity. That integrity is essential to the preservation of order in the Middle East. The British government has informed us that, owing to its own difficulties, it can no longer extend financial or economic aid to Turkey. As in the case of Greece, if Turkey is to have the assistance it needs, the United States must supply it. We are the only country able to provide that help.

I am fully aware of the broad implications involved if the United States extends assistance to Greece and Turkey, and I shall discuss these implications with you at this time. One of the primary objectives of the foreign policy of the United States is the creation of conditions in which we and other nations will be able to work out a way of life free from coercion. This was a fundamental issue in the war with Germany and Japan. Our victory was won over countries which sought to impose their will, and their way of life, upon other nations. . . .

At the present moment in world history nearly every nation must choose between alternative ways of life. The choice is too often not a free one. One way of life is based upon the will of the majority, and is distinguished by free institutions, representative government, free elections, guarantees of individual liberty, freedom of speech and religion, and freedom from political oppression. The second way of life is based upon the will of a minority forcibly imposed upon the majority. It relies upon terror and oppression, a controlled press and radio, fixed elections, and the suppression of personal freedoms.

I believe that it must be the policy of the United States to support free peoples who are resisting attempted subjugation by armed minorities or by outside pressures.

I believe that we must assist free peoples to work out their own destinies in their own way.

I believe that our help should be primarily through economic and financial aid which is essential to economic stability and orderly political processes.

The world is not static, and the status quo is not sacred. But we cannot allow changes in the status quo in violation of the Charter of the United Nations by such methods as coercion, or by such subterfuges as political infiltration. In helping free and independent nations to maintain their freedom, the United States will be giving effect to the principles of the Charter of the United Nations.

It is necessary only to glance at a map to realize that the survival and integrity of the Greek nation are of grave importance in a much wider situation. If Greece should fall under the control of an armed minority, the effect upon its neighbor, Turkey, would be immediate and serious. Confusion and disorder might well spread throughout the entire Middle East. Moreover, the disappearance of Greece as an independent state would have a profound effect upon those countries in Europe whose peoples are struggling against great difficulties to maintain their freedoms and their independence while they repair the damages of war.

It would be an unspeakable tragedy if these countries, which have struggled so long against overwhelming odds, should lose that victory for which they sacrificed so much. Collapse of free institutions and loss of independence would be disastrous not only for them but for the world. Discouragement and possibly failure would quickly be the lot of neighboring peoples striving to maintain their freedom and independence.

Should we fail to aid Greece and Turkey in this fateful hour, the effect will be far reaching to the West as well as to the East.

We must take immediate and resolute action. I therefore ask the Congress to provide authority for assistance to Greece and Turkey in the amount of $400,000,000 for the period ending 30 June 1948. In requesting these funds, I have taken into consideration the maximum amount of relief assistance which would be furnished to Greece out of the $350,000,000 which I recently requested that the Congress authorize for the prevention of starvation and suffering in countries devastated by the war.

In addition to funds, I ask the Congress to authorize the detail of American civilian and military personnel to Greece and Turkey, at the request of those countries, to assist in the tasks of reconstruction, and for the purpose of supervising the use of such financial and material assistance as may be furnished. . . .

This is a serious course upon which we embark. I would not recommend it except that the alternative is much more serious. The United States contributed $341,000,000,000 towards winning World War II. This is an investment in world freedom and world peace. The assistance that I am recommending for Greece and Turkey amounts to little more than 1 tenth of 1 percent of this investment. It is only common sense that we should safeguard this investment and make sure that it was not in vain. The seeds of totalitarian regimes are nurtured by misery and want. They spread and grow in the evil soil of poverty and strife. They reach their full growth when the hope of a people for a better life has died.

We must keep that hope alive.

The free peoples of the world look to us for support in maintaining their freedoms. If we falter in our leadership, we may endanger the peace of the world. And we shall surely endanger the welfare of our own nation.

Great responsibilities have been placed upon us by the swift movement of events.

I am confident that the Congress will face these responsibilities squarely.

Study Question

What did Truman mean when he referred to "armed minorities or outside pressures"?

Joseph McCarthy

American suspicions regarding Soviet intentions in the postwar world seemed to be confirmed by the events of the period 1945 to 1949. When, in 1949, Mao Zedong's communist forces defeated Nationalist China, paranoia in the United States ran rampant. Senator Joseph R. McCarthy (1908–1957), a Republican from Wisconsin, emerged as one of the most radical anti-communists in the United States government. "McCarthyism" reached its height in the early 1950s, as politicians, writers, intellectuals, and actors were brought before the House Un-American Activities Committee and accused of being communist sympathizers. In 1954,

when McCarthy accused the United States Army of harbouring Communists, the Army fought back and forced McCarthy to defend his groundless accusations. In December 1954 the United States Senate voted 67 to 22 to censure McCarthy. In the following speech, made before the US Senate on 20 February 1950,[1] McCarthy began his crusade against what he believed to be the "Reds" in the US government.

Document Source: Joseph McCarthy, "On Communists in Government," *Major Speeches and Debates of Senator Joe McCarthy Delivered in the United States Senate, 1950–1951* (Washington, DC: US Government Printing Office, 1953), 7–8, 11–14.

On Communists in Government

Ladies and gentlemen, tonight as we celebrate the one hundred and forty-first birthday of one of the greatest men in American history, I would like to be able to talk about what a glorious day today is in the history of the world. As we celebrate the birth of this man who with his whole heart and soul hated war, I would like to be able to speak of peace in our time, of war being outlawed, and of world-wide disarmament. These would be truly appropriate things to be able to mention as we celebrate the birthday of Abraham Lincoln. . . .

Five years after a world war has been won, men's hearts should anticipate a long peace, and men's minds should be free from the heavy weight that comes with war. But this is not such a period—for this is not a period of peace. This is a time of the "cold war." This is a time when all the world is split into two vast, increasingly hostile armed camps—a time of a great armaments race. . . .

Six years ago, at the time of the first conference to map out the peace—Dumbarton Oaks[2]—there was within the Soviet orbit 180,000,000 people. Lined up on the antitotalitarian side

there were in the world at that time roughly 1,625,000,000 people. Today, only six years later, there are 800,000,000 people under the absolute domination of Soviet Russia—an increase of over 400 per cent. On our side, the figure has shrunk to around 500,000,000. In other words, in less than six years the odds have changed from 9 to 1 in our favor to 8 to 5 against us. This indicates the swiftness of the tempo of Communist victories and American defeats in the cold war. As one of our outstanding historical figures once said, "When a great democracy is destroyed, it will not be because of enemies from without, but rather because of enemies from within."

The truth of this statement is becoming terrifyingly clear as we see this country each day losing on every front.

At war's end we were physically the strongest nation on earth and, at least potentially, the most powerful intellectually and morally. Ours could have been the honor of being a beacon on the desert of destruction, a shining living proof that civilization was not yet ready to destroy itself.

Unfortunately, we have failed miserably and tragically to arise to the opportunity.

The reason why we find ourselves in a position of impotency is not because our only powerful potential enemy has sent men to invade our shores, but rather because of the traitorous actions of those who have been treated so well by this Nation. It has not been the less fortunate or members of minority groups who have been selling this Nation out, but rather those who have had all the benefits that the wealthiest nation on earth has had to offer—the finest homes, the finest college education, and the finest jobs in Government we can give.

This is glaringly true in the State Department. There the bright young men who are born with silver spoons in their mouths are the ones who have been the worst. . . .

Now I know it is very easy for anyone to condemn a particular bureau or department in general terms. Therefore, I would like to cite one rather unusual case—the case of a man who has done much to shape our foreign policy.

When Chiang Kai-shek was fighting our war, the State Department had in China a young man named John S. Service. His task, obviously, was not to work for the communization of China. Strangely, however, he sent official reports back to the State Department urging that we torpedo our ally Chiang Kai-shek and stating, in effect, that communism was the best hope of China.

Later, this man—John Service—was picked up by the Federal Bureau of Investigation for turning over to the Communists secret State Department information. Strangely, however, he was never prosecuted. However, Joseph Grew, the Under Secretary of State, who insisted on his prosecution, was forced to resign. Two days after Grew's successor, Dean Acheson, took over as Under Secretary of State, this man—John Service—who had been picked up by the FBI and who had previously urged that communism was the best hope of China, was not only reinstated in the State Department but promoted. And finally, under Acheson, placed in charge of all placements and promotions.

Today, ladies and gentlemen, this man Service is on his way to represent the State Department and Acheson in Calcutta—by far and away the most important listening post in the Far East. . . .

Then there was a Mrs Mary Jane Kenny, from the Board of Economic Warfare in the State Department, who was named in an FBI report and in a House committee report as a courier for the Communist Party while working for the Government. And where do you think Mrs Kenny is—she is now an editor in the United Nations Document Bureau. . . .

This, ladies and gentlemen, gives you somewhat of a picture of the type of individuals who have been helping to shape our foreign policy. In my opinion the State Department, which is one of the most important government departments, is thoroughly infested with Communists.

I have in my hand 57 cases[3] of individuals who would appear to be either card carrying

"I HAVE HERE IN MY HAND ----"

American political cartoonist Herb Block captures the hysterical nature of McCarthy's accusations.

A 1954 Herblock Cartoon, © The Herb Block Foundation.

members or certainly loyal to the Communist Party, but who nevertheless are still helping to shape our foreign policy. . . .

This brings us down to the case of one Alger Hiss who is more important not as an individual any more, but rather because he is so representative of a group in the State Department. . . .

If time permitted, it might be well to go into detail about the fact that Hiss was Roosevelt's chief advisor at Yalta when Roosevelt was admittedly in ill health and tired physically and mentally. . . .

According to the then Secretary of State Stettinius, here are some of the things that Hiss helped to decide at Yalta. (1) The establishment of a European High Commission; (2) the treatment of Germany—this you will recall was the conference at which it was decided that we would occupy Berlin with Russia occupying an area completely circling the city, which, as you know, resulted in the Berlin airlift which cost 31 American lives; (3) the Polish question; . . . 6) Iran; (7) China—here's where we gave away Manchuria; (8) Turkish Straits question; (9) international trusteeships; (10) Korea. . . .

As you hear this story of high treason, I know that you are saying to yourself, "Well, why doesn't the Congress do something about it?" Actually, ladies and gentlemen, one of the important reasons for the graft, the corruption, the dishonesty, the disloyalty, the treason in high Government positions—one of the most important reasons why this continues is a lack of moral uprising on the part of the 140,000,000 American people. In the light of history, however, this is not hard to explain.

It is the result of an emotional hang-over and a temporary moral lapse which follows every war. It is the apathy of evil which people who have been subjected to the tremendous evils of war feel. As the people of the world see mass murder, the destruction of defenseless and innocent people, and all of the crime and lack of morals which go with war, they become numb and apathetic. It has always been thus after war.

However, the morals of our people have not been destroyed. They still exist. This cloak of numbness and apathy has only needed a spark to rekindle them. Happily, this spark has finally been supplied.

As you know, very recently the Secretary of State proclaimed his loyalty to a man [Hiss] guilty of what has always been considered as the most abominable of all crime—of being a traitor to the people who gave him a position of great trust. The Secretary of State in attempting to justify his continued devotion to the man who sold out the Christian world to the atheistic world, referred to Christ's Sermon on the Mount as a justification and reason therefore, and the reaction of the American people to this would have made the heart of Abraham Lincoln happy.

When this pompous diplomat in striped pants, with a phony British accent, proclaimed to the American people that Christ on the Mount endorsed communism, high treason, and betrayal of a sacred trust, the blasphemy was so great that it awakened the dormant indignation of the American people.

He has lighted the spark which is resulting in a moral uprising and will end only when the whole sorry mess of twisted, warped thinkers are swept from the national scene so that we may have a new birth of national honesty and decency in Government.

Notes

1. McCarthy had already given a more radical version of this speech to the Women's Club in Wheeling, West Virginia, on 9 February.
2. This was the conference that ultimately led to the creation of the United Nations.
3. In the Wheeling speech McCarthy claimed that there were in fact 205 names on his list and brandished a piece of paper as apparent proof. There was, however, no such list and pundits have suggested that he was holding up his laundry list.

Study Question

How much *specific* evidence is contained in McCarthy's speech?

Central Committee of the All-Union Communist Party

The propaganda war between the United States and Soviet Union accelerated in the early 1950s, exacerbated by Stalin's growing paranoia and rising Cold War tensions. New regulations dictated the nature of Soviet press coverage of the ongoing Cold War, placing particular emphasis on the peaceful nature of Soviet foreign policy and the superiority of socialism over capitalism.

The directive which follows was issued to all newspapers by the Central Committee of the Communist Party in September 1952, just six months before Stalin's death.

Document Source: Rossiskii Tsentr Khraneniia i Izucheniia Dokumentov Noveishei Istorii (RTsKhIDNI), Fond 17, op.132, d.507, ll.18–19; obtained and translated by Nigel Gould-Davies. Cold War International History Project: http://digitalarchive.wilsoncenter.org/document/110399

Shortcomings of the Press

[September 1952]

Draft
RESOLUTION OF THE CC VKP(b)[1]
On shortcomings in the treatment of the struggle for peace by the press

The CC VKP(b) notes that serious shortcomings and mistakes have been permitted of late in the coverage of the struggle for peace in a series of central and local newspapers and journals.

Comprehensive and thorough propaganda of the struggle for peace and of the successes of the movement of supporters of peace is frequently substituted in the press by the publication of superficial materials full of pacifist arguments. The movement of supporters of peace is often portrayed in these materials as an organization of people who hate all war, and not as a force that is capable of averting imperialist war and of giving a decisive rebuff to imperialist aggressors. Certain newspapers and journals, in explaining the peaceful character of the foreign policy of the Soviet Union, inadequately mobilize Soviet people to raise their vigilance against the intrigues of imperialist aggressors, weakly link the struggle for peace with the might of the Soviet Union, and are carried away by outward symbols, publishing images of doves, primitive drawings and pacifistic stories and poems that have little value. In the press the basic theses of Leninism on the origin and character of wars under imperialism are explained in insufficient depth, the designs of the Americo-English imperialists who are conducting an aggressive policy of unleashing a new war are poorly unmasked, and the profound contradictions in the camp of the imperialist aggressors are not properly reflected.

The CC VKP(b) resolves:

1. To oblige the editorial staff of the central and local newspapers, and also the staff of social-political and literary-artistic journals, to eliminate the shortcomings in the propaganda of the struggle for peace noted in this resolution.

2. To require the editorial staff of newspapers and journals to improve the coverage of the struggle for peace, bearing in mind the necessity of raising the political and labour activity of the masses and their vigilance against the intrigues of imperialist

aggressors, and of mobilizing the workers to selfless labour, overfulfillment of production plans, and improvement of work in all spheres of economic and cultural construction. In the press it is necessary to unmask the criminal machinations of the war hawks—their mendacious, ostensible peacefulness in word, their aggressive measures and plans in deed. The successes of the movement of supporters of peace and the growth of the forces of the international camp of peace, democracy and socialism should be fully reflected in the pages of newspapers and journals. It is necessary to explain that the Soviet peace-loving foreign policy relies on the might of the Soviet state and, that reinforcing its might with their creative labour, Soviet people are strengthening the security of the people of our country and the cause of peace in the whole world, and that a new world war, if it is unleashed by the imperialist aggressors, can lead only to the collapse of the capitalist system and its replacement by the socialist system.

3.   To instruct the Department of Propaganda and Agitation of the CC VKP(b) and the Foreign Policy Commission of the CC VKP(b) to carry out the following measures:

a)   to conduct a meeting of editors of central newspapers and of social-political and literary-artistic journals, to discuss measures for eliminating shortcomings

in the coverage in the press of the struggle for peace.

b)   jointly with the All-Union Society for the Dissemination of Political and Scientific Knowledge to organize the reading of lectures explaining the Marxist-Leninist teaching on the character, sources, and causes of wars, on the significance of an organized front of peace in the struggle for the preservation of peace against those who seek to ignite a new war, on the sharpening of the general crisis of capitalism in the postwar period, and on other subjects.

4.   To oblige *Gospolitzdat*[2] in the next one to two months to publish in mass editions works of Lenin and Stalin devoted to Marxist-Leninist teachings on wars, on the defence of the fatherland, and on the struggle for peace.

Notes

1. CC VKP(b) stands for Central Committee of the All-Union Communist Party (Bolsheviks); in late 1952 this would be renamed Communist Party of the Soviet Union (CPSU).
2. *Gospolitzdat* was the publishing arm of the Communist Party.

Study Question

Based on the points raised in the "Iron Curtain Speech" and "Truman Doctrine," how accurate is the claim in this directive that the Americans and British were waging a new "war" against the Soviet Union?

Nikita Khrushchev

In February 1956 Nikita Khrushchev seized the opportunity to develop his own support base by presenting himself as the one man willing to speak out against Stalin. Khrushchev later acknowledged that the "secret" *speech was leaked to several outside Communist Parties, including the Polish Communist Party, which in turn passed the document along to the American intelligence community. The speech had a profound impact on the communist world. In the Soviet Union it ushered in the era of de-Stalinization; in Eastern Europe it triggered nationalist uprisings; and, in the United States it led to a brief thaw in relations between the two superpowers.*

Document Source: Nikita Khrushchev, "Special Report to the 20th Congress of the Communist Party of the Soviet Union," *The New Leader* (1956): 57–9, 512–21, & 565. Available at http://www.marxists .org/archive/khrushchev/1956/02/24.htm

Secret Speech

Comrades! In the report of the Central Committee of the Party at the XXth Congress, in a number of speeches by delegates to the Congress, as also formerly during the plenary CC/CPSU sessions, quite a lot has been said about the cult of the individual and about its harmful consequences.

After Stalin's death the Central Committee of the Party began to implement a policy of explaining concisely and consistently that it is impermissible and foreign to the spirit of Marxism-Leninism to elevate one person, to transform him into a superman possessing supernatural characteristics akin to those of a god. Such a man supposedly knows everything, sees everything, thinks for everyone, can do anything, is infallible in his behaviour.

Such a belief about a man, and specifically about Stalin, was cultivated among us for many years.

The objective of the present report is not a thorough evaluation of Stalin's life and activity. Concerning Stalin's merits, an entirely sufficient number of books, pamphlets and studies had already been written in his lifetime. The role of Stalin in the preparation and execution of the Socialist Revolution, in the Civil War, and in the fight for the construction of Socialism in our country is universally known. Everyone knows this well. At the present we are concerned with a question which has immense importance for the Party now and for the future—with how the cult of the person of Stalin has been gradually growing, the cult which became at a certain specific stage the source of a whole series of exceedingly serious and grave perversions of

Party principles, of Party democracy, of revolutionary legality . . .

The great modesty of the genius of the revolution, Vladimir Ilyich Lenin, is known. Lenin had always stressed the role of the people as the creator of history, the directing and organizational role of the Party as a living and creative organism, and also the role of the Central Committee. . . .

While ascribing great importance to the role of the leaders and organizers of the masses, Lenin at the same time mercilessly stigmatized every

Nikita Khrushchev listens to debates in the United Nations General Assembly in September 1960.

U.S. News and World Report Magazine Photograph Collection. Courtesy of the Library of Congress, Prints and Photographs Division (LC-USZ62-134155).

manifestation of the cult of the individual, inexorably combated the foreign-to-Marxism views about a "hero" and a "crowd" and countered all efforts to oppose a "hero" to the masses and to the people. . . .

During Lenin's life the Central Committee of the Party was a real expression of collective leadership of the Party and of the nation. Being a militant Marxist-revolutionist, always unyielding in matters of principle, Lenin never imposed by force his views upon his co-workers. He tried to convince; he patiently explained his opinions to others. Lenin always diligently observed that the norms of Party life were realized, that the Party statute was enforced, that the Party congresses and the plenary sessions of the Central Committee took place at proper intervals.

In addition to the great accomplishments of V.I. Lenin for the victory of the working class and of the working peasants, for the victory of our Party and for the application of the ideas of scientific Communism to life, his acute mind expressed itself also in this, that he detected in Stalin in time those negative characteristics which resulted later in grave consequences. Fearing for the future fate of the Party and of the Soviet nation, V.I. Lenin made a completely correct characterization of Stalin, pointing out that it was necessary to consider the question of transferring Stalin from the position of the Secretary General because of the fact that Stalin is excessively rude, that he does not have a proper attitude toward his comrades, that he is capricious and abuses his power.

In December 1922, in a letter to the Party Congress, Vladimir Ilyich wrote: "After taking over the position of Secretary General Comrade Stalin accumulated in his hands immeasurable power and I am not certain whether he will be always able to use this power with the required care."

This letter—a political document of tremendous importance, known in the Party history as Lenin's "testament"—was distributed among the delegates to the XXth Party Congress. You have read it, and will undoubtedly read it again more than once. You might reflect on Lenin's plain words, in which expression is given to Vladimir Ilyich's anxiety concerning the Party, the people, the State, and the future direction of Party policy.

Vladimir Ilyich said: "Stalin is excessively rude, and this defect, which can be freely tolerated in our midst and in contacts among us Communists, becomes a defect which cannot be tolerated in one holding the position of the Secretary General. Because of this, I propose that the comrades consider the method by which Stalin would be removed from this position and by which another man would be selected for it, a man, who above all, would differ from Stalin in only one quality, namely, greater tolerance, greater loyalty, greater kindness and a more considerate attitude toward the comrades, a less capricious temper, etc.". . .

These negative characteristics of his developed steadily and during the last years acquired an absolutely insufferable character.

As later events have proven, Lenin's anxiety was justified: in the first period after Lenin's death Stalin still paid attention to his advice, but later he began to disregard the serious admonitions of Vladimir Ilyich.

When we analyze the practice of Stalin in regard to the direction of the Party and of the country, when we pause to consider everything which Stalin perpetrated, we must be convinced that Lenin's fears were justified. The negative characteristics of Stalin, which, in Lenin's time, were only incipient, transformed themselves during the last years into a grave abuse of power by Stalin, which caused untold harm to our Party.

We have to consider seriously and analyze correctly this matter in order that we may preclude any possibility of a repetition in any form whatever of what took place during the life of Stalin, who absolutely did not tolerate collegiality in leadership and in work, and who practiced brutal violence, not only toward everything which opposed him, but also toward that which seemed, to his capricious and despotic character, contrary to his concepts.

Stalin acted not through persuasion, explanation, and patient cooperation with people, but by imposing his concepts and demanding absolute submission to his opinion. Whoever opposed this concept or tried to prove his viewpoint, and the correctness of his position, was doomed to removal from the leading collective and to subsequent moral and physical annihilation. This was especially true during the period following the XVIIth Party Congress, when many prominent Party leaders and rank-and-file Party workers, honest and dedicated to the cause of Communism, fell victim to Stalin's despotism. . . .

It was determined that of the 139 members and candidates of the Party's Central Committee who were elected at the XVIIth Congress, 98 persons, i.e., 70 per cent, were arrested and shot (mostly in 1937–38). (*Indignation in the hall.*) What was the composition of the delegate to the 17th Congress? It is known that 80 per cent of the voting participants of the 17th Congress joined the Party during the years of conspiracy before the Revolution and during the civil war; i.e. meaning before 1921. By social origin the basic mass of the delegates to the Congress were workers (60 per cent of the voting members).

For this reason, it was inconceivable that a congress so composed would have elected a Central Committee a majority of whom would prove to be enemies of the party. . . .

The same fate met not only the Central Committee members, but also the majority of the delegates to the XVIIth Congress. Of 1,966 delegates with either voting or advisory rights, 1,108 persons were arrested on charges of anti-revolutionary crimes, i.e., decidedly more than a majority. This very fact shows how absurd, wild and contrary to common sense were the charges of counter-revolutionary crimes made out, as we now see against a majority of participants at the XVIIth Congress. (*Indignation in the hall.*)

We should recall that the XVIIth Party Congress is historically known as the Congress of Victors. Delegates to the Congress were active participants in the building of our socialist state, many of them suffered and fought for Party interests during the pre-revolutionary years in the conspiracy and at the Civil War fronts; they fought their enemies valiantly and often nervelessly looked into the face of death. How then can we believe that such people could prove to be "two-faced" and had joined the camps of the enemies of socialism during the era after the political liquidation of Zinovievites, Trotskyites and rightists and after the great accomplishments of socialist construction?

This was the result of the abuse of power by Stalin, who began to use mass terror against Party cadres. . . .

Comrades: We must abolish the cult of the individual decisively, once and for all; we must draw the proper conclusions concerning both ideological-theoretical and practical work.

We are absolutely certain that our Party, armed with the historical resolutions of the XXth Congress, will lead the Soviet people along the Leninist path to new successes, to new victories. (*Tumultuous, prolonged applause*).

Long live the victorious banner of our Party—Leninism! (*Tumultuous, prolonged applause ending in ovation. All rise.*)

Study Question

What, according to Khrushchev, were the most serious crimes of the Stalin era?

Robert McNamara

In 1961 President John F. Kennedy appointed Robert McNamara (1916–2009), the newly designated president of the Ford Motor Company, as his Secretary of Defense. McNamara held the post from 1961 until 1968, during which time he helped to shape America's policy in Vietnam. Like Kennedy, McNamara had virtually no foreign policy experience when he joined the government. Though McNamara would later have serious reservations about American involvement in Vietnam, in 1961, he endorsed many of the common assumptions about the dangers of non-involvement. In particular, McNamara repeated the common argument that non-intervention would lead to the rapid spread of communist influence throughout Southeast Asia.*

Document Source: "Memorandum for the President by McNamara, 8 November 1961." From Gareth Porter, ed., *Vietnam: A History in Documents* (New York: Meridian Books, 1979), 224–5.

Memorandum for the President, 8 November 1961

The basic issue framed by the Taylor Report is whether the US shall:

a. Commit itself to the clear objective of preventing the fall of South Vietnam to Communism, and

b. Support this commitment by necessary immediate military actions and preparations for possible later actions.

The Joint Chiefs, Mr Gilpatric, and I have reached the following conclusions:

1. The fall of South Vietnam to Communism would lead to the fairly rapid expansion of Communist control, or complete accommodation to Communism, in the rest of mainland Southeast Asia and in Indonesia. The strategic implications are wide and, particularly in the Orient, would be extremely serious.

2. The chances are against, probably sharply against, preventing that fall by measures short of the introduction of US forces on a substantial scale. We accept General Taylor's judgment that the various measures proposed by him in short are useful but will not in themselves do the job of restoring confidence and setting Diem on the way to winning his fight.

3. The introduction of a US force of the magnitude of an initial 8,000 men in a flood relief context will be of great help to Diem. However, it will not convince the other side (whether the shots are called from Moscow, Peiping[1] or Hanoi) that we mean business. Moreover, it probably will not tip the scales decisively. We would be almost certain to get increasingly mired down in an inconclusive struggle.

4. The other side can be convinced we mean business only if we accompany the initial force introduction by a clear commitment to the full objective stated above, accompanied by a warning through some channel to Hanoi that continued support of the Viet Cong will lead to punitive retaliation against North Vietnam.

5. If we act in this way, the ultimate possible extent of our military commitment must

be faced. The struggle may be prolonged and Hanoi and Peiping may intervene overtly. In view of the logistic difficulties faced by the other side, we can assume that the maximum US forces required on the ground in Southeast Asia will not exceed 6 divisions, or about 205,000 men, (CINC-PAC Plan 32–59, Phase IV). Our military posture is, or, with the addition of more National Guard or regular Army divisions, can be made, adequate to furnish these forces without serious interference with our present Berlin plans.

6. To accept the stated objective is of course a most serious decision. Military force is not the only element of what must be a most carefully coordinated set of actions. Success will depend on factors many of which are not within our control—notably the conduct of Diem himself and other leaders in the area. Laos will remain a major problem. The domestic political implications of accepting the objective are also grave, although it is our feeling that the country will respond better to a firm initial position than to courses of action that lead us in only gradually, and that in the meantime are sure to involve casualties. The over-all effect on Moscow and Peiping will need careful weighing and may well be mixed; however, permitting South Vietnam to fall can only strengthen and encourage them greatly.

In sum:

a. We do not believe major units of US forces should be introduced in South Vietnam unless we are willing to make an affirmative decision on the issue stated at the start of this memorandum.

b. We are inclined to recommend that we do commit the US to the clear objective of

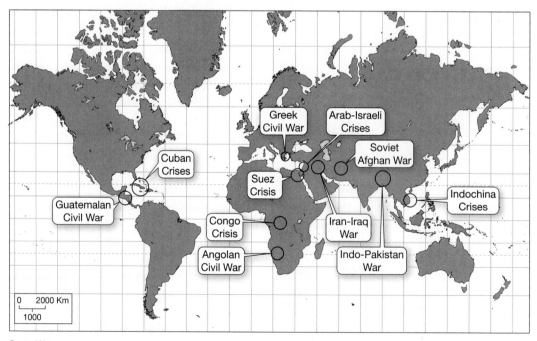

Proxy Wars

preventing the fall of South Vietnam to Communism and that we support this commitment by the necessary military actions.

c. If such a commitment is agreed upon, we support the recommendations of General Taylor as the first steps toward its fulfillment.

Note

1. Beijing.

Study Question

List the major concerns evident in this document. How many of them have to do with the situation inside Vietnam itself?

John F. Kennedy

John F. Kennedy (1917–1963) was elected US president in November 1960 as the Cold War entered a new phase. The paranoia of the McCarthy era had begun to recede, but tensions with the Soviets, under Nikita Khrushchev, remained high. In 1961 alone, Kennedy faced crises in Berlin, Cuba, Vietnam, and the Congo, none of which were resolved to his satisfaction. Thus, Kennedy's determination to take the lead in space exploration and to put a man on the moon—first proposed to Congress in May 1961—can be tied to his need for a clear foreign policy victory over the Soviets. The following speech was delivered in September 1962 at Rice University in Houston, Texas.

Document Source: John F. Kennedy, "On the Space Race," Speech at Rice University, Houston TX. 12 September 1962. *Public Papers of the Presidents of the United States*, Vol. 1, 1962, 669–70.

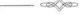

On the Space Race

. . . We meet at a college noted for knowledge, in a city noted for progress, in a state noted for strength, and we stand in need of all three, for we meet in an hour of change and challenge, in a decade of hope and fear, in an age of both knowledge and ignorance. The greater our knowledge increases, the greater our ignorance unfolds.

Despite the striking fact that most of the scientists that the world has ever known are alive and working today, despite the fact that this Nation's own scientific manpower is doubling every 12 years in a rate of growth more than three times that of our population as a whole, despite that, the vast stretches of the unknown and the unanswered and the unfinished still far outstrip our collective comprehension.

No man can fully grasp how far and how fast we have come, but condense, if you will, the 50,000 years of man's recorded history in a time span of but a half-century. Stated in these terms, we know very little about the first 40 years, except at the end of them advanced man had learned to use the skins of animals to cover them. Then about 10 years ago, under this standard, man emerged from his caves to construct other kinds of shelter. Only five years ago man learned to write and use a cart with wheels. Christianity began less than two years ago. The printing press came this year, and then less than two months ago, during this whole 50-year span of human history, the steam engine provided a new source of power. Newton explored the meaning of gravity. Last month electric lights and telephones and automobiles and airplanes became available. Only last week did we develop penicillin and television and nuclear power, and now if America's new spacecraft succeeds in reaching Venus, we will have literally reached the stars before midnight tonight.

This is a breathtaking pace, and such a pace cannot help but create new ills as it dispels old, new ignorance, new problems, new dangers. Surely the opening vistas of space promise high costs and hardships, as well as high reward. . . .

Those who came before us made certain that this country rode the first waves of the industrial revolution, the first waves of modern invention, and the first wave of nuclear power, and this generation does not intend to founder in the backwash of the coming age of space. We mean to be a part of it—we mean to lead it. For the eyes of the world now look into space, to the moon and to the planets beyond, and we have vowed that we shall not see it governed by a hostile flag of conquest, but by a banner of freedom and peace. We have vowed that we shall not see space filled with weapons of mass destruction, but with instruments of knowledge and understanding.

Yet the vows of this Nation can only be fulfilled if we in this Nation are first, and, therefore, we intend to be first. In short, our leadership in science and industry, our hopes for peace and security, our obligations to ourselves as well as others, all require us to make this effort, to solve these mysteries, to solve them for the good of all men, and to become the world's leading space-faring nation.

We set sail on this new sea because there is new knowledge to be gained, and new rights to be won, and they must be won and used for the progress of all people. For space science, like nuclear science and all technology, has no conscience of its own. Whether it will become a force for good or ill depends on man, and only if the United States occupies a position of pre-eminence can we help decide whether this new ocean will be a sea of peace or a new terrifying theater of war. I do not say that we should or will go unprotected against the hostile misuse of space any more than we go unprotected against the hostile use of land or sea, but I do say that space can be explored and mastered without feeding the fires of war, without

repeating the mistakes that man has made in extending his writ around this globe of ours.

There is no strife, no prejudice, no national conflict in outer space as yet. Its hazards are hostile to us all. Its conquest deserves the best of all mankind, and its opportunity for peaceful cooperation may never come again. But why, some say, the moon? Why choose this as our goal? And they may well ask why climb the highest mountain? Why, 35 years ago, fly the Atlantic? Why does Rice play Texas?

We choose to go to the moon. We choose to go to the moon in this decade and do the other things, not because they are easy, but because they are hard, because that goal will serve to organize and measure the best of our energies and skills, because that challenge is one that we are willing to accept, one we are unwilling to postpone, and one which we intend to win, and the others, too.

It is for these reasons that I regard the decision last year to shift our efforts in space from low to high gear as among the most important

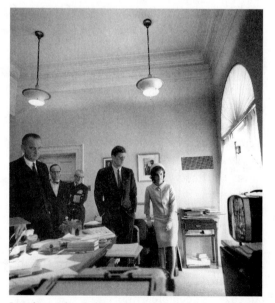

President John F. Kennedy, Jackie Kennedy, and Vice-President Lyndon Johnson watch Mercury astronaut Alan Shepard travel into space.

John F. Kennedy Presidential Library and Museum.

decisions that will be made during my incumbency in the office of the Presidency. . . .

To be sure, we are behind, and will be behind for some time in manned flight. But we do not intend to stay behind, and in this decade, we shall make up and move ahead.

The growth of our science and education will be enriched by new knowledge of our universe and environment, by new techniques of learning and mapping and observation, by new tools and computers for industry, medicine, the home as well as the school. Technical institutions, such as Rice, will reap the harvest of these gains.

And finally, the space effort itself, while still in its infancy, has already created a great number of new companies, and tens of thousands of new jobs. Space and related industries are generating new demands in investment and skilled personnel, and this city and this state, and this region, will share greatly in this growth. What was once the furthest outpost on the old frontier of the West will be the furthest outpost on the new frontier of science and space. Houston, your city of Houston, with its Manned Spacecraft Center, will become the heart of a large scientific and engineering community. During the next five years the National Aeronautics and Space Administration expects to double the number of scientists and engineers in this area, to increase its outlays for salaries and expenses to $60 million a year; to invest some $200 million in plant and laboratory facilities; and to direct or contract for new space efforts over $1 billion from this center in this city. . . .

. . . I think we're going to do it, and I think that we must pay what needs to be paid. I don't think we ought to waste any money, but I think we ought to do the job. And this will be done in the decade of the Sixties. It may be done while some of you are still here at school at this college and university. It will be done during the terms of office of some of the people who sit here on this platform. But it will be done. And it will be done before the end of this decade.

And I am delighted that this university is playing a part in putting a man on the moon as part of a great national effort of the United States of America.

Many years ago the great British explorer George Mallory, who was to die on Mount Everest, was asked why did he want to climb it. He said, "Because it is there."

Well, space is there, and we're going to climb it, and the moon and the planets are there, and new hopes for knowledge and peace are there. And, therefore, as we set sail we ask God's blessing on the most hazardous and dangerous and greatest adventure on which man has ever embarked.

Thank you.

Study Question

Which elements of Kennedy's argument can be seen to have been influenced by Cold War concerns?

Web Resources

The Diefenbunker: Canada's Cold War Museum/Musée canadien de la Guerre froide
    http://www.diefenbunker.ca/
Harry S. Truman Library & Museum: Ideological Foundations of the Cold War
    http://www.trumanlibrary.org/whistlestop/study_collections/coldwar
Cold War International History Project
    http://www.wilsoncenter.org/index.cfm?fuseaction=topics.home&topic
    _id=1409
The National Security Archive: George Washington University
    http://www.gwu.edu/~nsarchiv

Recommended Reading

Ray Bradbury, *Fahrenheit 451* (New York: Simon & Schuster, 2003). *Fahrenheit 451* is a futuristic 1953 novel touching on the censorship of thought, the power of the state, and the unquestioning acceptance of authority. It tells of one man's struggle with the temptation to discover the past through his access to banned books, and of the resistance movement that resorts to memorizing books to prevent their contents from being forgotten.

Ha Jin, *War Trash* (New York: Pantheon, 2004). Set in 1951, *War Trash* is based on historical accounts of Chinese POWs held by the Americans during the Korean War. The POWs find themselves longing for home, but that home was being profoundly transformed by Mao's revolution. The main character, Yu Yuan, acts as a translator in the POW camps and finds himself trapped between Communist and Nationalist POW factions.

Arthur Miller, *The Crucible* (New York: Penguin, 2003). Arthur Miller's 1953 play is based on the historical events and people involved in the 1692 Salem witch trials. It stands as a powerful allegory for the McCarthy era anti-communist paranoia and hysteria; Miller himself was called to testify before the House Un-American Activities Committee (HUAC). *The Crucible* examines the consequences of political policy based on a misplaced sense of good and evil.

B.F. Skinner, *Walden Two* (New York: Prentice Hall, 1976). A fictional work, drawn heavily from the author's theories of behaviourism, *Walden Two* focuses on a modern utopian community where problems are solved through the scientific study of human behaviour.

John Wyndham, *The Day of the Triffids* (Madison, WI: Turtleback Books, 2004). Survivors of an apocalyptic event discover that the earth is now dominated by triffids—human creations that have set out to destroy their human prey. Wyndham's 1951 novel relates to the Cold War, the development of atomic energy, paranoia with respect to Soviet intentions, and the potentially devastating consequences of bio-engineering.

Recommended Viewing

Den Pobedivshey Strany [*A Day in the Country of Victory*] (USSR, 1947). Director: Ilya Kopalin/Irina Setkina. This 68-minute documentary-style film was intended to capture a single day, 14 August 1947, in the lives of typical Soviet citizens in order to provide a visual endorsement of life under the Stalinist system, with typical propaganda images of industry, agriculture, and the military.

Red Menace (USA, 1949). Director: R.G. Springsteen. *Red Menace* remains the classic American propaganda film about the horrors of communist infiltration. It demonstrates all of the stereotypes of the era regarding the communist menace to the United States and to the rest of the "free world."

Invasion of the Body Snatchers (USA, 1956). Director: Don Siegel (B&W). *Invasion of the Body Snatchers* can be seen both as a reflection and condemnation of the anti-communist blacklisting actions of the McCarthy era, and as a reflection and denunciation of the conformity of 1950s suburbia. Siegel's original bleak ending was replaced by the studio, but can now be seen in restored director's cuts of the film.

Dr Strangelove (UK/USA, 1964). Director: Stanley Kubrick (B&W). An outstanding satire of the Cold War paranoia, Kubrick's classic black comedy captures the essential absurdity of mutual assured destruction. Faced with an imminent Armageddon resulting from the actions of a madman, the film focuses on the resulting attempts to prevent the destruction.

Hearts and Minds (USA, 1974). Director: Peter Davis (Documentary). This controversial documentary was released just as the United States withdrew its forces from Vietnam, prior to the fall of Saigon. It contains news footage and interviews with veterans and politicians and focuses on the disastrous "hearts & minds" strategy and the reasons for the near-total failure to achieve this.

The Boys in Company C (USA/Hong Kong, 1977). Director: Sidney J. Furie. *The Boys in Company C* is considered to be one of the most accessible Vietnam war movies. Made in 1977, when tensions about the war remained high, its themes include the futility of the war, demoralization of soldiers, war's impact on idealism, weakness of leadership, and problems of strategy and tactics.

The Atomic Café (USA, 1982). Director: Kevin Rafferty (Documentary). *The Atomic Café*—which was created from 1950s American propaganda film clips—exposes the lies and misinformation propagated by the American government. It remains a strongly relevant commentary on the gullibility of citizens in the face of an ongoing government propaganda barrage.

When Father Was Away On Business (Yugoslavia/Spain, 1985). Director: Emir Kusturica. The political tension of the time period after the break between Stalin and Tito is captured through the eyes of a child whose father has been sentenced to hard labour. The film depicts the subsequent struggles of the fatherless family to maintain their reputation and cope with the day-to-day trials of existence. Kusturica received the Palme d'Or at Cannes in 1985 for this film.

10

China and Japan:
The Re-emergence of Asian Power

At the end of the Pacific War the nation of Japan was utterly devastated. Its economy had been ruined, by the combined cost of fighting over a massive area, the impact of the US strategic bombing campaign, and by poorly chosen economic policies during the war. Japan had been stripped of its colonial empire, had lost most of its army and navy, and was occupied by the United States Army. Subsequently, the emperor was forced to renounce all claims to divinity—the traditional source of his power and respect—and was reduced to a symbolic figurehead. China, meanwhile, had successfully staved off the Japanese forces that had first entered the country in 1931, only to find itself immediately embroiled in a devastating civil war between the governing Nationalist forces and the increasingly popular Communists. Thus, in 1945, neither nation seemed poised to emerge as a major power in the postwar world.

Ultimately the Chinese Communists emerged victorious in their civil war due to a combination of military skill, careful planning, and fortuitous timing; simultaneously poor decision-making and disastrous economic policies undermined the authority of the Nationalist government. Once in power, though, the Communists, under Mao Zedong, faced a multitude of internal and external difficulties. Overt western hostility and a strained relationship with the Soviet Union meant that the Chinese Communist Party (CCP) could count on only irregular external assistance. Meanwhile, the nation had been economically, politically, and socially devastated by nearly two decades of war. An initial move towards rapid heavy industrialization and full collectivization was halted when its toll on the rural areas of China became evident; however, more moderate types of economic reform, though successful in practice, were viewed by more radical members of the Party as a retreat from the revolutionary goals of the Chinese Communist Party.

The perceived threat to the revolutionary aims of the movement, combined with a fear of ongoing bureaucratism and loss of revolutionary momentum, led to the Great Proletarian Cultural Revolution in 1966 and a draconian crackdown on all "bourgeois" influences. In turn, this led to an additional period of socio-economic upheaval as Mao sought to rein in the more extremist elements in the Communist Party. Mao's death in 1976 resulted in a succession struggle that once more postponed any substantial recovery from the disruptions of the late 1960s.

Mao addresses supporters in December 1944. The CCP had gained tremendous popularity in Northern China by this time.

Courtesy of the Franklin D. Roosevelt Library.

The situation stabilized in the late 1970s when Deng Xiaoping announced his intentions to modernize and strengthen the Chinese economy while building closer ties with the nations of the West. In 1980 four coastal cities were designated as special economic zones—areas where capitalist practices were permitted—in order to facilitate this interaction. Deng's successors continued to implement his plan for modernization, and the changes culminated in China's entry into the World Trade Organization in 2001. While China's economic success is indisputable, its political structure has changed little despite localized efforts to bring about a somewhat more representative system.

The American occupation authorities shaped Japan's postwar development profoundly. Under their supervision a new constitution was created in 1947 that confirmed the status of the Emperor as a symbolic figure and created a British-style parliamentary democracy. Universal suffrage was entrenched, as was a new human rights code. The large monopolies, which had fuelled prewar economic growth and which had benefited greatly from wartime expansionism, were dissolved and the rights of unions were guaranteed. Finally, Japan was prohibited from maintaining anything more than a civil defence force.

With the outbreak of the Korean War in 1950, the United States came to view Japan as the only barrier to the ongoing spread of communism in Asia. This led to a rapid shift in focus: from punishing Japan for past transgressions to rebuilding the nation as quickly as possible, under the umbrella of American military protection. Restrictions on economic monopolies were lifted and Japan gained access to the massive American market for its exports. Internally, a high savings rate and low labour costs allowed large-scale government investment in production for export, rather than domestic consumption. Despite the oil crisis of the 1970s and a global turn towards economic protectionism, Japan's economy continued to grow. By 1985 nearly ten per cent of the world's exports were produced by Japan. However, despite the "economic miracle" of the postwar era, by the 1990s Japan's economy began to falter. Productivity declined, unemployment rose, and government deficits soared while successive leaders attempted to shore up unprofitable ventures. By the end of the century the close relationship between government, industry, and banks, which had been so beneficial during the economic boom, became a dangerous liability.

The documents in this section provide an overview of the key developments in both China and Japan. Mao Zedong's views are presented in a speech delivered at the end of the Pacific War, as he contemplated the best approach to defeating the remnants of imperialism and feudalism which continued to restrict China's development. The catastrophic impact of the Cultural Revolution is discussed in Fox Butterfield's interview with Lihua. Excerpts from Deng Xiaoping's speeches reveal his approach to transforming China in the wake of Mao's death. Finally, one woman's view of the failure of the democratic reform movement of the late 1980s is presented in Chai Ling's account of the Tiananmen Square uprising.

Turning to Japan, the Security Treaty which shaped so much of Japan's postwar development is included here. Political scientist Chitoshi Yanaga analyzes the reasons behind Japan's rapid economic recovery and success in the 1960s, while Prime Minister Kakuei Tanaka reflects on the changing international situation facing Japan in the mid-1970s. This chapter concludes with an excerpt from the controversial *New History* textbook, which was published in Japan by an ultra-nationalist group and which led to violent anti-Japanese riots across China.

Mao Zedong

The Chinese Communist Party (CCP) experienced a series of setbacks during its rise to power, including Chiang Kai-shek's attacks during the Northern Expedition and the encirclement campaigns that destroyed the Jiangxi Soviet. However, as the CCP came to be seen as the more effective fighting force during the Sino–Japanese War, its popularity began to increase. Still, Mao Zedong (1893–1976) was aware that the threat of the Guomindang

and the foreign imperialists remained. In June 1945, even as the Sino–Japanese War continued, Mao gave the following speech in order to explain the strategy of the Chinese Communist Party with respect to its two primary enemies: imperialism and feudalism.

Document Source: Mao Zedong, "The Foolish Old Man Who Removed the Mountains." From *Selected Readings from the Work of Mao Tse-tung* (Peking: Foreign Languages Press, 1967), 260–2, 295–6.

The Foolish Old Man Who Removed the Mountains

We have had a very successful congress. We have done three things. First, we have decided on the line of our Party, which is boldly to mobilize the masses and expand the people's forces so that, under the leadership of our Party, they will defeat the Japanese aggressors, liberate the whole people and build a new-democratic China. Second, we have adapted the new Party Constitution. Third, we have elected the leading body of the Party— the Central Committee. Henceforth our task is to lead the whole membership in carrying out the Party line. Ours has been a congress of victory, a congress of unity. The delegates have made excellent comments on the three reports. Many comrades have undertaken self-criticism; with unity as the objective unity has been achieved through self-criticism. This congress is a model of unity, of self-criticism, and of inner-Party democracy.

When the congress closes, many comrades will be leaving for their posts and the various war fronts. Comrades, wherever you go, you should propagate the line of the congress and, through the members of the Party, explain it to the broad masses.

Our aim in propagating the line of the congress is to build up the confidence of the whole Party and the entire people in the certain triumph of the revolution. We must first raise the political consciousness of the vanguard so that, resolute and unafraid of sacrifice, they will surmount every difficulty to win victory. But this is not enough; we must also arouse the political consciousness of the entire people so that they may willingly and gladly fight together with us for victory. We should fire the whole people with the conviction that China belongs not to the reactionaries but to the Chinese people. There is an ancient Chinese fable called "The Foolish Old Man Who Removed the Mountains." It tells of an old man who lived in northern China long, long ago and was known as the Foolish Old Man of North Mountain. His house faced south and beyond his doorway stood the two great peaks, Taihang and Wangwu, obstructing the way. He called his sons, and hoe in hand they began to dig up these mountains with great determination. Another graybeard, known as the Wise Old Man, saw them and said derisively, "How silly of you to do this! It is quite impossible for you few to dig up those two huge mountains." The Foolish Old Man replied, "When I die, my sons will carry on; when they die, there will be my grandsons, and then their sons and grandsons, and so on to infinity. High as they are, the mountains cannot grow any higher and with every bit we dig, they will be that much lower. Why can't we clear them away?" Having refuted the Wise Old Man's wrong view, he went on digging every day, unshaken in his conviction. God was moved by this, and he sent down two angels, who carried the mountains away on their backs. Today, two big mountains lie like a dead weight on the Chinese people. One is imperialism, the other is feudalism. The Chinese Communist Party has long made up its mind to dig them up. We must persevere and work unceasingly, and we, too, will touch God's heart. Our God is none other than the masses of the Chinese people. If they stand up and dig together with us, why can't these two mountains be cleared away?

Yesterday, in a talk with two Americans who were leaving for the United States, I said that the US government was trying to undermine us and this would not be permitted. We oppose the US government's policy of supporting Chiang Kai-shek against the Communists. But we must draw a distinction, firstly, between the people of the United States and their government and, secondly, within the US government between the policy-makers and their subordinates. I said to these two Americans, "Tell the policy-makers in your government that we forbid you Americans to enter the Liberated Areas because your policy is to support Chiang Kai-shek against the Communists, and we have to be on our guard. You can come to the Liberated Areas if your purpose is to fight Japan, but there must first be an agreement. We will not permit you to nose around everywhere. Since Patrick J. Hurley has publicly declared against cooperation with the Chinese Communist Party, why do you still want to come and prowl around in our Liberated Areas?"

The US government's policy of supporting Chiang Kai-shek against the Communists shows the brazenness of the US reactionaries. But all the scheming of the reactionaries, whether Chinese or foreign, to prevent the Chinese people from achieving victory is doomed to failure. The democratic forces are the main current in the world today, while reaction is only a counter-current. The reactionary counter-current is trying to swamp the main current of national independence and people's democracy, but it can never become the main current. Today, there are still three major contradictions in the old world, as Stalin pointed out long ago: first, the contradiction between the proletariat and the bourgeoisie in the imperialist countries; second, the contradiction between the various imperialist powers, and third, the contradiction between the

Mao Zedong meets with US Ambassador Patrick J. Hurley at Mao's Yanan headquarters, during discussions of the postwar CPP/Nationalist relationship, 27 August 1945.

Courtesy of the National Archives (NWDNS-111-SC-360599), http://research.archives.gov/description/531400

colonial and semi-colonial countries and the imperialist metropolitan countries. Not only do these three contradictions continue to exist but they are becoming more acute and widespread. Because of their existence and growth, the time will come when the reactionary anti-Soviet, anti-Communist and anti-democratic counter-current still in existence today will be swept away.

At this moment two congresses are being held in China, the Sixth National Congress of the Kuomintang and the Seventh National Congress of the Communist Party. They have completely different aims: the aim of one is to liquidate the Communist Party and all the other democratic forces in China and thus to plunge China into

darkness; the aim of the other is to overthrow Japanese imperialism and its lackeys, the Chinese feudal forces, and build a new-democratic China and thus to lead China to light. Those two lines are in conflict with each other. We firmly believe that, led by the Chinese Communist Party and guided by the line of its Seventh Congress, the Chinese people will achieve complete victory, while the Kuomintang's counter-revolutionary line will inevitably fail.

> **Study Question**
>
> In what ways did Mao craft this speech so as to appeal to a variety of different audiences?

Fox Butterfield

As China entered the 1960s Mao Zedong had lost both his position as Head of State and most of his influence over policy-making, though he remained head of the Chinese Communist Party. Under Deng Xiaoping, Zhou Enlai, and Liu Shaoqi, China moved towards a more moderate economic and social policy which, while still emphasizing heavy industry and centralized planning, acknowledged the need from some level of material incentives. Gradually Mao became convinced that reactionary elements were seizing control of the revolution and that a massive revitalization was necessary. Thus in 1966, Mao launched an all-out war on "capitalist" elements

in the Party and the country, calling this the Great Proletarian Cultural Revolution. In the process, Party leaders, intellectuals, and professionals found themselves at the mercy of the Red Guards—revolutionary students entrusted to carry out the revitalization of the Chinese Revolution. Families such as that of Lihua found their lives turned upside down as they were forced into the rural areas for "rehabilitation." Lihua's story is told by a journalist, Fox Butterfield (b. 1939), who interviewed her over a period of several months in Beijing in 1979.

Document Source: Fox Butterfield, *China: Alive in a Bitter Sea* (New York: Bantam Books, 1982), 113–15.

Lihua

She was only six years old when it happened. Until then Lihua had lived in a spacious apartment in Peking with her three older brothers, a younger sister, her father, who was a scientist, and her mother, a nurse. They thought of themselves with pride as what the Chinese call intellectuals,

the carriers of the great tradition. Her mother used to tell the children about her own grandfather, who had passed one of the imperial exams under the Qing dynasty before the turn of the century and had held a sinecure job in the court in Peking.

But they had a neighbour who was jealous of

them. He was a worker and a Communist Party member, in Chinese terms a good class status. But he drank and smoked a lot, his wife was unemployed, and he had a hard time supporting their five children. In 1966, at the start of the Cultural Revolution, the neighbour moved quickly to organize a radical faction in their apartment building in support of Mao. His new position enabled him to examine Lihua's father's confidential dossier in the Party's files; in it he found her father had once been briefly a member of the Kuomintang before 1949 when he was a student. That was enough to convict him. A rally was held; Lihua's father was judged a "hidden counterrevolutionary," and he was stripped of his teaching post.

"Red Guards came to search our house, they confiscated everything," she recalled. "They took my father's books, my mother's jewelry, her college photo albums, our furniture. Then they built a bonfire in the yard outside and burned everything."

"That was the end of my childhood," Lihua said.

Afterward, the Public Security Bureau ordered her entire family to move to a village in a remote part of Hunan province, eight hundred miles south of Peking. It was punishment for her father's supposed past sins. Lihua's ancestors had come from the village, God Mountain, but neither her mother nor father ever lived there, and no one in the family knew how to farm. Six teenage Red Guards accompanied the family on the three-day train trip to make sure they got there.

"When we arrived, the local cadres took away the few things we had left, our clothes and our bedding. They left us only what we had on our backs." The family was put in the village schoolhouse, a small one-room building with holes in the walls where the windows should have been and a roof that leaked. There was no furniture. Lihua had to learn to sleep on the mud floor. The school had already been closed by the Cultural Revolution. The teacher had been arrested as a reactionary.

Mao's enemies are publicly shamed by Red Guards, 26 January 1967.

New York World-Telegram and Sun Newspaper Photograph Collection. Courtesy of the Library of Congress, Prints and Photographs Division (LC-USZ62-134168 DLC), http://www.loc.gov/pictures/item/2004669933/

"The peasants and the cadres made my parents parade through the streets every day for several weeks," she related. "They hung a placard around my father's neck, they made him kneel down to confess his crimes, and they beat both my father and mother with iron bars."

"A person is made of flesh. If you beat them long enough, they will die." Within a month her mother was dead and her father was left deaf and unable to use his right arm.

"My mouth is very stupid because I didn't go to school, but these are a few of the facts."

Lihua recounted this story the first time we met in September 1979 on the steps of the Peking Municipal Party Committee Headquarters, a functional gray-concrete building. I had gone there when I heard there were a number of petitioners from the countryside standing outside the Party office trying to present their grievances to the city authorities. It was one of those periods when China's leaders temporarily relaxed their control.[1] Some young factory workers and students took advantage of the slack to put up wall posters or print unofficial journals criticizing the regime, what we foreign correspondents came to call the "democracy movement." Thousands of other people materialized from the countryside asking to have their own personal cases reexamined. The Chinese referred to them as *shang-fang*, meaning they were "entreating a higher level for help." Lihua was one of these. . . . She talked in a calm, dispassionate voice, almost as if all this had happened to someone else, but her story soon gathered a crowd. . . .

"I would walk thirty li [ten miles] up to the hills at sunrise every day, then back that evening. Sometimes I had to carry a hundred pounds, almost twice my weight. But I was inexperienced and often cut myself with the ax," she said. When I looked down at her hands, there were long scars on the backs of both hands and a gash down the middle finger of her left hand from the tip of the nail to the first joint. "We didn't have enough money to pay for a doctor to stitch it," she explained. The village, as part of a commune, had a cooperative medical program, but families of landlords[2] were not eligible to join.

"In that first year, our clothes soon became like tattered pieces of paper. I had to teach myself how to sew for the family by taking apart our old clothes and then putting them back together."

"I was born into the new society," she went on, using a Chinese expression for the years after the Communists' victory in 1949. "I grew up under the Red flag and at first I didn't understand how such things could happen. But gradually I came to realize that I represent many thousands of people. It is just like in the old feudal society before Liberation. We Chinese must still *chi-ku*, 'eat bitterness.' Nothing has really changed."

"As humans, we should have rights, the right to a job, to get an education, but the cadres often treat us like dogs and pigs," she said. . . .

Notes

1. The first era of rehabilitations occurred shortly after Deng Xiaoping came to power.
2. Those who were banished from the cities were assumed to be part of the landlord class, that is, bourgeois exploiters of the peasantry.

Study Question

In what ways does the experience of Lihua's family provide insight into the nature of the Cultural Revolution?

Deng Xiaoping

By the end of the 1970s Deng Xiaoping (1904–1997) had emerged as the successor to Mao Zedong. Recognizing the damage that the Cultural Revolution had wrought, Deng took a more pragmatic approach to governing China. Building upon initiatives introduced by Zhou Enlai, he aimed to modernize the country's industrial sector, its agriculture, its scientific and technological base, and its military. Economic progress would be the key to a successful future.

Thus, Deng launched a tightly controlled experiment in which capitalist principles and foreign investment were introduced in specific coastal cities, known as Special Economic Zones (SEZ). In the two speeches which follow, made in 1980 and 1981, Deng discusses economic development and the relationship between China and the United States.

Document Source: Deng Xiaoping, *Selected Works of Deng Xiaoping*, Vol. 2 (Beijing: Foreign Languages Press, 1984), etext.

Speeches on the Economy and on Foreign Relations

12 April 1980

Over the past 30 years since the founding of the People's Republic, we have laid the basic socialist foundation in agriculture, industry, and other areas. But we have a major problem, that is, we have wasted some time and our productive forces have developed too slowly. All revolution is designed to remove obstacles to the development of the productive forces.

Since socialism is superior to capitalism, socialist countries should be able to develop their economies more rapidly than capitalist countries, improving their people's living standards gradually and becoming more powerful. We have suffered some setbacks in this respect.

The objective of achieving the four modernizations was actually put forth by Chairman Mao and announced by Premier Zhou in his report on government work. But how did the Gang of Four[1] respond? They said that it was better to be poor under socialism than to be rich under capitalism. It seemed to them that socialism meant pauperism. Marxists have always held that socialism is superior to capitalism and that socialist countries should be able to develop their productive forces more rapidly than capitalist countries. Lin Biao and the Gang of Four totally deviated from the cardinal principles of Marxism-Leninism and Mao Zedong Thought.

Being a large country, China should play a more important role in the world, but owing to its limited strength, it cannot play a greater role. In the final analysis, what we should do is try to promote China's development. It is not enough just to say we are poor, and actually, we are very poor. Such a status quo is far from being commensurate with the standing of a great nation such as ours. Therefore, starting last year, we shifted our focus onto economic development. We should unequivocally continue to do so. Developing the economy is a new endeavour for us, for which we must pay a price. We are exploring ways to develop the economy more rapidly and we have confidence that we can do so. We must emancipate our minds and we should do so even in answering the question as to what socialism is. If the economy remains stagnant and the people's living standards remain at a very low level for a long period of time, we cannot say that we are building socialism.

4 January 1981

We hope that after assuming the presidency, Mr Ronald Reagan will make new contributions to the development of Sino-US relations. It was the Republican Party that turned a new page in Sino-US relations during the administration of Mr Richard Nixon and Henry Kissinger. We will always remember it was Mr Nixon who was determined to improve Sino-US relations during his presidency. When Jimmy Carter served as President, Sino-US relations witnessed new development. . . . On our part, we hope that Sino-US relations will continue to develop. Frankly speaking, however, we were really disturbed by certain statements Mr Reagan made in his election platform. When George Bush visited China, we said to him that we understood that statements made in election campaigns in his country might not necessarily be put into practice and that we would pay close attention to what actions Mr Reagan takes after assuming office. When China and the United States established diplomatic relations in 1979, they settled the main question, the Taiwan question, and the United States recognized Taiwan as part of China.

Only by settling this question could the two countries establish new relations and continue to develop them. The Taiwan question should be considered an issue of the past, but now it has been brought up again. We asked Mr Bush to pass on to Mr Reagan our clear-cut position on this question.

We have noticed that the American media and the statements of some people convey four viewpoints concerning this question. These viewpoints, if not clarified, are likely to cause regression in Sino-US relations.

According to the first viewpoint, China is a very weak and poor country and has backward equipment, so it is a country that is of little importance and not worth a great deal of attention. This is by no means a minor issue, but a matter of judgment about the world's balance of power. We have always admitted that we are a weak and poor country. Nevertheless, China has its own advantages, that is, a vast territory and a large population. However, it is true that China is poor and has backward equipment. But we do have a sober estimate of our strength. We enjoy the advantages of being a vast country with a large population and we refuse to be misled by fallacies. . . .

I reiterate that we sincerely hope Sino-US relations will not stagnate, but will continue to develop. We pay close attention to the speeches given by a President both during the election campaign and prior to his assumption of office, and we formulate a certain understanding according to these speeches. However, we shall attach great importance to the actions taken by a new administration after it assumes office. What I have just said represents the official position of the Chinese government. I deem it highly important and necessary to let our American friends clearly understand the position of the Chinese government.

Note

1. Lin Biao, former head of the People's Liberation Army, and the Gang of Four (which included Mao's wife, Jiang Qing), were rivals to succeed Mao.

Study Question

Based upon these speeches how would you characterize Deng Xiaoping's ideological orientation?

Chai Ling

In the early 1980s as Deng Xiaoping sought to modernize Chinese industry by introducing carefully state-controlled elements of capitalism, he also endorsed reforms in agriculture, science and technology, and national defence. However, some observers pushed for a fifth area of modernization: the introduction of democracy. By 1987, influenced by an increasing awareness of western ideas, university students began to hold demonstrations in favour of greater political freedom and reforms such as a free press. These protests culminated in May and June 1989 with a massive demonstration at Tiananmen Square. On the night of 4 June 1989 rural army units[1] were brought into Beijing to suppress the students and remove all traces of their protest. Chai Ling (b. 1966) commanded the student headquarters at the Square. The following radio address was delivered on June 8th.

Document Source: Ming Pao News Reporters and Photographers, June Four: A Chronicle of the Chinese Democratic Uprising, transl. Jin Jiang and Qin Zhou (Fayetteville, AK: University of Arkansas Press, 1989), 151–5.

June Four: A Chronicle of the Chinese Democratic Uprising

It is now four o'clock in the afternoon of June the eighth, nineteen eighty-nine. My name is Chai Ling. I was the chief commander of the student headquarters in Tiananmen Square. I am still alive.

I think that I am best qualified to relate the happenings in the Square during the time between June 2 and June 4. I feel obliged to tell the truth to everybody here, and through you to every fellow citizen, every Chinese.

About ten o'clock on the night of June 2 came the first signal of the massacre: a police car ran over four innocent people. Three of them died. Then we found some soldiers unloading guns and army uniforms and distributing them to the students and civilians around them. We were very suspicious of their actions, so we collected those materials and forwarded them to the police. We have kept the receipts as evidence. The third signal arrived at 2:10 p.m. June 3 at Liubukou and Xinhuaman Gate when armed police attacked our students and civilians. The students had been standing on top of carts and crying out through loudspeakers. They were shouting: "The People's police must love the people!" and "The People's police do not beat people." The students had hardly finished the words when one student got kicked in the belly by a policeman who climbed up the cart. The policeman yelled "Who the hell loves you!" and gave him another blow on the head. The young man fell down at once.

Let me explain our operation in the Square. I was the chief commander. We had set up a broadcasting station that mainly reported the news of the hunger strike. I was always there directing the students' actions in the Square. There were, of course, other people at the station, people like Li Fu, Feng Congde, etc. We constantly received emergency information about students and civilians being beaten and injured in different parts of the Square.

Things became worse and worse as the time dragged from eight, to nine, to ten o'clock. At least ten news reports about people being attacked by the military were received in this period of time. We held a news conference for the reporters on the site. Unfortunately there were very few foreign correspondents, probably because they had been confined to their hotels by the military. We were also told that their rooms had been searched. Only one or two foreign press personnel managed to enter the Square.

The headquarters issued a statement. We put forward one single slogan, which was, "Overthrow the Li Peng government."[2]

At nine o'clock, all the students in Tiananmen Square stood up, raised their right hands, and pledged: "In order to push forward the democratic process of our motherland, to realize prosperity in our country, to avoid a handful of conspirators draining our great motherland, and to save the 1.1 billion Chinese from losing their lives in white terror, I pledge to use my young life to defend Tiananmen and to defend the republic. My head may be cut off, the blood may flow, but Tiananmen Square must not be lost. I will fight until the last person falls.". . .

All of us were very tired. The four hunger strikers went to the military to try to negotiate. They found an officer who claimed to be responsible and told him that the students would withdraw from the Square on the condition that the army guaranteed the safety of the students. Meanwhile, the student leaders in the Square decided to withdraw after asking the opinions of the other students. However, right before we could pass the decision to our students, the troops broke their promise. Armed with helmets and machine guns, they charged onto the third level of the platform of the Monument. Our loudspeakers were crushed instantly. They were now firing at us on the people's monument, the Monument to the People's Heroes. The students came down the monument in tears. We were all crying in retreat.

People shouted at us, "Don't cry!" The students replied that we would return to the Square again, because it was our square. Later we learned that some of us still held illusions about this government and its troops. They thought the troops mainly wanted to force them to leave the Square. Fatigue had lulled them to sleep in their tents; tanks knocked their tents down and ground their bodies apart. Some estimated a death toll of 200; others said 4,000. I simply have no idea how many died in the massacre. But I know for sure that the members of the Worker's Independent Association all got killed. They were about 20 or 30 people.

It was said that while the students were discussing the issue of withdrawing from the Square or not, the armed forces poured gas over the tents, padded coats, and dead bodies of the students and then set them on fire. They planned to wash the Square later so that no trace of killing could be exposed to the public. The symbol of our democratic movement, the Goddess of Liberty, was likewise crushed.

Holding hands together, we walked around the Mao Tse-tung Memorial Hall trying to find an exit on the west or the south side of the Square. We found about ten thousand soldiers in helmets sitting on the ground south of the Memorial Hall. The students shouted "dogs!" and "fascists!" at them. When we left toward the west, we saw column after column of troops running together in Tiananmen Square. The civilians shouted to them "Dogs!" "Fascists!" "Beasts!" The soldiers did not even glance at us. They ran as fast as they could toward the centre. When we passed by Liubukou, where one of the first bloody conflicts took place, the student leaders conscientiously walked in the front line. Debris, such as broken and burnt garbage bins, was everywhere. Between Liubukou and Changanjian Street, we saw vehicles damaged by fire, broken bricks and tiles left to remind us of the fierce fight the previous day, but no corpses. Later we learned that the troops collected the bodies that had fallen to the ground while they had forced their way forward. The bodies, some still alive, were dumped onto buses or tricycles, leaving no chance for the injured people to survive. They did their utmost to hide their crimes.

We wanted to stand up, to demonstrate, and to return to the Square again, but all the people around tried to dissuade us. . . .

On the way to Xidan, we saw a woman wailing. Her child had been killed. A little distance further, we saw four corpses, all civilians. Everyone we saw on our way to our schools had tears in his eyes. One civilian said to us angrily, "Are we buying state bonds to allow them more funds to manufacture more bullets to kill our own children and innocent people?" More information came to us from different sources, such as fellow students and civilians. It boiled down to one single truth—the government troops were butchers and were slaughtering people. They had fired rocket guns at the residential houses along Changanjie Avenue at about two AM. They were trying to block the tanks. He saw a small girl waving her arms at the tanks that were coming in her direction. The tanks ran over and ground her into pieces. My friend was holding two students by their arms. One bullet hit the student on the right in the arm and he fell down. Shortly afterwards, another hit the student on the left. My friend said, "I believe that death was only a tenth of an inch away from me."

We saw a woman looking for her son. She gave us his name and told us that he was alive yesterday. "Is he still there?" Many people were looking for relatives and friends. As we walked toward our schools, we found some office buildings hanging big posters supporting the "right" decisions of the Central Committee of the Communist Party. We got very angry, so some of us tore the slogan down and burned it.

All through the night the radio was broadcasting the message that "the military forces were moved to Beijing to quell a handful of rioters and to help the capital to restore order." I think that I am in a position to determine whether we are rioters at all. Now, every Chinese who has a conscience please put your hand on your heart and think about this: How can young students be considered rioters when all they did was sit together on the platform of the monument? If those who shot at us are animals and beasts, those who sit in front of the cameras or on television screens are worse. They have degenerated to such a rotten base that they are not ashamed to tell lies. Just as we were leaving the Square, a tank ran after us with tear gas bombs knocking down several students, but it didn't care. It drove over students' bodies. It crushed their legs and their necks. Their bodies can never be put together again. Now, who are the rioters? You tell me!

We put on cotton masks because the tear gas was drying up our throats. We walked on and on, mourning our friends who had sacrificed their young lives. They are gone forever.

We finally got back to the Beijing University campus. The university had prepared accommodations for the students who came to Beijing to join us. But none of us wanted bed or food. We were very, very sad. We are the survivors. Many of our friends died on the Square. They won't be coming back again. They will stay on Changanjie Avenue forever.

Our return to Beijing University marked the forced ending of the peaceful petition that started in the form of a hunger strike on 13 May 1989, and continued in the form of a sit-down through 4 June 1989. Later information came that, on the night of 3 June, Li Peng issued three mandates: First, the army was authorized to shoot. Second, armoured carriers were to move at full speed, and Tiananmen Square was to be cleared before the dawn of 4 June. Third, every leader and organizer of the movement was to be persecuted without mercy.

Friends, this is a chaotic government, but it is still moving troops to Beijing and it is still ruling the country. The Beijing massacre has just started. Gradually it will spread to the whole of China; it may have started in other parts of China already. Friends, let us have confidence in the future. The darkest period of the night comes right before the dawn. A real people's republic will be born in the awakening to the fascist suppression. This is a life-or-death moment for the Chinese nation. Arise, Chinese people. Arise, every citizen who has a conscience. The last victory surely belongs to you. It will not be long before the downfall comes to the government headed by Yang Shangkun, Li Peng, Wang Zheng, and Bo Yibo!

Down with fascism!

Down with the military rulers!

Victory to the people!

Long live the Republic!

Note

1. Rural military units were utilized because of the fear that the troops normally stationed in Beijing would refuse to fire on the demonstrators.
2. Although Deng Xiaoping remained the acknowledged leader of China, protesters widely blamed Premier Li Peng for the crackdown on pro-democracy movements.

Study Question

Why did the Chinese government react with such violence to the student protests?

Governments of Japan and the United States

On 8 September 1951, representatives of the United States government and Japanese Prime Minister Shigeru Yoshida signed an indefinite security treaty that bound the United States to ensure Japanese defence. This agreement served as an addendum to the final treaty of peace between Japan and the Allied Powers signed earlier the same day, and to the post-war Japanese Constitution that had, in Article 9, restricted Japan's ability to maintain land, sea, or air forces with offensive capabilities. The treaty is followed by a brief note that reminded the Japanese of the requirement to provide support to UN forces engaged in the Korean War.

Document Source: Joyakushu, 30–6. Japan's Foreign Relations-Basic Documents Vol. 1, 444–8. http://www.ioc.u-tokyo.ac.jp/~worldjpn/documents/texts/docs/19510908.T2E.html

Security Treaty between Japan and the United States of America

Japan has this day signed a Treaty of Peace with the Allied Powers. On the coming into force of that Treaty, Japan will not have the effective means to exercise its inherent right of self-defense because it has been disarmed.

There is danger to Japan in this situation because irresponsible militarism has not yet been driven from the world. Therefore Japan desires a Security Treaty with the United States of America to come into force simultaneously with the Treaty of Peace between Japan and the United States of America.

The Treaty of Peace recognizes that Japan as a sovereign nation has the right to enter into collective security arrangements, and further, the Charter of the United Nations recognizes that all nations possess an inherent right of individual and collective self-defense.

Japanese representatives leave the USS *Missouri* after signing the instruments of surrender, 2 September 1945. Japan was now an occupied nation, subject to American political, economic, and military control.

Courtesy of the National Archives (NWDNS-80-D-472629).

In exercise of these rights, Japan desires, as a provisional arrangement for its defense, that the United States of America should maintain armed forces of its own in and about Japan so as to deter armed attack upon Japan.

The United States of America, in the interest of peace and security, is presently willing to maintain certain of its armed forces in and about Japan, in the expectation, however, that Japan will itself increasingly assume responsibility for its own defense against direct and indirect aggression, always avoiding any armament which could be an offensive threat or serve other than to promote peace and security in accordance with the purposes and principles of the United Nations Charter.

Accordingly, the two countries have agreed as follows:

Article I

Japan grants, and the United States of America accepts, the right, upon the coming into force of the Treaty of Peace and of this Treaty, to dispose United States land, air, and sea forces in and about Japan. Such forces may be utilized to contribute to the maintenance of international peace and security in the Far East and to the security of Japan against armed attack from without, including assistance given at the express request of the Japanese Government to put down large-scale internal riots and disturbances in Japan, caused through instigation or intervention by an outside power or powers.

Article II

During the exercise of the right referred to in Article I, Japan will not grant, without the prior consent of the United States of America, any bases or any rights, powers or authority whatsoever, in or relating to bases or the right of garrison or of maneuver, or transit of ground, air, or naval forces to any third power.

Article III

The conditions which shall govern the disposition of armed forces of the United States of America in and about Japan shall be determined by administrative agreements between the two Governments.

Article IV

This Treaty shall expire whenever in the opinion of the Governments of Japan and the United States of America there shall have come into force such United Nations arrangements or such alternative individual or collective security dispositions as will satisfactorily provide for the maintenance by the United Nations or otherwise of international peace and security in the Japan Area.

Article V

This Treaty shall be ratified by Japan and the United States of America and will come into force when instruments of ratification thereof have been exchanged by them at Washington.

IN WITNESS WHEREOF the undersigned Plenipotentiaries have signed this Treaty.

DONE in duplicate at the city of San Francisco, in the Japanese and English languages, this eighth day of September, 1951.

FOR JAPAN:
Shigeru Yoshida

FOR THE UNITED STATES OF AMERICA:
Dean Acheson
John Foster Dulles
Alexander Wiley
Styles Bridges

NOTES EXCHANGED BETWEEN PRIME MINISTER YOSHIDA AND SECRETARY OF STATE ACHESON AT THE TIME OF THE SIGNING OF THE SECURITY TREATY BETWEEN JAPAN AND THE UNITED STATES OF AMERICA.

Excellency:
Upon the coming into force of the Treaty of Peace

signed today, Japan will assume obligations expressed in Article 2 of the Charter of the United Nations which requires the giving to the United Nations of "every assistance in any action it takes in accordance with the present Charter."

As we know, armed aggression has occurred in Korea, against which the United Nations and its members are taking action. There has been established a unified command of the United Nations under the United States pursuant to Security Council Resolution of July 7, 1950, and the General Assembly, by Resolution of February 1, 1951, has called upon all states and authorities to lend every assistance to the United Nations action and to refrain from giving any assistance to the aggressor. With the approval of SCAP, Japan has been and now is rendering important assistance to the United Nations action in the form of facilities and services made available to the members of the United Nations, the Armed Forces of which are participating in the United Nations action.

Since the future is unsettled and it may unhappily be that the occasion for facilities and services in Japan in support of United Nations action will continue or recur, I would appreciate confirmation, on behalf of your Government, that if and when the forces of a member or members of the United Nations are engaged in any United Nations action in the Far East after the Treaty of Peace comes into force, Japan will permit and facilitate the support in and about Japan, by the member or members, of the forces engaged in such United Nations action; the expenses involved in the use of Japanese facilities and services to be borne as at present or as otherwise mutually agreed between Japan and the United Nations member concerned. In so far as the United States is concerned the use of facilities and services, over and above those provided to the United States pursuant to the Administrative Agreement which will implement the Security Treaty between the United States and Japan, would be at United States expense, as at present.

Accept, Excellency, the assurances of my most distinguished consideration.

DEAN ACHESON
September 8, 1951.
His Excellency
Shigeru Yoshida,
Prime Minister of Japan

> **Study Question**
>
> Which elements of the Security Treaty and its resultant obligations can be seen as an infringement on Japanese sovereignty?

Chitoshi Yanaga

Chitoshi Yanaga (1903–1985) was born in Hawaii but was sent to Japan to study as a child. As a result he witnessed one of the most important eras in Japan's modernization—the age of massive industrialization and the beginning of Japanese imperialism. Returning to the United States in his twenties, Yanaga earned a doctoral degree in political science from Berkeley. After the Second World War, he taught at Yale and conducted research into the relationship between Japanese business, education, and politics. His 1968 study on big business during the Japanese "economic miracle" is said to have influenced American policy towards Japan. In the following excerpt Yanaga discusses the interrelationship among business, politics, education, and banking in Japan.

Document Source: Chitoshi Yanaga, "Big Business in Japanese Politics." From Chitoshi Yanaga, *Big Business in Japanese Politics* (New Haven: Yale University Press, 1968), 15–26 & 38–9.

Big Business in Japanese Politics

One of the characteristics of Japanese society is the existence of a number of rather exclusive groupings. Most of these are primary groups in which intimacy is achieved through submersion of individuality to the extent of not even using individual names. This strong familial orientation is reflected in the practice of addressing a domestic or waitress as *nesan* (older sister). Such cliques or groups provide the oasis of the power structure. In the prewar period, power was exercised by three distinct cliques, the financial (*zaibatsu*), bureaucratic (*kambatsu*), and military (*gumbatsu*), but in the postwar period the military and the financial cliques have ceased to exist. Only the bureaucratic clique has retained its power. Zaibatsu has been superseded by *zaikai* (the business leader clique). Two other groups . . . have come into prominence, namely, the extended family clique (*keibatsu*) and the university clique (*gakubatsu*).

There is no question that the most intimate group is the extended family clique, whose foundation is a combination of kinship and marital ties. The growth of the influence of this group has been conspicuous in postwar Japan. Although no longer recognized as a basic legal unit, the family is still the touchstone of social success. The importance of family background or connections in achieving success in almost any field has not diminished. On the contrary, it seems to have increased greatly. More than ever, family status (*iegara*) and pedigree (*kenami*) are necessary qualifications for membership in high society and for achieving a position of prestige and influence in business and politics, even in academic life.

Candidates for important posts are judged on the basis of family ties. When a new governor of the Bank of Japan was appointed in late 1964, press and public approval was on the basis of the appointee's family background rather than on his ability, which was widely recognized. If one's pedigree is not the best, it is always possible to improve it by marrying into the right family. Such ties are widely sought, especially in the business community. Chances for such marriages are greatly enhanced for men who have acquired a quality education, such as graduation from the prestigious Tokyo University, which is open to all solely on the basis of ability. Bright young graduates of the best universities are always in demand as husbands for daughters of influential business and political leaders. When one already has a good pedigree, it is possible to improve it socially and financially by acquiring a degree from an elite school. Marital ties are often established to enhance the position, prestige, and power of the families as well as the individuals involved. It is also possible to enhance the social status of the family through the centuries-old practice of adoption, which continues to flourish in Japan. . . .

Intimate personal relationships are based on shared experiences, and no shared experiences compare with those of college years for forming lifelong friendships. . . . The unique character of the university clique is responsible for the influence wielded by the graduates of Tokyo University in business, politics, and government as well as in higher education, science, technology, and medicine. Ever since its establishment in 1886, Tokyo University has inculcated in its students a strong sense of elitism and leadership. In light of the incredibly difficult entrance examinations, it is not surprising that its graduates feel superior, even though in many instances such an attitude is not justified in terms of academic achievement. The university was founded specifically for the purpose of training government officials. Upon graduation, its early graduates were given the privilege of immediate appointment, without examination, to the newly created higher civil service. This established a tradition of administrative elitism; until the end of World War I the cream of the Tokyo Imperial University graduates went into government service. In no time the university had established undisputed supremacy in higher education. It attracted the best students from all over the nation, and students have been flocking to it ever since.

Tōdai—as Tokyo University is commonly known—is in a sense a most exclusive club, membership in which establishes eligibility for the highest positions in the realm. Of the ten postwar prime ministers between 1945 and 1965, seven were Tōdai graduates (Shidehara, Katayama, Ashida, Yoshida, Hatoyama, Kishi, and Satō). . . .

One of the most distinctive features of Japan's power structure is the extraordinarily high concentration of power wielders in Tokyo. Here, in the world's largest city, a supermetropolis of over eleven million people and the seat of the national government, are located the main offices of practically all the major corporations, making it the business, banking, financial, transportation, communication, publishing, and mass media center of Japan. All political parties, labour unions, and trade associations have their national headquarters here. The leading universities, research institutes, museums, art galleries, theatres, radio and television broadcasting systems, and the country's six largest newspapers are located in Tokyo. All major political and economic decisions are made in this city. It is as if Washington, DC, New York, Chicago, Philadelphia, Pittsburgh, Boston, and Detroit were rolled into one.

Such a concentration of power is unknown in the United States. To create an analogous situation, it would be necessary to locate the head offices of America's hundred largest corporations in Washington, DC, together with their presidents, board chairmen, and directors, many of whom would be related by marriage not only to each other but to influential political leaders and government administrators. Furthermore these top-level executives would, for the most part, claim the same alma mater, belong to the same country clubs, have ready access to government offices, maintain daily contact with government officials by phone or over the luncheon table, enjoy intimate relations with influential senators and congressmen, and also serve on government advisory bodies and administrative commissions. The impact of this sort of concentration of political, economic, and social power on the governing process can indeed be far-reaching. . . .

Unlike the old zaibatsu, which dominated the prewar economic scene under a system of highly centralized family control through holding companies, the new postwar big business structure is composed of enterprise groups. These groups are of two kinds: those organized around the former zaibatsu and using the old names (Mitsubishi with 38 separate corporations and a research institute; Mitsui with 22 corporations; Sumitomo with 15 corporations) and those held together by large banks (Fuji, formerly Yasuda; Dai Ichi; and the Industrial Bank of Japan, through which the enterprises in both groups manage their financing).

These groups, known as *keiretsu*, cannot be described in American business terms. They are not really monopolies, since they compete with each other strongly and no one group completely dominates a given field. Actually they are horizontal groups of companies, each group containing many varied industries as well as a bank, a trust company, insurance companies, a trade company (or companies), and a real estate company. Member companies tend to cooperate with other companies within the group and to compete with companies outside the group. When entering new fields such as atomic energy or petrochemicals, where investment requirements are beyond the capability of any one company in the group, several or most members will combine to finance the venture jointly. The groups vary in cohesiveness. With each group, the bank is the primary though not the sole source of banking support. The group's trading company handles the sales, particularly export trading, and the purchase of raw materials, but not exclusively. Policy coordination is achieved through presidents' clubs which meet periodically.

These enterprise groups represent the post-war restructuring of big business on the basis of common interests, the better to cope with common problems in such fields as production, sales, and financing.

Study Question

Why was the interlocking system of *batsu* so effective in the late 1950s and 1960s? What are the dangers of such a system?

Kakuei Tanaka

Kakuei Tanaka (1918–1993) served as Japan's prime minister from 1972 until 1974. As with every other postwar prime minister to this time, Tanaka belonged to the Liberal Democratic Party. This era was characterized by a series of dramatic changes. The US war in Indochina was entering its final phase, with Richard Nixon already committed to the withdrawal of American forces; a vastly improved relationship between the US and China fundamentally changed the regional balance of power; and, Japan's economy for the first time began to show signs of slowing under the weight of rapidly increasing oil prices. As well, the continued presence and behaviour of US forces on Okinawa and in other areas had become a key source of friction between Japan and the US. The excerpt which follows comes from a 1974 speech in which Tanaka discusses his views on the defence of Japan and on international relations.

Document Source: Kakuei Tanaka, "Japanese Policies to Improve Understanding, 21 January 1974," *Vital Speeches of the Day*, 40(9) (15 February 1974): 268–73.

Japanese Policies to Improve Understanding

Since the year before last, I have travelled to the United States, the Eurasian continent, and Southeast Asia. Through such official tours, I have become convinced that a détente in . . . Asia is, as in Europe, being attained within the framework of the existing international order. We will continue to maintain the minimum defense capacity necessary for a self defense, and also uphold the Japan-US security system. The government will make further efforts to obtain understanding and support on [sic] a broad range of people concerning defense matters.

We will submit new bills to the present Diet to radically strengthen the various measures for the stabilization of the life of people in the areas surrounding the facilities and the areas of self-defense forces and US forces in Japan. We will also seriously tackle the problem of realigning the facilities and areas now being used by the US forces.

As for the defense appropriations for fiscal 1974, we held them within the necessary minimum by taking fully into account the present situations in and outside the country. . . .

The international situation is becoming ever more diversified and the world as a whole is now in search of a new order, politically and economically. Accordingly, the circumstances surrounding our country have never been more complex and austere. At such a time as this, it is particularly important for us to improve mutual understanding with other countries and increase cooperation with them. Recently, I visited five nations of Asia after having visited earlier the United States, China, West Europe, and the Soviet Union, because I wanted to determine for myself how our foreign policy should be from a global point of view and what is our responsibility to the international community.

I had long hoped to visit Asian nations at the

The postwar relationship between Japan and the US was symbolized by this 1971 visit by Emperor Hirohito and Empress Nagaka to the United States during the Nixon presidency.

Courtesy of National Archives, Richard Nixon Library, http://research.archives.gov/description/194382

earliest opportunity and, by deepening friendship with them as an intimate neighbor to open "A New Page" in our relations with these countries, I tried, to the best of my ability, to search ways for fostering and reinforcing "good neighboring relations sharing equally the benefits of peace and prosperity" with them. I saw with my own eyes and heard with my own ears complaints and criticisms concerning our relations with the Asian nations and the economic activities of Japanese enterprises in those countries. In their midst I felt strongly that although mutual understanding and cooperation are extremely important to countries and peoples, these things [are] easier said than done.

It is not as easy as we think to grasp accurately what international cooperation means and have that understanding reflected in the steps taken by the nation and the conduct of each of its citizens.

As a homogeneous people, the 100,000,000 citizens of Japan within their island country have no ethnic conflicts, no religious or language disputes.

Thus, we have been able to concentrate our efforts solely on rehabilitation and construction. In this respect we may be regarded as extremely fortunate among the nations of the world. At the same time, it is because of this peculiarity that we have yet a great deal to learn and criticize ourselves for in the areas of international cooperation and dealings with other peoples. The exclusive, narrow-minded manner of pursing national interests, which may have been overlooked and justified to some extent in the process of rehabilitation in the midst of the ruins immediately after our defeat in war, is not only no longer internationally valid but also a possible source of misfortune. Today, we must listen with an open mind to just criticisms of us, rectify what ought to be rectified, and try to maintain and augment an exchange and relationship of mutual benefit based on a long-term perspective only when we judge not with our own yardstick, become good neighbors to the other Asian nations and share both pain and pleasure with them, can we contribute to the establishment of an everlasting peace in Asia.

Thus I am making a plea for a review of ourselves in terms of "people." In terms of "things," I realized ever more strongly, through the summit meetings I held with the countries I visited, that we have a relationship of complementing each other with the other Asian nations. We need the cooperation of the Asian nations and they, too, expect a great deal of our cooperation for their nation-building. In order to live up to their expectations, we must alter our assistance programs for these countries, including a qualitative improvement of official development assistance. To be more specific, we will augment our assistance in the areas of agriculture, medical care, education, and communications in the interest of the improvement of the welfare of the masses of these countries, and relax the terms for government loans and expand the limits for giving grants. For the purpose of promoting international cooperation, the government decided to appoint a state minister without portfolio and to establish an international cooperation agency, thus improving the system for cooperation between the government and private quarters. . . .

The many difficult problems that lie before us are of a kind never experienced by our predecessors. It is impossible to find prescriptions for solving them in the textbooks of the past.

We built the road to rehabilitation which [sic] sharing what little we had and enduring the painful trials in the midst of the postwar privation. There is no reason why this same nation in this age of incomparably greater affluence than in those years cannot overcome the immediate difficulties, no matter how trying they may be. If we contend for short-ranged interests out of selfishness and fall into mutual distrust, it would be a great misfortune for all of us. And it is the responsibility of government to avoid such a situation, to resolve the anxiety of people, and to cope with the current difficulties. . . .

Going through a turning point is accompanied by great difficulties and pain. If the government and people make joint efforts to cooperate with each other on the firm basis of parliamentary democracy, it is possible, I am convinced, for us to overcome the trials of today and bring about a new era of cooperation and solidarity. I sincerely ask for the understanding and cooperation of all Japanese people.

Study Question

According to Tanaka, what were the greatest challenges facing Japan in the early 1970s?

Society for History Textbook Reform

Though China and Japan normalized diplomatic relations in 1972, unresolved issues—many of them related to the events of the Sino-Japanese War—continued to cause tensions between the two nations. Unlike Germany, which made a series of highly public gestures to atone for its wartime crimes, successive Japanese governments largely refused to revisit the events of 1937–1945. Periodic efforts to force issues such as the Nanjing massacre into the public realm were dismissed by Japan as attempts by the Chinese government to distract its own citizens from domestic problems. Eventually, when compensation was made to some groups affected by Japanese war crimes, ultra-nationalists in Japan decried the effort to "shame" their country. The perception that Japanese schoolchildren were being taught to hate their own country led, in 2004, to calls from the far right for a new, patriotic history. Subsequently, the Society for History Textbook Reform published its New History in 2005. The excerpts included here cover the wartime period.[1]

Document Source: Japanese Society for History Textbook Reform, *New History* (Tokyo: Fusosha, 2005), 49–54. Used with permission.

New History

From the Marco Polo Bridge Incident to War with China

Tension between Japan and China heightened when Japanese troops established a pro-Japan government in the Hebei region, which adjoins Manchuria. The Japanese were motivated by the desire to preserve their interests in Manchuria and gain access to natural resources. At that time, 5,000 Japanese soldiers were stationed near Beijing, in accordance with a treaty concluded after the Boxer Rebellion (the Western powers concluded similar treaties with China). On July 7, 1937, shots were fired at Japanese soldiers while they were engaged in maneuvers near Marco Polo Bridge (located outside Beijing). By the next day, this incident (the **Marco Polo Bridge Incident**) had escalated into hostilities with Chinese troops. The incident was of relatively small magnitude, and efforts were made to resolve it locally. But Japan decided to send a large number of troops to China when the Nationalist government issued an emergency mobilization order. These events marked the beginning of a war that lasted for eight long years.

Full-Scale War with China

In August 1937, two Japanese soldiers, one an officer, were shot to death in Shanghai (the hub of foreign interests). After this incident, the hostilities between Japan and China escalated. Japanese military officials thought Chiang Kai-shek would surrender if they captured Nanking, the Nationalist capital; they occupied that city in December.[*2] But Chiang Kai-shek had moved his capital to the remote city of Chongqing. The conflict continued. . . .

Japan Constrained by Economic Blockade

Seeking a source of petroleum, Japan approached the Netherlands about obtaining oil from Indonesia (a Dutch colony), but was rejected. Japan was cornered economically by the ABCD (American, British, Chinese and Dutch) encirclement.

Negotiations intended to break the impasse in Japan–US relations opened in Washington, DC in April 1941, but were not successful. In July, units from the Japanese Army and Navy entered Saigon (now Ho Chi Minh City) in what is referred to as the "advance into southern French Indochina." Saigon was a militarily strategic location, destined to serve as the base for Japan's southern advance. The Americans, sensing a crisis, immediately retaliated by freezing Japanese assets in the US and imposing an embargo on petroleum exports to Japan. In August, British and American officials conferred on board ship in the Atlantic, and issued the Atlantic Charter, which stated both nations' war objectives. According to the charter, neither nation would seek territorial expansion, nor desired redefinition of national borders; both nations expressed their respect for ethnic self-determination. Japan–US negotiations continued, but made no progress. In November, the US sent a note to the Japanese demanding the unconditional withdrawal of all troops from China and Indochina (the Hull Note). The Japanese government, interpreting the Hull Note as an ultimatum, decided to go to war with the US. . . .

The Greater East Asian War (Pacific War)

Describe the course of the Greater East Asian War.

Attack on Pearl Harbor
On December 8, 1941, the Japanese Navy bombed Pearl Harbor in Hawaii, inflicting damage that destroyed most of the US Pacific Fleet. The objectives of this operation were to destroy the main American fleet, and take command of the Pacific Ocean away from the Americans. On the same day, Japanese Army units landed in

Malaysia, defeated the British troops there, and advanced toward Singapore.

Japan declared war on the US and Great Britain, maintaining that this was a war of survival and self-defense, and naming it the **Greater East Asian War**. Germany and Italy also declared war on the US. World War II developed into a conflict whose battles were waged all over the world, pitting the Axis nations (Japan, Germany, and Italy) against the Allies (the US, Great Britain, the Netherlands, the Soviet Union, and China).

Most of the people of Japan, who learned of the outbreak of war through the news media, were intoxicated by reports of victory after victory. The US government told the American people that the assault on Pearl Harbor was a cowardly act, calling it a "sneak attack" because it had occurred before the note indicting that Japan–US talks were handed over [sic]. The Pearl Harbor attack was a military success, but it served to unite the American people (who had previously been opposed to the war) against Japan behind the battle cry, "Remember Pearl Harbor!"

The Fortunes of War Turn Against Japan

Japan's initial victories were dazzling. Once they had landed on the Malay Peninsula, Japanese troops destroyed the British fortress in Singapore (located at the southern tip of the Malay Peninsula) in only 70 days. Partly because the Allied forces were unprepared, the Japanese quickly occupied all of Southeast Asia.

But in 1942, Japan's Combined Fleet was defeated by the US Navy in the Battle of Midway. Japan lost four aircraft carriers in that conflict. It was at this point that the Americans began to gain the upper hand. Japan lost command of the Pacific, and its supply line was cut off. American submarines sank countless Japanese supply ships. The gap between Japanese and American productivity became increasingly obvious. Faced with shortages of weapons and ammunition, Japanese soldiers experienced unimaginable suffering. But officers and enlisted men alike fought fiercely and bravely.

The Assembly of Greater East-Asiatic Nations and the Nations of Asia

What was the significance of Japan's war to the peoples of Asia?

Hope of Independence Spreads Throughout Asia

Japan's initial victories encouraged the peoples of Southeast Asia and India, and instilled in them the hope that they too might achieve independence. Sweeping Japanese military success in Southeast Asia could not have been accomplished without local assistance. The Japanese captured Indian soldiers fighting for Great Britain. It was from the ranks of those prisoners of war that the Indian National Army was formed. Its members marched alongside Japanese troops as they advanced to India. Armies were formed in Indonesia and Burma as well, under Japanese guidance.

The Assembly of Greater East-Asiatic Nations

In November 1943, Japan sponsored the **Assembly of Greater East-Asiatic Nations**. The purpose of the assembly, held in Tokyo, was to seek the cooperation of the nations of Asia in the war effort, and to demonstrate solidarity with other East Asian nations. At the Assembly, a joint declaration (**Joint Declaration of the Assembly of Greater East-Asiatic Nations**) was issued in response to the Atlantic Charter. It spoke of the autonomy and independence of all nations, economic progress achieved through cooperation, and the eradication of racial discrimination. Following the assembly, Japan issued clearer explanations of its reason for waging war: the building of a **Greater East Asian Co-Prosperity Sphere**, from which the Western powers would be excluded. . . .

[Related Information]

Japanese Actions Inspire the Peoples of Asia

Japanese soldiers drove out the forces of Western Europe, which had colonized the nations of Asia for many years. They surprised us, because we didn't think we could possibly beat the white man, and they inspired us with confidence. They awakened us from our long slumber, and convinced us to make the nation of our ancestors our own nation once again.

We cheered the Japanese soldiers as they marched through the Malay Peninsula. When we saw the defeated British troops fleeing, we felt an excitement we had never experienced before. (*Excerpt from the writings of Raja Dato Nong Chik, leader of the Malaysian independence movement and former member of the Malaysian House of Representatives*)

Notes

1. The *New History* is laid out like many textbooks, with study questions and supplemental material (listed here as "related information").

2. [*New History* note] *At this time, many Chinese soldiers and civilians were killed or wounded by Japanese troops (the Nanking Incident). Documentary evidence has raised doubts about the actual number of victims claimed by the incident. The debate continues even today.

Study Question

When the *New History* was published it led to violent anti-Japanese protests throughout China. In what ways could the excerpts here be seen to have contributed to these demonstrations?

Web Resources

John Fairbank Memorial Chinese History Virtual Library
    http://www.cnd.org/fairbank
Mao Tse-tung (Zedong) Internet Library
    http://www.marx2mao.com/Mao/Index.html
Historical Text Archive: Japan
    http://historicaltextarchive.com/links.php?action=links&cid=5&sid=13
World History Archives: The History of East Asia
    http://www.hartford-hwp.com/archives/55/index.html

Recommended Reading

China

Dai Sijie, *Balzac and the Little Chinese Seamstress* (New York: Anchor, 2002). *Balzac and the Little Chinese Seamstress* is the tale of two friends who have been exiled to a remote mountain village for re-education. The novel, set during the Cultural Revolution, examines the survival skills that the friends develop as well as the lessons they learn from their horrific experience. The author himself experienced re-education and was exiled to France in 1984.

Mo Yan, *Big Breasts and Wide Hips* (New York: Arcade Publishing, 2004). Mo Yan's controversial novel covers a broad sweep of Chinese history, from the late Qing years to the post-Mao era. The book—divided into seven chapters, representing each major time period—focuses on strong female characters, including the central character of Mother. The book won awards in the People's Republic, but was quickly banned for its "immorality."

Wang Meng, *Bolshevik Salute* (Washington, DC: University of Washington Press, 1990). *Bolshevik Salute* is a fictionalized version of Wang's life as a devoted follower of the revolution in Mao's China. Wang was purged in the anti-Rightist Campaign of 1957 and rehabilitated in 1979; the story explores alienation, political identity, and betrayal.

After his rehabilitation Wang served as China's Minister of Culture, but was removed in 1989 following the Tiananmen Square demonstrations.

Yu Hua, *To Live: A Novel* (New York: Anchor, 2003). Set during the revolutionary transformation of Chinese society, *To Live* follows one ordinary man, Fugui, through his life as a member of the landlord class, then as a soldier, then a simple farmer, as the turmoil of China's transformation affects him and his family over some 30 years.

Japan

Saiichi Maruya, *Singular Rebellion* (New York: Kodansha America, 1990). Set in 1969, the year of student rebellions, *Singular Rebellion* tells the story of one businessman whose single act of rebellion is to marry a younger woman. Maruya examines the consequences that follow from that one decision.

Haruki Murakami, *The Wind-up Bird Chronicle* (New York: Vintage, 1998). Murakami's novel explores postwar Japanese society and the pivotal issue of identity. The author examines the underside of modern Japan, reflecting back through the prewar period and the experience of war, to the repressed memory, the guilt, and the general state of modern society.

Recommended Viewing

China

River Without Buoys (China, 1983). Director: Wu Tianming. Filmed in the early years of the Deng Xiaoping era, as the aftereffects of the Cultural Revolution were still being felt, Wu's film deals with the devastation caused by the Cultural Revolution. The film's symbolic story focuses on a group of refugees fleeing persecution by raft only to be faced by a series of challenges from the river itself.

The Blue Kite (China/Hong Kong, 1993). Director: Tian Zhuangzhuang. Focusing on the fate of one family between the early 1950s and late 1960s, Tian Zhuangzhuang shows the human impact of the campaigns to remake China including the Rectification Movement, the Great Leap Forward, and the Cultural Revolution.

Good Men, Good Women (Japan/Taiwan, 1995). Director: Hou Hsiao-Hsien. *Good Men, Good Women*—loosely based on actual events—is set in Taiwan, after Chiang Kai-shek fled Mainland China. It highlights the US-backed anti-Communist campaign launched by Chiang Kai-shek in the early 1950s, and the subsequent unwillingness of the Taiwanese government to address this period in its history.

To Live (Hong Kong, 1994). Director: Zhang Yimou. The film adaptation of Yu Hua's novel follows the fate of Fugui and his wife Jiazhen from the 1940s to the 1970s. Despite the fact that the film was banned in Mainland China for its depiction of life under the Communist regime, film critics have noted that its message is somewhat less bleak than that of the novel.

Japan

Night and Fog in Japan (Japan, 1960). Director: Nagisa Oshima. *Night and Fog in Japan* is an examination of left-wing politics in Japan, centred on opposition to the US–Japan Security Treaty. It reveals the divisions inherent on the left and their inability to bring about real changes in Japanese society. It also provides insights into postwar Japanese politics and society, as well as the complex reactions to American occupation.

Asia Rising (UK/USA, 1999). Director: Bill Treharne Jones/WGBH Boston/BBC (Documentary). This documentary examines the postwar rise of Korea and Japan to global economic power, focusing on the economic "miracles" in both countries and the path taken to achieve that success in the 1950s and 1960s.

11

Anti-colonial Movements and Independence

The economic realities following the Second World War dictated that the massive colonial empires of the past would have to be broken up. Given the pressing domestic demands for postwar rebuilding, the major European colonial powers were simply unable to sustain substantial overseas ventures. Despite a vociferous pro-imperial lobby, postwar British leaders were among the first to commit to a pro-independence policy for their colonies in South Asia. In Africa, however, British policy was markedly less favourable towards immediate independence.

French, Dutch, and Belgian leaders showed an even greater reluctance to acknowledge colonial demands for independence and preferred to view their colonies, and their inherent economic obligations, as an integral part of their

Road construction in Congo after independence. Projects such as this demonstrated the UN's desire to ensure a successful transition to independence.

Courtesy of the United Nations Photo Library (74797/UN/DPI/B. Zarov).

territorial sovereignty. As a result, a series of costly wars for independence occurred in the 1950s and 1960s. France, for example, became embroiled in destructive conflicts in Indochina and Algeria, the combination of which would eventually lead to the collapse of the Fourth Republic.

Within the colonies the early decolonization movement was viewed, for the most part, with enthusiasm. Western-educated elites would assume control and govern largely in the traditions established by the former colonizers; rapid industrialization and ambitious education programs were seen as the key to a prosperous future. This enthusiasm, however, did not last. The colonial era had created and magnified a series of barely contained tensions. After the colonizers left, economic grievances, boundary disputes, problems of ethnicity often related to the post-colonial distribution of power, and any number of related issues served to destabilize the newly independent governments. Military intervention intended to contain these conflicts often undermined any chance for successful civilian governance.

Calls for an end to the massive colonial empires that had dominated the prewar world predated the Second World War. However, the war and the resultant burdens placed upon colonized peoples served to crystalize and intensify earlier demands for independence. Calls for an immediate end to colonial occupation emerged even as the war continued, especially in Asia.

The documents in this chapter begin with a draft resolution—subsequently revised and moderated—proposed by Mohandas Gandhi that demanded the immediate removal of British troops in India so that the nation could pursue a future free of British colonial control. While the wartime response to Gandhi's demands was swift and draconian, postwar British leaders generally conceded that Great Britain could no longer afford to hold onto its rebellious colony in South Asia. A speech by Clement Attlee summarizes the pro-independence view. Jawaharlal Nehru captures both the promise of independence for India and the clear obstacles which would have to be confronted and Syed Abul A'ala Maududi assesses the challenge of replacing western institutions with Islamic ones in newly independent Pakistan.

Turning to France, Prime Minister Paul Ramadier argues vehemently that colonialism must continue because it was providing innumerable benefits to the colonized peoples. In response, groups such as the National Liberation Front (FLN) in Algeria emerged, determined to fight for freedom from colonial rule. Sekou Touré assesses the aftermath of the French colonial era in Guinea.

Struggles to confront the legacy of colonialism were evident in other parts of the world too. Some nations, such as Cuba, had experienced not only a lengthy period of direct colonial rule, but also had to come to terms with the impact of more informal neo-colonial relationships that had developed after independence. A speech by Fidel Castro points out the many problems created by both Spanish and, subsequently, American involvement in Cuba. The documents in this chapter conclude with the 1960 United Nations declaration which called on all nations immediately to relinquish their colonial possessions.

Mohandas K. Gandhi

Mohandas Gandhi (1869–1948) was born in Porbander. He was educated as a barrister in Britain and practised law in South Africa where he developed the essential elements of his later campaign for Indian independence—non-violent non-cooperation (satya-graha). Gandhi returned to India in 1915 and, despite his own non-violent philosophy, campaigned in support of the British war effort. However, at the end of the war the British curtailed civil liberties in India in order to control the growing independence movement, and these

actions culminated in the deaths of hundreds of Indians during the Amritsar Massacre (see Chapter Two). Resistance to British rule gradually escalated until, in 1942, Gandhi demanded that the British "Quit India." The document that follows is the text of Gandhi's origin-al "Quit India" resolution. This draft was rejected by the All-India Congress Working Committee in favour of a more moderate version submitted by Jawaharlal Nehru.

Document Source: Mohandas K. Gandhi, "Quit India Resolution." Available online: http://www.ibiblio.org/pha/policy/1942/420427a.html

"Quit India" Draft Resolution

Whereas the British War Cabinet proposals by Sir Stafford Cripps have shown up British imperialism in its nakedness as never before, the All-India Congress Committee has come to the following conclusions:

The committee is of the opinion that Britain is incapable of defending India. It is natural that whatever she does is for her own defence. There is the eternal conflict between Indian and British interest. It follows that their notions of defence would also differ.

The British Government has no trust in India's political parties. The Indian Army has been maintained up till now mainly to hold India in subjugation. It has been completely segregated from the general population, who can in no sense regard it as their own. This policy of mistrust still continues, and is the reason why national defence is not entrusted to India's elected representatives.

Japan's quarrel is not with India. She is war-ring against the British Empire. India's participa-tion in the war has not been with the consent of the representatives of the Indian people. It was purely a British act. If India were freed, her first step would probably be to negotiate with Japan.

The Congress is of the opinion that if the

British withdrew from India, India would be able to defend herself in the event of the Japanese, or any aggressor, attacking India.

The committee is, therefore, of the opinion that the British should withdraw from India. The plea that they should remain in India for the pro-tection of the Indian princes is wholly untenable. It is an additional proof of their determination to maintain their hold over India. The princes need have no fear from an unarmed India.

The question of majority and minority is the creation of the British Government, and would disappear on their withdrawal.

For all these reasons, the committee appeals to Britain, for the sake of her own safety, for the sake of India's safety and for the cause of world peace, to let go her hold on India, even if she does not give up all her Asiatic and African possessions.

This committee desires to assure the Japanese Government and people that India bears no enmity, either toward Japan or toward any other nation. India only desires freedom from all alien domination. But in this fight for freedom the committee is of the opin-ion that India, while welcoming universal sympathy, does not stand in need of foreign military aid.

India will attain her freedom through her non-violent strength, and will retain it likewise. Therefore, the committee hopes that Japan will not have any designs on India. But if Japan attacks India, and Britain makes no response to its appeal, the committee will expect all those who look to the Congress for guidance to offer complete non-violent non-cooperation to the Japanese forces, and not to render any assistance to them. It is no part of the duty of those who are attacked to render any assistance to the attacker. It is their duty to offer complete non-cooperation.

It is not difficult to understand the simple principle of nonviolent non-cooperation:

First, we may not bend the knee to an aggressor, or obey any of his orders.

Second, we may not look to him for any favours nor fall to his bribes, but we may not bear him any malice nor wish him ill.

Third, if he wishes to take possession of our fields we will refuse to give them up, even if we have to die in an effort to resist him.

Fourth, if he is attacked by disease, or is dying of thirst and seeks our aid, we may not refuse it.

Fifth, in such places where British and Japanese forces are fighting, our non-cooperation will be fruitless and unnecessary.

At present, our non-cooperation with the British Government is limited. Were we to offer them complete non-cooperation when they are actually fighting, it would be tantamount to bringing our country deliberately into Japanese hands. Therefore, not to put any obstacle in the way of the British forces will often be the only way of demonstrating our non-cooperation with the Japanese.

Neither may we assist the British in any active manner. If we can judge from their recent attitude, the British Government do not need any help from us beyond our non-interference. They desire our help only as slaves.

It is not necessary for the committee to make a clear declaration in regard to a scorched-earth policy. If, in spite of our nonviolence, any part of

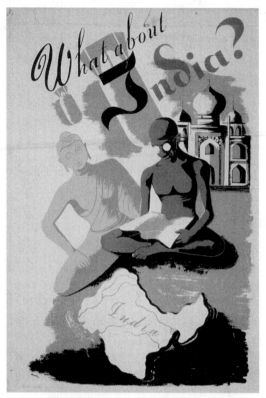

A wartime poster uses key images from India's past and present to question its future direction.

Courtesy of the Library of Congress, Prints and Photographs Division (LC-USZC2-803).

the country falls into Japanese hands, we may not destroy our crops or water supply, etc., if only because it will be our endeavour to regain them. The destruction of war material is another matter, and may, under certain circumstances, be a military necessity. But it can never be the Congress policy to destroy what belongs, or is of use, to the masses.

Whilst non-cooperation against the Japanese forces will necessarily be limited to a comparatively small number, and must succeed if it is complete and genuine, true building up of swaraj [self-government] consists in the millions of India wholeheartedly working for a constructive program. Without it, the whole nation cannot rise from its age-long torpor.

Whether the British remain or not, it is our duty

always to wipe out our unemployment, to bridge the gulf between the rich and the poor, to banish communal strife, to exorcise the demon of untouchability, to reform the Dacoits [armed bandits] and save the people from them. If scores of people do not take a living interest in this nation-building work, freedom must remain a dream and unattainable by either non-violence or violence.

Foreign soldiers: The committee is of the opinion that it is harmful to India's interests, and dangerous to the cause of India's freedom, to introduce foreign soldiers in India. It therefore appeals to the British Government to remove these foreign legions, and henceforth stop further introduction. It is a crying shame to bring foreign troops in, in spite of India's inexhaustible manpower, and it is proof of the immorality that British imperialism is.

> **Study Question**
>
> If Britain had removed all foreign soldiers in India, as Gandhi's version of the proposal demanded, how might this have affected the Indian independence movement?

Clement Attlee

Great Britain was devastated at the end of the Second World War. The nation was deeply in debt and many areas had been destroyed by wartime bombardment. Under such circumstances domestic needs had to take precedence over international commitments. Thus, on 15 March 1946 Labour Prime Minister Clement Attlee (1883–1967) announced that Britain was granting India's wish for independence. In the following speech

before the House of Commons, Attlee summarized the problems and the potential inherent in an independent India. Within Britain, especially among Conservative MPs, a substantial degree of opposition remained to granting India complete independence.

Document Source: Clement Attlee, "Debates of the House of Commons, 15 March 1946." From Clement Attlee. *Parliamentary Debates of the House of Commons*, 15 March 1946, HMSO 420, 1418–23.

Debates of the House of Commons, 15 March 1946

I have had a fairly close connection with this problem now for nearly 20 years, and I would say there have been faults on all sides, but at this time we should be looking to the future rather than harking back to the past. This alone I would say to hon. Members, that it is no good applying the formulae of the past to the present position. The temperature of 1946 is not the temperature of 1920 or of 1930 or even of 1942. The slogans of an earlier day are discarded. Indeed, sometimes words that seemed at that time to Indians to express the height of their aspirations are now set on one side, and other words, other ideas, are substituted. Nothing increases more the pace of public opinion than a great war. Everyone who had anything to do with this question in the early days between the wars knows what an effect the war of 1914–18 had on Indian aspirations and Indian ideals. A tide which runs slowly in peace becomes in wartime vastly accelerated, and especially directly after a war, because that tide is to some extent banked up during the war.

I am quite certain that at the present time the tide of nationalism is running very fast in India and, indeed, all over Asia. One always has to remember that India is affected by what happens elsewhere in Asia. I remember so well, when I was on the Simon Commission,[1] how it was borne in upon us what an effect the challenge that had been thrown out by

Japan at that time had had on the Asiatic people. The tide of nationalism that at one time seemed to be canalized among a comparatively small proportion of the people of India—mainly a few of the educated classes—has tended to spread wider and wider. I remember so well, indeed, I think we put it in the Simon Commission Report, that although there were great differences in the expression of nationalist sentiment between what are called the extremists and the moderates, and although in many circumstances there might be such a stress on communal claims as might seem almost to exclude the conception of nationalism, yet we found that Hindu, Muslim, Sikh or Mahrattah,[2] the politician or civil servant—among all of them that conception of nationalism had been growing stronger and stronger. Today I think that national idea has spread right through and not least, perhaps, among some of those soldiers who have given such wonderful service in the war. I should like today therefore, not to stress too much the differences between Indians. Let us all realize that whatever the difficulties, whatever the divisions may be, there is this underlying demand among all the Indian peoples. . . .

The right hon. Gentleman stressed the great part India played during the war. It is worthwhile recording that twice in 25 years India has played a great part in the defeat of tyranny. Is it any wonder that today she claims—as a nation of 400 million people that has twice sent her sons to die for freedom—that she should herself have freedom to decide her own destiny? My colleagues are going to India with the intention of using their utmost endeavours to help her to attain that freedom as speedily and fully as possible. What form of Government is to replace the present regime is for India to decide; but our desire is to help her to set up forthwith the machinery for making that decision. There we are met sometimes with the initial difficulty of getting that machinery set up. We are resolved that machinery shall be set up and we seek the utmost cooperation of all Indian leaders to do so. . . .

India herself must choose what will be her future Constitution; what will be her position in the world. I hope that the Indian people may elect to remain within the British Commonwealth. I am certain that she will find great advantages in doing so. In these days the demand for complete, isolated nationhood apart from the rest of the world, is really outdated. Unity may come through the United Nations, or through the Commonwealth, but no great nation can stand alone without sharing in what is happening in the world. But if she does so elect, it must be by her own free will. The British Commonwealth and Empire is not bound together by the chains of external compulsion. It is a free association of free peoples. If, on the other hand, she elects for independence, in our view she has the right to do so. It will be for us to help to make the transition as smooth and easy as possible.

We should be conscious that the British have done a great work in India. We have united India and given her that sense of nationalism which she so very largely lacked over the previous centuries. She has learned from us principles of democracy and justice. When Indians attack our rule, they base their attack, not on Indian principles, but on the basis of standards derived from Britain. I was struck the other day in the United States, at a dinner where I met a number of distinguished Americans, including a very distinguished Indian, where the talk was turning on the way in which principles worked out here, have been applied to the continent of America. It was pointed out that America had a great heritage from Britain. My Indian friend said to me, "You know the Americans sometimes forget there is another great nation that has also inherited these principles and traditions, and that is India. We feel that we have a duty, a right, and a privilege because we also bring to the world and work those very principles that you evolved in Britain."

I am well aware, when I speak of India, that I speak of a country containing a congeries of races, religions, and languages, and I know well all the difficulties thereby created. But those difficulties can only be overcome by Indians. We are very mindful of the rights of minorities and minorities should be able to live free from fear. On the other hand, we cannot allow a minority to place a veto on the advance of the majority. . . .

In conclusion, may I stress again the crucial nature of the task before us? This problem is of vital importance not only to India and the British Commonwealth and Empire, but to the world. There is this immense nation, set in the midst of Asia, an Asia which has been ravaged by war. Here we have the one great country that has been seeking to apply the principles of democracy. I have always hoped myself that politically India might be the light of Asia. It is a most unfortunate circumstance that, just at the time when we have to deal with these great political issues, there should be grave economic difficulties and, in particular, very grave anxiety over India's food supply. The House knows that His Majesty's Government are deeply concerned in this problem, and my right hon. Friend the Minister of Food is at the present time in the United States with an Indian delegation. We shall do our utmost to help

her. At the present moment I do not think I should say anything on the social and economic difficulties to which the right hon. Gentleman referred except this: I believe that those economic and social difficulties can only be solved by the Indians themselves, because they are so closely bound up with the whole Indian way of life and outlook. Whatever we can do to assist, we shall do. My right hon. Friends are going out to India resolved to succeed and I am sure everyone will wish them "God speed". . . .

Notes

1. The Simon Commission was dispatched to India in 1927 to report upon the state of government at the time and to suggest a future constitution for India. The Commission contained no Indian members.
2. The Mahrattah are descendants of an ethnic group that once ruled the southern tip of India (the Tamil region).

Study Question

Did Britain have any option other than to grant independence to India?

Jawaharlal Nehru

By the end of the Second World War, Jawaharlal Nehru had emerged as the clear leader of the Indian National Congress. With the decision to partition the country into predominantly Hindu and Muslim areas under the Mountbatten Plan, Nehru was poised to become the first prime minister of India on 15 August 1947. The following speech was delivered on the evening before independence became official. Even as he spoke Nehru was aware that tremendous violence had broken out as a result of the rapid partition of the country and the resulting movement of population.

Document Source: Jawaharlal Nehru, Jawaharlal Nehru, "A Tryst with Destiny," speech to the Constituent Assembly, August 14, 1947.

Tryst With Destiny, 14 August 1947

Long years ago we made a tryst with destiny, and now the time comes when we shall redeem our pledge, not wholly or in full measure, but very substantially.

At the stroke of the midnight hour, when the

world sleeps, India will awake to life and freedom. A moment comes, which comes but rarely in history, when we step out from the old to the new, when an age ends, and when the soul of a nation, long suppressed, finds utterance.

It is fitting that at this solemn moment we take the pledge of dedication to the service of India and her people and to the still larger cause of humanity.

At the dawn of history India started on her unending quest, and trackless centuries are filled with her striving and the grandeur of her success and her failures. Through good and ill fortune alike she has never lost sight of that quest or forgotten the ideals which gave her strength. We end today a period of ill fortune and India discovers herself again.

The achievement we celebrate today is but a step, an opening of opportunity, to the greater triumphs and achievements that await us. Are we brave enough and wise enough to grasp this opportunity and accept the challenge of the future?

Freedom and power bring responsibility. The responsibility rests upon this assembly, a sovereign body representing the sovereign people of India. Before the birth of freedom we have endured all the pains of labour and our hearts are heavy with the memory of this sorrow. Some of those pains continue even now. Nevertheless, the past is over and it is the future that beckons to us now.

That future is not one of ease or resting but of incessant striving so that we may fulfil the pledges we have so often taken and the one we shall take today. The service of India means the service of the millions who suffer. It means the ending of poverty and ignorance and disease and inequality of opportunity.

The ambition of the greatest man of our generation has been to wipe every tear from every eye. That may be beyond us, but as long as there are tears and suffering, so long our work will not be over.

And so we have to labour and to work, and work hard, to give reality to our dreams. Those dreams are for India, but they are also for the world, for all the nations and peoples are too closely knit together today for anyone of them to imagine that it can live apart.

Peace has been said to be indivisible; so is freedom, so is prosperity now, and so also is

Indian Prime Minister Jawaharlal Nehru visits the United States in 1949, two years after India gained its independence. Future Prime Minister Indira Gandhi, Nehru's daughter, stands to the right of her father.
Department of State. Courtesy of the Harry S. Truman Library.

disaster in this one world that can no longer be split into isolated fragments.

To the people of India, whose representatives we are, we make an appeal to join us with faith and confidence in this great adventure. This is no time for petty and destructive criticism, no time for ill will or blaming others. We have to build the noble mansion of free India where all her children may dwell.

The appointed day has come—the day appointed by destiny—and India stands forth again, after long slumber and struggle, awake, vital, free and independent. The past clings on to us still in some measure and we have to do much before we redeem the pledges we have so often taken. Yet the turning point is past, and history begins anew for us, the history which we shall live and act and others will write about.

It is a fateful moment for us in India, for all Asia and for the world. A new star rises, the star of freedom in the east, a new hope comes into being, a vision long cherished materialises. May the star never set and that hope never be betrayed!

We rejoice in that freedom, even though clouds surround us, and many of our people are sorrow-stricken and difficult problems encompass us. But freedom brings responsibilities and burdens and we have to face them in the spirit of a free and disciplined people.

On this day our first thoughts go to the architect of this freedom, the father of our nation, who, embodying the old spirit of India, held aloft the torch of freedom and lighted up the darkness that surrounded us.

We have often been unworthy followers of his and have strayed from his message, but not only we but succeeding generations will remember this message and bear the imprint in their hearts of this great son of India, magnificent in his faith and strength and courage and humility. We shall never allow that torch of freedom to be blown out, however high the wind or stormy the tempest.

Our next thoughts must be of the unknown volunteers and soldiers of freedom who, without praise or reward, have served India even unto death.

We think also of our brothers and sisters who have been cut off from us by political boundaries and who unhappily cannot share at present in the freedom that has come. They are of us and will remain of us whatever may happen, and we shall be sharers in their good and ill fortune alike.

The future beckons to us. Whither do we go and what shall be our endeavour? To bring freedom and opportunity to the common man, to the peasants and workers of India; to fight and end poverty and ignorance and disease; to build up a prosperous, democratic and progressive nation, and to create social, economic and political institutions which will ensure justice and fullness of life to every man and woman.

We have hard work ahead. There is no resting for any one of us till we redeem our pledge in full, till we make all the people of India what destiny intended them to be.

We are citizens of a great country, on the verge of bold advance, and we have to live up to that high standard. All of us, to whatever religion we may belong, are equally the children of India with equal rights, privileges and obligations. We cannot encourage communalism or narrow-mindedness, for no nation can be great whose people are narrow in thought or in action.

To the nations and peoples of the world we send greetings and pledge ourselves to cooperate with them in furthering peace, freedom and democracy.

And to India, our much-loved motherland, the ancient, the eternal and the ever-new, we pay our reverent homage and we bind ourselves afresh to her service. Jai Hind.

Study Question

According to Nehru's assessment, what was the single greatest problem facing India at this point in its history?

Syed Abul A'ala Maududi

Syed Abul A'ala Maududi (1903–1979) was a Pakistani political theorist and the founder of Jamaat-e-Islami, a party dedicated to the creation of an Islamic state in Pakistan. Maududi travelled widely and his works have been translated into a number of languages. He believed firmly in the reestablishment of Islamic law in Pakistan; however, he envisioned a gradual and carefully planned transition from the British system to one based upon sharia law. The following comments on Islamic law in Pakistan were presented in a 1948 speech.

Document Source: Abul A'ala Maududi, *The Islamic Law and its Introduction in Pakistan* (Lahore: Islamic Publications Limited, 1948), 43–50.

Islamic Law in Pakistan

If we really wish to see our Islamic ideals translated into reality, we should not overlook the basic law of nature that all stable and far-reaching changes in the collective life of a people come about gradually. The more sudden a change, the more short-lived it generally turns out to be. For a permanent change it is necessary that it should be free from extremist bias and unbalanced approach.

The best example of this gradual change is the revolution brought about by the Holy Prophet (peace be on him) in Arabia. One who is acquainted, even superficially, with the history of the Prophet's achievements knows that he did not enforce the entire body of Islamic laws all at once. Instead of that, the society was prepared gradually for their enforcement. He started his efforts for reform by inculcating belief in the fundamentals of Islam, namely, the unity of God, the Life after Death and the institution of Prophethood and by inducing the people to live a life of righteousness and piety. Those who accepted this message were trained by him to believe in and practice the Islamic Way of Life. When this was achieved to a considerable degree, the Prophet (peace be on him) went a step further and established an Islamic State in Madinah with the object of making the entire life of the country conform to the Islamic pattern. After gaining political power and taking the reins of administration in his hands, he (peace be on him) started an all-out campaign for the regeneration and the reconstruction of the collective life of the community on Islamic concepts of life: an end for which he had been heretofore endeavoring by means of preaching and persuasion only. . . .

Coming to our own times and our own country, Pakistan, if we wish to promulgate Islamic Law here, it would mean nothing less that the demolition of the entire structure erected by our British masters and the erection of a new one in its place. It is obvious that this cannot be achieved by just an official

proclamation or a parliamentary bill, because it is a stupendous task and demands a good deal of hard and systematic work according to a well-thought-out and all-embracing program. For instance, we need a thorough reorientation of our educational system. At present, we find two kinds of educational institutions running simultaneously in our country, namely, the old, religious "madrasahs" and the modern, secular schools, colleges, and universities. None of them can produce people needed to run a modern Islamic State. The old-fashioned schools are steeped in conservatism to such an extent that they have lost all touch with the modern world. Their education has lost all contact with the practical problems of life and has thus become barren and lifeless. It cannot, therefore, produce people who might be able to serve, for instance, as judges and magistrates of a progressive modern state. As for our modern, secular institutions, they produce people who are ignorant of even a rudimentary knowledge of Islam and its laws. Moreover, we can hardly find such persons among those whose mentality has not been affected by the poisonous content and the thoroughly materialistic bias of modern, secular education.

There is yet another difficultly. The Islamic law has not been in force for the last century or so. Consequently our legal code has become stagnant and has lagged behind the time, while our urgent need is to bring it in level with the latest developments of the modern age. Obviously, this would require a considerable amount of hard work.

There is, however, an even bigger hurdle. Living under the domination of an alien power and deprived of the Islamic influences for a long time, the pattern of our moral, cultural, social, economic, and political life has undergone a radical change, and is at present far removed from the Islamic ideals. Under such circumstances it cannot be fruitful, even if it were possible, to change the legal structure of the country all at once, because then the general pattern of life and the legal structure will be poles apart, and the legal change will have to suffer the fate of a sapling planted in an uncongenial soil and facing a hostile environment. It is, therefore, inevitable that the required reform should be gradual and the changes in the laws should be effected in such a manner as to balance favorably the change in the moral, educational, social, cultural, and political life of the nation.

But making a pretext of this reasonable consideration for gradation in change, some people plead for the establishment of a secular state for the time being. They argue that when an Islamic atmosphere is created, an Islamic state will automatically come into existence and the enforcement of Islamic law will follow in its natural course. Such statements are absolutely fallacious and misleading. The question is: Who will build up the required Islamic atmosphere? Can an irreligious state, with Westernized people at its helm, do this job? Will the persons well-versed only in running bars and night-clubs and movie-houses spend their energies in constructing and maintaining mosques? If the answer is in the affirmative it will indeed be a unique experience of its kind in human history: ungodliness fostering godliness so that it might ultimately be supplanted by the latter! . . .

If we reflect for a moment and consider the examples quoted above to support the principle of gradual change in the transformation of collective life, we can very well understand that a system of life, whether Islamic or un-Islamic, can be brought into existence only when the goal is unmistakably clear and a definite plan is chalked out for the achievement of that goal.

The Islamic revolution brought about by the Holy Prophet (peace be on him) was the outcome of years of toil—years spent in producing men suitable for the cause and in changing the outlook of the people by propagating the teachings of Islam. And above all, the entire administrative machinery of the small city state of Madinah was utilized for the regeneration of the society and the creation of a new civilization. Thus was the ground prepared for the enforcement of the Islamic laws.

The Britishers too, could succeed in bringing about their cherished changes in India only because the reins of government were in their hands and because they knew the proper method of transforming the collective life of a people. They had a definite goal and a clear plan. They worked incessantly for it and at last succeeded in establishing a legal system which was in conformity with their ideology and culture. But still some people are under the delusion that a building can be erected without architects or by those who are neither competent nor willing to do the job!

> **Study Question**
>
> What are the largest obstacles to the creation of a modern Islamic State, such as that envisioned by Maududi?

Paul Ramadier

Most nations in postwar Europe considered imperial obligations to be a cost that they could no longer afford. However, postwar French governments, including those on the left, stridently defended their right to re-occupy their colonial possessions. The following speech to the National Assembly was made by Socialist Prime Minister Paul Ramadier (1888–1961) on 18 March 1947. There are various references throughout the speech to "applause from the right" and so on. In the French National Assembly deputies are seated from right to left (from conservative to communist) according to their political ideology. Shortly after this speech deputies from the French Communist Party (PCF) were expelled from government.

Document Source: Paul Ramadier, "Speech to the National Assembly, 1947," in Tony Smith, *The End of the European Empire* (Lexington, MA: D.C. Heath, 1975).

Speech to the National Assembly

The Prime Minister (Ramadier): Ladies and gentlemen, two things are certain, affirmed by all and should be considered as unanimous conclusions of this debate.

The first is that France must stay in Indochina, that her succession there is not in question and that she must carry out there her civilizing work. *(Applause from the left, centre, and right.)*

The second is that the old ways are over. They have been criticized; they have been praised. There have assuredly been excesses. There have also been glorious pages written. A work has been accomplished which no one can deny, least of all probably those in the ranks of our opponents who came to gain their culture from our hands. *(Applause from the same benches.)* These are two certain facts, two established principles. Faced with the situation in Indochina we have wanted to have a policy of understanding. . . . Perhaps we have been carried away too quickly by the events; we have treated, we have negotiated. For almost a year, from March 6 until the morning of December 19, we have not ceased to negotiate.

The Overseas Minister (Moutet): Very good!

The Prime Minister: And then, on the 19th of December, we were obliged to recognize that the negotiations, even the accords, did not settle everything and that certain acts of violence, of savagery, tore up all the accords and ruined any thought of conciliation.

I have here, ladies and gentlemen, photographs of the mutilated bodies found in the burned-out houses of Hanoi. But perhaps more than any other act of savagery, the total destruction of the Pasteur Institute is the symbol of a wild, destructive will which is not, I am sure, that of the Vietnamese people, but of certain men.[1]

We were then obliged to fight.

Everyone has accepted this struggle, from the time of Léon Blum's Government just as at the moment, on January 21, when I made my declaration before the National Assembly.[2] *(Applause from the left, centre, and right.)*

At that time I said: "We cannot accept that the peace be disturbed. We must protect the life and the goods of those Frenchmen, foreigners and our Indochinese friends who put their confidence in French liberty. We must assure the security of our forts, reestablish essential communications and insure the security of the people who seek refuge with us."

This we have done.

The Government has sent the necessary reinforcements. We have sent them in force and as fast as we could. Not all have yet left. The departures continue. But already we can confirm the results.

And it is here that I want to render homage to our Far East Expeditionary Forces, to those soldiers who fight in a climate they are not used to, with a French faith which allows them to hold and to advance under the most difficult circumstances.

They have shown their heroism. France should express her gratitude. *(Prolonged applause from the left, centre, and right. The deputies seated on those benches rise.)*

(Numerous voices from the right and centre call to the extreme left [i.e., to the Communists] "Get up!" From the centre: "It is a disgrace to remain seated!")

René Pleven: I see that the Minister of Defence [Billoux, a Communist] has not risen. *(Exclamations from the extreme left.)*

Florimond Bonte [Communist]: It is we who defend the lives of our soldiers. We are not at your command! *(Exclamations from the right.)*

The President: The Prime Minister has the floor. It is to him alone at this time to express the sentiment of the Assembly and the country.

The Prime Minister: France should render

homage to those who have fallen. France should render homage to those who fight and who continue to fight. (*Applause from the left, centre, and right. The deputies seated on those benches rise again.*)

Fernand Bouxom: France rises!

The Prime Minister: She can proudly recognize the results obtained. We were speaking of forts it was necessary to open, of communication lines to reestablish along the Chinese border between Langson and the sea. Communications have been reestablished. From Hanoi to Haiphong, the road is open. A clever and audacious operation launched by troops from Tourane and a detachment from Savanaket have permitted us to rejoin the Mekong to the sea. Recently, on Government orders, Nam-Dinh has been cleared of the enemy. (*Applause to the left, centre, and right.*)

There is no solution but a political solution. Now we must build. And we know what it is we must build. We know because the Constitution says it. . . . Within the framework of the French Union we are going to create and organize an association of nations and peoples who will put or coordinate in common their resources and their efforts in order to develop their respective civilizations, increase their well-being, and insure their security. Not domination, not subjugation: association. We are not masters who have spoken as masters. We want to be instructors and counsellors. We are associates. This implies that we respect the independence of peoples. The preamble of the Constitution prescribes it: "Faithful to her traditional mission, France intends to guide the peoples for whom she has responsibility into freedom to administer themselves and conduct their own affairs democratically."

That is why, last 21 January, I stated before you: independence within the framework of the French Union, that is the right to conduct and administer democratically their own affairs, to choose their government, to fix the framework in which the Vietnamese people want to live. We expressed no preference. We were not going to impose our views. We recognize, we proclaim, we assure liberty—entirely and completely.

I also said: union of the three Vietnamese countries if the Vietnamese people wish, and I should have added, in the manner they wish. We know without question that the Vietnamese peoples have a feeling of their common culture and history, as well as of their differences, and that they want at once a certain unity and a certain flexibility within this unity. We want to respect their will just as we want to have respected the will of those other peoples, the Cambodians, the Laotians and the Montagnards. Here we are the servants of liberty, and the cause of the French Union and of French influence is tied to this cause of liberty. . . .

From xenophobia, that mindless hatred of the foreigner, we have everything to fear because it is negative and rests upon hatred. But from patriotism we have nothing to fear so long as we remember to respect the liberty of others. In Vietnam we will see new republics built with new liberties knowing, after all, that if the word liberty can be spoken in the Far East it is because France spoke it there first. (*Applause from the left, centre, and right.*) But this cannot be realized except within the framework of the French Union which, in addition to such broad freedom, implies mutual obligations as well. The 62nd Article of the French Constitution states that "the members of the French Union will pool all their resources in order to guarantee the defence of the entire Union. The Government of the Republic shall see to the coordination of these resources and to the direction of the policy appropriate to prepare and assure this defence."

That is to say that all these countries share a common foreign policy and military defence and that the French Republic is charged in the interest of all to direct them.

Most probably this was not clearly indicated in the Treaty of March 6. The Constitution had not then been approved; it had not even been written. Today there is no longer any question of the framework of the Treaty of March 6.[3] We can only be bound by the framework of the new Constitution which offers the possibility of a constructive effort. . . .

In order for this work to be accomplished, it is first of all necessary that France—that all of France—wants it and that it not be the policy of a majority against a minority, but the policy of France, wanted by her Assembly, wanted by her Parliament. . . . I address [the Communists]: this is our policy. It is the policy of freedom. It is the policy of the French Union. You accept this policy or you refuse it: here is the issue. *(Sharp applause from the left, centre, and right.)* . . .

Notes

1. The acts of violence to which Ramadier refers occurred in December 1946 following the 23 November bombardment of Haiphong by the French fleet in November. The French actions caused several thousand civilian casualties.
2. The Declaration was made when Ramadier was sworn in as Prime Minister.
3. The Treaty of 6 March 1946 recognized the Republic of Vietnam under Ho Chi Minh as a free state, but within the French Union.

Study Question

Did countries that gained their independence through violent struggle gain any advantages over those countries whose independence was granted peacefully?

Front de Libération Nationale (FLN)

French involvement in Algeria dated back to the 1830s, though total control over the country was not achieved until much later. During this period many European settlers had arrived in Algeria exacerbating tensions with the country's predominantly Muslim population. As in many colonized countries, resistance movements had emerged in the 1920s and 1930s, often led by French-educated Algerians. Eventually, several resistance movements combined into the National Liberation Front (FLN). Guided by an ideology that combined Algerian nationalism with a strongly socialist orientation, the FLN was eventually successful in its

quest for independence. The Proclamation below, dated 1 November 1954, announces the formation of the FLN and its primary goals. In 1958 the new French government of Charles de Gaulle indicated that it would consider the possibility of granting greater autonomy to Algeria. In 1962 a referendum produced almost unanimous support for independence; however, over one million people who were not sympathetic to the FLN subsequently fled to France.

Document Source: Front de Libération Nationale (FLN), Proclamation, 1 November 1954; http://www.marxists.org/history/algeria/1954/proclamation.htm

Proclamation, 1 November 1954

To the Algerian people

To the Militants of the National Cause

To you who are called upon to judge us, the Algerian people in a general way, the militants more particularly, our purpose in distributing this proclamation is to enlighten you concerning the profound reasons which have impelled us to act by revealing to

you our program, the meaning of our action, and the cogency of our views, the goal of which remains National Independence within the North African framework. Our wish as well is to help you avoid the confusion maintained by imperialism and its corrupt political and administrative agents.

Before all else, we consider that after decades of struggle the National Movement has reached its final stage of realization. In fact, as the goal of the revolutionary movement is to create all the favorable conditions needed for the launching of operations for liberation, we believe that internally the people are united behind the sign of independence and action; and externally the climate of détente is favorable for the settling of minor problems (among them ours) with the support of our Arab and Muslim brothers above all. The events in Morocco and Tunisia are significant in this regard, and profoundly mark the process of the liberation struggle in North Africa. It is worth noting that for quite some time we have been, in this regard, precursors in the unity of action, unfortunately never realized among the three countries.

Today, many are resolutely engaged on this path and we, relegated to the rear, suffer the fate of those who events have passed by. It is thus that our national movement, overwhelmed by years of *immobilisme* and routine, poorly oriented, deprived of the indispensable support of public opinion, and overtaken by events, has progressively disintegrated, to the great satisfaction of colonialism, which thinks it has carried off its greatest victory in its struggle against the Algerian vanguard. The hour is serious.

Facing this situation, which risks becoming irreparable, a group of young leaders and conscious activists, rallying around it the majority of the healthy and decisive elements, has judged that the moment has arrived to move the National Movement out of the impasse into which it was backed by personal struggles and fights over influence, in order to launch it, at the side of the Moroccan and Tunisian brothers, into the true revolutionary struggle.

To this end, we insist on specifying that *we are independent of the two clans* that are fighting over power. Placing national interest above all petty and erroneous considerations of personality and prestige, in conformity with revolutionary principles, our action is directed solely against colonialism, our only blind and obstinate enemy, which has always refused to grant the least freedom by peaceful means.

These are, we think, sufficient reasons for a movement of renewal to present itself under the name of NATIONAL LIBERATION FRONT, releasing itself in this way from all possible compromises, and offering the possibility to all Algerian patriots of all social classes, of all the purely Algerian parties and movements, to integrate themselves into the struggle for liberation, without any other consideration. . . .

In order to reach these objectives, the National Liberation Front will have two essential tasks to carry out simultaneously: an internal action, on the fronts of politics and action, and an external action, with the goal of the making of the Algerian problem a reality for the entire world, with the support of all our natural allies.

This is a heavy task which necessitates the mobilization of all national energy and resources. It is true that the struggle will be long, but the result is certain.

In the last place, in order to avoid all false interpretations and subterfuges, in order to prove our real desire for peace, to limit the number of human lives lost and the amount of blood spilled, we propose to French authorities an honorable platform of discussion, if these latter are animated by good faith and recognize once and for all in the people they subjugate the right to dispose of themselves:

1. The opening of negotiations with the authorized spokesmen of the Algerian people on the basis of the recognition of sovereignty through Algerian liberation, one and indivisible.

2. The creation of a climate of confidence through the liberation of all political prisoners, the lifting of all measures of exception, and the ceasing of all pursuit of the fighting forces.

3. The recognition of Algerian nationality by an official declaration abrogating the edicts, decrees and laws making Algeria a "French land," which is a denial of the History, the geography, the language, the religion, and the mores of the Algerian people.

In return:

1. French cultural and economic interests, honestly acquired, will be respected, as will persons and families.
2. All Frenchmen wishing to remain in Algeria will have the choice between their nationality of origin, in which case they will be considered foreigners vis-à-vis the laws in place, or they will opt for Algerian nationality, in which case they will be considered such in rights and obligations.
3. The bonds between France and Algeria will be defined and will be the object of an agreement between the two powers on the basis of equality and mutual respect.

Algerian[s]! We invite you to think over our above Charter. Your obligation is to join with it in order to save our country and restore to it its freedom. The National Liberation Front is your front. Its victory is yours.

As for us, resolved to pursue the struggle, sure of your anti-imperialist sentiments, we give the best of ourselves to the Fatherland.

The Secretariat

> **Study Question**
>
> References within this proclamation hint at the problems which would beset Algeria after independence. Which of these problems stand out?

Ahmed Sekou Touré

Sekou Touré (1922–1984) was born in French West Africa at the height of French colonial domination of the region. He was educated in a French school and was familiar with the works of Marx and Lenin (note his comments below regarding the loss of identity that accompanied his French education). After gaining a leading position in the movement for independence, Touré was able to convince his fellow Guineans to reject an offer of autonomy within the French Union, *and successfully obtained full independence for his country. As President, Touré was criticized for the authoritarian manner by which he ruled his country; however, he was highly regarded by leaders of the more radical civil rights organizations in the United States. The following analysis of the "African problem" was published in 1960.*

Document Source: Sekou Touré, "The Republic of Guinea," *International Affairs*, 36(2), (April 1960): 168–73.

The Republic of Guinea

The African problem is both simple and complex, and many nations, groups, and parties are facing the kind of new problems with which Guinea is now faced. Africa is a geographical and a human entity but, both morally and spiritually, it is more diverse than any other. It is therefore essential to discuss the problems that have to be solved in that context. It is impossible for me, either in writing or in lectures, to present these problems objectively. But it is possible to present a context, though it will necessarily contribute an

incomplete image of my country, a country that some of you probably knew before I was born.

The essential factor that I want to bring out is the extent to which we, in Africa, are conditioned by our way of life. Our country is backward and has gone through three distinct stages. First, there was the stage of pre-colonization, in which our organization was communal. Each group had its own customs, its own concepts of economic organization, its own philosophy. It had its own sketchy form of civilization. But the important thing is that this civilization was our own. Like other parts of the world, our countries knew insecurity and famine and went through the kind of struggle which is common to the whole human race. To satisfy their material and moral needs people had to use what means they found at hand. They had few contacts with the outside world.

In the second stage, with the arrival of outsiders, these contacts were established. At first they were economic, then social, cultural, and political. During this period our original way of life was interrupted and modified by our contact with other civilizations. Sometimes the evolution characteristic of the first stage was arrested, sometimes it became more dynamic; in any case life was changed. Above all, it was diverted from its normal course. In my grandparents' time, ethnic, language, and tribal divisions gave way to divisions on a territorial basis. African lands became colonies whose frontiers no longer respected the natural divisions which, though not watertight, had formerly—whether, for instance, in Senegal, in Sudan, or in Guinea—had a real existence.

These countries are inhabited by the same races and have the same civilization. Their essential characteristics are those of the entire African continent. But the colonizers had their own methods. The first change that they made, the modification of frontiers, was a negative contribution. The second, the linking of the African economy to the world economy, was more dynamic. It brought many changes. It helped to increase markets and provided more social opportunities. Yet social development could not progress very far, because the natural basis, the popular basis, was lacking. The new social organization also created new problems. Education brought us into contact with new cultures. A certain number of us assimilated the civilization of other countries, and the result was that Africa became culturally divided. May I quote a personal example? I find myself more at home with French friends than with my own elder brother who has never been to school.

Colonization meant that opportunities of advancement were open to a small African élite, but the cost was the creation of deep divisions between us.

Materially, there was progress. But the happiness of man does not come merely from material things. It comes from the harmonious development of material and spiritual elements. The risk was that a moral vacuum would be created, that we should become déclassés, educated, but at home nowhere.

This is the negative contribution of Colonialism. Evolution, which in the pre-colonial era was vertical, now became horizontal. The different areas of Africa evolved inharmoniously, along different lines. It was a period of unification, military, administrative, and cultural unification, when laws were applied throughout a whole territory. The result was to create a positive sense of belonging to a larger community than that of the family or the tribe. But it also had the negative result that the unified system was ill-adapted to meet the real diversity of needs. There was a consequent distortion.

During this phase, individual Africans benefited from new possibilities of evolution. At first, they welcomed assimilation, because education revealed new horizons. But these horizons were always receding. The original aim was to achieve equality between rulers and ruled. But, too often, Africans found, say, when elected to the Assembly, that their problems were as far as ever from a solution. Another phase followed, during which trade unions, students' associations, ex-servicemen's organizations, cultural organizations, and political parties were formed. They constituted an affirmation of the African personality.

This is not a complete picture, but it is a picture of something that we feel deeply, even if we cannot always express these feelings articulately.

There followed a third stage, in which we realized that individual expressions of our personality were not enough. We had to find collective forms of association because, as individuals, we could not achieve our objective, which was the expression of the African personality. This stage is the most important, but the most difficult to describe. Africans believe that the dynamic period of colonialism gave Africa a positive means of action. Our struggle for independence is not negative. We want to retain the positive contribution of colonialism, the increased contacts and the increased possibilities of exchange that it brought. But we want to eliminate its negative aspects. Africa has, we believe, potentialities for economic expansion, and we believe that independence will be a factor making for stabilization. We do not believe that independence will bring a Paradise on earth. We are conscious of our need to unite, and independence is, for us, a means to that end. We are realists. We want to increase our understanding of, and our cooperation with, other peoples, to liquidate the disequilibrium that has been created in Africa.

Man, as a human being, must fulfill himself. If we cannot create the necessary conditions for ourselves, we must create them for those who will come after us. This is the real moving force of African nationalism. You can afford to oppose nationalism, because you have gone through this stage. We have not. That is the tragedy of our situation. What we want is to have laws that are the expression of our own people, and this they have not always been. An imposed system, however good it may be, is never valued as much as one that one has created for oneself. What is lacking is human dignity.

Of course, we in Guinea have our problems. Our country includes many tribes, speaking some twenty different languages. This is a problem which has to be tackled. It is no good shutting one's eyes to the fact of our internal divisions; it is better to tackle them head on. We must organize the country. At first there has naturally been opposition, but in two, or three, or five years our people will have forgotten this.

We want to be responsible for our own lives. One can always give one's brother good advice, but he may prefer to make his own mistakes. That is the African psychology, and it is another reason why we are nationalists. Whatever people may say, nationalism is psychologically inevitable and we are all nationalists. What we Africans are seeking is justice and equality. Let me give you an example of what I mean. An employer may decide to pay a wage of 1,000 francs, even though he knows that the minimum wage is only 500 francs. Everybody will be happy at getting double the rate. But if there is inequality between one worker and another the whole relationship within the group will be affected. This is a human problem that the employer does not understand. He sees only that he is paying double rates. But what the African is interested in is equality.

> **Study Question**
>
> What does Touré consider to be the positive legacies of colonial rule? Negative?

Fidel Castro

The following speech was delivered by Fidel Castro (b. 1926) to a massive gathering of Cuban people in Havana in September 1960. A little over eighteen months had elapsed since Castro's forces had toppled the Batista regime, during which time his policy towards the United States had remained relatively moderate. However, this speech marked the first clear statement of Castro's new socialist policy and his increasingly hostile view of American attempts to undermine the Cuban revolution. The speech provides an overview of the desperate situation facing the people of Cuba and its new government after the overthrow of Batista.

Document Source: Fidel Castro, "On the Exploitation of the Cuban Nation." From *Obra Revolucionaria*, 22 (Havana, 6 September 1960), 15–20.

On the Exploitation of the Cuban Nation

Citizens: It is obvious that each of you, from where you are sitting, is completely unable to see the vast size of the crowd which has gathered this afternoon. It is a true sea of humanity which stretches into the distance on both sides of the Civic Plaza.

For us, the men of the revolutionary government, who have seen many popular gatherings, this one is so huge that it impresses us deeply and helps to show us the vast responsibility which you and we carry upon our shoulders.

The people have gathered today to discuss important matters, particularly those of an international nature. But why has no one remained at home? Why has this been the largest gathering our people have held since the triumph of the revolution? Why? Because our people know what they are defending, our people know what battle they are waging. And as our people know that they are waging a great struggle for their survival and triumph, and since our people are a combative and a courageous people—that is why Cubans are present here.

And it is said that today, when we are going to discuss the same questions as were discussed in Costa Rica, the 21 American foreign ministers are not seated here. It is very sad that they are not present, so that they could have a chance to see the people they condemned at the Costa Rica meeting. It is sad that they are not here, so they could see how different the diplomatic language of the foreign ministries and the language of the peoples are!

There, however, our foreign minister spoke on behalf of our people. But those who heard him, the majority of those who were gathered there, did not represent their peoples. If there, in Costa Rica, men representing the true interests and feelings of the peoples of America, particularly the peoples of Latin America, had gathered there, never could a statement such as that issued against the interests of an American people and against the interests of all the brotherly peoples of America have been drafted.

And what were they discussing there? There they were playing with the destiny of our country, there they were whitewashing the aggressions against our country. There they were sharpening the dagger which the criminal hand of Yankee imperialism wants to drive into the heart of the Cuban fatherland!

But why did they want to condemn Cuba? What has Cuba done to be condemned? What has our people done to merit the Costa Rica Declaration? Our people have done nothing but break their chains! Our people have done nothing, harming no other people and taking nothing from any other people, than to fight for a better destiny. Our people have wanted only to be free, our people have wanted only to live from their

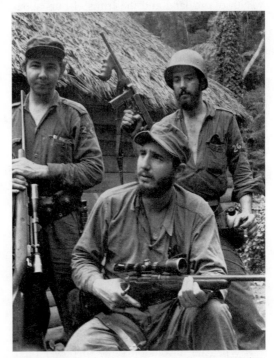

A young Fidel Castro during the guerrilla campaign in Cuba's Sierra Maestra mountains.

Image © Corbis

own works, and our people have wanted nothing but to live from the fruits of their efforts. Our people have wanted nothing except to have what is theirs, that what is produced from their land, that what is produced with their blood, that what is produced with their sweat should be theirs.

The Cuban people have only wanted the decisions guiding their conduct to be theirs, that the flag with the solitary star which flutters over our fatherland should be theirs and theirs alone! They wanted their laws to be their own, their natural wealth to be their own, their democratic and revolutionary institutions to be their own. They wanted their fate to be their own, a fate in which no interest, no oligarchy and no government, however powerful it might be, would have a right to interfere.

And it must be our freedom, because it has cost us much sacrifice to win it. Sovereignty must be ours and complete, because our people have been fighting for sovereignty for a century. The wealth of our land and the fruits of our labour must be ours, because our people have had to sacrifice much for this and all that has been created has been created by the people, and all there is here of wealth has been produced by our people, through their sweat and their labour.

Our people had a right to be a free people one day. Our people had a right to govern their own destiny one day. Our people had a right to expect one day to have a government which would not defend the foreign monopolies, which would not defend the privileged interests, which would not defend the exploiters, but which would put the interests of the people and their fatherland above the interests of the greedy foreigners, a government which would put the interests of the people, the interests of the peasants, the interests of the workers, the interests of the young people and children, the interests of the women and the old people above the interests of the privileged and the exploiters.

When the revolution came to power on 1 January 1959, just a little more than a year and a half ago, what was there in our country? What

was there in our fatherland but tears, blood, misery, and sweat? What was there for the peasants in our country? What was there for the children? What was there for the workers here? What was there in Cuba for the humble families? What prevailed in our fatherland until that day?

The most inhuman exploitation, abuse, injustice, systematic plunder of public funds by greedy politicians, had prevailed, the systematic exploitation of our national wealth by foreign monopolies, inequality and discrimination, lies and deceit, submission to foreign ambitions and poverty had prevailed. Hundreds and hundreds of thousands of families lived without hope in their humble huts. Hundreds and hundreds of thousands of children were without schools. More than a half a million Cubans were without work. And black Cubans had less opportunity than anyone to find work. The rural people lived in compounds. The sugar cane workers were employed only a few months a year and they and their children suffered hunger the rest of the time. Vice, gambling and all that goes with it prevailed in our country. The farmer was exploited, the fisherman was exploited, the worker was exploited—the vast majority of the people were exploited.

Nothing was ever done for the people. No measures of justice were ever undertaken to free the people from hunger, from their poverty, from their pain and suffering, to free you, the Cuban citizens, to free you, men and women, old people and children, to free you, this vast multitude which has gathered here, to free the Cuban nation, to do something for it, to make something good of it—absolutely nothing was done.

And the people, helpless, had to tolerate it. The people had to pay the highest rents in the world in our fatherland. The people had to pay the highest electrical rates in the world in our fatherland. The people had to pay for telephone services as dictated by the interests of a foreign company which extracted concessions from a tyrannical government, while the blood of our heroic student youth was still warm in the courtyards of the Presidential Palace.

The monetary reserves of the nation were down to only 70 million. Our country, in unequal trade with the United States, had paid out a billion dollars more than we had been paid for our goods in ten years. There were no factories. Who would establish factories for the hundreds of thousands of Cubans who were without work? There were no plans for agriculture, no plans for industry. Who would concern himself with establishing industries? And the people, what could they do? What could the sugar worker do? What could the sugar cane farmer do? What could the worker do? The worker had only his miserable wage, the piece of bread which he could not always provide to his starving children. The profits were carried off by the foreign monopolies, the profits were accumulated by the owners. The profits were accumulated by the interests which grew fat off the labor of the people. And this money was either kept indefinitely in the banks or was spent on all kinds of luxuries. Mainly, it went abroad.

Who would establish factories for the hundreds of thousands of Cubans who were without work? And as the Cuban population was growing, and as each year more than 50,000 young people came of age, what were they to live on? What was the growing population of our fatherland to live on? How were the peasants, the children of the peasants, to live when they had neither work nor land? How was a people which was growing, and whose growth was much more rapid than the increase in its industry and its economy supposed to live?

The people lacked every kind of opportunity. The son of a peasant, or of a worker, or of any humble family, could hardly hope to become a professional one day—a doctor, an engineer, an architect, or a university technician. There were children of poor families who by dint of great sacrifice managed to complete higher studies, but the vast majority of the children of our families often even lacked the opportunity to learn their letters, and there were entire regions in Cuba where there had never been a teacher. Our people had access

to nothing but work, if they could find it! For our people, only the worst was available. For our people, there were never any sports fields, never any streets, never any parks, and there were many places where if there was a park, some citizens—the black ones—were not allowed.

This was what the revolution inherited when it came to power: an economically underdeveloped country, a people which had been the victim of every kind of exploitation. This was what the revolution found at the end of its heroic and bloody struggle. And revolutions are not undertaken to leave things as they were. Revolutions are undertaken to correct all the injustices. Revolutions are not undertaken to protect and promote privileges. Revolutions are undertaken to aid those who need to be aided. Revolutions are undertaken to establish justice, to put an end to abuse, to put an end to exploitation. And our revolution was undertaken for this, and to this end those who fell gave their lives, and to achieve this goal so many sacrifices were made.

The revolution came to correct matters in our fatherland. The revolution came to do what each Cuban had been asking to have done for so long. When any helpless Cuban citizen analyzed life in our country and the picture presented by national life, he said: "This must be corrected. This needs correcting, one day this must be changed." And the more optimistic said: "One day this will be changed."

To correct matters in their country, Cubans had been fighting for a long time. But there was a greater force which prevented us from correcting things in our country. This force was the imperialist penetration of the United States in our fatherland. It was this force which frustrated our full independence. It was this force which prevented Calixto Garcia and his brave soldiers in Santiago de Cuba from succeeding. It was this force which prevented the liberation army from undertaking revolution in the early days of the republic. It was this force which determined the destiny of our fatherland from the very first. It was this force which permitted the seizure of the natural resources and the best lands of our fatherland by foreign interests. It was this force which appropriated the right to intervene in our country's affairs. It was this force which crushed so many revolutionary efforts. It was this force which was always associated with everything negative, everything reactionary, and everything abusive in our country. It was this force which prevented an earlier revolution in our fatherland, and it is this force which is trying to prevent us from correcting things in our country now. This is the force which maintained the tyranny. This is the force which trained the hired ruffians of the tyranny, which armed the soldiers of the tyrant, which provided weapons, planes, and bombs to the tyrant's regime, in order to keep our people under the worst kind of oppression. This force has been the main enemy of development and progress in our country. This force has been the main cause of our evils. This force has dedicated itself to the failure of the Cuban revolution. This force is trying to ensure that the war criminals will return, that the exploiters will return, that the monopolies will return, that the large estate owners will return, that misery will return, that oppression will return to our country.

Cubans must see with full clarity that imperialism is the force to which we refer, that it is trying to prevent our people from achieving full development. They must understand that this force does not want you, the Cubans, to achieve a higher standard of living. It does not want your children educated, it does not want our workers to profit from the fruits of their labour. It does not want our peasants to enjoy the fruits of their land. It does not, in a word, want our people to be able to grow, to be able to work, and to have a better destiny.

Our people have not had an opportunity in the past to understand these great truths. The truth was concealed from our people. Our people were miserably deceived. Our people were kept divided and confused. Our people have never had an opportunity to discuss these matters of an international nature. The people did not know a word of what was being said by the American Ambassador to the government leaders. The people did not know a word of what the foreign ministers were saying, the people counted for nothing. The people were not gathered together to learn about their problems. The people were not gathered together to be guided or to be told the truth. The destinies of our peoples were decided by the US Foreign Minister, our people counted for nothing in the destiny of the country.

Could Cuba continue to resign itself to this fate? Could Cubans continue to tolerate this system? What have the Cubans done? All they have done is to rebel against all this. All the Cubans have done is to free themselves from all this.

Study Question

According to Castro, in what ways had Cuba been damaged by its neo-colonial relationship with the United States?

United Nations

On 14 December 1960 the United Nations General Assembly adopted Resolution 1514: Declaration on the Granting of Independence to Colonial Countries and Peoples. Though the process of decolonization was well underway by 1960, numerous peoples remained under colonial or neo-colonial rule. Thus the Declaration has been invoked on many occasions in support of nascent independence movements. The contemporary reader should recall, however, that a General Assembly resolution carries little weight under international law.

Document Source: United Nations, UN Declaration on Colonial Independence. Available online: http://www.un.org/en/decolonization/declaration.shtml

UN Declaration on Colonial Independence

The General Assembly

Mindful of the determination proclaimed by the peoples of the world in the Charter of the United Nations to reaffirm faith in fundamental human rights, in the dignity and worth of the human person, in the equal rights of men and women and of nations large and small, and to promote social progress and better standards of life in larger freedom,

Conscious of the need for the creation of conditions of stability and well-being and peaceful and friendly relations based on respect for the principles of equal rights and self-determination of all peoples, and of universal respect for, and observance of, human rights and fundamental freedoms for all without distinction as to race, sex, language, or religion,

Recognizing the passionate yearning for freedom in all dependent peoples and the decisive role of such peoples in the attainment of their independence,

Aware of the increasing conflicts resulting from the denial of or impediments in the way of the freedom of such peoples, which constitute a serious threat to world peace,

Considering the important role of the United Nations in assisting the movement for independence in Trust and Non-Self-Governing Territories,

Recognizing that the people of the world ardently desire the end of colonialism in all its manifestations,

Convinced that the continued existence of colonialism prevents the development of international economic cooperation, impedes the social, cultural, and economic development of dependent peoples and militates against the United Nations ideal of universal peace,

Affirming that peoples may, for their own ends, freely dispose of their natural wealth and resources without prejudice to any obligations arising out of international economic cooperation, based upon the principle of mutual benefit, and the international law,

Believing that the process of liberation is irresistible and irreversible and that, in order to avoid serious crises, an end must be put to colonialism and all practices of segregation and discrimination associated therewith,

Welcoming the emergence in recent years of a large number of dependent territories into freedom and independence, and recognizing the increasingly powerful trends towards freedom in such territories which have not yet attained independence,

Convinced that all peoples have an inalienable right to complete freedom, the exercise of their sovereignty and the integrity of their national territory,

Solemnly proclaims the necessity of bringing to a speedy and unconditional end colonialism in all its forms and manifestations;

And to this end

Declares that:

1. The subjection of peoples to alien subjugation, domination, and exploitation constitutes a denial of fundamental human rights, is contrary to the Charter of the United Nations and is an impediment to the promotion of world peace and cooperation.

2. All peoples have the right to self-determination; by virtue of that right they freely determine their political status and freely pursue their economic, social and cultural development.

3. Inadequacy of political, economic, social, or educational preparedness should never serve as a pretext for delaying independence.

4. All armed action or repressive measures of all kinds directed against dependent peoples shall cease in order to enable them to exercise peacefully and freely their right

to complete independence, and the integrity of their national territory shall be respected.

5. Immediate steps shall be taken, in Trust and Non-Self-Governing Territories or all other territories which have not yet attained independence, to transfer all powers to the peoples of those territories, without any conditions or reservations, in accordance with their freely expressed will and desire, without any distinction as to race, creed, or colour, in order to enable them to enjoy complete independence and freedom.

6. Any attempt aimed at the partial or total disruption of the national unity and the territorial integrity of a country is incompatible with the purposes and principles of the Charter of the United Nations.

7. All States shall observe faithfully and strictly the provisions of the Charter of the United Nations, the Universal Declaration of Human Rights, and the present Declaration on the basis of equality, noninterference in the internal affairs of all States, and respect for the sovereign rights of all peoples and their territorial integrity.

Study Question

Despite its positive intent, are there elements of the UN Declaration that could be seen as leading to future regional or global instability?

Web Resources

African History on the Internet: Colonial Period
    http://www-sul.stanford.edu/depts/ssrg/africa/history/hiscolonial.html
Internet African History Sourcebook
    http://www.fordham.edu/halsall/africa/africasbook.html
History in Focus: Empire
    http://www.history.ac.uk/ihr/Focus/Empire/index.html
Political Discourse: Theories of Colonialism and Post-colonialism
    http://www.postcolonialweb.org/poldiscourse/discourseov.html

Recommended Reading

André Brink, *A Dry White Season* (New York: Penguin, 1984). Brink is an Afrikaner author whose powerful novel exposes many of the injustices of the apartheid system. *A Dry White Season*—set against the Soweto Riots in 1976—tells the story of a white Afrikaner who attempts to explain the disappearance of a black friend.

Graham Greene, *The Quiet American* (New York: Penguin, 1996). American involvement in Indochina, particularly during the final days of French rule, forms the backdrop for the 1955 novel, *The Quiet American*. The novel is sympathetic towards the Vietminh guerrillas and seems prophetic in its look at the consequences of early American activities in the region.

Rohinton Mistry, *A Fine Balance* (New York: Vintage, 2001). Mistry's Giller Prize-winning novel takes place in India in 1975–6 during the state of emergency declared by Indira Gandhi. Social policies, including forced sterilization, corruption, violence, and caste discrimination, form the backdrop as the characters try to find a "fine balance between hope and despair."

V.S. Naipaul, *A Bend in the River* (New York: Vintage, 1989). Set in Kisangani on the Congo River, a young merchant of Indian descent sets out to make his fortune in post-colonial Zaire. The novel takes place during Mobutu's attempt to forge a new identity for Zaire as the country experienced spiralling poverty, ethnic conflict, and government corruption. *A Bend in the River* raises complex questions of identity, traditional values, modernity, and post-colonial power structures.

Khushwant Singh, *Train to Pakistan* (New York: Grove Press, 1990). In 1947 a small village on the proposed border with Pakistan finds itself immersed in the panic of partition. Traditionally peaceful relations between Hindu and Muslim are strained as the devastating consequences of forcible separation become clear. Singh's novel provides a sensitive look at the tension and violence wrought by the decision to partition India.

M.G. Vassanji, *The In-Between World of Vikram Lall* (New York: Knopf, 2003). The story of a third-generation Indian child growing up in East Africa, caught between the world of Africans and the world of Europeans, experiences the Mau Mau rebellion, post-independence government, the colonial legacy, corruption, and finally, exile.

Recommended Viewing

Cry, the Beloved Country (UK, 1951). Director: Zoltan Korda (B&W). Shot on location in South Africa when the apartheid system was consolidating its grip on the country, Korda provides a powerful examination of systemic racism and its consequences in the 1940s.

The Battle of Algiers (Algeria/Italy, 1966). Director: Gilberto Pontecorvo. This film provides a highly sympathetic account of the FLN's struggle to liberate Algeria from French rule. The film, which was banned in France for several years, captures the motivations and radical tactics utilized by the FLN, and later adopted by many other groups around the world.

Cry Freedom (UK/USA, 1987). Director: Richard Attenborough. In *Cry Freedom* Attenborough recreates the friendship between white South African journalist Donald Woods and the black anti-apartheid activist Stephen Biko, the struggle to investigate Biko's death, and the difficulty of keeping Biko's anti-apartheid message alive.

Long Night's Journey Into Day (USA, 2000). Directors: Frances Reid/Deborah Hoffmann. (Documentary). This 90-minute documentary examines the workings of the Truth and Reconciliation Commission in South Africa. It follows four of the Commission's cases as the perpetrators attempt to reconcile with the families of their victims.

The Quiet American (USA/Australia, 2002). Director: Phillip Noyce. Much of the history in *The Quiet American* is played out in the background, but this adaptation of Graham Greene's novel still offers an interesting look at the level of American involvement prior to the French defeat in Indochina. In particular, the film exposes the early years of CIA involvement in Vietnamese politics.

12

The Postwar Era in
the Middle East

Postwar development in the Middle East must be understood in the context of prewar policy, as well as the events of the Second World War. The creation of League of Nations Mandates throughout the region, in the wake of the First World War, had intensified pre-existing conflicts and created new ones. The British White Paper of 1939 endeavoured to contain some of these tensions by severely limiting emigration to the Mandate of Palestine. In retrospect the timing of these emigration restrictions could not have been worse. Hitler was poised to begin his expansion into Eastern Europe and had already predicted in January 1939 that, in the event of another war, it would be the Jews of Europe who would pay the ultimate price.

By 1945, Soviet and American troops had liberated the remaining concentration and extermination camps and the pressure to settle Jewish survivors and refugees was growing. In the Mandate of Palestine anti-British sentiment was becoming increasingly violent, with organizations such as Irgun using increasingly effective terror tactics against the British authorities. The British government, facing problems at home and in its empire, chose to hand the situation off to the United Nations, which ultimately devised a proposal to create two states—one Arab and one Jewish—in the area. The immediate result was the 1948 Arab–Israeli War, the end of which saw the State of Israel substantially strengthened and the Arab forces weakened and divided. At least 700,000 refugees fled the area during the 1948 war, creating an ongoing conflict over the right of those refugees to return to Palestine. Meanwhile the remaining League Mandates in the area, including Transjordan, Syria, and Lebanon, also broke free of their mandatory overlords in the immediate aftermath of the Second World War.

The events taking place in the postwar Middle East also played out in the context of the Cold War. Though both the US and the Soviet Union supported the creation of the State of Israel, over the years the Americans increasingly supported the Israelis, whereas the Soviets backed the Arab States. Thus, periodic conflicts in the region threatened to evolve into catastrophic superpower clashes, particularly in the 1950s and 1960s.

The documents in this chapter begin with the profound impact of the creation of the State of Israel and the conflicts which followed. The MacDonald White Paper of 1939 sets the stage for the events that followed in the second half of the twentieth century. The reader can also refer to the documents in Chapter Eight for more on the discussions which led to the creation of the State of Israel. The postwar history of the Middle East was also shaped by the emergence of a new and powerful advocate of Arab nationalism: Gamal Abdel Nasser. Nasser's views on regional development are evident in his speech on the nationalization of the Suez Canal in 1956. With the events of 1956 setting the stage for further conflict, the next two documents examine the consequences of the 1967 Six-Day War and the seizure of the Occupied Territories. UN Resolution 242 discusses international opinion on the war; the Palestine National Charter presents the opinions of some of the inhabitants of the occupied territories.

Some of the optimism of the mid-1970s is captured in Golda Meir's remarks on Egyptian president Anwar Sadat's visit to Israel in 1977. As well, the joint US/USSR statement on peace in the Middle East provides insight into the pressure exerted by both superpowers to resolve the endless cycle of violence in the region. However, despite the achievement of peace between Egypt and Israel in 1978, the major concerns of the Palestinians remained unresolved. This led to the creation of increasingly radical groups, such as Hamas, in the 1980s. Excerpts from the Hamas Covenant provide insight into the organization's ideology in 1988. The late Edward Said speaks of the possibility of "truth and reconciliation" between Israel and the Palestinians in the wake of the accords of the early 1990s. The chapter concludes with Saddam Hussein's address to his armed forces on the eve of the 2003 American invasion of Iraq.

Government of Great Britain

In late 1938 the British Government invited representatives of both the Arab and Jewish populations of Palestine to a discussion of future British policy in the region. Neither the Arab nor the Jewish representatives were willing to accept the British government proposals and, as a result, the Government proceeded unilaterally to impose a new policy for the Mandate of Palestine. This new policy was embodied in the White Paper of 1939.

Document Source: Government of Great Britain, *The British White Paper of 1939*. Available online: http://avalon.law.yale.edu/20th_century/brwh1939.asp

The White Paper of 1939

The Mandate for Palestine, the terms of which were confirmed by the Council of the League of Nations in 1922, has governed the policy of successive British Governments for nearly 20 years. It embodies the Balfour Declaration and imposes on the Mandatory four main obligations. . . .

There is no dispute regarding the interpretation of one of these obligations, that touching the protection of and access to the Holy Places and religious buildings or sites. The other three main obligations are generally as follows:

To place the country under such political,

administrative, and economic conditions as will secure the establishment in Palestine of a national home for the Jewish People. To facilitate Jewish immigration under suitable conditions, and to encourage, in cooperation with the Jewish Agency, close settlement by Jews on the Land.

To safeguard the civil and religious rights of all inhabitants of Palestine, irrespective of race and religion, and, whilst facilitating Jewish immigration and settlement, to ensure that the rights and position of other sections of the population are not prejudiced.

To place the country under such political, administrative, and economic conditions as will secure the development of self-governing institutions.

The Royal Commission and previous commissions of Enquiry have drawn attention to the ambiguity of certain expressions in the Mandate, such as the expression "a national home for the Jewish people," and they have found in this ambiguity and the resulting uncertainty as to the objectives of policy a fundamental cause of unrest and hostility between Arabs and Jews. His Majesty's Government are convinced that in the interests of the peace and well-being of the whole people of Palestine a clear definition of policy and objectives is essential. The proposal of partition recommended by the Royal Commission would have afforded such clarity, but the establishment of self-supporting independent Arab and Jewish States within Palestine has been found to be impracticable. It has therefore been necessary for His Majesty's Government to devise an alternative policy which will, consistent with their obligations to Arabs and Jews, meet the needs of the situation in Palestine. . . .

Section I. "The Constitution"

It has been urged that the expression "a national home for the Jewish people" offered a prospect that Palestine might in due course become a Jewish State or Commonwealth. His Majesty's Government do not wish to contest the view, which was expressed by the Royal Commission, that the Zionist leaders at the time of the issue of the Balfour Declaration recognized that an ultimate Jewish State was not precluded by the terms of the Declaration.[1] But, with the Royal Commission, His Majesty's Government believe that the framers of the Mandate in which the Balfour Declaration was embodied could not have intended that Palestine should be converted into a Jewish State against the will of the Arab population of the country. That Palestine was not to be converted into a Jewish State might be held to be implied in the passage from the Command Paper of 1922, which reads as follows:

> Unauthorized statements have been made to the effect that the purpose in view is to create a wholly Jewish Palestine. Phrases have been used such as that "Palestine is to become as Jewish as England is English." His Majesty's Government regard any such expectation as impracticable and have no such aim in view. Nor have they at any time contemplated . . . the disappearance or the subordination of the Arabic population, language, or culture in Palestine. They would draw attention to the fact that the terms of the (Balfour) Declaration referred to do not contemplate that Palestine as a whole should be converted into a Jewish National Home, but that such a Home should be founded IN PALESTINE.

But this statement has not removed doubts, and His Majesty's Government therefore now declare unequivocally that it is not part of their policy that Palestine should become a Jewish State. They would indeed regard it as contrary to their obligations to the Arabs under the Mandate, as well as to the assurances which have been given to the Arab people in the past, that the Arab population of Palestine should be made the subjects of a Jewish State against their will. . . .

In the recent discussions the Arab delegations have repeated the contention that Palestine was included within the area in which Sir Henry

McMahon, on behalf of the British Government, in October 1915, undertook to recognize and support Arab independence. The validity of this claim, based on the terms of the correspondence which passed between Sir Henry McMahon and the Sharif of Mecca, was thoroughly and carefully investigated by the British and Arab representatives during the recent conferences in London. Their report, which has been published, states that both the Arab and the British representatives endeavoured to understand the point of view of the other party but that they were unable to reach agreement upon an interpretation of the correspondence. There is no need to summarize here the arguments presented by each side. His Majesty's Government regret the misunderstandings which have arisen as regards some of the phrases used. For their part they can only adhere, for the reasons given by their representatives in the Report, to the view that the whole of Palestine west of Jordan was excluded from Sir Henry McMahon's pledge, and they therefore cannot agree that the McMahon correspondence forms a just basis for the claim that Palestine should be converted into an Arab State.

His Majesty's Government are charged as the Mandatory authority "to secure the development of self-governing institutions" in Palestine. Apart from this specific obligation, they would regard it as contrary to the whole spirit of the Mandate system that the population of Palestine should remain forever under Mandatory tutelage. It is proper that the people of the country should as early as possible enjoy the rights of self-government that are exercised by the people of neighbouring countries. His Majesty's Government are unable at present to foresee the exact constitutional forms which government in Palestine will eventually take, but their objective is self government, and they desire to see established ultimately an independent Palestine State. It should be a State in which the two peoples in Palestine, Arabs, and Jews, share authority in government in such a way that the essential interests of each are shared. . . .

In the light of these considerations His Majesty's Government make the following declaration of their intentions regarding the future government of Palestine:

The objective of His Majesty's Government is the establishment within 10 years of an independent Palestine State in such treaty relations with the United Kingdom as will provide satisfactorily for the commercial and strategic requirements of both countries in the future. The proposal for the establishment of the independent State would involve consultation with the Council of the League of Nations with a view to the termination of the Mandate.

The independent State should be one in which Arabs and Jews share government in such a way as to ensure that the essential interests of each community are safeguarded.

The establishment of the independent State will be preceded by a transitional period throughout which His Majesty's Government will retain responsibility for the country. During the transitional period the people of Palestine will be given an increasing part in the government of their country. Both sections of the population will have an opportunity to participate in the machinery of government, and the process will be carried on whether or not they both avail themselves of it.

As soon as peace and order have been sufficiently restored in Palestine steps will be taken to carry out this policy of giving the people of Palestine an increasing part in the government of their country, the objective being to place Palestinians in charge of all the Departments of Government, with the assistance of British advisers and subject to the control of the High Commissioner. Arab and Jewish representatives will be invited to serve as heads of Departments approximately in proportion to their respective populations. The number of Palestinians in charge of Departments will be increased as circumstances permit until all heads of Departments are Palestinians, exercising the administrative and advisory functions, which are presently performed by British officials. When that stage is reached consideration will be given to the question of converting the Executive Council into a Council of Ministers with a consequential change in the status and functions of the Palestinian heads of Departments. . . .

Section II. "Immigration"

Under Article 6 of the Mandate, the Administration of Palestine, "while ensuring that the rights and position of other sections of the population are not prejudiced," is required to "facilitate Jewish immigration under suitable conditions." Beyond this, the extent to which Jewish immigration into Palestine is to be permitted is nowhere defined in the Mandate. But in the Command Paper of 1922 it was laid down that for the fulfilment of the policy of establishing a Jewish National Home:

> it is necessary that the Jewish community in Palestine should be able to increase its numbers by immigration. This immigration cannot be so great in volume as to exceed whatever may be the economic capacity of the country at the time to absorb new arrivals. It is essential to ensure that the immigrants should not be a burden upon the people of Palestine as a whole, and that they should not deprive any section of the present population of their employment.

In practice, from that date onwards until recent times, the economic absorptive capacity of the country has been treated as the sole limiting factor, and in the letter which Mr Ramsay MacDonald, as Prime Minister, sent to Dr Weizmann in February 1931 it was laid down as a matter of policy that economic absorptive capacity was the sole criterion. This interpretation has been supported by resolutions of the Permanent Mandates Commissioner. But His Majesty's Government do not read either the Statement of Policy of 1922 or the letter of 1931 as implying that the Mandate requires them, for all time and in all circumstances, to facilitate the immigration of Jews into Palestine subject only to consideration of

the country's economic absorptive capacity. Nor do they find anything in the Mandate or in subsequent Statements of Policy to support the view that the establishment of a Jewish National Home in Palestine cannot be effected unless immigration is allowed to continue indefinitely. If immigration has an adverse effect on the economic position in the country, it should clearly be restricted; and equally, if it has a seriously damaging effect on the political position in the country, that is a factor that should not be ignored. Although it is not difficult to contend that the large number of Jewish immigrants who have been admitted so far have been absorbed economically, the fear of the Arabs that this influx will continue indefinitely until the Jewish population is in a position to dominate them has produced consequences which are extremely grave for Jews and Arabs alike and for the peace and prosperity of Palestine. . . .

Jewish immigration during the next five years will be at a rate, which, if economic absorptive capacity permits, will bring the Jewish population up to approximately one third of the total population of the country. Taking into account the expected natural increase of the Arab and Jewish populations, and the number of illegal Jewish immigrants now in the country, this would allow the admission, as from the beginning of April this year, of some 75,000 immigrants over the next five years. These immigrants would, subject to the criterion of economic absorptive capacity, be admitted as follows:

For each of the next five years a quota of 10,000 Jewish immigrants will be allowed on the understanding that a shortage one year may be added to the quotas for subsequent years, within the five year period, if economic absorptive capacity permits.

In addition, as a contribution towards the solution of the Jewish refugee problem, 25,000 refugees will be admitted as soon as the High Commissioner is satisfied that adequate provision for their maintenance is ensured, special consideration being given to refugee children and dependents. . . .

After the period of five years, no further

Jewish immigration will be permitted unless the Arabs of Palestine are prepared to acquiesce in it.

His Majesty's Government are determined to check illegal immigration, and further preventive measures are being adopted. The numbers of any Jewish illegal immigrants who, despite these measures, may succeed in coming into the country and cannot be deported will be deducted from the yearly quotas. . . .

Note

1. See the Balfour Declaration and McMahon Correspondence in Chapter Three.

Study Question

Would the Palestinian state envisioned by the creators of the White Paper have produced a workable solution to the ongoing regional instability?

Gamal Abdel Nasser

Gamal Abdel Nasser (1918–1970) was a leading advocate of pan-Arab nationalism and a staunch opponent of the creation of the State of Israel. He came to power in Egypt in 1952 in a military coup that deposed the unpopular monarchy of Farouk I. After establishing a one-party state and repressing his strongest opposition—the Muslim Brotherhood— Nasser launched an ambitious set of reforms designed to establish Egypt as a regional power independent of all foreign influence. To this end Nasser proclaimed non-alignment in the Cold War and pursued funding for a massive dam on the Nile River that would generate revenue for Egyptian industrialization. He was also determined to remove the British presence in the Suez Canal Zone. The speech that follows was delivered on 26 July 1956, and announced the nationalization of the canal company.

Document Source: *Notes et études documentaires: Écrits et Discours du colonel Nasser.* Dir. de publ. La Documentation française. n° 2.206. Paris: La Documentation française, 20.08.1956. Tracey Kinney, trans.

On the Fifth Year of the Revolution

Citizens,

On this day, we observe the fifth year of the Revolution. We have spent four years fighting. We have fought to rid ourselves of the traces of the past, of imperialism and despotism, the traces of foreign occupation and domestic despotism.

Today, in welcoming the fifth year of the Revolution, we are stronger than ever and our will is strengthened. We have fought and we have won. We depended upon ourselves and we achieved the objectives set forth by the Revolution with determination, strength, and power, the achievements for which our ancestors fought and for which our children were sacrificed. We

fight and we sense that we have triumphed in strengthening our principles of dignity, freedom, and greatness, in establishing an independent state, a truly independent state, with political and economic independence.

Looking forward we know well that our fight is not over. Indeed, it is not easy to build our power amidst imperialist and international conspiracies. It is not easy to achieve our political and economic independence without a continuing struggle. We have before us a series of struggles so that we might live in dignity.

Today we have the opportunity to lay the foundations for dignity and freedom and, in the future, we will always aim to consolidate these foundations and to make them even stronger and more solid.

Imperialism has tried by all means possible to undermine our Arab nationalism. It tried to disperse us and to separate us, and for that, it has created Israel, the work of imperialism. . . .

Egypt in the World

Since Egypt declared its political freedom and independence, the whole world has fixed eyes upon it. The whole world watches Egypt and the Arabs. Formerly, we wasted our time in the offices of ambassadors and extraordinary envoys, but to-day, after we have united to create a national front against imperialism and foreign intervention, those who would disdain us began to fear us.

The voice of Egypt has grown stronger internationally and the value of Arabs has become greater. . . .

Economic Independence

. . . In 1952 we were certain to achieve our political independence; but we firmly believed that political independence could never be achieved fully without the aid of and in partnership with economic independence.

We worked to achieve the removal [of foreign influence] by all means possible: by gentleness and force; by negotiations and discussions. . . . Once we reached those complicit in imperialism, the occupier realized that he could not remain in a land surrounded by enemies. And so he left. . . .

The Development of Production

We have not neglected economic independence: because we were firmly convinced that political independence could not be achieved without

The Middle East in the Late 1990s

economic independence. Therefore, we have given our full attention to the development of production, relying solely on ourselves and on our own means. We managed to increase national revenue by 16 per cent between 1952 and 1954, and by a similar proportion between 1954 and 1956.

After the celebrations of freedom, I said that Egypt would forget the past and extend a hand to all those who would be peaceful with her and equally to those who would be hostile. I also declared that Egyptian policy comes from the heart of Egypt and not from London or from Washington, or from elsewhere. I also said that we were willing to co-operate with anyone providing that this is not to the detriment of Egypt and its interests. . . .

The History of Weapons

In 1952, we started talking about weapons. They told us: we will not give you weapons if you do not sign the Common Defence Pact and this would mean that a British mission would come here and take charge of all of the actions of the Egyptian military.

We answered that we do not like military missions and that we are aware that they have but one objective: to weaken the army and make it powerless.

We said that we want an Egyptian army representing the principles proclaimed in the Revolution. We want a strong and powerful military and we will not allow our army to be placed under the command of a few foreign officers, Americans, or others. The army must work for the people and in the interests of the people.

We told them we wanted to buy weapons with our own money and that we did not want anything in the way of support; but this they did not want. They wanted to give us weapons as a means to establish our slavery and undermine our sovereignty.

After that the struggle over the Canal began and each of you knows how much we have sacrificed and how many of our people have died on the field of honour in the course of these battles over the Canal.

The English have left. They have evacuated and the glory comes not in the negotiations and the discussions, but in the blood that was shed like water in the Canal, of so many dead. The fight was bitter and violent but is it over?

No, today the struggle continues against the accomplices of the imperialists. These accomplices are everywhere, in every country, and they act without weapons. . . .

The Nationalization of the Canal

. . . History repeats itself, but it is not possible for us to allow this history to repeat itself in Egypt. We are all here today to put an absolute end to this sinister past and if we ourselves turn to the past, it is for the sole purpose of destroying it utterly. We will not allow the Suez Canal to exist as a state within a state. Today, the Suez Canal is an Egyptian company. . . .

Poverty is no disgrace, but the exploitation of a people is.

We will resume our rights [to the Canal Company] because these funds are ours and this canal is owned by Egypt. The Company is an Egyptian joint stock company, and the canal was dug by 120,000 Egyptians, who died during its creation. We will build the High Dam and we will gain all the rights that we have lost. We will maintain our aspirations and our goals. The £35 million of company cash, we will take for the benefit of Egypt.

So I say to you today, dear citizens, by building the High Dam, we will build a fortress of honour and glory and demolishing our humiliation. We declare that Egypt in its entirety is one, a united and inseparable national entity. Egypt will fight to the last drop of blood to build its nation. We will give no opportunities to the forces of occupation to execute their plans, and with our own arms we will build a strong Egypt, and this is why today I have set forth the Government's agreement on the nationalization of the Canal Company. . . .

"We will proceed to destroy once and for all the traces of occupation and exploitation. After a hundred years each one has recovered his rights, and today we build our edifice by demolishing the state that lived within our state; the Suez Canal is for the benefit of Egypt and not for exploitation. The nationalization of the Suez Canal is now a fait accompli: our funds have been returned and we have £35 million in shares. . . . We must all work and produce, despite the plots against us. . . ."

In four years, we have felt that we have become stronger and more courageous, and as we were able to dethrone the king on July 26, on the same day we nationalize the Suez Canal Company. We realize some of our aspirations and we begin building a healthy and strong country.

No sovereignty exists in Egypt apart from the Egyptian people, one people who are advancing on the road of construction and industrialization, in one bloc against any aggressor and against the plots of the imperialists. We are realizing, moreover, many of our aspirations, and are building our nation effectively because no longer is there anyone meddling in our affairs. We are now free and independent.

Note

1. See the Balfour Declaration and McMahon Correspondence in Chapter Three.

> **Study Question**
>
> Does Nasser make an effective case for the nationalization of the Suez Canal Company?

United Nations Security Council/ Palestine National Council

During the course of the Six-Day War in June 1967, Israeli forces moved into a number of Palestinian territories, including the Golan Heights, East Jerusalem, the West Bank, and the Gaza Strip. Both the Americans and the Soviets—concerned primarily with the stability of the Middle East—backed a resolution in the United Nations Security Council calling for the withdrawal of Israeli occupation forces to pre-1967 lines. To date Resolution 242 has not been enforced. Given the ineffectiveness of Resolution 242, the Palestinian people found themselves surrounded by a vastly strengthened Israeli State. As well, thousands of additional refugees had been forced to flee across the borders into neighbouring Arab states. A number of movements dedicated to liberating the Palestinian people from Israeli occupation formed among these refugees. The Palestinian National Charter summarized the basic aims of many such groups in July 1968. The Charter itself follows Resolution 242.

Document Sources: United Nations Security Council, "Resolution 242, 22 November 1967"; available online:http://avalon.law.yale.edu/20th_century/un242.asp; Palestine National Council, *Palestinian National Charter*. Available online: http://avalon.law.yale.edu/20th_century/plocov.asp; http://www.un.int/wcm/content/site/palestine/pid/12362

Resolution 242, 22 November 1967

The Security Council,

Expressing its continuing concern with the grave situation in the Middle East,

Emphasizing the inadmissibility of the acquisition of territory by war and the need to work for a just and lasting peace in which every state in the area can live in security.

Emphasizing further that all member states in their acceptance of the Charter of the United Nations have undertaken a commitment to act in accordance with Article 2 of the Charter,

1. *Affirms* that the fulfillment of Charter principles requires the establishment of a just

and lasting peace in the Middle East which should include the application of both the following principles:

(i) Withdrawal of Israeli armed forces from territories of recent conflict;

(ii) Termination of all claims or states of belligerency, and respect for and acknowledgement of the sovereignty, territorial integrity and political independence of every state in the area and their right to live in peace within secure and recognized boundaries free from threats or acts of force;

2. *Affirms* further the necessity

   (a) For guaranteeing freedom of navigation through international waterways in the area;

   (b) For achieving a just settlement of the refugee problem;

   (c) For guaranteeing the territorial inviolability and political independence of every state in the area, through measures including the establishment of demilitarized zones;

3. *Requests* the Secretary General to designate a special representative to proceed to the Middle East to establish and maintain contacts with the states concerned in order to promote agreement and assist efforts to achieve a peaceful and accepted settlement in accordance with the provisions and principles in this resolution.

4. *Requests* the Secretary General to report to the Security Council on the progress of the efforts of the special representative as soon as possible.

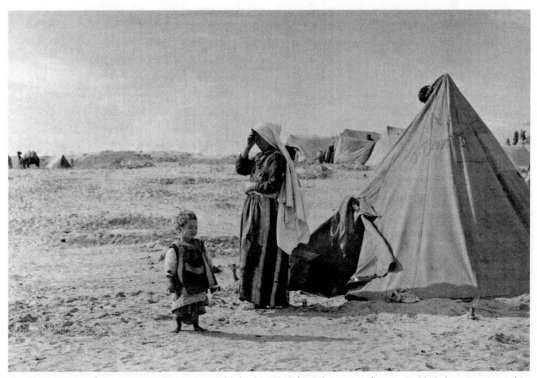

The Khan Younis refugee camp in Gaza was established in 1949 for Palestinian refugees. In 2010 the UN estimated its population at more than 72,000.

Courtesy of the United Nations Photo Library (20758 UN/DPI).

The Palestinian National Charter

1. Palestine is the homeland of the Arab Palestinian people; it is an indivisible part of the greater Arab homeland, and the Palestinian people are an integral part of the Arab nation.

2. Palestine, with the boundaries it had during the British Mandate, is an indivisible territorial unit.

3. The Palestinian Arab people possess the legal right to their homeland and to self-determination after the completion of the liberation of their country in accordance with their wishes and entirely of their own accord and will.

4. The Palestinian identity is a genuine, essential, and inherent characteristic; it is transmitted from fathers to children. The Zionist occupation and the dispersal of the Palestinian Arab people, through the disasters which befell them, do not make them lose their Palestinian identity and their membership in the Palestinian community, nor do they negate them.

5. The Palestinians are those Arab nationals who, until 1947, normally resided in Palestine regardless of whether they were evicted from it or have stayed there. Anyone born, after that date, of a Palestinian father—whether inside Palestine or outside it—is also a Palestinian.

6. The Jews who had normally resided in Palestine until the beginning of the Zionist invasion are considered Palestinians.

7. There is a Palestinian community and that it has material, spiritual, and historical connection with Palestine are indisputable facts. It is a national duty to bring up individual Palestinians in an Arab revolutionary manner. All means of information and education must be adopted in order to acquaint the Palestinian with his country in the most

profound manner, both spiritual and material, that is possible. He must be prepared for the armed struggle and ready to sacrifice his wealth and his life in order to win back his homeland and bring about its liberation.

8. The phase in their history, through which the Palestinian people are now living, is that of national struggle for the liberation of Palestine. Thus the conflicts among the Palestinian national forces are secondary, and should be ended for the sake of the basic conflict that exists between the forces of Zionism and of colonialism on the one hand, and the Palestinian Arab people on the other. . . .

9. Armed struggle is the only way to liberate Palestine. Thus it is the overall strategy, not merely a tactical phase. The Palestinian Arab people assert their absolute determination and firm resolution to continue their armed struggle and to work for an armed popular revolution for the liberation of their country and their return to it. They also assert their right to normal life in Palestine and to exercise their right to self-determination and sovereignty over it.

10. Commando action constitutes the nucleus of the Palestinian popular liberation war. This requires its escalation, comprehensiveness, and the mobilization of all the Palestinian popular and educational efforts and their organization and involvement in the armed Palestinian revolution. . . .

11. The Palestinians will have three mottoes: national (wataniyya) unity, national (qawmiyya) mobilization, and liberation.

12. The Palestinian Arab people believe in Arab unity. In order to contribute their share toward the attainment of that objective, however, they must, at the present stage of

their struggle, safeguard their Palestinian identity and develop their consciousness of that identity, and oppose any plan that may dissolve or impair it.

13. Arab unity and the liberation of Palestine are two complementary goals, the attainment of either of which facilitates the attainment of the other. . . .

14. The destiny of the Arab nation, and indeed Arab existence itself, depend upon the destiny of the Palestine cause. From this interdependence springs the Arab nation's pursuit of, and striving for, the liberation of Palestine. The people of Palestine play the role of the vanguard in the realization of this sacred (qawmi) goal.

15. The liberation of Palestine, from an Arab viewpoint, is a national duty and it attempts to repel the Zionist and imperialist aggression against the Arab homeland, and aims at the elimination of Zionism in Palestine. Absolute responsibility for this falls upon the Arab nation—peoples and governments—with the Arab people of Palestine in the vanguard. Accordingly, the Arab nation must mobilize all its military, human, moral, and spiritual capabilities to participate actively with the Palestinian people in the liberation of Palestine. . . .

16. The liberation of Palestine, from a spiritual point of view, will provide the Holy Land with an atmosphere of safety and tranquility, which in turn will safeguard the country's religious sanctuaries and guarantee freedom of worship and of visit to all, without discrimination of race, colour, language, or religion. Accordingly, the people of Palestine look to all spiritual forces in the world for support.

17. The liberation of Palestine, from a human point of view, will restore to the Palestinian individual his dignity, pride, and freedom. Accordingly, the Palestinian Arab people look forward to the support of all those who believe in the dignity of man and his freedom in the world.

18. The liberation of Palestine, from an international point of view, is a defensive action necessitated by the demands of self-defence. Accordingly, the Palestinian people, desirous as they are of the friendship of all people, look to freedom-loving and peace-loving states for support in order to restore their legitimate rights in Palestine, to re-establish peace and security in the country, and to enable its people to exercise national sovereignty and freedom.

19. The partition of Palestine in 1947 and the establishment of the state of Israel, are entirely illegal, regardless of the passage of time, because they were contrary to the will of the Palestinian people and to their natural right in their homeland, and inconsistent with the principles embodied in the Charter of the United Nations; particularly the right to self-determination.

20. The Balfour Declaration, the Mandate for Palestine, and everything that has been based upon them, are deemed null and void. Claims of historical or religious ties of Jews with Palestine are incompatible with the facts of history and the true conception of what constitutes statehood. Judaism, being a religion, is not an independent nationality. Nor do Jews constitute a single nation with an identity of its own; they are citizens of the states to which they belong.

21. The Arab Palestinian people, expressing themselves by the armed Palestinian revolution, reject all solutions which are substitutes for the total liberation of Palestine and reject all proposals aiming at the liquidation of the Palestinian problem, or its internationalization.

22. Zionism is a political movement organically associated with international imperialism and antagonistic to all action for liberation

and to progressive movements in the world. It is racist and fanatic in its nature, aggressive, expansionist, and colonial in its aims, and fascist in its methods. Israel is the instrument of the Zionist movement, and the geographical base for world imperialism placed strategically in the midst of the Arab homeland to combat the hopes of the Arab nation for liberation, unity, and progress. Israel is a constant source of threat vis-à-vis peace in the Middle East and the whole world. Since liberation of Palestine will destroy the Zionist and imperialist presence and will contribute to the establishment of peace in the Middle East, the Palestinian people look for the support of all the progressive and peaceful forces and urge them all, irrespective of their affiliations and beliefs, to offer the Palestinian people all aid and support in their just struggle for the liberation of their homeland.

Study Questions

1. To what extent was Resolution 242 a realistic solution to the situation in the Middle East after the Six-Day War?
2. Is "armed struggle the only way to liberate Palestine"? Why or why not?

Golda Meir

Golda Meir (1898–1978) served in a number of capacities in the Israeli government, including as minister of labour, foreign minister, and, eventually, prime minister from 1969 until 1974. Although Israel emerged victorious in the Yom Kippur War in 1973, Meir's leadership in the weeks leading up to the war was criticized by many in the country. However, she remained a prominent figure in politics even after her resignation. In 1977 she delivered the first speech in the Israeli parliament (the Knesset), marking the historic visit of Egyptian president Anwar Sadat (1918–1981).

Document Source: Remarks by Mrs Golda Meir to President Sadat in the Knesset—21 November 1977; Israeli Ministry of Foreign Affairs, Vols. 4–5: 1977–1979; http://www.mfa.gov.il

Remarks to President Sadat

Mr President, I'm sure that from the moment your plane landed at Lydda Airport, and as you drove through the streets of Jerusalem, you must have felt, in all your encounters with the many people who turned out to meet you—the little children; the mothers with babies in their arms; the old people; the people who were born in this country, the second, third, fourth and fifth generations, and those who have come recently—that all, without exception, were overjoyed to see you in our Land.

When asked, many years ago, when I thought that peace would come to this region to our country and to our neighbouring countries—I said: I do not know the date, but I do know under what conditions it will come—when there will be a leader, a great leader of an Arab country. He will wake up one morning and feel sorry for his own people, for his own sons who have fallen in battle, and that day will be the beginning of peace between us.

Mr President, we have a saying in Hebrew: "zchut rishonim." In English, this means "the privilege of being the first." I congratulate you, Mr President, that you are privileged to be the first great Arab leader of the greatest country among our neighbours to come to us, with courage and determination, despite so many difficulties, for the sake of your sons, as well as for the sake of ours; for the sake of all mothers who mourn sons that fell in battle. . . .

You have come telling us that, from now on, you are prepared to live in peace with us. I can assure you, Mr President, that as far as we are concerned, the desire for peace, the hope of peace and the dream of peace have never left the hearts of a single one of us. We have come back to this country to live in peace. We have come back to this country to live. We have come back to this country to create. In this room, you will see people who, for the first time in their lives, have climbed hills and planted trees in this country; who, for the first time, have gone down to the desert—it was considered a desert, a God-forsaken land and have made it green, so that our children can live and play everywhere in it. . . . All this we have done for peace—to live in peace; to live, but to live in peace.

Mr President, we listened to you last night and we heard your appeal for peace. When I was in office, and I am sure this was true for everyone who preceded me and for those who succeeded me in office—I hoped that the day would come when we could meet with a leader of one of the Arab countries and hold a discussion with him. . . .

Of course, we must all realize that the path leading to peace may be a difficult one, but not as difficult as that path which leads to war. What Israel wants—what this group with which you are meeting today has wanted, from the very beginning, is territorial compromise, in accordance with the programme it adopted immediately after the war of 1967. As a matter of fact, Israel has made and accepted compromises ever since 1947. . . .

We will not go into history today, but what we want to tell you is that we were, and are, prepared for territorial compromise on all our borders—with one condition: these borders will give us security, and protect us from danger, so that we will never be in need, God forbid, at any time, of help from abroad in order to defend ourselves. We have never sought such help from others;

Egyptian President Anwar Sadat and Israeli Prime Minister Menachem Begin in 1978 at the announcement of the successful outcome of the Camp David Accords. US News and World Report Magazine Photograph Collection.
Courtesy of the Library of Congress, Prints and Photographs Division (LC-DIG-ppmsca-09792).

nobody has ever come to defend us. The blood that has been shed, to our sorrow, has been our own. We don't want to shed the blood of others.

With us today is Mr Rabin. After the war of 1967, he was awarded an Honorary degree by the Hebrew University of Jerusalem and, in his words of acceptance, as Chief of Staff, he said: "Here is the Israeli army that came back victorious. It came back a sad army, despite its victory; sad because of our men who fell, but also because of our sons who were compelled to shoot others." These two things we do not want: we do not want to be shot at—and, believe me—we do not want to shoot others.

Therefore, we want borders within which, when we do sign peace treaties, all Israelis will be assured that they live in security, without having to rely on international guarantees. I do not think we will need these when we have peace—neither we shall need them, nor you. But we must have borders that will enable us—if, God forbid, something should happen in the future—to defend ourselves. Territorial compromise—yes, but not compromise with our security! Each country, each nation, will decide its security requirements. When we talk of territorial compromise, it is essential that we remember this.

Mr President. We, the People of Israel, are the last to be insensitive to the sorrow of others. We have never said that we want the Palestinian Arabs to remain as they are—in camps, in misery, dependent on charity. We do not wish to be dependent upon others, nor do we wish them to be dependent upon others. Had it been within our power, there would never have been a problem of this kind. Of course, we realize that there are Palestinian Arabs and we believe there is a solution, one that is both good for them and safe for us.

Because we believe this, we believe also that there is no connection between our opposition to another state between us and Jordan—a Palestinian state which would be small, probably not viable and perhaps forced to expand—and between our awareness of the need to solve the problem of the Palestinian Arabs. Our opposition to another state is based on Israel's most vital security requirements. Mr President, should we agree to the establishment of such a state, there would be only ten miles between the Mediterranean and the borders of this state. You cannot expect us to feel secure within such borders.

Of course, we favour a solution for the Palestinian Arabs, and believe that in the programme of this group gathered here today with you, such a solution exists. This programme, formulated prior to the elections and still valid to this day, states that in our peace treaty with Jordan, there must be a solution for the Palestinian Arabs, so the camps may be wiped out and become a thing of the past. But not at the expense of Israel's security. If there were no solution, it would be a terrible problem for us. But there is a solution to this problem too.

Therefore, we say to you, Mr President, that, while we do not agree with everything you said last night—surely, this does not surprise you—we deeply appreciate your call for peace, and believe in your sincere desire for it, just as I hope you believe in our sincere desire for it. Now, let us go forward. Even if we do not reach agreement on everything this morning, let us, at least, conclude one thing: the beginnings that you have made, with such courage and with such hope for peace, must go on, continuing face-to-face between ourselves and you, so that even an old lady like myself will live to see the day—yes, you always call me an old lady—and regardless of whoever signs on Israel's behalf, I want to live to see that day—that peace reigns between you and us, peace between ourselves and all our neighbours.

And, Mr President, as a grandmother to a grandfather, may I give you a little present for your new grand-daughter, and thank you for the present you have given me.

Study Question

Under what circumstances could Israel enjoy the security of which Golda Meir speaks here?

Joint US/Soviet Statement

By 1977 several wars had been fought over the presence of the State of Israel—in 1948, 1956, 1967, and 1973. All had threatened to embroil the superpowers, due to the nature of the Cold War alliance system. The framework below reflects the determination of both the United States, under President Jimmy Carter, and the Soviet Union, under Leonid Brezhnev, to avoid further conflicts in the region.

Document Source: Joint US/Soviet Statement on Peace, 29 September 1977. Israeli Ministry of Foreign Affairs, Vols. 4–5: 1977–1979; http://www.mfa.gov.il

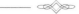

Peace in the Middle East, September 1977

Having exchanged views regarding the unsafe situation which remains in the Middle East, United States Secretary of State Cyrus Vance and member of the Politburo of the Central Committee of the CPSU, Minister for Foreign Affairs of the USSR, A.A. [Andrei] Gromyko have the following statement to make on behalf of their countries, which are Co-Chairmen of the Geneva Peace Conference[1] on the Middle East:

1. Both governments are convinced that vital interests of the peoples of this area as well as the interests of strengthening peace and international security in general urgently dictate the necessity of achieving as soon as possible a just and lasting settlement of the Arab–Israeli conflict. This settlement should be comprehensive, incorporating all parties concerned and all questions.

   The United States and the Soviet Union believe that, within the framework of a comprehensive settlement of the Middle East problem, all specific questions of the settlement should be resolved, including such key issues as withdrawal of Israeli armed forces from territories occupied in the 1967 conflict; The resolution of the Palestinian question including ensuring the legitimate rights of the Palestinian people; Termination of the state of war and establishment of normal peaceful relations on the basis of mutual recognition of the principles of sovereignty, territorial integrity, and political independence.

   The two governments believe that, in addition to such measures for ensuring the security of the borders between Israel and the neighboring Arab states as the establishment of demilitarized zones and the agreed stationing in them of UN troops or observers, international guarantees of such borders as well as of the observance of the terms of the settlement can also be established, should the contracting parties so desire. The United States and the Soviet Union are ready to participate in these guarantees, subject to their constitutional processes.

2. The United States and the Soviet Union believe that the only right and effective way for achieving a fundamental solution to all aspects of the Middle East problem in its entirety is negotiations within the framework of the Geneva Peace Conference, specially convened for these purposes, with participation in its work of the representatives of all the parties involved in the conflict including those of the Palestinian people, and legal and contractual formalization of the decisions reached at the conference.

In their capacity as Co-Chairmen of the Geneva Conference, the US and the USSR affirm their intention through joint efforts and in their contacts with the parties concerned to facilitate in every way the resumption of the work of the conference not later than December 1977. The Co-Chairmen note that there still exist several questions of a procedural and organizational nature which remain to be agreed upon by the participants to the conference.

3. Guided by the goal of achieving a just political settlement in the Middle East and of eliminating the explosive situation in this area of the world, the US and the USSR appeal to all the parties in the conflict to

understand the necessity for careful consideration of each other's legitimate rights and interests and to demonstrate mutual readiness to act accordingly.

Note

1. The Geneva Peace Conference was convened in 1973 to reach a solution to the conflict between Israel and the Arab States. Though the Geneva process failed, it did set the stage for the successful Israeli–Egyptian accord signed at Camp David in 1978.

> **Study Question**
>
> Why were both the United States and the Soviet Union determined to push Israel and Egypt towards a peace settlement in the mid-1970s?

Hamas

Hamas was founded in 1987 in the wake of repeated failures to achieve a peaceful resolution to conflicts between Israelis and Palestinians. Unlike organizations such as the Palestine Liberation Organization (PLO), which include strongly secular elements, Hamas calls for the creation of an Islamic Palestinian State. In 2006, in an election deemed by international observers to be both free and fair, Hamas gained a majority of seats in the Palestinian National Authority. Hamas is viewed by many Palestinians to be less corrupt than Fatah, its major rival, and more reliable in terms of providing basic social services in the West Bank and Gaza. Most western nations, however, regard Hamas as a terrorist organization. The fundamental goals of Hamas are clearly evident in the following excerpts from the group's 1988 Covenant.

Document Source: Hamas, The Covenant of the Islamic Resistance Movement, 1988; http://avalon.law.yale.edu/20th_century/hamas.asp

Covenant of the Islamic Resistance Movement, 1988

In The Name Of The Most Merciful Allah

"Ye are the best nation that hath been raised up unto mankind: ye command that which is just, and ye forbid that which is unjust, and ye believe in Allah. And if they who have received the scriptures had believed, it had surely been the better for them: there are believers among them, but the greater part of them are transgressors. They shall not hurt you, unless with a slight hurt; and if they fight against you, they shall turn their backs to you, and they shall not be helped. They are smitten with vileness wheresoever they are found; unless they obtain security by entering into a treaty with Allah, and a treaty with men; and they draw on themselves indignation from Allah, and they are afflicted with poverty. This they suffer, because they disbelieved the signs of Allah, and slew the prophets unjustly; this, because they were rebellious, and transgressed" (Al-Imran, verses 109–111).

"Israel will exist and will continue to exist until Islam will obliterate it, just as it obliterated others before it" (The Martyr, Imam Hassan al-Banna, of blessed memory).

"The Islamic world is on fire. Each of us should pour some water, no matter how little, to extinguish whatever one can without waiting for the others." (Sheikh Amjad al-Zahawi, of blessed memory).

In The Name Of The Most Merciful Allah

Introduction

Praise be unto Allah, to whom we resort for help, and whose forgiveness, guidance and support we seek; Allah bless the Prophet and grant him salvation, his companions and supporters, and to those who carried out his message and adopted his laws—everlasting prayers and salvation as long as the earth and heaven will last. Hereafter: O People:

Out of the midst of troubles and the sea of suffering, out of the palpitations of faithful hearts and cleansed arms; out of the sense of duty, and in response to Allah's command, the call has gone out rallying people together and making them follow the ways of Allah, leading them to have determined will in order to fulfill their role in life, to overcome all obstacles, and surmount the difficulties on the way. Constant preparation has continued and so has the readiness to sacrifice life and all that is precious for the sake of Allah.

Thus it was that the nucleus (of the movement) was formed and started to pave its way through the tempestuous sea of hopes and expectations, of wishes and yearnings, of troubles and obstacles, of pain and challenges, both inside and outside.

When the idea was ripe, the seed grew and the plant struck root in the soil of reality, away from passing emotions, and hateful haste. The Islamic Resistance Movement emerged to carry out its role through striving for the sake of its Creator, its arms intertwined with those of all the

Residents of Gaza check voters lists in advance of the 2006 election which brought Hamas to power.
Image © Shawn Baldwin/Corbis.

fighters for the liberation of Palestine. The spirits of its fighters meet with the spirits of all the fighters who have sacrificed their lives on the soil of Palestine, ever since it was conquered by the companions of the Prophet, Allah bless him and grant him salvation, and until this day.

This Covenant of the Islamic Resistance Movement (Hamas), clarifies its picture, reveals its identity, outlines its stand, explains its aims, speaks about its hopes, and calls for its support, adoption and joining its ranks. Our struggle against the Jews is very great and very serious. It needs all sincere efforts. It is a step that inevitably should be followed by other steps. The Movement is but one squadron that should be supported by more and more squadrons from this vast Arab and Islamic world, until the enemy is vanquished and Allah's victory is realized.

Thus we see them coming on the horizon "and you shall learn about it hereafter" "Allah hath written, Verily I will prevail, and my apostles: for Allah is strong and mighty" (The Dispute, verse 21).

"Say to them, This is my way: I invite you to Allah, by an evident demonstration; both I and he who followeth me; and, praise be unto Allah! I am not an idolator" (Joseph, verse 107).

Hamas (means) *strength and bravery* (according to) Al-Mua'jam al-Wasit: c1. . . . .

Article Four

The Islamic Resistance Movement welcomes every Moslem who embraces its faith, ideology, follows its programme, keeps its secrets, and wants to belong to its ranks and carry out the duty. Allah will certainly reward such one.

Article Six

The Islamic Resistance Movement is a distinguished Palestinian movement, whose allegiance is to Allah, and whose way of life is Islam. It strives to raise the banner of Allah over every inch of Palestine, for under the wing of Islam followers of all religions can coexist in security and safety where their lives, possessions and rights are concerned. In the absence of Islam, strife will be rife, oppression spreads, evil prevails and schisms and wars will break out.

How excellent was the Moslem poet, Mohamed Ikbal, when he wrote: "If faith is lost, there is no security and there is no life for him who does not adhere to religion. He who accepts life without religion, has taken annihilation as his companion for life."

Article Seven

. . . The Islamic Resistance Movement is one of the links in the chain of the struggle against the Zionist invaders. It goes back to 1939, to the emergence of the martyr Izz al-Din al Kissam and his brethren the fighters, members of Moslem Brotherhood. It goes on to reach out and become one with another chain that includes the struggle of the Palestinians and Moslem Brotherhood in the 1948 war and the Jihad operations of the Moslem Brotherhood in 1968 and after.

Moreover, if the links have been distant from each other and if obstacles, placed by those who are the lackeys of Zionism in the way of the fighters obstructed the continuation of the struggle, the Islamic Resistance Movement aspires to the realisation of Allah's promise, no matter how long that should take. . . .

Article Eight

Allah is its target, the Prophet is its model, the Koran its constitution: Jihad is its path and death for the sake of Allah is the loftiest of its wishes. . . .

Article Fifteen

The day that enemies usurp part of Moslem land, Jihad becomes the individual duty of every Moslem. In face of the Jews' usurpation of Palestine, it is compulsory that the banner of Jihad be raised. To do this requires the diffusion of Islamic consciousness among the masses, both on the regional, Arab and Islamic levels. It is necessary to instill the spirit of Jihad in the heart of the nation so that they would confront the enemies and join the ranks of the fighters.

It is necessary that scientists, educators and teachers, information and media people, as well as the educated masses, especially the youth and sheikhs of the Islamic movements, should take part in the operation of awakening (the masses). It is important that basic changes be made in the school curriculum, to cleanse it of the traces of ideological invasion that affected it as a result of the orientalists and missionaries who infiltrated the region following the defeat of the Crusaders at the hands of Salah el-Din (Saladin). The Crusaders realized that it was impossible to defeat the Moslems without first having ideological invasion pave the way by upsetting their thoughts, disfiguring their heritage and violating their ideals. Only then could they invade with soldiers. This, in its turn, paved the way for the imperialistic invasion that made Allenby declare on entering Jerusalem: "Only now have the Crusades ended." General Guru stood at Salah el-Din's grave and said: "We have returned, O Salah el-Din." Imperialism has helped towards the strengthening of ideological invasion, deepening, and still does, its roots. All this has paved the way towards the loss of Palestine.

It is necessary to instill in the minds of the Moslem generations that the Palestinian problem is a religious problem, and should be dealt with on this basis. Palestine contains Islamic holy sites. In it there is al-Aqsa Mosque which is bound to the great Mosque in Mecca in an inseparable bond as long as heaven and earth speak of Isra (Mohammed's midnight journey to the seven heavens) and Mi'raj (Mohammed's ascension to the seven heavens from Jerusalem).

"The bond of one day for the sake of Allah is better than the world and whatever there is on it. The place of one's whip in Paradise is far better than the world and whatever there is on it. A worshipper's going and coming in the service of Allah is better than the world and whatever there is on it" (As related by

al-Bukhari, Moslem, al-Tarmdhi and Ibn Maja).

"I swear by the holder of Mohammed's soul that I would like to invade and be killed for the sake of Allah, then invade and be killed, and then invade again and be killed" (As related by al-Bukhari and Moslem). . . .

Article Twenty-Seven

The Palestinian Liberation Organization is the closest to the heart of the Islamic Resistance Movement. It contains the father and the brother, the next of kin and the friend. The Moslem does not estrange himself from his father, brother, next of kin or friend. Our homeland is one, our situation is one, our fate is one and the enemy is a joint enemy to all of us.

Because of the situations surrounding the formation of the Organization, of the ideological confusion prevailing in the Arab world as a result of the ideological invasion under whose influence the Arab world has fallen since the defeat of the Crusaders and which was, and still is, intensified through orientalists, missionaries and imperialists, the Organization adopted the idea of the secular state. And that is how we view it.

Secularism completely contradicts religious ideology. Attitudes, conduct and decisions stem from ideologies.

That is why, with all our appreciation for The Palestinian Liberation Organization—and what it can develop into—and without belittling its role in the Arab–Israeli conflict, we are unable to exchange the present or future Islamic Palestine with the secular idea. The Islamic nature of Palestine is part of our religion and whoever takes his religion lightly is a loser.

"Who will be adverse to the religion of Abraham, but he whose mind is infatuated?" (The Cow, verse 130).

The day the Palestinian Liberation Organization adopts Islam as its way of life, we will become its soldiers, and fuel for its fire that will burn the enemies.

Until such a day, and we pray to Allah that it will be soon, the Islamic Resistance Movement's stand towards the PLO is that of the son towards his father, the brother towards his brother, and the relative to relative, suffers his pain and supports him in confronting the enemies, wishing him to be wise and well-guided.

"Stand by your brother, for he who is brotherless is like the fighter who goes to battle without arms. One's cousin is the wing one flies with—could the bird fly without wings?"

Study Question

In what ways does the Covenant highlight the divisions among the Palestinian factions?

Edward Said

Edward Said (1935–2003) received his early education in Jerusalem and Cairo, continuing on to Princeton and Harvard to pursue both undergraduate and graduate work. Said claimed to have become a political activist in 1969 when Golda Meir declared that there "are no Palestinian people." He immediately set out to prove her wrong. *Thereafter Said became one of the foremost spokesmen for the Palestinian cause. Yet, as the following article, written in 1999, demonstrates, he was most certainly not uncritical of the Palestinian Authority.*

Document Source: Edward Said, "Truth and Reconciliation." From *Al-Ahram Weekly On-line*, Issue No. 412, 14–20 January 1999.

Truth and Reconciliation

Given the collapse of the Netanyahu government over the Wye peace agreement, it is time once again to question whether the entire peace process begun in Oslo in 1993 is the right instrument for bringing peace between Palestinians and Israelis. It is my view that the peace process has in fact put off the real reconciliation that must occur if the 100-year war between Zionism and the Palestinian people is to end. Oslo set the stage for separation, but real peace can come only with a bi-national Israeli–Palestinian state.

This is not easy to imagine. The Zionist–Israeli narrative and the Palestinian one are irreconcilable. Israelis say they waged a war of liberation and so achieved independence; Palestinians say their society was destroyed, most of the population evicted. And, in fact this irreconcilability was already quite obvious to several generations of early Zionist leaders and thinkers, as of course it was to all the Palestinians.

"Zionism was not blind to the presence of Arabs in Palestine," writes the distinguished Israeli historian Zeev Sternhell in his recent book, *The Founding Myths of Israel*. "Even Zionist figures who had never visited the country knew that it was not devoid of inhabitants. At the same time, neither the Zionist movement abroad nor the pioneers who were beginning to settle the country could frame a policy toward the Palestinian national movement. The real reason for this was not a lack of understanding of the problem but a recognition of the insurmountable contradictions between the basic objectives of the two sides. If Zionist intellectuals and leaders ignored the Arab dilemma, it was chiefly because they knew that this problem had no solution within the Zionist way of thinking."

Ben Gurion, for instance, was always clear: "There is no example in history," he said in 1944, "of a people saying we agree to renounce our country, let another people come and settle here and outnumber us." Another Zionist leader, Berl Katznelson, also had no illusions that the opposition between Zionist and Palestinian aims could ever be surmounted. And binationalists like

Martin Buber, Judah Magnes, and Hannah Arendt were fully aware of what the clash would be like, if it ever came to fruition, as of course it did.

Vastly outnumbering the Jews, Palestinian Arabs during the period after the 1917 Balfour Declaration and the British Mandate always refused anything that would compromise their dominance. It's unfair to berate the Palestinians retrospectively for not accepting partition in 1947. Until 1948, Zionists held only about seven per cent of the land. Why, the Arabs said when the partition resolution was proposed, should we concede 55 per cent of Palestine to the Jews who were a minority in Palestine? Neither the Balfour Declaration nor the mandate ever specifically conceded that Palestinians had political, as opposed to civil and religious, rights in Palestine. The idea of inequality between Jews and Arabs was therefore built into British, and subsequently Israeli and United States, policy from the start.

The conflict appears intractable because it is a contest over the same land by two peoples who believed they had valid title to it and who hoped that the other side would in time give up or go away. One side won the war, the other lost, but the contest is as alive as ever. We Palestinians ask why a Jew born in Warsaw or New York has the right to settle here (according to Israel's Law of Return) whereas we, the people who lived here for centuries, cannot. After 1967, the issue between us was exacerbated. Years of military occupation have created in the weaker party anger, humiliation, and hostility.

To its discredit, Oslo did little to change the situation. Arafat and his dwindling number of supporters were turned into enforcers of Israeli security, while Palestinians were made to endure the humiliation of dreadful and noncontiguous "homelands" that make up only about nine per cent of the West Bank and 60 per cent of Gaza. Oslo required us to forget and renounce our history of loss, dispossessed by the very people who have taught everyone the importance of not forgetting the past. Thus we are the victims of the victims, the refugees of the refugees. . . .

The effort to separate has occurred simultaneously and paradoxically with the effort to take more and more land, which in turn has meant that Israel has acquired more and more Palestinians. In Israel proper, Palestinians number about one million, almost 20 per cent of the population. Among Gaza, East Jerusalem, and the West Bank, which is where the settlements are the thickest, there are almost 2.5 million more Palestinians. Israel has built an entire system of "by-passing" roads, designed to go around Palestinian towns and villages, connecting settlements and avoiding Arabs. But so tiny is the land area of historical Palestine, so closely intertwined are Israelis and Palestinians, despite their inequality and antipathy, that clean separation simply won't, can't really occur or work. It is estimated that by 2010 there will be demographic parity. What then?

Clearly, a system of privileging Israeli Jews will satisfy neither those who want an entirely homogenous Jewish state nor those who live there but are not Jewish. For the former, Palestinians are an obstacle to be disposed of somehow; for the latter, being Palestinians in a Jewish polity means forever chafing at inferior status. But Israeli Palestinians don't want to move; they say they are already in their country and refuse any talk of joining a separate Palestinian state, should one come into being. Meanwhile, the impoverishing conditions imposed on Arafat are making it difficult to subdue the highly politicised people of Gaza and the West Bank. These Palestinians have aspirations for self-determination that, contrary to Israeli calculations, show no sign of withering away. It is also evident that as an Arab people—and, given the despondently cold peace treaties between Israel and Egypt and Israel and Jordan, this fact is important—Palestinians want at all costs to preserve their Arab identity as part of the surrounding Arab and Islamic world.

For all this, the problem is that Palestinian self-determination in a separate state is unworkable, just as unworkable as the principle of separation between a demographically mixed, irreversibly connected Arab population without sovereignty and a Jewish population with it. The question, I believe, is not how to devise means for persisting in trying to separate them but to see whether it is possible for them to live together as fairly and peacefully as possible.

What exists now is a disheartening, not to say, bloody, impasse. Zionists in and outside Israel will not give up on their wish for a separate Jewish state; Palestinians want the same thing for themselves despite having accepted much less from Oslo. Yet in both instances the idea of a state for "ourselves" simply flies in the face of the facts: short of ethnic cleansing or mass transfer as in 1948 there is no way for Israel to get rid of the Palestinians or for Palestinians to wish Israelis away. Neither side has a viable military option against the other, which, I am sorry to say, is why both opted for a peace that so patently tries to accomplish what war couldn't. . . .

Violence, hatred, and intolerance are bred out of injustice, poverty, and a thwarted sense of political fulfillment. Last fall, hundreds of acres of Palestinian land were expropriated by the Israeli army from the village of Umm Al-Fahm, which isn't in the West Bank but inside Israel. This drove home the fact that, even as Israeli citizens, Palestinians are treated as inferior, as basically a sort of underclass existing in a condition of apartheid. . . .

In the West Bank, Jerusalem, and Gaza, the situation is deeply unstable and exploitative. Protected by the army, Israeli settlers (almost 350,000 of them) live as extraterritorial, privileged people with rights that resident Palestinians do not have. (For example, West Bankers cannot go to Jerusalem, and 70 per cent of the territory is still subject to Israeli military law, with their land available for confiscation.) Israel controls Palestinian water resources and security, as well as exits and entrances. Even the new Gaza Airport is under Israeli security control. One doesn't need to be an expert to see that this is a prescription for extending, not limiting, conflict. Here the truth must be faced, not avoided or denied.

There are Israeli Jews today who speak candidly about "post-Zionism," insofar as, after 50 years of Israeli history, classic Zionism has neither provided a solution to the Palestinian presence, nor an exclusively Jewish presence. I see no other way than to begin now to speak about sharing the land that has thrust us together, sharing it in a truly democratic way, with equal rights for each citizen. There can be no reconciliation unless both peoples, two communities of suffering, resolve that their existence is a secular fact, and that it has to be dealt with as such. This does not mean a diminishing of Jewish life as Jewish life or surrendering Palestinian Arab aspirations and political existence. On the contrary, it means self-determination for both peoples. But that does mean being willing to soften, lessen, and finally give up special status for one people at the expense of the other. . . .

The initial step, however, is a very difficult one to take. Israeli Jews are insulated from the Palestinian reality; most of them say that it does not really concern them. I remember the first time I drove from Ramallah into Israel: it was like going straight from Bangladesh into southern California. Yet reality is never that near. My generation of Palestinians, still reeling from the shock of losing everything in 1948, find it nearly impossible to accept that their homes and farms were taken over by another people. I see no way of evading the fact that in 1948 one people displaced another, thereby committing a grave injustice. Reading Palestinian and Jewish history together not only gives the tragedy of the Holocaust and of what subsequently happened to the Palestinians their full force but also reveals how, in the course of interrelated Israeli and Palestinian life since 1948, one people, the Palestinians, have borne a disproportional share of the pain and loss.

Religious and right-wing Israelis and their supporters have no problem with such a formulation. Yes, they say, we won, but that's how it should be. This land is the land of Israel not of anyone else. I heard those words from an Israeli soldier guarding a bulldozer that was destroying a West Bank Palestinian field (its owner helplessly watching) in order to expand a by-pass road.

But they are not the only Israelis. For others, who want peace as a result of reconciliation, there is dissatisfaction both with the religious parties' increasing hold on Israeli life and Oslo's unfairness and frustrations. Many such Israelis demonstrate energetically against their government's Palestinian land expropriations and house demolitions. So one senses a healthy willingness to look elsewhere for peace than in land-grabbing and suicide-bombs.

For some Palestinians, because they are the weaker party, the losers, giving up on a full restoration of Arab Palestine is giving up on their own history. Most others, however, especially my children's generation, are sceptical of their elders and look more unconventionally toward the future, beyond conflict and unending loss. . . .

The beginning is to develop something entirely missing from both Israeli and Palestinian realities today: the idea and practice of citizenship, not of ethnic or racial community, as the main vehicle for coexistence. In a modern state, all its members are citizens by virtue of their presence and the sharing of rights and responsibilities. Citizenship therefore entitles an Israeli Jew and a Palestinian Arab to the same privileges and resources. A constitution and a bill of rights thus become necessary for getting beyond square one of the conflict, since each group would have the same right to self-determination; that is, the right to practice communal life in its own (Jewish or Palestinian) way, perhaps in federated cantons, a joint capital in Jerusalem, equal access to land and inalienable secular and juridical rights. Neither side should be held hostage to religious extremists.

> **Study Question**
>
> Said notes that, "[t]he conflict appears intractable because it is a contest over the same land by two peoples who believed they had valid title to it and who hoped that the other side would in time give up or go away." Given this, how does one approach "peace and reconciliation"?

Saddam Hussein

Saddam Hussein (1937–2006) was a member of the secular socialist Ba'ath Party in Iraq. An early convert to pan-Arab nationalism, Hussein ruled Iraq as a one-party state from 1979 until 2003. In 1980 Hussein triggered a costly war with neighbouring Iran, during which his government was heavily supported by western countries; however, an invasion of Kuwait in 1990 brought a swift, if limited, reprisal from a broad coalition of forces, including for the first time since the end of the Cold War members of the former Soviet bloc. In the aftermath of the 9/11 attacks, the United States sought to place blame on Hussein's Iraq despite the absence of evidence linking either Hussein or the Ba'athists to al-Qaeda. By early 2003, when Hussein delivered the speech that follows, it was clear that the United States was planning a military campaign against Iraq.

Document Source: Saddam Hussein, Speech to the Armed Forces 6 January 2003; available at http://www.guardian.co.uk/world/2003/jan/06/iraq1

Speech to the Armed Forces

In the Name of Allah, The Merciful, The Compassionate, Remember thy Lord inspired the angels (with the message): "I am with you: give firmness to the Believers: I will instill terror into the hearts of the Unbelievers: smite ye above their necks and smite all their finger tips off them."

This is because they contended against Allah and His Messenger: if any contend against Allah and His Messenger, Allah is strict in punishment. Thus (will it be said): "Taste ye then of the (punishment): for those who resist Allah, is the penalty of the Fire." . . .

Our great people . . . the valiant men of our Armed forces. On previous occasions, we have said that our view of our history in Iraq, which is also our view of our history as a nation, is that it is tantamount to faith. This is because history, to our nation and people, is not merely a register of contextual activities. It is rather a record of sacrifices made in blood in order for the nation to preserve its qualities and maintain its role, and in order for our people as well to remain as such.

What raises history and elevates it to the status of belief is the fact that the sacred blood shed in the most crucial situations for our nation to assert its traits, and its mission to augment its everlasting contribution to humanity, has been the blood of the Mujahideen who loved Allah and would therefore not hesitate to carry out, their missions as designated by Allah, the Almighty, along with the honour they had in carrying the Call of the Message of Heaven to mankind as a whole, after spreading it in their own great nation.

This is how the faithful people of our nation view history, and this is how we have read our history and believed in its meanings, and have hence stressed that our history is not merely a series of events, as in the case in the history of a lot of activities and situations in life for other nations and peoples.

History is rather the reservoir in which exist, and from whose depth we derive, the laws that elevate the nation to assume its great mission for humanity, having attained the sublime status of communication with Allah, as a nation of loving, chosen believers, who are confident and obedient to the commands of the Almighty; a nation conscious of its great mission of faith both nationally and on the level of humanity, which is extended from the essence of the tenets established throughout its eternal history and the wealth of values adorning the landmarks of distinction along its mission. . . .

History, which you have treated as a glorious faith, returns now carrying all the values and requirements of faith and generous sacrifice in order to strengthen its principles and the edifice of your glorious community on the basis of those principles.

History is the doctrine of the present that is linked to the spirit and values of the glorious past. Its spirit and high effect exist in you, valiant men and women. Hence our celebration of the 6th of January every year, as a historic mission of the struggle and Jihad of our heroic armed forces and faithful people, on the basis of the same values already referred to, now that you have reaffirmed these meanings through your faith and stands, through the blood shed by those martyred or wounded amongst us, and through the suffering and resilience of our prisoners of war. So this has become a day for us to recall all these meanings as we celebrate and honour the day every year.

The celebration is unlike any other, because this one of honour and renewal of our pledge to the Almighty before ourselves, our people and armed forces, and our nation and humanity, as a people and army of Mujahideen, men and women who have established the foundation for this faith in the depth of our blood and suffering, and in our treatment of the spirit of history, whereby we recall history in our sacrifices and our readiness as followers of a rich and glorious Faith at present and in the future as well. . . .

If anyone attempts to intimidate you, the people of Iraq, repel him and tell him that he is a small midget while we belong to a nation of glorious Faith, a great nation and an ancient people who have, through their civilization, taught the human race as a whole what man was yet to know. We are the offsprings of the sword and the pen; and, in the Name of Allah, we shall fear no one in defending our right, and shall continue our march on the path drawn by Allah, in order to achieve the tasks assigned to us by the Almighty. . . .

We salute the Palestinian people of heroic mujahideen as well as every hero and heroine amongst the champions of self-sacrifice who confront the zionest [sic] aggression with their lives and thus foil the wrong ideas of the American administrations which have acted in alliance with their artificial zionist creation in the crimes they perpetrate and the shame they reap.

Glorious and sublime are our martyrs in Palestine, Iraq and the nation as a whole.

Long live Palestine, free and Arab, from the sea to the river.

Long live Great Iraq and its valiant army of Mujahideen.

Long live our glorious Arab nation. . . .

Iraq is not the only target in this confusion, even if the noise is meant to intimidate us and to cover the aggression to be decided by the enemy whenever the devil so instructs him. The objective is rather to subject the Arab Gulf area to a full, complete, and physical occupation through which to achieve many goals. These include political interference and military intervention in the countries of the region in a manner unaccustomed before, with a view to securing complete control over their resources.

The enemy is preparing now to control entry to the Red Sea and the gate-ways to the Arab Sea, with a view to ensuring enemy interests and security for the zionist entity, while securing transport lines for oil and military shipments there. The enemy is in full coordination with the zionist entity in this respect, and has achieved a lot of what it wanted to see achieved in order to cover the weaknesses of its agencies, as exposed before the US public opinion, vis-à-vis the events of the 11th of September 2001 and the weakness, or indeed near-collapse, of the United States economy.

The enemy has been trying to divert the American people's attention from these facts, the details of which are being sought by many conscientious people there. This includes the failure of the policy of the United States towards the Palestinian question and the rights of the people of Palestine, the failure of US policies in the world in general, with anger and hatred being generated amongst peoples everywhere against those policies, as well as the failure of the US military policy in Afghanistan in the face of local resistance there. . . .

Nothing will therefore be more disappointing and discouraging to the enemy than for our people to be prepared, after relying on Allah, for any further confrontation expected with the enemy in addition to the aggression already perpetrated on a daily basis, while maintaining our life for the present and the future, building, building, and building . . . with great optimism and conviction that the future is secured by firm adherence to Faith. . . .

Study Question

What, according to Hussein, were the main goals of Iraq's enemies?

Web Resources

Columbia University Libraries: Middle East and Islamic Studies
> http://www.columbia.edu/cu/lweb/indiv/mideast/cuvlm
Yale University Library: Research Guide to Middle East Politics
> http://www.library.yale.edu/neareast/politics2.html
University of Exeter: Arabic, Islamic, and Middle Eastern Resources
> http://as.exeter.ac.uk/library/subjectguides/arabandislamicstudies/usingthe internet/arabicandislamicresources/
Harvard University Center for Middle Eastern Studies
> http://cmes.hmdc.harvard.edu/research

Recommended Reading

S.Y. Agnon, *Only Yesterday* (Princeton, NJ: Princeton University Press, 2002). *Only Yesterday* focuses on Jewish emigration to Palestine during the early twentieth century. The central character, Isaac Kumer, arrives in Palestine amidst the devotees of Zionism and the ultra-Orthodox Jews who reject Zionist ideology. His own rootlessness, the inability to establish an identity in his new homeland, and absurd twists of fate lead Kumer to question his long-held beliefs.

Ghassan Kanafani, *Men in the Sun* (Boulder, CO: Lynne Rienner Publishers, 1998). *Men in the Sun*—set in 1958—is the story of three Palestinians who attempt to escape to Kuwait in order to guarantee their survival. Three generations recollect the Palestinian experience beginning with the war in 1948, offering thoughts on national identity, the refugee question, and survival itself.

Abdelrahman Munif, *Cities of Salt* (New York: Vintage, 1989). Set in an unidentified Gulf State that the author calls Mooran, *Cities of Salt* is often seen as a veiled allusion to the history of Saudi Arabia. The novel traces the development of "Mooran" from Bedouin times to the discovery of oil and its consequences, including the negative effects of Western influence in the Gulf region.

Leon Uris, *Exodus* (New York: Doubleday, 1958). *Exodus* is Uris's fictionalized account of the founding of the state of Israel. The novel introduces the reader to many of the key themes in the postwar history of the region, including the struggle to move displaced Jewish refugees to Palestine, the role of groups such as Haganah, and the fate of newly arrived refugees in the region. The novel was subsequently made into a film of the same name in 1960.

A.B. Yehoshua, *Mr Mani* (Fort Washington, PA: Harvest Books, 1993). The story of six generations of the Mani family, from 1848 to 1982, is told through a series of conversations. Yehoshua's novel touches on many of the key events in European and Israeli Jewish history, with numerous intersecting plot lines, as it moves backwards from contemporary Israel to nineteenth century Athens.

Recommended Viewing

Escape from Iran: The Canadian Caper (Canada/USA, 1981). Director: Lamont Johnson. This made-for-television co-production examines the 1979 Iranian hostage crisis. The film provides a clear picture of the role of Canadian ambassador Ken Taylor and his staff in orchestrating the hostage rescue.

Occupied Palestine (Palestine, 1981). Director: David Koff (Documentary). *Occupied Palestine* is an Israeli-made documentary that focuses on the Palestinian plight from the perspective of the Palestinians. The film was intended to balance what the director believed to be the one-sided depiction of Palestinians in the American media.

Tsahal (Israel/France, 1994). Director: Claude Lanzmann (Documentary). *Tsahal* is one of three films in Lanzmann's trilogy exploring Jewish life in the twentieth century (*Shoah* and *Pourquoi Israel* are the others). This documentary focuses on the founding of the Israeli state and the role of the military in society and politics.

Munich (USA, 2005). Director: Stephen Spielberg. Spielberg's film focuses on the five Mossad agents chosen to assassinate the surviving members of Black September who perpetrated the massacre of Israeli athletes at the 1972 Munich Olympics.

Argo (USA, 2012). Director: Ben Affleck. Affleck's *Argo* tells a fictionalized version of the 1979 Iranian hostage crisis, focusing on the circumstances of the hostage rescue. The film concentrates on the role of the CIA in the rescue and was criticized by some for downplaying the Canadian role in the rescue.

13

Post-colonial Legacies

The vast majority of nationalist leaders who led their countries to independence in the 1950s and 1960s were firmly committed to the promotion of rapid economic modernization. Prompted by economic advisors from the former colonial powers, a number of leaders envisioned their nations following the same path to economic prosperity as the western nations before them: modernization and industrialization would bring future prosperity, even if they required short-term sacrifices.

However, a number of obstacles needed to be overcome if the newly independent nations were to achieve economic success. The economic infrastructure left over from the colonial era was frequently outdated and, even if it could be modernized, had been designed to suit the needs of the colonizer, not the colonized peoples. In addition, a majority of former colonies still relied on the production of cash crops and had developed little in the way of secondary or tertiary economic sectors. Neither the United States nor the Soviet Union encouraged the recently independent nations to change their economic orientation. In fact, both superpowers encouraged the development of subservient or neo-colonial relationships in the formerly colonized regions of the world.

Even in nations such as India, where genuine economic development did take place, additional factors frequently prevented any substantial progress. Most important, population growth often became an insurmountable obstacle to national prosperity. The conditions for massive population growth had been established in the colonial era: internal warfare had largely ended, nutrition and health-care had improved, and the food supply had become more consistent. Thus death rates declined while birth rates, for the most part, remained high. In the immediate post-colonial period, inexperienced leaders struggled to address the demands of an ever-increasing population. As population growth in the rural areas outstripped the available land and employment opportunities, mass migrations to urban areas ensued. Because the cities generally lacked the rapidly expanding industrial sectors that had absorbed a similar influx during the Industrial Revolution in the west, the cities often became dead ends for rural migrants. Impoverished urban areas then became a further drain on the already over-taxed rural economies that people were attempting to escape. The net effect was a general decline in the standard of living and increasing unpopularity for the governments that seemed unable, or unwilling, to redress the worsening situation.

The documents in this chapter address some of the issues discussed above, primarily from the perspective of the formerly colonized peoples. The chapter opens with Che Guevara's vision for Cuban development in the wake of the successful overthrow of Fulgencio Batista. Frantz Fanon's analysis of post-colonial elites follows. Patrice Lumumba reflects on both the problems and potential inherent in Congo as independence approaches. A country study compiled by the *Atlantic Monthly* identifies numerous sources of conflict in 1964 Rwanda. Kwame Nkrumah meanwhile places much of the blame for post-independence turmoil on the persistence of neo-colonialism. To counter this, Julius Nyerere, post-independence leader of Tanzania, advocates a radical form of self-reliance. Mu'ammar al-Qadhafi's *Green Book* looks to socialism to solve Libya's ongoing economic and social difficulties. Huey Newton focuses attention on areas where independence had yet to be achieved, while Rami Chhabra's interview with Indira Gandhi examines the complex issue of population control.

Ernesto "Che" Guevara

K'ung Mai and Ping An, two journalists from the People's Republic of China, interviewed Che Guevara (1928–1967) on 18 April 1959. At this time Guevara was the second-most powerful man in Cuba, after Fidel Castro, and had been appointed head of both the National Institute for Agrarian Reform and of Cuba's new national bank. As such, he was well aware of the

desperate financial situation facing Cuba. This interview was summarized on Beijing Radio and a few excerpts appeared in Chinese newspapers in 1959.

Document Source: Ernesto Che Guevara, "A New Old Interview." From Ernesto Che Guevara Archive; http://www.marxists.org/archive/guevara/1959/04/18-abs.htm. Hispanic American Historical Review, August 1966. William Ratliff, translator.

A New Old Interview

Reporter: Will you please tell us how Cuba achieved her revolutionary victory?

Guevara: Certainly. Let us begin at the time I joined the 26th of July Movement in Mexico. Before the dangerous crossing on the Granma[1] the views on society of the members of this organization were very different. I remember, in a frank discussion within our family in Mexico, I suggested we ought to propose a revolutionary program to the Cuban people. I have never forgotten how one of the participants in the attack on the Moncada army camp responded at that time. He said to me: "Our action is very simple. What we want to do is to initiate a coup d'état. Batista pulled off a coup and in only one morning took over the government. We must

make another coup and expel him from power. . . . Batista has made a hundred concessions to the Americans, and we will make one hundred and one." At that time I argued with him, saying that we had to make a coup on the basis of principle and yet at the same time understand clearly what we would do after taking over the government. That was the thinking of a member of the first stage of the 26th of July Movement. Those who held the same view and did not change left our revolutionary movement later and adopted another path.

From that time on, the small organization that later made the crossing on the Granma encountered repeated difficulties. Besides the never-ending suppression by the Mexican authorities, there was also a series of internal problems, like those people who were adventurous in the beginning but later used this pretext and that to break away from the military expedition. Finally at the time of the crossing on the Granma there remained only eighty-two men in the organization. The adventurous thought of that time was the first and only catastrophe encountered within the organization during the process of starting the uprising. We suffered from the blow. But we gathered together again in the Sierra Maestra. For many months the manner of our life in the mountains was most irregular. We climbed from one mountain peak to another, in a drought, without a drop of water. Merely to survive was extremely difficult.

The peasants who had to endure the persecution of Batista's military units gradually began to change their attitude toward us. They fled to us for refuge to participate in our guerrilla units. In this way our rank and file changed from city people to peasants. At that same time, as the peasants began to participate in the armed struggle for freedom of rights and social justice, we put forth a correct slogan—land reform. This slogan mobilised the oppressed Cuban masses to come forward and fight to seize the land. From this time on the first great social plan was determined, and it later became the banner and primary spearhead of our movement.

It was at just this time that a tragedy occurred in Santiago de Cuba; our Comrade Frank País was killed. This produced a turning point in our revolutionary movement. The enraged people of Santiago on their own poured into the streets and called for the first politically oriented general strike. Even though the strike did not have a leader, it paralyzed the whole of Oriente Province. The dictatorial government suppressed the incident. This movement, however, caused us to understand that working class participation in the struggle to achieve freedom was absolutely essential! We then began to carry out secret work among the workers, in preparation for another general strike, to help the Rebel Army seize the government.

The victorious and bold secret activities of the Rebel Army shook the whole country; all of the

people were stirred up, leading to the general strike on April 9 last year. But the strike failed because of a lack of contact between the leaders and the working masses. Experience taught the leaders of the 26th of July Movement a valuable truth: the revolution must not belong to this or that specific clique, it must be the undertaking of the whole body of the Cuban people. This conclusion inspired the members of the movement to work their hardest, both on the plains and in the mountains. At this time we began to educate our forces in revolutionary theory and doctrine. This all showed that the rebel movement had already grown and was even beginning to achieve political maturity. . . .

Every person in the Rebel Army remembered his basic duties in the Sierra Maestra and other areas: to improve the status of the peasants, to participate in the struggle to seize land, and to build schools. Agrarian law was tried for the first time; using revolutionary methods we confiscated the extensive possessions of the officials of the dictatorial government and distributed to the peasants all of the state-held land in the area. At this time there rose up a peasant movement, closely connected to the land, with land reform as its banner. . . .

To carry out thoroughly the law providing for the abolition of the latifundia[2] system will be the concern of the peasant masses themselves. The present State Constitution provides for mandatory

Ernesto "Che" Guevara in 1964. Guevara was involved with revolutionary groups around the world by 1964.

Image © Michael Nicholson/Corbis

monetary compensation whenever land is taken away, and land reform under it will be both sluggish and difficult. Now after the victory of the revolution, the peasants who have achieved their freedom must rise up in collective action and democratically demand the abolition of the latifundia system and the carrying out of a true and extensive land reform.

Reporter: What problems does the Cuban Revolution now face, and what are its current responsibilities?

Guevara: The first difficulty is that our new actions must be engaged in on the old foundations. Cuba's anti-people regime and army are already destroyed, but the dictatorial social system and economic foundations have not yet been abolished. Some of the old people are still working within the national structure. In order to protect the fruits of the revolutionary victory and to enable the unending development of the revolution we need to take another step forward in our work to rectify and strengthen the government. Second, what the new government took over was a rundown mess. When Batista fled he cleaned out the national treasury, leaving serious difficulties in the national finances. . . . Third, Cuba's land system is one in which latifundistas hold large amounts of land, while at the same time many people are unemployed. . . . Fourth, there is still racial discrimination in our society which is not beneficial to efforts to achieve the internal unification of the people. Fifth, our house rents are the highest in the world; a family frequently has to pay over a third of its income for rent. To sum up, the reform of the foundations of the economy of the Cuban society is very difficult and will take a long time.

In establishing the order of society and in democratizing the national life, the new government has adopted many positive measures. We have exerted great effort to restore the national economy. For example, the government has passed a law lowering rents by fifty per cent. Yesterday a law regulating beaches was passed to cancel the privileges of a small number of people who occupy the land and the seashores. . . .

Most important is the land reform law, which will soon be promulgated. Moreover, we will found a National Land Reform Institute. Our land reform here is not yet very penetrating; it is not as thorough as the one in China. Yet it must be considered the most progressive in Latin America. . . .

Reporter: How will Cuba struggle against domestic and foreign reactionary enemies? What are the prospects of the revolution?

Guevara: The Cuban Revolution is not a class revolution, but a liberation movement that has overthrown a dictatorial, tyrannical government. The people detested the American-supported Batista dictatorial government from the bottoms of their hearts and so rose up and overthrew it. The revolutionary government has received the broad support of all strata of people because its economic measures have taken care of the requirements of all and have gradually improved the livelihood of the people. The only enemies remaining in the country are the latifundistas and the reactionary bourgeoisie. They oppose the land reform that goes against their own interests. These internal reactionary forces may get in league with the developing provocations of the foreign reactionary forces and attack the revolutionary government.

The only foreign enemies who oppose the Cuban Revolution are the people who monopolize capital and who have representatives in the United States State Department. The victory and continuous development of the Cuban Revolution has caused these people to panic. They do not willingly accept defeat and are doing everything possible to maintain their control over the Cuban government and economy and to block the great influence of the Cuban Revolution on the people's struggles in the other Latin American countries. . . .

Our revolution has set an example for every other country in Latin America. The experience and lessons of our revolution have caused the mere talk of the coffee houses to be dispersed like smoke. We have proved that an uprising can begin even when there is only a small group of fearless men with a resolute will; that it is only necessary to gain the support of the people who can then compete with, and in the end defeat, the regular disciplined army of the government. It is also necessary to carry out a land reform. This is another experience that our Latin American brothers ought to absorb. On the economic front and in agricultural structure they are at the same stage as we are.

The present indications are very clear that they are now preparing to intervene in Cuba and destroy the Cuban Revolution. The evil foreign enemies have an old method. First they begin a political offensive, propagandizing widely and saying that the Cuban people oppose Communism. These false democratic leaders say that the United States cannot allow a Communist country on its coastline. At the same time they intensify their economic attack and cause Cuba to fall into economic difficulties. Later they will look for a pretext to create some kind of dispute and then utilize certain international organizations they control to carry out intervention against the Cuban people. We do not have to fear an attack from some small neighbouring dictatorial country, but from a certain large country, using certain international organizations and a certain kind of pretext in order to intervene and undermine the Cuban Revolution. . . .

Notes

1. The boat that carried Che Guevara, Fidel Castro, and their allies to Cuba was named the *Granma*. The vessel ran aground off the coast of Cuba forcing Castro's men into the water and leading to heavy casualties from Batista's forces on the shoreline.
2. The system of landholding in Cuba before the revolution. The latifundia system was characterized by an intensive concentration of land in the hands of a few landowners.

Study Question

Why would Guevara believe that reforming the land-holding system was the key to all future development in Cuba?

Frantz Fanon

In The Wretched of the Earth, *Frantz Fanon (1925–1961), a French-trained psychiatrist and opponent of colonial control, addressed the issue of neo-colonialism and its impact upon newly independent nations. Fanon, however, defined neo-colonialism in much broader terms than many of his contemporaries,* *indicting not only the former colonial overlords, but also many of the new indigenous leaders who had replaced them.* The Wretched of the Earth *was published in 1961, the year of Fanon's death.*

Document Source: Frantz Fanon, *The Wretched of the Earth*, transl. Constance Farrington (Paris: Présence Africaine, 1963), 112–15.

The Collaborating Class in Neo-Colonialism

History teaches us clearly that the battle against colonialism does not run straight away along the lines of nationalism. For a very long time the native devotes his energies to ending certain definite abuses: forced labour, corporal punishment, inequality of salaries, limitation of political rights, etc. This fight for democracy against the oppression of mankind will slowly leave the confusion of neo-liberal universalism to emerge, sometimes laboriously, as a claim to nationhood. It so happens that the unpreparedness of the educated classes, the lack of practical links between them and the mass of the people, their laziness, and, let it be said, their cowardice at the decisive moment of the struggle will give rise to tragic mishaps. . . .

This traditional weakness, which is almost

congenital to the national consciousness of underdeveloped countries, is not solely the result of the mutilation of the colonized people by the colonial regime. It is also the result of the intellectual laziness of the national middle class, of its spiritual penury, and of the profoundly cosmopolitan mould that its mind is set in.

The national middle class which takes over power at the end of the colonial regime is an underdeveloped middle class. It has practically no economic power, and in any case it is in no way commensurate with the bourgeoisie of the mother country which it hopes to replace. In its willful narcissism, the national middle class is easily convinced that it can advantageously replace the middle class of the mother country. But that same independence which literally drives it into a corner will give rise within its ranks to catastrophic reactions, and will oblige it to send out frenzied appeals for help to the former mother country. The university and merchant classes which make up the most enlightened section of the new state are in fact characterized by the smallness of their number and their being concentrated in the capital, and the type of activities in which they are engaged: business, agriculture, and the liberal professions. Neither financiers nor industrial magnates are to be found within this national middle class. The national bourgeoisie of underdeveloped countries is not engaged in production, nor in invention, nor building, nor labour; it is completely canalized into activities of the intermediary type. Its innermost vocation seems to be to keep in the running and to be part of the racket. The psychology of the national bourgeoisie is that of the businessman, not that of a captain of industry; and it is only too true that the greed of the settlers and the system of embargoes set up by colonialism has hardly left them any other choice.

Under the colonial system, a middle class which accumulates capital is an impossible phenomenon. Now, precisely, it would seem that the historical vocation of an authentic national middle class in an underdeveloped country is to repudiate its own nature insofar as it is bourgeois, that is to say insofar as it is the tool of capitalism, and to make itself the willing slave of that revolutionary capital which is the people.

In an underdeveloped country an authentic national middle class ought to consider as its bounden duty to betray the calling fate has marked out for it, and to put itself to school with the people; in other words to put at the people's disposal the intellectual and technical capital that it has snatched when going through the colonial universities. But unhappily we shall see that very often the national middle class does not follow this heroic, positive, fruitful, and just path; rather, it disappears with its soul set at peace into the shocking ways—shocking because anti-national—of a traditional bourgeoisie, of a bourgeoisie which is stupidly, contemptibly, cynically bourgeois.

The objective of nationalist parties as from a certain given period is, we have seen, strictly national. They mobilize the people with slogans of independence, and for the rest leave it to future events. When such parties are questioned on the economic program of the State that they are clamoring for, or on the nature of the regime which they propose to install, they are incapable of replying, because, precisely, they are completely ignorant of the economy of their own country.

The economy has always developed outside the limits of their knowledge. They have nothing more than an approximate, bookish acquaintance with the actual and potential resources of their country's soil and mineral deposits; and therefore they can only speak of these resources on a general and abstract plane. After independence this underdeveloped middle class, reduced in numbers and without capital, which refuses to follow the path of revolution, will fall into deplorable stagnation. It is unable to give free rein to its genius, which formerly it was wont to lament, though rather too glibly, was held in check by colonial domination. The precariousness of its resources and the paucity of its managerial class forces it back for years into an artisanal economy. From its point of view, which is inevitably a very limited one, a national economy is an economy based on what may be called local products. Long speeches will be made about the artisan class. Since the middle classes find it impossible to set up factories that would be more profit-earning both for themselves and for the country as a whole, they will surround the artisan class with a chauvinistic tenderness in keeping with the new awareness of national dignity, and which moreover will bring them in quite a lot of money. This cult of local products and this incapability to seek out new systems of management will be equally manifested by the bogging down of the national middle class in the methods of agricultural production which were characteristic of the colonial period.

The national economy of the period of independence is not set on a new footing. It is still concerned with the ground-nut harvest, with the cocoa crop, and the olive yield. In the same way there is no change in the marketing of basic products, and not a single industry is set up in the country. We go on sending out raw materials; we go on being Europe's small farmers, who specialize in unfinished products. . . .

As regards internal affairs and in the sphere of institutions, the national bourgeoisie will give equal proof of its incapacity. In a certain number of underdeveloped countries the parliamentary game is faked from the beginning. Powerless economically, unable to bring about the existence of coherent social relations, and standing on the principle of its domination as a class, the bourgeoisie chooses the solution that seems to it the easiest, that of the single party. It does not yet have the quiet conscience and the calm that economic power and the control of the state machine alone can give. It does not create a State that reassures the ordinary citizen, but rather one that rouses his anxiety.

The State, which by its strength and discretion ought to inspire confidence and disarm and lull everybody to sleep, on the contrary seeks to impose itself in spectacular fashion. It makes a display, it jostles people and bullies them, thus intimating to the citizen that he is in continual danger. The single party is the modern form of the dictatorship of the bourgeoisie, unmasked, unpainted, unscrupulous, and cynical.

It is true that such a dictatorship does not go very far. It cannot halt the processes of its own contradictions. Since the bourgeoisie has not the economic means to ensure its domination and to throw a few crumbs to the rest of the country; since, moreover, it is preoccupied with filling its pockets as rapidly as possible but also as prosaically as possible, the country sinks all the more deeply into stagnation. And in order to hide this stagnation and to mask this regression, to reassure itself and to give itself something to boast about, the bourgeoisie can find nothing better to do than to erect grandiose buildings in the capital and to lay out money on what are called prestige expenses.

The national bourgeoisie turns its back more and more on the interior and on the real facts of its undeveloped country, and tends to look towards the former mother country and the foreign capitalists who count on its obliging compliance. As it does not share its profits with the people, and in no way allows them to enjoy any of the dues that are paid to it by the big foreign companies, it will discover the need for a popular leader to whom will fall the dual role of stabilizing the regime and of perpetuating the domination of the bourgeoisie. The bourgeois dictatorship of underdeveloped countries draws its strength from the existence of a leader. We know that in the well-developed countries the bourgeois dictatorship is the result of the economic power of the bourgeoisie. In the underdeveloped countries on the contrary the leader stands for moral power, in whose shelter the thin and poverty-stricken bourgeoisie of the young nation decides to get rich. The people who for years on end have seen this leader and heard him speak, who from a distance in a kind of dream have followed his contests with the colonial power, spontaneously put their trust in this patriot. Before independence, the leader generally embodies the aspirations of the people for independence, political liberty, and national dignity. But as soon as independence is declared, far from embodying in concrete form the needs of the people in what touches bread, land, and the restoration of the country to the sacred hands of the people, the leader will reveal his inner purpose: to become the general president of that company of profiteers impatient for their returns which constitutes the national bourgeoisie.

Study Question

In what ways, according to Fanon, have post-colonial leaders been responsible for the problems facing their nations?

Patrice Lumumba and Graham Heath

Patrice Lumumba (1925–1961) was part of a very small Congolese middle class by virtue of his education at a Protestant school and his job as a postal clerk. He emerged as a key figure in the movement for greater independence from Belgian rule in the 1950s. Unlike his rivals, Lumumba emphasized a common Congolese nationalism, as well as a pan-African focus. At independence, in 1960, Lumumba was elected the country's first prime minister, but was immediately faced with a Belgian-backed secessionist movement in the wealthy Katanga province. Despite UN intervention, the situation in Congo spiralled out of control and, facing a political stalemate, Lumumba eventually accepted aid from the Soviet Union. Shortly thereafter the United States authorized a plot to assassinate Lumumba. In the end, however, he was captured by Belgian forces and turned over to his Congolese rivals who executed him. Lumumba had begun writing an analysis of the Congolese situation in 1956–57, prior to independence. The work was not published, however, until the manuscript was located and translated after his death. The excerpt which follows discusses the possibility of a cooperative approach to independence.

Document Source: Patrice Lumumba, *Congo: My Country*, transl. Graham Heath (London: Pall Mall Press, 1962), 145–52.

Congo: My Country

To My Congolese Compatriots

What should be our attitude towards the complex and agonising problems which confront us and which involve the future of our country? It must be one of calm, level-headedness, correct behaviour, impartiality, objectivity, justice, patience, perseverance, constant faith and continuity of effort and action. We must not give way to discouragement if we are to complete our difficult journey with its many hazards, disappointments and rebuffs.

Problems exist, and will continue to exist, as long as the world exists. The solution of these problems often depends on many factors which are not always evident to us. Let us not always jump to the conclusion that these problems are due to ill-will on the part of the authorities or of our rulers.

Every time that we évolués[1] discuss these problems, we must think of the mass of our fellow-Africans, for our task, like that of the Government of the country, is to concern ourselves not with a single class but with the population as a whole.

Let us not stand aloof from our brothers because they are less educated, less cultured, less fortunate than ourselves; this would create an unfortunate gulf between us. We want to bridge the gulf which separates us from the Whites but we must not create another one behind us. Who will work for them if we abandon them? May they not one day turn against us? Our concern must be not to satisfy personal ambitions but to achieve the harmonious development of all Africans. We must give up any activities which may cause cleavages within our society.

Our success depends above all on our unity. This can only be achieved if we manage to rid our minds of excessive clannishness, to face up together to our patriotic duty and, above all, to be aware of the absolute necessity for each one of us to achieve the harmonious development of the Congo by means of a united and unselfish effort.

The reforms which we are seeking must be achieved in a spirit of agreement and harmony. Anyone who plans rebellion or conspiracy will endanger the country and bring it into disrepute.

It is easy enough to shout slogans, to sign manifestos, but it is quite a different matter to build, manage, command, spend days and nights seeking the solution of problems.

Some Europeans of the less desirable kind exploit the credulity of the still largely uneducated Africans by urging them to claim immediate independence; they go so far as to suggest that autonomy will never be obtained without the spilling of blood, that all the Western countries had to fight in order to obtain their independence and that the Congolese must do the same if they wish to free themselves from the Belgians. This is indeed a sad state of mind!

We must reject these ideas, from whatever source they may come. The Congo will obtain its independence with dignity and not with barbarism. Civilisation and war are incompatible.

Some nations may have obtained their independence by means of atom bombs and bloody wars, but we shall obtain ours by words, by intelligence, by reason. It would be an act of the greatest barbarism, an act of banditry, to sacrifice human lives, the lives of our fellow-countrymen who are

so dear to us, in our zeal for independence. No, the Congo shall not be kept on apron strings. Let us spare our country this misfortune, which humanity would hold against us. Instead of imitating other warlike nations, we shall give them an object lesson.

This is no childish phrase. There is no moral justification for war, with its slaughter and pillage, and those who commit such barbarous acts, except under extreme provocation, do not deserve the name of civilised people whether they be white, yellow or red. . . .

Let us tell the Belgians frankly what we want, opening our hearts to them and they will do the same to us. Frankness and sincerity must be the keynote of our mutual relations in this freely contracted Belgo-Congolese marriage, because those qualities are indispensable if the union is to be a lasting one. Let us give up all tendencies to hypocrisy in dealing with Europeans. Many Congolese tell the Europeans not what they think or feel in the depths of their heart but what they think the Europeans would like them to say. We must realise that the Europeans who devote themselves to our problems have no desire for flattery or excessive and hypocritical praise, nor is this in their interest. On the contrary, they want to be told frankly what our problems are. How can they get to know us, find a solution for our troubles or correct our judgments (many of us do in fact still lack reasoning powers) if we conceal our true thoughts from them? There are many people who say that one should never tell the truth to a European because this will not be appreciated and your frankness will later cost you dear. It is, of course, a fact that some of us have suffered and still do sometimes suffer for our frankness and sincerity, either because we have boldly put forward a valid point of view which is not accepted by the Europeans concerned, or because we have defended a just cause; but that is no reason to lose heart, to take refuge in silence or, worst of all, to dull our wits by hypocrisy . . . This dumbness is a serious handicap to the liberation of our minds because, instead of discovering the truth and correcting our false judgments, we remain prisoners of ignorance and fear—very often imaginary fear.

There is no question of saying everything that comes into our heads; that would be stupid. The essential point is not to violate truth and commonsense. We must set ourselves to search ceaselessly for truth in all its forms. Truth is the only means by which we can contribute to our spiritual and intellectual development. . . .

Let us not always have our hands outstretched to receive, but always make a personal effort to obtain what we want. We shall achieve nothing by folding our arms, indulging in perpetual lamentations and recriminations or philosophising over a glass of beer. We shall never achieve anything except by working feverishly, struggling fiercely for our existence, and searching for constructive solutions. Life on this earth is hard, very hard, and bristles with difficulties; it often requires sacrifices.

Civilisation is not handed out like alms; nor can it be poured into men as one pours water into a bottle; it must be acquired by personal effort.

We must sacrifice all that we have in order to teach and educate our children, for the future of the Congo is in their hands; we must be very exacting in regard to them, watching over their studies, their outings and their walks, keeping in close touch with their teachers, so as to bring to light and remedy in good time any difficulties in their school life, and we must subject them to very severe discipline. . . .

We must not continue to live like spoilt children, always awaiting magnificent gifts. We must take action so that the Congo shall not lag behind the other countries of Africa in regard to education and political emancipation; we must realize that this emancipation depends on a real maturity of its citizens.

When the Congo has its own technicians in every trade, its doctors, agricultural specialists, engineers, businessmen, geologists, administrators, contractors, skilled workers (this does not mean that we have no skilled workers at present; I am referring here to highly qualified workers like those to be found in the big factories in Europe), social workers, nurses and mid-wives, then and then only can we talk of independence or autonomy, because we shall then be strong enough, intellectually, technically, and materially, to administer the country on our own if necessary.

Some Congolese like to keep on recalling past errors. But what is gained by this? Virtually nothing. Let us leave to the past what belongs to the past and look at the future from another angle.

No one denies that these mistakes have been made. They were errors due to inexperience. But we must remember that those who made these mistakes, the pioneers of colonisation, were not saints and had not the gift of infallibility. Yet it is to these brave pioneers of the Free State, these heroes who obtained little or no benefit from their labours, that we owe our present position.

These pioneers of the Free State left their fair country to answer the call of conscience; they left behind them their families, their closest friends, their pleasures, in order to cross the seas and rescue us from chaos and from the yoke of the man-hunting pirates; they crossed trackless and perilous country to establish lines of communication. These humanitarians, who lived in the greatest discomfort and shared our sorrows and our food, were closer to us than the "modernists" of the epoch of refrigerators and American cars.

Some of them, worn out and demoralised by countless disappointments, undoubtedly made some mistakes, but are not those mistakes outweighed by the immense amount of good which has been achieved and is in the process of achievement?

No human activity is entirely free from blemishes and mistakes. It is often these blemishes and mistakes which show the correct route to be followed in the future. . . . people who claim that the Whites are in Africa solely to exploit the Blacks seem to be mistaken in their judgment. There are, of course, some who exploit the Blacks but it is wrong to claim that all Europeans exploit the Blacks.

Is the African to show ingratitude by reviling

the pioneers of the civilising process who sleep their last sleep in this country which they loved and served? Certainly not. We must not lay ourselves open to such a charge.

When we pass the graves of these heroes who gave their lives for our safety, and thanks to whom we can now utter the words "independence—autonomy," let us be silent for a few moments and bow our heads respectfully in their memory. Together with our fellow countrymen they gave their lives for the defence of the country. May the mingled blood of the Belgians and Congolese,

which was spilt in their common struggle and formed an undying bond of friendship, cement Belgo-Congolese friendship for ever.

Note

1. Africans who had received a European education and who had been integrated into the European colonial system.

> **Study Question**
>
> To what extent do the sentiments expressed here support or undermine the claims made by Frantz Fanon in the previous document?

The Atlantic Monthly

In June 1964 The Atlantic Monthly *published a country report on Rwanda. It contained a detailed overview of Rwanda's twentieth century history and offered insights into the tensions between Rwanda's competing ethnic groups. The report concluded by identifying ongoing sources of conflict that would continue throughout the 1960s. Many of the claims in* this report have since been challenged by Africanists who argue that the tribal divisions enumerated below were much more a creation of the colonial period than they were a product of earlier African history.

Document Source: The Atlantic Report, "Rwanda 1964." From "The Atlantic Report: Rwanda," *The Atlantic Monthly*, 213(6) (June 1964), 26–33.

Rwanda 1964

The Central African Republic of Rwanda lies isolated and landlocked between the Nile and Congo River basins some 1,000 miles from the Indian Ocean and 1,600 miles from the Atlantic. It is roughly the size of Vermont and has the highest population density in Africa South of the Sahara (245 persons per square mile) and the lowest per capita income ($50 per year).

Rwanda has always known population pressure on scant resources; yet, in the midst of this scarcity one sector of its population evolved a highly intricate society, which has today fallen apart. The consequences of the destruction of that society and the attempt to replace it with another lie at the root of Rwanda's present tragic situation.

The population of Rwanda is divided into

three distinct tribal groups sharing a common language. The pygmoid Twa constitute less than one per cent of the population and are rarely seen, being hunters and forest dwellers. The short, stocky, Bantu, Negroid Hutu represent 85 per cent of the population. They were the first to fell Rwanda's forest, to clear the brush, and to cultivate. They never evolved a centralized political system, and their reliance on small units formed around clan chiefs made them highly vulnerable to invasion.

Some four centuries ago a tall, slender, haughty, exquisitely aristocratic people known as the Tutsi conquered Rwanda through a combination of force and persuasion.[1] Although they never constituted more than 15 per cent of the population, their hierarchical organization, built around a king known as the Mwami, their development of specialized warrior castes, and above all their possession of cattle enabled them to dominate the Hutu. Reputed to have originated in Ethiopia or the Nile Valley, the Tutsis were the outer fringe of a great southbound pastoral migration.

The Tutsi Sacred Cows

The Tutsi promised protection and cattle to individual Hutu, who in turn accepted the Tutsi as their lords to whom they owed personal services and a portion of their crops, and who eventually secured possession of all cattle and land. Each

Rwanda's main tribal groups cross many of the national boundaries depicted in this map.

Tutsi was the client of another Tutsi patron, the Mwami being at the pinnacle.

This feudal system was justified by an elaborate ideology which had as its essential premise the fundamental inequality of human beings. . . .

This legend reflects the reality of four centuries of Tutsi domination whereby a small and highly self-conscious minority indulged in the pleasures of a distinct leisure class through the exploitation of the Hutu majority. The basis of this exploitation was the cow. The highly exotic, sleek long-horned *Ndanga* cattle were the only recognized form of wealth, and Hutus could obtain them only by serving their Tutsi masters, who could at any time break the relationship and regain all the cattle they had lent to their clients.

It was not until 1894 that the first European entered Rwanda. Four years later Rwanda and the neighboring Tutsi kingdom of Burundi came under German rule. Both countries had first been allotted to Germany at the Berlin Conference in 1885, during the colonial scramble for Africa.

At the end of the First World War Belgium acquired a League of Nations mandate for Rwanda as partial compensation for war reparations which Germany would be unlikely to be able to pay. The Belgians continued the German system of indirect rule, relying upon the Mwami and the Tutsi officialdom and confining administrative posts and education to the Tutsi elite.

While never directly attacking the basis of Tutsi rule, the colonial period set in motion forces which led to its eventual destruction. Foremost among these forces was Christianity, which preached the equality of all men in the eyes of Christ. The Catholics took an early lead and soon converted the Mwami and his court; through the Church the Hutus could aspire to status, education, and authority, which were denied them elsewhere. The introduction of cash cropping and cultivation of Arabica coffee provided Hutu peasants with an income and lessened their reliance on their Tutsi masters. Finally, because of population pressures,

thousands of Hutus migrated to neighboring territories, where some were exposed to and returned with ideas of democracy and majority rule.

The sudden attainment of political independence by the former Belgian Congo, and United Nations pressure on the Belgians, who exercised a trusteeship for Rwanda, caused political activity in Rwanda to spurt. It was obvious that unless the Hutus seized power before the Belgians left, an independent Rwanda in Tutsi hands would forever enslave the Hutu. Yet the Hutus were handicapped by their lack of education and experience and their inborn submissiveness.

The Rise of the Hutus

On 24 July 1959, the 46-year-old Mwami Rudahigwa died suddenly under mysterious circumstances without having designated his successor. This proved the occasion for the decisive clash between the Tutsi and the embryonic Parmehutu, the political organization of the Hutu, led by Gregoire Kayibanda, former seminary student, guide at the Brussels World's Fair, and editor of the Catholic newspaper. While the Tutsis quickly installed the Mwami's nephew as the new king and prepared a terrorist campaign against leading Hutu politicians, the Hutu masses staged an uprising under Parmehutu direction. The Mwami was deposed and fled the country along with thousands of other Tutsi refugees, and a provisional Hutu government was installed.

Two extremely bitter years followed, during which a United Nations-supervised referendum resulted in an 80 per cent victory for the Parmehutu Party and the decisive rejection of the monarchy. Periodic fighting between Hutus and Tutsis continued, and additional thousands of refugees fled the country.

Meanwhile, in neighboring Burundi, to which Rwanda was linked by a customs and monetary union, the 64-year-old Mwami Mwambutsa used the political skills garnered through 50 years on the throne to hold his country and Tutsi rule together. While Rwanda achieved independence on 1 July 1962, as a republic, Burundi remained a monarchy, and ideological strains caused relations between the two countries to deteriorate rapidly.

Among the 100,000 Tutsis who fled Rwanda prior to its independence and the 250,000 who remained behind, there are many who refuse to face a life of permanent exile or to accept Hutu rule. Four centuries of domination have led them to believe that they are superior to the humble, submissive, and physically inferior Hutu. Among the hard-core exiles a secret terrorist organization known as the Inyenzi was formed. This became the focus of counterrevolutionary activity directed at overthrowing the Rwanda government and restoring the monarchy. . . .

Invasion by Refugees

This period of calm has been rudely and decisively shattered by three invasion attempts mounted by the Inyenzi. The first of these occurred on 25 November 1963, when 3,000 Tutsi refugees in Burundi began a march toward the Rwanda border to "return to their homeland." The marchers included old men, women, and children, as well as three truckloads of arms. The marchers were spotted by missionaries and UN refugee officials, and the Burundi government intervened to turn them back.

The second invasion attempt occurred on 20 December 1963, one day after the conclusion of a conference between the Rwanda and Burundi governments in which they agreed to dissolve their customs and monetary union. The invaders struck this time at Nemba on the Rwanda-Burundi border. They were armed only with homemade rifles, spears, and bows and arrows, and first attacked a Rwanda military base under construction, where they seized light arms and two jeeps. The invaders then proceeded north toward Kigali, the smallest and probably worst-defended capital in the world, with a population of 4,500 and one paved street. They advanced to

within 12 miles of Kigali before they were intercepted by the Rwanda Garde Nationale. The invaders fled, suffering heavy losses, after a battle waged with modern weapons but highly reminiscent of an intertribal skirmish.

The Rwanda government was panic-stricken by the news of the second invasion attempt. Rwanda's mountainous terrain, lack of village life, and open borders make it ideal for terrorist operations. The 1,000-man Garde Nationale had its hands full defending the capital and the border posts, and the defense of the country would have had to rely on the civilian Hutu population taking up arms.

The government took two measures to guard the country against further invasion and internal subversion (the second group of invaders had made contact with local Tutsis). Prominent Tutsis throughout Rwanda were arrested and herded to government prisons, where after severe beatings the majority were released. However, all those whose names had been found on a list of people whom the invaders planned to install as government officials were shot. This list had been taken off the body of a Congolese mercenary killed while fighting with the invaders.

The second measure was to send a minister to each of Rwanda's ten prefectures to organize the "self-defense" of the civilian population with the aid of the local prefect and the elected burgomasters. The individual situation in each prefecture and the attitude of local officials, rather than government policy, caused the subsequent massive reprisals and massacres of the local Tutsi population which have been so widely reported.

The worst slaughter took place in Gikongoro prefecture, where the dense tropical forest provides an open border with Burundi. Here, word had been received that Kigali had fallen and the former Mwami restored. Local Tutsis had for several days prior to the invasion been boasting of their hopes of returning to power and had been congregating around the former royal residence, located in this prefecture. Whether spontaneously or upon the orders of local officials, the Hutu population arose against the Tutsis in this prefecture.

The most reliable estimates of the numbers killed are between 10,000 and 14,000. The population used any weapons nearby, mostly hoes and long knives for cutting grass, resulting in hideous atrocities. Bodies were dumped into rivers and streams, left alongside roads to be scavenged by wild animals, and buried in mass graves.

Elsewhere in Rwanda timely action averted tragedy. Thus, in Kibungo prefecture on the Tanganyikan border the Catholic White Fathers prevailed upon the local authorities not to excite the Hutu population. The result was relative calm; Hutu and Tutsi celebrated Christmas mass together, and local Tutsis turned over to the authorities an Inyenzi invader hiding among them. Yet the White Fathers were convinced that had a single Tutsi hut been burned, all the Tutsis in the prefecture would have fled.

There was never a government policy of genocide against the Tutsi. Beginning on Christmas Eve, 6,000 Tutsis, including 5,300 women and children, fled into Uganda, with 13,000 head of cattle. No attempt was made by the Rwanda government to interfere with this defenseless horde or even larger masses of refugees who fled into Burundi, the Congo, and Tanganyika. Other thousands of Tutsis took refuge in Catholic mission stations within Rwanda, where they believed they would be safe because of Catholic influence in the government. While the government tried to induce these internal refugees to return to their homes, it took no action against them.

A third invasion attempt occurred at Kizinga on the Uganda border on 27 December. At this point 500 well-armed Tutsis, coming mostly from the Congo, were met by a force of the Rwanda Garde Nationale, which had been alerted for several days to expect an attack. The invaders were repulsed; more than 300 were killed, and the others were taken prisoner by Ugandan officials.

A Call for UN Help

This invasion attempt prompted the Rwanda government to cable U Thant for UN assistance. Max Dorsinville, personal representative of U Thant in the Congo, arrived in Kigali on 1 January and spent several days in the country before going on to Burundi. His failure to protest vociferously or threaten international action enabled the reprisals to continue, and they were not brought under control until mid-January, largely as a result of pressure from Catholic and Protestant authorities and foreign embassies within Rwanda. Meanwhile, the world remained almost totally uninformed since Radio Rwanda is too weak to be heard outside the Country and Rwanda has no newspapers except a monthly bulletin in Kinyarwanda.

Today Rwanda remains in a state of constant military alert, with passes required for traveling within the Country and military roadblocks maintained on the principal roads. The effects of the invasions and of the security situation have been disastrous for the Rwanda economy. The cash sector, dependent almost entirely on exports of coffee, is dying, and the standard of living has fallen markedly. The subsistence sector continues to supply adequate foodstuffs, although malnutrition is widespread. Rwanda hopes to create its own currency, although its foreign-exchange reserves are depleted and its balance-of-payments deficit is chronic. Only Belgian and other external aid and technicians are keeping the non-subsistence sector of the economy alive.

The 150,000 Tutsi refugees huddled along Rwanda's borders provide a constant security threat and a fertile ground for Inyenzi agitation. Their presence makes life impossible for the Tutsis remaining in Rwanda, who are regarded as suspect by the Rwanda government.

Urgent measures are required to prevent Rwanda from erupting again into violence and to restore hope to its crippled economy. Among these are military measures to control the refugees and prevent further invasion attempts by the Inyenzi. The neighboring governments of Uganda, Tanganyika, and the Congo are using the limited military means at their disposal toward these ends, and the Burundi government is under pressure to do likewise. Also required is external assistance to enable the permanent resettlement of the refugees in the neighboring countries, where fortunately there is ample unused arable land.

Finally, even if the Tutsi question is resolved, Rwanda still faces a galloping population increase threatening its meagre resources. The strength of Catholicism within Rwanda and the traditional high regard for children rule out artificial methods of population control. Meanwhile, at the present rate the population will double within 23 years, and unless a long-term economic plan is implemented

to increase agricultural productivity and bring additional lands into cultivation, the only alternative will be a return to pre-colonial Malthusian methods of population control. This can be averted if economic planning, technical assistance, and external aid to the total sum of $8 to $10 million a year are forthcoming. Otherwise, Rwanda is likely to remain on the world's conscience.

Note

1   The physical differences between Hutu and Tutsi are overstated in the article.

> **Study Question**
>
> What were the primary sources of conflict in Rwanda in 1964, according to this article?

Kwame Nkrumah

Kwame Nkrumah (1909–1972) became deeply involved in the struggle for African decolonization during his studies in the US and Great Britain. Despite being arrested by the British in 1950, he won election to the Ghanaian parliament while in prison. In 1951, after the British had determined that Ghana would obtain independence, he was released and allowed to take his seat in parliament. In 1952 Nkrumah became the country's first prime minister. He declared Ghana's independence in 1957 and, in 1960,

proclaimed the nation a republic. In 1964, after seeing many of his development policies fail, Nkrumah appointed himself "President for Life" and began to rule in an increasingly authoritarian manner. In the excerpt below, from 1965, Nkrumah argued that Ghana's lack of success, and the problems facing other post-colonial states, was due primarily to the persistence of neo-colonialism in sub-Saharan Africa.

Document Source: Kwame Nkrumah, *Neo-Colonialism: The Last Stage of Imperialism* (London: Nelson, 1965), i–ix.

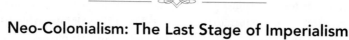

Neo-Colonialism: The Last Stage of Imperialism

The neo-colonialism of today represents imperialism in its final and perhaps its most dangerous stage. In the past it was possible to convert a country upon which a neo-colonial regime had been imposed—Egypt in the nineteenth century is an example—into a colonial territory. Today this process is no longer feasible. Old-fashioned colonialism is by no means entirely abolished. It

still constitutes an African problem, but everywhere on the retreat. Once a territory has become nominally independent it is no longer possible, as it was in the last century, to reverse the process. Existing colonies may linger on, but no new colonies will be created. In place of colonialism as the main instrument of imperialism we have today neo-colonialism.

The essence of neo-colonialism is that the State which is subject to it is, in theory, independent and has all the outward trappings of international sovereignty. In reality its economic system and thus its political policy is directed from the outside.

The methods and form of this direction can take various shapes. For example, in an extreme case the troops of the imperial power may garrison the territory of the neo-colonial State and control the government of it. More often, however, neo-colonialist control is exercised through economic or monetary means. The neo-colonial State may be obliged to take the manufactured products of the imperialist power to the exclusion of competing products from elsewhere. Control over government policy in the neo-colonial State may be secured by payments towards the cost of running the State, by the provision of civil servants in positions where they can dictate policy, and by monetary control over foreign exchange through the imposition of a banking system controlled by the imperial power.

Where neo-colonialism exists the power exercising control is often the State which formerly ruled the territory in question, but this is not necessarily so. For example, in the case of South Vietnam the former imperial power was France, but neo-colonial control of the State has now gone to the United States. It is possible that neo-colonial control may be exercised by a consortium of financial interests which are not specifically identifiable with any particular State. The control of the Congo by great international financial concerns is a case in point.

American Vice-President Richard Nixon attends Ghana's independence ceremonies in 1957.

National Archives, 306-rnt-12-16, http://www.archives.gov/publications/prologue/1999/winter/us-and-ghana-1957-1966-1.html

The result of neo-colonialism is that foreign capital is used for the exploitation rather than for the development of the less developed parts of the world. Investment under neo-colonialism increases rather than decreases the gap between the rich and the poor countries of the world.

The struggle against neo-colonialism is not aimed at excluding the capital of the developed world from operating in less-developed countries. It is aimed at preventing the financial power of the developed countries being used in such a way as to impoverish the less developed.

Nonalignment, as practised by Ghana[1] and many other countries, is based on cooperation with all States whether they be capitalist, socialist, or have a mixed economy. Such a policy, therefore, involves foreign investment from capitalist countries, but it must be invested in accordance with a national plan drawn up by the government of the nonaligned State with its own interests in mind. The issue is not what return the foreign investor receives on his investments. He may, in fact, do better for himself if he invests in a non-aligned country than if he invests in a neo-colonial one. The question is one of power. A State in the grip of neo-colonialism is not master of its own destiny. It is this factor which makes neo-colonialism such a serious threat to world peace. The growth of nuclear weapons has made out-of-date the old-fashioned balance of power which rested upon the ultimate sanction of a major war. Certainty of mutual destruction effectively prevents either of the great power blocs from threatening the other with the possibility of a worldwide war, and military conflict has thus become confined to "limited war." For these neo-colonialism is the breeding ground.

Such wars can, of course, take place in countries which are not neo-colonialist controlled. Indeed their object may be to establish in a small but independent country a neo-colonialist regime. The evil of neo-colonialism is that it prevents the formation of those large units which would make impossible "limited war." To give one example: if Africa was united, no major power bloc would attempt to subdue it by limited war because from the very nature of limited war, what can be achieved by it is itself limited. It is only where small States exist that it is possible, by landing a few thousand marines or by financing a mercenary force, to secure a decisive result.

The restriction of military action of "limited wars" is, however, no guarantee of world peace and is likely to be the factor which will ultimately involve the great power blocs in a world war, however much both are determined to avoid it.

Limited war, once embarked upon, achieves a momentum of its own. Of this, the war in South Vietnam is only one example. It escalates despite the desire of the great power blocs to keep it limited. While this particular war may be prevented from leading to a world conflict, the multiplication of similar limited wars can only have one end—world war and the terrible consequences of nuclear conflict.

Neo-colonialism is also the worst form of imperialism. For those who practice it, it means power without responsibility and for those who suffer from it, it means exploitation without redress. In the days of old-fashioned colonialism, the imperial power had at least to explain and justify at home the actions it was taking abroad. In the colony those who served the ruling imperial power could at least look to its protection against any violent move by their opponents. With neo-colonialism neither is the case.

Above all, neo-colonialism, like colonialism before it, postpones the facing of the social issues which will have to be faced by the fully developed sector of the world before the danger of world war can be eliminated or the problem of world poverty resolved.

Neo-colonialism, like colonialism, is an attempt to export the social conflicts of the capitalist countries. The temporary success of this policy can be seen in the ever-widening gap between the richer and the poorer nations of the world. But the internal contradictions and conflicts of neo-colonialism make it certain that it cannot endure as a permanent world policy. How it should be brought to an end is a problem that should be studied above all, by the developed nations of the world, because it is they who will feel the full impact of the ultimate failure. The longer it continues the more certain it is that its inevitable collapse will destroy the social system of which they have made it a foundation.

Note

1. The policy of non-alignment was pioneered by Nehru's India and Nkrumah's Ghana; the idea was to side with neither the United States nor the Soviet Union during the Cold War in the hopes of creating a powerful third bloc.

Study Question

Based upon all of the arguments presented in this chapter, was neo-colonialism primarily to blame for the problems that emerged after independence, or were the actions of indigenous elites equally or more responsible?

Julius Nyerere

In February 1967, Tanzanian President Julius Nyerere (1922–1999) announced a new policy direction. Tanzania would become an egalitarian socialist society, based upon cooperative agriculture. Nyerere emphasized self-sufficiency, the need to break away from foreign aid and investment, and placed new emphasis on education and literacy. Economic cooperation, racial and tribal harmony, and self-sacrifice would characterize Nyerere's Tanzania. The following declaration, made in Arusha and published in

the March 1967 edition of Africa Report, *summarizes these views. Despite his vision for his country, when Nyerere retired in 1985, Tanzania was still one of the most impoverished nations in the world. Some people might consider this a failure on Nyerere's part; however, Tanzania was also politically and socially stable and had one of the highest literacy rates in sub-Saharan Africa.*

Document Source: Julius Nyerere, "The Arusha Declaration," *Africa Report* (March 1967), 11–13.

The Arusha Declaration

It is obvious that in the past we have chosen the wrong weapon for our struggle, because we chose money as our weapon. We are trying to overcome our economic weakness by using the weapons of the economically strong—weapons which in fact we do not possess. By our thoughts, words, and actions it appears as if we have come to the conclusion that without money we cannot bring about the revolution we are aiming at. It is as if we have said, "Money is the basis of development. Without money there can be no development.". . .

It is stupid to rely on money as the major instrument of development when we know only too well that our country is poor. It is equally stupid, indeed it is even more stupid, for us to imagine that we shall rid ourselves of our poverty through foreign financial assistance rather than our own financial resources. . . .

Let us therefore always remember the following. We have made a mistake to choose money, something which we do not have, to be our major instrument of development. We are mistaken when we imagine that we shall get money from foreign countries, firstly because, to say the truth, we cannot get enough money for our development and, secondly, because even if we could get it, such complete dependence on outside help would have endangered our independence and the other policies of our country.

Because of our emphasis on money, we have made another big mistake. We have put too much emphasis on industries. Just as we have said "Without money there can be no development," we also seem to say "industries are the basis of development." This is true. The day when we have lots of money we shall be able to say we are a developed country.

The mistake we are making is to think that development begins with industries. It is a mistake because we do not have the means to establish many modern industries in our country. We do not have either the necessary finances or the technical know-how. It is not enough to say that we shall borrow the finances and the technicians from other countries to come and start the industries. The answer to this is the same one we gave earlier, that we cannot get enough money, and borrow enough technicians to start all the industries we need. And even if we could get the necessary assistance, dependence on it could interfere with our policy of socialism. The policy of inviting a chain of capitalists to come and establish industries in our country might succeed in giving us all the industries we need, but it would also succeed in preventing the establishment of socialism unless we believe that without first building capitalism, we cannot build socialism. . . .

The development of a country is brought about by people, not by money. Money, and the wealth it represents, is the result and not the basis of development. . . .

A great part of Tanzania's land is fertile and gets sufficient rains. Our country can produce various crops for home consumption and for export. We can produce food crops (which can be exported if we produce in large quantities) such as maize, rice, wheat, beans, and groundnuts. And we can produce such cash crops as sisal, cotton, coffee, tobacco, pyrethrum, and tea. Our land is also good for grazing cattle, goats, sheep, and for raising chickens; we can get plenty of fish from our rivers, lakes, and from the sea. All of our farmers are in areas which can produce two or three or even more of the food and cash crops enumerated above, and each farmer could increase his production so as to get more food or more money. And because the main aim of development is to get more food, and more money for our other needs, our purpose must be to increase production of these agricultural crops. This is in fact the only road through which we can develop our country—in other words, only by increasing our production of these things can we get more food and more money for every Tanzanian.

Everybody wants development, but not everybody understands and accepts the basic requirements for development. The biggest requirement is hard work. Let us go to the villages and talk to our people and see whether or not it

East African Heads of Government Conference in 1964. Left to right: Julius Nyerere (Tanzania), Milton Obote (Uganda), and Jomo Kenyatta (Kenya).

Image © Bettman/Corbis.

is possible for them to work harder.

In towns, for example, the average paid worker works seven and a half or eight hours a day for six or six and a half days a week. This is about 45 hours a week, excluding two or three weeks leave every year. This means that an urban worker works for 45 hours a week in 48 to 50 weeks a year.

For a country like ours, these are really quite short working hours. In other countries, even those which are more developed than we are, people work for more than 45 hours a week. It is not normal for a young country to start with such a short working week. The normal thing is to begin with long working hours and decrease them as the country becomes more and more prosperous. By starting with such short working hours and asking for even shorter hours, we are in fact imitating the more developed countries. And we shall regret this imitation. . . .

It would be appropriate to ask our farmers, especially the men, how many hours a week and how many weeks a year they work. Many do not even work for half as many hours as the wage earner does. The truth is that in the villages the women work very hard. At times they work for 12 or 14 hours a day. They even work on Sundays and public holidays. Women who live in the villages work harder than anybody else in Tanzania. But the men who live in villages (and some of the women in towns) are on leave for half of their life. The energies of the millions of men in the villages and thousands of women in the towns which are at present wasted in gossip, dancing, and drinking, are a great treasure which could contribute more toward the development of our country than anything we could get from rich nations. . . .

The second condition of development is the use of intelligence. Unintelligent hard work would not bring the same good results as the two combined. Using a big hoe instead of a small one; using a plough pulled by oxen instead of an ordinary hoe; the use of fertilizers; the use of insecticides; knowing the right crop for a particular season or soil; choosing good seeds for planting; knowing the right time for planting, weeding, etc.; all these things show the use of knowledge and intelligence. And all of them combine with hard work to produce more and better results.

The money and time we spend on passing on this knowledge to the peasants are better spent and bring more benefits to our country than the money and the great amount of time we spend on other things which we call development. . . .

None of this means that from now on we will not need money or that we will not start industries or embark upon development projects which require money. Furthermore, we are not saying that we will not accept, or even that we shall not look for, money from other countries for our development. This is not what we are saying. We will continue to use money; and each year we will use more money for the various development projects than we used the previous year because this will be one of the signs of our development.

What we are saying, however, is that from now on we shall know what is the foundation and what is the fruit of development. Between money and people it is obvious that the people and their hard work are the foundation of development, and money is one of the fruits of that hard work.

From now on we shall stand upright and walk forward on our feet rather than look at this problem upside down. Industries will come and money will come, but their foundation is the people and their hard work, especially in agriculture. This is the meaning of self-reliance.

Study Question

What are the strengths and weaknesses of a policy of self-reliance such as that envisioned here?

Mu'ammar al-Qadhafi

Mu'ammar al-Qadhafi (1942–2011) took part in a coup that overthrew the Libyan monarchy in 1969. He led Libya until his death in 2011, assuming a variety of titles during that time. Qadhafi was a strong supporter of pan-Arabism and a political ideology that he referred to as "Islamic socialism." In the 1970s and 1980s Qadhafi's Libya was a strong supporter of international terrorist organizations, leading to both UN and US sanctions. In the latter years of his rule,

Qadhafi paid large sums in compensation to victims of terrorism in order to free his country from these restrictions. The following excerpt from Qadhafi's Green Book *was written in 1978 and discusses the importance of socialist ownership.*

Document Source: The Green Book by Mu'ammar al-Qadhafi. This translation was published by the Public Establishment for Publishing, Advertising and Distribution in Tripoli, Libya; http://zadishefreeman.com/images/Muammar-Qaddafi-Green-Book-Eng.pdf

The Green Book

Land

Land is no one's property. But everyone has the right to use it, to benefit from it by working, farming or pasturing. This would take place throughout a man's life and the lives of his heirs, and would be through his own effort without using others with or without wages, and only to the extent of satisfying his own needs.

If possession of land is allowed, only those who are living there have a share in it. The land is permanently there, while, in the course of time, users change in profession, in capacity and in their presence.

The purpose of the new socialist society is to create a society which is happy because it is free. This can be achieved through satisfying the material and spiritual needs of man, and that, in turn, comes about through the liberation of these needs from outside domination and control.

Satisfaction of these needs must be attained without exploiting or enslaving others, or else, it will contradict the purpose of the new socialist society.

Man in the new society works for himself to guarantee his material needs, or works for a socialist corporation in whose production he is a partner, or performs a public service to the society which provides his material needs.

Economic activity in the new socialist society is productive activity for the satisfaction of material needs. It is not unproductive activity or an activity which seeks profit in order, after satisfying material needs, to save the surplus. That is impossible under the rules of the new socialism.

The legitimate purpose of the individual's economic activity is solely to satisfy his needs. For the wealth of the world has limits at each stage as does the wealth of each individual society. Therefore no individual has the right to carry out economic activity in order to acquire more of that wealth than is necessary to satisfy his needs, because the excess amount belongs to other individuals. He has the right to save from his needs and from his own production but not from the efforts of others nor at the expense of their needs. For if we allow economic activity to extend beyond the satisfaction of needs, one person will only have more than his needs by preventing another from obtaining his. The savings which are in excess of one's needs are another person's share of the wealth of society.

To allow private production for the purpose of acquiring savings that exceed the satisfaction of needs is exploitation itself, as in permitting the use of others to satisfy your own needs or to get more than your own needs. This can be done by exploiting a person to satisfy the needs of others and making savings for others at the expense of his needs.

Work for a wage is, in addition to being an enslavement of man as mentioned before, work without incentives because the producer is a wage-worker rather than a partner.

Whoever works for himself is certainly devoted to his productive work because his incentive to production lies in his dependence on his private work to satisfy his material needs. Also whoever works in a socialist corporation is a partner in its production. He is, undoubtedly, devoted to his productive work because the impetus for devotion to production is that he gets a satisfaction of his needs through production. But whoever works for a wage has no incentive to work.

Work for wages failed to solve the problem of increasing and developing production. Work, either in the form of services or production, is continually deteriorating because it rests on the shoulders of wage-workers.

Examples of Labour for Wages for Society, of Labour for Wages for a Private Activity, and Labour for No Wage

First Example
(a) A worker who produces ten apples for society. Society gives him one apple for his production. The apple fully satisfies his needs.
(b) A worker who produces ten apples for society. Society gives him one apple for his production. The apple is not enough to satisfy his needs.

Second Example
A worker who produces ten apples for another person and gets a wage of less than the price of one apple.

Third Example
A worker who produces ten apples for himself.

The Conclusion
The first (a) will not increase his production for whatever the increase might be, he will only get an apple for himself. It is what satisfies his needs. Thus all those working for such a society are always psychologically apathetic.

The first (b) has no incentive to production itself, for he produces for the society without obtaining satisfaction of his needs. However he has to continue to work without incentive because he is forced to submit to the general conditions of work throughout the society. That is the case with members of that society.

The second does not initially work to produce. He works to get wages. Since his wages are not enough to satisfy his needs, he will either search for another master and sell him his work at a better price or he will be obliged to continue the same work just to survive. The third is the only one who produces without apathy and without coercion. In the socialist society, there is no possibility for private production exceeding the satisfaction of individual needs, because satisfaction of needs at the expense of others is not allowed.

As the socialist establishments work for the satisfaction of the needs of society, the third example explains the sound basis of economic production. However, in all conditions, even in bad ones, production continues for survival. The best proof is that in capitalist societies production accumulates and expands in the hands of a few owners who do not work but exploit the efforts of toilers who are obliged to produce in order to survive. However, *The Green Book* not only solves the problem of material production but also prescribes the comprehensive solution of the problems of human society so that the individual may be materially and spiritually liberated . . . a final liberation to attain his happiness. . . .

Study Question
Consider the logic of Qadhafi's three examples. What are the flaws in the logic? What are the strengths?

Huey P. Newton

The struggle to end colonialism in Africa coincided with the civil rights movement in the United States, leading many American civil rights advocates to call for a joint liberation effort. Huey Newton (1942–1989), one of the founders of the Black Panther movement,[1] drew his inspiration from the teachings of Marx, Lenin, Che Guevara, and Mao Zedong. The following excerpt ties the

northern civil rights movement to the independence struggle in Mozambique. It was written in October 1971, a period in which the Panther movement, under constant attack by the FBI, began to split into factions.

Document Source: Huey P. Newton, "Uniting against a Common Enemy," in David Hilliard and Donald Weise, eds, *The Huey P. Newton Reader* (New York: Seven Stories Press, 2002), 236–40.

Uniting Against a Common Enemy

On the continent of Africa there are people who look like us. They are Black. We are brothers because our struggle is common. We have both suffered under White racism and under oppression. This is why we should not let the reactionaries of the world be the only ones communicating across the waters and masses of land. We have a common interest to serve, and therefore, we can learn from each other. What happens here affects our brothers in Africa; what happens in Africa affects us. The United States has seen to this. But this is good. We can learn to fight together, though separated.

There is a place in Africa called Mozambique. It lies on Africa's eastern shore, in the southern portion of the continent. It is a rich land, like most in Africa. In 1498 (six years after Columbus' famous "discovery") the Portuguese invader (if you remember, your elementary school books credit him as an "explorer") Vasco da Gama violated the shores of Mozambique. The rest of the troops landed seven years later, in 1505. From that point on the Portuguese have dominated the economy and lives and the culture of the Mozambican people. Their national language became, and still is, Portuguese. To this day, the Portuguese lay claim to Mozambique, referring to "Portuguese" Mozambique.

This, of course, is not in agreement with our brothers and sisters in Mozambique. Mozambique

is their home. They are not the invaders. Of course, the people of Mozambique have made many attempts throughout their long history of Portuguese colonial oppression to rid themselves of their chains. However, the most powerful and successful struggle is presently being waged under the guidance of the revolutionary organization FRELIMO (Front for the Liberation of Mozambique). The people support FRELIMO, for FRELIMO is of the people and is organizing struggle in the true interest of all the people. . . .

Today, FRELIMO, under the wise leadership of President Machel,[2] is guiding the people of Mozambique toward greater and final victory. But today, naturally, the attacks of the combined forces of the United States, Portugal, Germany, France, and Britain are even more fierce: constant bombings and many ground attacks take place. However, there is a more intricate, but ultimately more vicious, plan in the making, headed primarily by the United States. They plan to build, for the Portuguese, a large hydroelectric dam. The site for the dam is in the liberated Tete Province in Cahora Bassa, along the Zambesi [sic] River, bordering racist Rhodesia. Its purpose is to not only give financial aid to impoverished Portugal but to be used as a key part in a plot with South Africa to launch a political, diplomatic, and military offensive upon all of Africa. A familiar name to us is General Electric. The General Electric Company has spent millions to aid in building the Cahora Bassa Dam. Altogether, the United States and others have agreed to invest 500 million dollars in the dam, which is capable of producing 18.4 billion kilowatts of electricity. Also, in regard to this Cahora Bassa Dam, late FRELIMO President Mondlane once said, "They say it will enable them to settle one million Whites in Mozambique within 10 years . . . to form a great white barrier across Southern Africa."

If we believe that we are brothers with the people of Mozambique, how can we help? They need arms and other material aid. We have no weapons to give. We have no money for materials. Then how do we help? Or, how can they help our struggle? They cannot fight for us. We cannot fight in their place. We can each narrow the territory that our common oppressor occupies. We can liberate ourselves, learning from and

teaching each other along the way. But the struggle is one; the enemy is the same. Eventually, we and our brothers in Mozambique, in all of Africa, throughout the world, can discuss a world without boundaries or national ties. We will have a human culture, a human language, the earth will be all our territory, serving all our interests; serving the interest of all people.

Notes

1. The group's full name was the Black Panther Party for Self-Defense.
2. Samora Machel (1933–1986) was a revolutionary leader who played a key role in FRELIMO's fight for independence. He was named the country's first president at independence in 1975.

> **Study Question**
>
> What were the main obstacles to the achievement of independence for Mozambique, according to this article?

Rami Chhabra

Rami Chhabra is a prominent Indian journalist who has been a strong advocate for the rights of women. She reported on many of Indira Gandhi's press conferences and was appointed by Prime Minister Rajiv Gandhi to the Ministry of Health and Family Welfare in 1986. She has also served on a number of committees on population control. The interview that follows took place in September 1980 after Indira Gandhi returned for a third term as prime minister and after her highly controversial attempt to impose a program of mandatory sterilization in the mid-1970s.

Document Source: Rami Chhabra, "Population Policy in India: Two Comments," *Population and Development Review,* 1(1) (March 1981): 168–71.

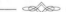

An Interview with Indira Gandhi

Q. Madam Prime Minister, what priorities does your Government accord to the Family Planning Programme?

A. Our Government was the very first in the whole world which took it up as an official programme and that shows how important it is to us. As you know our population has grown

enormously; we add an Australia every year.

Q. Mrs Gandhi, do you see any alternative for economic viability for the nation in the face of failure to curb population growth rate to a manageable proportion?

A. The real answer, of course, is development from both angles: first the development to provide what the people need, to open up areas, and, secondly, because development itself curbs families. I mean people who reach a particular standard are more conscious of their duty to the child. That is, they want something more for their children than they had; and, therefore, they themselves think about smaller families. But ultimately, of course, size of the population has to be tackled at various levels not just through development, but through persuasion of the people.

Q. Because development itself would be denied if we cannot control the situation to the manageable proportions.

A. Well, it is a bit of a circle. But, for instance, take places like Punjab where there has been agricultural progress or industrial areas or even a place like Kerala which has educational progress, there the birth-rate has gone down.

Q. Mrs Gandhi, would you say that even more important in its place within the economic perspective is the question of family planning being the primary concern of the fundamental right of the woman not to be denied options in her life and of the child not to be born into a situation where it is just in a position of neglect?

A. Why leave out the father? I agree with the view that [the] human rights aspect of it is very important, especially of course for the woman because she has the entire burden of child bearing and child rearing and yet her opinion is hardly ever asked for; nor is there much consideration for her welfare. And, unfortunately the child is [the] one who suffers from this. Today birth should be a matter of choice [by] both parents so that they feel responsible for the child and give it its due rights.

Q. But, given the importance of family planning, would you say, like national security, it should be part of the minimum national consensus, i.e. above party politics and we should be willing to promote this national consensus for the country?

A. Well, obviously a subject like family planning should be above any controversy. But, as you have noticed in the past years, there have been certain parties and groups which have done tremendous propaganda against this, telling people of one religion that they will be exterminated and the others that their numbers were going down and they will be in difficulty; besides, of course, all the propaganda that was done about sterilization. Because we do not believe in coercion; we think that there should be persuasion. But this must be done on a massive educational scale and unless everybody is in favour it will take a very long time and may defeat the whole purpose of it.

Q. But, knowing the very low, totally ineffective performance that there has been in the Family Planning Programme in the last few years, what steps is your Government now proposing to take to revitalize the programme?

A. I think we have to involve not just the department that is in charge of this, but

US President Richard Nixon meets with Indira Gandhi in August 1969.

Courtesy of the National Archives, Richard Nixon Library, http://research.archives.gov/description/194651

the whole population, specially [especially] schools, the whole youth movement, women's organizations, other institutions which are concerned with any type of social welfare. I mean everybody gets into it to create the right atmosphere; and you find that village women are ready or any woman for that matter, not just one. One part which is very important is that we must ensure better health, because if there is any chance of children dying more, then people will not be willing to risk that. So, they must be ensured better health, education, and of course, even employment later on. It is part of national planning as a whole.

Q.   Madam Prime Minister, would you be in favour of systematically linking emphasis on family planning incentives? You know the tax structure on the one hand and all the collective inputs on the other so that a system of reciprocal responsibility can be established between the State and the people.

A.   Well, this idea is a very complicated matter and it has been discussed many times; and previously we did give some incentives and some disincentives. I do not know how well it worked. It has to be gone into.

Q.   Are you willing to examine the issue?

A.   I am willing to examine it.

Q.   And also would you feel there is a need for review of the law in order to see how it can be made more supporting to the family planning effort? You know a moral framework can be created within which incentives for family planning are decided upon and not struck down as discriminatory.

A.   I do not know whether you can create a moral climate legally. That is a question of changing attitudes to life.

Q.   And finally, Mrs Gandhi, may I ask you, since a great deal of research has pointed out women's education, women's employment, raising of women's status is important for fertility decline to take place, quite apart from the fact that this is badly needed in the country itself. Is your Government contemplating any particular steps for bringing up the status of women?

A.   We are doing a great deal. We have to start at the bottom, i.e., the girls; and I think a great deal is being done now to help girls to continue with their education and not drop out as they have been doing.

Study Question

According to Indira Gandhi, what were the necessary steps to achieving substantial population control?

Web Resources

Guide to Research in Post-colonial Theory
    http://www.libraries.iub.edu/index.php?pageId=1001063
Decolonization
    http://www.fordham.edu/halsall/mod/modsbook51.html
University of Pennsylvania: African Studies Center
    http://www.africa.upenn.edu/AS.html
Latin American Network Information Center
    http://www1.lanic.utexas.edu
Handbook of Latin American Studies Online
    http://lcweb2.loc.gov/hlas/hlashome.html

Recommended Reading

Chinua Achebe, *Anthills of the Savannah* (London: Heinemann, 1987). Achebe's first novel to be set in post-colonial Africa provides a fictionalized look at the problems of nation-building, the corrupting nature of political power, and the persistence of tradition amidst a rapidly modernizing world.

Isabel Allende, *The House of the Spirits* (New York: Bantam, 1986). Allende's novel, set in an unidentified Latin American country, spans several generations of the Trueba family and their struggles: between landlords and tenants, rich and poor, Marxist and Conservative. Throughout, the constant role of the military in government is evident.

Gabriel Garcia Marquez, *The Autumn of the Patriarch* (New York: HarperCollins Perennial Classics, 1999). Garcia Marquez's 1975 novel takes place in a Caribbean country following the death of a dictator and the subsequent end of his long reign. The novel examines the mythical status attained by some dictators, the ever-present military junta, corruption, and the oppression of nations living under a carefully constructed system of terror.

Ngugi wa Thiong'o, *Petals of Blood* (Harmondsworth: Penguin, 2005). Written in the 1970s, *Petals of Blood* is set in post-colonial Kenya and examines the frustrations and disappointments that followed the granting of independence. The novel touches on greed and corruption, as well as the pressures of globalization.

Recommended Viewing

The Killing Fields (UK, 1984). Director: Roland Joffé. Set in Cambodia during the genocidal era of the Khmer Rouge, *The Killing Fields* is based on the true story of Dith Pran, who was captured by the Khmer Rouge and imprisoned in the "re-education camps." The film also tells some of the political history of the notorious Khmer Rouge.

Guelwaar (Senegal/France, 1993). Director: Ousmane Sembene. *Guelwaar* illustrates the complexities of life in post-colonial Senegal, highlighting the religious conflicts between Catholics and Muslims, bureaucratic corruption and its impact on the nation, and the nature of foreign aid and its impact. Underlying the film is the story of AIDS in Africa.

Lumumba (France/Belgium/Germany/Haiti, 2000). Director: Raoul Peck. *Lumumba* is a dramatization of the life and work of Patrice Lumumba. The film focuses on Lumumba's struggles to organize resistance in Congo and then to control the forces that had been unleashed. The film ends with Congo's destructive civil war, the events of which laid the foundation for the region's disastrous state today.

Thirteen Days (USA, 2000). Director: Roger Donaldson. *Thirteen Days* recreates the events surrounding the thirteen days in October when the United States and the Soviets clashed over the placement of missiles in Cuba. The film captures the extreme tension of the era, the conflict between "doves" and "hawks," and the very real possibility of nuclear war.

Comandante (USA, 2003). Director: Oliver Stone (Documentary). Unprecedented access to Fidel Castro—over thirty hours of interviews—allowed Stone to create this 90-minute documentary. Despite the restrictions placed on Stone, the film still provides an excellent look at life in Cuba today. *Comandante* saw limited release in the United States due to Stone's perceived sympathy for Castro.

Che (USA/France/Spain, 2008). Director: Steven Soderbergh. Soderbergh's two-part biopic covers the planning for and ultimate success of the Cuban Revolution and Che's capture and death in Bolivia.

14

Ideological Change and Radical Movements

The postwar era was characterized by a series of revolts against established authorities. The civil rights movement in the United States was the first of these to attain global prominence. Beginning in the mid-1950s all forms of segregation came under attack across the southern states. Influential leaders such as Dr Martin Luther King, Jr, and Malcolm X focused global media attention on the plight of African-Americans. Ill-considered and violent reprisals by southern authorities soon brought the weight of worldwide disapproval against southern segregationists. Eventually federal legislation against the discriminatory practices in the South was imposed. The attention of the civil rights leaders turned next to the desperate economic conditions of African-Americans in the northern urban ghettos. However, the civil rights movements made far less progress in this area.

Young activists who rejected the assumptions and prejudices of the previous generation proved to be one of the most important driving forces of the civil rights movement. The youth movement quickly evolved into a much broader protest against false democracy, false gods, capitalist exploitation, imperialism, the military-industrial complex, and many other issues. Spurred on by intellectual theories on alienation and the absence of meaning in modern existence, the protest movements spread to Britain, France, West Germany, Canada, Japan, and other countries. By May 1968 a student occupation of the main campus at the University of Paris led to a sympathy strike by more than half of the French workforce. Though the student movements eventually subsided they contributed greatly to discrediting, albeit temporarily, the conservative postwar political elites and their governments. Unsurprisingly, the forces of conservatism made a dramatic comeback in the late 1970s and early 1980s—most particularly in Great Britain and the United States.

Alongside the youth and civil rights movement and building on the so-called "first wave" of feminist thought, the 1960s and 1970s also saw the emergence of a substantial women's movement. Because of economic changes that led to an increasing number of women joining the workforce and seeking higher education, the women's movement focused, initially, on basic civil rights: equal pay for equal work, the right to contraception, and equality under the law. However, more radical women's groups, often inspired by Marxist ideals, called for an end to all gender-based exploitation and the punishment of those who continued to inflict such abuse. Divisions among conservative, liberal, and radical feminists often served to undermine the effectiveness of the women's movement, though substantive changes were accomplished in some areas. Simultaneous to the emergence of the women's movement, the first steps towards gay rights began in the late 1960s. Though far less effective in terms of changing legislation, the early gay rights movements did succeed in raising awareness of the injustices directed against the gay community and, in 1974, homosexuality was removed from the 7th Printing of the American Psychological Association's *Diagnostic and Statistical Manual*, thereby acknowledging for the first time that homosexuality was not a mental disorder.

The documents in this chapter present the views of a number of key civil rights authors and activists. The chapter opens with Simone de Beauvoir's seminal 1949 work on feminism, which precedes the more radical Marxist-inspired views of the New York-based Redstockings group. Turning to the movement for African-American equality, Dr Martin Luther King, Jr's famous "I Have a Dream" speech, made at the height of the civil rights movement during the 1963 March on Washington reflects the ambitions of the mainstream civil rights movement; the 1966 platform of the Black Panther Party reveals the degree of radicalization caused by the failure to achieve many of King's fundamental goals. British Labour MP Roy Jenkins' groundbreaking speech on homosexuality, delivered in 1966, both illustrates and challenges many of the prevailing views on homosexuals. A 1969 letter by author Edmund White provides insight into the events surrounding the 1969 Stonewall riots in the United States. The views of student activists are evidenced in the 1962 Port Huron Statement written by members of Students for a Democratic Society (SDS). The more radical platform of the Youth International Party (Yippies)—as presented during the trial of the so-called Chicago Seven—concludes the chapter.

Simone de Beauvoir

Simone de Beauvoir (1908–1986) was raised in Paris and studied philosophy at the Sorbonne. She taught at a number of small colleges in the early 1930s until she began writing full-time. In 1949 de Beauvoir published The Second Sex, *a philosophical and historical examination of the subjugation of women. De Beauvoir was heavily influenced by Jean-Paul Sartre's existentialist philosophies. In* The Second Sex *she argued that women could free themselves from their second class status by recognizing their oppression and by working for economic freedom and advancement.* The Second Sex *was translated into English and published in 1953.*

Document Source: Simone de Beauvoir, *The Second Sex*, transl. Constance Borde and Sheila Malovany-Chevallier (New York, NY: Vintage Books, 1949/2009), Chapter 10.

The Second Sex

In one sense, her whole existence is a waiting since she is enclosed in the limbo of immanence and contingency and her justification is always in someone else's hands: she is waiting for a tribute, men's approval, she is waiting for love, she is waiting for gratitude and her husband's or lover's praise; she expects to gain from them her reasons to exist, her worth, and her very being. She awaits

Simone de Beauvoir in 1947, shortly before the publication of *The Second Sex*.

Image © Pictorial Press Ltd./Alamy

her subsistence from them; whether she has her own checkbook or receives the money her husband allocates to her every week or month, he has to have been paid, obtained the raise for her to pay the grocer or buy a new dress. She awaits men's presence: her economic dependence puts her at his disposal; she is only one element of masculine life, whereas the man is her whole life; the husband has occupations outside the home, the woman endures his absence every day; it is the lover—even if passionate—who decides on the separation and meetings according to his obligations. In bed, she awaits the male's desire; she awaits—sometimes anxiously—her own pleasure. The only thing she can do is to be late for the date the lover set up; or not to be ready at the time the husband fixed; this is the way she asserts the importance of her own occupations, she claims her independence, she becomes the essential subject for a moment while the other passively submits to her will. But this is meager revenge; no matter how determined she might be to make men stew, she will never compensate for the infinite hours

she has spent being subjected to and watching out and hoping for the male's goodwill.

In general, while more or less acknowledging men's supremacy and accepting their authority, worshipping their idols, she will contest their reign tooth and nail; hence the famous "contrariness" for which she is so often criticized; as she does not possess an autonomous domain, she cannot put forward truths or positive values different from those that males assert; she can only negate them. Her negation is more or less systematic depending on her particular balance of respect and resentment. But the fact is, she knows all the fault lines of the masculine system and she hastens to denounce them. . . .

It is understandable why, from this perspective, woman objects to masculine logic. Not only does it have no bearing on her experience, but she also knows that in men's hands reason becomes an insidious form of violence; their peremptory affirmations are intended to mystify her. They want to confine her in a dilemma: either you agree or you don't; she has to agree in the name of the whole system of accepted principles: in refusing to agree, she rejects the whole system; she cannot allow herself such a dramatic move; she does not have the means to create another society: yet she does not agree with this one. Halfway between revolt and slavery, she unwillingly resigns herself to masculine authority. He continuously uses force to make her shoulder the consequences of her reluctant submission. He pursues the chimera of a freely enslaved companion: he wants her to yield to him as yielding to the proof of a theorem; but she knows he himself has chosen the postulates on which his vigorous deductions are hung; as long as she avoids questioning them, he will easily silence her; nevertheless, he will not convince her, because she senses their arbitrariness. Thus will he accuse her, with stubborn irritation, of being illogical: she refuses to play the game because she knows the dice are loaded. . . .

Rejecting logical principles and moral imperatives, skeptical about the laws of nature, woman lacks a sense of the universal; the world seems to her a confused collection of individual cases; this is why she more readily accepts a neighbor's gossip than a scientific explanation; she doubtless respects the printed book, but this respect skims along the written pages without grasping the content; by contrast, the anecdote told by an unknown person waiting in a line or in a drawing room instantly takes on overwhelming authority; in her domain, everything is magic; outside, everything is mystery; she is ignorant of the criterion for credibility; only immediate experience convinces her: her own experience or another's, as long as it is forcefully affirmed. As for herself, she feels she is a special case because she is isolated in her home and has no active contact with other women; she always expects destiny and men to make an exception in her favor; she believes in whatever insights come her way far more than in reasoning that is valid for everyone; she readily admits that they have been sent by God or by some obscure world spirit; in relation to misfortunes or accidents, she calmly thinks, "That can't happen to me," or else she imagines, "I'll be the exception": she enjoys special favors; the storekeeper will give her a discount, the policeman will let her go to the head of the line; she has been taught to overestimate the value of her smile, but no one told her that all women smiled. It is not that she thinks herself more special than her neighbor: it is that she does not make comparisons; for the same reason experience rarely proves her wrong: she suffers one failure, then another, but she does not add them up.

This is why women do not succeed in building up a solid "counter-universe" where they can defy males; they sporadically rant against men in general, they tell stories about the bedroom or childbirth, they exchange horoscopes and beauty secrets. But to truly build this "world of grievances" that their resentment calls for, they lack conviction; their attitude to man is too ambivalent. Indeed, he is a child, a contingent and vulnerable body, an innocent, an unwanted drone, a mean tyrant, an egotist, a vain man: and he is also the liberating hero, the divinity who sets the standards. His desire is a gross appetite, his embraces a degrading chore: yet his ardor and virile force are also a demiurgic energy. When a woman ecstatically utters, "This is a man!" she is evoking both the sexual vigor and the social effectiveness of the male she admires: in both are expressed the same creative sovereignty; she does not think he can be a great artist, a grand businessman, a general, or a chief without being a great lover: his social success is always a sexual attraction; inversely, she is ready to recognize genius in the man who satisfies her. . . .

Man lives in a coherent universe that is a thought reality. Woman struggles with a magic reality that does not allow thinking: she escapes through thoughts lacking real content. Instead of assuming her existence, she contemplates in the heavens the pure Idea of her destiny; instead of acting, she erects her statue in her imagination; instead of reasoning, she dreams. From here comes the fact that while being so "physical," she is also so artificial, while being so terrestrial, she can be so ethereal. Her life is spent scrubbing pots and pans, and it is a marvelous romance; vassal to man, she believes she is his idol; debased in her flesh, she exalts Love. Because she is condemned to know only life's contingent facticity, she becomes priestess of the Ideal.

This ambivalence is marked by the way woman deals with her body. It is a burden: weakened by the species, bleeding every month, passively propagating, for her it is not the pure instrument of her grasp on the world but rather an opaque presence; it is not certain that it will give her pleasure, and it creates pains that tear her apart; it contains threats: she feels danger in her "insides." Her body is "hysterical" because of the close connection between endocrine secretions and nervous and sympathetic systems commanding muscles and viscera; it expresses reactions the woman refuses to accept: in sobs, convulsions, and vomiting, her body escapes her; it betrays her; it is her most intimate reality, but it is a shameful reality that she keeps hidden. And yet it is her marvelous double; she contemplates it in the mirror with amazement; it is the promise of happiness, a work of art, a living statue; she shapes it, adorns it, displays it. When she smiles into the mirror, she forgets her carnal contingence; in love's embrace, in motherhood, her image disappears. But often, dreaming about herself, she is surprised to be both that heroine and that flesh.

Nature symmetrically provides her with a double face: it supplies the stew and incites mystical effusions. In becoming a housewife and mother, woman gave up her free getaways into fields and woods, she preferred the calm cultivation of the kitchen garden, she tamed flowers and put them in vases: yet she is still exalted by moonlights and sunsets. In the terrestrial fauna and flora, she sees food and ornamentation before all; yet a sap flows

that is generosity and magic. Life is not only immanence and repetition: it is also a dazzling face of light; in flowering meadows, it is revealed as Beauty. In tune with nature by the fertility of her womb, woman also feels swept by the breath that animates her and is spirit. And insofar as she is unsatisfied and feels like the uncompleted and unlimited girl, her soul will then rush forward on endlessly unwinding roads toward limitless horizons. Slave to her husband, children, and home, she finds it intoxicating to be alone, sovereign on the hillside; she is no longer spouse, mother, housewife, but a human being; she contemplates the passive world: and she recalls that she is a whole consciousness, an irreducible freedom.

Study Question

What does de Beauvoir mean when she says that women "lack a sense of the universal"?

Redstockings

In the 1960s and 1970s feminism incorporated a wide range of ideological positions around the world. In the United States and Europe a number of groups adopted Marxist theories; yet rather than see economic exploitation as the root of all social and political relationships, radical feminist groups saw gender exploitation as the foundation of all other relationships. The Redstockings group was founded in 1969 in New York City by Canadian-born Shulamith Firestone (1945–2012) and New York native Ellen Willis (1941–2006); in 1970 Redstockings expanded to San Francisco.[1] Firestone

would go on to write one of the most influential Marxist-inspired feminist tracts, The Dialectic of Sex: The Case for Feminist Revolution. *In it she argued that child-bearing was the crux of women's oppression and that technological advances could eventually free women from this enslavement. The 1969 Redstockings Feminist Manifesto clearly demonstrates the reworking of Marxist ideology and its resulting radical implications.*

Document Source: Redstockings, "A Feminist Manifesto," in Miriam Schneir, ed., *Feminism in Our Times: The Essential Writings, World War II to the Present* (New York/Toronto: Vintage Books, 1994), 127–9.

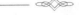

A Feminist Manifesto

I. After centuries of individual and preliminary political struggle, women are uniting to achieve this final liberation from male supremacy. Redstockings is dedicated to building their

unity and winning our freedom.

II. Women are an oppressed class. Our oppression is total, affecting every facet of our lives. We are exploited as sex objects, breeders, domestic servants, and cheap labour. We are considered inferior beings, whose only purpose is to enhance men's lives. Our humanity is denied. Our prescribed behaviour is enforced by the threat of physical violence.

Because we have lived so intimately with our oppressors, in isolation from each other, we have been kept from seeing our personal suffering as a political condition. This creates the illusion that a woman's relationship with her man is a matter of interplay between two unique personalities, and can be worked out individually. In reality, every such relationship is a *class* relationship, and the conflicts between individual men and women are *political* conflicts that can only be solved collectively.
III. We identify the agents of our oppression as men. Male supremacy is the oldest, most basic form of domination. All other forms of exploitation and oppression (racism, capitalism, imperialism, and the like) are extensions of male supremacy: men dominate women, a few men dominate the rest. All power structures throughout history have been male-dominated and male-oriented. Men have controlled all political, economic, and cultural institutions and backed up this control with physical force. They have used their power to keep women in an inferior position. *All men* receive economic, sexual, and psychological benefits from male supremacy. *All men* have oppressed women.

Opponents of the Equal Rights Amendment rally outside the White House in Washington, DC, February 1977.

U.S. News and World Report Magazine Photograph Collection. Courtesy of the Library of Congress, Prints and Photographs Division (LC-U9-33889A-31/31A).

IV. Attempts have been made to shift the burden of responsibility from men to institutions or to women themselves. We condemn these arguments as evasions. Institutions alone do not oppress; they are merely tools of the oppressor. To blame institutions implies that men and women are equally victimized, obscures the fact that men benefit from the subordination of women, and gives men the excuse that they are forced to be oppressors. On the contrary, any man is free to renounce his superior position provided that he is willing to be treated like a woman by other men.

We also reject the idea that women consent to or are to blame for their own oppression. Women's submission is not the result of brainwashing, stupidity, or mental illness but of continual, daily pressure from men. We do not need to change ourselves, but to change men.

The most slanderous evasion of all is that women can oppress men. The basis for this illusion is the isolation of individual relationships from their political context and the tendency of men to see any legitimate challenge to their privileges as persecution.
V. We regard our personal experience, and our feelings about that experience, as the basis for an analysis of our common situation. We cannot rely on existing ideologies as they are all products of male supremacist culture. We question every generalization and accept none that are not confirmed by our experience.

Our chief task at present is to develop female class consciousness through sharing experience and publicly exposing the sexist foundation of all our institutions. Consciousness-raising is not "therapy," which implies the existence of individual solutions and falsely assumes that the male-female relationship is purely personal, but the only method by which we can ensure that our program for liberation is based on the concrete realities of our lives.

The first requirement for raising class consciousness is honesty, in private and in public, with ourselves and other women.

VI. We identify with all women. We define our best interest as that of the poorest, most brutally exploited woman.

We repudiate all economic, racial, educational, or status privileges that divide us from other women. We are determined to recognize and eliminate any prejudices we may hold against other women.

We are committed to achieving internal democracy. We will do whatever is necessary to ensure that every woman in our movement has an equal chance to participate, assume responsibility, and develop her political potential.

VII. We call on all our sisters to unite with us in struggle.

We call on all men to give up their male privileges and support women's liberation in the interests of our humanity and their own.

In fighting for our liberation we will always take the side of women against their oppressors. We will not ask what is "revolutionary" or "reformist," only what is good for women.

The time for individual skirmishes has passed. This time we are going all the way.

Note

1. In 1973 Redstockings incorporated as a non-profit, educational, and scientific organization for the furtherance of the women's liberation movement.

> **Study Question**
>
> Which elements of the Redstockings' manifesto would be likely to attract support to the movement?

Martin Luther King, Jr

Martin Luther King, Jr (1929–1968), was born in Atlanta, Georgia, at the height of racial segregation. He graduated from Morehouse College with a BA and went on to study theology at Crozer Theological Seminary in Pennsylvania. He ultimately graduated from Boston University in 1955 with a doctoral degree in theology. An ordained minister since 1948, King became pastor of the Dexter Avenue Baptist Church in Montgomery, Alabama, in 1954. It was during this time that King became actively involved in the civil rights movement, participating in the Montgomery Bus Boycott, the Selma to Montgomery March, and eventually founding the Southern Christian Leadership Conference (SCLC). He headed the SCLC, which advocated non-violent social change, until his death in 1968. The following speech was one of King's most famous, delivered at the March on Washington in 1963.

I Have a Dream

I am happy to join with you today in what will go down in history as the greatest demonstration for freedom in the history of our nation.

Five score years ago, a great American, in whose symbolic shadow we stand today, signed the Emancipation Proclamation. This momentous decree came as a great beacon light of hope to millions of Negro slaves who had been seared in the flames of withering injustice. It came as a joyous daybreak to end the long night of captivity.

But one hundred years later, the Negro still is not free. One hundred years later, the life of the Negro is still sadly crippled by the manacles of segregation and the chains of discrimination. One hundred years later, the Negro lives on a lonely island of poverty in the midst of a vast ocean of material prosperity. One hundred years later, the Negro is still languished in the corners of American society and finds himself in exile in his own land. So we have come here today to dramatize a shameful condition.

In a sense we've come to our nation's Capital to cash a check. When the architects of our republic wrote the magnificent words of the Constitution and the Declaration of Independence, they were signing a promissory note to which every American was to fall heir.

This note was a promise that all men, yes, black men as well as white men, would be guaranteed the unalienable rights of life, liberty, and the pursuit of happiness.

It is obvious today that America has defaulted on this promissory note insofar as her citizens of color are concerned. Instead of honoring this sacred obligation, America has given the Negro people a bad check; a check which has come back marked "insufficient funds."

But we refuse to believe that the bank of justice is bankrupt. We refuse to believe that there are insufficient funds in the great vaults of opportunity of this nation. So we have come to cash this check—a check that will give us upon demand the riches of freedom and the security of justice.

We have also come to this hallowed spot to remind America of the fierce urgency of now. This is no time to engage in the luxury of cooling off or to take the tranquilizing drug of gradualism.

Now is the time to make real the promises of democracy. Now is the time to rise from the dark and desolate valley of segregation to the sunlit path of racial justice. Now is the time to lift our nation from the quicksands of racial injustice to the solid rock of brotherhood. Now is the time

Coretta Scott King and Martin Luther King meet New York City mayor Robert Wagner in 1964.

New York World-Telegram and the Sun Newspaper Photograph Collection. Courtesy of the Library of Congress, Prints and Photographs Division (LC-USZ62-120210).

to make justice a reality for all of God's children.

It would be fatal for the nation to overlook the urgency of the moment. This sweltering summer of the Negro's legitimate discontent will not pass until there is an invigorating autumn of freedom and equality. Nineteen sixty-three is not an end, but a beginning. Those who hope that the Negro needed to blow off steam and will now be content will have a rude awakening if the nation returns to business as usual. There will be neither rest nor tranquility in America until the Negro is granted his citizenship rights. The whirlwinds of revolt will continue to shake the foundations of our nation until the bright day of justice emerges.

But there is something that I must say to my people who stand on the warm threshold which leads into the palace of justice. In the process of gaining our rightful place we must not be guilty of wrongful deeds. Let us not seek to satisfy our thirst for freedom by drinking from the cup of bitterness and hatred. We must forever conduct our struggle on the high plane of dignity and discipline. We must not allow our creative protest to degenerate into physical violence. Again and again we must rise to the majestic heights of meeting physical force with soul force.

The marvelous new militancy which has engulfed the Negro community must not lead us to a distrust of all white people, for many of our white brothers, as evidenced by their presence here today, have come to realize that their destiny is tied up with our destiny. And they have come to realize that their freedom is inextricably bound to our freedom. We cannot walk alone.

And as we walk, we must make the pledge that we shall march ahead. We cannot turn back. There are those who are asking the devotees of civil rights, "When will you be satisfied?"

We can never be satisfied as long as the Negro is the victim of the unspeakable horrors of police brutality.

We can never be satisfied as long as our bodies, heavy with the fatigue of travel, cannot gain lodging in the motels of the highways and the hotels of the cities.

We cannot be satisfied as long as the Negro's basic mobility is from a smaller ghetto to a larger one.

We can never be satisfied as long as our children are stripped of their selfhood and robbed of their dignity by signs stating "for whites only."

We cannot be satisfied as long as a Negro in Mississippi cannot vote and a Negro in New York believes he has nothing for which to vote.

No, no, we are not satisfied, and we will not be satisfied until justice rolls down like waters and righteousness like a mighty stream.

I am not unmindful that some of you have come here out of great trials and tribulations. Some of you have come fresh from narrow jail cells. Some of you have come from areas where your quest for freedom left you battered by the storms of persecution and staggered by the winds of police brutality. You have been the veterans of creative suffering. Continue to work with the faith that unearned suffering is redemptive.

Go back to Mississippi, go back to Alabama, go back to South Carolina, go back to Georgia, go back to Louisiana, go back to the slums and ghettos of our northern cities, knowing that somehow this situation can and will be changed. Let us not wallow in the valley of despair.

I say to you today, my friends, so even though we face the difficulties of today and tomorrow, I still have a dream. It is a dream deeply rooted in the American dream.

I have a dream that one day this nation will rise up and live out the true meaning of its creed: "We hold these truths to be self-evident; that all men are created equal."

I have a dream that one day on the red hills of Georgia the sons of former slaves and the sons of former slave owners will be able to sit down together at the table of brotherhood.

I have a dream that one day even the state of Mississippi, a state sweltering with the heat of injustice, sweltering with the heat of oppression, will be transformed into an oasis of freedom and justice.

I have a dream that my four little children will one day live in a nation where they will not be judged by the color of their skin but by the content of their character.

I have a dream today.

I have a dream that one day down in Alabama, with its vicious racists, with its governor having his lips dripping with the words of interposition and nullification, that one day right down in Alabama little black boys and black girls will be able to join hands with little white boys and white girls as sisters and brothers.

I have a dream today.

I have a dream that one day every valley shall be exalted, every hill and mountain shall be made low, the rough places will be made plain, and the crooked places will be made straight, and the glory of the Lord shall be revealed, and all flesh shall see it together.

This is our hope. This is the faith that I will go back to the South with. With this faith we will be able to hew out of the mountain of despair a stone of hope. With this faith we will be able to transform the jangling discords of our nation into a beautiful symphony of brotherhood.

With this faith we will be able to work together, to pray together, to struggle together, to go to jail together, to stand up for freedom together, knowing that we will be free one day.

This will be the day when all of God's children will be able to sing with new meaning, "My country 'tis of thee, sweet land of liberty, of thee I sing. Land where my fathers died, land of the Pilgrims' pride, from every mountainside, let freedom ring."

And if America is to be a great nation, this must become true. So let freedom ring from the prodigious hilltops of New Hampshire. Let freedom ring from the mighty mountains of New York. Let freedom ring from the heightening Alleghenies of Pennsylvania.

Let freedom ring from the snow-capped Rockies of Colorado. Let freedom ring from the curvaceous slopes of California. But not only that; let freedom ring from the Stone Mountain of Georgia. Let freedom ring from Lookout Mountain of Tennessee.

Let freedom ring from every hill and molehill of Mississippi. From every mountainside, let freedom ring.

And when this happens, and when we allow freedom ring, when we let it ring from every village and every hamlet, from every state and every city, we will be able to speed up that day when all of God's children, black men and white men, Jews and gentiles, Protestants and Catholics, will be able to join hands and sing in the words of the old Negro spiritual, "Free at last! Free at last! Thank God Almighty, we are free at last!"

Study Question

What are the strongest elements of King's argument?

Black Panther Party

The Black Panther Party was founded in Oakland, California, in October 1966 to advance the cause of African-American civil rights. Its platform and program were co-written by Huey P. Newton and Bobby Seale (b. 1936), though Newton is believed to have written most of the final document. The rules that *follow the ten-point program were added gradually over time. They conclude with the Three Rules of Discipline and Eight Points for Attention of the Chinese People's Liberation Army (PLA). In the platform, the Three Rules and Eight points are reversed and slightly modified to fit the circumstances in the United States in the late 1960s. The Black Panthers were heavily influenced by Marxist and Maoist theory and the party itself was structured as a revolutionary vanguard.*

Document Source: Huey P. Newton, *War against the Panthers: A Study of Repression in America*—Doctoral Dissertation: UC Santa Cruz, 1980, Appendix A (Platform & Program); www.marxists.org (Rules). Used by permission of the Dr Huey P. Newton Foundation.

Platform and Program

What We Want, What We Believe

1. We want freedom. We want power to determine the destiny of our Black community.

We believe that Black people will not be free until we are able to determine our own destiny.

2. We want full employment of our people.

We believe that the federal government is responsible and obligated to give every man employment or a guaranteed income. We believe that if the White American businessmen will not give full employment, then the means of production should be taken from the businessmen and placed in the community so that the people of the community can organize and employ all of its people and give a high standard of living.

3. We want an end to the robbery by the white man of our Black community.

We believe that this racist government has robbed us and now we are demanding the overdue debt of forty acres and two mules. Forty acres and two mules [were] promised 100 years ago as restitution for slave labour and mass murder of Black people. We will accept the payment in currency, which will be distributed to our many communities. The Germans are now aiding the Jews in Israel for the genocide of the Jewish people. The Germans murdered six million Jews. The American racist has taken part in the slaughter of over 50 million Black people; therefore, we feel that this is a modest demand that we make.

4. We want decent housing fit for shelter of human beings.

We believe that if the White landlords will not give decent housing to our Black community, then the housing and the land should be made into cooperatives so that our community, with government aid, can build and make decent housing for its people.

5. We want education for our people that exposes the true nature of this decadent American society. We want education that teaches us our true history and our role in the present-day society.

We believe in an educational system that will give to our people a knowledge of self. If a man does not have knowledge of himself and his position in society and the world, then he has little chance to relate to anything else.

6. We want all Black men to be exempt from military service.

We believe that Black people should not be forced to fight in the military service to defend a racist government that does not protect us. We will not fight and kill other people of color in the world who, like Black people, are being victimized by the White racist government of America. We will protect ourselves from the force and violence of the racist police and the racist military, by whatever means necessary.

7. We want an immediate end to police brutality and murder of Black people.

We believe we can end police brutality in our Black community by organizing black self-defense groups that are dedicated to defending our Black community from racist police oppression and brutality. The Second Amendment to the Constitution of the United States gives a right to bear arms. We therefore believe that all Black people should arm themselves for self-defense.

8. We want freedom for all Black men held in federal, state, county and city prisons and jails. We believe that all Black people should be released from the many jails and prisons because they have not received a fair and impartial trial.

9. We want all Black people when brought to trial to be tried in court by a jury of their peer group or people from their Black communities, as defined by the Constitution of the United States. We believe that the courts should follow the United States Constitution so that Black people will receive fair trials. The 14th Amendment of the US Constitution gives a man a right to be tried by his peer group. A peer is a person from a similar economic, social, religious, geographical, environmental, historical, and racial background. To do this the court will be forced to select a jury from the Black community from which the Black defendant came. We have been, and are being, tried by all-White juries that have no understanding of the "average reasoning man" of the Black community.

10. We want land, bread, housing, education, clothing, justice, and peace.[1] When, in the course of human events, it becomes necessary for one people to dissolve the political bands which have connected them with another, and to assume, among the powers of the earth, the separate and equal station to which the laws of nature and nature's God entitle them, a decent respect to the opinions of mankind requires that they should declare the causes which impel them to the separation.

We hold these truths to be self-evident, that all men are created equal; that they are endowed by their Creator with certain unalienable rights; that among these are life, liberty, and the pursuit of happiness. That, to secure these rights, governments are instituted among men, deriving their just powers from the consent of the governed; that, whenever any form of government becomes destructive of these ends, it is the right of the people to alter or to abolish it, and to institute a new government, laying its foundation on such principles, and organizing its powers in such form, as to them shall seem most likely to effect their safety and happiness. Prudence, indeed, will dictate that governments long established should not be changed for light and transient causes; and, accordingly, all experience hath shown, that mankind are more disposed to suffer, while evils are sufferable, than to right themselves by abolishing the forms to which they are accustomed. But, when a long train of abuses and usurpations, pursuing invariably the same object, evinces a design to reduce them under absolute despotism, it is their right, it is their duty, to throw off such government, and to provide new guards for their future security.

Rules of the Black Panther Party

Every member of the BLACK PANTHER PARTY throughout this country of racist America must abide by these rules as functional members of this party. CENTRAL COMMITTEE members, CENTRAL STAFFS, and LOCAL STAFFS, including all captains subordinate to either national, state, and local leadership of the BLACK PANTHER PARTY will enforce these rules. Length of suspension or other disciplinary action necessary for violation of these rules will depend on national decisions by national, state or state area, and local committees and staffs where said rule or rules of the BLACK PANTHER PARTY WERE VIOLATED.

Every member of the party must know these verbatim by heart. And apply them daily. Each member must report any violation of these rules to their leadership or they are counter-revolutionary and are also subjected to suspension by the BLACK PANTHER PARTY.

The rules are:

1. No party member can have narcotics or weed in his possession while doing party work.
2. Any party member found shooting narcotics will be expelled from this party.
3. No party member can be DRUNK while doing daily party work.
4. No party member will violate rules relating to office work, general meetings of the BLACK PANTHER PARTY, and meetings of the BLACK PANTHER PARTY ANYWHERE.
5. No party member will USE, POINT, or FIRE a weapon of any kind unnecessarily or accidentally at anyone.
6. No party member can join any other army force other than the BLACK LIBERATION ARMY.
7. No party member can have a weapon in his possession while DRUNK or loaded off narcotics or weed.
8. No party member will commit any crimes against other party members or BLACK people at all, and cannot steal or take from the people, not even a needle or a piece of thread.
9. When arrested BLACK PANTHER MEMBERS will give only name, address, and will sign nothing. Legal first aid must be understood by all Party members.
10. The Ten-Point Program and platform of the BLACK PANTHER PARTY must be known and understood by each Party member.
11. Party Communications must be National and Local.
12. The 10-10-10-program should be known by all members and also understood by all members.
13. All Finance officers will operate under the jurisdiction of the Ministry of Finance.
14. Each person will submit a report of daily work.
15. Each Sub-Section Leader, Section Leaders, and Lieutenants, Captains must submit Daily reports of work.
16. All Panthers must learn to operate and service weapons correctly.
17. All Leadership personnel who expel a member must submit this information to the Editor of the Newspaper, so that it will be published in the paper and will be known by all chapters and branches.
18. Political Education Classes are mandatory for general membership.
19. Only office personnel assigned to respective offices each day should be there. All others are to sell papers and do Political work out in the community, including Captains, Section Leaders, etc.
20. COMMUNICATIONS—all chapters must submit weekly reports in writing to the National Headquarters.
21. All Branches must implement First Aid and/or Medical Cadres.
22. All Chapters, Branches, and components of the BLACK PANTHER PARTY must submit a monthly Financial Report to the Ministry of Finance, and also the Central Committee.
23. Everyone in a leadership position must read no less than two hours per day to keep abreast of the changing political situation.
24. No chapter or branch shall accept grants, poverty funds, money or any other aid from any government agency without contacting the National Headquarters.
25. All chapters must adhere to the policy and the ideology laid down by the CENTRAL COMMITTEE of the BLACK PANTHER PARTY.
26. All Branches must submit weekly reports in writing to their respective Chapters.

8 Points of Attention

1) Speak politely.
2) Pay fairly for what you buy.
3) Return everything you borrow.

4) Pay for anything you damage.

5) Do not hit or swear at people.

6) Do not damage property or crops of the poor, oppressed masses.

7) Do not take liberties with women.

8) If we ever have to take captives do not ill-treat them.

3 Main Rules of Discipline

1) Obey orders in all your actions.

2) Do not take a single needle or a piece of thread from the poor and oppressed masses.

3) Turn in everything captured from the attacking enemy.

Note

1. Alternate versions of the 10th point include the following: "And as our major political objective, a United Nations-supervised plebiscite to be held throughout the black colony in which only black colonial subjects will be allowed to participate, for the purpose of determining the will of black people as to their national destiny." This was, however, omitted from the version of the document that Newton included in his Ph.D. dissertation.

Study Question

Martin Luther King's vision of non-violent social change was often frustrated by groups such as the Black Panthers who argued that non-violence would accomplish little against such powerful opponents. What were the strengths and weaknesses of the two approaches?

Roy Jenkins

Welsh-born Roy Jenkins (1920–2003) was a Labour Party Member of Parliament. He held a number of key posts including that of Home Secretary from 1965 to 1967. During this time Jenkins was instrumental in advancing policies that supported the legalization of abortion, the abolition of capital punishment, and the decriminalization of homosexuality—all with the aim of creating what he called a more "civilized society."

The following speech on the Sexual Offences Bill was delivered on 11 February 1966 and is considered one of the watershed moments in a nearly ten-year process to decriminalize homosexuality in Great Britain. The bill passed in 1967 and, thereafter, homosexuality was no longer regarded as a criminal offence under the law.

Document Source: Roy Jenkins, *Essays and Speeches*, ed. Anthony Lester (London: Collins, 1967), 256–8.

Homosexuality Has Existed in All Societies

In order that there should be no misunderstanding, from the beginning I would not wish to conceal from the House that should this Motion be divided upon, I propose to go into the Lobby in support of the Bill and so, I understand, by an entirely individual process of decision, would the three other Home Office Ministers who sit in this House.

Perhaps I may make an attempt to deal with what appear to me to be some misunderstandings about the basic problem of homosexuality. Homosexuality has existed in all societies at all periods of history and in all cultures. It has sometimes been condemned, it has sometimes been condoned, and at times it has even been encouraged, but it has never been suppressed. From country to country at the present time, the laws relating to homosexuality vary considerably, although I believe that in Western Europe only the Federal Republic of Germany has a provision similar to our own.

There is no evidence either from history or geography that the incidence of homosexuality varies with the laws against homosexuality. It is more deep-seated a problem than that. There is certainly no evidence, as far as I am aware, that the relaxation of the law which took place in Austria, for example, in 1960, or in Sweden in 1942, led to any increase in the practice of homosexuality. Certainly no attempt has been made during the debate to produce any evidence to support such a proposition.

The extent of the problem in this and in other countries is without doubt considerable. No one can know exactly what is the incidence, but probably the best estimates which have been made vary between suggesting that one male in 20 and one male in 40 is in some sense an active homosexual.[1] The spread is much more even than is sometimes imagined. It is not concentrated in any particular social classes or occupational groups but goes fairly evenly throughout the community. It follows from this incidence and spread that the majority of homosexuals are not exhibitionist freaks—although there are some of these, as there are some among heterosexuals—but ordinary citizens who do normal jobs, in many cases usefully and unobtrusively, in some cases with great distinction.

Homosexual inclinations are not often a matter of choice for the individual. Occasionally they may be, but this is the exception rather than the rule. In general it is, I am convinced, an involuntary deviation. But according to most medical opinion—I know that there are some differences about this—and certainly according to the Wolfenden Committee, it is not a disease in a sense of being, in the majority of cases, subject to medical treatment.[2] It is more in the nature of a disability than a disease and, of course, it is a grave disability for the individual. It leads to a great deal of loneliness and unhappiness and to a heavy weight of guilt and shame. It greatly reduces the chance of the individual finding a stable and lasting emotional relationship.

The question which we have to answer today is whether, in addition, the disability, provided it involves no corruption of minors and no public indecency, should remain subject to the rigours of the criminal law. Do we serve any useful and proper public purpose by keeping it so?

The Wolfenden Committee distinguished three possible main reasons why some people might answer "Yes" to this question. The first was that homosexual behaviour might be held to menace the health of society. The second was that it might have damaging effects upon family life. The third was that a man who indulges in homosexual practices with another man might turn to indulging in them with boys.

The first proposition, that homosexual behaviour menaces the health of society, is necessarily, I think the House is bound to agree, a somewhat vague concept. The Wolfenden Committee said that it heard no evidence to support this view. On the second point, that such behaviour might have a damaging effect upon family life, the Committee found that it might well do that but so also, it must be added, can female homosexuality and so, indeed, do some forms of heterosexual conduct. It still remains to be proved that the harm is diminished by singling out this particular form of conduct for punishment by the criminal law while other forms of conduct equally damaging to family life are not so treated. . . .

On the third point—that conduct with other adults might lead on to similar conduct with boys—the Committee was authoritatively informed by a large number of witnesses that this seldom happens. Indeed, the Committee held that the relaxation of the law relating to adults might well give more, and not less, protection to minors. It would, indeed, be difficult to see why a relaxation of the law relating to one category of offence, accompanied by a stiffening of the penalties relating to the other category of offence, that with minors, about which we are all concerned, could possibly lead people to switch from the one which had become legal to the other which remained illegal and against which, indeed, the penalties had been increased. Therefore, these grounds, I think it may be held, do not add up to a justification of the present law.

> **Study Question**
>
> To what extent does Jenkins' speech still reflect the prejudices of his era against homosexuality?

Notes

1. Estimating prevalence remains highly contentious; current studies place the figure between 5 and 10 percent of the human population.
2. The Wolfenden Committee (actually, The Departmental Committee on Homosexual Offences and Prostitution) produced a report in 1957 that recommended decriminalizing homosexuality.

Edmund White

Edmund White (b. 1940) is the author of numerous books and essays, both fictional and non-fictional, including the 1977 work The Joy of Gay Sex. *He lived in both New York and San Francisco in the late 1960s and early 1970s and thus witnessed firsthand the emergence of the American gay rights movement. In the letter that follows, written to his friends Ann and Alfred Corn, White describes the police raids on* the Stonewall Inn in Greenwich Village, New York, *which began on 28 June 1969, and the increasingly radical response from the gay community. White also touches on the alliances which developed between gay activists and their supporters.*

Document Source: Lisa Grunwald and Stephen Adler, eds. *Letters of the Century: America 1900–1999* (New York: The Dial Press, A Division of Random House, 1999), 489–91.

Letter to Ann and Alfred Corn, 8 July 1969

Dear Ann and Alfred,

Well, the big news here is Gay Power. It's the most extraordinary thing. It all began two weeks ago on a Friday night. The cops raided the Stonewall, that mighty Bastille which you know has remained impregnable for three years, so brazen and so conspicuous that one could only surmise that the Mafia was paying off the pigs handsomely. Apparently, however, a new public official, Sergeant Smith, has taken over the Village, and he's a peculiarly diligent lawman. In any event, a mammoth paddy wagon, as big as a school bus, pulled up to the Wall and about ten cops raided the joint. The kids were all shooed into the street; soon other gay kids and straight spectators swelled the ranks to, I'd say, about a thousand people. Christopher Street was completely blocked off and the crowds swarmed from the *Voice* office down to the Civil War hospital.

As the Mafia owners were dragged out one by one and shoved into the wagon, the crowd would let out Bronx cheers and jeers and clapping. Someone shouted "Gay Power," others took up the cry——and then it dissolved into giggles. A few more gay prisoners—bartenders, hatcheck boys—a few more cheers, someone starts singing "We Shall Overcome"—and then they started camping on it. A drag queen is shoved into the wagon; she hits the cop over the head with her purse. The cop clubs her. Angry stirring in the crowd. The cops, used to the cringing and disorganization of the gay crowds, snort off. But the crowd doesn't disperse. Everyone is restless, angry, and high-spirited. No one has a slogan, no one even has an attitude, but something's brewing.

Some adorable butch hustler boy pulls up a parking meter, mind you, out of the pavement, and uses it as a battering ram (a few cops are still inside the Wall, locked in). The boys begin to pound at the heavy wooden double doors and windows; glass shatters all over the street. Cries of "Liberate the

Bar." Bottles (from hostile straights?) rain down from the apartment windows. Cries of "We're the Pink Panthers." A mad Negro queen whirls like a dervish with a twisted piece of metal in her hand and breaks the remaining windows. The door begins to give. The cop turns a hose on the crowd (they're still within the Wall). But they can't aim it properly, and the crowd sticks. Finally the door is broken down and the kids, as though working to a prior plan, systematically dump refuse from the waste cans into the Wall, squirting it with lighter fluid, and ignite it. Huge flashes of flame and billows of smoke.

Now the cops in the paddy wagon return, and two fire engines pull up. Clubs fly. The crowd retreats.

Saturday night, the pink panthers are back full force. The cops form a flying wedge at the Greenwich Avenue end of Christopher and drive the kids down towards Sheridan Square. The panthers, however, run down Waverly, up Gay Street, and come out <u>behind</u> the cops, kicking in a chorus line, taunting, screaming. Dreary middle-class East Side queens stand around disapproving but fascinated, unable to go home, as though torn between their class loyalties, their desire to be respectable, and their longing for freedom. Sheridan Square is cordoned off by the cops. The United Cigar store closes, Riker's closes, the deli closes. No one can pass through the square; to walk up Seventh Avenue, you must detour all the way to Bleeker.

A mad left-wing group of straight kids called the Crazies is trying to organize gay kids, point out that Lindsay is to blame (the Crazies want us to vote for Procaccino, or "Prosciutto," as we call him). A Crazy girl launches into a tirade against Governor Rockefeller, "Whose Empire," she cries, "Must Be Destroyed." Straight Negro boys put their arms around me and say we're comrades (it's okay with me—in fact, great, the first camaraderie I've felt with blacks in years). Mattachine (our NAACP) hands out leaflets about "what to do if arrested." Some man from the Oscar Wilde bookstore hands out a leaflet describing to newcomers what's going on. I give

a stump speech about the need to radicalize, how we must recognize "we're part of a vast rebellion of all the repressed." Some jeers, some cheers. Charles Burch plans to make a plastique to hurl at cops.

Sunday night, the Stonewall, now reopened—though one room is charred and blasted, all lights are smashed, and only a few dim bulbs are burning, no hard liquor being sold—the management posts an announcement: "We appreciate all of you and your efforts to help, but the Stonewall believes in peace. Please end the riots. We believe in peace." Some kids, nonetheless, try to turn over a cop car. Twelve are arrested. Some straight toughs rough up some queens. The queens beat them up. Sheridan Square is again blocked off by the pigs. That same night a group of about 75 vigilantes in Queens chops down a wooded part of a park as vengeance against the perverts who are cruising in bushes. "They're endangering our women and children." *The Times*, which has scarcely mentioned the Sheridan Square riots (a half column, very tame) is now so aroused by the <u>conservation</u> issue that it blasts the "vigs" for their malice toward <u>nature</u>.

Wednesday. The *Voice* runs two front-page stories on the riots, both snide, both devoted primarily to assuring readers that the authors are straight.

This last weekend, nothing much happened because it was the Fourth of July and everyone was away. Charles Burch has decided it's all a drag. When he hears that gay kids are picketing Independence Hall in Philly because they're being denied their constitutional rights, he says: "But of course, the Founding Fathers didn't intend to protect <u>perverts</u> and <u>criminals</u>." Who knows what will happen this weekend, or this week? I'll keep you posted.

Otherwise, nothing much. I've been going out with a mad boy who tried to kill me last Friday. He's very cute, and I'm sure it'd be a kick, but I think I'll take a rain check on the death scene. . . .

I miss you both frightfully. No more fun dinners, no endless telephone conversations, no

sharing of exquisite sensations, gad, it's awful.
Love,
Ed

Study Question

What does White's letter reveal about divisions within the gay community?

Students for a Democratic Society

Among the many student groups founded in the United States in the 1960s, Students for a Democratic Society (SDS) was among the most important. At its height in 1968 SDS teach-ins and occupations were attracting tens of thousands of demonstrators on university campuses across the country. Ultimately the group split into several factions, the most radical of which—the Weather Underground—launched a *campaign of urban guerrilla warfare against targets connected to the US Government. Today, however, SDS is most often remembered for its founding doctrine, embodied in the Port Huron Statement of 1962. The statement laid out a vision for a participatory democracy which many believe still holds merit.*

Document Source: Office of Senator Tom Hayden: http://www.h-net. org/~hst306/documents/huron.html. Used with permission.

Port Huron Statement

We are people of this generation, bred in at least modest comfort, housed now in universities, looking uncomfortably to the world we inherit.

When we were kids the United States was the wealthiest and strongest country in the world: the only one with the atom bomb, the least scarred by modern war, an initiator of the United Nations that we thought would distribute Western influence throughout the world. Freedom and equality for each individual, government of, by, and for the people—these American values we found good, principles by which we could live as men. Many of us began maturing in complacency.

As we grew, however, our comfort was penetrated by events too troubling to dismiss. First, the permeating and victimizing fact of human degradation, symbolized by the Southern struggle against racial bigotry, compelled most of us from silence to activism. Second, the enclosing fact of the Cold War, symbolized by the presence of the Bomb, brought awareness that we ourselves, and our friends, and millions of abstract "others" we knew more directly because of our common

peril, might die at any time. We might deliberately ignore, or avoid, or fail to feel all other human problems, but not these two, for these were too immediate and crushing in their impact, too challenging in the demand that we as individuals take the responsibility for encounter and resolution.

While these and other problems either directly oppressed us or rankled our consciences and became our own subjective concerns, we began to see complicated and disturbing paradoxes in our surrounding America. The declaration "all men are created equal. . ." rang hollow before the facts of Negro life in the South and the big cities of the North. The proclaimed peaceful intentions of the United States contradicted its economic and military investments in the Cold War status quo.

We witnessed, and continue to witness, other paradoxes. With nuclear energy whole cities can easily be powered, yet the dominant nation states seem more likely to unleash destruction greater than that incurred in all wars of human history. Although our own technology is destroying old and creating new forms of social organization, men still tolerate meaningless work and idleness. While two-thirds of mankind suffers undernourishment, our own upper classes revel amidst superfluous abundance. Although world population is expected to double in 40 years, the nations still tolerate anarchy as a major principle of international conduct and uncontrolled exploitation governs the sapping of the earth's physical resources. Although mankind desperately needs revolutionary leadership, America rests in national stalemate, its goals ambiguous and tradition-bound instead of informed and clear, its democratic system apathetic and manipulated rather than "of, by, and for the people."

Not only did tarnish appear on our image of American virtue, not only did disillusion occur when the hypocrisy of American ideals was discovered, but we began to sense that what we had originally seen as the American Golden Age was actually the decline of an era. The worldwide outbreak of revolution against colonialism and imperialism, the entrenchment of totalitarian states, the menace of war, overpopulation, international disorder, super technology—these trends were testing the tenacity of our own commitment to democracy and freedom and our abilities to visualize their application to a world in upheaval.

Our work is guided by the sense that we may be the last generation in the experiment with living. But we are a minority—the vast majority of our people regard the temporary equilibriums of our society and world as eternally-functional parts. In this is perhaps the outstanding paradox: we ourselves are imbued with urgency, yet the message of our society is that there is no viable alternative to the present. Beneath the reassuring tones of the politicians, beneath the common opinion that America will "muddle through," beneath the stagnation of those who have closed their minds to the future, is the pervading feeling that there simply are no alternatives, that our times have witnessed the exhaustion not only of Utopias, but of any new departures as well. Feeling the press of complexity upon the emptiness of life, people are fearful of the thought that at any

moment things might thrust out of control. They fear change itself, since change might smash whatever invisible framework seems to hold back chaos for them now. For most Americans, all crusades are suspect, threatening. The fact that each individual sees apathy in his fellows perpetuates the common reluctance to organize for change. The dominant institutions are complex enough to blunt the minds of their potential critics, and entrenched enough to swiftly dissipate or entirely repel the energies of protest and reform, thus limiting human expectancies. Then, too, we are a materially improved society, and by our own improvements we seem to have weakened the case for further change. . . .

In a participatory democracy, the political life would be based in several root principles:

- that decision-making of basic social consequence be carried on by public groupings;
- that politics be seen positively, as the art of collectively creating an acceptable pattern of social relations;
- that politics has the function of bringing people out of isolation and into community, thus being a necessary, though not sufficient, means of finding meaning in personal life;
- that the political order should serve to clarify problems in a way instrumental to their solution; it should provide outlets for the expression of personal grievance and aspiration; opposing views should be organized so as to illuminate choices and facilitate the attainment of goals; channels should be commonly available to related men to knowledge and to power so that private problems—from bad recreation facilities to personal alienation—are formulated as general issues.

The economic sphere would have as its basis the principles:

- that work should involve incentives worthier than money or survival. It should be educative, not stultifying; creative, not mechanical; selfdirect [sic], not manipulated, encouraging independence; a respect for others, a sense of dignity and a willingness to accept social responsibility, since it is this experience that has crucial influence on habits, perceptions, and individual ethics;
- that the economic experience is so personally decisive that the individual must share in its full determination;
- that the economy itself is of such social importance that its major resources and means of production should be open to democratic participation and subject to democratic social regulation.

Like the political and economic ones, major social institutions—cultural, education, rehabilitative,

and others—should be generally organized with the well-being and dignity of man as the essential measure of success.

In social change or interchange, we find violence to be abhorrent because it requires generally the transformation of the target, be it a human being or a community of people, into a depersonalized object of hate. It is imperative that the means of violence be abolished and the institutions—local, national, international—that encourage nonviolence as a condition of conflict be developed.

These are our central values, in skeletal form. It remains vital to understand their denial or attainment in the context of the modern world.

> **Study Question**
>
> What are the strengths and weaknesses of the SDS vision of participatory democracy (including its economic and social dimensions)?

The Chicago Seven Trial Transcript

By 1968, antiwar movements, civil rights movements, and protest groups had combined to create an explosive atmosphere in the United States. During the 1968 Democratic Party Convention in Chicago, protesters clashed violently with massive numbers of police and national guardsmen called out by Chicago Mayor Richard Daley. A number of high-profile protesters were arrested and charged with crossing state lines for the purpose of inciting a riot. The ensuing "Chicago Seven Trial" made a mockery of the American judicial

system, as this excerpt from the testimony of Abbot Howard "Abbie" Hoffman (1936–1989) demonstrates. In February 1970 the defendants were found guilty and sentenced to five years in prison. On appeal all of the sentences were overturned and a subsequent inquiry blamed police over-reaction for all of the violence that took place at the convention. The trial transcripts were collected and published in 1970.

Document Source: Judy Clavir and John Spitzer, eds., *The Conspiracy Trial* (Indianapolis, IN: Bobbs-Merrill Co., 1970), 344–60.

Testimony of Abbie Hoffman

Mr Weinglass: Will you please identify yourself for the record?[1]

The Witness: My name is Abbie. I am an orphan of America.

Mr Schultz: Your Honor, may the record show it is the defendant Hoffman who has taken the stand?

The Court: Oh, yes. It may so indicate.

The Witness: Well, it is not really my last name.

Mr Weinglass: Abbie, what is your last name?

The Witness: Well, there is some confusion about it because, well, my grandfather, he was a Russian Jew, and he decided to protest the anti-Semitism in the Russian Army and he slew—

Mr Schultz: Objection. If the defendant has a last name, let him state it, but not—

The Court: All we want to know, sir, is your last name.

The Witness: My slave name is Hoffman. My real name is Shaboysnakoff. I can't spell it.

The Court: There is a lawyer who has filed his appearance in the name of Abbie Hoffman for you. You gave him your name as Abbie Hoffman, did you not?

The Witness: Well, no. It was the Government's idea and the name was Abbott Howard.

Mr Weinglass: Where do you reside?

The Witness: I live in Woodstock Nation.

Mr Weinglass: Will you tell the Court and jury where it is?

The Witness: Yes. It is a nation of alienated young people. We carry it around with us as a state of mind in the same way as the Sioux Indians carried the Sioux nation around with them. It is a nation dedicated to cooperation versus competition, to the idea that people should have better means of exchange than property or money, that there should be some other basis for human interaction. It is a nation dedicated to—

The Court: Just where it is, that is all.

The Witness: It is in my mind and in the minds of my brothers and sisters. It does not consist of property or material but, rather, of ideas and certain values. We believe in a society—

The Court: No, we want the place of residence, if he has one, place of doing business, if you have a business. Nothing about philosophy or India, sir. Just where you live, if you have a place to live. Now you said Woodstock. In what state is Woodstock?

The Witness: It is in the state of mind, in the mind of myself and my brothers and sisters. It is a conspiracy. Presently, the nation is held captive, in the penitentiaries of the institutions of a decaying system.

Mr Weinglass: Can you tell the Court and jury your present age?

The Witness: My age is 33. I am a child of the 60s.

Mr Weinglass: When were you born?

The Witness: Psychologically, 1960.

The Chicago Seven: Lee Weiner, John Froines, Abbie Hoffman, Rennie Davis, Jerry Rubin, Tom Hayden, Dave Dellinger, Chicago, 5 November 1969. Photograph Richard Avedon.

Mr Schultz: Objection, if the Court please. I move to strike the answer.

Mr Weinglass: What is the actual date of your birth?

The Witness: 30 November 1936.

Mr Weinglass: Between the date of your birth, 30 November 1936, and 1 May 1960, what if anything occurred in your life?

The Witness: Nothing. I believe it is called an American education.

Mr Schultz: Objection.

The Court: I sustain the objection.

The Witness: Huh.

Mr Weinglass: Abbie, could you tell the Court and jury—

Mr Schultz: His name isn't Abbie. I object to this informality.

Mr Weinglass: Can you tell the Court and jury what is your present occupation?

The Witness: I am a cultural revolutionary. Well, I am really a defendant—full-time.

Mr Weinglass: What do you mean by the phrase "cultural revolutionary"?

The Witness: Well, I suppose it is a person who tries to shape and participate in the values, and the mores, the customs and the style of living of new people who eventually become inhabitants of a new nation and a new society through art and poetry, theatre, and music.

Mr Weinglass: What have you done yourself to participate in that revolution?

The Witness: Well, I have been a rock and roll singer. I am a reporter with the Liberation News Service. I am a poet. I am a film maker. I made a movie called "Yippies² Tour Chicago or How I Spent My Summer Vacation." Currently, I am negotiating with United Artists and MGM to do a movie in Hollywood. I have written an extensive pamphlet on how to live free in the city of New York. I have written two books, one called *Revolution for the Hell of It* under the pseudonym Free, and one called, *Woodstock Nation*.

Mr Weinglass: Taking you back to the spring of 1960, approximately May 1, 1960, will you tell the Court and jury where you were?

Mr Schultz: 1960?

The Witness: That's right.

Mr Schultz: Objection.

The Court: I sustain the objection.

Mr Weinglass: Your Honor, that date has great relevance to the trial. May 1, 1960, was this witness's first public demonstration. I am going to bring him down through Chicago.

The Court: Not in my presence, you are not going to bring him down. I sustain the objection to the question.

The Witness: My background has nothing to do with my state of mind?

The Court: Will you remain quiet while I am making a ruling? I know you have no respect for me. . . .

The Court: I will let the witness tell about this asserted conversation with Mr Rubin on the occasion described.

Mr Weinglass: What was the conversation at that time?

The Witness: Jerry Rubin told me that he had come to New York to be project director of a peace march in Washington that was going to march to the Pentagon in October, October 21. He said that the peace movement suffered from a certain kind of attitude, mainly that it was based solely on the issue of the Vietnam war. He said that the war in Vietnam was not just an accident but a direct by-product of the kind of system, a capitalist system in the country, and that we had to begin to put forth new kinds of values, especially to young people in the country, to make a kind of society in which a Vietnam war would not be possible. . . . I said that the Pentagon was a five-sided evil symbol in most religions and that it might be possible to approach this from a religious point of view. If we got large numbers of people to surround the Pentagon, we could exorcize it of its evil spirits. So I had agreed at that point to begin working on the exorcism of the Pentagon demonstration. . . .

Mr Weinglass: Now, drawing your attention to the first week of December 1967, did you have occasion to meet with Jerry Rubin and the others?

The Witness: Yes.

Mr Weinglass: Will you relate to the Court and jury what the conversation was?

The Witness: Yes. We talked about the possibility of having demonstrations at the Democratic Convention in Chicago, Illinois, that was going to be occurring that August. I am not sure that we knew at that point that it was in Chicago. Wherever it was, we were planning on going. Jerry Rubin, I believe, said that it would be a good idea to call it the Festival of Life in contrast to the Convention of Death, and to have it in some kind of public area, like a park or something, in Chicago. One thing that I was very particular about was that we didn't have any concept of leadership involved. . . .

Mr Weinglass: The document that is before you, D-222 for identification, what is that document?

The Witness: It was our initial call to people to describe what Yippie was about and why we were coming to Chicago.

Mr Weinglass: Now, Abbie, could you read the entire document to the jury.

The Witness: It says: "A STATEMENT FROM YIP! Join us in Chicago in August for an international festival of youth, music, and theater. Rise up and abandon the creeping meatball! Come all you rebels, youth spirits, rock minstrels, truth-seekers, peacock-freaks, poets, barricade-jumpers, dancers, lovers and artists! It is summer. It is the last week in August, and the NATIONAL DEATH PARTY meets to bless Lyndon Johnson. We are there! There are 50,000 of us

dancing in the streets, throbbing with amplifiers and harmony. We are making love in the parks. We are reading, singing, laughing, printing newspapers, groping, and making a mock convention, and celebrating the birth of FREE AMERICA in our own time. Everything will be free. Bring blankets, tents, draft-cards, body-paint, Mr Leary's Cow, food to share, music, eager skin, and happiness. The threats of LBJ, Mayor Daley, and J. Edgar Freako will not stop us. We are coming! We are coming from all over the world! The life of the American spirit is being torn asunder by the forces of violence, decay, and the napalm-cancer fiend. We demand the Politics of Ecstasy! We are the delicate spores of the new fierceness that will change America. We will create our own reality, we are Free America! And we will not accept the false theater of the Death Convention. We will be in Chicago. Begin preparations now! Chicago is yours! Do it!" . . .

Mr Weinglass: Now, will you read for the Court and jury the eighteen demands first, then the postscript.

The Witness: I will read it in the order that I wrote it. "Revolution toward a free society, Yippie, by A. Yippie. This is a personal statement. There are no spokesmen for the Yippies. We are all our own leaders. We realize this list of demands is inconsistent. They are not really demands. For people to make demands of the Democratic Party is an exercise in wasted wish fulfillment. If we have a demand, it is simply and emphatically that they, along with their fellow inmates in the Republican Party, cease to exist. We demand a society built along the alternative community in Lincoln Park, a society based on humanitarian cooperation and equality, a society which allows and promotes the creativity present in all people and especially our youth.

"Number one. An immediate end to the war in Vietnam and a restructuring of our foreign policy which totally eliminates aspects of military, economic and cultural imperialism; the withdrawal of all foreign based troops and the abolition of military draft.

"Two. An immediate freedom for Huey Newton of the Black Panthers and all other black people; adoption of the community control concept in our ghetto areas; an end to the cultural and economic domination of minority groups.

"Three. The legalization of marijuana and all other psychedelic drugs; the freeing of all prisoners currently imprisoned on narcotics charges.

"Number four. A prison system based on the concept of rehabilitation rather than punishment.

"Five. A judicial system which works towards the abolition of all laws related to crimes without victims; that is, retention only of laws relating to crimes in which there is an unwilling injured party: i.e. murder, rape, or assault.

"Six. The total disarmament of all the people beginning with the police. This includes not only guns but such brutal vices as tear gas, Mace, electric prods, blackjacks, billy clubs, and the like.

"Seven. The abolition of money, the abolition of pay housing, pay media, pay transportation, pay food, pay education, pay clothing, pay medical health, and pay toilets.

"Eight. A society which works towards and actively promotes the concept of full unemployment, a society in which people are free from the drudgery of work, adoption of the concept 'Let the machines do it.'[3]

"Number ten. A program of ecological development that would provide incentives for the decentralization of crowded cities and encourage rural living.

"Eleven. A program which provides not only free birth control information and

devices, but also abortions when desired.

"Twelve. A restructured educational system which provides a student power to determine his course of study, student participation in over-all policy planning; an educational system which breaks down its barriers between school and community; a system which uses the surrounding community as a classroom so that students may learn directly the problems of the people.

"Number thirteen. The open and free use of the media; a program which actively supports and promotes cable television as a method of increasing the selection of channels available to the viewer.

"Fourteen. An end to all censorship. We are sick of a society that has no hesitation about showing people committing violence and refuses to show a couple fucking.

"Fifteen. We believe that people should fuck all the time, any time, wherever they wish. This is not a programmed demand but a simple recognition of the reality around us.

"Sixteen. A political system which is more streamlined and responsive to the needs of all the people regardless of age, sex, or race; perhaps a national referendum system conducted via television or a telephone voting system; perhaps a decentralization of power and authority with many varied tribal groups, groups in which people exist in a state of basic trust and are free to choose their tribe.

"Seventeen. A program that encourages and promotes the arts. However, we feel that if the free society we envision were to be sought for and achieved, all of us would actualize the creativity within us; in a very real sense we would have a society in which every man would be an artist.

"And eighteen was left blank for anybody to fill in what they wanted. It was for these reasons that we had come to Chicago, it was for these reasons that many of us may fight and die here. We recognize this as the vision of the founders of this nation. We recognize that we are America; we recognize that we are free men. The present-day politicians and their armies of automatons have selfishly robbed us of our birthright. The evilness they stand for will go unchallenged no longer. Political pigs, your days are numbered. We are the second American Revolution. We shall win.

"yippie."

Mr Weinglass: When you used the words "fight and die here," in what context were you using those words?

The Witness: It is a metaphor. That means that we felt strongly about our right to assemble in the park and that people should be willing to take risks for it. It doesn't spell it out because people were capable of fighting in their own way and making their own decisions and we never would tell anyone specifically that they should fight, fistfight.

Mr Weinglass: Did you during the week of the Convention and the period of time immediately before the Convention tell any person singly or in groups that they should fight in the park?

Mr Schultz: Objection.

The Court: I sustain the objection. . . .

Mr Weinglass: Abbie Hoffman, prior to coming to Chicago, from April 1968 on to the week of the Convention, did you enter into an agreement with David Dellinger, John Froines, Tom Hayden, Jerry Rubin, Lee Weiner, or Rennie Davis, to come to the city of Chicago for the purpose of encouraging and promoting violence during the Convention week?

The Witness: An agreement?

Mr Weinglass: Yes.

The Witness: We couldn't agree on lunch.

Mr Weinglass: I have no further questions.

Notes

1. Leonard Weinglass (1933–2011) and William Kunstler (1919–1995) were the defence lawyers for the Chicago Seven; Richard Schultz was the assistant US attorney prosecuting the case against Hoffman and the others.
2. "Yip" or "Yippies" was short for the "Youth International Party."
3. Point Nine was omitted from the transcript but it reads: "A conservation program geared towards preserving our natural resources and committed to the elimination of pollution from our air and water."

Study Question

What do you believe was accomplished by the more radical protest movements such as the Yippies?

Web Resources

The King Center (Martin Luther King, Jr)
   http://www.thekingcenter.org
Sixties Project: Primary Document Archive
   http://www2.iath.virginia.edu/sixties/HTML_docs/Resources/Primary.html
Library of Congress: Civil Rights Resource Guide
   http://www.loc.gov/rr/program/bib/civilrights/external.html
Internet Women's History Sourcebook
   http://www.fordham.edu/halsall/women/womensbook.html

Recommended Reading

Anthony Burgess, *A Clockwork Orange* (New York: W.W. Norton, 1986). In a futuristic London, where gangs of teenage "droogs" commit random unspeakably violent acts, the central character, Alex, is captured and imprisoned. An experimental hospital treatment modifies his behaviour in such a way as to "free" him from his violent nature; however, the cost of freedom is the loss of free will. The conditioning is eventually reversed. Note that the 1962 British version of the novel contains a final, optimistic chapter in which Alex turns 21 and, having escaped adolescence, freely chooses to abandon his violent ways. This ending was omitted from most American editions of the novel, as well as from the film.

Joseph Heller, *Catch-22* (New York: Simon & Schuster, 1996). Set in Second World War Italy, *Catch-22* (written in 1961) is a satirical and surrealist commentary on the essential insanity of war. The war is seen through the eyes of bombardier John Yossarian as he struggles to stay alive in the face of the omnipresent bureaucracy that demands he demonstrate his insanity—the precondition of getting out of the military—by continuing to fly dangerous missions.

Hermann Hesse, *Steppenwolf* (New York: Picador, 2002). Although written in 1927, the 1960s counterculture movement idolized Hesse's *Steppenwolf*. The novel tells the story of one man's struggle between a life of bourgeois peace and order, and one of action, instinct, and impulse. Hesse's central message concerns the need to focus on one's inner voice, and reject the dictates of the external world: "There is no reality except the one contained within us."

Jack Kerouac, *On the Road* (New York: Penguin, 1991). The classic novel of the Beat Generation, written in 1957, tells a fictionalized version of Kerouac's cross-country travels and his meetings with counter-culture icons such as Allen Ginzberg and William Burroughs. Kerouac's themes include dropping out, sex, drugs, mysticism, energy, speed, and freedom.

J.D. Salinger, *The Catcher in the Rye* (New York: Little, Brown and Company, 1991). Considered the essential novel of youth alienation and coming of age, Holden Caulfield runs away to 1940s New York with its jazz scene, ambivalent sexuality, alcohol, prostitution, and violence. Loneliness and alienation are intensified by his experiences, leading to a complete breakdown.

Kurt Vonnegut. 1969. *Slaughterhouse Five* (New York: Delacorte Press, 1994). *Slaughterhouse Five* is a science fiction/fantasy novel drawn, in part, from the author's experiences as a POW during the firebombing of Dresden. (Vonnegut survived, sheltered under a slaughterhouse.) The novel recounts Billy Pilgrim's journey through time, over the course of which he encounters the dangers of technology, the butchery of war, and the risk of blind obedience.

Recommended Viewing

In the Year of the Pig (USA, 1968). Director: Emile de Antonio (Documentary). This controversial 1968 documentary—often considered the forerunner of contemporary investigative documentaries—attempted to uncover the truth behind the ongoing war in Vietnam. The film, using archival footage and interview, is both intensely anti-war and anti-American.

Easy Rider (USA, 1969). Director: Dennis Hopper. Perhaps the best known of the 1960s "anti-establishment" films, *Easy Rider* highlights the youth culture, hippies, drug culture, and music of the era. Shot on location in documentary style, the film also touches on the rampant poverty and prejudice of 1960s America.

Stammheim (West Germany, 1986). Director: Reinhard Hauff. Hauff's fictionalized account of the West German Baader–Meinhof group (Red Army Faction) of the late 1960s and early 1970s tackles the issue of anti-military, anti-corporate terrorism and its consequences. It also reveals the complexities of German–American relations during the Cold War and the level of support for radical groups using terrorist tactics.

Mississippi Burning (USA, 1988). Director: Alan Parker. *Mississippi Burning* is a highly fictionalized dramatization of the 1964 Klu Klux Klan murders of three white civil rights activists. It captures the climate of hatred in the southern United States and the determination to prevent the civil rights movement from gaining any ground.

The Laramie Project (USA, 2002). Director: Moisés Kaufman. *The Laramie Project* is the film version of Kaufman's stage play about the vicious murder of gay university student Matthew Sheppard. The film re-enacts some of the events leading to Sheppard's murder, the town's reaction, and the subsequent debates about hate crime legislation.

Milk (USA, 2008). Director: Gus van Sant. Van Sant recreates the life of Harvey Milk, a community leader and vocal advocate for gay rights in the 1970s and the first openly gay official elected to the municipal government in San Francisco. The film includes some archival footage of Milk's later speeches.

15

The End of the Cold War and Its Aftermath

Eastern European countries made several failed attempts to break away from the control of the Soviet Union throughout the 1950s and 1960s; Poland and Hungary rebelled in 1956, Czechoslovakia in 1968. On each occasion the Soviet Union used its military superiority to re-impose control over the rebellious satellite states. However, even as the Soviets re-asserted control, some concessions—particularly on economic matters—were made to the defiant Eastern bloc nations. These compromises, and the potential for greater freedoms in the future, sustained an active underground opposition movement in the region.

The mere presence of dissent would likely never have achieved independence for Eastern Europe. However, by the late 1970s, the economy of the Soviet Union was severely overburdened by the accelerated military spending necessary to keep pace with the United States. Increasingly the Soviets sacrificed the basic needs of

Gorbachev and Reagan at the White House on 8 December 1987, signing the INF treaty to reduce immediate-range nuclear weapons.

Courtesy of the Ronald Reagan Library.

their own citizens in order to maintain their global commitments. By the early 1980s alarming statistics showed that infant mortality was increasing and longevity declining. The Soviet economy was simply no longer able to deliver essential services such as health care and, as a result, the quality of Soviet life declined. Meanwhile, nepotism and corruption grew, especially within the massive Communist Party bureaucracy. The death of Leonid Brezhnev in 1982 brought few immediate changes, but it was clear that the present situation could not continue.

By March 1985 the situation in the Soviet Union was desperate. The aged leaders of the Communist Party had little choice but to move in a new direction under the leadership of the Politburo's youngest member, the then 54-year-old Mikhail Gorbachev. Gorbachev had long since concluded that the time for small changes had passed and that only radical reforms could preserve the Leninist system while moving the USSR into the post-industrial age. Over the next three years Gorbachev unleashed the widest array of reforms that the Soviet Union had seen since the 1920s. Peaceful co-existence was sought with the West through arms limitation talks, new economic initiatives were designed to make Soviet goods competitive in the world markets, political openness was encouraged, and it was made clear that the Soviets would no longer invest monies in propping up the unpopular governments of Eastern Europe.

The immediate result of the latter decision was open demonstrations of dissatisfaction throughout Eastern Europe. Lacking Soviet military backing, communist governments across the region crumbled. Unpopular governments were overthrown in Poland, Hungary, East Germany, Bulgaria, Czechoslovakia, Rumania, and Yugoslavia. The early jubilation, however, proved short-lived, as the end of single-party states did not automatically solve the major problems facing the former Soviet satellites. The collapse of communism saw a resurgence of multi-party democratic systems that tended to form along traditional ethnic and religious lines. Elsewhere, weak coalition governments struggled with the transition to capitalism and suffered hyperinflation, massive unemployment, and social dislocation as the conversion proceeded. Nonetheless, over time, states such as Poland and Hungary would undergo remarkable recoveries from the ravages of the Soviet era and the post-Soviet transition. In the Soviet Union itself, few of Gorbachev's reforms were unfolding as planned. Angry consumers resented the removal of subsidies from basic foodstuffs, managers resented the new requirements to demonstrate profitability, advocates of democratic political reforms demanded Gorbachev move faster while old-guard communists argued that he had already gone too far. Gradually it became evident that Gorbachev was unable to control the forces he had unleashed and few in the Soviet Union were distressed when a coup d'état in August 1991 left Gorbachev with vastly reduced powers. By the end of 1991 the Soviet Union had disintegrated and in its place the more loosely affiliated Commonwealth of Independent States (CIS) emerged.

Beyond the Soviet bloc, the removal of the restraining influence of Cold War alliances produced opportunities for some and catastrophes for others. In South

Africa, the loss of American support contributed to the crumbling of the Apartheid regime and the rise to power of Nelson Mandela. However, in Yugoslavia, the loss of American aid contributed to the reemergence of deeply rooted ethnic tensions and, ultimately, to the ongoing disintegration of the Yugoslav State. For Cuba, the end of the neo-colonial relationship with the Soviet Union brought both new challenges and new opportunities to plot an independent course.

The documents in this section introduce a variety of views on the latter years of the Cold War and the period of transition thereafter, beginning with Leonid Brezhnev's thoughts on the danger posed by the Solidarity Movement in Poland, as well as Václav Havel's hope that the quiet stirrings of dissent visible in the 1980s would eventually combine into a potent force for reform. As well, we see Mikhail Gorbachev's analysis of the situation facing the Soviet Union in the mid-1980s and Aleksandr Solzhenitsyn's suggestions for rebuilding Russia after the collapse of the USSR. Nelson Mandela addresses both the challenges and the promise of South African development in the aftermath of the Cold War. A portion of the report on Hungary's successful transition to a democratic capitalist system and its readiness for membership in the EU follows. Aleksander Kwaśniewski similarly reflects on Poland's successes since 1989, as well as those problems which remained. The darker side of the post-Cold War world is evidenced in Robert Donia's testimony before the International Criminal Tribunal for the Former Yugoslavia (ICTFY). Finally, Raúl Castro reflects on Cuba's efforts to remedy its economic problems while preserving its socialist nature.

Leonid Brezhnev

Leonid Brezhnev (1906–1982) rose to power in the Soviet Union following the dismissal of Nikita Khrushchev. Despite officially sharing power with Aleksei Kosygin, Brezhnev emerged as the de facto Soviet leader after advocating a harsh crackdown on dissent in Prague, Czechoslovakia, in 1968. Brezhnev's tenure coincided with the aging of the Soviet political leadership and the gradual decay of the country's infrastructure. Outsiders began to speak of a "gerontocracy"—rule by old men. Brezhnev was responsible for the generally improved relations with the United States that characterized the early 1970s, but he also mired the USSR in an unwinnable situation in Afghanistan after 1978. The transcript that follows records Brezhnev's comments during a telephone conversation in 1981 with key Polish leaders following the emergence of the Solidarity Movement under Lech Walesa.

Document Source: SAPMDB, ZPA, J IV 2/202-550, first published in CWIHP Special Working Paper 1. Cold War International History Project Digital Archive; digitalarchive.wilsoncenter.org/document/112799

The Threat from Solidarity, 15 September 1981

"Hello, Stanislaw![1] They told me that you want to speak with me. Please go ahead." . . .

"I listened to your remarks. It seems to me that you're still under the sway of certain illusions.

"I discussed the situation in Poland with you and Wojciech [Jaruzelski] in the Crimea roughly a month ago. At that point there was already more than enough basis for disquiet. Since then, in our view, the situation has become even more alarming. I'll say this candidly: you should wake up again and think about who is controlling the situation in Poland. Has the fulcrum of power there already changed? The leaders of Solidarity are acting so brazenly that you cannot help but ask yourself this question.

"Solidarity's congress and the whole atmosphere around it attest that Solidarity openly aspires to the role of a political party, a party with an anti-Communist bent. The results of the first round of the Congress, in our view, amounted to a declaration of war against the PZPR and the socialist regime.

"Of course this in no way was a congress of workers. Even according to Solidarity's own information, only 25 per cent of the delegates were workers. More than a quarter of the delegates were representatives of the counterrevolutionary organizations KSS-KOR and Confederation for an Independent Poland. And it was not the interests of the working class that preoccupied the participants in this gathering. Instead they focused on how to humiliate the PZPR and the government and force them to their knees.

"At the Congress, as you know, the question was raised about possibly removing from Solidarity's statutes the provisions about the leading role of the party and recognition of Poland's international alliances. These are provisions in your Constitution. This means that attacks have begun against the constitutional bases of society.

"Solidarity has decided not to confine itself solely to Poland. It is attempting to impose its subversive ideas on neighboring states and to interfere in their internal affairs. That's the only way one can view the 'Appeal to the Peoples of Eastern Europe,' which was adopted by Solidarity's Congress. There aren't many words in that document, but they all make the same point. The authors of the document would like to foment disturbances in the socialist countries and stir up groups of various renegades. I don't know what you've decided to do about this

provocative escapade, but we believe it is essential to give it the rebuff it deserves.

"Solidarity is not limiting itself to slogans and appeals. It is in fact making preparations, including military preparations, to seize power. According to reports filtering in from the West, Solidarity is creating 'combat groups,' whose task is to terrorize Communists and patriots. This is just what fascists do in creating brigades of stormtroopers. According to the same reports, Solidarity is initiating courses for new draftees in the Polish Army. How can this be tolerated? If fresh troops come in imbued with anti-socialist and anti-Soviet preconceptions, you might quickly find that the army disintegrates.

"One position after another is being transferred to Solidarity's control. The legitimately appointed directors of enterprises are being removed without any prior arrangement. Solidarity is calling the shots at more than half of the large factories and is creating there what it calls 'organs of self-management.'

"In rural areas there have been instances of the unauthorized seizure of state and co-operative farmland by private peasants. Solidarity reacted viciously when the mass media featured criticism of its actions, and they are now seeking to take complete control of the media.

"It is painful to speak about the frenzy of anti-Sovietism that has now engulfed Poland. How can you let this go unpunished? How can you tolerate instances of psychological and physical terror against Communists and all others who want to work honestly? As an ultimatum, the opposition continually demands that the elections to the Sejm and the People's Councils be moved up. Their ultimate goal is, through 'peaceful means,' to destroy the economic and political foundations of the socialist order.

"I will not refer to many other things, which are no less alarming. These things must be at least as well known to you as they are to us. It is understandable why at the recent plenums, including the third, many members of the newly formed Central Committee were speaking with great alarm about the situation. They demanded not only bold words but decisive actions from the PZPR leadership.

"Their concerns are understandable. The impudent leaders of Solidarity openly declare that their organization is already the leading force in society. . . .

"We request that you inform us, the leadership of a fraternal party, the CPSU, what you intend to do.

"In practical terms, we have nothing to add to the recommendations we already provided to you about how to get out of the crisis, including the recommendations in the letter of 5 June and during the meeting in the Crimea on 14 August. These recommendations and advice remain in force.

"Both then and now we have been convinced that if you do nothing to offset the appeals of the insolent Solidarity, you will open the way to counterrevolution. In our view, it is essential not to delay any further in gearing up the party for a decisive and uncompromising struggle against the counterrevolution. And when the very fate of socialism is at stake, you can't limit yourself to only one form or another of struggle.

"I believe it is important to emphasize, once again, that in today's complicated world situation, the course of events in Poland is forcing the socialist commonwealth to confront the ever thornier question of how to maintain security in the center of Europe. If Poland is ruled by Solidarity, who will guarantee the inviolability of the commonwealth's vital lines of communication that pass through the PPR, including strategic lines of communication? How could we, the participants in the Warsaw Pact, ensure the preservation of the results of the Second World War, which were codified in well-known political and international legal documents?

"I want to emphasize, once again, Stanislaw, that the fate of socialism in Poland and the outcome of the political struggle in your country profoundly affect all the fraternal countries. . . ."

Note

1. Stanislaw Kania was the general secretary of the Polish Communist Party (PZPR) at the time of this conversation; Brezhnev also makes reference to Wojciech Jaruzelski, then prime minister and soon to become Kania's replacement as General Secretary.

> **Study Question**
>
> Brezhnev highlights a number of issues which directly threaten the Soviet system. Based on your reading of this document, what are the most damaging concerns?

Václav Havel

Václav Havel (1936–2011) rose to prominence during the 1960s as an opponent of the Soviet system imposed upon Czechoslovakia after the Second World War. He played an active role during the Prague Spring (1968) and his writings in defence of Eastern European independence would lead to numerous arrests and a four-and-a-half year prison term. Havel continued to publish anti-Soviet literature throughout the 1970s and 1980s. In 1989, when the USSR granted full independence to the satellite states, Havel was elected as the first president of Czechoslovakia. He remained president during the peaceful separation of the Czechoslovakian Federation into two states and served until February 2003. In the following excerpt from an interview with exiled journalist Karel Hvížd'ala, originally published in 1986, Havel responds to questions regarding the potential for reform in the 1980s.

Document Source: Václav Havel, *Disturbing the Peace*, transl. Paul Wilson (New York: Knopf, 1990).

Disturbing the Peace

Hvížd'ala: Do you see a grain of hope anywhere in the 1980s?

Havel: I should probably say first that the kind of hope I often think about (especially in situations that are particularly hopeless, such as prison) I understand above all as a state of mind, not a state of the world. Either we have hope within us or we don't; it is a dimension of the soul, and it's not essentially dependent on some particular observation of the world or estimate of the situation. Hope is not prognostication. It is an orientation of the spirit, an orientation of the heart; it transcends the world that is immediately experienced, and is anchored somewhere beyond its horizons. . . .

Hope, in this deep and powerful sense, is not the same as joy that things are going well, or willingness to invest in enterprises that are obviously headed for early success, but, rather, an ability to work for something because it is good, not just because it stands a chance to succeed. The more unpropitious the situation in which we demonstrate hope, the deeper that hope is. Hope is definitely not the same thing as optimism. It is not the conviction that something will turn out well, but the certainty that something makes sense, regardless of how it turns out. . . .

That was by way of introduction; now to answer your question about the state of the world and the kind of hopeful phenomena I see in it. Here too, I think you can find modest grounds for hope. I leave it to those more qualified to decide what can be expected from Gorbachev and, in general, "from above"—that is, from what is happening in the sphere of power. I have never fixed my hopes there; I've always been more interested in what was happening "below," in what could be expected from "below," what could be won there, and what defended. All power is power over someone, and it always somehow responds, usually unwittingly rather than deliberately, to the state of mind and the behavior of those it rules over. One can always find in the behavior of power a reflection of what is going on "below." No one can govern in a vacuum. The exercise of power is determined by thousands of interactions between the world of the powerful and that of the powerless, all the more so because these worlds are never divided by a sharp line: everyone has a small part of himself in both.

Having said that, if I try to look unbiasedly at what is going on "below," I must say that here too I find a slow, imperceptible, yet undoubted and undoubtedly hopeful movement. After seventeen years of apparent stagnation and moribundity, the situation is rather different now. If we compare how society behaves now, how it expresses itself, what it dares to do—or, rather, what a significant minority dares to do—with how it was in the early seventies, those differences must be obvious. People seem to be recovering gradually, walking straighter, taking a renewed interest in things they had so energetically denied themselves before. New islands of self-awareness and self-liberation are appearing, and the connections between them, which were once so brutally disrupted, are multiplying. A new generation, not traumatized by the shock of the Soviet occupation, is maturing: for them, the invasion is history and Dubček is what Kramář,[1] for example, was to my generation. Something is happening in the social awareness, though it is still an undercurrent as yet, rather than something visible.

And all of this brings subtle pressure to bear on the powers that govern society. I'm not thinking now of the obvious pressure of public criticism coming from dissidents, but of the invisible kinds of pressure brought on by this general state of mind and its various forms of expression, to which power unintentionally adapts, even in the act of opposing it. One is made aware of these things with special clarity when one returns from prison and experiences the sharp contrast between the situation as he had fixed it in his mind before his arrest, and the new situation at the moment of his return. I have observed this in my own case, and others have had the same experience. Again and again, we were astonished at all the new things that were going on, the greater risks people were taking, how more freely they were behaving, how much greater and less hidden was their hunger for truth, for a truthful word, for genuine values. . . .

But things are different now from the way they were a few years ago, right in the midst of the so-called dissident or Chartist milieu as well. And although those in power have not altered their view of the Charter, they have still had to get used to it. Today it is a firm part of social life here, even though its position is marginal, one that society perceives more as the final horizon of its relationships or the final focus of various values than as an immediate challenge, something to be emulated. Today it is hard to imagine a time when the Charter did not exist, and when one does try to imagine it, it evokes a feeling of vacuum and moral relativity.

Or take VONS.[2] Few of us were arrested and sent to prison for working in the "anti-state center." When that happened, VONS did not cave in; others immediately filled in and continued the work. We didn't cave in either; we served our sentences, and VONS is here to this day, working energetically on, and

apparently no one thinks anymore of prosecuting it for what it does. It still officially remains an "antistate organization" (an epithet those in power are too vainglorious to withdraw), but by insisting on it, they have turned it into a worthless phrase: what kind of an "antistate organization" is it that can go on publicly functioning for nine years? In a sense, our jail sentences gained us the right to run VONS.

To outside observers, these changes may seem insignificant. "Where are your ten-million-strong trade unions?" they may ask. "Where are your members of parliament? Why does Husák not negotiate with you? Why is the government not considering your proposals and acting on them?" But for someone from here who is not completely indifferent, these are far from insignificant changes; they are the main promise of the future, since he has long ago learned not to expect it from anywhere else.

I can't resist concluding with a question of my own. Isn't the reward of all those small but hopeful signs of movement this deep, inner hope that is not dependent on prognoses, and which was the primordial point of departure in this unequal struggle? Would so many of those small hopes have "come out" if there had not been this great hope "within," this hope without which it is impossible to live in dignity and meaning, much less find the will for the "hopeless enterprise" which stands at the beginning of most good things?

Notes

1. Karel Kramář (1860–1937) was instrumental in gaining Czech independence from the Austro-Hungarian Empire.
2. VONS: The Committee for the Defence of the Unjustly Prosecuted (*Vybor na obranu nespravedlive stihanych*).

Study Question

What are the "small but hopeful signs" that Havel sees in Czechoslovakia and elsewhere in the 1980s?

Mikhail Gorbachev

Mikhail Gorbachev (b. 1931) joined the Communist Party of the Soviet Union in 1952 and then rose steadily through the ranks of the party bureaucracy. With degrees in law and agriculture, Gorbachev joined the Central Committee of the CPSU in 1971 and became the youngest member in the history of the Politburo in 1980. The death of Konstantin Chernenko in March 1985 and the desperate social and economic situation in the Soviet Union opened the way for Gorbachev to be elected General Secretary of the Communist Party of the Soviet Union. This speech, given at the closing of the 27th Congress of the Communist Party in 1986, was one of Gorbachev's most candid regarding the many challenges facing the USSR in the mid-1980s.

Document Source: Mikhail Gorbachev, "On the Closing of the 27th Congress of the CPSU." From Mikhail Gorbachev, General Secretary of the CPSU Central Committee, "Closing Speech to the 27th CPSU Central Committee, 6 March 1986," Moscow: 1986, 82–9.

On the Closing of the 27th Congress of the CPSU

Dear Comrades,

The 27th Congress is about to close.

It is up to history to give an objective evaluation of its importance. But already today we can say: the Congress has been held in an atmosphere of Party fidelity to principle, in a spirit of unity, exactingness, and Bolshevik truth; it has frankly pointed out shortcomings and deficiencies, and made a profound analysis of the internal and external conditions in which our society develops. It has set a lofty moral and spiritual tone for the Party's activity and for the life of the entire country.

Coming to this rostrum, delegates put all questions frankly, and did not mince words in showing what is impeding our common cause, what is holding us back. Not a few critical statements were made about the work of all links of the Party, of government and economic organizations, both at the centre and locally. In fact, not a single sphere of our life has escaped critical analysis. All this, comrades, is in the spirit of the Party's finest traditions, in the Bolshevik spirit.

More than sixty years ago, when summing up the discussion on the Political Report of the RCP(B) Central Committee to the 11th Party Congress, Lenin expressed a thought that is of fundamental importance. He said: "All the revolutionary parties that have perished so far, perished because they became conceited, because they failed to see the source of their strength and were afraid to discuss their weaknesses. We, however, shall not perish, because we are not afraid to discuss our weaknesses and will learn to overcome them."

It is in this way, in Lenin's way, that we have acted here at our Congress. And that is the way we shall continue to act!

The Congress has answered the vital questions that life itself has put before the Party, before society, and has equipped every Communist, every Soviet citizen, with a clear understanding of the coming tasks. It has shown that we were right when we advanced the concept of socioeconomic acceleration at the April 1985 Plenary Meeting. The idea of acceleration imbued all our pre-Congress activity. It was at the centre of attention at the Congress. It was embodied in the Political Report of the Central Committee, the new edition of the Party Programme, and the amendments to the Party Rules, as well as in the Guidelines for the Economic and Social Development of the USSR for the 12th Five-Year Plan Period and for the Period Ending in the Year 2000. These documents were wholeheartedly endorsed and approved by the delegates to the Congress.

The adopted and approved general line of the Party's domestic and foreign policy—that of the country's accelerated socioeconomic development, and of consolidating world peace—is the main political achievement of the 27th CPSU Congress. From now on it will be the law of life for the Party, for its every organization, and a guide to action for Communists, for all working people.

We are aware of the great responsibility to history that the CPSU is assuming, of the huge load it has taken on by adopting the strategy of acceleration. But we are convinced of the vital necessity of this strategy. We are confident that this strategy is a realistic one. Relying on the inexhaustible potentials and advantages of socialism, on the vigorous creative activity of the people, we shall be able to carry out all the projected objectives.

To secure the country's accelerated socio-economic development means to provide new powerful stimuli to the growth of the productive forces and to scientific and technological progress through the improvement of socialism's economic system, and to set in motion the tremendous untapped potentials of our national economy.

To secure acceleration means conducting an active and purposeful social policy by closely linking the improvement of the working people's well-being with the efficiency of labour, and by combining all-round concern for people with the consistent implementation of the principles of social justice.

To secure acceleration means to provide scope for the initiative and activity of every working person, every work collective, by deepening democracy, by steadily developing the people's socialist self-government, and by ensuring more openness in the life of the Party and society.

To secure acceleration means to bring ideological and organizational work closer to the people and direct it towards the elimination of difficulties and the practical solution of our tasks

US President Ronald Reagan stands with Mikhail Gorbachev in Red Square, May 1988, during the Moscow Summit.
Courtesy of the Ronald Reagan Library.

by associating this work more closely with the actual problems of life, by getting rid of hollow verbiage and didacticism, and by increasing people's responsibility for their job.

Comrades, we can and must accomplish all this! The CPSU is entering the post-Congress period better organized, more cohesive, more efficient, with a well-considered long-term policy. It is determined to act with purpose, aware of all the complexity, the great scope and novelty of the tasks it faces, undaunted by difficulties and obstacles.

It is up to us to reach every Soviet citizen and bring home the essence and spirit of the Congress decisions. Not only must we explain the basic concepts of the Congress; we must also organize in practice all work in line with present-day demands.

Very many interesting proposals were made and many profound thoughts expressed at our

Congress and in the pre-Congress period. They must be carefully examined, and everything valuable and useful should be put into effect.

The most important thing now is to convert the energy of our plans into the energy of concrete action. This idea was very well expressed by a delegate to our Congress, Vasily Gorin, chairman of a Belgorod collective farm.

"All over the country," he said, "in every work collective, a difficult but, we are sure, irreversible process of renovation and reconstruction is now under way. It passes through the hearts and minds of Soviet people and calls for complete dedication on the part of each and everyone. Above all in their work."

Yes, comrades, acceleration and radical changes in all spheres of our life are not just a slogan but a course that the Party will follow firmly and undeviatingly.

Many delegates noted that departmentalism, localism, paper work, and other bureaucratic practices are a big obstacle to what is new and progressive. I wish to assure you, comrades, that the Central Committee will resolutely eliminate all the obstacles standing in the way of accelerating socioeconomic progress, strengthen discipline and order, and create the organizational, moral, and material pre-requisites for the maximum development of creative activity, bold search, and socialist enterprise. I am confident that this will meet with broad and active support on the part of the entire Party and of all working people.

The Party committees, from top to bottom, are the organizers of the work of implementing the instructions of the Congress. What we now need are a concrete, businesslike, and consistent style of work, unity of words and deeds, use of the most effective ways and means, a thorough consideration of people's opinions, and efficient coordination of the actions of all social forces.

Sluggishness, formalism, indifference, the habit of letting good ideas get bogged down in empty, and endless roundabout discussions and attempts to "adjust to readjustment" must be completely overcome.

One of the main conclusions of the Congress is that all Party committees should act as genuine bodies of political leadership. In the final analysis, the success of all our efforts to implement the general line of the 27th Party Congress will be determined by the conscious participation of the broadest masses of the people in building communism. Everything depends on us, comrades! The time has come for vigorous and united actions. The Party calls on every Communist, every Soviet citizen, to join actively in the large-scale work of putting our plans into practice, of perfecting Soviet society, of renovating our socialist home.

Comrades, the Congress has strongly reaffirmed that socialism and peace, and peace and constructive endeavour, are indivisible. Socialism would fail to carry out its historic mission if it did not lead the struggle to deliver mankind from the burden of military threats and violence. The main goal of Soviet policy is security and a just peace for all nations. We regard the struggle against war and military preparations, against the propagation of hatred and violence as an inseparable part of the democratization of all international relations, of the genuine normalization of the political climate in the world.

In one respect the nuclear danger has put all states on an equal footing: in a big war nobody will be able to stand aside or to profit from the misfortunes of others. Equal security is the imperative of the times. Ensuring this security is becoming increasingly a political issue, one that can be resolved only by political means. It is high time to replace weapons by a more stable foundation for the relations among states. We see no alternative to this, nor are we trying to find one.

Unfortunately, however, in the international community there are still some who lay claims to a special security, one that is suited only to themselves. This is illustrated by the thinking in Washington. Calls for strength are still in fashion there, and strength continues to be regarded as the most convincing argument in world politics.

It looks as though some people are simply afraid of the possibility that has appeared for a serious and long-term thaw in Soviet-American relations and in international relations as a whole.

This is not the first time we have come up against this kind of situation. Now, too, the militaristic, aggressive forces would of course prefer to preserve and perpetuate the confrontation. But what should we do, comrades? Slam the door? It is possible that this is just what we are being pushed into doing. But we very clearly realize our responsibility for the destinies of our country and for the destinies of the world. We do not intend, therefore, to play into the hands of those who would like to force mankind to get used to the nuclear threat and to the arms race.

Soviet foreign policy is oriented towards a search for mutual understanding, towards dialogue, and the establishment of peaceful coexistence as the universal norm in relations among states. We have both a clear idea of how to achieve this and a concrete programme of work for maintaining and consolidating peace.

The Soviet Union is acting and will continue to act in the world arena in an open and responsible way, energetically and in good faith. We intend to work persistently and constructively to eliminate nuclear weapons, radically to limit the arms race, and to build reliable international security that is equal for all countries. A mandate to preserve peace and to curb the arms race resounded forcefully in speeches by delegates to our Congress. The Party will unswervingly carry out this mandate.

We call on the leaders of countries that have a different social system to take a responsible approach to the key issue of world politics today: the issue of war and peace.

The leadership of the CPSU and the Soviet state will do its utmost to secure for our people the opportunity to work under the conditions of freedom and a lasting peace. As reaffirmed by the Congress, our Party and the Soviet Union have many allies, supporters and partners abroad in the struggle for peace, freedom, and the progress of mankind.

We are sincerely happy to see here the leaders of the socialist countries. Allow me, on behalf of the Congress, wholeheartedly to thank the Communist Parties and peoples of these countries for their solidarity with the CPSU and the Soviet Union!

For a number of the fraternal parties in socialist countries this is also a congress year. The problems and tasks that the very course of history has set before the ruling Communist Parties are similar in many respects. And by responding to them, each party contributes to the treasure-chest of world socialism's combined experience. We wish you every success, dear friends!

The CPSU is grateful for the warm greetings addressed to it by the representatives of communist, revolutionary-democratic, socialist and social-democratic parties, of democratic, liberation, and anti-war forces, and movements. We highly appreciate their understanding and support of the idea advanced by the Congress of establishing a comprehensive system of international security and the plan for eliminating nuclear arms before the end of the century. The CPSU is convinced that they are consonant with the true interests of all nations, all countries and all humanity.

Comrades, our Congress has shown that at the present stage, which is a turning point in our country's social development, the Leninist Party is equal to its historic tasks. On behalf of the delegates representing our entire Party I should like to say from this rostrum that we Communists set great store by the confidence placed in us by the workers, the farmers, the intelligentsia, by all Soviet people. We put above all else the interests of the people, of our Motherland, of socialism, and peace. We will spare neither effort nor energy to translate into life the decisions of the 27th Congress of the Communist Party of the Soviet Union.

Study Question

According to Gorbachev what are the most pressing problems facing the USSR in 1985?

Aleksandr Solzhenitsyn

Aleksandr Solzhenitsyn (1918–2008) was one of the best-known critics of the Soviet system. The Gulag Archipelago—published in 1973—chronicled his own experiences in the gulags and work camps of the USSR between 1945 and 1956. Solzhenitsyn sought to expose the devastating effects of the Stalinist era throughout his career. He was awarded the Nobel Prize for Literature in 1970. Between 1974 and

1994 Solzhenitsyn lived in exile in the United States, though his interest in and concern for the fate of his homeland remained strong. Rebuilding Russia, his blueprint for reviving the Russian nation, was published as a pamphlet in the Soviet Union in 1990 and then reissued as a short book in 1991.

Document Source: Aleksandr Solzhenitsyn, *Rebuilding Russia*, transl. Alexis Kilmoff (New York: Farrar, Straus, & Giroux, Inc., 1991).

Rebuilding Russia

Time has finally run out for communism.

But its concrete edifice has not yet crumbled.

And we must take care not to be crushed beneath its rubble instead of gaining liberty.

At the End of Our Endurance

Can there still be anyone among us who is unaware of our troubles, covered up though they are by mendacious statistics? For seventy years in labored pursuit of a purblind and malignant Marxist-Leninist utopia, we have lost a full third of our population—lives yielded up to the executioner or squandered in the ineptly, almost suicidally waged "Patriotic War." We have forfeited our earlier abundance, destroyed the peasant class together with its settlements, deprived the raising of crops of its whole purpose and the soil of its ability to yield a harvest, while flooding the land with man-made seas and swamps. The environs of our cities are befouled by the effluents of our primitive industry, we have poisoned our rivers, lakes, and fish, and today we are obliterating our last resources of clean water, air, and soil, speeding the process by the addition of nuclear death, further supplemented by the storage of Western radioactive wastes for money. Depleting

our natural wealth for the sake of grandiose future conquests under a crazed leadership, we have cut down our luxuriant forests and plundered our earth of its incomparable riches—the irreplaceable inheritance of our great-grandchildren—in order to sell them off abroad with uncaring hand. We have saddled our women with backbreaking, impossibly burdensome labor, torn them from their children, and have abandoned the children themselves to disease, brutishness, and a semblance of education. Our health care is utterly neglected, there are no medicines, and we have even forgotten the meaning of a proper diet. Millions lack housing, and a helplessness bred of the absence of personal rights permeates the entire country. And throughout all this we cling to only one thing: that we not be deprived of unlimited drunkenness.

Human beings are so constituted that we can put up with such ruination and madness even when they last a lifetime, but God forbid that anyone should dare to offend or slight our *nationality*! Should that occur, nothing can restrain us in our state of chronic submission: with furious courage we snatch up stones, clubs, spears, and guns and fall upon our neighbors, intent on murder and arson. Such is man: nothing has the capacity to convince us that our hunger, our poverty, our early deaths, the degeneration of our children—that any of these misfortunes can take precedence over national pride.

And that is why, in this attempt to propose some tentative steps toward our recovery and reconstruction, we are forced to begin, not with our unendurable wounds or debilitating suffering, but with a response to such questions as: How will the problem of the nationalities be approached? And within what geographical boundaries shall we heal our afflictions or die? And only thereafter shall we turn to the healing process itself.

Urgent Measures for the Russian Union

After three-quarters of a century we have all grown so poor, so tainted, and so filled with despair, that many of us are ready to give up, and it seems that the intercession of heaven alone can save us.

But miracles do not descend upon those who make no effort on their own behalf.

The fate of our children, our will to live, our millennial history, and the spirit of our ancestors, which must surely have been transferred to us in some fashion—all these things together will help us find the strength to prevail.

We may have been granted no time for reflecting upon the best-suited paths of development, no time to put together a reasoned program, and we may have no choice other than racing around frantically, plugging leaks, while imperative demands close in upon us, each one clamoring for priority. Yet we must preserve presence of mind and the wisdom of circumspection in our choice of initial measures.

I cannot presume to enumerate all these steps by myself; this must be done by a council drawing on the clearest practical minds and the best available energies. All things cry out for help in our present-day economy, and we simply cannot go on without pointing them in the right direction. Our people must urgently be made aware of the meaning of work, after half a century when no one could

Aleksandr Solzhenitsyn during his exile in the United States.
Photo by Sergei Guneyev/Time Life Pictures/Getty Images.

see any advantage to putting forth an effort—which is why nobody is available to raise crops or tend the cattle. Millions are inhabiting spaces that cannot be called homes, or are forced to spend decades in filthy dormitories. Dire poverty stalks the elderly and the handicapped. Our once magnificent expanses are befouled by industrial dumps and scarred by vehicle tracks due to lack of roads. Nature, disdained so ungratefully by us, is taking its revenge, and the radioactive blotches from Chernobyl and elsewhere are spreading ominously.

On top of all this, must we now prepare to resettle those compatriots who are losing their places of residence? Yes, unavoidably so.

Wherever shall we find the money?

But, then, how long shall we continue supplying and propping up the tyrannical regimes we have implanted the world over, regimes which are incapable of supporting themselves and which are nothing if not insatiable squanderers of our wealth: Cuba, Vietnam, Ethiopia, Angola, North Korea. We mind everyone's business, after all, and the above list is far from complete, with thousands of our "advisers" roaming about in all sorts of unlikely places. And after all the blood spilled in Afghanistan, isn't it a shame to let that country go? So, should we not dole out money there as well?. . . All this adds up to tens of billions each year.

He who cuts off *all this* at one fell stroke will deserve to be called a patriot and a true statesman.

How long and for what purpose must we keep producing ever more types of offensive weapons? And why the naval presence in all the world's oceans? Do we wish to seize the planet? The cost of all this escalates to hundreds of billions yearly. This, too, must be cut off without delay. The space program can also wait.

There is, furthermore, the preferential supplying of Eastern Europe with our ever-exploited raw materials. But we've had our stint of living together as a "socialist camp," and enough is enough. We rejoice for the countries of Eastern Europe, may they thrive in freedom, but let them pay for everything at world prices.

But what if this is not enough? Then we must stop reckless capital investment in industries that do not show signs of recovery.

There are, finally, the unimaginably huge assets of the Communist Party, a topic of much recent discussion. They certainly did manage to appropriate a lot of goods from the population over seventy years, and to use it for their pleasure. Of course, there is no way to get back all that has been wasted, scattered, and plundered, but let them at least return what is left: the buildings, resorts, special farms, and publishing houses. . . .

And the whole army of appointive bureaucrats, that parasitic multimillion-strong governing apparatus which inhibits all living forces in the nation—with their high salaries, various benefits, and special stores—we shall feed no more! Let them earn what they can by engaging in useful labor. Under the new order, eighty percent of the ministries and committees will also become unnecessary.

So that the money will come from all these sources.

> **Study Question**
>
> Would the reforms Solzhenitsyn suggested have substantially helped the former Soviet Union to recover?

Nelson Mandela

Nelson Rolihlahla Mandela (1918–2013) graduated in 1942 with a law degree and soon after joined the African National Congress (ANC). Beginning in 1948 Mandela was active in the fight against the segregation policies introduced by Daniel Malan's National Party. Mandela was first arrested, then acquitted in the 1950s. He was arrested again in 1962 and sentenced to hard labour. A 1964 trial on charges of treason brought a sentence of life in prison. Rather than disappearing into the South African penal system, Mandela gained a wide international audience

during his years in jail. In February 1990 he was released and in 1991 assumed the leadership of the ANC. In 1993 he accepted the Nobel Peace Prize on behalf of all South Africans. On 24 May 1994, just three weeks after winning the first open election in South African history, Nelson Mandela addressed the parliament in Cape Town, summarizing both the state of the nation and the changes needed to ensure a successful transition to majority rule in South Africa.

Document Source: Nelson Mandela, "State of the Nation Address, 1994"; http://www.info.gov.za/speeches/1994/170595002.htm

State of the Nation Address, 24 May 1994

Madame Speaker and Deputy Speaker, President of the Senate and Deputy President, Deputy Presidents, Chief Justice, Distinguished members of the National Assembly and the Senate, Provincial Premiers, Commanders of the Security Forces, Members of the Diplomatic Corps, Esteemed guests, Comrades, Ladies and gentlemen.

The time will come when our nation will honour the memory of all the sons, the daughters, the mothers, the fathers, the youth and the children who, by their thoughts and deeds, gave us the right to assert with pride that we are South Africans, that we are Africans and that we are citizens of the world.

The certainties that come with age tell me that among these we shall find an Afrikaner woman who transcended a particular experience and became a South African, an African and a citizen of the world. Her name is Ingrid Jonker.[1]

She was both a poet and a South African. She was both an Afrikaner and an African. She was both an artist and a human being.

In the midst of despair, she celebrated hope. Confronted with death, she asserted the beauty of life.

In the dark days when all seemed hopeless in our country, when many refused to hear her resonant voice, she took her own life.

To her and others like her, we owe a debt to life itself. To her and others like her, we owe a commitment to the poor, the oppressed, the wretched and the despised.

In the aftermath of the massacre at the anti-pass demonstration in Sharpeville she wrote that:

The child is not dead
the child lifts his fists against his mother
who shouts Africa!. . .
The child is not dead
Not at Langa nor at Nyanga
nor at Orlando nor at Sharpeville
nor at the police post at Philippi

where he lies with a bullet through his brain. . .
the child is present at all assemblies and
law-giving
the child peers through the windows of houses
and into the hearts of mothers
this child who only wanted to play in the sun at
Nyanga
is everywhere
the child grown to a man treks on through all
Africa
the child grown to a giant journeys
over the whole world
without a pass!

And in this glorious vision, she instructs that our endeavours must be about the liberation of the woman, the emancipation of the man and the liberty of the child.

It is these things that we must achieve to give meaning to our presence in this chamber and to give

Nelson Mandela's Inaugural Address, 1994. The ANC had dominated the first free election in South Africa's modern history, gaining 63 per cent of the vote.

Courtesy of the United Nations Photo Library (186835 UN/DPI/C. Sattleburger).

purpose to our occupancy of the seat of government.

And so we must, constrained by and yet regardless of the accumulated effect of our historical burdens, seize the time to define for ourselves what we want to make of our shared destiny.

The government I have the honour to lead and I dare say the masses who elected us to serve in this role, are inspired by the single vision of creating a people-centred society.

Accordingly, the purpose that will drive this government shall be the expansion of the frontiers of human fulfilment, the continuous extension of the frontiers of the freedom.

The acid test of the legitimacy of the programmes we elaborate, the government institutions we create, the legislation we adopt must be whether they serve these objectives.

Our single most important challenge is therefore to help establish a social order in which the freedom of the individual will truly mean the freedom of the individual.

We must construct that people-centred society of freedom in such a manner that it guarantees the political and the human rights of all our citizens.

As an affirmation of the government's commitment to an entrenched human rights culture, we shall immediately take steps to inform the Secretary General of the United Nations that we will subscribe to the Universal Declaration of Human Rights.

We shall take steps to ensure that we accede to the International Covenant on Civil and Political Rights, the International Covenant on Social and Economic Rights and other human rights instruments of the United Nations.

Our definition of the freedom of the individual must be instructed by the fundamental objective to restore the human dignity of each and every South African.

This requires that we speak not only of political freedoms.

My government's commitment to create a people-centred society of liberty binds us to the pursuit of the goals of freedom from want,

freedom from hunger, freedom from deprivation, freedom from ignorance, freedom from suppression and freedom from fear.

These freedoms are fundamental to the guarantee of human dignity. They will therefore constitute part of the centrepiece of what this government will seek to achieve, the focal point on which our attention will be continuously focused. . . .

My government is equally committed to ensure that we use this longer period properly fully to bring into the decision-making processes organs of civil society.

This will include the trade union movement and civic organisations, so that at no time should the government become isolated from the people. At the same time, steps will be taken to build the capacity of communities to manage their own affairs.

Precisely because we are committed to ensuring sustainable growth and development leading to a better life for all, we will continue existing programmes of fiscal rehabilitation.

We are therefore determined to make every effort to contain real general government consumption at present levels and to manage the budget deficit with a view to its continuous reduction.

Similarly, we are agreed that a permanently higher general level of taxation is to be avoided.

To achieve these important objectives will require consistent discipline on the part of both the central and the provincial governments.

Furthermore, this disciplined approach will ensure that we integrate the objectives of our Reconstruction and Development Plan within government expenditure and not treat them as incidental to the tasks of government, marginalised to the status of mere additions to the level of expenditure.

There are major areas of desperate need in our society.

As a signal of its seriousness to address these, the government will, within the next 100 days, implement various projects under the direct supervision of the President. Let me briefly mention these.

Children under the age of six and pregnant

mothers will receive free medical care in every state hospital and clinic where such need exists. Similarly, a nutritional feeding scheme will be implemented in every primary school where such need is established. A concrete process of consultation between the major stakeholders in this area will be organised immediately.

A programme is already being implemented to electrify 350,000 homes during the current financial year.

A campaign will be launched at every level of government, a public works programme designed and all efforts made to involve the private sector, organised labour, the civics and other community organisations to rebuild our townships, restore services in rural and urban areas, while addressing the issue of job creation and training, especially for our unemployed youth.

Many details of the overall reconstruction and development plan remain to be discussed, agreed and put in place. But I believe that the broad outline I have given and the immediate initiatives I have mentioned, will allow you to share my joy at the progress already made by the Government of National Unity with regard to this important matter.

We shall carry out this plan within the context of a policy aimed at building a strong and growing economy which will benefit all our people. . . .

The Government is determined forcefully to confront the scourge of unemployment, not by way of handouts but by the creation of work opportunities.

The Government will also deal sensitively with the issue of population movements into the country, to protect our workers, to guard against the exploitation of vulnerable workers and to ensure friendly relations with all countries and peoples.

The Government is also taking urgent measures to deal firmly with drug trafficking some of which is carried out by foreign nationals who are resident in the country.

We must end racism in the workplace as part of our common offensive against racism in general. No more should words like Kaffirs,

Hottentots, Coolies, Boy, Girl, and Baas be part of our vocabulary. . . .

Below I mention some of the work in which the relevant governments are already involved to translate these objectives into reality.

The Government will take steps to ensure the provision of clean water on the basis of the principle of water security for all and the introduction of proper sanitation sensitive to the protection of the environment.

We are determined to address the dire housing shortage in a vigorous manner, acting together with the private sector and the communities in need of shelter.

Health also remains a fundamental building block of the humane society we are determined to create through the implementation of the Reconstruction and Development Programme.

We must address the needs of the aged and disabled, uplift disadvantaged sectors such as the women and the youth, and improve the lives of our people in the rural communities and the informal settlements.

We must invest substantial amounts in education and training and meet our commitment to introduce free and compulsory education for a period of at least 9 years. Everywhere we must reinculcate the culture of learning and of teaching and make it possible for this culture to thrive.

We must combat such social pathologies as widespread poverty, the break down of family life, crime, alcohol and drug abuse, the abuse of children, women and the elderly, and the painful reality of street children. We are giving urgent attention to the long waiting lists for the payment of social grants which have developed in some areas, owing to lack of funds.

I am especially pleased that we have a ministry dedicated to the issue of the environment. Its work must impact on many aspects of national activity and address the question of the well-being of society as a whole and the preservation of a healthy environmental future even for generations not yet born.

As we began this address, we borrowed the words of Ingrid Jonker to focus on the plight of the children of our country.

I would now like to say that the Government will, as a matter of urgency, attend to the tragic and complex question of children and juveniles in detention and prison.

The basic principle from which we will proceed from now onwards is that we must rescue the children of the nation and ensure that the system of criminal justice must be the very last resort in the case of juvenile offenders.

I have therefore issued instruction to the Departments concerned, as a matter of urgency, to work out the necessary guidelines which will enable us to empty our prisons of children and to place them in suitable alternative care. This is in addition to an amnesty for various categories serving prisoners as will be effected in terms of what I said in my Inauguration Address two weeks ago.

In this context, I also need to make the point that the Government will also not delay unduly with regard to attending to the vexed and unresolved issue of an amnesty for criminal activities carried out in furtherance of political objectives.

We will attend to this matter in a balanced and dignified way. The nation must come to terms with its past in a spirit of openness and forgiveness and proceed to build the future on the basis of repairing and healing.

The burden of the past lies heavily on all of us, including those responsible for inflicting injury and those who suffered.

Following the letter and the spirit of the Constitution, we will prepare the legislation which will seek to free the wrongdoers from fear of retribution and blackmail, while acknowledging the injury of those who have been harmed so that the individual wrongs, injuries, fears and hopes affecting individuals are identified and attended to.

In the meantime, summoning the full authority of the position represent, we call on all concerned not to take any steps that might, in any way, impede or compromise the processes of reconciliation which the impending legislation will address.

The problem of politically motivated violence is still with us. We depend on our country's security forces to deal with this problem using all resources at their disposal. In this, and in their efforts to deal especially with criminal violence, they have our personal support and confidence.

We have also directed that all relevant ministries should engage the structures set up in terms of the National Peace Accord so that these can be invigorated to pursue their noble mission in the context of the changed circumstances in our country.

The Government will otherwise not spare any effort in ensuring that our security forces enjoy the standing they deserve of being accepted by all our people the defenders of our sovereignty, our democratic system, the guarantors of a just peace within the country and the safety and security of all citizens and their property.

Let me also take this opportunity to reiterate our assurance to the rest of the public service that the Government is firmly committed to the protection of the rights of all members of this service.

We are also determined to work with the organizations of the service to ensure that we have the democratic, non-racial, non-sexist, honest, and accountable corps of public servants which members of the Public Service themselves desire.

In this context, we must also make the observation that the Government will not waver from the principle of achieving parity in remuneration and conditions of service among all workers in the public sector.

The youth of our country are the valued possession of the nation. Without them there can be no future. Their needs are immense and urgent. They are at the centre of our reconstruction and development plan.

To address them, acting with the youth themselves, the Government will engage the representative organizations of the youth and other formations, among other things to look at the siting of a broad-based National Commission on Youth Development among the structures of Government. . . .

Tomorrow, on Africa Day, the dream of Ingrid Jonker will come to fruition. The child grown to a man will trek through all Africa. The child grown to a journey will journey over the whole world—without a pass!

Tomorrow, on Africa Day, our new flag will be hoisted in an historic ceremony at the OUA Headquarters in Addis Ababa, with the OUA having already agreed to accept us as its latest member.

Tomorrow, on Africa Day, the UN Security Council will meet to lift the last remaining sanctions against South Africa and to position the world organization to relate to our country as an honoured, responsible and peace-loving citizen.

As such, the Government is involved in discussion to determine what our contribution could be to the search for peace in Angola and Rwanda, to the reinforcement of the peace process in Mozambique, to the establishment of a new world order of mutually beneficial cooperation, justice, prosperity and peace for ourselves and for the nations of the world.

Yesterday the Cabinet also decided to apply for our country to join the Commonwealth. This important community of nations is waiting to receive us with open arms.

We have learnt the lesson that our blemishes speak of what all humanity should not do. We understand this fully that our glories point to the heights of what human genius can achieve.

In our dreams we have a vision of all our country at play in our sportsfields and enjoying deserved and enriching recreation in our theatres, galleries, beaches, mountains, plains, and game parks, in conditions of peace, security and comfort.

Our road to that glorious future lies through collective hard work to accomplish the objective of creating a people-centred society through the implementation of the vision contained in our reconstruction and development plan.

Let us all get down to work!

Note

1. Ingrid Jonker (1933–1965) was an Afrikaner poet whose work opposed the discrimination and prejudice of the Apartheid system.

> **Study Question**
>
> The details of reform laid out by Nelson Mandela in 1994 were enormously ambitious. Based on this speech, what were the most important changes that had to be achieved?

European Commission[1]

After the collapse of the Soviet bloc in the late 1980s and early 1990s, many Eastern European leaders concluded that membership in the European Union (EU) would ease the transition to market economies and democratic governance. As one of the countries best prepared for the post-Cold War transition, Hungary was also among the first nations to begin discussions, in 1990, regarding joining the EU. Its membership was approved in 2002, with the accession date set for May 2004 assuming that Hungarians voted in favour in a nation-wide referendum to be held in 2003. In the end, approximately 84 per cent of people voted in favour, though the turnout for the election was less than 50 per cent of eligible voters. The report of the European Commission that is excerpted below was drafted in 1997 and provided a general assessment of Hungary's suitability for membership—including an overview of its economic, political, social, and cultural development to that point.

Document Source: Commission Opinion on Hungary's Application for Membership of the European Union, Brussels, 15 July 1997; http://ec.europa.eu/enlargement/archives/pdf/dwn/opinions/hungary/hu-op_en.pdf

Opinion on Hungary's Application for Membership in the EU

Democracy and the Rule of Law

The far-reaching reform in October 1989 of the Hungarian Constitution of 1949, which gave rise to the new Constitution of December 1990, led to a smooth transition to a parliamentary democracy. Parliament is still working on the revision of the Constitution.

The Hungarian institutions work smoothly, the various authorities being mindful of the limits of their powers and of the need for cooperation. . . .

Elections have taken place in free and fair conditions. A centre-left coalition won in 1994. . . taking over from the conservative coalition which had been successful at the previous general elections in 1990. Hungary presents the characteristics of a democracy the smooth working of which allows the peaceful alternation of political power.

Parliament functions satisfactorily: its powers are respected and the opposition plays a full part in its activities. . . .

The central institutions of the State function smoothly.

The public administration is still facing certain difficulties: salaries and wages are still low compared with earnings in the private sector and there are certain shortcomings in the training system. The Government has tried to improve the situation by increasing civil servants' pay using the resources made available by the manpower reduction programmes.

There have been a number of cases of corruption in the Hungarian police in the last few years and its effectiveness in combating organised crime has also been called into question (as when in November 1996 top national and local police officials were removed from their posts following a number of violent settlements of account in Budapest). . . .

Civil and Political Rights

Access to justice is guaranteed in Hungary, in particular by very easily accessible appeal procedures and relatively well-developed legal aid machinery. The rights of the defence seem to be properly covered, except in the case of certain categories of foreigners and gypsies, who have difficulty in asserting their rights before the law.

The death penalty was abolished in 1990 in all circumstances.

The right not to be arbitrarily arrested is assured since no citizen can remain in detention for over 72 hours without being charged.

All citizens aged 18 or over have the right to vote.

Freedom of association and peaceful assembly are also guaranteed; evidence of this includes the increase in the number of non-governmental organisations from 8,396 in 1989 to 44,167 in 1995.

Freedom of expression is assured by the Constitution, which prohibits censorship and guarantees journalists' rights.

The public sector still plays a very large role in the media, with a monopoly of television and a dominant position in radio (only one private national channel). The Prime Minister controls, in particular, the budget given to the channels. The question of the opposition's access to the media arose during the campaign preceding the 1994 elections. The lack of legislation on this matter applicable to all the media does not give the opposition all the appropriate guarantees for fair access to new channels resulting from future privatisation. This sector is still not open to foreign operators. Under the Law of December 1995, however, the Government launched an invitation to tender in December 1996 for the establishment of a private channel to start broadcasting from 1 September 1997. The regulatory body (ORTT), which under the Law of December 1995 is responsible for issuing operating licences for private channels, is made up of representatives of all the political formations present in Parliament.

The right of ownership is guaranteed and ex-propriation must be in the public interest, with fair prior compensation. For people previously expropriated, the Government has introduced a system of partial compensation with coupons for the purchase of rural property and real estate. A 1990 law provided for restoring to the church the property which the Communist regime had taken away from it. An October 1996 decree provided for the restoration of property to the families of victims of the Holocaust through a Foundation set up for that purpose.

The Hungarian legislation in force limits for-eigners' right of ownership of agricultural land to a maximum of 300 ha. A bill before Parliament provides for possible foreign investment in public bodies which own agricultural land. The land register is computerised and at present covers virtually all the land, with almost 99 per cent of the 7.5 million deeds of ownership having been registered.

Respect for privacy is assured by the need to obtain a warrant from the judicial authorities before property can be searched or telephone communications tapped.

As Hungary acceded to the Geneva Convention on refugees only in respect of refugees from other European countries and has still not provided satisfactory access to justice and shelter for these people, the situation regarding political refugees seemed worrying, but the Government has put a bill before Parliament abolishing geographical restrictions on the application of the Geneva Convention and has agreed to close the Kirstarcsa[2] refugee camp, which had been very strongly criticised by the United Nations High Commissioner for Refugees.

A number of organisations have reported cases of inhumane, degrading treatment by the police with no steps having been systematically taken to punish the perpetrators. There have also been instances of such treatment in the prisons, despite the steps recently taken by the Hungarian authorities. . . .

Minorities represent some 6 per cent of the population (4 to 5 per cent gypsies (Roma) and the remainder are mainly German, Slovaks, Croats, and Romanians).

There are first of all a number of international standards to ensure the protection of minorities. Hungary ratified the Framework Convention on minorities in September 1995 and subscribes to the principles of Recommendation 1201 of the Parliamentary Assembly of the Council of Europe providing for the recognition of collective rights for minorities, although this text is not legally binding. . . .

The gypsies (Roma) have a special place. The Hungarian Government's report on the situation regarding the national and ethnic minorities approved by Parliament in March 1997 recognises that the gypsies (Roma) are still frequently subjected to attacks and discriminatory measures and considers that the situation is in danger of worsening over the next few years. The same document states that present legislation does not make it possible effectively to prevent the outbreak of "ethnic conflicts" of which the gypsies (Roma) are victims.

Their social situation is often very difficult. According to the government report on this matter, inequality of opportunity between the gypsies (Roma) and the rest of the Hungarian population has increased in recent years, while the standard of education of the gypsies (Roma) has improved. Similarly, the unemployment rate among this population is four to five times that of the national average and life expectancy is ten years less than for the rest of the population. This situation can largely be explained by sociological factors. The gypsies (Roma) are also subject to discrimination on the labour market.

The Hungarian Government has undertaken to implement a programme to reduce the inequality of opportunities between the gypsies (Roma) and the rest of the population.

The Council for coordinating matters

concerning the gypsies has since the end of 1995 been supervising all the action taken by the various state institutions in this area. The Committee for the Gypsy Programme, established in March 1996, examines the political and social problems encountered by the gypsy community, under the direct authority of the Prime Minister. This community benefits from the protective provisions of the 1993 Law and has 477 local governments for minorities.

General Evaluation

The Hungarian institutions work smoothly, the various authorities being mindful of the limits of their powers and of the need for cooperation. Elections have taken place in free and fair conditions and have allowed a switch in political power in 1990 and 1994. The opposition plays the customary part in the operation of the institutions.

There are no major problems regarding observance of fundamental rights in the country. The rights of minorities are guaranteed and protected.

Although some improvement is still needed, progress has been made in the form of measures recently taken by the government to ensure justice and protection for the Roma (gypsies). Efforts to combat corruption need to be made more effective.

Hungary presents the characteristics of a democracy with stable institutions which guarantee the rule of law, human rights, and respect for, and the protection of, minorities.

Notes

1. The European Commission is the executive body of the European Union.
2. The Kirstarcsa (Kerepestarcsa) refugee camp was used to detain any person deemed to have entered Hungary illegally between 1989 and 1995. The camp closed in 1995 after groups such as Amnesty International exposed the extremely poor conditions in the camp as well as the denial of basic rights to the persons interned there.

Study Question

What, according to this report, are the most important elements of a democratic state?

Aleksander Kwaśniewski

Aleksander Kwaśniewski (b. 1954) served as president of Poland for ten years, between 1995 and 2005, after replacing Solidarity leader Lech Walesa, whose popularity plummeted amidst the economic turmoil of the post-Soviet era transition. As the economy gradually recovered, Kwaśniewski concentrated on the establishment of a new constitution for Poland, and on negotiating his country's entry into both NATO

and the European Union. The following is an excerpt from a speech delivered to members of the government in January 1998. Despite concerns regarding Kwaśniewski's far left politics, he was elected to a second term as president in 2000.

Document Source: Aleksander Kwaśniewski, *We Won the Future: 10 Years of Presidency of Aleksander Kwaśniewski—Addresses, Interviews, Documents* (Warsaw: Amicus Europae, 2008), 182–5.

We Won the Future

The other issue is the economic growth, which I treat as the main thing. The past two years were a period of economic growth and I am convinced that Poland can afford its continuation and make

it a sound foundation for solving the numerous problems we are facing. Considering this, I am open to all proposals, which will consolidate the economic growth in Poland, which will change the structure of the economy into a more effective one. I am open to the proposals, which will augment the competitiveness of Polish economy, which will help solve our social problems especially such as unemployment, poverty, or bridging the civilizational gap, which still exists between the highly developed countries and Poland. An extremely important thing—and I mentioned it in my election programme and will assess government proposals from this angle—are the costs of the reform and spreading them so that no social group could have the feeling of being deprived of chances or handicapped. . . .

As far as the economic issues are concerned, I would like to assure you that I would cooperate with the government also in case of those decisions, which raised controversies in recent time. As I said, I am ready to seriously talk about the social insurance system and its reform, which will take up the difficult problem of uniformed services. I think that 1998 offers enough time to think about such a formula, which would be acceptable from the point of view of the comprehensive social insurance system and which would not be received by the uniformed services sector as budgetary saving done at their cost. I realise that the problem has many economic and social aspects. I reiterate my offer of a serious dialogue on this issue.

The situation is similar in the case of other laws, which will consolidate the economic growth and which will spur the indispensable restructuring of the Polish economy. I inform you that a team of economic advisers headed by Prof. Marek Belka will cooperate with me. I think that this is a good place to elaborate such standpoints, which would not raise controversies on the government–president line. My most sincere care is to maintain the economic growth and take up such actions, which would protect Poland against crisis phenomena, which are known also in our part of Europe. . . .

I would also like to inform Mr prime minister and all ministers about my special interest, stemming from the role the president plays in the system of the state, in such areas as social policy, education, and culture. I would like to count on cooperation with competent ministers in seeking solutions, which would modernise these areas. It seems to me that Poland, after the great success of the eight years of transformation should now start realising a more ambitious and difficult task: to be competitive, cope with the competition, which, in my opinion, will be a major sign of the twenty-first century. And we, without good education, education in the first place, without high level of science, high level of culture, will be in a difficult situation. That is why I think that independently of all the overwhelming current problems it is necessary to deal with things of such cardinal importance as the educational reform. It seems to me that here we should focus our attention and invite different social communities and political groupings to cooperation. If we want to be competitive, we need a grand reform of the educational system; the strengthening of Polish science and recognition that culture may also be an element of the Polish image and Polish competitiveness. This is not a supplement; it can be a strong point and the main argument we shall usher in to the European structures.

This requires not only discussion but also outlays in the first place. It requires understanding when one talks about money, about the organisational structures and about people. I would like to assure you that, in this respect, there will be support on my part. Esteemed ladies and gentlemen, I understand social policy broadly not only as a reform of social insurance and health service system but also as the problem of housing, the handicapped and poor communities and the problem of imbalance, which in Poland is an undeniable fact. I proceed from the Koszalin province and I observe how this level of imbalance is intensifying instead of dying out. It seems, therefore, that the current social policy in Poland, especially in the context of the administrative reform must take into account this major problem of growing imbalance between the individual regions and communities. Without finding statutory, economic solutions we shall soon—I stress soon—find ourselves in a situation far more dramatic than Italy, where there is the rich north on the one hand, and the still backward south, on the other. In Poland, the differences are growing rather than diminishing. I would like to know the opinion of the government what could and should be done in this respect. (. . .)

> **Study Question**
>
> What does Kwaśniewski see as the key to Poland's success as the country moves into the twenty-first century?

Robert J. Donia

Robert J. Donia (b. 1945) is a specialist in Modern Balkan History and a Research Associate in the Center for Russian, East European, and Eurasian Studies at the University of Michigan. He has published a number of works on the complex history of the Balkan region, focusing in particular on the relationships among the region's many divergent peoples. Donia has served as an expert witness before the International Criminal Tribunal for the Former Yugoslavia (ICTY) at The Hague on a number of occasions. The excerpt that follows was taken from Donia's overview of the History of Bosnia-Herzegovina which was prepared for the ICTY in August 2001.

Document Source: Robert J. Donia, "Bosanski Šamac and the History of Bosnia and Herzegovina – Statement of Expert Witness Presented to the International Criminal Tribunal for the Former Yugoslavia" 14 August 2001, evidence #IT95-9 Simic et al; ICTY Court Records http://icr.icty.org

Ethnic Cleansing

"From advocating Serbian control over all areas inhabited by Serbs to expelling the non-Serbian population from such areas is but a small step," noted Tadeusz Mazowiecki, the former Polish Prime Minister who served as Special Rapporteur of the UN Commission on Human Rights for the former Yugoslavia. Serbian armed forces joined with SDS[1] local authorities to take that step in the first months of the war that began in 1992. After visiting the region in August and October 1992, Mazowiecki and those accompanying him reported that "massive and systematic violations of human rights" were underway in BH[2], conducted principally in areas that were under Serbian control.

"The term ethnic cleansing refers to the elimination by the ethnic group exercising control over a given territory of members of other ethnic groups," according to Mazowiecki's report.

While noting that a variety of means were used to cleanse Serb-controlled territory of non-Serbs, certain methods were widely used:

> replacement by extremists of those elected representatives who refused to cooperate with ethnic cleaning [sic], harassment, discrimination, beatings, torture, summary executions, expulsions, forced crossing of the confrontation line, confiscation of property, dismissal from work, intimidation, destruction of mosques . . .

The report linked these practices to:

> political objectives formulated and pursued by Serbian nationalists, namely ensuring Serbian control over all territories inhabited by significant numbers of Serbs, as well as adjacent

territories assimilated to them owing to logistical and military considerations.

It was frequent practice, according to this and other reports, for the Serbian military forces to direct artillery and mortar fire at civilian towns and villages prior to an incursion by infantry troops or paramilitary forces. The attacks were often justified by alleged shooting at a Serbian patrol or other aggression emanating from the settlement being attacked. Those who did not flee were often subjected to identity checks and ordered to turn in their arms. Homes of Muslims and Croats were searched and sometimes torched, and on several occasions local non-Serb leaders were forced to make statements on local radio stations announcing a change of authority and urging local citizens not to resist. Some Muslims and Croats were summarily executed; others were put in buses and taken to camps; and others were allowed to remain. Some became hostages to be held for an "exchange of prisoners" with the ABiH or HVO.[3]

A legal regimen was frequently introduced to assure compliance by the remaining population and control by the Serbian authorities. Mark Mazower has described this as a "bureaucratic dimension reminiscent of National Socialist occupation policy during the Second World War." Laws were designed to limit the movement of non-Serbs, provide stern punishments for those who had abandoned their homes, and redistribute the property of those who had fled. Not all of these policies were implemented everywhere, but most of them have been noted at many locations that were purged of non-Serbs by 1993.

Military takeover, particularly when followed by the ethnic cleansing of territory, gave important strategic advantages to the conquerors. International negotiators typically began the peacemaking process by seeking a cease-fire along existing lines of confrontation, and then advanced peace settlement plans based on a combination of military holdings and the ethnic composition of the territories concerned. Since no western power appeared ready to alter military holdings by force of arms, international peacemaking efforts relied more on existing conquests and the good will of the parties than on

UN Protection Force in Vukovar, Croatia, July 1992. The limited mandate of the UN force crippled its ability to contain the ethnic unrest in the Balkans.

Courtesy of the United Nations Photo Library (159206 UN/DPI/S. Whitehouse).

credible threats of armed intervention. Although the International Conference on the Former Yugoslavia was committed in principle to the return of refugees to their homes, in practice ethnic cleansing significantly weakened the claims of rival groups to reclaim that territory.

The importance of conquest and cleansing became starkly evident in the peace agreement that ended the Croatian war, signed on 2 January 1992 between the JNA[4] and Croatia with the mediation of former US Secretary of State Cyrus Vance. The territorial division followed closely the lines of confrontation and interposed UN peacekeeping forces between the rival military forces while providing for a reversal of ethnic cleansing only at a future date. Thus the nature

of internationally-sponsored negotiations gave a substantial benefit to any armed formation with the temerity to sponsor or engage in widespread ethnic cleansing in the wake of military conquest.

Notes

1. The Serbian Democratic Party (SDS) in Bosnia-Herzegovina.
2. Bosnia-Herzegovina.
3. ABiH: Army of the Republic of Bosnia-Herzegovina; HVO: Croatian Defence Council.
4. JNA: Yugoslav National Army.

Study Question

In what ways can the international response described here be seen to have facilitated ethnic cleansing?

Raúl Castro

Raúl Castro (b. 1931) assumed the presidency of Cuba in 2008, when illness forced his brother, Fidel, to step down from his day-to-day governing functions. Of the two brothers, it was Raúl who was first attracted to socialist doctrines as a student in Havana. He was jailed for almost two years after a failed effort to topple the Batista government in 1953, but played a pivotal role in the revolution that culminated in Batista's exile on 1 January 1959. Despite the perception that Raúl was the more doctrinaire of

the Castro brothers, his tenure has been characterized by a number of increasingly bold reform programs designed to transform Cuba's economy without sacrificing the nation's fundamentally socialist orientation. The following excerpt from an April 2011 speech addresses some of the difficulties of modernization, especially economic reform.

Document Source: Raúl Castro Ruz, "Closing Remarks at the 6th Party Congress, 21 April 2011"; http://en.cubadebate.cu/opinions/2011/04/21/closing-remarks-raul-castro-ruz-party-congress-cuba

Closing Remarks at the 6th Party Congress, 21 April 2011

Dear Fidel,
Comrades,
We have come to the end of this Congress after intensive working sessions where the Cuban communists have discussed and adopted the Guidelines of the Economic and Social Policy of the Party and the Revolution, the Central Report and various resolutions on the main issues examined.

I think that the best and most productive

way to commemorate the 50th Anniversary of the Victory over the Playa Girón (Bay of Pigs) mercenary invasion, on a day like this 19 April 1961, is precisely this excellent Party Congress. This meeting comes to an end more than five months after the onset of the Guidelines discussions. This was a profoundly democratic and transparent process whose indisputable protagonist was our people under the Party's leadership. . . .

The updating of the economic model is not a miracle that can happen overnight like some people believe. Its full development will only be attained gradually in the course of five years for it requires a conscientious work of planning and co-ordination both in legal terms and in the thorough training of all those involved in its implementation.

It will also be necessary to work intensively providing the people with adequate information on every measure adopted while, at the same time, keeping our feet and ears firmly on and attentively to the ground, to be able to overcome the obstacles we encounter, and to quickly rectify the mistakes we make in implementation.

We are convinced that the main enemy we are confronting and shall confront will be our own inefficiencies and that an endeavor of such a great significance to the future of our country cannot be tackled recklessly or hastily. We will make every change required, as Fidel indicated in his *Reflections* published yesterday, but we will do it at the adequate pace mindful of our objective conditions and always with our people's support and understanding. We will never risk our most powerful weapon: the unity of our nation in support of the Revolution and its programs.

Chauvinism aside, I think that Cuba is one of the few countries in the world in which conditions exist to transform its economic model and leave the crisis behind while avoiding social trauma. First of all because our patriotic people know that their force stems from their monolithic unity, the justice of their cause and military training as well as from their high instruction and pride in their history and revolutionary roots.

We shall advance resolutely despite the US blockade and the adverse conditions prevailing in the international market, which among other things, limit Cuba's access to financial sources and expose it to the oil prices spiral that impinges on the prices of the rest of the raw materials and food. Simply put, everything that we purchase abroad is more expensive.

Barely a few months into the year 2011 and the data already show that the additional cost of imports for this year amounts to over 800 millions USD. This is just on account of price increases and only to buy the same quantities planned; therefore, we will be forced to make adjustments to the plan adopted last December, as soon as this Congress is over.

At the moment, saving all kinds of resources is one of the main things that our country can do to preserve our income since there is still irrational spending and huge reserves of efficiency remain untapped. We should work on this with much common sense and political sensitivity.

Despite the existing acceptable situation to this date concerning the delivery of fallow lands in usufruct, in compliance with Legislative Decree No. 259 of 2008, there are still thousands and thousands of hectares of arable land waiting for those willing to produce what our people and the national economy keep demanding and that can be grown in our farmland to replace the increasingly expensive imports of a number of products that are today benefiting foreign suppliers instead of our farmers. . . .

In order to succeed, the first thing we need to change in the life of the Party is its mentality, which as a psychological barrier will, in my opinion, be more difficult to overcome for it is tied to many years of repeated dogmas and obsolete criteria. It will also be indispensable to correct mistakes and to shape, with rationality and firm principles, a comprehensive vision of the future that will guarantee the preservation and development of Socialism under the present circumstances.

In terms of the cadre policy, the election of the new Central Committee, its Secretariat and Political Bureau, and their presentation this morning, constitute a first step towards compliance with the agreements reached at this Congress, particularly with respect to the beginning of a gradual process of renovation and rejuvenation of the cadre in different governmental and political positions. At the same time, the gender and racial composition of these organs has been considerably improved.

The Central Committee is now made up by 115 members; 48 of them are women, for a 41.7 per cent. This is more than three times the 13.3 per cent proportion obtained in the previous Congress. The number of black and mixed blood people is 36, which accounts for 31.3 per cent of the total, and 10 per cent higher than before. . . .

On a day like this, our gratitude goes to the current socialist countries for their continuous cooperation and support during these years of hard battles and sacrifices.

Our brothers and sister in the Third World, especially those from Latin America and the Caribbean, who are making great efforts to transform the legacy of centuries of colonial domination, should know that they can always count on our solidarity and support.

Our fraternal greetings also go to the communist parties and other progressive forces all over the planet fighting restlessly with the deep conviction that a better world is possible.

I also wish to express the recognition of the Cuban people to all those governments that every year claim, with their voices and votes at the United Nations, for the removal of the economic, commercial, and financial blockade imposed on Cuba by the United States. . . .

Study Question

To what extent do the problems identified by Castro, mirror those identified by his brother in the 1960 speech included in Chapter Eleven?

Web Resources

US Intelligence and the End of the Cold War
> https://www.cia.gov/library/center-for-the-study-of-intelligence/kent-csi/vol44no3/html/v44i3a02p.htm

Cold War International History Project
> http://wilsoncenter.org/program/cold-war-international-history-project

Communism: End of an Era
> http://news.bbc.co.uk/hi/english/static/special_report/1999/09/99/iron_curtain/default.htm

Nelson Mandela Centre of Memory
> http://www.nelsonmandela.org

Recommended Reading

Milan Kundera, *Ignorance: A Novel* (New York: Perennial, 2003). The central themes of *Ignorance*, set in post-communist Prague, concern the experience of exile and homecoming, and the nature of memory and identity. As in his other works, Kundera focuses on the nature of perceptions and their impact on reality.

Andrei Makine, *Requiem for a Lost Empire* (Washington, DC: Washington Square Press, 2003). Makine's novel spans the entire history of the Soviet Empire, from the Bolshevik Revolution in 1917 to the fall of communism. The narrative is told over three generations of fathers and sons and their experiences of collectivization, the Second World War, the Cold War and its intrigues, and finally, the last years of the USSR.

Ralph Peters, *Flames of Heaven* (Mechanicsburg, PA: Stackpole Books, 2003). Peters's novel examines life during the final years of the failing Soviet Union through the eyes of a disaffected Latvian artist and a decorated veteran of the Afghan war. The story moves from East Germany to Latvia to Uzbekistan amidst political turmoil and the potential threat of Islamic fundamentalism.

Irene Zabytko, *The Sky Unwashed* (Chapel Hill, NC: Algonquin Books, 2000). *The Sky Unwashed* is a documentary novel set amidst the 1986 disaster at Chernobyl and the chaos that followed in small villages across Ukraine. Disorganized evacuations lead many survivors to return home to the contaminated villages, frustrated with the bureaucratic response and struggling to find a way to survive.

Recommended Viewing

Czlowiek Z Zelaza [*Man of Iron*] (Poland, 1981). Director: Andrzej Wajda. In a combination of documentary and fictional footage, actors and real political figures (Lech Walesa appears briefly) tell the story of the Gdansk shipyard labour activists and the formation of the Solidarity movement.

Red Dawn (USA, 1984). Director: John Milius. *Red Dawn*, though built on an absurd plot involving a joint Soviet–Cuban invasion of the United States, captures much of the renewed anti-communist paranoia of the Reagan era.

Death of Apartheid (UK, 1995). Director: Stephen Clarke. *Death of Apartheid* is a made-for-TV film which tells the story of Nelson Mandela's release from prison, the final days of the Apartheid system, and the election of the ANC.

Wag the Dog (USA, 1997). Director: Barry Levinson. In the post–Cold War world an American president attempts to divert attention from an impending scandal by creating a fictitious war with Albania. Levinson's film provides a powerful commentary on the power of media spin-doctors, the gullibility of the average citizen, and the nation's general lack of geopolitical knowledge.

Good Bye Lenin (Germany, 2002). Director: Wolfgang Becker. This insightful film is set in East Germany during the fall of communism. As Westernization rushes into the East Bloc, one man attempts to maintain the illusion of life under the old socialist regime in order to preserve his mother's health. Becker underscores the divide between East and West, while reflecting on the complex question of identity in newly reunified Germany.

The Fog of War (USA, 2003). Director: Errol Morris (Documentary). This documentary, based in part on Robert McNamara's memoir *In Retrospect*, tells the story of President John F. Kennedy's former Secretary of Defense. The film reflects on the beliefs of the early 1960s on Vietnam, the subsequent realization that the United States had made a number of key mistakes, and the lessons that must be learned from this and applied to future foreign policy.

Mañana (Cuba, 2006). Director: Alejandro Moya. Moya's 2006 film provides the audience with a look at the lives, aspirations, and excesses of Cubans in the early 2000s. Moya financed *Mañana* outside of official channels and is considered one of Cuba's most important independent filmmakers.

16

One World—One People

In the aftermath of the Second World War the power of technology to transform human existence—even to destroy human existence—was evident as never before. Entire nations lay in ruins, devastated by "conventional" aerial bombardment and, in the case of Hiroshima and Nagasaki, by atomic weapons. Once the Soviets successfully tested an atomic bomb in 1949—several years ahead of the schedule predicted by US military analysts—the nuclear arms race began in earnest. New, more powerful weapons such as the hydrogen bomb soon followed, some designed for tactical use, as in the case of the neutron bomb, which was intended to target humans while leaving buildings and infrastructure intact. The stability attained when the US and Soviets achieved a state of Mutual Assured Destruction (MAD) did little to reassure the ordinary citizen living in a bipolar world.

Spurred in part by the looming spectre of nuclear annihilation and also by the dramatic images of the planet Earth provided by the space program, attention in the 1960s increasingly turned to environmental issues. The 1962 publication of Rachel Carson's seminal work *Silent Spring* raised new and troubling questions regarding the long-term effects of the use of the chemical pesticide DDT. Thus the first "environmentalists" focused primarily on the impact of chemicals on the environment and on the question of nuclear testing. Groups such as the Don't Make a Wave Committee (later renamed Greenpeace) attempted to interrupt planned nuclear tests. Meanwhile, major chemical companies such as Dow and Monsanto soon became targets of both antiwar protestors—due to the widespread use of chemical defoliants such as Agent Orange in Vietnam—and of the first environmental groups. Subsequently, many of these organizations broadened their focus to other pressing environmental issues, such as pollution, acid rain, and ozone depletion.

As the twenty-first century dawned, however, the increasing pace of globalization brought a renewed concern for the fate of the planet—now burdened with a population soon to exceed seven billion. Corporations had extended their reach around the world, seeking cheap labour and, often, lax environmental regulations, to the detriment of many of Earth's peoples. While the impact of oil spills and toxic chemical leaks made headlines around the world, no single issue attracted greater public and scientific attention than the concern over global climate change. Numerous scientific studies pointed to a pattern of climate change beginning during the industrial revolution and accelerating during the twentieth century. Critics countered that the global climate has always passed through cycles of heating and warming, but the alarming melting of polar ice caps at the turn of the century gave new weight to scientific claims regarding climate change.

Thus the environmental groups found common ground with anti-globalization forces. The readings in this chapter focus on the development of the environmental movement, and on the interconnections between globalization and the environment. The passage from *Silent Spring* introduces the reader to Rachel Carson's ground-breaking research on DDT. Rex Weyler recalls the origins and evolution of the group that would become Greenpeace. Excerpts from the report on the Bhopal disaster highlight the horrendous human toll of toxic chemical spills. The 1987 Brundtland Report was one of the first to assess the relationship between economic development and environmental impact. Five years later, in 1992, the Rio Earth Summit translated many of the issues raised by the Brundtland Report into a concrete set of principles designed to balance environmental protection against the need for economic development. The relationship between globalization and the environment is evident in the final four documents which make up this chapter: an analysis of race, poverty, and globalization by john a. powell and S.P. Udayakumar, Robert Kaplan's thoughts on the global power of the corporation, Al Gore's Nobel Prize acceptance speech, and, finally, Stephen Hawking's arguments for a return to space.

Rachel Carson

Rachel Carson (1907–1964) was a biologist and naturalist by training. Her work on river and ocean ecosystems in the 1940s led to an increasing awareness of the impact of synthetic pesticide use. Carson's concern for the environment was crystallized in 1957 by a US Department of Agriculture (USDA) campaign to eliminate fire-ants. Carson argued that the effects of the pesticides used had been inadequately researched. Her 1962 monograph Silent Spring *assessed the human and animal toll of widespread pesticide use. Despite sustained attacks from chemical companies and their political representatives, the book contributed to the successful ban on the pesticide DDT in 1972.*

Document Source: Rachel Carson, *Silent Spring* (New York: Fawcett Crest, 1962), chapter two.

Silent Spring

The problem whose attempted solution has brought such a train of disaster in its wake is an accompaniment of our modern way of life. Long before the age of man, insects inhabited the earth—a group of extraordinarily varied and adaptable beings. Over the course of time since man's advent, a small percentage of the more than half a million species of insects have come into conflict with human welfare in two principal ways: as competitors for the food supply and as carriers of human disease.

Disease-carrying insects become important where human beings are crowded together, especially under conditions where sanitation is poor, as in time of natural disaster or war or in situations of extreme poverty and deprivation. Then control of some sort becomes necessary. It is a sobering fact, however, as we shall presently see, that the method of massive chemical control has had only limited success, and also threatens to worsen the very conditions it is intended to curb.

Under primitive agricultural conditions the farmer had few insect problems. These arose with the intensification of agriculture—the devotion of immense acreages to a single crop. Such a system set the stage for explosive increases in specific insect populations. Single-crop farming does not take advantage of the principles by which nature works; it is agriculture as an engineer might conceive it to be. Nature has introduced great variety into the landscape, but man has displayed a passion for simplifying it. Thus he undoes the built-in checks and balances by which nature holds the species within bounds. One important natural check is a limit on the amount of suitable habitat for each species. Obviously then, an insect that lives on wheat can build up its population to much higher levels on a farm devoted to wheat than on one in which wheat is intermingled with other crops to which the insect is not adapted.

The same thing happens in other situations. A generation or more ago, the towns of large areas of the United States lined their streets with the noble elm tree. Now the beauty they hopefully created is threatened with complete destruction as disease sweeps through the elms, carried by a beetle that would have only limited chance to build up large populations and to spread from tree to tree if the elms were only occasional trees in a richly diversified planting.

Another factor in the modern insect problem is one that must be viewed against a background of geologic and human history: the spreading of thousands of different kinds of organisms from their native homes to invade new territories. . . .

The importation of plants is the primary agent in the modern spread of species, for animals have almost invariably gone along with the plants. . . . In new territory, out of reach of the restraining hand of the natural enemies that kept down its numbers in its native land, an invading plant or animal is able to become enormously abundant. Thus it is no accident that our most troublesome insects are introduced species.

These invasions, both the naturally occurring and those dependent on human assistance, are likely to continue indefinitely. Quarantine and massive chemical campaigns are only extremely expensive ways of buying time. We are faced . . . "with a life-and-death need not just to find new technological means of suppressing this plant or that animal"; instead we need the basic knowledge of animal populations and their relations to their surroundings that will "promote an even balance and damp down the explosive power of outbreaks and new invasions."

Much of the necessary knowledge is now available but we do not use it. We train ecologists in our universities and even employ them in our governmental agencies but we seldom take their advice. We allow the chemical death rain to fall as though there were no alternative, whereas in fact there are many, and our ingenuity could soon discover many more if given opportunity.

Have we fallen into a mesmerized state that makes us accept as inevitable that which is inferior or detrimental, as though having lost the will or the vision to demand that which is good? Such thinking, in the words of the ecologist Paul Shepard, "idealizes life with only its head out of water, inches above the limits of toleration of the corruption of its own environment . . . Why should we tolerate a diet of weak poisons, a home in insipid surroundings, a circle of acquaintances who are not quite our enemies, the noise of motors with just enough relief to prevent insanity? Who would want to live in a world which is just not quite fatal?"

Yet such a world is pressed upon us. The crusade to create a chemically sterile, insect-free world seems to have engendered a fanatic zeal on the part of many specialists and most of the so-called control agencies. On every hand there is evidence that those engaged in spraying operations exercise a ruthless power. . . .

It is not my contention that chemical insecticides

Rachel Carson collecting specimens of marine life in the Florida Keys in 1955.

Courtesy US Fish and Wildlife Service National Digital Library.

must never be used. I do contend that we have put poisonous and biologically potent chemicals indiscriminately into the hands of persons largely or wholly ignorant of their potentials for harm. We have subjected enormous numbers of people to contact with these poisons, without their consent and often without their knowledge. . . .

I contend, furthermore, that we have allowed these chemicals to be used with little or no advance investigation of their effect on soil, water, wildlife, and man himself. Future generations are unlikely to condone our lack of prudent concern for the integrity of the natural world that supports all life.

Study Question

What does Carson believe to be the most important causes of the dependence on chemicals such as DDT to eradicate insect populations?

Rex Weyler

Rex Weyler (b. 1947) is a journalist and activist who has been involved in the Canadian environmental movement since the early 1970s. He took part in many of the early campaigns of Greenpeace and served on the board of the Greenpeace Foundation, as well as working as a photographer for the organization from 1974 to 1979. In the 2007

article which follows, Weyler recalls the context in which concern for the environment first emerged, as well as the events leading to the creation of the Greenpeace Foundation and its first anti-nuclear testing campaigns.

Document Source: Rex Weyler, "Waves of Compassion: The Founding of Greenpeace. Where Are They Now?" *Utne Reader*, October 9, 2007.

Waves of Compassion

I arrived in Vancouver, on the west coast of Canada, in the spring of 1972 as a fugitive of American justice, a draft-resister with the FBI on my trail and intimidating my family to give me up. I faced 25 years in prison had they caught me. My wife of six months, Glenn, and I slept by the furnace in the cellar of a Vancouver shelter set up for war objectors on 7th Avenue near Fir Street. We had our sleeping bags, a change of clothes, 47 dollars, and a wrinkled piece of paper with the names of

Canadian peace activists who might help us.

Unitarian minister and University librarian Mac Elrod and his wife Norma took us in and introduced us to the local pacifist crowd. I found a job as reporter and photographer at the *North Shore News* community newspaper. While covering a local story, I met Bree Drummond who was sitting in a platform, high in a cottonwood tree to save it from being felled for a parking lot by North Vancouver maintenance crews. Her boyfriend,

Rod Marining, was a wild Yippie environment-alist who had helped stop the construction of a Four Seasons Hotel at the entrance to Vancouver's magnificent Stanley Park by declaring the land "All Season Park" and camping out on the site until the developers gave up. He also had sailed for the Aleutian Island of Amchitka to protest a US atomic bomb test there as a member of the Don't Make A Wave Committee that had changed its name to the "Greenpeace Foundation" that spring.

Rod introduced me to Bob Hunter from Winnipeg, clearly the hippest young journalist in the city, writing a daily column in the Vancouver *Sun* in which he explained Gestalt Therapy, de-scribed peyote ceremonies, introduced edgy psych-ologists like R.D. Laing, and quoted famed ecologist Rachel Carson. Hunter had written a brilliant novel, *Erebus*, and a profound, post-McLuhan analysis of media and social consciousness, *Storming of the*

Mind. He had also sailed on the protest boat with the Don't Make a Wave Committee. He had a beard, long hair, and a large leather bag over his shoul-der, filled with newspaper clippings, books, and his own journal in which he wrote incessantly. I liked him right away, traveled in similar media circles, and began sharing beer and philosophy with him at the Cecil Hotel pub. Now, three decades later, the Cecil is a glitzy strip bar, but in the early 1970s it was a pool hall and hangout for Vancouver radicals and intelligentsia. Greenpeace had no public office at this time. We sat near the pay-phone to conduct both our journalist and activist business. . . .

It was here in the pub that Dr Paul Spong, a sci-entist at the Vancouver Aquarium, appeared in 1974 promoting his radical idea that we should put our lives on the line to save the whales. The anti-war ac-tivists were skeptical at first, but Spong's idea would soon change the face of this little band of radicals.

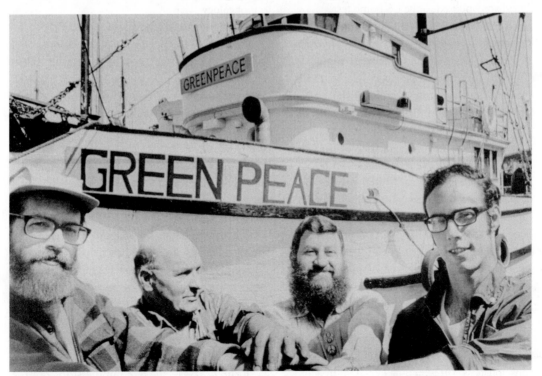

Preparing to sail from Vancouver to Amchitka Island to protest nuclear testing in 1971. From left to right: Jim Bohlen, John Cormack, Erving Stowe, and Paul Cote.

Image © Bettman/Corbis.

On an Ocean Named for Peace

In 1969 in Vancouver hippies and revolutionaries mixed gleefully in the redbrick coffee houses of Gastown, and in the rainbow-painted organic juice bars of tree-lined Kitsilano near the University of British Columbia. "Revolutions," says Hunter, "start at the outer fringes of the empire, in this case the American Empire." When the US announced that summer that they were going to test a 1.2 megaton nuclear bomb on the Aleutian Island of Amchitka, Vancouver peaceniks, love children, American draft dodgers, and Marxist revolutionaries began to agitate. In September 1969 Hunter warned in his newspaper column of "a distinct danger that the tests might set in motion earthquakes and tidal waves which could sweep from one end of the Pacific to the other". This image of the tidal wave captured the imagination of Canadians opposed to the US bomb test.

Three decades later Hunter recalls, "In Vancouver at that time there was a convergence of hippies, draft dodgers, Tibetan monks, sea dogs, artists, radical ecologists, rebel journalists, Quakers, and expatriate Yanks in the one major city that happened to be closest to Amchitka Island, where the US wanted to explode a bomb. Greenpeace was born of all of this."

Vancouver lawyer Hamish Bruce read Hunter's columns and called the reporter. Bruce wanted to start an organization called the "Green Panthers". Hunter and Bruce became fast friends. They plotted to establish the Green Panthers as the ecological equivalent of the Black Panthers, whose leader, Fred Hampton, Hunter had interviewed in Chicago. "Our idea," says Bruce today, "was that ecology was the sleeping giant, the issue that was ultimately going to rock the world."

At that time, Hunter was writing his third book, *Storming of the Mind*, about the "new holistic consciousness," in which he declares "In ecology we see the new consciousness finding its roots". Hunter predicted that continued environmental

deterioration would lead to the rise of "the Green Panthers or their equivalent," and he advocated "the hoisting of the green flag."

On 2 October, when the US detonated the bomb at Amchitka, a mob from Vancouver stormed the US border, closing it to traffic for two hours. A banner placed at the border crossing read: "Don't Make a Wave" in reference to the potential tidal wave. In January 1970 the protestors moved to the US Embassy and "liberated" Granville Street in downtown Vancouver. The seeds of Greenpeace were in these crowds. Hippies on bicycles milled among the anti-bomb protestors, stopping cars and delivering speeches about ecology.

Among the protestors was freelance journalist Ben Metcalfe, who had a radio program on the CBC. Metcalfe, on his own initiative, had placed 12 billboard signs in Vancouver that read:

Ecology
Look it up. You're involved.

"It's hard to imagine now," says Metcalfe, "but in those days most people had no idea what the word ecology meant. I was doing environmental stories on my radio program and I started a campaign to stop the Skagit River Dam. In the winter of 1969 and 1970, the US bomb tests were the hot story. The night we closed the US border, Hunter and Hamish Bruce were there, and Jim and Marie Bohlen." . . .

. . . Marie Bohlen, inspired by the Quaker boat the Golden Rule, suggested to Jim one morning over coffee that someone should "just sail a boat up there and confront the bomb." Moments later, in one of the synchronous events that would characterize the evolution of Greenpeace, a Vancouver *Sun* reporter phoned for an update on the Sierra Club's plans to protest the bomb. "Before I knew it," recalls Jim Bohlen, "I was telling them we were sailing a boat into the test zone."

The next day, the *Sun* ran the story, but the Sierra Club had not officially ratified the action, so at the next Don't Make a Wave meeting, the ad hoc group adopted the plan. Typical of those days, the anti-war crowd parted with the V-sign, saying "peace". A quiet 23-year-old Canadian carpenter, union organizer, and ecologist, Bill Darnell, who rarely spoke at the meetings, added sheepishly "Make it a green peace."

"The term had a nice ring to it," Hunter recalls. "It worked better in a headline than The Don't Make a Wave Committee. We decided to find a boat and call it *Greenpeace*.". . .

These twelve souls headed off across the Gulf of Alaska for Amchitka Island, making landfall on Akutan Island on September 26. The Greenpeace was immediately seized by the US Coast Guard for landing without permission and escorted back to Sand Point, Alaska, where they paid a fine and were released. The bomb test was then postponed until November, but the boat charter with Captain Cormack ran out at the end of October.

"We found out in Sand Point," recalls Metcalfe, "that the voyage was getting media attention in Canada and the US. Demonstrations had occurred in every major Canadian city." Twenty members of the Coast Guard vessel *Confidence*, which seized the Greenpeace boat, signed a letter saying "what you are doing is for the good of all mankind." The protestors sensed that they were having an impact, but there was a fierce battle among the crew. Hunter wanted to continue on to Amchitka, while Bohlen and Metcalfe felt they had done their job and should head home. Bohlen took charge and instructed Cormack to head for Vancouver. At Kodiak Fineberg left the boat and Rod Marining joined. In the meantime, the Don't Make A Wave Committee chartered a larger, faster Canadian minesweeper, renamed *Greenpeace Too*. The two boats met in Union Bay, BC where, Simmons, Cummings, Marining, and Birmingham joined the second boat, headed for Amchitka.

"During the voyage," Hunter remembers, "Metcalfe, Bohlen, and I discussed replacing Irving Stowe as the leader. But Stowe had control of Don't Make a Wave, so I suggested we start a new organization called Greenpeace." When they returned, Hunter, Moore, and Bruce founded The Whole Earth Church, using the Greenpeace emblem and Moore's now famous line from the voyage, "A flower is your brother." The Whole Earth Church espoused that "all forms of life are inter-related. Any form of life which goes against the natural laws of interdependency has fallen from the State of Grace known as ecological harmony." Members of the Church were asked to "assume their rightful role as Custodians of the Earth."

It was during this voyage that Hunter read *Warriors of the Rainbow* by William Willoya and Vinson Brown, which recounts the Cree Indian prophecy that one day, when the earth was poisoned by humans, a group of people from all nations would band together to defend nature. "Well, this is us, I thought right away," Hunter remembers. "We're the Warriors of the Rainbow."

Study Question

Based on Weyler's recollections, how do you believe that the circumstances in Vancouver in the late 1960s and early 1970s contributed to the development of the environmental movement?

Indian Council of Medical Research

The 1984 toxic chemical leak in Bhopal, India focused global attention on the potential environmental impact of multinational corporations located in developing countries. Investigations conducted after the *disastrous release of methyl isocyanate gas revealed a litany of abuses, not least of which was the location of the plant within a heavily populated area, as well as inadequate safety training, monitoring, and* containement protocols. *The official death toll now stands at 3,787 people, but many sources acknowledge that hundreds of thousands of people have suffered lasting effects from their exposure to the gas. Union Carbide eventually paid $470 million in compensation.*

The site remains profoundly contaminated.

Document Source: Indian Council of Medical Research, "Health Effects of the Toxic Gas Leak from the Union Carbide Methyl Isocyanate Plant: Technical Report on Population Based Long Term Epidemiological Studies (1985–1994)," Bhopal Gas Disaster Research Centre (1994): 46–50.

Bhopal Report: Summary and Conclusions

1. The Bhopal Gas Disaster—the worst industrial accident of the world—occurred on the night of 2nd/3rdDecember, 1984, in Bhopal—the capital city of the state of Madhya Pradesh in Central India, at the Pesticide Plant owned by an American Multinational, the Union Carbide Corporation. Approximately, 40 tons of highly toxic liquid Methyl Isocyanate (MIC—boiling point 39.1°C) was stored in Tank 610. The toxic material, under conditions of extremely high temperature and pressure generated inside the tank suddenly escaped in a gaseous form over a period of two to three hours into the atmosphere, while all monitoring devices and safety mechanisms had failed. It was estimated that what actually escaped into the atmosphere was a mixture of MIC and other products of chemical reaction triggered off inside the Tank 610.

2. It was estimated that of the total population of over 8 lac[1], about 5 lac were exposed to the Toxic Gas(es), inhaling it either inside their houses or outside in the streets as they panicked out of their houses for safety. The Gases condensed on contact with cold air, and due to [the] phenomenon of atmospheric inversion settled down on the ground. It then evaporated and gradually spread in the atmosphere to low wind velocity and affected the human, animal and plant life. The MIC Plant was located in a densely populated, highly congested part of Bhopal. Out of the total population, nearly 1.6 lac people present within a radius of three km from the Factory were exposed presumably to a higher concentration of gas and also perhaps for a longer period of time. The maximum number of deaths occurred in them and 85 per cent

of these in the first three days. The estimates placed the number of dead persons at 2,000 and dead cattle around 1,000.

3. Early autopsy studies unequivocally established asphyxia as the immediate cause of death, resulting from acute lung injury, chemical pneumonia, and acute respiratory distress syndrome (ARDS) and other toxic effects like anoxic brain damage. During subsequent autopsies, extensive pulmonary oedema and exudative lesions were noted. Still later, i.e., from four months to one year and beyond, diffuse interstitial pulmonary fibrosis could be detected.

Further, the toxicological studies in the survivors clearly established the presence of elevated levels of "cyanide" in many of the victims, alongside evidence of Carbamoylation or binding of MIC to the end terminal valine residue of circulating haemoglobin and possibly myoglobin. Both factors could account for the cherry red discoloration of the lungs and viscera, as also the blood gas disturbances. The demonstration of the toxic chemicals viz., MIC or its related compounds in the blood of victims in Bhopal, is from all accounts a unique and unprecedented event in the annals of Chemical Disasters. Similarly, there was every likelihood that N-Carbamoylation of end-terminal residue of myoglobin could have occurred, although it is not easy to explain the muscle weakness which was dramatically reversed by administration of sodium thiosulphate. The possibility of S-Carbamoylation of SH groups of muscle enzymes like cholinesterase and aldolase remain unanswered.

4. The survivor population in large numbers suffered from multisystem morbidities, particularly the

respiratory, ophthalmic, and gastrointestinal systems.

(a) In the "Acute Phase" i.e., immediately following the Toxic Gas inhalation, the prevalence rates for the different clinical findings were : breathlessness—99 per cent; cough—90 per cent, pain chest—40 per cent, irritation of upper respiratory tract (choking)—46 per cent, extreme muscle weakness—25 per cent, apathy (listlessness) —21 per cent, hypersomnolesence—16 per cent, coma—7 per cent, loss of appetite—92 per cent, nausea and vomiting—52 per cent, eye irritation, lacrimation, swelling, blepharospasm—86 per cent, tachycardia—54 per cent, fever—2 per cent, Chest radiographs also showed extensive abnormalities.

(b) In the "Subacute Phase" i.e., one to three months post-exposure, majority of the already affected population continued to suffer from respiratory symptoms of breathlessness, cough, chest pain etc., which did not correlate well with the chest radiograph or lung function studies. The latter showed in a proportion of the symptomatics, evidence of obstructive, restrictive, or combined impairment. A significant proportion of them also continued to suffer from gastrointestinal, psychiatric symptoms, and muscle weakness. In most patients who had eye symptoms in the acute phase, the lesions had healed with no evidence of progressive loss of vision.

(c) In the "Chronic Phase," i.e., after three months of the exposure, a very large number of people continued to suffer from

respiratory, gastrointestinal, ophthalmic, psychiatric symptoms, and muscle weakness. With passage of time, the prevalence rates and intensity of clinical signs and symptoms gradually decreased. However, even five years after the Toxic Gas exposure, several thousand exposees daily attended the hospital and clinics seeking medical relief.

(d) Of the 2,566 pregnancies at the time of the gas exposure, 373 ended in abortions, 82 still births, both incidences being higher than in other parts of the country. This is known to happen following any major life threatening disasters. . . .

Conclusions

1. The Bhopal Gas Disaster was entirely man made because: (a) If the Union Carbide Pesticide Factory did not have any habitation within 4 km radius, nobody would have been hurt; (b) If Methyl Isocyanate had not been stored for such a long time (rather unusual) the accident could have been averted; (c) If the monitoring and safety devices had been maintained, the accident would have been averted. . . .

Note

1. Lac (*lakh*) is a unit of measure equivalent to 100,000. So 8 lac would be 800,000.

> **Study Question**
>
> Why do the authors conclude that the disaster at Bhopal was "a unique and unprecedented event"?

Gro Harlem Brundtland

In 1983 then UN Secretary General Javier Pérez de Cuéllar established a special commission to propose a new strategy for sustainable global development by the year 2000. He entrusted Norway's Prime

Minister Gro Harlem Brundtland (b. 1939) with the task of chairing what was to be called the World Commission on Environment and Development (WCED). Brundtland's previous tenure as Norway's environment minister made her ideally suited to the task of chairing the WCED. She is currently one of The Elders—a small group of global leaders commissioned by Nelson Mandela to use their collective expertise in politics, economics, human rights, and social issues to address some of the world's most difficult issues.

Excerpts from the 1987 report of the WCED on the environment, sustainability, and human impacts, which came to be known as the Brundtland Report, follow.

Document Source: Gro Harlem Brundtland/World Commission on Environment and Development, Our Common Future: From One Earth to One World (March 1987); http://www.un-documents.net/wced-ocf.htm

Our Common Future

1. In the middle of the twentieth century, we saw our planet from space for the first time. Historians may eventually find that this vision had a greater impact on thought than did the Copernican revolution of the sixteenth century, which upset the human self-image by revealing that the Earth is not the centre of the universe. From space, we see a small and fragile ball dominated not by human activity and edifice but by a pattern of clouds, oceans, greenery, and soils. Humanity's inability to fit its activities into that pattern is changing planetary systems, fundamentally.

Many such changes are accompanied by life-threatening hazards. This new reality, from which there is no escape, must be recognized—and managed.

2. Fortunately, this new reality coincides with more positive developments new to this century.

We can move information and goods faster around the globe than ever before; we can produce more food and more goods with less investment of resources; our technology and science gives us at least the potential to look deeper into and better understand natural systems. From space, we can see and study the Earth as an organism whose health depends on the health of all its parts. We have the power to reconcile human affairs with natural laws and to thrive in the process. In this our cultural and spiritual heritages can reinforce our economic interests and survival imperatives.

3. This Commission believes that people can build a future that is more prosperous, more just, and more secure. Our report, *Our Common Future*, is not a prediction of ever increasing environmental decay, poverty, and hardship in an ever more polluted world among ever decreasing resources. We see instead the possibility for a new era of economic growth, one that must be based on policies that sustain and expand the environmental resource base. And we believe such growth to be absolutely essential to relieve the great poverty that is deepening in much of the developing world.

4. But the Commission's hope for the future is conditional on decisive political action now to begin managing environmental resources to ensure both sustainable human progress and human survival. We are not forecasting a future; we are serving a notice—an urgent notice based on the latest and best scientific evidence—that the time has come to take the decisions needed to secure the resources to sustain this and coming generations. We do not offer a detailed blueprint for action, but instead a pathway by which the peoples of the world may enlarge their spheres of cooperation.

I. The Global Challenge

1. Successes and Failures

5. Those looking for success and signs of hope can find many: infant mortality is falling; human life expectancy is increasing; the proportion of the world's adults who can read and write is climbing; the proportion of children starting school is rising; and global food production increases faster than the population grows.

6. But the same processes that have produced these gains have given rise to trends that the planet and its people cannot long bear. These have

traditionally been divided into failures of "development" and failures in the management of our human environment. On the development side, in terms of absolute numbers there are more hungry people in the world than ever before, and their numbers are increasing. So are the numbers who cannot read or write, the numbers without safe water or safe and sound homes, and the numbers short of woodfuel with which to cook and warm themselves. The gap between rich and poor nations is widening—not shrinking—and there is little prospect, given present trends and institutional arrangements, that this process will be reversed.

7. There are also environmental trends that threaten to radically alter the planet, that threaten the lives of many species upon it, including the human species. Each year another 6 million hectares of productive dryland turns into worthless desert. Over three decades, this would amount to an area roughly as large as Saudi Arabia. More than 11 million hectares of forests are destroyed yearly, and this, over three decades, would equal an area about the size of India. Much of this forest is converted to low-grade farmland unable to support the farmers who settle it. In Europe, acid precipitation kills forests and lakes and damages the artistic and architectural heritage of nations; it may have acidified vast tracts of soil beyond reasonable hope of repair. The burning of fossil fuels puts into the atmosphere carbon dioxide, which is causing gradual global warming. This "greenhouse effect" may by early next century have increased average global temperatures enough to shift agricultural production areas, raise sea levels to flood coastal cities, and disrupt national economies. Other industrial gases threaten to deplete the planet's protective ozone shield to such an extent that the number of human and animal cancers would rise sharply and the oceans' food chain would be disrupted, industry and agriculture put toxic substances into the human food chain and into underground water tables beyond reach of cleansing. . . .

2. The Interlocking Crises

11. Until recently, the planet was a large world in which human activities and their effects were neatly compartmentalized within nations, within sectors (energy, agriculture, trade), and within broad areas of concern (environment, economics, social). These compartments have begun to dissolve. This applies in particular to the various global "crises" that have seized public concern, particularly over the past decade. These are not separate crises: an environmental crisis, a development crisis, an energy crisis. They are all one.

12. The planet is passing through a period of dramatic growth and fundamental change. Our human world of 5 billion must make room in a finite environment for another human world. The population could stabilize at between 8 and 14 billion sometime next century, according to UN projections. More than 90 per cent of the increase will occur in the poorest countries, and 90 per cent of that growth in already bursting cities.

13. Economic activity has multiplied to create a $13 trillion world economy, and this could grow five to tenfold in the coming half century. Industrial production has grown more than fiftyfold over the past century, four-fifths of this growth since 1950. Such figures reflect and presage profound impacts upon the biosphere, as the world invests in houses, transport, farms, and industries. Much of the economic growth pulls raw material from forests, soils, seas, and waterways.

14. A mainspring of economic growth is new technology, and while this technology offers the potential for slowing the dangerously rapid consumption of finite resources, it also entails high risks, including new forms of pollution and the introduction to the planet of new variations of life forms that could change evolutionary pathways. Meanwhile, the industries most heavily reliant on environmental resources and most heavily polluting are growing most rapidly in the developing world, where there is both more urgency for growth and less capacity to minimize damaging side effects.

The World Commission on Environment and Development first met in October 1984 and published its Report 900 days later, in April 1987. Over those few days:

- The drought-triggered, environment-development crisis in Africa peaked, putting 36 million people at risk, killing perhaps a million.
- A leak from a pesticides factory in Bhopal, India killed more than 2,000 people and blinded and injured over 200,000 more.
- Liquid gas tanks exploded in Mexico City, killing 1,000 and leaving thousands more homeless.
- The Chernobyl nuclear reactor explosion sent nuclear fallout across Europe, increasing the risks of future human cancers.
- Agricultural chemicals, solvents, and mercury flowed into the Rhine River during a warehouse fire in Switzerland, killing millions of fish and threatening drinking water in the Federal Republic of Germany and the Netherlands.
- An estimated 60 million people died of diarrhoeal diseases related to unsafe drinking water and malnutrition; most of the victims were children.

15. These related changes have locked the global economy and global ecology together in new ways. We have in the past been concerned about the impacts of economic growth upon the environment. We are now forced to concern ourselves with the impacts of ecological stress—degradation of soils, water regimes, atmosphere, and forests upon our economic prospects.

We have in the more recent past been forced to face up to a sharp increase in economic interdependence among nations. We are now forced to accustom ourselves to an accelerating ecological interdependence among nations. Ecology and economy are becoming ever more interwoven locally, regionally, nationally, and globally into a seamless net of causes and effects.

16. Impoverishing the local resource base can impoverish wider areas: deforestation by highland farmers causes flooding on lowland farms; factory pollution robs local fishermen of their catch. Such grim local cycles now operate nationally and regionally. Dryland degradation sends environmental refugees in their millions across national borders. Deforestation in Latin America and Asia is causing more floods, and more destructive floods, in downhill, downstream nations. Acid precipitation and nuclear fallout have spread across the borders of Europe. Similar phenomena are emerging on a global scale, such as global warming and loss of ozone. Internationally traded hazardous chemicals entering foods are themselves internationally traded. In the next century, the environmental pressure causing population movements may increase sharply, while barriers to that movement may be even firmer than they are now.

17. Over the past few decades, life-threatening environmental concerns have surfaced in the developing world. Countrysides are coming under pressure from increasing numbers of farmers and the landless. Cities are filling with people, cars, and factories. Yet at the same time these developing countries must operate in a world in which the resources gap between most developing and industrial nations is widening, in which the industrial world dominates in the rule-making of some key international bodies and in which the industrial world has already used much of the planet's ecological capital. This inequality is the

planet's main "environmental" problem; it is also its main "development" problem.

18. International economic relationships pose a particular problem for environmental management in many developing countries. Agriculture, forestry, energy production, and mining generate at least half the gross national product of many developing countries and account for even larger shares of livelihoods and employment. Exports of natural resources remain a large factor in their economies, especially for the least developed. Most of these countries face enormous economic pressures, both international and domestic, to overexploit their environmental resource base.

> **Study Question**
>
> Of all of the challenges identified, which would be the most difficult to remedy? Which could readily be achieved?

United Nations

Spurred by events such as the disaster in Bhopal as well as the environmental destruction caused by the Exxon Valdez *oil spill off the coast of Alaska in 1989, environmentalists, politicians, and activists met in 1992 in Rio de Janeiro, Brazil, at the United Nations Conference on Environment and Development, known more commonly as the Earth Summit. The Conference produced a wide-ranging declaration of principles designed to protect the environment while encouraging development. However, fully twenty years later most participants in the 2012 Rio Summit agreed that only minimal progress had been made on the original goals. The 27 principles agreed upon at Rio are included below.*

Document Source: United Nations, *Report of the United Nations Conference on Environment and Development,* Vol. 1 (New York: United Nations, 1993), 3–8. http://www.un.org/documents/ga/conf151/aconf15126-1annex1.htm

Rio Declaration on Environment and Development

Principle 1

Human beings are at the centre of concerns for sustainable development. They are entitled to a healthy and productive life in harmony with nature.

Principle 2

States have, in accordance with the Charter of the United Nations and the principles of international law, the sovereign right to exploit their own resources pursuant to their own environmental and developmental policies, and the responsibility to ensure that activities within their jurisdiction or control do not cause damage to the environment of other States or of areas beyond the limits of national jurisdiction.

Principle 3

The right to development must be fulfilled so as to equitably meet developmental and environmental needs of present and future generations.

Principle 4

In order to achieve sustainable development, environmental protection shall constitute an integral part of the development process and cannot be considered in isolation from it.

Principle 5

All States and all people shall cooperate in the essential task of eradicating poverty as an indispensable requirement for sustainable development, in order to decrease the disparities in standards of living and better meet the needs of the majority of the people of the world.

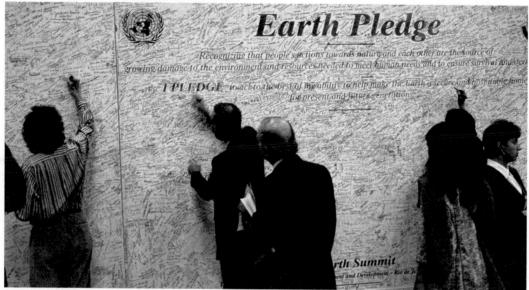

Participants at the 1992 Earth Summit in Rio sign a pledge to preserve the earth.

Courtesy of the United Nations Photo Library (281390/UN/DPI/Tom Prendergast)

Principle 6

The special situation and needs of developing countries, particularly the least developed and those most environmentally vulnerable, shall be given special priority. International actions in the field of environment and development should also address the interests and needs of all countries.

Principle 7

States shall cooperate in a spirit of global partnership to conserve, protect, and restore the health and integrity of the Earth's ecosystem. In view of the different contributions to global environmental degradation, States have common but differentiated responsibilities. The developed countries acknowledge the responsibility that they bear in the international pursuit of sustainable development in view of the pressures their societies place on the global environment and of the technologies and financial resources they command.

Principle 8

To achieve sustainable development and a higher quality of life for all people, States should reduce and eliminate unsustainable patterns of production and consumption and promote appropriate demographic policies.

Principle 9

States should cooperate to strengthen endogenous capacity-building for sustainable development by improving scientific understanding through exchanges of scientific and technological knowledge, and by enhancing the development, adaptation, diffusion, and transfer of technologies, including new and innovative technologies.

Principle 10

Environmental issues are best handled with the participation of all concerned citizens, at the relevant level. At the national level, each individual shall have appropriate access to information concerning the environment that is held by public authorities, including information on hazardous materials and activities in their communities, and the opportunity to participate in decision-making processes. States shall facilitate and encourage public awareness and participation by making information widely available. Effective access to judicial and administrative proceedings, including redress and remedy, shall be provided.

Principle 11

States shall enact effective environmental legislation. Environmental standards, management objectives, and priorities should reflect the environmental and developmental context to which they apply. Standards applied by some countries may be inappropriate and of unwarranted economic and social cost to other countries, in particular developing countries.

Principle 12

States should cooperate to promote a supportive and open international economic system that would lead to economic growth and sustainable development in all countries, to better address the problems of environmental degradation. Trade policy measures for environmental purposes should not constitute a means of arbitrary or unjustifiable discrimination or a disguised restriction on international trade. Unilateral actions to deal with environmental challenges outside the jurisdiction of the importing country should be avoided. Environmental measures addressing transboundary or global environmental problems should, as far as possible, be based on an international consensus.

Principle 13

States shall develop national law regarding liability and compensation for the victims of pollution and other environmental damage. States shall also cooperate in an expeditious and more determined manner to develop further international law regarding liability and compensation for adverse effects of environmental damage caused by activities within their jurisdiction or control to areas beyond their jurisdiction.

Principle 14

States should effectively cooperate to discourage or prevent the relocation and transfer to other States of any activities and substances that cause severe environmental degradation or are found to be harmful to human health.

Principle 15

In order to protect the environment, the precautionary approach shall be widely applied by States according to their capabilities. Where there are threats of serious or irreversible damage, lack of full scientific certainty shall not be used as a reason for postponing cost-effective measures to prevent environmental degradation.

Principle 16

National authorities should endeavour to promote the internalization of environmental costs and the use of economic instruments, taking into account the approach that the polluter should, in principle, bear the cost of pollution, with due regard to the public interest and without distorting international trade and investment.

Principle 17

Environmental impact assessment, as a national instrument, shall be undertaken for proposed activities that are likely to have a significant adverse impact on the environment and are subject to a decision of a competent national authority.

Principle 18

States shall immediately notify other States of any natural disasters or other emergencies that are likely to produce sudden harmful effects on the environment of those States. Every effort shall be made by the international community to help States so afflicted.

Principle 19

States shall provide prior and timely notification and relevant information to potentially affected States on activities that may have a significant adverse transboundary environmental effect and shall consult with those States at an early stage and in good faith.

Principle 20

Women have a vital role in environmental management and development. Their full participation is therefore essential to achieve sustainable development.

Principle 21

The creativity, ideals, and courage of the youth of the world should be mobilized to forge a global partnership in order to achieve sustainable development and ensure a better future for all.

Principle 22

Indigenous people and their communities, and other local communities, have a vital role in environmental management and development because of their knowledge and traditional practices. States should recognize and duly support their identity, culture, and interests and enable their effective participation in the achievement of sustainable development.

Principle 23

The environment and natural resources of people under oppression, domination, and occupation shall be protected.

Principle 24

Warfare is inherently destructive of sustainable development. States shall therefore respect international law providing protection for the environment in times of armed conflict and cooperate in its further development, as necessary.

Principle 25

Peace, development, and environmental protection are interdependent and indivisible.

Principle 26

States shall resolve all their environmental disputes peacefully and by appropriate means in accordance with the Charter of the United Nations.

Principle 27

States and people shall cooperate in good faith and in a spirit of partnership in the fulfilment of the principles embodied in this Declaration and in the further development of international law in the field of sustainable development.

Study Question

Between 1992 and 2012, what were the largest barriers to the achievement of the principles enumerated at the Earth Summit?

S.P. Udayakumar and john a. powell

S.P. Udayakumar (b. 1959) was a research associate and co-director of programs at the Institute on Race and Poverty, University of Minnesota, Minneapolis. He currently runs the South Asian Community Center for Education and Research (SACCER) at Nagercoil, Tamil Nadu, India. American civil liberties scholar john a. powell (b. 1947) has held numerous academic positions during his career.

Most recently he was appointed director of the Haas Diversity Research Center at the University of California, Berkeley. The following article, written in 2000, examines many of the worst effects of globalism, especially on people of colour.

Document Source: S.P. Udayakumar and john a. powell, "Race, Poverty, and Globalization." From Global Exchange. Available online: http://www.globalexchange.org/resources/econ101/globalization

Race, Poverty, and Globalization

The world economy is in a state of what is commonly viewed as unprecedented growth. But with this growth has come dangerous and destructive economic disparity. On the one hand, we see the "impressive" economy in the Northern Hemisphere, particularly in the United States, where Silicon Valley, a region of 2.3 million people, has produced tens of thousands of millionaires, with 64 new ones every day. There are regular US reports of historically low unemployment rates, labor shortages, and booming economy.

On the other hand, many people of color, particularly those in the Southern Hemisphere, do not have enough food to eat, resulting in malnutrition and disease. They face growing inflation while their governments, which used to subsidize some aspects of their marginal living, are urged to stop subsidies for food and adopt a more market-oriented economics. Many workers in these economies are trapped in poor working conditions with low pay. Women are often expected to do back-breaking farm and domestic work, with few rights or benefits. Yet many of the fiscal policies pushed onto developing countries and adopted in northern countries exacerbate the problem of the most marginal while celebrating the wealth of the rich.

In the North as well, people of color often find themselves being left farther and farther behind. Even as states in the US and the nation as a whole report budget surpluses, we seem unable or unwilling to provide adequate housing for the growing number of working-class and homeless families, to repair the physical structure of schools that house low-income students of color, or to provide social services or medical attention for those most in need.

Sweatshops that employ people of color working as virtual slave laborers are tolerated—even encouraged—as part of the new world trade. The public space people of color and marginal groups are most dependent on—whether it is public hospitals, schools, parks, or a social welfare system—is constantly attacked as inconsistent with the needs of capital and the market. Indeed, we are encouraged to remake public space to mimic private space with a market, anti-democratic orientation where we are consumers, not citizens.

How are these disparate conditions related to globalism, and why are people of color under the most severe threat from this process? Certainly, other people are also under a threat from this globalization process, and some would assert that democracy and capitalism itself may be undone by this process if it is not checked. To answer the above question and to understand why minorities and other marginal populations are most at risk, it is first necessary to better understand what globalism is, particularly the type of globalism that dominates today's markets.

What Is Globalism?

In the most general sense, globalism refers to the process in which goods and services, including capital, move more freely within and among nations. As globalism advances, national boundaries become more and more porous, and to some extent, less and less relevant.

Since many of our early industries, such as steel, were location-sensitive, there was a natural limitation to globalization. To be sure, some things remain location-sensitive, but mobility is the trend. It is assumed that liberalizing laws and structures, so that goods and services can become more globally focused, will produce more wealth, and indeed this seems to be true. Using this general understanding of globalism and globalization, it would be accurate to say this process has been developing and growing for well over a hundred years.

But there have been many changes in the globalization process in the last two decades that makes it distinct from earlier incarnations. The major thing being traded in today's global market is information and capital itself, rather than commodities or other products. Technological change allows capital to move almost instantaneously. Changes in monetary policies, as well as in what is being traded and the importance of capital, have created a global market distinctively different from previous eras. Earlier products and capital were more rooted to a place. Today, many of the things traded and produced in the global market, such as knowledge and computer technology, are extremely mobile or rootless.

The United States has emerged as the only world superpower. This has allowed the US tremendous influence in setting the terms for global trade. The style of globalism pushed by the United States has favored the free movement and protection of capital, while being at best indifferent and at worst hostile to the more place-dependent labor. It is the dual relationship of mobile capital and fixed, unorganized, and unprotected labor that has created the conditions for capital to dominate. This has been greatly enhanced by the US position toward organized labor and capital. While the US has been aggressive in protecting capital both at home and abroad, it has encouraged both the weakening of organized labor and removing protections for workers.

While both Japan and Europe have aggressively pushed for globalism, each has been more willing to protect labor, the environment, and certain markets—at least within their own borders. It is the United States that has consistently been the most radical on liberalizing capital and protecting it as it moves across boundaries, and the most hostile to protecting labor and fragile markets. Protecting labor expresses itself not only in strong unions and workers' benefits but also in a strong social welfare system. The United States has purposefully moved toward weaker labor unions, as well as an anemic social welfare system. It has used the globalism it advocates as justification for keeping workers' jobs insecure, pay, and benefits relatively low. Workers are told that pushing hard for benefits will cause capital to leave to another location in the country or the world where workers are willing to work for less with fewer benefits.

The United States and the international organizations over which it has substantial influence, such as the International Monetary Fund, have demanded protection of capital and encouraged or tolerated the suppression of labor and the environment in the weaker southern countries. Capital is actively being directed to markets with low wages, where workers are sometimes abused, and labor organizations suppressed. The wealth this globalism is creating is being forcefully subsidized by vulnerable workers and the environment, especially in the Southern Hemisphere. This logic is then used to weaken the position of labor in the North, as we are required to compete with unorganized, suppressed labor in the South.

While sweatshops and slave labor may attract capital investments, what about the futures of black welfare mothers in Detroit or the Aborigines in Australia, who need government assistance to take advantage of, say, the educational system? How or why does US-style globalism affect their needs? US-style globalism not only attempts to suppress labor, but also seeks to suppress social welfare systems and support for public expenditures that do not directly benefit the expansion of capital. The social welfare system and other public services, such as schools, social services in the North, and food subsidies in the South, are supported through taxes, and taxes reduce short-term benefits to capital.

In the North, it is women and minorities who are most dependent on the public sector. These racial and gender correlations make it all the easier to attack the legitimacy of taxation for this purpose. Taxes are seen as undesirable because they reduce profits and interfere with the market. But the public space, including the welfare system, can only be supported by the public in the form of taxes. Whether we are talking about education or other public services, we are encouraged to believe that they should be as limited as possible and made to mimic the market. Those who cannot thrive in the market environment without help, especially if they are people of color, are seen as free-loaders and illegitimate. In many ways, much of the public space in the United States becomes associated with people of color.

Goodbye, Democratic Vision?

Public purposes and civic goods—to the extent they are even recognized—are no longer to be achieved through public institutions but are to be privatized. The democratic vision associated with public functions is to be abandoned or seriously curtailed in favor of the ideal of efficiency. There is an abiding belief that democracy must be limited because it interferes with the private decisions of market experts, thereby reducing wealth and capital. And anything that is perceived as interfering with the growth of capitalism—be it the social welfare system, labor unions, civil rights, or government programs—is being curtailed, while government policies and structures that protect capital, including the military, are enhanced.

Although proponents of this style of globalism purport to support democracy, it is only in a role subservient to capital. In the United States, we are softly encouraged to vote, while being constantly reminded that in these global matters that shape our everyday life, we have no say. We are told that no city, state, or nation can or should try to influence this powerful but uncontrollable process. We are reminded that one can regulate capital, and any attempt to do so will hurt the economy.

The deregulation of capital is made to appear both good and natural. Our attention is drawn away from the fact that there are powerful organizations supported by the US government's leadership that protect and facilitate the flow of capital. These institutions include the World Bank, International Development Association, International Finance Corporation, International

Monetary Fund, World Trade Organization, etc.

Unfortunately, there are no organizations of equal stature to protect the interests of workers, racial minorities, the environment, or women and children. There are, of course, several treaties and international instruments dealing with some of these issues, such as the Convention on International Trade in Endangered Species, Convention on the Elimination of All Forms of Discrimination Against Women, Declaration on the Rights of Persons Belonging to National or Ethnic, Religious or Linguistic Minorities, and so forth.

However, they are nearly impotent, compared with the institutions with far-reaching and substantial goals of protecting capital. When citizens try to raise such issues, it is simply asserted that making working conditions or the environment part of trade agreements would unduly interfere with free trade. American-style globalism has not just transformed the flow of capital, it has transformed the role of government and the meaning of citizenship.

People are now brought together as consumers but kept apart as citizens. The transformed role of government is not to protect citizens or the precious safety net of public space but to protect and facilitate the flow of capital. So today we speak of free markets but not of free labor. We speak of an expanding global market, but a diminishing public space, and we hardly speak at all of citizen participation and justice. This is an authoritarian vision where armies police people and nations, so capital might be free.

It is very doubtful that capital, despite advances in technology, would be nearly as mobile as it is without the nationally brokered agreements that have the force of law and the coercive power of the state behind them. But while capital relies on the government to do its bidding, we enjoy freedom as individuals without the power that only comes from the collective action of informed citizens. While it might be true that cities and states, and certainly private individuals, can do little to influence globalism, it is clearly false that nations, especially the United States, are powerless in the face of globalism.

Undermining Social Movements

During the last part of the 20th century, the Civil Rights Movement, the women's movement, and the environmental movement advanced their claims for inclusion and justice. An attack on the public role of the state is a powerful strategy to limit the aspirations of these groups. They are made impotent in a forum where wealth, not votes, dictates policies. These groups are marginalized in an economic arena that transforms the market, with decisions made behind closed doors, and not in public and civic spaces.

Destruction of the public space also results in a decline of the public voice. In the United States, this decline in the role and scope of democracy in the relationship to the market occurred just when the Civil Rights Movement began to make significant gains in securing for blacks and other minorities real access to the political process.

This article, then, is not an attack on globalism per se but on the excess and undemocratic nature of the US-style globalism popular now, which is particularly hostile to people of color and other marginal groups. This style of globalism disempowers average Americans in every way, except as consumers. Globalization has been happening for over a century and will continue. It must be re-envisioned to appropriately protect capital, but also to protect labor, the environment, and people of color. These concerns must be seen as interrelated,

not as separate. Furthermore, we must create the necessary international structures with transparency and accountability in order to make this vision a reality and to develop suitable remedies for the plight of marginalized peoples. These steps should not be seen as hostile to business, but as an appropriate cost of doing business in a justice-oriented and sustainable global economy.

Despite the rhetoric about the unmitigated good that can come from US-style globalism, there is an increasing call to look more closely at the process as it relates to people and the environment throughout the world. Some assert that US-style globalism threatens democracy. Others argue that this style of globalism threatens capitalism itself. We think that both claims may be right.

We believe it is critical to look more closely at what globalism means for people in general and people of color in particular. Given its more recent history of developing a social compact that includes all people, the United States should not be championing a style of globalism that is blind to the needs of some sectors. If this process continues, we are likely to permanently re-inscribe a subordinated, life-threatening status for people of color all over the globe and rationalize it with an invisible hand. We can change this by working to make the invisible visible.

> **Study Question**
>
> According to the authors, anything that interferes with the growth and expansion of capitalism is under attack. Upon what basis do they make this claim?

Robert Kaplan

Robert D. Kaplan (b.1952) is a senior national correspondent for The Atlantic Monthly *and the author of a number of books based on his reporting from the some of the world's most embattled regions. In "World Government," first published in 1997, Kaplan considers the issue of globalization and the impact of an*

increasingly interconnected world where corporations know few restrictions and traditional concepts of boundaries and nation-states are beginning to lose their meaning.

Document Source: Robert Kaplan, *The Coming Anarchy* (New York: Random House, 2000), 43–50.

World Government

Authoritarian or hybrid regimes, no matter how illiberal, will still be treated as legitimate if they can provide security for their subjects and spark economic growth. And they will easily find acceptance in a world driven increasingly by financial markets that know no borders.

For years idealists have dreamed of a "world government." Well, a world government has been emerging—quietly and organically, the way vast developments in history take place. I do not refer to the United Nations, the power of which, almost by definition, affects only the poorest countries. After its peace-keeping failures in Bosnia and Somalia—and its $2 billion failure to make Cambodia democratic—the UN is on its way to becoming a supranational relief agency. Rather, I refer to the increasingly dense ganglia of international corporations and markets that are becoming the unseen arbiters of power in many countries. It is much more important nowadays for the leader of a developing country to get a hearing before corporate investors at the World Economic Forum than to speak before the UN General Assembly. Amnesty International now briefs corporations, just as it has always briefed national governments. Interpol officials have spoken about sharing certain kinds of intelligence with corporations. The Prime Minister of Malaysia, Mahathir Mohamad, is recognizing the real new world order (at least in this case) by building a low-tax district he calls a "multimedia super-corridor," with two new cities and a new airport designed specifically for international corporations. The world's most efficient peacemaking force belongs not to the UN or even to the great powers but to a South African corporate mercenary force called Executive Outcomes,[1] which restored relative stability to Sierra Leone in late 1995. (This is reminiscent of the British East India Company, which raised armies transparently for economic interests.) Not long after Executive Outcomes left Sierra Leone, where only 20.7 per cent of adults can read, that country's so-called model democracy

crumbled into military anarchy, as Sudan's model democracy had done in the late 1980s.

Of the world's hundred largest economies, 51 are not countries but corporations. While the 200 largest corporations employ less than three-fourths of one per cent of the world's work force, they account for 28 per cent of world economic activity. The 500 largest corporations account for 70 per cent of world trade. Corporations are like the feudal domains that evolved into nation-states; they are nothing less than the vanguard of a new Darwinian organization of politics. Because they are in the forefront of real globalization while the overwhelming majority of the world's inhabitants are still rooted in local terrain, corporations will be free for a few decades to leave behind the social and environmental wreckage they create—abruptly closing a factory here in order to open an unsafe facility with a cheaper work force there. Ultimately, as technological innovations continue to accelerate and the world's middle classes come closer together, corporations may well become more responsible to the cohering global community and less amoral in the course of their evolution toward new political and cultural forms.

For instance, ABB Asea Brown Boveri Ltd. is a $36 billion-a-year multinational corporation divided into 1,300 companies in 140 countries; no one national group accounts for more than 20 per cent of its employees. ABB's chief executive officer, Percy Barnevik, recently told an interviewer that this diversity is so that ABB can develop its own "global ABB culture—you might say an umbrella culture." Barnevik explains that his best managers are moved around periodically so that they and their families can develop "global personalities" by living and growing up in different countries. ABB management teams, moreover, are never composed of employees from any one country. Barnevik says that this encourages a "cross-cultural glue." Unlike the multiculturalism of the left, which masks individual deficiencies through collective—that is, ethnic or racial—self-esteem, a multinational corporation like ABB has created a diverse multicultural environment in which individuals rise or fall completely on their own merits. Like the hybrid regimes of the present and future, such an evolving corporate community can bear an eerie resemblance to the oligarchies of the ancient world. "Decentralization goes hand in hand with central monitoring," Barnevik says.

The level of social development required by democracy as it is known in the West has existed in only a minority of places—and even there only during certain periods of history. We are entering a troubled transition, and the irony is that while we preach our version of democracy abroad, it slips away from us at home.

Note

1. Executive Outcomes was disbanded in 1999 when South Africa passed a new anti-mercenary law. However, it is reported that some of EO's members continue to operate in new organizations.

> **Study Question**
>
> Do international corporations make up a new "world government"?

Albert Gore

In 2007 Al Gore (b. 1948) and the United Nations Intergovernmental Panel on Climate Change (IPCC) were named joint recipients of the Nobel Peace Prize for their efforts to raise awareness of man-made global climate change. Gore's environmental activism dates back to the mid-1970s, but he was able to reach a wider audience in the 1990s when he served as US President Bill Clinton's vice-president (1993–2001). After a failed bid for the presidency in 2000, Gore renewed his focus on environmental issues via a series of public lectures that would eventually become the monograph and documentary film An Inconvenient Truth.

Document Source: Albert Gore, "Nobel Lecture," Oslo, 10 December 2007. C. Nobel Foundation: http://www.nobelprize.org/nobel_prizes/peace/laureates/2007/gore-lecture_en.html

Nobel Lecture

We, the human species, are confronting a planetary emergency—a threat to the survival of our civilization that is gathering ominous and destructive potential even as we gather here. But there is hopeful news as well: we have the ability to solve this crisis and avoid the worst—though not all—of its consequences, if we act boldly, decisively and quickly.

However, despite a growing number of honorable exceptions, too many of the world's leaders are still best described in the words Winston Churchill applied to those who ignored Adolf Hitler's threat: "They go on in strange paradox, decided only to be undecided, resolved to be irresolute, adamant for drift, solid for fluidity, all powerful to be impotent."

So today, we dumped another 70 million tons of global-warming pollution into the thin shell of atmosphere surrounding our planet, as if it were an open sewer. And tomorrow, we will dump a slightly larger amount, with the cumulative concentrations now trapping more and more heat from the sun.

As a result, the earth has a fever. And the fever is rising. The experts have told us it is not a passing affliction that will heal by itself. We asked for a second opinion. And a third. And a fourth.

And the consistent conclusion, restated with increasing alarm, is that something basic is wrong.

We are what is wrong, and we must make it right.

Last September 21, as the Northern Hemisphere tilted away from the sun, scientists reported with unprecedented distress that the North Polar ice cap is "falling off a cliff." One study estimated that it could be completely gone during summer in less than 22 years. Another new study, to be presented by US Navy researchers later this week, warns it could happen in as little as seven years.

Seven years from now.

In the last few months, it has been harder and harder to misinterpret the signs that our world is spinning out of kilter. Major cities in North and South America, Asia and Australia are nearly out of water due to massive droughts and melting glaciers. Desperate farmers are losing their livelihoods. Peoples in the frozen Arctic and on low-lying Pacific islands are planning evacuations of places they have long called home. Unprecedented wildfires have forced a half million people from their homes in one country and caused a national emergency that almost brought down the government in another. Climate refugees have migrated into areas already inhabited by people with different cultures, religions, and traditions, increasing the potential for conflict. Stronger storms in the Pacific and Atlantic have threatened whole cities. Millions have been displaced by massive flooding in South Asia, Mexico, and 18 countries in Africa. As temperature extremes have increased, tens of thousands have lost their lives. We are recklessly burning and clearing our forests and driving more and more species into extinction. The very web of life on which we depend is being ripped and frayed.

We never intended to cause all this destruction, just as Alfred Nobel never intended that dynamite be used for waging war. He had hoped his invention would promote human progress. We shared that same worthy goal when we began burning massive quantities of coal, then oil and methane. . . .

We also find it hard to imagine making the massive changes that are now necessary to solve the crisis. And when large truths are genuinely inconvenient, whole societies can, at least for a time, ignore them. Yet as George Orwell reminds us: "Sooner or later a false belief bumps up against solid reality, usually on a battlefield." . . .

Indeed, without realizing it, we have begun to wage war on the earth itself. Now, we and the earth's climate are locked in a relationship familiar to war planners: "Mutually assured destruction."

More than two decades ago, scientists calculated that nuclear war could throw so much debris and smoke into the air that it would block life-giving sunlight from our atmosphere, causing a "nuclear winter." Their eloquent warnings here in Oslo helped galvanize the world's resolve to halt the nuclear arms race.

Now science is warning us that if we do not quickly reduce the global warming pollution that is trapping so much of the heat our planet normally radiates back out of the atmosphere, we are in danger of creating a permanent "carbon summer."

As the American poet Robert Frost wrote, "Some say the world will end in fire; some say in ice." Either, he notes, "would suffice."

But neither need be our fate. It is time to make peace with the planet.

We must quickly mobilize our civilization with the urgency and resolve that has previously been seen only when nations mobilized for war. These prior struggles for survival were won when leaders found words at the 11th hour that released a mighty surge of courage, hope and readiness to sacrifice for a protracted and mortal challenge.

These were not comforting and misleading assurances that the threat was not real or imminent; that it would affect others but not ourselves; that ordinary life might be lived even in the presence of extraordinary threat; that Providence could be trusted to do for us what we would not do for ourselves.

No, these were calls to come to the defense of the common future. They were calls upon the courage, generosity, and strength of entire peoples, citizens of every class and condition who were ready to stand against the threat once asked to do so. Our enemies in those times calculated that free people would not rise to the challenge; they were, of course, catastrophically wrong.

Now comes the threat of climate crisis—a threat that is real, rising, imminent, and universal. Once again, it is the 11th hour. The penalties for ignoring this challenge are immense and growing, and at some near point would be unsustainable and unrecoverable. For now we still have the power to choose our fate, and the remaining question is only this: Have we the will to act vigorously and in time, or will we remain imprisoned by a dangerous illusion?

Mahatma Gandhi awakened the largest democracy on earth and forged a shared resolve with what he called "Satyagraha"—or "truth force."

In every land, the truth—once known—has the power to set us free.

Truth also has the power to unite us and bridge the distance between "me" and "we," creating the basis for common effort and shared responsibility.

There is an African proverb that says, "If you want to go quickly, go alone. If you want to go far, go together." We need to go far, quickly.

We must abandon the conceit that individual, isolated, private actions are the answer. They can and do help. But they will not take us far enough without collective action. At the same time, we must ensure that in mobilizing globally, we do not invite the establishment of ideological conformity and a new lock-step "ism."

That means adopting principles, values, laws, and treaties that release creativity and initiative at every level of society in multifold responses originating concurrently and spontaneously.

This new consciousness requires expanding the possibilities inherent in all humanity. The innovators who will devise a new way to harness the sun's energy for pennies or invent an engine that's carbon negative may live in Lagos or Mumbai or Montevideo. We must ensure that entrepreneurs and inventors everywhere on the globe have the chance to change the world.

When we unite for a moral purpose that is manifestly good and true, the spiritual energy unleashed can transform us. The generation that defeated fascism throughout the world in the 1940s found, in rising to meet their awesome challenge, that they had gained the moral authority and long-term vision to launch the Marshall Plan, the United Nations, and a new level of global cooperation and foresight that unified Europe and facilitated the emergence of democracy and prosperity in Germany, Japan, Italy and much of the world. One of their visionary leaders said, "It is time we steered by the stars and not by the lights of every passing ship." . . .

We must understand the connections between the climate crisis and the afflictions of poverty, hunger, HIV/AIDS and other pandemics. As these problems are linked, so too must be their solutions. We must begin by making the common rescue of the global environment the central organizing principle of the world community. . . .

We have everything we need to get started, save perhaps political will, but political will is a renewable resource.

So let us renew it, and say together: "We have a purpose. We are many. For this purpose we will rise, and we will act."

Study Question

Why does Gore warn that the establishment of a "lock-step-ism" such as "environmentalism" is the wrong approach to solve the global environmental crisis?

Stephen Hawking

Stephen Hawking (b. 1942) is a world-renowned theoretical physicist from Great Britain. He has worked on questions relating to cosmology and quantum gravity for over forty years and has also authored a number of popular works, including A Brief History of Time, aimed at making his theories accessible to a broader audience. The speech that follows was part of NASA's 50th Anniversary Lecture Series and was delivered in April 2008.

Document Source: Stephen Hawking, "Why We Should Go into Space," 21 April 2008: http://www.nasa.gov/50th/NASA_lecture_series/hawking.html

Why We Should Go into Space

Why we should go into space. What is that justification for spending all that effort and money on getting a few lumps of moon rock? Aren't there better causes here on Earth?

In a way, the situation was like that in Europe before 1492. People might well have argued that it was a waste of money to send Columbus on a wild goose chase. Yet, the discovery of the new world made a profound difference to the old. Just think, we wouldn't have had a Big Mac or a KFC. *[Laughter.]*

Spreading out into space will have an even greater effect. It will completely change the future of the human race and maybe determine whether we have any future at all.

It won't solve any of our immediate problems on Planet Earth, but it will give us a new perspective on them and cause us to look outwards and inwards. Hopefully, it would unite us to face a common challenge.

This would be a long-term strategy, and by long term, I mean hundreds or even thousands of years. We could have a base on the Moon within 30 years or reach Mars in 50 years and explore the moons of the outer planets in 200 years. By "reach," I mean with man or, should I say, person space flight.

We have already driven Rover and landed a probe on Titan, a moon of Saturn, but if one is considering the future of the human race, we have to go there ourselves.

Going into space won't be cheap, but it will take only a small proportion of world resources. NASA's budget has remained roughly constant in real terms since the time of the Apollo landings, but it has decreased from 0.3 per cent of US GDP

Stephen Hawking visits the Kennedy Space Center in 2007 in preparation for a zero gravity flight.

NASA//Kim Shiflett.

in 1970 to 0.12 per cent now.

Even if we were to increase the international budget 20 times to make a serious effort to go into space, it would only be a small fraction of world GDP.

There will be those who argue that it would be better to spend our money solving the problems of this planet, like climate change and pollution, rather than wasting it on a possibly fruitless search for a new planet.

I am not denying the importance of fighting climate change and global warming, but we can do that and still spare a quarter of a per cent of world GDP for space. Isn't our future worth a quarter of [a] per cent?

We thought space was worth a big effort in the sixties. In 1962, President Kennedy committed the US to landing a man on the Moon by the end of the decade. This was achieved just in time by the Apollo 11 mission in 1969.

The space race helped to create a fascination with science and led to great advances in technology, including the first large-scale integrated circuits which are the basis of all modern computers.

However, after the last Moon landing in 1972, with no future plans for further manned space flight, public interest in space declined. This went along with a general dissention with science in the West because, although it had brought great benefits, it had not solved the social problems that increasingly occupied public attention.

A new manned space flight program would do a lot to restore public enthusiasm for space and for science generally.

Robotic missions are much cheaper and may provide more scientific information, but they don't catch the public imagination in the same way, and they don't spread the human race into space which I am arguing should be our long-term strategy.

A goal of a base on the Moon by 2020 and of a man landing on Mars by 2025 would reignite a space program and give it a sense of purpose in the same way that President Kennedy's Moon target did in the 1960s.

A new interest in space would also increase the public standing of science generally. The low esteem in which science and scientists are held is having serious consequences. We live in a society that is increasingly governed by science and technology, yet fewer and fewer young people long to go into science. . . .

Can we exist for a long time away from the Earth? Our experience with the ISS, the International Space Station, shows that it is possible for human beings to survive for many months away from Planet Earth. However, the zero gravity aboard it causes a number of undesirable physiological changes and weakening of the bones, as well as creating practical problems with liquids, et cetera.

One would, therefore, want any long-term base for human beings to be on a planet or moon. By digging into the surface, one would get thermal insulation and protection from meteors and cosmic rays. The planet or moon could also serve as a source of the raw materials that would be needed if the extraterrestrial community was to be self-sustaining independently of Earth.

What are the possible sites of a human colony in the solar system? The most obvious is the Moon. It is close by and relatively easy to reach. We have already landed on it and driven across it in a buggy.

On the other hand, the Moon is small and without atmosphere or a magnetic field to deflect the solar radiation particles, like on Earth. There is no liquid water, but there may be ice in the craters at the north and south poles. A colony on the Moon could use this as a source of oxygen with power provided by nuclear energy or solar panels. The Moon could be a base for travel to the rest of the solar system.

Mars is the obvious next target. It is half as far, again, as the Earth from the Sun and so receives half the warmth. It once had a magnetic field, but it decayed 4 billion years ago, leaving Mars without protection from solar radiation. It stripped Mars of most of its atmosphere, leaving it with only 1 per cent of the pressure of the Earth's atmosphere.

However, the pressure must have been

higher in the past because we see what appear to be runoff channels and dried-up lakes. Liquid water cannot exist on Mars now.

It would vaporize in the near-vacuum. This suggests that Mars had a warm wet period during which life might have appeared either spontaneously or through panspermia.[1] There is no sign of life on Mars now, but if we found evidence that life had once existed, it would indicate that the probability of life developing on a suitable planet was fairly high. . . .

What about beyond the solar system? Our observations indicate that a significant fraction of stars have planets around them. So far, we can detect only giant planets like Jupiter and Saturn, but it is reasonable to assume that they will be accompanied by smaller Earth-like planets. Some of these will lay in the (inaudible) zone where the distance from the stars is the right range for liquid water to exist on their surface.

There are around a thousand stars within 30 lightyears of Earth. If 1 per cent of each had Earth-size planets in the [inaudible] zone, we would have 10 candidate new worlds. We can revisit it with current technology, but we should make interstellar a long-term aim. By long term, I mean over the next 200 to 500 years. The human race has existed as a separate species for about 2 million years. Civilization began about 10,000 years ago, and the rate of development has been steadily increasing.

If the human race is to continue for another million years, we will have to boldly go where no one has gone before.

Thank you for listening.

Note

1. Panspermia: microorganisms with the potential to generate life under favourable conditions.

> **Study Question**
>
> What is the basis for Hawking's claim that the colonization of space will be essential to human survival?

Web Resources

The Eisenhower Archives: Sputnik and the Space Race
   http://www.eisenhower.archives.gov/research/online_documents/sputnik.html
NASA (National Aeronautics and Space Administration)
   http://www.nasa.gov
Library of Congress: The Environment
   http://www.loc.gov/rr/scitech/selected-internet/environment.html
Intergovernmental Panel on Climate Change
   http://www.ipcc.ch

Recommended Reading

Isaac Asimov, I, Robot (New York: Bantam Spectra, 2008). Originally nine short stories published in 1950, Asimov's I, Robot considers questions of morality, responsibility, and humanity through the lens of robotic "life."
Rachel Carson, Silent Spring (Boston: Houghton Mifflin, 2002). Carson's groundbreaking work examines the consequences of the uncontrolled use of pesticides on the natural environment. The book is considered to be one of the seminal works of the 1960s environmental movement.

Michael Crichton, *State of Fear* (New York: HarperCollins, 2005). Crichton's *State of Fear* focuses on an environmental organization planning a series of eco-terrorist attacks around the world in order to bring environmental issues to global attention. The book openly challenges the theory of man-made climate change.

Frank Herbert, *Dune* (New York: Ace Books, 1999). Herbert's 1965 novel, which takes place thousands of years in the future after humans have populated much of the universe, raises questions about the relationship between humans and animals, greed, expansionism, ecology, and human nature.

Amulya Malladi, *A Breath of Fresh Air* (New York: Ballantine Books, 2002). Malladi's novel takes place in the aftermath of the 1984 release of toxic methyl isocyanate gas in Bhopal, India. The novel confronts the reader with both the immediate and long-term effects of the disaster.

Kim Stanley Robinson, *The Mars Trilogy* (New York: Spectra, 1993). Written in three volumes (*Red Mars*, *Green Mars*, *Blue Mars*), Robinson's trilogy focuses on the first settlement of Mars and the resulting consequences of transforming the natural environment of Mars to make it suitable for human habitation.

Recommended Viewing

Silkwood (US, 1983). Director: Mike Nichols. Nichols's film retells the true story of Karen Silkwood, who was killed under mysterious circumstances in 1974 just before she was scheduled to meet with a *New York Times* reporter about conditions at the Kerr-McGee plutonium fuel plant in Oklahoma where she worked. The plant closed in 1975 but the site remained contaminated for many years.

The Rainbow Warrior Conspiracy (Australia, 1989). Director: Chris Thomson. This Australian drama examines the events leading up to the sinking of the Greenpeace flagship by agents of the French intelligence service in 1985.

Who Killed the Electric Car (US, 2006). Director: Chris Paine. Paine's documentary focuses on the electric cars developed in the 1990s and the chain of events that led to their elimination by the mid-2000s.

An Inconvenient Truth (US, 2006). Director: Davis Guggenheim. The documentary based on Al Gore's environmental slide show. Though attacked for bias and over-simplification by elements of the popular media, Gore's film resonated with its audience in a way that few documentaries ever have before, bringing worldwide attention to the climate crisis.

Flow: For Love of Water (US/France, 2008). Director: Irena Salina. Salina's film focuses on the commoditization of water in the twenty-first century and the resulting impact on politics, economics, and human rights. The film addresses the potential outcome of corporate ownership of water rights.

WALL-E (US, 2008). Director: Andrew Stanton. Stanton's animated film presents a world abandoned by its inhabitants after being rendered uninhabitable by mounds of discarded trash. WALL-E is the robot tasked with cleaning up the planet so that humans—who have become almost immobilized by the technologies that make their lives easier—can return.

17

History in the Making: Into the Twenty-First Century

In the concluding chapter of *Conflict and Cooperation*, the documents introduce a number of the key issues that seem poised to shape the twenty-first-century world. Many analysts, including Benjamin Barber whose work opens the chapter, have argued that the two most powerful forces acting upon the contemporary world are the impulse towards globalism[1]—as evidenced by the increasing power of multinational corporations and international organizations—and the simultaneous trend towards ever further fragmentation—the collapse of nation-states and the emergence of sub-state actors. While the overall direction may remain uncertain, it is evident that the confident predictions of a world dominated by liberal democracies advanced by writers such as Francis Fukuyama in the wake of the Cold War have been largely disproven by the increasing global influence of the People's Republic of China, post-Soviet Russia, and other nations.

While it is clearly too early to identify the main themes that will define the twenty-first century, there can be little doubt that the century's first decade was profoundly influenced by the 11 September 2001 terrorist attacks on the United States and the subsequent American interventions in Afghanistan and Iraq. In the immediate aftermath of 9/11 there was an unprecedented level of global support and sympathy for the US and its efforts to eradicate the threat posed by al-Qaeda. However, the subsequent invasion of Iraq and the revelation that US officials had manipulated evidence to build support for the invasion led many nations to refuse further assistance. The presence of a new wave of American troops in the Middle East also brought about a further radicalization among America's existing enemies. Finally, the debt generated by two long and costly wars, as well as a series of more localized interventions, contributed to the devastating economic crisis that gripped the US at the end of the first decade of the new century.

With the US mired in a series of overlapping crises, the influence of new international powers became increasingly clear. As of 2005 China held the second largest total of currency reserves in the world; was the third largest trading nation; and produced some 15 per cent of all US imports. In 2006 Chinese industry employed 83 million workers, with another 100 million able to move into the industrial sector should demand increase. India's emergence as a major economic power has been somewhat less dramatic than China's, but it is no less important. The German Development Institute (DIE) has predicted that by the year 2020 India will occupy China's current role in the global economy. Thus both countries have become increasingly important actors on the international stage.

While some countries undoubtedly benefited from an era of free markets and globalization, other regions of the world struggled with the impact of neo-liberal economics. This has led to the formation of new organizations, such as Mercosur in South America, designed to integrate a number of regional economies in order to create a more powerful and competitive trading bloc. Meanwhile, progress towards genuinely democratic regimes has been mixed. In Russia democracy is clearly in retreat, as new measures have been introduced to limit freedom of the press, to control the electoral process, and to limit free speech. On the other hand, the events of the Arab Spring, which began in December 2010, generated tremendous optimism for a regional turn away from dictatorial regimes across the Middle East and North Africa. Two and a half years later the picture is far less optimistic as constitutional reforms in several countries have either stalled or at least failed to deliver on the ambitious goals of the protesters. In other countries even the most minimal progress has been blocked and, in the case of Syria, a bloody civil war continues between the regime of Bashar al-Assad and those who seek to remove him from power. In both Tunisia, where the movement began, and Egypt, the democratic elections brought about by the Arab Spring initially brought Islamist governments to power. This, in turn, led to the 2013 return to military rule in Egypt.

The documents in this chapter attempt to capture both the potential inherent in the twenty-first century world, and its most serious challenges. The chapter opens with an excerpt from Benjamin Barber's monograph, *Jihad versus McWorld*. One of the worst consequences of global fragmentation can be seen in Philip Gourevitch's *We Wish to Inform You that Tomorrow We Will be Killed with Our Families*. John Updike recalls the shock of the 9/11 attacks and the sense that the world had been profoundly changed at that moment. Many of the grievances that motivated al-Qaeda are explained by Osama bin Laden in a 2004 speech. Stephen Lewis cautions that the global preoccupation with retaliatory wars was taking vital attention away from one of the twenty-first century's most important crises: HIV/AIDS in Africa. Turning to South America, Hugo Chávez reflects on the problems of neo-liberalism and the possibility of a brighter future. Similarly, Dilma Rousseff underscores the many areas that will require attention as Brazil seeks to consolidate its economic growth and development. Vladimir Putin reviews the many security challenges in the twenty-first century world and, finally, Hu Jintao reflects on the legacy of the Chinese Communist Party (CCP) after 90 years in power.

Note

1. "Globalism" is used here rather than "globalization" since the latter tends to have a more exclusively economic connotation.

Benjamin Barber

Benjamin Barber, born in 1939, is a Senior Research Scholar at The Graduate Center, CUNY, founder of the Interdependence Movement, and Walt Whitman Professor Emeritus at Rutgers University. He has been active in a number of non-governmental organizations dedicated to supporting democracy. He was an external advisor to President Bill Clinton and Vermont Governor Howard Dean, and has consulted on and directed a number of pieces for television on political topics. Barber is the author of 17 books, including Strong Democracy, An Aristocracy of Everyone, *and* Jihad versus McWorld. *The ideas that were developed more fully in* Jihad versus McWorld *originally appeared in a 1992 article for the* Atlantic Monthly. *Excerpts from that article follow.*

Document Source: Published originally in *The Atlantic Monthly*, 269(3) (March 1992), 53–65.

Jihad versus McWorld

Just beyond the horizon of current events lie two possible political futures—both bleak, neither democratic. The first is a retribalization of large swaths of humankind by war and bloodshed: a threatened Lebanonization of national states in which culture is pitted against culture, people against people, tribe against tribe—a Jihad in the name of a hundred narrowly conceived faiths against every kind of interdependence, every kind of artificial social cooperation and civic mutuality. The second is being borne in on us by the onrush of economic and ecological forces that demand integration and uniformity and that mesmerize the world with fast music, fast computers, and fast food—with MTV, Macintosh, and McDonald's, pressing nations into one commercially homogenous global network: one McWorld tied together by technology, ecology, communications, and commerce. The planet is falling precipitantly apart AND coming reluctantly together at the very same moment.

These two tendencies are sometimes visible in the same countries at the same instant: thus Yugoslavia, clamoring just recently to join the New Europe, is exploding into fragments; India is trying to live up to its reputation as the world's largest integral democracy while powerful new fundamentalist parties like the Hindu nationalist Bharatiya Janata Party . . . are imperiling its hard-won unity. States are breaking up or joining up: the Soviet Union has disappeared almost overnight, its parts forming new unions with one another or with like-minded nationalities in neighboring states. The old interwar national state based on territory and political sovereignty looks to be a mere transitional development.

The tendencies of what I am here calling the forces of Jihad and the forces of McWorld operate with equal strength in opposite directions, the one driven by parochial hatreds, the other by universalizing markets, the one re-creating ancient subnational and ethnic borders from within, the other making national borders porous from without. They have one thing in common: neither offers much hope to citizens looking for practical ways to govern themselves democratically. If the global future is to pit Jihad's centrifugal whirlwind against McWorld's centripetal black hole, the outcome is unlikely to be democratic—or so I will argue.

McWorld, or the Globalization of Politics

Four imperatives make up the dynamic of McWorld: a market imperative, a resource imperative, an information-technology imperative, and an ecological imperative. By shrinking the world and diminishing the salience of national borders, these imperatives have in combination achieved a considerable victory over factiousness and particularism, and not least of all over their most virulent traditional form—nationalism. It is the realists who are now Europeans, the utopians who dream nostalgically of a resurgent England or Germany, perhaps even a resurgent Wales or Saxony. Yesterday's wishful cry for one world has yielded to the reality of McWorld.

THE MARKET IMPERATIVE. Marxist and Leninist theories of imperialism assumed that the quest for ever-expanding markets would in time compel nation-based capitalist economies to push against national boundaries in search of an international economic imperium. Whatever else has happened to the scientistic predictions of Marxism, in this domain they have proved farsighted. All national economies are now vulnerable to the inroads of larger, transnational markets within which trade is free, currencies are convertible, access to banking is open, and contracts are enforceable under law. In Europe, Asia, Africa, the South Pacific, and the Americas such markets are eroding national sovereignty and giving rise to entities—international banks, trade associations, transnational lobbies like OPEC and Greenpeace, world news services like CNN and the BBC, and multinational corporations that increasingly lack a meaningful national identity—that neither reflect nor respect nationhood as an organizing or regulative principle.

The market imperative has also reinforced the quest for international peace and stability, requisites of an efficient international economy. Markets are enemies of parochialism, isolation, fractiousness, war. Market psychology attenuates the psychology of ideological and religious cleavages and assumes a concord among producers and consumers—categories that ill fit narrowly conceived national or religious cultures. Shopping has little tolerance for blue laws, whether dictated by pub-closing British paternalism, Sabbath-observing Jewish Orthodox fundamentalism, or no-Sunday-liquor-sales Massachusetts puritanism. . . .

Common markets demand a common language, as well as a common currency, and they produce common behaviors of the kind bred by cosmopolitan city life everywhere. Commercial pilots, computer programmers, international bankers, media specialists, oil riggers, entertainment celebrities, ecology experts, demographers, accountants, professors, athletes—these compose a new breed of men and women for whom religion, culture, and nationality can seem only marginal elements in a working identity. . . .

THE RESOURCE IMPERATIVE. Democrats once dreamed of societies whose political autonomy rested firmly on economic independence. The Athenians idealized what they called autarky, and tried for a while to create a way of life simple and austere enough to make the polis genuinely self-sufficient. To be free meant to be independent of any other community or polis. . . .

The dream of autarky briefly engrossed nineteenth-century America as well, for the underpopulated, endlessly bountiful land, the cornucopia of natural resources, and the natural barriers of a continent walled in by two great seas led many to believe that America could be a world unto itself. Given this past, it has been harder for Americans than for most to accept the inevitability of interdependence. But the rapid depletion of resources even in a country like ours, where they once seemed inexhaustible, and the maldistribution of arable soil and mineral resources on the planet, leave even the wealthiest societies ever more resource-dependent and many other nations in permanently desperate straits.

Every nation, it turns out, needs something another nation has; some nations have almost nothing they need.

THE INFORMATION-TECHNOLOGY IMPERATIVE. Enlightenment science and the technologies derived from it are inherently universalizing. They entail a quest for descriptive principles of general application, a search for universal solutions to particular problems, and an unswerving embrace of objectivity and impartiality.

Scientific progress embodies and depends on open communication, a common discourse rooted in rationality, collaboration, and an easy and regular flow and exchange of information. Such ideals can be hypocritical covers for power-mongering by elites, and they may be shown to be wanting in many other ways, but they are entailed by the very idea of science and they make science and globalization practical allies.

Business, banking, and commerce all depend on information flow and are facilitated by new communication technologies. The hardware of these technologies tends to be systemic and integrated—computer, television, cable, satellite, laser, fiber-optic, and microchip technologies combining to create a vast interactive communications and information network that can potentially give every person on earth access to every other person, and make every datum, every byte, available to every set of eyes. If the automobile was, as George Ball once said (when he gave his blessing to a Fiat factory in the Soviet Union during the Cold War), "an ideology on four wheels," then electronic telecommunication and information systems are an ideology at 186,000 miles per second—which makes for a very small planet in a very big hurry. . . .

THE ECOLOGICAL IMPERATIVE. The impact of globalization on ecology is a cliché even to world leaders who ignore it. We know well enough that the German forests can be destroyed by Swiss and Italians driving gas-guzzlers fueled by leaded gas. We also know that the planet can be asphyxiated by greenhouse gases because Brazilian farmers want to be part of the twentieth century and are burning down tropical rain forests to clear a little land to plough, and because Indonesians make a living out of converting their lush jungle into toothpicks for fastidious Japanese diners, upsetting the delicate oxygen balance and in effect puncturing our global lungs. Yet this ecological consciousness has meant not only greater awareness but also greater inequality, as modernized nations try to slam the door behind them, saying to developing nations, "The world cannot afford your modernization; ours has wrung it dry!"

Each of the four imperatives just cited is transnational, transideological, and transcultural. Each applies impartially to Catholics, Jews, Muslims, Hindus, and Buddhists; to democrats and totalitarians; to capitalists and socialists. The Enlightenment dream of a universal rational society has to a remarkable degree been realized—but in a form that is commercialized, homogenized, depoliticized, bureaucratized, and, of course, radically incomplete, for the movement toward McWorld is in competition with forces of global breakdown, national dissolution, and centrifugal corruption. These forces, working in the opposite direction, are the essence of what I call Jihad.

Jihad, or the Lebanonization of the World

OPEC, the World Bank, the United Nations, the International Red Cross, the multinational corporation . . . there are scores of institutions that reflect globalization. But they often appear as ineffective reactors to the world's real actors: national states and, to an ever greater degree, subnational factions in permanent rebellion against uniformity and integration—even the kind represented by universal law and justice. The headlines feature these players regularly: they are cultures, not countries; parts, not wholes; sects, not religions; rebellious factions and dissenting minorities at war not just with globalism but with the traditional nation-state. Kurds, Basques, Puerto Ricans, Ossetians, East Timoreans, Québécois, the Catholics of Northern Ireland, Abkhasians, Kurile Islander Japanese, the Zulus of Inkatha, Catalonians, Tamils, and, of course, Palestinians—people without countries, inhabiting nations not their own, seeking smaller worlds within borders that will seal them off from modernity.

A powerful irony is at work here. Nationalism was once a force of integration and unification, a movement aimed at bringing together disparate clans, tribes, and cultural fragments under new, assimilationist flags. But as Ortega y Gasset noted more than sixty years ago, having won its victories, nationalism changed its strategy. In the 1920s, and again today, it is more often a reactionary and divisive force, pulverizing the very nations it once helped cement together. The force that creates nations is "inclusive," Ortega wrote in *The Revolt of the Masses*. "In periods of consolidation, nationalism has a positive value, and is a lofty standard. But in Europe everything is more than consolidated, and nationalism is nothing but a mania." . . .

This mania has left the post–Cold War world smoldering with hot wars; the international scene is little more unified than it was at the end of the Great War, in Ortega's own time. There were more than thirty wars in progress last year, most of them ethnic, racial, tribal, or religious in character, and the list of unsafe regions doesn't seem to be getting any shorter. Some new world order!

The aim of many of these small-scale wars is to redraw boundaries, to implode states and resecure parochial identities: to escape McWorld's dully insistent imperatives. The mood is that of Jihad: war not as an instrument of policy but as an emblem of identity, an expression of community, an end in itself. Even where there is no shooting war, there is fractiousness, secession, and the quest for ever smaller communities. Add

to the list of dangerous countries those at risk: In Switzerland and Spain, Jurassian and Basque separatists still argue the virtues of ancient identities, sometimes in the language of bombs. . . .

The passing of communism has torn away the thin veneer of internationalism (workers of the world unite!) to reveal ethnic prejudices that are not only ugly and deep-seated but increasingly murderous. Europe's old scourge, anti-Semitism, is back with a vengeance, but it is only one of many antagonisms. It appears all too easy to throw the historical gears into reverse and pass from a Communist dictatorship back into a tribal state.

Among the tribes, religion is also a battlefield. ("Jihad" is a rich word whose generic meaning is "struggle"—usually the struggle of the soul to avert evil. Strictly applied to religious war, it is used only in reference to battles where the faith is under assault, or battles against a government that denies the practice of Islam. My use here is rhetorical, but does follow both journalistic practice and history.) Remember the Thirty Years War? Whatever forms of Enlightenment universalism might once have come to grace such historically related forms of monotheism as Judaism, Christianity, and Islam, in many of their modern incarnations they are parochial rather than cosmopolitan, angry rather than loving, proselytizing rather than ecumenical, zealous rather than rationalist, sectarian rather than deistic, ethnocentric rather than universalizing. As a result, like the new forms of hypernationalism, the new expressions of religious fundamentalism are fractious and pulverizing, never integrating. This is religion as the Crusaders knew it: a battle to the death for souls that if not saved will be forever lost. . . .

Study Question

For which of the two scenarios—Jihad or McWorld—does Barber make a more compelling case?

Philip Gourevitch

Philip Gourevitch (b. 1961) is a staff writer at The New Yorker *magazine. He travelled to Rwanda in 1995, one year after the genocide that killed some-where near 800,000 people, mostly Tutsis, in a mat-ter of a few months. After several more trips into the region Gourevitch published* We Wish to Inform You That Tomorrow We Will Be Killed with Our Families *in 1998. One of the book's central themes concerns the absence of western intervention during* *the genocide, despite the presence of a small UN peacekeeping force, under Canadian General Roméo Dallaire, who called repeatedly for assistance in the face of the escalating massacres. Another theme, more clearly illustrated in the excerpt below, concerns the human capacity for evil.*

Document Source: Philip Gourevitch, *We Wish to Inform You That Tomorrow We Will Be Killed with Our Families: Stories from Rwanda* (New York: Farrar, Straus, & Giroux, Inc., 1998).

We Wish to Inform You That Tomorrow We Will Be Killed with Our Families

In the province of Kibungo, in eastern Rwanda, in the swamp and pastureland near the Tanzanian border, there's a rocky hill called Nyarubuye with a church where many Tutsis were slaughtered in mid-April of 1994. A year after the killing I went to Nyarubuye with two Canadian military officers. We flew in a United Nations helicopter, traveling low over the hills in the morning mists, with the banana trees like green starbursts dense over the slopes. The uncut grass blew back as we dropped into the center of the parish schoolyard. A lone solider materialized with his Kalashnikov, and shook our hands with stiff, shy formality. The Canadians pre-sented the paperwork for our visit, and I stepped up into the open doorway of a classroom.

At least fifty mostly decomposed cadavers covered the floor, wadded in clothing, their be-longings strewn about and smashed. Macheted skulls had rolled here and there.

The dead looked like pictures of the dead. They did not smell. They did not buzz with flies. They had been killed thirteen months earlier, and they hadn't been moved. Skin stuck here and there over the bones, many of which lay scat-tered away from the bodies, dismembered by the killers, or by scavengers—birds, dogs, bugs. The more complete figures looked a lot like people, which they were once. A woman in a cloth wrap printed with flowers lay near the door. Her flesh-less hip bones were high and her legs slightly spread, and a child's skeleton extended between them. Her torso was hollowed out. Her ribs and spinal column poked through the rotting cloth. Her head was tipped back and her mouth was open: a strange image—half agony, half repose.

I had never been among the dead before. What to do? Look? Yes. I wanted to see them, I suppose; I had come to see them—the dead had been left unburied at Nyarubuye for memorial purposes—and there they were, so intimately exposed. I didn't need to see them. I already knew, and be-lieved, what had happened in Rwanda. Yet looking at the buildings and the bodies, and hearing the silence of the place, with the grand Italianate basil-ica standing there deserted, and beds of exquisite, decadent, death-fertilized flowers blooming over the corpses, it was still strangely unimaginable. I mean one still had to imagine it.

Those dead Rwandans will be with me forever, I expect. That was why I had felt compelled to come to Nyarubuye: to be stuck with them—not with their experience, but with the experience of looking at them. They had been killed there, and they were dead there. What else could you really see at first? The Bible bloated with rain lying on top of one corpse or, littered about, the little woven wreaths of thatch which Rwandan women wear as crowns to balance the enormous loads they carry on their heads, and the water gourds, and the Converse tennis sneaker stuck somehow in a pelvis. . . .

A few weeks earlier, in Bukavu, Zaire, in the giant market of a refugee camp that was home to many Rwandan Hutu militiamen, I had watched a man butchering a cow with a machete. He was quite expert at his work, taking big precise strokes that made a sharp hacking noise. The rallying cry to the killers during the genocide was "Do your work!" And I saw that it *was* work, this butchery; hard work. It took many hacks—two, three, four, five hard hacks—to chop through the cow's leg. How many hacks to dismember a person?

Considering the enormity of the task, it is tempting to play with theories of collective madness, mob mania, a fever of hatred erupted into a mass crime of passion, and to imagine the blind orgy of the mob, with each member killing one or two people. But at Nyarubuye, and at thousands of other sites in this tiny country, on the same days of a few months in 1994, hundreds of thousands of Hutus had worked as killers in regular shifts. There was always the next victim, and the next. What sustained them, beyond the frenzy of the first attack, through the plain physical exhaustion and mess of it?

The pygmy in Gikongoro said that inhumanity is part of nature and that we must go against nature to get along and have peace. But mass violence, too, must be organized; it does not occur aimlessly. Even mobs and riots have a design, and great and sustained destruction requires great ambition. It must be conceived as the means toward achieving a new order, and although the idea behind that new order may be criminal and objectively very stupid, it must also be compellingly simple and at

Victims of the Rwandan genocide. A number of memorial sites have been created in post-genocide Rwanda.
REUTERS/Peter Andrews.

the same time absolute. The ideology of genocide is all of those things, and in Rwanda it went by the bald name of Hutu Power. For those who set about systematically exterminating an entire people—even a fairly small and unresisting subpopulation of perhaps a million and a quarter men, women, and children, like the Tutsis in Rwanda—blood lust surely helps. But the engineers and perpetrators of a slaughter like the one just inside the door where I stood need not enjoy killing, and they may even find it unpleasant. What is required above all is that they want their victims dead. They have to want it so badly that they consider it a necessity.

So I still had much to imagine as I entered the classroom and stepped carefully between the remains. These dead and their killers had been neighbors, schoolmates, colleagues, sometimes friends, even in-laws. The dead had seen their killers training as militias in the weeks before the end, and it was well known that they were training to kill Tutsis; it was announced on the radio, it was in the newspapers, people spoke of it openly. The week before the massacre at Nyarubuye, the killing began in Rwanda's capital, Kigali. Hutus who opposed the Hutu Power ideology were publicly denounced as "accomplices" of the Tutsis and were among the first to be killed as the extermination got under way. In Nyarubuye, when Tutsis asked the Hutu Power mayor how they might be spared, he suggested that they seek sanctuary at the church. They did, and a few days later the mayor came to kill them. . . .

The killers killed all day at Nyarubuye. At night they cut the Achilles tendons of survivors and went off to feast behind the church, roasting cattle looted from their victims in big fires, and drinking beer. (Bottled beer, banana beer—Rwandans may not drink more beer than other Africans, but they drink prodigious quantities of it around the clock.) And, in the morning, still drunk after whatever sleep they could find beneath the cries of their prey, the killers at Nyarubuye went back and killed again. Day after day, minute to minute, Tutsi by Tutsi: all across Rwanda, they worked like that. "It was a process," Sergeant Francis said. I can see that it happened, I can be told how, and after nearly three years of looking around Rwanda and listening to Rwandans, I can tell you how, and I will. But the horror of it—the idiocy, the waste, the sheer wrongness—remains uncircumscribable. . . .

"Every survivor wonders why he is alive," Abbé Modeste, a priest at the cathedral in Butare, Rwanda's second-largest city, told me. Abbé Modeste had hidden for weeks in his sacristy, eating communion wafers, before moving under the desk in his study, and finally into the rafters at the home of some neighboring nuns. The obvious explanation of his survival was that the RPF had come to the rescue. But the RPF didn't reach Butare till early July, and roughly seventy-five per cent of the Tutsis in Rwanda had been killed by early May.

In this regard, at least, the genocide had been entirely successful: to those who were targeted, it was not death but life that seemed an accident of fate.

"I had eighteen people killed at my house," said Etienne Niyonzima, a former businessman who had become a deputy in the National Assembly. "Everything was totally destroyed—a place of fifty-five meters by fifty meters. In my neighborhood they killed six hundred and forty-seven people. They tortured them, too. You had to see how they killed them. They had the number of everyone's house, and they went through with red paint and marked the homes of all the Tutsis and of the Hutu moderates. My wife was at a friend's, shot with two bullets. She is still alive, only"—he fell quiet for a moment—"she has no arms. The others with her were killed. The militia left her for dead. Her whole family of sixty-five in Gitarama were killed." Niyonzima was in hiding at the time. Only after he had been separated from his wife for three months did he learn that she and four of their children had survived. "Well," he said, "one son was cut in the head with a machete. I don't know where he went." His voice weakened, and caught. "He disappeared." Niyonzima clicked his tongue, and said, "But the others are still alive. Quite honestly, I don't understand at all how I was saved."

Laurent Nkongoli attributed his survival to "Providence, and also good neighbors, an old woman who said, 'Run away, we don't want to see your corpse.'" Nkongoli, a lawyer, who had become the vice president of the National Assembly after the genocide, was a robust man, with a taste for double-breasted suit jackets and lively ties, and he moved, as he spoke, with a brisk determination. But before taking his neighbor's advice, and fleeing Kigali in late April of 1994, he said, "I had accepted death. At a certain moment this happens. One hopes not to die cruelly, but one expects to die anyway. Not death by machete, one hopes, but with a bullet. If you were willing to pay for it, you could often ask for a bullet. . . .

"Rwandan culture is a culture of fear," Nkongoli went on. "I remember what people said." He adopted a pipey voice, and his face took on a look of disgust: 'Just let us pray, then kill us,' or 'I don't want to die in the street, I want to die at home.'" He resumed his normal voice. "When you're that resigned and oppressed you're already dead. It shows the genocide was prepared for too long. I detest this fear. These victims of genocide had been psychologically prepared to expect death just for being Tutsi. They were being killed for so long that they were already dead."

I reminded Nkongoli that, for all his hatred of fear, he had himself accepted death before his neighbor urged him to run away. "Yes," he said. "I got tired in the genocide. You struggle so long, then you get tired."

Every Rwandan I spoke with seemed to have a favorite, unanswerable question. For Nkongoli, it was how so many Tutsis had allowed themselves to be killed. For François Xavier Nkurunziza, a Kigali lawyer, whose father was Hutu and whose mother and wife were Tutsi, the question was how so many Hutus had allowed themselves to kill. Nkurunziza had escaped death only by chance as he moved around the country from one hiding place to another, and he had lost many family members.

"Conformity is very deep, very developed here," he told me. "In Rwandan history, everyone obeys authority. People revere power, and there isn't enough education. You take a poor, ignorant population, and give them arms, and say, 'It's yours. Kill.' They'll obey. The peasants, who were paid or forced to kill, were looking up to people of higher socio-economic standing to see how to behave. So the people of influence, or the big financiers, are often the big men in the genocide. They may think that they didn't kill because they didn't take life with their own hands, but the people were looking to them for their orders. And, in Rwanda, an order can be given very quietly."

As I traveled around the country, collecting accounts of the killing, it almost seemed as if, with the machete, the *masu*—a club studded with nails—a few well-placed grenades, and a few bursts of automatic-rifle fire, the quiet orders of Hutu Power had made the neutron bomb obsolete. . . .

Study Question

Based upon the author's account, what were the most important factors that facilitated genocide in Rwanda?

John Updike

John Updike (1932–2009) was one of the best-known American writers and literary critics of the twentieth century. After beginning his career at The New Yorker magazine in the late 1950s, he wrote prodigiously for the next five decades. In 2001, after witnessing the destruction of the World Trade Center towers from the rooftop of a New York apartment, *he joined a number of other prominent writers and intellectuals to reflect on the experience and its consequences. Their observations were published in The New Yorker on 24 September 2001, less than two weeks after the attacks.*

Document Source: John Updike, "Talk of the Town," *The New Yorker,* September 24, 2001.

11 September 2001

Suddenly summoned to witness something great and horrendous, we keep fighting not to reduce it to our own smallness. From the viewpoint of a tenth-floor apartment in Brooklyn Heights, where

I happened to be visiting some kin, the destruction of the World Trade Center twin towers had the false intimacy of television, on a day of perfect reception. A four-year-old girl and her babysitter called from the library, and pointed out through the window the smoking top of the north tower, not a mile away. It seemed, at that first glance, more curious than horrendous: smoke speckled with bits of paper curled into the cloudless sky, and strange inky rivulets ran down the giant structure's vertically corrugated surface. The W.T.C. had formed a pale background to our Brooklyn view of lower Manhattan, not beloved, like the stony, spired midtown thirties skyscrapers it had displaced as the city's tallest, but, with its pre-postmodern combination of unignorable immensity and architectural reticence, in some lights beautiful. As we watched the second tower burst into ballooning flame (an intervening building had hidden the approach of the second airplane), there persisted the notion that, as on television, this was not quite real; it could be fixed; the technocracy the towers symbolized would find a way to put out the fire and reverse the damage.

And then, within an hour, as my wife and I watched from the Brooklyn building's roof, the south tower dropped from the screen of our viewing; it fell straight down like an elevator, with a tinkling shiver and a groan of concussion distinct across the mile of air. We knew we had just witnessed thousands of deaths; we clung to each other as if we ourselves were falling. Amid the glittering impassivity of the many buildings across the East River, an empty spot had appeared, as if by electronic command, beneath the sky that, but for the sulfurous cloud streaming south toward the ocean, was pure blue, rendered uncannily pristine by the absence of jet trails. A swiftly expanding burst of smoke and dust hid the rest of lower Manhattan; we saw the collapse of the second tower only on television, where the footage of hellbent airplane, exploding jet fuel, and imploding tower was played and replayed, much rehearsed moments from a nightmare ballet.

The nightmare is still on. The bodies are beneath the rubble, the last-minute cell-phone calls—remarkably calm and loving, many of them—are still being reported, the sound of an airplane overhead still bears an unfamiliar menace, the thought of boarding an airplane with our old blasé blitheness keeps receding into the past. Determined men who have transposed their own lives to a martyr's afterlife can still inflict an amount of destruction that defies belief. War is conducted with a fury that requires abstraction—that turns a planeful of peaceful passengers, children included, into a missile the faceless enemy deserves. The other side has the abstractions; we have only the mundane duties of survivors—to pick up the pieces, to bury the dead, to take more precautions, to go on living.

American freedom of motion, one of our prides, has taken a hit. Can we afford the openness that lets future kamikaze pilots, say, enroll in Florida flying schools? A Florida neighbor of one of the suspects remembers him saying he didn't like the United States: "He said it was too lax. He said, 'I can go anywhere I want to, and they can't stop me.'" It is a weird complaint, a begging perhaps to be stopped. Weird, too, the silence of the heavens these days, as flying has ceased across America. But fly again we must; risk is a price of freedom, and walking around Brooklyn Heights that afternoon, as ash drifted in the air and cars were few and open-air lunches continued as usual on Montague Street, renewed the impression that, with all its failings, this is a country worth fighting for. Freedom, reflected in the street's diversity and daily ease, felt palpable. It is mankind's elixir, even if a few turn it to poison.

The next morning, I went back to the open vantage from which we had watched the tower so dreadfully slip from sight. The fresh sun shone on the eastward façades, a few boats tentatively moved in the river, the ruins were still sending out smoke, but New York looked glorious.

Study Question

Updike argues that America's freedom of movement was a casualty of 9/11. More than a decade after the events of September 11, have other freedoms been affected by the attacks in the United States? Have any of these been reclaimed?

Osama bin Laden

Osama bin Laden (1957–2011) was born in Riyadh, Saudi Arabia. His father was a wealthy businessman, with close ties to the Saudi monarchy. Sources on his education often provide conflicting information, but it is possible that bin Laden completed a degree in either civil engineering or public administration. He travelled to Afghanistan in either the late 1970s or early 1980s and began working with US-backed mujahedeen factions. After the Soviet withdrawal he founded al-Qaeda ("The

Base") and was responsible for a number of subsequent terrorist attacks on targets identified as sympathetic to the United States. Many analysts point to the first Gulf War as the key to bin Laden's hatred of the US. The following speech by bin Laden in 2004 explains the motives behind the 11 September 2001 attack on targets inside the US.

Document Source: Osama bin Laden, Speech on American Policy, October 2004: Available online: http://www.aljazeera.com/archive/2004/11/200849163336457223.html

Speech on American Policy, October 2004

Praise be to Allah who created the creation for his worship and commanded them to be just and permitted the wronged one to retaliate against the oppressor in kind. To proceed:

Peace be upon he who follows the guidance: People of America this talk of mine is for you and concerns the ideal way to prevent another Manhattan, and deals with the war and its causes and results.

Before I begin, I say to you that security is an indispensable pillar of human life and that free men do not forfeit their security, contrary to Bush's claim that we hate freedom.

If so, then let him explain to us why we don't strike for example—Sweden? And we know that freedom-haters don't possess defiant spirits like those of the 19—may Allah have mercy on them.[1]

No, we fight because we are free men who don't sleep under oppression. We want to restore freedom to our nation, just as you lay waste to our nation. So shall we lay waste to yours.

No one except a dumb thief plays with the security of others and then makes himself believe he will be secure. Whereas thinking people, when disaster strikes, make it their priority to look for its causes, in order to prevent it happening again.

But I am amazed at you. Even though we are

in the fourth year after the events of September 11th, Bush is still engaged in distortion, deception, and hiding from you the real causes. And thus, the reasons are still there for a repeat of what occurred.

So I shall talk to you about the story behind those events and shall tell you truthfully about the moments in which the decision was taken, for you to consider.

I say to you, Allah knows that it had never occurred to us to strike the towers. But after it became unbearable and we witnessed the oppression and tyranny of the American/Israeli coalition against our people in Palestine and Lebanon, it came to my mind.

The events that affected my soul in a direct way started in 1982 when America permitted the Israelis to invade Lebanon and the American Sixth Fleet helped them in that. This bombardment began and many were killed and injured and others were terrorised and displaced.

I couldn't forget those moving scenes, blood and severed limbs, women and children sprawled everywhere. Houses destroyed along with their occupants and high rises demolished over their residents, rockets raining down on our home without mercy.

The situation was like a crocodile meeting a helpless child, powerless except for his screams. Does the crocodile understand a conversation that doesn't include a weapon? And the whole world saw and heard but it didn't respond.

In those difficult moments many hard-to-describe ideas bubbled in my soul, but in the end they produced an intense feeling of rejection of tyranny, and gave birth to a strong resolve to punish the oppressors.

And as I looked at those demolished towers in Lebanon, it entered my mind that we should punish the oppressor in kind and that we should destroy towers in America in order that they taste some of what we tasted and so that they be deterred from killing our women and children.

And that day, it was confirmed to me that oppression and the intentional killing of innocent women and children is a deliberate American policy. Destruction is freedom and democracy, while resistance is terrorism and intolerance.

This means the oppressing and embargoing to death of millions as Bush Sr did in Iraq in the greatest mass slaughter of children mankind has ever known, and it means the throwing of millions of pounds of bombs and explosives at millions of children—also in Iraq—as Bush Jr did, in order to remove an old agent and replace him with a new puppet to assist in the pilfering of Iraq's oil and other outrages.

So with these images and their like as their background, the events of September 11th came as a reply to those great wrongs, should a man be blamed for defending his sanctuary?

Is defending oneself and punishing the aggressor in kind, objectionable terrorism? If it is such, then it is unavoidable for us.

This is the message which I sought to communicate to you in word and deed, repeatedly, for years before September 11th.

And you can read this, if you wish, in my interview with Scott in *Time Magazine* in 1996, or with Peter Arnett on CNN in 1997, or my meeting with John Weiner in 1998.

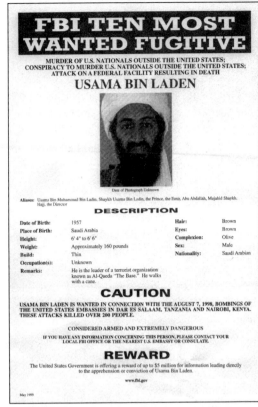

The "Most Wanted" poster created by the FBI for Osama bin Laden in 1999.

Department of Justice, Federal Bureau of Investigation. Courtesy of the Office of Public Affairs, Fugitive Publicity Office.

You can observe it practically, if you wish, in Kenya and Tanzania and in Aden. And you can read it in my interview with Abdul Bari Atwan, as well as my interviews with Robert Fisk.

The latter is one of your compatriots and co-religionists and I consider him to be neutral. So are the pretenders of freedom at the White House and the channels controlled by them able to run an interview with him? So that he may relay to the American people what he has understood from us to be the reasons for our fight against you?

If you were to avoid these reasons, you will have taken the correct path that will lead America to the security that it was in before September

11th. This concerned the causes of the war.

As for its results, they have been, by the grace of Allah, positive and enormous, and have, by all standards, exceeded all expectations. This is due to many factors, chief among them, that we have found it difficult to deal with the Bush administration in light of the resemblance it bears to the regimes in our countries, half of which are ruled by the military and the other half which are ruled by the sons of kings and presidents.

Our experience with them is lengthy, and both types are replete with those who are characterized by pride, arrogance, greed and misappropriation of wealth. This resemblance began after the visits of Bush Sr to the region.

At a time when some of our compatriots were dazzled by America and hoping that these visits would have an effect on our countries, all of a sudden he was affected by those monarchies and military regimes, and became envious of their remaining decades in their positions, to embezzle the public wealth of the nation without supervision or accounting.

So he took dictatorship and suppression of freedoms to his son and they named it the Patriot Act, under the pretense of fighting terrorism. In addition, Bush sanctioned the installing of sons as state governors, and didn't forget to import expertise in election fraud from the region's presidents to Florida to be made use of in moments of difficulty.

All that we have mentioned has made it easy for us to provoke and bait this administration. All that we have to do is to send two mujahidin to the furthest point east to raise a piece of cloth on which is written al-Qaida, in order to make the generals race there to cause America to suffer human, economic, and political losses without their achieving for it anything of note other than some benefits for their private companies.

This is in addition to our having experience in using guerrilla warfare and the war of attrition to fight tyrannical superpowers, as we, alongside the mujahidin, bled Russia for 10 years, until it went bankrupt and was forced to withdraw in defeat.

All Praise is due to Allah.

So we are continuing this policy in bleeding America to the point of bankruptcy. Allah willing, and nothing is too great for Allah. . . .

Note

1. Bin Laden is referring to the 19 hijackers who were part of the September 11th attacks.

> **Study Question**
>
> Based on bin Laden's speech, what were the most important motivations for the attacks on the United States?

Stephen Lewis

Stephen Lewis (b. 1937) was the UN Secretary-General's Special Envoy for HIV/AIDS in Africa from 2001 until 2006. Prior to accepting this position Lewis had been the Deputy Executive Director of UNICEF (1995 to 1999) and Canada's Ambassador to the United Nations (1984–1988), and prior to that the leader of the NDP opposition in Ontario in the 1970s. As UN Special Envoy, Lewis undertook to focus western attention on the crisis unfolding in AIDS-stricken Sub-Saharan Africa. The following is an excerpt of a briefing he gave to the United Nations on 8 January 2003. But even as he delivered this speech, global attention was being increasingly focused on the imminent US attack on Iraq.

Document Source: Stephen Lewis, "UN Briefing on HIV/AIDS in Africa." From Stephen Lewis, "Text of UN Briefing by Stephen Lewis on HIV/AIDS in Africa." Available online: http://www.worldrevolution.org/article/279

UN Briefing on HIV/AIDS in Africa

Last month, I spent two weeks touring four countries in Southern Africa: Lesotho, Zimbabwe, Malawi, and Zambia. The primary purpose was to view the link between hunger and AIDS. I want to look back at that visit, because little will have changed between then and now (except, perhaps, that things will have deteriorated further), and then look forward to the prospects for addressing the pandemic in 2003.

At the outset, however, let me express, yet again, the fundamental conviction I have every time I visit Africa: there is no question that the pandemic can be defeated. No matter how terrible the scourge of AIDS, no matter how limited the capacity to respond, no matter how devastating the human toll, it is absolutely certain that the pandemic can be turned around with a joint and Herculean effort between the African countries themselves and the international community.

I am weary to the point of exasperated impatience at the endless expressions of doubt about Africa's resolve and Africa's intentions and Africa's capacities. The truth is that all over the continent, even in the most extreme of circumstances, such as those which prevail today in the four nations I visited, Africans are engaged in endless numbers of initiatives and projects and programmes and models which, if taken to scale, if generalized throughout the country, would halt the pandemic, and prolong and save millions of lives.

What is required is a combination of political will and resources. The political will is increasingly there; the money is not. A major newspaper in the United States, reflecting on the paucity of resources, used the startling phrase "murder by complacency." I differ in only one particular: it's mass murder by complacency.

You will forgive me for the strong language. But as we enter the year 2003, the time for polite, even agitated, entreaties is over. This pandemic cannot be allowed to continue, and those who watch it unfold with a kind of pathological equanimity must be held to account. There may yet come a day when we have peacetime tribunals to deal with this particular version of crimes against humanity.

As bad as things are in Southern Africa—and they are terrible—every country I visited exhibited particular strengths and hopes.

The little country of Lesotho has a most impressive political leadership, but is absolutely impoverished. If it had some significant additional resources, with which to build capacity, it could begin to rescue countless lives. I vividly remember the Prime Minister of Lesotho saying to me "We're told repeatedly by donors that we don't have capacity. I know we have no capacity; give us some help and we'll build the capacity." It's worth remembering that Lesotho has a population greater than that of Namibia and Botswana, but it has nowhere near the same pockets of wealth. It has, however, one of the highest prevalence rates for HIV[1] on the continent . . . higher than Namibia; almost as high as Botswana . . . and is fatally compromised in its response by the lack of resources.

Zimbabwe, whatever the levels of political turbulence, has created a sturdy municipal infrastructure for the purpose of dealing with AIDS. You will know that for the last couple of years, Zimbabwe has had a three per cent surtax on corporate and personal income, devoted to work on AIDS. A good part of that money has been channelled down to district and village level, through a complex array of committees and structures which actually get the money to the grassroots. It's visible in the work of youth peer educators, outreach workers, and home care through community-based and faith-based organizations. . . .

In Malawi, we may be about to see the most interesting of experiments in the provision of anti-retroviral treatment in the public sector. The Government of Malawi had originally intended to treat 25,000 people based on receipt of monies from the Global Fund. They then realized that the calculation of 25,000 was based on the purchase of patent drugs, but now that it is possible to purchase generic drugs, the numbers eligible for treatment could rise to 50,000. . . .

Zambia, whatever the difficulties—and they are overwhelming—is emerging from the bleak and dark ages of denial into the light of recognition. The bitter truth is that in the regime of the previous President, nothing was done. He spent his time disavowing the reality of AIDS, and hurling obstacles in the way of those who were desperate to confront the pandemic. I can recall personally attending an annual OAU Summit on behalf of UNICEF, and sitting down with the then President Chiluba, and asking him what he intended to do about AIDS, and he simply wouldn't talk to me about it. Well there's a new President in Zambia. And although he's been in place for only one year, everyone agrees that there's a dramatic change in the voice of political leadership around the subject of AIDS.

The fact is that in every country, even under the most appalling of human circumstance, there are signs of determination and hope. Whether they can be harnessed in the name of social change will be known in the year 2003. God knows, there are incredible hurdles to leap.

If I am to extract from my trip those aspects that made the greatest impression on me, they are six in number.

First, there is absolutely no doubt that hunger and AIDS have come together in a Hecate's[2] brew of horror. We saw it everywhere. How could it be otherwise? In Malawi, for example, analysis of the data shows that 50 per cent of poor households are affected by chronic illness due to HIV/AIDS. You can't till the soil, grow the crops, feed the family, when disease stalks the land. Add to that the reality of erratic rainfall and drought, and WFP and the broader UN family have a hugely daunting job.

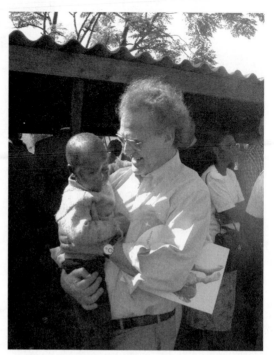

Stephen Lewis in Zimbabwe during his travels as a UN Special Envoy for HIV/AIDS in Africa.

© WFP/ Brenda Barton

I think the nadir was reached for me in the paediatric ward of the University Teaching Hospital in Lusaka.[3] The infants were clustered, stick-thin, three and four to a bed, most so weakened by hunger and ravaged by AIDS (a prevalence rate in the nutrition section of the ward of 56 per cent . . . in the respiratory section of the ward, 72 per cent), that they really had no chance. We were there for 45 minutes. Every 15 minutes, another child died, awkwardly covered with a sheet, then removed by a nurse, while the ward was filled with the anguished weeping of the mothers. A scene from hell.

Second, I couldn't help but feel, on occasion, that we were witnessing the grinding down of a society. We've all imagined the catastrophe, but no one wanted to believe that it could happen. The fact that the agricultural sector is beginning to decay could simply be a harbinger of worse to come. My own sense is that education is on the brink. In all of the countries, teachers were dead, teachers were dying, teachers were ill and away from school, children, especially girls, were being taken out of school to tend to sick and dying parents, children who had lost their parents to AIDS weren't in school because they couldn't afford the school fees. It felt, in every instance, as though the education sector was under siege. In Zambia, they lost 1,967 teachers in 2001, over two thousand teachers in 2002; the Teacher's Colleges are graduating fewer than one thousand a year. In parts of Malawi, HIV-positive teachers are estimated at over 30 per cent. How can education be sustained?

Or maybe the collapse of agriculture and education are happening simultaneously, and we fasten on agriculture simply because the human damage is visible and immediate. If you don't eat for five days, the consequence is far more dramatic than being out of school for five days. In Malawi they've done an analysis of the impact of AIDS on four different Ministries, and the erosion in each, in human terms, to a lesser or greater degree, is inescapable. It's necessary to recognize that even at a prevalence rate of 15 or 20 per cent . . . the incessant, irreversible, cumulative death of so many productive members of society means, ultimately, that things fall apart. When Chinua Achebe wrote his novel of that title several decades ago, little did he know that it would be the mantra of whole societies. I wouldn't discount the possibility, 10 or 15 years down the road, of failed states.

Third, one of the saddest manifestations of a society coming apart at the seams, is the growing rate of sexual abuse of children and adolescents. I was frankly jolted by what we were told. Whether it was the plight of orphans in the mountains of Lesotho, or outreach workers telling gruesome stories, *sotto voce*, as we traveled in Zimbabwe, or the evidence we absorbed in Zambia, there seems little doubt that sexual assaults on children have reached shocking proportions. It's so bad in Zambia that a trio of women parliamentarians are actually introducing a private member's bill to counter "child defilement." . . .

It appears to happen to orphans especially.

As they are moved from place to place, more and more distant from their origins, they become increasingly vulnerable to sexual abuse. Ironically, and bitterly, they also therefore become ever more vulnerable to HIV transmission.

Fourth, I've never before felt the impact of orphans so strongly. It struck me again that we have obvious ways of dealing with most other aspects of the pandemic, but dealing with the astronomic number of orphans is a new phenomenon for which the world has no evident solution. Public health has confronted and subdued terrible contagions of communicable disease at other moments in human history. One day, the same will be true for AIDS. But we've never before confronted the selective destruction of parents that leaves such a mass of orphans behind.

And it's necessary, I think, to recognize that the extended family, and the willing community, can never fully cope with the numbers. The result is the present and escalating reality of orphan street children, of orphan gangs, of orphan delinquency, as hordes of kids, torn from their familial roots, wander the continent, bewildered, lonely, disenfranchised from reality, angry, acting out, unable to relate to normal life. Some have already reached adulthood; they've had no love, no nurturing . . . how do they bring up their own children? And in the meantime, they can be a high-risk group, posing a collective threat to social stability.

Fifth, if women are at the center of the pandemic, as they are, acutely vulnerable to infection on the one hand, doing all the care-giving for the sick and the orphans on the other, we saw precious little evidence of efforts at women's empowerment, sexual autonomy or gender equality. And there was certainly no effort whatsoever to relieve their unfair share of the burden. In fact, male hegemony was ubiquitous. On my return trip later this month, I intend to focus on what is being done to imbed the human rights of women in each country, such that they can save their lives.

Finally, the issue of antiretroviral treatment

came up constantly and everywhere. Every single group of People Living With HIV/AIDS pounded the demand home in unrelenting fashion. There is a crescendo of rage and desperation which governments will ignore at their peril. In Malawi, the prospect of 50,000 people eligible for treatment in the foreseeable future brings a strong quotient of hope. But in Zambia, the amorphous prospect of perhaps ten thousand people entering into treatment, over time, the eligibility criteria not yet known, prompts nothing but anger. And in Zimbabwe and Lesotho, where treatment is at the earliest stage of discussion, there is a festering despair among those who need it now.

What has changed is the maturity, vehemence, and confidence of the organizations of People Living With HIV/AIDS. Time and again we met activists who know everything there is to know about CD4 counts and viral loads; they know the cost of generic drugs; they know about the treatment regimens; they know that WHO [World Health Organization] has undertaken to have three million people in treatment by 2005; they know that the rich members of society vault down to South Africa for treatment, while the poor remain helplessly behind; they know about Doha and intellectual property rights and the WTO; they know, from bitter experience, about all the false political promises. Increasingly, we're dealing with sophistication and determination in equal measure.

When I met with the group of People Living With HIV/AIDS in Lusaka, they presented me with a powerful and encyclopedic brief, a small part of which read as follows: ". . . for each day that passes without people accessing treatment we attend funerals. People die. We hear a hundred reasons

for not providing people with treatment. For each reason given, lives are lost. The government must realize that it has a responsibility to provide health care for its people. Any government that fails to put in place measures to ensure the health of its citizens is not a government worth its name. Such governments should resign. If it does not do so, then people are justified to remove it by any means necessary. The right to life and dignity should not be a preserve of the rich and powerful.

"What we are seeing in Zambia is a microcosm of what is happening globally. The HIV/AIDS crisis is not a crisis of lack of resources. It is a crisis of lack of conscience. It is the obscene gap between the haves and the have-nots that is driving this holocaust. . . ."

People living with HIV/AIDS are in a race against time. What they never imagined was that over and above the virus itself, there would be a new adversary, and that adversary would be a war.

Notes

1. In 2004 Lesotho's HIV infection rate was 28.9 per cent. By 2009 it had dropped to 23.6 per cent.
2. Hecate (Hecuba) was regarded in Greece as a goddess of magic. Over the years she became associated with the dark side of magic.
3. The capital of Zambia.

> **Study Question**
>
> "The HIV/AIDS crisis is not a crisis of lack of resources. It is a crisis of lack of conscience. It is the obscene gap between the haves and the have-nots that is driving this holocaust." What does Lewis mean by this?

Hugo Chávez

Hugo Chávez (1954–2013) was elected president of Venezuela in 1998, and took office in 1999. He had previously attempted, unsuccessfully, to topple the repressive government of Carlos Andrés Pérez, inspired by an ideology he called Bolivarianism developed during his university days and based on the actions of Latin American liberator Simón Bolívar. After taking office Chávez spoke out against globalization and the economic policies supported by organizations such as the IMF and World Bank, while promoting regional economic cooperation and socialist policies at home. The Group of 15 (G-15) works to coordinate policy among developing nations around the world. Chavez delivered the speech which follows in 2004, as

Venezuela played host to the G-15 summit in 2004.

Document Source: Hugo Chávez, "Speech on the Opening of the G-15 Summit, 2004," Caracas, Venezuela; Source: http://www.venezuelanalysis.com/analysis/381

Speech on the Opening of the G-15 Summit, 2004

. . . Welcome to this land washed by the waters of the Atlantic Ocean and the Caribbean Sea, crossed by the magnificent Orinoco River. A land crowned by the perpetual snow of the Andean mountains. . . !

A land overwhelmed by the never-ending magic of the Amazon forest and its millenary chants. . . !

Welcome to Venezuela, the land where a patriotic people has taken over again the banners of Simon Bolivar, its Libertador, whose name is well known beyond these frontiers!

. . . In his letter to Jamaica in 1815, Bolivar [wrote] . . .

I wish one day we would have the opportunity to install there an august congress with the representatives of the Republics, Kingdoms, and Empires to debate and discuss the highest interests of Peace and War with the countries of the other three parts of the world.

Bolivar reveals himself as an anti-imperialist leader, in the same historic perspective that 140 years after that insightful letter at Kingston materialized in the Bandung Conference in April 1955. Inspired by Nehru, Tito y [and] Nasser, a group of important leaders gathered at this conference to face great challenges and expressed their wish of not being involved in the East–West conflict and rather work together toward national development. This was the first key milestone: the first Afro-Asian conference, the immediate precedent of the Non-Aligned Countries that gathered 29 Heads of State and from which the "Conscience of the South" was born.

Two events of great political significance occurred in the '60s: the creation of the Non-Aligned Movement in Belgrade in 1961 and the Group of the 77 in 1964[1]: Two milestones and a clear historic trend: the need of the self-awareness of the South and of acting together in a world reality characterized by imbalance and unequal exchange. . . .

All those struggles, ideas and proposals sunk in the Neo-liberal Flood and the world began to witness the so-called "end of History" and the triumphant chant of the Neo-liberal Globalization, which today, besides an objective reality, is a weapon of manipulation intended to force us to passiveness faced to an Economic World Order that excludes our South countries and condemns them to the never-ending role of producers of wealth and recipients of leftovers.

Never before had the world such a tremendous scientific-technical potential, such a capacity to generate wealth and well-being. Authentic technological wonders that have made any place in the world to be always close with regard to distances and communications have not been capable of bringing well-being for everybody, but only for a meager 15 per cent living in the countries of the North.

Globalization has not brought the so-called interdependence, but an increase in dependency. Instead of wealth globalization, there is poverty wide spreading. Development has not become general, or been shared. To the contrary, the abysm between North and South is now so huge, that the unsustainability of the current economic order and the blindness of the people who try to justify continuing to enjoy opulence and waste, are evident.

The face of this world economic order of globalization with a neo-liberal sign is not only

[the] Internet, virtual reality, or the exploration of the space.

This face can also be seen, and with a greater dramatic character in the countries of the South, in the 790 millions of people who are starving, 800 millions of illiterate adults, 654 millions of human beings who live today in the south and who will not grow older than 40 years of age. This is the harsh and hard face of the work economic order dominated by the Neoliberalism and seen every year in the south, the death of over 11 millions of boys and girls below 5 years of age caused by illnesses that are practically always preventable and curable and who die at the appalling rate of over 30 thousand every day, 21 every minute, 10 each 30 seconds. In the South, the proportion of children suffering of malnutrition reaches up to 50 per cent in quite a few countries, while according to the FAO, a child who lives in the First World will consume throughout his or her life, the equivalent to what 50 children consume in an underdeveloped country.

The great possibilities that a globalization of solidarity and true cooperation could bring to all people in the world through the scientific-technical wonders, has been reduced by the neo-liberal model to this grotesque caricature full of exploitation and social injustice. . . .

We are, dear friends, in Latin America, the favourite scenario of the neo-liberal model in the past decades. Here, neoliberalism reached the status of a dogma and was applied with greatest severity. . . .

Dear friends:

I saw with my own eyes, a day like today but exactly 15 years ago, the 27th of February 1989, when an intense day of protest broke out on the streets of Caracas against the neo-liberal package of the International Monetary Fund and ended in a real massacre known as "The Caracazo"[2]. . . .

The [neoliberal] model recommended the most strict financial liberalization and exchange freedom to achieve a greater influx of foreign capitals and greater stability. But in neo-liberal years the financial crises have been more intense and frequent than ever before, the external regional debts non-existent at the end of the Second World War amounts today to 750 billion dollars, the per capita highest debt in the world and in several countries is equal to more than half the GDP. Only between 1990 and the year 2002, Latin America made external debt payments amounting to 1 trillion 528 billions of dollars, which duplicates the amount of the current debt and represented an annual average payment of 118 billions. That is, we pay the debt every 6.3 years, but this evil burden continues to be there, unchanging and inextinguishable.

It is a never-ending debt!! . . .

The neo-liberal model promised that after a painful adjustment period necessary to deprive the State of its regulatory power over economy and liberalize trade and finance, wealth would spread over Latin America and the long-lasting history of poverty and underdevelopment would be left behind. But the painful and temporary adjustment became permanent and appears to become everlasting. The results cannot be concealed.

Taking 1980 as the conventional year of the commencement of the neo-liberal cycle, by that time around 35 per cent of the Latin American population were poor. Two decades thereafter, 44 per cent of Latin American men and women are poor. Poverty is particularly cruel to children. It is a sad reality that in Latin America most of the poor people are children and most children are poor. In the late 90s, the Economic Commission for Latin America reported that 58 per cent of children under 5 were poor, as well as 57 per cent of children with ages ranging from 6 to 12.

Poverty among children and teenagers tends to reinforce and perpetuate inequalities of access to education, as shown by a survey conducted by the Inter-American Development Bank on 15 countries where householders in 10 per cent of the population with the highest income had an average schooling of 11 years, whereas among householders in 30 per cent of the lowest income population such average was 4 years. . . .

This exploitation model has turned Latin America and the Caribbean into a social bomb ready to explode, should anti-development, unemployment and poverty keep increasing. . . .

Thanks to the heroic struggle against colonialism, the developing countries broke the economic and social order condemning them to the condition of exploited colonies. Colonialism was not defeated by the accumulations of tears of sorrow or by the repentance of colonialists, but by centuries of heroic fights for independence and sovereignty in which the resistance, tenacity and sacrifice of our peoples worked wonders.

Here, in South America, this year we are precisely commemorating 180 years of the heroic deeds of Ayacucho battle, where people joined and became a liberating army after almost 20 years of revolutionary wars under the bright leadership of José de San Martin, Bernardo O'Higgins, José Inacio Abreu e Lima, Simon Bolivar and Antonio José de Sucre,

sending away the Spanish empire hitherto extended from the warm Caribbean beaches to the cold lands of Patagonia, thus ending 300 years of colonialism.

Today, vis-à-vis the obvious failure of neoliberalism and the great threat that the International Economic Order represents for our countries, it is necessary to retake the Spirit of the South. . . .

Ladies and Gentlemen, thank you very much.

Notes

1. Both organizations attempted to counter the dominant bipolar Cold War world and to allow developing countries to gain greater global influence.
2. Security forces killed a large number of Venezuelans protesting against neo-liberal economic reforms on 27 February 1989.

> **Study Question**
>
> What, according to Chavez, are the most important consequences of neo-liberal economic policies in South America?

Dilma Vana Rousseff

After two rounds of voting in October 2010, Dilma Vana Rousseff (b. 1947) was elected President of Brazil, replacing the immensely popular Luiz "Lula" da Silva. Rousseff had held several positions within da Silva's government including Minister for Mines and Energy, and Chief of Staff. Like da Silva, Rousseff belongs to the left-leaning Workers' Party (PT), but unlike post-Chávez Venezuela, remains firmly committed to a liberal democratic model of government.

In the 1970s Rousseff was imprisoned and tortured for her opposition to the military dictatorship that controlled the country from 1964 until 1985. The speech that follows was a portion of Rousseff's Inaugural Address in 2011.

Document Source: Presidency of the Federative Republic of Brazil; available at http://www2.planalto.gov.br/imprensa/discursos/speech-delivered-by-the-president-of-the-republic-of-brazil-dilma-rousseff-before-the-national-congress-during-the-constitutional-oath-ceremony

Inaugural Address—Brasília, 1 January 2011

My Dear Brazilians,

By the sovereign decision of the people, today will be the first time that the Presidential sash encircles the shoulders of a woman.

I am immensely honored by this choice the Brazilian people have made, and I recognize the

historic significance of this decision.

I also recognize that the green and yellow silk of the Presidential sash may appear to be soft, but it carries with it an enormous responsibility for the nation.

To take on this responsibility, I have with me the strength and the example of the Brazilian woman. I open my heart to receive, at this moment, a spark of her immense energy.

And I know that my presidential term must involve the most generous interpretation of this brave vote that the people have made: after electing a man of the people, of the working class, to the presidency, they have decided to call on a woman to take the helm in the country's destiny.

I am here to open doors so that in the future many other women can also be President; so that, today, all Brazilian women may feel proud and happy to be themselves.

I am not here to boast of my own life story, but rather to praise the life of every Brazilian woman. My greatest commitment, I repeat, is to honoring our women, protecting our most vulnerable people, and governing for everyone.

I am here, above all, to carry on the greatest process of affirmation that this country has experienced in recent times.

I am here to consolidate the transforming work of President Luiz Inácio Lula da Silva, with whom I have had the most vigorous political experience of my life and the privilege of serving the country, at his side, for the last few years.

He is a President who changed the way our Brazilian people were governed and led them to believe more in themselves and in the future of the country.

The greatest tribute I can pay him is to broaden and take forward his government's achievements. To recognize, believe and invest in the strength of our people was the greatest lesson that President Lula bequeaths to all of us.

Under his leadership, we Brazilians crossed over to another shore, another time in our history.

My mission now is to consolidate this passage and to advance along the path taken by a nation that generates such wide-ranging opportunities. . . .

We are living through one of the best periods of our nation's life: millions of jobs are being created; our growth rate has more than doubled and we have ended a long period of dependence

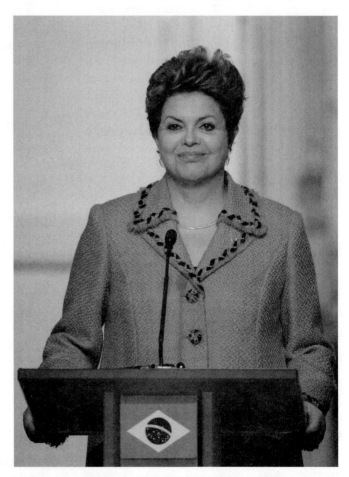

Brazilian president Dilma Vana Rousseff addresses the 67th General Assembly of the United Nations in New York City in 2012.

© Christian Liewig/Liewig Media Sports/Corbis

on the International Monetary Fund, at the same time as overcoming our external debt.

Above all, we have cut our historical social debt, rescuing millions of Brazilians from the tragedy of extreme poverty and helping millions of others to join the middle classes. But in a country as complex as ours, we always have to wish for more, discover more, create innovative new directions and always seek new solutions.

It is only thus that we can guarantee that those who have seen improvements in their lives will be able to accomplish still more; and to prove to those who are still struggling to emerge from destitution that they will indeed change their lives and reach a new level, with the help of the government and of all society.

That we can, in fact, be one of the most developed and least unequal nations in the world—a country with a solid and entrepreneurial middle class; a vibrant and modern democracy, full of social commitment, political liberty and creativity.

My Dear Brazilians,

To face these great challenges we have to maintain the foundations that guaranteed our arrival at this point.

But, equally, we must include new tools and new values.

In politics, reform is an indeclinable and urgent task to bring about changes in legislation so that our young democracy can move forward, strengthen the direction taken by political parties and fine-tune our institutions, restoring values and providing more transparency in all types of public activity.

To make the current cycle of growth last, it is necessary to guarantee stability, especially price stability, and to go on ironing out the wrinkles that still hold back our economy's dynamism. We need to facilitate production and stimulate our people's entrepreneurial capacity, from the large corporations down to the small local businesses, from big agribusiness to family-run smallholdings.

We cannot, therefore, put off implementing a set of measures that will modernize the taxation system, led by the principle of simplification and rationality. The intensive use of information technology should be put at the service of an increasingly efficient system that is marked by its respect for the tax-payer.

Valuing our industry and increasing its strength in exportation will be an ongoing target. The competitiveness of our agriculture and our livestock, which makes Brazil a major exporter of quality products to every continent, deserves all our attention. In the most productive sectors the internationalization of our corporations is already well underway.

Support for our big exporters is not incompatible with providing incentives, development and support for smallholders and micro-businesses. Small companies are responsible for the greatest number of permanent jobs in our country. They will merit ongoing tax and credit policies.

Giving value to regional development is also imperative in a country of continental dimensions. We must sustain the vibrant economy of the North-East; preserve, respect and develop the biodiversity of Amazonia in the North; and provide conditions for the extraordinary agricultural production of the Middle-West, the industrial output of the South-East and the vigor and pioneering spirit of the South.

First, however, it is vital to create real and effective conditions that can better use and realize the potential that lies in the immense creative and productive energy of the Brazilian people.

In the social arena, inclusion will only be fully reached with the universalization and improvement of essential services. This is one decisive and irrevocable step toward consolidating and broadening the great achievements obtained by our people during President Lula's government.

It is therefore essential that we undertake a

renovating, effective and integrated action among the federal, state and municipal governments, especially in the areas of health, education and security, as is the express wish of the families and the Brazilian population.

My Dear Brazilians,

My government's most determined fight will be to eradicate extreme poverty and create opportunities for all.

We have seen significant social mobility during President Lula's two terms. But poverty still exists to shame our country and prevent us from affirming ourselves fully as a developed people.

I will not rest while there are Brazilians who have no food on their tables, while there are desperate families on the streets, while there are poor children abandoned to their own devices. Family unity lies in food, peace and happiness. This is the dream I will pursue!

This is not the isolated task of one government, but a commitment to be embraced by all society. For this, I humbly ask for the support of public and private institutions, of all the parties, business entities and workers, the universities, our young people, the press and all those who wish others well.

Overcoming extreme poverty demands that a long period of growth is given priority. It is growth that generates the jobs needed for current and future generations.

It is growth, together with strong social programs, that will enable us to vanquish inequality in income and in regional development.

This means—and I repeat—maintaining economic stability as a value. Our recent culture involves the conviction that inflation disorganizes the economy and erodes the worker's income. It is absolutely certain that we will not allow this poison to return to corrode our economic fabric and castigate the poor. . . .

We will not make the slightest concession to rich countries' protectionism, which suffocates any hope of overcoming poverty in so many nations that strive to do so through their production efforts.

We will continue working to improve the quality of public spending.

Brazil has opted, throughout its history, to build a State that provides basic services and social welfare.

This involves high costs for the whole of society, but it also means that everyone is guaranteed a pension and universal health and education services. Therefore, improving public services is also imperative as we improve our government spending. . . .

Study Question

According to Rousseff, what are the keys to maintaining a level of prosperity in Brazil?

Vladimir Putin

Vladimir Putin (b. 1952) was Boris Yeltsin's handpicked successor as president of the Russian Federation. He served two terms as president, from 2000 to 2008, enjoying exceptionally high approval ratings, and was subsequently chosen as Russia's prime minister when term limits prevented him from continuing to serve as president. Putin's critics pointed to an increasing loss of democratic rights in Russia, repression of the media, and rampant corruption. However, under his tenure Russia's economy expanded—driven by high oil and *gas prices—and its power in the world recovered substantially. In 2012, Putin returned to the presidency after an election which was widely criticized for having been manipulated to ensure his victory. The speech which follows was delivered at a conference on international security in Munich, Germany, in 2007.*

Document Source: Vladimir Putin, "Speech at the 43rd Munich Conference on Security Policy, 2007," Munich Conference on Security Policy: http://archive.kremlin.ru/eng/speeches/2007/02/10/0138_type82912type82914type82917type84779_118123.shtml

Speech at the 43rd Munich Conference on Security Policy, 2007

Thank you very much dear Madam Federal Chancellor, Mr Teltschik, ladies and gentlemen!

I am truly grateful to be invited to such a representative conference that has assembled politicians, military officials, entrepreneurs and experts from more than 40 nations.

This conference's structure allows me to avoid excessive politeness and the need to speak in round-about, pleasant but empty diplomatic terms. This conference's format will allow me to say what I really think about international security problems. . . .

Therefore, it is well known that international security comprises much more than issues relating to military and political stability. It involves the stability of the global economy, overcoming poverty, economic security, and developing a dialogue between civilisations.

This universal, indivisible character of security is expressed as the basic principle that "security for one is security for all." As Franklin D. Roosevelt said during the first few days that the Second World War was breaking out: "When peace has been broken anywhere, the peace of all countries everywhere is in danger."

These words remain topical today. Incidentally, the theme of our conference—global crises, global responsibility—exemplifies this.

Only two decades ago the world was ideologically and economically divided and it was the huge strategic potential of two superpowers that ensured global security.

This global stand-off pushed the sharpest economic and social problems to the margins of the international community's and the world's agenda. And, just like any war, the Cold War left us with live ammunition, figuratively speaking. I am referring to ideological stereotypes, double standards and other typical aspects of Cold War bloc thinking.

The unipolar world that had been proposed after the Cold War did not take place either.

The history of humanity certainly has gone through unipolar periods and seen aspirations to world supremacy. And what hasn't happened in world history?

However, what is a unipolar world? However one might embellish this term, at the end of the day it refers to one type of situation, namely one centre of authority, one centre of force, one centre of decision-making.

It is a world in which there is one master, one sovereign. And at the end of the day this is pernicious not only for all those within this system, but also for the sovereign itself because it destroys itself from within. . . .

I consider that the unipolar model is not only unacceptable but also impossible in today's world. And this is not only because if there was individual leadership in today's—and precisely in today's—world, then the military, political and economic resources would not suffice. What is even more important is that the model itself is flawed because at its basis there is and can be no moral foundations for modern civilisation.

Along with this, what is happening in today's world—and we just started to discuss this—is a tentative effort to introduce precisely this concept into international affairs, the concept of a unipolar world.

And with which results?

Unilateral and frequently illegitimate actions have not resolved any problems. Moreover, they have caused new human tragedies and created new centres of tension. Judge for yourselves: wars as well as local and regional conflicts have not diminished. . . . And no less people perish in these conflicts—even more are dying than before. Significantly more, significantly more!

Today we are witnessing an almost uncontained hyper use of force—military force—in international relations, force that is plunging the world into an abyss of permanent conflicts. As a result we do not have sufficient strength to find a comprehensive solution to any one of these conflicts. Finding a political settlement also becomes impossible.

We are seeing a greater and greater disdain for the basic principles of international law. And independent legal norms are, as a matter of fact, coming increasingly closer to one state's legal system. One state and, of course, first and foremost the United States, has overstepped its national borders in every way. This is visible in the economic, political, cultural and educational policies it imposes on other nations. Well, who likes this? Who is happy about this?

In international relations we increasingly see the desire to resolve a given question according to so-called issues of political expediency, based on the current political climate.

And of course this is extremely dangerous. It results in the fact that no one feels safe. I want to emphasize this—no one feels safe! Because no one can feel that international law is like a stone wall that will protect them. Of course such a policy stimulates an arms race.

The force's dominance inevitably encourages a number of countries to acquire weapons of mass destruction. Moreover, significantly new threats—though they were also well-known before—have appeared, and today threats such as terrorism have taken on a global character.

I am convinced that we have reached that decisive moment when we must seriously think about the architecture of global security.

And we must proceed by searching for a reasonable balance between the interests of all participants in the international dialogue. Especially since the international landscape is so varied and changes so quickly—changes in light of the dynamic development in a whole number of countries and regions.

Madam Federal Chancellor already mentioned this. The combined GDP measured in purchasing power parity of countries such as India and China is already greater than that of the United States. And a similar calculation with the GDP of the BRIC countries—Brazil, Russia, India and China—surpasses the cumulative GDP of the EU. And according to experts this gap will only increase in the future.

There is no reason to doubt that the economic potential of the new centres of global economic growth will inevitably be converted into political influence and will strengthen multipolarity.

In connection with this the role of multilateral diplomacy is significantly increasing. The need for principles such as openness, transparency and predictability in politics is uncontested and the use of force should be a really exceptional measure, comparable to using the death penalty in the judicial systems of certain states.

However, today we are witnessing the opposite tendency, namely a situation in which countries that forbid the death penalty even for murderers and other, dangerous criminals are airily participating in military operations that are difficult to consider legitimate. And as a matter of fact, these conflicts are killing people—hundreds and thousands of civilians! . . .

But do we have the means to counter these threats? Certainly we do. It is sufficient to look at recent history. Did not our country have a peaceful transition to democracy? Indeed, we witnessed a peaceful transformation of the Soviet regime—a peaceful transformation! And what a regime! With what a number of weapons, including nuclear weapons! Why should we start bombing and shooting now at every available opportunity? Is it the case when without the threat of mutual destruction we do not have enough political culture, respect for democratic values and for the law?

I am convinced that the only mechanism that can make decisions about using military force as a last resort is the Charter of the United Nations. . . . The use of force can only be considered legitimate if the decision is sanctioned by the UN. And we do not need to substitute NATO or the EU for the UN. . . .

Dear ladies and gentlemen!

In conclusion I would like to note the following. We very often—and personally, I very often—hear appeals by our partners, including our European partners, to the effect that Russia should play an increasingly active role in world affairs.

In connection with this I would allow myself to make one small remark. It is hardly necessary to incite us to do so. Russia is a country with a history that spans more than a thousand years and has practically always used the privilege to carry out an independent foreign policy.

We are not going to change this tradition today. At the same time, we are well aware of how the world has changed and we have a realistic sense of our own opportunities and potential. And of course we would like to interact with responsible and independent partners with whom we could work together in constructing a fair and democratic world order that would ensure security and prosperity not only for a select few, but for all.

Thank you for your attention.

> **Study Question**
>
> Is Putin's argument against unipolarity convincing?

Hu Jintao

Hu Jintao (b. 1942) became General Secretary of the Communist Party of China in 2002 and was President of the People's Republic from 2003 to 2013. Identified by Deng Xiaoping as a potential leader in the early 1990s, Hu generally followed Deng's principles on modernization in China. Hu repeatedly used the phrase "hexie shehui" 和谐社会—*"harmonious society"—to describe his vision of a modern China in which all peoples live in harmony with one another and with the natural environment. In 2011, on the occasion of the ninetieth anniversary of the founding of the CCP, Hu reflected on the historical transformation of China.*

Document Source: Hu Jintao, "Speech at a Meeting Commemorating the 90th Anniversary of the Founding of the CCP," Xinhua News, 1 July 2011; http://news.xinhuanet.com/english2010/china/2011-07/01/c_13960505_2.htm

---

On the 90th Anniversary of the Founding of the Chinese Communist Party

Comrades and Friends,

Today, together with the entire Party and the people of all ethnic groups in China, we are holding this grand meeting here to commemorate the 90th anniversary of the founding of the Communist Party of China (CPC) and also to review the great course of China's development and progress and look ahead at the bright future of development and prosperity for the country.

The CPC was founded 90 years ago today, which was an epoch-making event in the history of the Chinese nation. From then on, the Chinese people embarked on the bright road of striving for independence and liberation and began the glorious pursuit of prosperity and strength for the country and themselves.

Over the past 90 years, Chinese Communists and the people of all ethnic groups in China have, through indomitable struggles, achieved major successes in revolution, development and reform. Today, a vibrant socialist China has emerged in the East, and the 1.3 billion Chinese people are forging ahead full of confidence under the great banner of socialism with Chinese characteristics to realize the great rejuvenation of the Chinese nation.

Comrades and Friends,

In the 170 plus years since the Opium War of 1840, our great country has weathered untold hardships, our great nation has waged earthshaking struggles, and our great people have scored splendid achievements in the annals of history.

Following the Opium War, China gradually became a semi-colonial and semi-feudal society, and foreign powers stepped up their aggression against China. The feudal rule became increasingly corrupt, the country was devastated by incessant wars and turbulence, and the Chinese people suffered from hunger, cold, and oppression. To salvage China from subjugation was an urgent mission for the Chinese nation. And the Chinese people faced the historic tasks of winning independence and liberation, and making China strong and prosperous.

In those dark years, in order to change the destiny of the Chinese nation, the Chinese people, led by many leading figures with lofty ideals, waged unyielding struggles to explore a new future against great odds. Not resigned to fate, the Chinese people launched one struggle after another, such as the Taiping Heavenly Kingdom Movement, the Reform Movement of 1898, and the Yihetuan Movement, but all these struggles ended in failure. The Revolution of 1911 led by Dr Sun Yat-sen put an end to the autocratic rule that had existed in China for several thousand years. This revolution greatly boosted China's social progress, but it did not change the country's nature as a semi-colonial and semi-feudal society or end the misery of the Chinese people. . . .

In 1921, the CPC was born in the process of integrating Marxism-Leninism with the Chinese workers' movement. The birth of the CPC was a natural product of the development of modern and contemporary Chinese history as well as the indomitable exploration of the Chinese people for survival of the nation. The birth of the CPC put the Chinese revolution on the right course, gave the Chinese people a powerful motivation, and created bright prospects for China's future development.

Over the past 90 years, our Party has united with and led the Chinese people in writing a grand epic in the history of human development on this ancient land of China, evidenced in three earthshaking events.

The first is that our Party, firmly relying on the people, completed the new-democratic revolution, winning national independence, and liberation of the people. The Party and the people fought through the Northern Expedition, the Agrarian Revolutionary War, the War of Resistance Against Japanese Aggression and the War of Liberation in 28 years, during which they defeated Japanese imperialist aggressors, overthrew the Kuomintang reactionary rule and established the People's Republic of China. With the founding of New China, the Chinese people became masters of their country and society and determined their own destiny. China achieved a great transition from a feudal autocracy that was several thousand years old to a people's democracy. Great unity and unprecedented solidarity of all ethnic groups were realized in China. The history of old China being a semi-colonial and semi-feudal society which was like a heap of loose sand was brought to an end once and for all. The unequal treaties imposed on China by imperialist powers and all the privileges they had in China were abolished. The Chinese people stood up, and the Chinese nation entered a new era of development and progress.

The second is that, firmly relying on the people, our Party completed the socialist revolution and established the basic socialist system. We creatively achieved the transition from New Democracy to socialism, therefore creating a socialist society for a quarter of the world's population in this large country in the East, and brought about the most extensive and profound social changes in Chinese history. We established industrial and economic systems that were independent and fairly complete, and we gained important experience of building socialism in China, a country with backward productive forces.

The third is that, firmly relying on the people, our Party carried out a great new revolution of reform and opening up, creating, upholding, and developing socialism with Chinese characteristics. Since the Third Plenary Session of the Eleventh CPC Central Committee, we have reviewed China's practices of building socialism and drawn on the experience of other countries. We have embarked on the path of reform and opening up with tremendous political and theoretical courage and courage in practice. Going through an arduous process of trial and error, we have formed the Party's basic theory, line, and platform and gained basic experience in the primary stage of socialism, established a socialist market economy, and constantly improved it, made China fully open, and made world-renowned progress in the socialist modernization drive.

These three major events reshaped the future and destiny of the Chinese people and the Chinese nation. They irreversibly ended the misery endured by China in modern times when it suffered from both domestic turmoil and foreign invasion and was poor and weak. They also irreversibly started the Chinese nation's historic march for development, growth, and great rejuvenation. They gave China, a civilization of over 5,000 years, a completely new look and created unimagined prospects for the great rejuvenation of the Chinese nation.

The profundity and the political and social impact of the changes that have taken place in Chinese society and in the destiny of the Chinese people over the past 90 years are rare in the history of human development.

What has happened shows that in the great cause of China's social development and progress since modern times, history and the people have chosen the CPC, Marxism, the socialist road, and the reform and opening up policy.

History has also fully shown that the CPC truly deserves to be called a great, glorious, and correct Marxist political party and the core force leading the Chinese people in breaking new ground in development. . . .

Comrades and Friends,

Ninety years ago, the CPC only had a few dozen members. Back then, China was a poor and backward country and its people were leading a miserable life. Today, the CPC has more than 80 million members. China is prospering and its people are living a happy life. All the achievements of the Party over the past 90 years have been made by the Party together with the people. We will never forget that the people are the real heroes.

We have every reason to be proud of what the Party and the people have achieved, but we have no reason to be complacent. We must not and will never rest on our laurels.

In the first half of this century, the Party will unite with and lead the people in accomplishing two grand goals: First, to build a moderately prosperous society of a higher level to the benefit of over one billion people by the centennial of the founding of the CPC and, second, to make China a prosperous, strong, democratic, culturally advanced, and harmonious modern socialist country by the centennial of the founding of New China. We have great responsibilities on our shoulders. All the comrades in the Party must keep in mind their historic missions, remain modest and prudent, guard against arrogance and rashness, and maintain the style of plain living and hard struggle. We should be eager to make changes and innovations and guard against rigid thinking and stagnation. We will not vacillate, relax our efforts, or act recklessly. And we will never be intimidated by risks or confused by distractions. We must unswervingly forge ahead along the path of socialism with Chinese characteristics and work even harder to unite with and lead the people of all ethnic groups in China in working for our happy life and the bright future of the Chinese nation.

Study Question

What does Hu list as the most important achievements of the CPC? What remains to be accomplished after 90 years?

Web Resources

Resources on Globalization
> http://www2.hawaii.edu/~fredr/glocon.htm#end

Global Gateway: World Culture and Resources
> http://international.loc.gov/intldl/intldlhome.html

Resources on the events of September 11, 2001
> http://www.nyu.edu/fas/projects/vcb/case_911/resources/web.html

Teaching with the News: A Guide to Current Issues in the Classroom
> http://www.choices.edu/resources/current.php

Recommended Reading

Richard Dawkins, *The God Delusion* (Boston: Houghton Mifflin, 2006). Dawkins examines contemporary religion, creationism, and the emergence of intelligent design arguments. Speaking from an atheist perspective, he links religion to war, racism, and fragmentation.

Mohsin Hamid, *The Reluctant Fundamentalist* (New York: Harcourt, 2007). Hamid's novel focuses on the life of a Princeton-educated Pakistani financial analyst and his experiences in New York before and after 9/11. The novel captures the atmosphere of suspicion and the racial tensions after the September 11 attacks, and their consequences.

Khaled Hosseini, *The Kite Runner* (New York: Riverhead Books, 2003). *The Kite Runner* is set in Afghanistan as the monarchy collapses and Soviet troops invade the country. The novel captures the power of tribal loyalties and their resulting, often disastrous, implications.

Kurt Vonnegut, *Timequake* (Berkley, Ca: Berkley Publishing Group, 1998). Part unfinished novel and part Vonnegut memoir, *Timequake* sees the universe move back ten years, forcing the world to relive the 1990s in exactly the same way. En route, Vonnegut reflects on numerous issues including war, the state of humanity, spirituality, and evolution.

Ruth Linnea Whitney, *Slim* (Dallas, TX: Southern Methodist University Press, 2003). Set in Africa at the onset of the AIDS epidemic, the novel examines the problems of dictatorship, patriarchal society, and indifference amidst a gradually rising awareness of the potential social, political, and economic devastation of the unchecked epidemic.

Recommended Viewing

Hotel Rwanda (France/USA, 2004). Director: Terry George. *Hotel Rwanda* is based on the life of Paul Rusesabagina, manager of a hotel in Kigali, who attempted to shelter hundreds of Tutsis and moderate Hutus during the 1994 genocide in Rwanda. The film captures the violence and intensity of the genocide.

The Corporation (Canada, 2003). Directors: Mark Achbar/Jennifer Abbott (Documentary). This Canadian-made documentary gained critical acclaim for its exploration of the "personality" of the corporation. The film examines the history of the corporation beginning in the nineteenth century, and the basis of its power under the law, as well as the current global power of corporations, their environmental impact, and the nature of global capitalism.

Fahrenheit 9/11 (USA, 2004). Director: Michael Moore (Documentary). Winner of the Palme d'Or at Cannes, Moore's controversial documentary focuses on the events of 11 September 2001, the Bush presidency, its questionable legitimacy, and the second Iraq War. The film examines political manipulation, the role of corporations in politics, US foreign policy, and the causes and impact of terrorism.

United 93 (USA, 2006). Director: Paul Greengrass. *United 93* follows the events surrounding the hijacking of the fourth airplane on 11 September 2001, on the plane and on the ground. Greengrass received praise for the film for its insights into the decisions of all of the parties involved.

World Trade Center (USA, 2006). Director: Oliver Stone. Based on actual events, the film follows the activities of two Port Authority police officers as they react to the chaos of the terrorist attacks on the World Trade Center. After entering the South Tower, the two men are trapped as the concourse collapses.

Charlie Wilson's War (USA, 2007). Director: Mike Nichols. Nichols's film examines the role of US Congressman Charlie Wilson in setting up American funding to the Afghan Mujahedeen during the era of Soviet involvement in Afghanistan. The film provides the background to the rise of the Taliban and subsequent developments as the Soviets withdrew in 1988 and 1989.

Shake Hands with the Devil (J'ai serré la main du diable) (Canada, 2007). Director: Roger Spottiswoode. Based on the book of the same name by Canadian general Roméo Dallaire, *Shake Hands with the Devil* recounts the days leading up to the genocide in Rwanda in 1994, Dallaire's frustrations with the United Nations apparatus, and the eventual unfolding of the genocide despite the presence of a small contingent of UN peacekeepers.

Battle in Seattle (France, 2008). Director: Stuart Townsend. *Battle in Seattle* effectively combines actual event footage with fictional portrayals of key characters involved in the November 1999 protests at the World Trade Organization meetings in Seattle. The film examines the impact on the city, as well as world opinion on globalization and public protest.

Zero Dark Thirty (USA, 2012). Director: Kathryn Bigelow. A winner of numerous awards, *Zero Dark Thirty* revolves around the ten-year hunt to find Osama bin Laden and the final confrontation between American forces and bin Laden in Pakistan. Bigelow's film generated a number of controversies, not least for appearing to condone the use of torture to elicit information on bin Laden's whereabouts.

Suggestions for Further Reading

1 | The World and the West

Adas, Michael P. 1989. *Machines as the Measure of Men: Science, Technology, and Ideologies of Western Dominance*. Ithaca, NY: Cornell University Press.

Conquest, Robert. 2001. *Reflections on a Ravaged Century*. New York: W.W. Norton.

Crosby, Alfred W. 1986. *Ecological Imperialism: The Biological Expansion of Europe, 900–1900*. New York: Cambridge University Press.

Ferguson, Niall. 2011. *Civilization: The West and the Rest*. New York: Penguin Press.

Goto, Kenichi. 2003. *Tensions of Empire: Japan and Southeast Asia in the Colonial and Postcolonial World*. Athens, OH: Ohio University Press.

Gran, Peter. 1996. *Beyond Eurocentrism: A New View of Modern World History*. New York: Syracuse University Press.

Headrick, Daniel. 1991. *The Invisible Weapon: Telecommunications and International Politics, 1851–1945*. New York: Oxford University Press.

Hobsbawm, E.J. 1996. *The Age of Extremes: A History of the World, 1914–1991*. London: Vintage.

McNeill, William H. 1963. *The Rise of the West: A History of the Human Community*. Chicago: University of Chicago Press.

Nolan, Mary. 2012. *The Transatlantic Century: Europe and America, 1890 to 2010*. Cambridge: Cambridge University Press.

Ponting, Clive. 1998. *Progress and Barbarism: The World in the Twentieth Century*. London: Chatto & Windus.

Teich, Mikuláš, and Roy Porter, eds. 1990. *Fin-De-Siècle and Its Legacy*. Cambridge: Cambridge University Press.

Tuchman, Barbara. 1966. *The Proud Tower: A Portrait of the World before the War, 1890–1914*. New York: Macmillan.

Von Laue, Theodore H. 1987. *The World Revolution of Westernization: The Twentieth Century in Global Perspective*. New York: Macmillan.

Watson, Peter. 2000. *A Terrible Beauty: A History of the People and Ideas that Shaped the Modern Mind*. London: Weidenfeld & Nicolson.

2 | Global Capitalism and Imperialism

Blue, Gregory, Martin Bunton, and Ralph Croizier, eds. 2002. *Colonialism and the Modern World: Selected Studies*. Armonk, NY: M.E. Sharpe.

Burbank, Jane, and Frederick Cooper, 2010. *Empires in World History: Power and the Politics of Difference*. Princeton, NJ: Princeton University Press.

Cooper, Frederick, and Ann Laura Stoler, eds. 1997. *Tensions of Empire: Colonial Cultures in a Bourgeois World*. Berkeley: University of California Press.

Curtin, Philip D. 1989. *Death by Migration: Europe's Encounter with the Tropical World in the Nineteenth Century*. New York: Cambridge University Press.

Ferro, Marc. 1997. *Colonization: A Global History*. London: Routledge.

Fieldhouse, D.K. 1999. *The West and the Third World: Trade, Colonialism, Dependence and Development*. Oxford: Blackwell.

Headrick, Daniel. 1988. *The Tentacles of Progress: Technology Transfer in the Age of Imperialism, 1850-1940*. New York: Oxford University Press.

Hobsbawm, E.J. 1987. *The Age of Empire, 1875–1914*. London: Vintage.

Johnson, Robert. 2003. *British Imperialism: Histories and Controversies*. New York: Palgrave Macmillan.

Porter, Andrew. 1994. *European Imperialism*. New York: St Martin's Press.

Said, Edward W. 1993. *Culture and Imperialism*. New York: Knopf.

Wolf, Eric. 1982. *Europe and the People Without History*. Berkeley, CA: University of California Press.

Young, Crawford. 1994. *The African Colonial State in Comparative Perspective*. New Haven: Yale University Press.

3 | War and Peace

First World War

Beckett, I.F.W. 2012. *The Making of the First World War*. New Haven: Yale University Press.

Dadrian, Vahakn N. 2003. *The History of the Armenian Genocide: Ethnic Conflict from the Balkans to Anatolia to the Caucasus*. Oxford: Berghahn Books.

Eksteins, Modris. 1989. *Rites of Spring: The Great War and the Birth of the Modern Age*. Toronto: Mariner Books.

Ferguson, Niall. 1999. *The Pity of War: Explaining World War I*. New York: Basic Books.

Herwig, Holger. 1996. *The First World War: Germany and Austria Hungary*. London: Arnold Publishers.

Joll, James. 2000. *The Origins of the First World War*. London: Longman.

Mackaman, Douglas, and Michael Mays, eds. 2000. *World War I and the Cultures of Modernity*. Jackson, MS: University Press of Mississippi.

Winter, Jay, Geoffrey Parker, and Mary R. Habeck, eds. 2000. *The Great War and the Twentieth Century*. New Haven, CT: Yale University Press.

Postwar Settlement

Ferrell, Robert H. 1985. *Woodrow Wilson and World War I*. New York: HarperCollins.

Macmillan, Margaret. 2002. *Paris 1919: Six Months that Changed the World*. New York: Random House.

Marks, Sally. 2002. *The Ebbing of European Ascendancy: An International History of the World, 1914–1945*. London: Arnold Publishers.

Northedge, F.S. 1986. *The League of Nations: Its Life and Times, 1920–1946*. Leicester: Leicester University Press.

Overy, R.J. 1994. *The Inter-war Crisis 1919–1939*. London/New York: Longman Publishing Group.

4 | The Appeal of Revolutionary Change

Beasley, W.G. 1987. *Rise of Modern Japan: Political, Economic and Social Change since 1850*. London: Palgrave Macmillan.

Bergere, Marie-Claire. 1989. *The Golden Age of the Chinese Bourgeoisie, 1911–1937*. Stanford: Cambridge University Press.

Bix, Herbert P. 2000. *Hirohito and the Making of Modern Japan*. New York: Perennial.

Brovkin, Vladimir N., ed. 1997. *The Bolsheviks in Russian Society: The Revolution and the Civil Wars*. New Haven, CT: Yale University Press.

Brown, Judith M. 1994. *India: The Origins of an Asian Democracy*. Oxford: Oxford University Press.

Eastman, Lloyd E. 1974. *The Abortive Revolution: China under Nationalist Rule, 1927–1937*. Cambridge, MA: Harvard University Press.

Eley, Geoff. 2002. *Forging Democracy: The History of the Left in Europe, 1850–2000*. Oxford: Oxford University Press.

Figes, Orlando. 1996. *People's Tragedy: The Russian Revolution, 1891–1924*. New York: Penguin.

Freeze, Gregory L., ed. 2002. *Russia: A History*. Oxford: Oxford University Press.

Goldman, Merle, and Leo Ou-Fan Lee, eds. 2002. *An Intellectual History of Modern China*. Cambridge/New York: Cambridge University Press.

Guha, Ramachandra, ed. 2011. *The Makers of Modern India*. Cambridge, MA: The Belknap Press of Harvard University Press.

Harding, Neil, 1996. *Leninism*. Basingstoke, UK: Palgrave Macmillan.

Inkster, Ian. 2001. *Japanese Industrialisation: Historical and Cultural Perspectives*. London/New York: Routledge.

Mamdani, Mahmoud. 1996. *Citizen and Subject: Contemporary Africa and the Legacy of Late Colonialism*. London: James Currey.

Narangoa, Li. 2003. *Imperial Japan and National Identities in Asia, 1895–1945*. London/New York: Routledge.

Nove, Alec. 1992. *Economic History of the USSR*. London: Penguin.

Perry, Elizabeth J. 2002. *Challenging the Mandate of Heaven: Social Protest and State Power in China*. Armonk, NY: M.E. Sharpe.

Schoppa, R. Keith. 2001. *Revolution and its Past: Identities and Change in Modern Chinese History*. Englewood Cliffs, NJ: Prentice Hall.

Service, Robert. 1999. *The Russian Revolution, 1900–1927*. New York: Palgrave Macmillan.

Spence, Jonathan D. 1999. *The Search for Modern China*. New York: W.W. Norton.

Stern, R.W. 1993. *Changing India: Bourgeois Revolution on the Subcontinent*. Cambridge: Cambridge University Press.

Wade, Rex A. 2001. *The Bolshevik Revolution and Russian Civil War*. Westport, CT: Greenwood Press.

Wheatcroft, Stephen G., ed. 2002. *Challenging Traditional Views of Russian History*. New York: Palgrave Macmillan.

Wolpert, Stanley A. 1984. *Jinnah of Pakistan*. New York: Oxford University Press.

Wong, R. Bin. 1998. *China Transformed: Historical Change and the Limits of European Experience*. Ithaca, NY: Cornell University Press.

5 | The Authoritarian Alternative

Beasley, W.G. 1987. *Japanese Imperialism, 1894–1945*. Oxford: Oxford University Press.

Bessel, Richard. 2004. *Nazism and War*. London: Modern Library.

Conquest, Robert. 1990. *The Great Terror: A Reassessment*. New York: Oxford University Press.

Gellately, Robert. 2001. *Backing Hitler: Consent and Coercion in Nazi Germany*. Oxford: Oxford University Press.

Gregor, A. James. 2012. *Totalitarianism and Political Religion: An Intellectual History*. Stanford, CA: Stanford University Press.

Laqueur, Walter. 1996. *Fascism: Past, Present, Future*. New York: Oxford University Press.

Larsen, Stein Ugelvik. 2001. *Fascism Outside Europe: The European Impulse against Domestic Conditions in the Diffusion of Global Fascism*. New York: Columbia University Press.

McCauley, Martin. 2003. *Stalin and Stalinism*. Harlow: Longman.

Paxton, Robert O. 2004. *The Anatomy of Fascism*. New York: Vintage.

Payne, Stanley G. 1995. *A History of Fascism, 1914–1945*. Madison, WI: University of Wisconsin Press.

Tismaneanu, Vladimir. 2012. *The Devil in History: Communism, Fascism, and Some Lessons of the Twentieth Century*. Berkeley, CA: University of California Press.

Todd, Allan. 2002. *The European Dictatorships: Hitler, Stalin, Mussolini*. Cambridge: Cambridge University Press.

Tucker, Robert. 1990. *Stalin in Power: The Revolution from Above*. New York: W.W. Norton.

Wiarda, Howard, and Harvey Kline, eds. 1990. *Latin American Politics and Development*, 3rd Edition. Boulder, CO: Westview Press.

6 | Global Depression

Balderston, Theo, ed. 2003. *The World Economy and National Economies in the Interwar Slump*. New York: Palgrave Macmillan.

Bernanke, Ben. 2000. *Essays on the Great Depression*. Princeton, NJ: Princeton University Press.

Clavin, Patricia. 2000. *The Great Depression in Europe, 1929–1939*. London: Palgrave Macmillan.

Heale, M.J. 1999. *Franklin D. Roosevelt—The New Deal and War*. London: Routledge.

Himmelberg, Robert F. 2001. *The Great Depression and the New Deal*. Westport, CT: Greenwood Press.

Kindleberger, Charles P. 1973. *The World in Depression 1929–1939*. London: University of California Press.

Klein, Maury. 2001. *Rainbow's End: The Crash of 1929*. New York: Oxford University Press.

Latham, A.J.H. 1981. *The Depression and the Developing World, 1914–1939*. London: Barnes and Noble Books.

Rothermund, Dietmar. 1996. *The Global Impact of the Great Depression, 1929–1939*. London: Routledge.

———. 1992. *India in the Great Depression, 1929–1939*. Columbia, MO: South Asia Publications.

Shiroyama, Tomoko. 2008. *China during the Great Depression: Market, State, and the World Economy, 1929–1937*. Cambridge, MA: Harvard University Asia Center.

7 | Global War and Genocide

Second World War

Calvocoressi, Peter, and Guy Wint. 1988. *Total War: The Story of World War II*. London: Penguin.

Chickering, Roger, and Stig Förster, eds. 2003. *The Shadows of Total War: Europe, East Asia, and the United States, 1919–1939*. Cambridge: Cambridge University Press.

Closmann, Charles E. 2009. *War and the Environment: Military Destruction in the Modern Age*. College Station: Texas A&M University Press.

Collingham, E.M. 2012. *The Taste of War: World War Two and the Battle for Food*. New York: Penguin Books.

Irye, Akira. 1987. *The Origins of the Second World War in Asia and the Pacific*. London: Longman.

Keegan, John. 1990. *The Second World War*. New York: Penguin.

Leibau, Heike, ed. 2010. *The World in World Wars: Experiences, Perceptions, and Perspectives from Africa and Asia*. Leiden, The Netherlands: Brill.

Overy, R.J. 1999. *The Road to War*. London/New York: Penguin.

Weinberg, Gerhard. 1994. *A World at Arms: A Global History of World War II*. Cambridge: Cambridge University Press.

Genocide

Bartov, Omer. 2000. *Mirrors of Destruction: War, Genocide, and Modern Identity*. New York: Oxford University Press.

Burleigh, Michael. 1997. *Ethics and Extermination: Reflections on Nazi Genocide*. Cambridge/New York: Cambridge University Press.

Gellately, Robert, and Ben Kiernan, eds. 2003. *The Specter of Genocide: Mass Murder in Historical Perspective*. Cambridge/New York: Cambridge University Press.

Hamerow, Theodore S. 2008. *Why We Watched: Europe, America, and the Holocaust*. New York: Norton.

Hilberg, Raul. 1992. *Perpetrators Victims Bystanders: The Jewish Catastrophe, 1933–1945*. New York: Perennial.

Jones, Adam, ed. 2004. *Genocide, War Crimes and the West: History and Complicity*. London/New York: Zed Books.

Valentino, Benjamin A. 2004. *Final Solutions: Mass Killing and Genocide in the Twentieth Century*. Ithaca, NY: Cornell University Press.

8 | A New World Order?

Aoi, Chiyuki, et al., eds. 2007. *Unintended Consequences of Peacekeeping Operations*. Tokyo/New York: United Nations University Press.

Bennett, Simon, and Éadaoin O'Brian, eds. 2012. *What Future for Human Rights in a Non-Western World*. London: Human Rights Consortium, School of Advanced Study, University of London.

Hamburg, David A. 2002. *No More Killing Fields: Preventing Deadly Conflict*. Lanham, MD: Rowman and Littlefield Publishers.

Hunnicutt, Susan. 2007. *The United Nations*. Detroit: Greenhaven Press.

James, Stephen. 2007. *Universal Human Rights: Origins and Development*. New York: LFB Scholarly Publishers.

Meyer, Howard N. 2002. *The World Court in Action: Judging among the Nations*. Lanham, MD: Rowman and Littlefield Publishers.

Mingst, Karen A. 2006. *The United Nations in the Twenty-First Century*. Boulder, CO: Westview.

Newman, Edward, and Roland Rich, eds. 2004. *The UN Role in Promoting Democracy: Between Ideals and Reality*. Tokyo/New York: United Nations University Press.

Parsons, Anthony. 1995. *From Cold War to Hot Peace: UN Interventions 1947–1994*. New York: Penguin.

Weiss, Thomas. 2007. *The Oxford Handbook on the United Nations*. New York: Oxford University Press.

9 | Origins and Implications of the Cold War

Alperovitz, Gar. 1997. *The Decision to Use the Atomic Bomb*. New York: Vintage.

Ash, Timothy Garton. 1993. *In Europe's Name: Germany and the Divided Continent*. London: Vintage.

Brands, H.W. 1993. *The Devil We Knew: Americans and the Cold War*. Oxford: Oxford University Press.

DePorte, Anton. 1987. *Europe between the Superpowers*. New Haven: Yale University Press.

Fried, Albert. 1997. *McCarthyism: The Great American Red Scare*. Oxford: Oxford University Press.

Fursenko, Aleksandr, and Timothy Naftali. 1998. *One Hell of a Gamble: Khrushchev, Castro and Kennedy, 1958–1964*. New York: W.W. Norton.

Gaddis, John. 1997. *We Now Know: Rethinking Cold War History*. Oxford: Oxford University Press.

Knight, Amy. 2006. *How the Cold War Began: The Igor Gouzenko Affair and the Hunt for Soviet Spies*. New York: Carroll & Graf.

Lowe, Keith. 2012. *Savage Continent: Europe in the Aftermath of World War II*. New York, NY: St Martin's Press.

Paterson, James. 1996. *Grand Expectations: The United States, 1945–74*. Oxford: Oxford University Press.

Rhodes, Richard. 1988. *The Making of the Atomic Bomb*. London: Simon & Schuster.

Smyser, W.R. 1999. *From Yalta to Berlin: The Cold War Struggle Over Germany*. New York: St Martin's Press.

Takaki, Ronald. 1995. *Hiroshima: Why America Dropped the Atomic Bomb*. New York: Bay Back Books.

Zubok, Vladislav, and Constantine Pleshakov. 1996. *Inside the Kremlin's Cold War: From Stalin to Khrushchev*. Cambridge, MA: Harvard University Press.

10 | China and Japan: The Re-emergence of Asian Power

Bailey, Paul. *Women and Gender in Twentieth-Century China*. Basingstoke: Palgrave Macmillan.

Benton, Gregor, and Lin Chun, eds. 2010. *Was Mao Really a Monster? The Academic Response to Chang and Halliday's Mao, the Unknown Story*. London/New York: Routledge.

Borthwick, Mark. 1998. *Pacific Century: The Emergence of Modern Pacific Asia*. Boulder, CO: Westview Press.

Dickson, Bruce J. 2003. *Red Capitalists in China: The Party, Private Entrepreneurs, and Prospects for Political Change*. Cambridge: Cambridge University Press.

Goldman, Merle, and Roderick MacFarquhar, eds. 1999. *The Paradox of China's Post-Mao Reforms*. Cambridge: Harvard University Press.

Gries, Peter Hays. 2004. *China's New Nationalism: Pride, Politics and Diplomacy*. Berkeley: University of California Press.

Gulliver, Katrina. 2011. *Modern Women in China and Japan: Gender, Feminism, and Global Modernity Between the Wars*. London: I.B. Tauris.

Hane, Mikiso. 2003. *Peasants, Rebels, and Outcastes: The Underside of Modern Japan*. Lanham, MD: Rowan and Littlefield Publishers.

Iriye, Akira, and Robert A. Wampler, eds. 2001. *Partnership: The United States and Japan, 1951–2001*. Tokyo: Kodansha International.

Kingston, Jeffrey. 2001. *Japan in Transformation, 1952–2000*. New York: Longman.

Moore, Thomas Geoffrey. 2002. *China in the World Market: Chinese Industry and International Sources of Reform in the Post-Mao Era*. New York: Cambridge University Press.

Nolan, Peter. 2003. *Transforming China: Globalization, Transition and Development*. London: Anthem Press.

Perry, Elizabeth J., and Mark Selden, eds. 2000. *Chinese Society: Change, Conflict and Resistance*. New York: Routledge.

Schlesinger, Jacob M. 1999. *Shadow Shoguns: The Rise and Fall of Japan's Postwar Political Machine*. Stanford, CA: Stanford University Press.

Schwartz, Frank J., and Susan J. Pharr, eds. 2003. *The State of Civil Society in Japan*. Cambridge: Cambridge University Press.

Vogel, Erza. 2011. *Deng Xiaoping and the Transformation of China*. Cambridge, MA: The Belknap Press of Harvard University Press.

11 | Anti-colonial Movements and Independence

Anderson, David M. 1992. *Policing and Decolonization: Politics, Nationalism and the Police, 1917–65*. Manchester: Manchester University Press.

Berger, Mark T. 2004. *The Battle for Asia: From Decolonization to Globalization*. London/New York: Routledge.

Betts, Raymond F. 2004. *Decolonization: Making of the Contemporary World*. New York: Routledge.

Brown, Judith M. 1989. *Gandhi: Prisoner of Hope*. New Haven, CT: Yale University Press.

Chafer, Tony. 2002. *The End of Empire in French West Africa: France's Successful Decolonization?* Oxford/New York: Berg Publishers.

Elkins, Caroline. 2004. *Imperial Reckoning: The Untold Story of Britain's Gulag in Kenya*. New York: Henry Holt and Company.

Grimal, Henri. 1979. *Decolonization: The British, French, Dutch, and Belgian Empires, 1919–1963*. Boulder, CO: Westview Press.

Hahn, Peter L., and Mary Ann Heiss, eds. 2001. *Empire and Revolution: The United States and the Third World since 1945*. Columbus, OH: Ohio State University Press.

Le Sueur, James D., ed. 2003. *The Decolonization Reader*. New York: Routledge.

Springhall, John. 2001. *Decolonization since 1945: The Collapse of European Overseas Empires*. New York: Palgrave Macmillan.

Wolpert, Stanley A. 2003. *A New History of India*, 7th Edition. New York: Oxford University.

12 | The Postwar Era in the Middle East

Bhutto, Benazir. 2008. *Reconciliation: Islam, Democracy, and the West*. New York: Harper.

Horowitz, Dan, and Moshe Lissak. 1989. *Trouble in Utopia: The Overburdened Polity of Israel*. Albany, NY: State University of New York Press.

Keddie, Nikki. 2007. *Women in the Middle East: Past and Present*. Princeton, NJ: Princeton University Press.

Lapidus, Ira M. 2002. *A History of Islamic Societies*. Cambridge/New York: Cambridge University Press.

Mottahedeh, Roy. 1985. *The Mantle of the Prophet: Religion and Politics in Iran*. New York: Simon & Schuster.

Nasr, Seyyed Vali Reza. 2006. *The Shia Revival: How Conflicts within Islam will Shape the Future*. New York: W.W. Norton.

Said, Edward. 1994. *The Politics of Dispossession: The Struggle for Palestinian Self-determination, 1969–1994*. New York: Vintage.

Saikal, Amin. 2003. *Islam and the West: Conflict or Cooperation?* New York: Palgrave Macmillan.

Yapp, Malcolm. 1991. *The Near East since the First World War*. London: Longman Group UK.

Zahan, Rosemary Said. 1989. *The Making of the Modern Gulf States*. London: Ithaca Press.

Zubaida, Sami. 2011. *Beyond Islam: A New Understanding of the Middle East*. London: I.B. Tauris.

13 | Post-colonial Legacies

Amin, Samir. 1973. *Neo-colonialism in West Africa*. New York: Monthly Review Press.

Clark, Nancy L., and William H. Worger. 2004. *South Africa: The Rise and Fall of Apartheid*. New York: Longman.

Cooper, Frederick. 2002. *Africa since 1940: The Past of the Present*. Cambridge: Cambridge University Press.

Dirks, Nicholas B. 2001. *Castes of Mind: Colonialism and the Making of Modern India*. Englewood Cliffs, NJ: Princeton University Press.

Donghi, Tulio Halperin. 1993. *The Contemporary History of Latin America*. Durham, NC: Duke University Press.

Esedebe, P. Olisanwuche. 1982. *Pan-Africanism: The Idea and the Movement, 1776–1963*. Washington, DC: Howard University Press.

Goodman, David. 1999. *Fault Lines: Journeys into the New South Africa*. Berkeley: University of California Press.

Hoogvelt, Ankie. 2001. *Globalization and the Postcolonial World: The New Political Economy of Development*. Baltimore, MD: Johns Hopkins University Press.

Iweriebor, Ehiedu. 1997. *The Age of Neo-colonialism in Africa: Essays on Domination and Resistance after Independence*. Ibadan: African Book Builders.

Perez, Louis A. 1995. *Cuba: Between Reform and Revolution*. Oxford: Oxford University Press.

Smith, Peter H. 1999. *Talons of the Eagle: Dynamics of US–Latin American Relations*, 2nd Edition. Oxford: Oxford University Press.

Werbner, Richard, and Terence Ranger, eds. 1996. *Postcolonial Identities in Africa*. London: Zed Books.

Wiarda, Howard, and Harvey Kline, eds. 1990. *Latin American Politics and Development*, 3rd Edition. Boulder, CO: Westview Press.

14 | Ideological Change and Radical Movements

Dierenfield, Bruce J. 2004. *The Civil Rights Movement*. New York: Longman.

Gitlin, Todd. 1993. *The Sixties: Years of Hope, Days of Rage*. New York: Bantam.

Hagan, John. 2001. *Northern Passage: American Vietnam War Resistors in Canada*. Cambridge, MA: Harvard University Press.

Isserman, Maurice, and Michael Kazin. 1999. *America Divided: The Civil War of the 1960s*. Oxford: Oxford University Press.

Klatch, Rebecca E. 1999. *A Generation Divided: The New Left, the New Right, and the 1960s*. Berkeley: University of California Press.

Kurlansky, Mark. 2003. *1968: The Year that Rocked the World*. New York: Ballantine Books.

Middlemas, Keith. 1995. *Orchestrating Europe: The Informal Politics of European Union 1973–1995*. London: Fontana Press.

Polenberg, Richard. 1993. *One Nation Divisible: Class, Race and Ethnicity in the United States since 1938*. New York: Peter Smith Publisher Inc.

Rosen, Ruth. 2000. *The World Split Open: How the Modern Women's Movement Changed America*. New York: Penguin.

15 | The End of the Cold War and Its Aftermath

Antohi, Sorin, and Vladimir Tismaneanu, eds. 2000. *Between Past and Future: The Revolutions of 1989 and their Aftermath*. Budapest: Central European University Press.

Brown, Archie. 2011. *The Rise and Fall of Communism*. New York: Ecco.

Fitzgerald, Frances. 2000. *Way Out There in the Blue: Reagan, Star Wars, and the End of the Cold War*. New York: Simon & Schuster.

Garthoff, Raymond. 1994. *The Great Transition: American Soviet Relations and the End of the Cold War*. Washington: Brookings Institution Press.

Glaser, Daryl, and David M. Walker, eds. 2007. *Twentieth-Century Marxism: A Global Introduction*. London/New York: Routledge.

Holm, Hans-Henrick, and Georg Sorensen. 1995. *Whose World Order: Uneven Globalization and the End of the Cold War*. Boulder, CO: Westview Press.

Howard, Marc Morjé. 2003. *The Weakness of Civil Society in Post-Communist Europe*. Cambridge: Cambridge University Press.

Morton, Jeffrey S., ed. 2004. *Reflections on the Balkan Wars: Ten Years after the Break-Up of Yugoslavia*. New York: Palgrave Macmillan.

Remnick, David. 1993. *Lenin's Tomb: The Last Days of the Soviet Empire*. London, UK: Vintage.

Suny, Ronald Gregor. 1993. *The Revenge of the Past: Nationalism, Revolution, and the Collapse of the Soviet Union*. Stanford: Stanford University Press.

Tsyganov, Andrei P. 2004. *Whose World Order? Russia's Perception of American Ideas after the Cold War*. Notre Dame, IN: University of Notre Dame Press.

16 | One World—One People

Bramwell, Anna. 1989. *Ecology in the Twentieth Century: A History*. New Haven, CT: Yale University Press.

Diamond, Jared. 2005. *Collapse: How Societies Choose to Fail or Succeed*. New York: Viking.

Ehrlich, Paul. 2008. *The Dominant Animal: Human Evolution and the Environment*. Washington DC: Island Press.

Flannery, Tim. 2006. *The Weather Makers: How We Are Changing the Climate and What It Means for Life on Earth*. Toronto: HarperCollins Canada.

Hård, Mikel. 2005. *Hubris and Hybrids. A Cultural History of Technology and Science*. New York: Routledge.

Horowitz, Roger and Arwen Mohun. 1998. *His and Hers: Gender, Consumption, and Technology*. Charlottesville, VA: University Press of Virginia.

McNeill, J.R. 2000. *Something New Under the Sun: An Environmental History of the Twentieth-Century World*. New York: W.W. Norton & Co.

Radkau, Joachim. 2008. *Nature and Power: A Global History of the Environment*. Washington, DC: German Historical Institute.

Strate, Lance. 2005. *The Legacy of McLuhan*. Cresskill, NJ: Hampton Press.

17 | History in the Making: Into the Twenty-First Century

Ali, Tariq. 2002. *The Clash of Fundamentalisms: Crusades, Jihads, and Modernity*. London: Verso.

Bakan, Joel. 2004. *The Corporation: The Pathological Pursuit of Profit and Power*. Toronto: Penguin Books Canada.

Barber, Benjamin. 1995. *Jihad vs. McWorld: How Globalism and Tribalism are Reshaping the World*. New York: Ballantine Books.

Black, Jeremy. 2004. *War and the New Disorder in the 21st Century*, rev. edition. New York/London: Continuum International Publishing Group.

Chomsky, Noam. 2003. *Hegemony or Survival: America's Quest for Global Dominance*. New York: Metropolitan Books.

Dyer, Gwynne. 2004. *Future: Tense: The Coming World Order?* Toronto: McClelland & Stewart.

Fernandez-Armesto, Felipe. 1995. *Millennium*. London: Free Press.

Frank, Andre Gunder. 1998. *Reorient: Global Economics in the Asian Age*. Berkeley: University of California Press.

Fukuyama, Francis. 2004. *State-Building: Governance and World Order in the 21st Century*. Ithaca, NY: Cornell University Press.

Kennedy, Paul. 1993. *Preparing for the Twenty-First Century*. New York: Vintage.

Landes, David S. 1998. *The Wealth and Poverty of Nations: Why Some Are So Rich and Some So Poor*. New York/London: W.W. Norton & Company.

Lukacs, John. 1993. *The End of the Twentieth Century and the End of the Modern Age*. New York: Ticknor and Fields.

Mazama, Ama. 2007. *Africa in the 21st Century: Toward a New Future*. London: Routledge.

Melvern, Linda. 2004. *Conspiracy to Murder: The Rwanda Genocide*. London/New York: Verso.

Orbinski, James. 2008. *An Imperfect Offering: Humanitarian Action in the Twenty-First Century*. Toronto: Doubleday Canada.

Veltmeyer, Henry, ed. 2004. *Globalization and Antiglobalization: Dynamics of Change in the New World Order*. Aldershot, Hants, UK: Ashgate Publishing.

Weitz, Eric D. 2003. *A Century of Genocide: Utopias of Race and Nation*. Princeton, NJ: Princeton University Press.

Acknowledgements

The Amur Society, "Anniversary Statement": From pp. 255–9 of *Sources of Japanese Traditions* volume two, Wm. Theodore de Bary, ed. Copyright 1958 Columbia University Press. Reprinted with permission of the publisher.

The Atlantic Monthly, "Rwanda 1964": © 1964 The Atlantic Media Co., as first published in *The Atlantic Monthly*. All rights reserved. Distributed by Tribune Media Services

Benjamin Barber, "Jihad versus McWorld": Published originally in *The Atlantic Monthly*, Volume 269 (3) (March 1992), 53–65. Benjamin Barber is president of the international NGO CivWorld and of the Interdependence Movement, Walt Whitman Professor Emeritus at Rutgers University, and the author of 19 books, including the classic *Strong Democracy*, the international best-seller *Jihad vs. McWorld*, and, forthcoming from Yale University Press, *If Mayors Ruled the World*.

Fox Butterfield, "Lihua": Excerpt from *China* by Fox Butterfield, copyright © 1982 by Fox Butterfield. Used by permission of Times Books, an imprint of Random House LLC. All rights reserved.

Rachel Carson, "Silent Spring": Excerpt from "The Obligation to Endure" from *Silent Spring* by Rachel Carson. Copyright © 1962 by Rachel L. Carson, renewed 1990 by Roger Christie. Reprinted by permission of Houghton Mifflin Harcourt Publishing Company. All rights reserved.

Raúl Castro, "Closing Remarks at the 6th Party Congress, 21 April 2011": Reprinted from www.cubadebate.cu

Chicago Seven Trial Transcript, "Testimony of Abbie Hoffman": Available at http://law2.umkc.edu/faculty/projects/ftrials/chicago7/hoffman.html

Li Dazhao, "The Victory of Bolshevism": Reprinted by permission of the publisher from *China's Response to the West: A Documentary Survey, 1839–1923*, by Ssu-yü Têng and John King Fairbank, pp. 246–9, Cambridge, Mass.: Harvard University Press, Copyright © 1954, 1979 by the President and Fellows of Harvard College. Copyright © renewed 1982 by Ssu-yü-Têng and John King Fairbank.

European Commission, "Opinion on Hungary's Application for Membership in the EU": © European Union, 1995–2013.

Evgeniia Ginzburg, "Journey into the Whirlwind": From *Journey into the Whirlwind* by Eugenia Semyonovna Ginzburg. Copyright © 1967 by Arnoldo Mondadori Editore. English translation Copyright © 1967 by Harcourt, Inc. Originally published as *Krutoj Mars rut* by Mondadori. Used by permission of Georges Borchardt, Inc., on behalf of the author.

Albert Gore, "Nobel Lecture": Copyright © The Nobel Foundation (2007). Source: Nobelprize.org

Philip Gourevitch, "We Wish to Inform You That Tomorrow We Will Be Killed with Our Families": Excerpts from Chapter 1 from *We Wish to Inform You That Tomorrow We Will Be Killed With Our Families* by Philip Gourevitch. Copyright © 1998 by Philip Gourevitch.

Vaclav Havel, "Disturbing the Peace": From *Disturbing the Peace* by Vaclav Havel, translation copyright 1990 by Vaclav Havel. Used by permission of Alfred A. Knoff, an imprint of the Knopf Doubleday Publishing Group, a division of Random House LLC. All rights reserved.

Roy Jenkins, "Homosexuality Has Existed in All Societies": From Roy Jenkins' speech to parliament, February 11, 1966, as cited in: Roy Jenkins, *Essays and Speeches*, ed. Anthony Lester (London: Collins, 1967), 257–8.

Robert Kaplan, "World Government": From *The Coming Anarchy: Shattering the Dreams of the Post Cold War*, by Robert D. Kaplan. Published by Random House. Copyright © 2000 by Robert Kaplan. Used by permission of Brandt & Hochman Literary Agents, Inc.

Victor *Klemperer*, "I Will Bear Witness": Excerpt from *I Will Bear Witness, Volume 1: A Dairy of the Nazi Years* by Victor Klemperer, translated by Martin Chalmers, translation copyright © 1998 by Martin Chalmers. Used by permission of Random House, an imprint of The Random House Publishing Group, a division of Random House LLC. All rights reserved.

Raymond Mikesell, "The Bretton Woods Debates": From Raymond F. Mikesell, *The Bretton Woods Debates: A Memoir*, Essays in International Finance No. 192, © March 1994. Reprinted by permission of the International Economics Section of Princeton University.

Benito Mussolini, "Fascist Doctrines": Extract *from Italian Fascisms from Pareto to Gentile* by Adrian Lyttleton, ed. Trans. By Douglas Parmee, reprinted by permission of Peters, Fraser, & Dunlop (www.petersfraserdunlop.com) on behalf of the Estate of Adrian Lyttleton. Published by Jonathan Cape. Reprinted by permission of The Random House Group Limited.

Huey P. Newton, "Uniting Against a Common Enemy": Excerpt from "Uniting Against a Common Enemy" from *The Huey P. Newton Reader*, edited by David Hilliard and Donald Weiss. Copyright © 2002 by Fredrick S. Newton and David Hilliard. Reproduced with the permission of The Permissions Company, Inc., on behalf of Seven Stories Press, www.sevenstories.com.

Lester B. Pearson, "On Peacekeeping": Selected text from speech: "On Peacekeeping" by Lester B. Pearson, 2 April 1965 (Address on Accepting the 2nd Temple University World Peace Award at the Founder's Dinner of the University's General Alumni Association) Philadelphia, PA.

Index

Note: Page numbers in boldface indicate the locations of primary
documents; page numbers in italics refer to illustrations.